ANNUAL REVIEW OF
POLITICAL SCIENCE

ANNUAL REVIEW OF POLITICAL SCIENCE

VOLUME 3, 2000

NELSON W. POLSBY, *Editor*
University of California, Berkeley

www.AnnualReviews.org   science@AnnualReviews.org   650-493-4400

ANNUAL REVIEWS
4139 El Camino Way • P.O. BOX 10139 • Palo Alto, California 94303-0139

ANNUAL REVIEWS
Palo Alto, California, USA

International Standard Serial Number: 1094-2939
International Standard Book Number: 0-8243-3303-9

TYPESET BY TECHBOOKS, FAIRFAX, VA
PRINTED AND BOUND IN THE UNITED STATES OF AMERICA

PREFACE

The production of an *Annual Review of Political Science* provides a good vantage point for the consideration of the discipline as a whole. Willy-nilly, it makes of our editorial board students of the history of the ideas that animate contemporary scholarly concerns, and provokes us to think about trends leading toward the future. One consequence of this perspective has been our interest in finding and publishing articles treating aspects of political science as case studies in the development and dissemination of ideas—not only in political philosophy, where studying "greats" is a settled tradition, but also in other branches of the discipline. Readers of these articles will note that social foundations of intellectual work—the communities that nurture scholarly innovation and conserve scholarly achievement—are not neglected and appear alongside accounts of ideas and their cultural and intellectual antecedents.

Such articles can provide an orientation to our diverse field not matched by any other publication. For example, one area that has received attention in early volumes has been British political science, with David Butler's review of the path-breaking Nuffield election studies, and Alan Ryan's introduction to Isaiah Berlin, along with Nöel Annan's beautiful evocation of the academic milieu in which Sir Isaiah flourished. In future volumes we anticipate articles on the influential English political philosopher Michael Oakeshott and on Sammy Finer's magnum opus, *The History of Government*. And we shall be following developments tracking changes in the British constitution.

British political scientists have recently appraised their contributions over the last century to political science in a volume sponsored by the British Academy.[1] They appear to be of more than one mind about whether there is—or ought to be—a distinctive national style of work setting them apart from their continental neighbors or from colleagues in the United States. No doubt there is something different, at least compared with the United States, about the university life that surrounds and sustains scholarship in the UK with its ancient traditions, short distances, and relatively small communities of scholars. Large political issues of conflict and harmony, unity and diversity, status and contract (for example) are bound to present themselves differently to at least part of the scholarly population in the UK compared with US scholars. But I know of no systematic exploration of the way these or other features of the social landscape affect the preoccupations, or the intellectual strategies, or the output of scholars who study politics. Perhaps

---

[1] Jack Hayward, Brian Barry, Archie Brown (eds), *The British Study of Politics in the 20th Century*, Oxford: 1999, published for the British Academy by Oxford University Press.

the piecemeal explorations provided by an *Annual Review* can begin to stimulate political scientists to look at this larger picture.

Nelson W. Polsby
Editor

RELATED ARTICLES

CONTENTS

Annu. Rev. Polit. Sci. 2000. 3:1–24

PREFERENCE FORMATION

James N. Druckman
*Department of Political Science, University of Minnesota, Minneapolis,
Minnesota 55455-0410; e-mail: druckman@polisci.umn.edu*

Arthur Lupia
*Department of Political Science, University of California, San Diego, La Jolla,
California 92093-0521; e-mail: alupia@ucsd.edu*

Key Words   belief formation, accessibility, on-line processing,
preference reversals, persuasion

■ **Abstract**   This review concerns political preferences—what they are and where
they come from. We begin by documenting the close relationship between processes of
preference formation and change. Rather than suddenly appearing, most preferences
emerge from interactions between individuals and their environment. This aspect of
preference formation poses a concrete challenge: to uncover the mechanics of these
interactions in important social contexts. We then describe political science research
that meets this challenge. We find an expansive literature that clarifies how phenomena
such as parties, campaigns, and the need to act strategically affect preferences. This
work provides many widely applicable insights.

INTRODUCTION

Why do people do what they do? An easy answer is that people do what they want.
But why do people want what they want? This question has fascinated intellectuals for centuries and continues to motivate researchers today. What scientists,
generally, and political scientists, in particular, have learned about the answer is
the topic of our review.

In what follows, we begin by defining what many scholars mean by "preference," paying particular attention to what scholars outside of political science have
discovered about the nature and origins of preferences. These discoveries clarify
how individuals transform the "great, blooming, buzzing confusion" of human
experience into preferences for objects such as candidates and policies (James
1890:488).

We then move to the core of the review: a description of political science
research relevant to preference formation. This core has two sections. The first
section focuses on the internal dynamics of preference formation. We compare and
contrast some of political science's most prominent approaches to explaining how

1094-2939/00/0623-0001$14.00

humans convert old and new information into political preferences. In the second section, we review work in political science that explores preference formation's external dynamics. This research shows how occurrences outside the brain affect preferences inside it. For example, when some political actors have an incentive to provide information strategically, others may face changed incentives for interpreting the information they receive (i.e. they must choose whom to believe). When factors such as strategic behavior affect the quantity or character of available information, they can also cause people to form different preferences. The point of the research we review is to clarify the dynamics of such effects.

Although our review is expansive, it is far from comprehensive. The size of the literature relevant to preference formation necessitates a focused presentation. The literature is broad not only because of widespread interest in the topic of preference formation but also because questions of preference formation and preference change are, for most practical purposes, the same. This kinship is well established in cognitive science and psychology, where differences between the formation and change of related ideas (e.g. concepts, attitudes) are considered differences of degree rather than of kind. In the context of political science, this same kinship unites research on topics as diverse as on-line processing, persuasion, and strategic communication under the common domain of research relevant to preference formation. It also suggests new avenues for future research on preference formation.

THE NATURE AND ORIGINS OF HUMAN PREFERENCES

> Theories of human cognition are ultimately theories of physical, biological systems. Our ability to describe human cognition in one way rather than another rests ultimately on the physical and biological nature of human beings. Furthermore, the fact that human beings are grounded in the world implies additional constraints that must be taken into account in constructing our theories. (Newell 1990:42)

To proceed to questions of preference formation, we need a working definition of "preference." We say working definition because there is no global agreement on a single definition of the term. Indeed, terms such as preferences, tastes, and values are often used interchangeably throughout the social sciences. We define a preference as a comparative evaluation of (i.e. a ranking over) a set of objects. A preference serves as a cognitive marker that reminds people how to interact with various aspects of their environment. Preferences are stored in memory and drawn on when people make decisions. When, for example, people say that they prefer Lincoln to Douglass, they identify an aspect of their environment that, in their mind, provides them with greater benefits than other environmental aspects.

In this section, we begin our review of research on preference formation by looking at insights from cognitive science. We do so not because cognitive science has had a direct influence on political science—it has not—but because it helps us to understand the nature and origins of preferences. We proceed by reviewing basic cognitive-science insights regarding the component parts of a preference—the objects of preference and comparative evaluations.

The Objects of Preference

> The amoeba cannot choose whether to categorize, it just does. The same is true at every level of the animal world. Animals categorize food, predators, possible mates, members of their own species, and so on. How animals categorize depends upon their sensing apparatus and their ability to move themselves and to manipulate objects. (Lakoff & Johnson 1999:17)

The objects of preference are aspects of the environment that are evaluated relative to one another. They can include observable, physically continuous phenomena (such as bowling balls) and unobservable, physically discontinuous phenomena (such as shared ideas).

The objects within a preference are those that a person can imagine as substitutable. For example, shoes and tofu are substitutes within many domains, including apparel, where most people prefer shoes, and eating, where most people prefer tofu. If people cannot imagine what eating shoes or wearing tofu would be like, then they cannot have such preferences.

The predominant view of human cognition for nearly 2000 years has been that the objects of preference (alternatively, the categories of phenomena over which preferences can be held) are strictly external. In recent years, the evidence against this view of cognition has been piling high. Consider, for example, colors. Most people prefer some colors to others, and many have a favorite. People treat colors as basic attributes of other objects. But are colors just out there in the world waiting to be evaluated by the next sentient being who comes along? The answer is no. Colors, as we know them, are as much human creations as they are exogenous characteristics of our surroundings.

As Churchland & Sejnowski (1992:221) explain, "[c]olor perception depends on wavelength, but it is not identical to wavelength." For example, a "red wagon may look red under a wide range of illuminations, including broad daylight, dusk, candle light, fluorescent light, and so forth, where the physical wavelengths actually impinging on the retina vary dramatically" (Churchland & Sejnowski 1992:221). It is more accurate to think of color perception as the product of an equilibrium between brain, body, and world. As Lakoff & Johnson (1999:23,25) explain,

> [C]olors do not exist in the external world. Given the world, our bodies and brains have evolved to create color. Our experience of color is created by a combination of four factors: wavelengths of reflected light, lighting conditions, and two aspects of our bodies: (1) the three kinds of color cones in our retinas, which absorb light of long, medium, and short wavelengths, and (2) the complex neural circuitry connected to those cones.... The

meaning of the word *red* cannot be just the relation between the word and something in the world (say, a collection of wavelengths of light or a surface reflectance).... It must make reference to the neural circuitry.

That we can communicate preferences and other phenomena based on the color "red" is a testament to similarities in our cognitive and perceptive architecture more than to any universal property of surface reflectance. Indeed, two people whose retinas reacted very differently to light could find it difficult to communicate color-related concepts effectively.

An important implication of such research is that personal experience affects the set of objects over which people have preferences. For example, some people prefer dogs to cats as pets. Some make further distinctions between kinds of dogs and kinds of cats, whereas others are indifferent to dog or cat breeds. Indeed, the extent to which people hold preferences over types of objects depends on their prior experiences with related objects. For example, people who are very distant from politics may have only a general dislike for politicians, whereas those whose well-being requires interactions with different types of politicians hold preferences with finer distinctions.

In sum, the objects of preference are not simply out in the world waiting to be ranked. They are, instead, objects that our perceptive capacity allows us to differentiate, that our experience gives us an incentive to differentiate and recall, and that our cognitive capacity allows us to remember and evaluate.

Where Comparative Evaluations Come From

Nature ... is heavily bound by achieved solutions to previously encountered problems. As a result, new cognitive garments seldom are made of whole cloth; usually they comprise hastily tailored amendments to old structures and strategies. (Clark 1997:81)

We contend that evaluations are based, in part, on beliefs; that beliefs are the product of interactions between brain, body, and world; and that understanding these interactions is the key to answering questions about preference formation. Indeed, explaining preference formation is the process of explaining how beliefs and evaluations emerge from correlations between what people experience and what they feel.

Preferences are rankings derived from comparative evaluations that psychologists call attitudes. We follow O'Keefe (1990:18) in defining an attitude as "a person's general evaluation of an object (where 'object' is understood in a broad sense, as encompassing persons, events, products, policies, institutions, and so on)." Attitudes are people's orientations toward objects.

Most objects have more than one recognizable attribute. As a result, many scholars think of evaluations in spatial terms—as multidimensional orientations toward objects. Many people, for example, like Bill Clinton's politics but not his penchant for extramarital affairs. We say that such people are "close" to Clinton on the political dimension, but "far" from him on the marital-ethics dimension.

Evaluations of multidimensional objects are based, in part, on evaluations of object attributes (see e.g. Fishbein 1963). Each attribute evaluation, in turn, is based on beliefs. A belief is a neurally held probability distribution over possible characteristics of an object attribute (Churchland & Sejnowski 1992, Kandel et al 1995). For example, an attribute of certain types of skies (e.g. cloudy and dark) is that they produce rain. People base preferences over objects (such as the beauty of different types of skies or the best time for a picnic) on their beliefs about object attributes, such as the likelihood of rain.

Beliefs about attributes, in turn, depend on information. Following convention in cognitive science, we define information as any data potentially relevant to interactions between the brain, the body and, in some cases, the environment. Beliefs, therefore, are the result of interactions between brain, body, and world. Learning is the process by which new information leads to a change in beliefs about attributes of the object being studied. Churchland & Sejnowski (1992:117) call learning "[A]dapting to the present on the evolutionary-tried assumption that the future resembles the past."

Having traced the ancestry of preference, we confront the question, "Where do particular preferences come from?" The recent literature in cognitive science suggests the following explanation.

From very early stages in fetal development, the brain receives information from and sends instructions to other parts of the body. Among the most important signals sent to the brain are those regarding pain. Put differently, "Biological cognition is highly selective, and it can sensitize an organism to whatever (often simple) parameters reliably specify states of affairs that matter to the specific life form ... [organisms] rely on simple cues that are specific to their needs, and ... profit by not bothering to represent other types in detail" (Clark 1997:25). Aspects of early brain-body communiqués are stored in the brain and become the basis for future instructions from the brain. Physically, much of this information is stored as growth in dendrites. The resultant neural network formed by dendritic growth then facilitates or inhibits the subsequent chemical and electrical transmissions that serve as the medium for future brain-body communications.

As the fetus develops, early brain-body communications come to correlate with variations in the fetal, and subsequently the infant, environment. Preferences for or against certain environmental aspects arise. The fetus and infant come to prefer (i.e. want to be near) the identifiable aspects of their environment that correlate with an increase in pleasure or a decrease in pain. "[F]or an infant, the subjective experience of affection is typically correlated with the sensory experience of warmth, the warmth of being held.... Universal early experiences lead to universal conflations..." (Lakoff & Johnson 1999:46).

As the infant learns that it can manipulate aspects of its environment (e.g. that crying induces parental attentiveness and that food can be thrown), it realizes the concept of choice. When sensorimotor skills develop, the infant has an incentive to compare a larger set of objects.

Early on, a child's preferences over most classes of objects are based on direct experiences. As Holland et al (1986:9) explain, the process "is (a) directed by problem solving activity and (b) based on feedback regarding the success or failure of predictions generated by the system." As children gain the ability to communicate, however, they begin to experience objects indirectly. Through stories, for example, children develop affinities for abstractions such as Peter Pan and fears of abstractions such as monsters. When sensorimotor and communicative organs develop fully, the architecture for all subsequent preference formation is in place. People can then begin to develop preferences for objects as abstract as political parties and constitutional forms.

Preference Change and Preference Formation

Many of the preferences that adults hold are different from those they held as children. Interactions with their environment cause these changes. However, the number of interactions is far greater than the number of changes. When do preferences change? And how different are the mechanics of preference change from the mechanics of preference formation?

To answer these questions, it is important to note that "preference change" can mean either of two things. First, we can change preferences between two types of objects, A and B, because we gain new information about the attributes of at least one type of object. (For example, when a child learns that certain dogs bite, her preference for playing with those dogs, relative to other things, may shift.) Second, we can decide that the objects formerly known as P are better treated as objects of distinct types P_1 and P_2.

In both cases, new information about an object attribute causes a change in the comparative evaluations of a class of objects. Preferences over "new" objects are examples of the second kind of change. However, when we encounter stimuli that are novel to us, we instantly form beliefs about them. These beliefs—and the preferences that follow—are not newly created; rather, they emerge from preferences and beliefs we have about objects with which we have interacted in the past. The objects we select from the past are those that we perceive to be similar to the novel stimulus.

Holland et al (1986) clarify the conditions under which such changes are most likely and the consequences of such change. The literal process they describe consists of rules of induction, but these rules are equivalent to conditions for belief change.

> "Two important kinds of triggering conditions are the failure of a prediction and the occurrence of some unusual event" (Holland et al 1986:80).

> "A new rule is built from the existing one by (a) augmenting the condition of the existing rule with additional unusual properties of the failure context and

(b) substituting the unexpected outcome as the action of the new rule" (Holland et al 1986:88).

"Thus, competition will favor those rules that (a) provide a description of the current situation, (b) have a history of past usefulness to the system, (c) produce the greatest degree of completeness of description and (d) have the greatest compatibility with other currently active information" (Holland et al 1986:49).

Seen from this perspective, the mechanics of preference formation and preference change are indistinguishable for most adults. Explaining preference formation means explaining how beliefs and attitudes emerge from correlations between what we observe and what we feel. From early in life, however, novel stimuli are understood by their relationship to stimuli that are more familiar. As a result, there is no difference between preference formation and preference change. New preferences emerge from existing ones (e.g. we learn that objects of type P are better treated as objects of type P_1 and P_2). "New" preferences are not created out of thin air; they evolve from refinements of existing preferences. Like many prominent psychological treatments of attitudes (e.g. Eagly & Chaiken 1993:219), this review treats the formation and the change of beliefs, evaluations, and preferences as identical.

Summary

The objects over which preferences are held are not necessarily external. Indeed, many of what we perceive to be objects are conceptual creations that result from an equilibrium between brain, body, and world. Preferences over classes of objects are rankings that are derived from evaluations, where evaluations depend on beliefs, and beliefs are the result of interactions between individuals and their surroundings.

This view of the cognitive underpinnings of preference formation is not without competitors or controversy (see e.g. Lakoff 1987; Clark 1993, 1997; McCauley 1996; Pinker 1997; Lakoff & Johnson 1999). It is, however, an increasingly dominant view that is well supported by empirical research on brain function and conceptual development in cognitive science, the neurosciences, and psychology.

Some observers object that this point of view poses the threat of subjectivism. If objects are not simply external and if preferences derive from previous associations, then perhaps everything about our world, including morality, is a matter of opinion. The evidence supporting such a conclusion, however, is slight. Researchers have discovered basic and universal properties of brain function and many higher-level behaviors (e.g. Kandel et al 1995). These similarities, combined with omnipresent forces of nature (e.g. laws of gravity), put an upper limit on the variance with which humans perceive the world and the differences in the preferences that they can hold. Such discoveries reinforce the foundation of systematic, generalizable, and scientific studies of preferences.

PREFERENCE FORMATION IN POLITICAL SCIENCE

Internal Processes

In this section, we describe attempts to characterize the internal process by which individuals convert information from their environment into evaluations of political objects. Because these attempts differ in their portrayals of how people treat new information, they generate different implications for how preferences form. This review is not comprehensive. Rather it focuses on ideas developed recently and cited frequently.

We begin by comparing and contrasting memory-based and on-line models of information processing. We end by discussing the implications of preference-reversal experiments for the more general study of preferences.

Memory-Based Models

Many social science models share the implicit assumption that preferences form through a memory-based process (Lodge et al 1990). The idea behind a memory-based model is that people base their evaluations on information that they retrieve from memory. For example, when called on to evaluate an object, people canvass their memories for information on object attributes and use what they find to form preferences.

In comprehensive memory-based models, an individual recalls all relevant information and integrates it into an overall evaluation. For example, when an individual receives information about a candidate (e.g. the candidate's issue positions), she files it away in long-term memory. Later, she retrieves the candidate's issue positions on a host of issues from long-term memory, weights the information according to its importance or relevance, and finally integrates it into an overall evaluation (see e.g. Fishbein & Ajzen 1975, Enelow & Hinich 1984).

Such models assume that people engage in an enormous amount of computation. This assumption contrasts with the widely held view of individuals—voters in particular—as having neither the motivation nor the ability to engage in an exhaustive memory search and weighting of evidence. Numerous scholars have attempted to rectify this apparent contradiction by offering memory-based models that assume less computation (e.g. van der Pligt & Eiser 1984).

For example, Kelley & Mirer (1974:574; also see Kelley 1983) argue that a voter forms his candidate preference by canvassing "his likes and dislikes of the leading candidates and major parties involved in an election. Weighing each like and dislike equally, he votes for the candidate toward whom he has the greatest net number of favorable attitudes, if there is such a candidate...." Using this model, Kelley & Mirer accurately predicted vote choice for approximately 88% of voters surveyed during presidential elections from 1952 through 1964.

More recent work presents actors who are even less computationally complex. Accessibility models, for example, portray people as basing preferences on small sets of considerations. Accessibility refers to the likelihood that a given consideration (or construct) will be retrieved from memory when forming a preference (e.g. Bruner 1957:135).[1] A large literature shows that people base many judgments on the considerations that are most accessible in memory (e.g. Higgins & King 1981, Wyer & Srull 1989, Fazio 1995). For example, if economic considerations happen to be accessible in a voter's mind, she will base her candidate preference on economic considerations; if, instead, foreign affairs considerations are accessible, then the voter will base her preference on foreign affairs considerations (Sherman et al 1990).

A prominent example of such a model in political science is that of Zaller (1992) and Zaller & Feldman (1992). Zaller argues that people form evaluations by "averaging across the considerations that are immediately salient or accessible to them" (1992:49), where a consideration is defined as "any reason that might induce an individual to decide a political issue one way or the other" (1992:40). In Zaller's model, people base their preferences on whichever considerations happen to come to the "top of the head" (i.e. whichever considerations happen to be accessible).

Which considerations are likely to float to the top? Zaller (1992:48) contends that "the more recently a consideration has been called to mind or thought about, the less time it takes to retrieve that consideration or related considerations from memory and bring them to the top of the head for use."

An important implication is that citizens are unlikely to have true attitudes (see e.g. Wilson & Hodges 1992, Zaller 1992:93, Kinder 1993:48; for an alternative view, see Kuklinski & Hurley 1996:134–38). In Zaller's model, citizens' preferences depend on whatever happens to be salient at the time of expression. For example, if an individual recently overheard a discussion about economic issues, then economic considerations may come to the top of the individual's head, and as a result, her expressed preference will be based largely on considerations of economic issues.

Accessibility models are widely and successfully applied throughout political science (e.g. Krosnick 1988, Aldrich et al 1989, Lau 1989, Ottati et al 1989, Tourangeau et al 1989, Johnston et al 1992, Chong 1993, Jacobs & Shapiro 1994, Cappella & Jamieson 1997, Price & Tewksbury 1997, Huckfeldt et al 1999). Iyengar & Kinder (1987) and Iyengar (1990, 1991) are particularly well known. They argue, for example, that when the television news emphasizes defense, then the accessibility of the defense issue increases in the minds of viewers. As a result, viewers base evaluations on the defense issue (see Krosnick & Brannon 1993 and Nelson et al 1997a for alternative views of the psychology of media effects).

---

[1]It is unclear when a consideration is sufficiently accessible for activation (see e.g. Fazio 1995:273). Accessibility is similar but not identical to Tversky & Kahneman's (1973) availability heuristic (Higgins & King 1981:71).

On-Line Models

Like the accessibility model, the on-line model of evaluation recognizes that memory limitations prevent people from engaging in an exhaustive information search every time they form a preference. However, the on-line model portrays people as overcoming this limitation in a very different way (see e.g. Hastie & Park 1986, Bassili 1989).

Instead of basing an evaluation on whichever considerations happen to come to mind, the on-line model suggests that people form and maintain a running "evaluation counter" of certain objects. When an individual encounters new information about such objects, she brings an affect-laden "evaluation counter" (i.e. running tally) into working memory, updates it using the new information, and restores the counter to long-term memory.

An important aspect of this model is that, after updating her evaluation, the individual may forget the information that affected the evaluation. When asked to express their evaluation, people simply retrieve the evaluation counter without searching for the information on which it was based. Lodge et al (1989:401) explain that the result may be "that people can often tell you how much they like or dislike a book, movie, candidate, or policy [because they maintain a running evaluation] but not be able to recount the specific whys and wherefores for their overall evaluation..." This is in sharp contrast to memory-based models, in which individuals do not maintain a running evaluation counter and instead base their evaluations on whatever information they happen to remember.

Lodge and his colleagues have been at the forefront of developing an on-line model of candidate evaluation. Their experiments show that subjects who engage in on-line processing base their candidate evaluations on information that enters their evaluation counter (over time) rather than the bits of information that happen to be available in memory at the time the evaluation is rendered. For example, a pro-choice, tough-on-crime voter may receive campaign information that a candidate supports abortion rights and strict federal crime laws. As a result, the voter accesses and updates her on-line evaluation of the candidate in a favorable direction, and then quickly forgets her reasons for doing so while restoring the on-line evaluation in long-term memory. At a later time, when the voter needs to evaluate the candidate (e.g. cast a vote), she simply retrieves the positive on-line evaluation and thus offers a favorable candidate evaluation, even if she does not remember the candidate's stances. Thus, there may be no relationship between what the voter remembers and whom the voter prefers, or the relationship may reflect post hoc rationalizations.

If people form their evaluations on-line, then researchers should not expect people to remember and report the reasons for their preferences. This has a number of implications (Lodge et al 1995, Lodge & McGraw 1995). First, if the on-line model is accurate, then we should be wary of using recall measures such as open-ended like-dislike questions and issue-position questions to understand the basis for citizens' preferences. These recall information measures may have no relationship to actual preferences, or they may be rationalizations for preferences.

Indeed, Rahn et al (1994b) argue that the likes and dislikes that Kelley & Mirer (1974) use to explain candidate preference are actually post hoc rationalizations for on-line evaluations formed over time (also see Lau 1982; Lodge & Stroh 1993:257–61; Lodge et al 1995:311, 319–20).

Second, if voters form evaluations on-line, then we cannot judge the impact of a campaign by assessing how much campaign material voters remember, since a voter may use campaign information to update her evaluation and then dispose of the information (Lodge et al 1995). Both these points contradict memory-based models, which contend that what an individual happens to remember forms the ingredients for what she prefers (Hastie & Park 1986).

The on-line model also suggests that individual preferences are less susceptible to sudden shifts (Krosnick & Brannon 1993:965) than accessibility models would imply. In sharp contrast to accessibility models, the on-line model largely maintains the traditional view of preferences as more stable phenomena (Zaller 1992:50).

Memory-Based Versus On-Line

When do people form evaluations on-line and when do they base their evaluations on what is available in memory? The most basic answer is that people form evaluations on-line when they believe that a judgment will probably be required later (Hastie & Park 1986:262). In contrast, when an individual encounters information without a specific processing goal, or if the goal is to remember as much as possible, then the individual will probably not form an on-line evaluation. Moreover, when an individual lacks the motivation for accuracy or the opportunity to engage in an extended memory search, she may simply base her evaluation on whatever information happens to be accessible (Fazio 1990).

Which type of processing takes place in political settings? Although both Zaller (1992:279) and Lodge (see McGraw et al 1990) acknowledge that people may use different types of processing at different times, they disagree on the prominence of each type of processing.[2] Zaller (1992:279) argues that "the on-line model is inappropriate in the domain of political attitudes..." (also see Zaller 1992:50), whereas Lodge et al (1995:321) argue for the on-line model when they state, "we believe there are many circumstances (political campaigns being a case in point) under which memory does not play a critical mediating role" (also see Lodge 1995:119).

A possible explanation for the differences between Lodge's and Zaller's claims is that Lodge focuses on candidate evaluation whereas Zaller focuses on survey response more generally. In the case of candidate evaluation, people may anticipate that a judgment will be required later (i.e. they know that they will have to vote), and so they form on-line evaluations. In contrast, most people do not anticipate

---

[2]Zaller and Lodge also recognize that the on-line versus memory-based distinction is not always clear (see e.g. Hastie and Pennington 1989).

answering survey questions, and thus, they cannot access on-line evaluations when a surveyor surprises them with a question (see Kinder 1998b:813–14).

There is also some evidence that on-line processing occurs more often among political sophisticates, whereas memory-based processing occurs more often among those with less political sophistication (McGraw et al 1990, McGraw & Pinney 1990, Rahn et al 1994b; also see Jarvis & Petty 1996). Rahn et al (1994a) show, however, that the effect of political sophistication is context-dependent. They find that sophisticates typically engage in on-line candidate evaluation, regardless of the context, whereas less sophisticated people engage in on-line candidate evaluation in less demanding contexts (e.g. candidates presenting information sequentially) and memory-based evaluation in more demanding contexts (e.g. a debate between two candidates).

Preference Reversals and Their Implications

We close this section with a brief description of, and comment on, the implications of experimental results documenting preference reversals. A common assumption in the social sciences, particularly in microeconomic models, is that the comparative evaluations in a preference have at least two properties (Kreps 1990:19–22; see e.g. Arrow 1951:12–14, Downs 1957:6, Riker & Ordeshook 1973:16, Morrow 1994:18). The first property is that an individual cannot strictly prefer Policy A to Policy B while also strictly preferring Policy B to Policy A. The second property is that preferences are transitive, so that if an individual prefers Policy A to Policy B and Policy B to Policy C, then she must also prefer Policy A to Policy C. A third commonly assumed property of preferences, which is related to the first property, is that preferences are invariant, meaning that "different representations of the same choice problem should yield the same preference" (Tversky & Kahneman 1987:69).

Whether and when preferences have these properties is a point of great contention. Fueling this debate is the existence of experimental subjects whose preferences violate transitivity or invariance assumptions (e.g. Tversky 1969, Lichtenstein & Slovic 1971, Grether & Plott 1979, Kahneman & Tversky 1979, Tversky & Kahneman 1987, Quattrone & Tversky 1988, Tversky & Thaler 1990, Rabin 1998). Perhaps the most widely cited example is that of Tversky & Kahneman (1981, 1987). These researchers show that when choosing between risky prospects, people prefer risk-averse alternatives when the consequences of their choices are framed in terms of gains, and they prefer risk-seeking alternatives when equivalent consequences are framed in terms of losses. This work is consistent with a large literature showing that people's preferences, as expressed in surveys, change with alterations in question wording, format, or placement (e.g. Mueller 1973, Sullivan et al 1978, Schuman & Presser 1981, Brady & Ansolabehere 1989, Bishop et al 1982, Sears & Lau 1983, Tourangeau et al 1989, Zaller 1992). These types of examples are often taken as evidence that preferences are neither stable nor invariant (e.g. Bartels 1998).

Such "preference reversal" results have had an important impact on how social scientists think about choice. However, the implications of these results, particularly the results of Tversky & Kahneman, for the formal study of preferences are often overinterpreted. Tversky & Kahneman's results provide clear examples of the fact that people's preferences depend on the information that they are given. Describe abstract objects (e.g. policies regarding a distant, fictional population) in terms of deaths caused and people rank them in one manner. Describe equivalent objects in terms of lives saved and people may rank them differently. But such demonstrations do not imply that people cannot, or do not regularly, hold transitive and invariant preferences in many political contexts (Sniderman 2000).

The preference reversal results reveal a problem in a more basic—and often unstated—assumption in many rational choice models, particularly older ones. The assumption is that preferences are fixed and exogenous (e.g. changes in information do not alter preferences). Tversky & Kahneman's results clearly show that such an assumption is not viable in many cases of substantive interest. This valuable insight complements Simon's (1979, 1985) effort to make formal modeling more cognitive. However, their results do not show that people are incapable of holding transitive and invariant preferences either generally or in many of the substantive contexts that political scientists care about.

Indeed, there are all kinds of preferences that appear to be stable and invariant for most people, including favorite political party, favorite religion, and favorite sexual orientation. For the many substantive domains in which information changes do not induce preference change, no external validity is sacrificed by using the traditional modeling assumptions.

In sum, experimental work on the relationship between preferences and information has produced some of the social sciences' most important recent findings. At a minimum, these findings have led scholars to ask more pointed and constructive questions about the role of preferences in social science models (see e.g. Lacy 1997).

External Influences

Attempts to change the beliefs and preferences of others are a primary means of political action. In this section, we review scholarship on how such attempts affect political preferences. We focus on two categories of such studies: studies of persuasion and studies of strategic communication.

The first category contains the literature on political persuasion. Research on persuasion is relevant to preference formation because the point of persuasion is to change another's beliefs. Recent research clarifies the conditions under which attempts to change the beliefs of others succeed. The seconds category contains a literature whose logical foundations are game theoretic. Contributors to this literature clarify the mechanics of belief change in situations where people have an incentive to be strategic in what they say. Because it answers questions such as

"How do people choose whom to believe?", this literature clarifies the extent to which preferences are affected by the actions of others.[3]

Persuasion Studies

Persuasion, defined as "human communication designed to influence others by modifying their beliefs, values, or attitudes" (Simons 1976:21), plays an important role in politics. As Mutz et al (1996a:1) explain, "Politics, at its core, is about persuasion. It hinges not just on whether citizens at any one moment in time tend to favor one side of an issue over another, but on the numbers of them that can be brought, when push comes to shove, from one side to the other or, indeed, induced to leave the sidelines in order to take a side."

Persuasion has long been the subject of scholarly inquiry (see e.g. Hovland & Weiss 1951–1952, Hovland et al 1953, McGuire 1985, Petty & Cacioppo 1986, O'Keefe 1990, Eagly & Chaiken 1993, Petty & Wegener 1998). In recent years, political scientists have joined the debate in increasing numbers (see e.g. Sniderman et al 1991, Zaller 1992, 1996, Bartels 1993, Lupia 1994, Popkin 1994, Mutz et al 1996a, Gibson 1998, Kinder 1998a, Lupia & McCubbins 1998). We organize our review of this literature in the manner suggested by Lasswell (1948), who asked, "Who says what to whom with what effect?" Lasswell's question reminds us that there are three component parts of a persuasive attempt: the recipient (whom), the message (what), and the source (who).

Recipient Effects   Sniderman et al (1991:8) explain, "People make up their minds in different ways." Theirs is among recent work that examines how individual differences affect the impact of new information on beliefs and evaluations. For example, some recipients are persuaded by messages that others find unpersuasive, and researchers of recipient effects want to know why.

Perhaps the most studied recipient characteristic is the amount of political information the recipient possesses, also known as the recipient's political awareness, expertise, involvement, knowledge, or sophistication (see e.g. Luskin 1987, Krosnick 1990, Sniderman et al 1990, Zaller 1992, Krosnick & Brannon 1993, Delli Carpini & Keeter 1996, Popkin & Dimock 2000). Many political scientists working in this area agree that (*a*) for one person to change another's beliefs, the information recipient must receive and accept the message (McGuire 1968, Zaller 1992); (*b*) the most aware individuals are more likely to receive new political information; and (*c*) the most aware individuals' beliefs are less likely to be changed by new information. The basis for this last point is the finding that well-informed (or highly aware) people are more likely to carefully and critically evaluate the messages they receive (see e.g. Zaller 1992, McGraw & Hubbard 1996, Cobb & Kuklinski 1997).

---

[3]Because of space limitations, this chapter does not describe research on persuasion in particular substantive domains such as mass media, or research on socialization (e.g. by neighbors and parents). See Kinder (1998a,b) for such reviews.

An increasingly common finding in this type of work is that people who are moderate in their awareness/information scores are the most likely to change their beliefs. These peoples' beliefs are thought to be more prone to change because they are more likely to receive new information than less aware persons and are more likely to be persuaded by new information than more aware persons. Zaller explains (1992:124) that "the relationship between awareness and attitude change may be nonmonotonic, that is, that persons at middle levels of awareness may be most likely to change" (also see Kinder 1998a:183–84, 1998b:812–15; Nelson et al 1997b:227).

The implications of this work for questions of preference formation are as follows. The best-informed and worst-informed persons in the population have stable beliefs and evaluations about a wide range of political objects. As a result, they have stable preferences as well. The preference stability of the best-informed persons comes from the fact that they are already very knowledgeable, which gives them the ability to generate internal counterarguments and limits the extent to which new information surprises them. The preference stability of the worst-informed persons comes from the fact that they receive little feedback about their current beliefs and, therefore, little stimulation for preference change. Other citizens' preferences are more susceptible to change.

Message Effects   How the content of a message affects the preferences of a listener can be difficult to study. Consider, for example, an attempt to determine how certain presidential phrasings affect the extent to which people prefer a president's actions. Such a determination requires researchers to somehow identify and separate all of the other environmental factors that could affect beliefs or preference changes. This task is not easy. As a result, such studies are not numerous, particularly in political science. However, some political scientists have designed clever ways to uncover message effects.

Cobb & Kuklinski (1997), for example, exposed experimental subjects to arguments about the North American Free Trade Agreement (NAFTA) and health care. For each issue, they varied the structure of the argument in multiple ways. In one of the variations, they exposed subjects to either an argument that was in favor of the policy (pro) or an argument that was against the policy (con). Cobb & Kuklinski (1997:115) find that "con arguments win the day." This is consistent with their expectation (1997:91) that when "making political decisions, [people] place more emphasis on avoiding potential losses than on obtaining potential gains" (also see Lau 1985). The status quo bias they find resembles findings elsewhere in the social sciences (e.g. Samuelson & Zeckhauser 1988).

These findings have important implications for the politics of preference formation. Chief among these implications is the attractiveness of "going negative" as a political strategy (e.g. Ansolabehere & Iyengar 1995). If people are more concerned about losses than gains, or if negative information about a particular candidate helps citizens draw finer distinctions between competing candidates, then citizens have a greater incentive to attend to negative information, and information providers have a greater incentive to supply negative information. Such incentives will change the stream of information available to many citizens in ways that increase the likelihood that negative information will be the platform from which preferences emerge.

Source Effects   Many political messages come from known sources, such as the President, a party leader, a prominent politician, a media figure, or an interest group. Unlike research on message effects, explorations of the dynamics of source effects are abundant. This work has demonstrated the effect of source characteristics such as the speaker's trustworthiness (Popkin 1994:47), public approval (Page et al 1987, Mondak 1993:195), insider status (Carmines & Kuklinski 1990:248), accuracy and objectivity (Iyengar & Kinder 1985), expert status (Page et al 1987), likeability (O'Keefe 1990:107; also see Brady & Sniderman 1985), party reputation (Iyengar & Valentino 2000), and ideology (Zaller 1992:47).

Kuklinski & Hurley (1994, 1996) provide a simple and effective example of such research. The researchers gave experimental subjects the following passage:

> We would like to get your reaction to a statement that [SPEAKER]
> recently made. He was quoted in the *New York Times* as saying that
> African-Americans must stop making excuses and rely much more on
> themselves to get ahead in society. Please indicate how much you agree
> or disagree with [SPEAKER]'s statement.

Respondents randomly received the statement either without attribution to a speaker or attributed to one of the following speakers: Ted Kennedy, George Bush, Clarence Thomas, or Jesse Jackson. Kuklinski & Hurley find that African-American respondents demonstrated significantly greater agreement with the statement when it was attributed to Jackson or Thomas than when it was attributed to Kennedy or Bush (or when no attribution was given). African-American respondents were much more persuaded when the statement came from an African-American source than when the same statement came from a Caucasian source. The ideology of the speaker had a far smaller effect.

Lupia & McCubbins (1998) use a series of models, laboratory experiments, and survey experiments to probe more deeply into how people acquire and process information in political settings. They prove that persuasion requires that the receiver perceive the speaker to be knowledgeable and to share her interests. The speaker's actual knowledge and interests, factors employed in many studies of persuasion, are of secondary importance. This result implies that the receiver's perception of the speaker's knowledge and interests are the fundamental source effects. All other speaker attributes—such as a speaker's attractiveness, party, race, likeability, ideology, or reputation—affect persuasion only if they affect the listener's perception of the speaker's knowledge or interests.

Lupia & McCubbins' many experiments put their most critical findings to the test. In a survey experiment, for example, they ask respondents whether they think spending money to build prisons is a good or bad idea. Before posing the question, however, they expose many of the respondents to a positive or negative endorsement by Rush Limbaugh or Phil Donahue. They find that respondents follow their endorser's advice when they perceive the endorser both to be knowledgeable and to share their interests. Further, it is these two variables that mediate persuasion and not likability, partisanship, or ideology. This and related laboratory experiments provide strong support for the conclusion that a receiver's perceptions of a speaker's interests and knowledge are primary factors in determining whether phenomena such as speeches, advertisements, or threats from abroad will affect the preferences of their intended audiences.

Strategic Communication Studies

Outside of political science, most empirical studies of preferences take place in a laboratory environment. Many of these studies follow the rules of the experimental paradigm so dominant in psychology, in which the experimenter picks the stimulus and the sole point of the experiment is to measure the subject's response. Although such studies are very informative, many political contexts differ in an important way.

In politics, many people provide information to others in an explicit attempt to change beliefs, attitudes, or preferences. When a speaker wants to express an idea, there are often multiple ways to frame the issue at hand and choices to be made about the amount of information to provide. If such speakers base their choice of what to say on an audience's likely reaction, we say that the speakers have chosen their words strategically.

When speakers choose their words strategically, two things happen. First, the content and amount of available information can change. Second, recipients of such information may have an incentive to process it differently. As a result, when speakers choose their words strategically, it can affect the information received, and consequently the preferences held, by the recipients.

Untangling the implications of strategic behavior for preference formation is tricky. An emerging branch of scholarship in political science, however, has provided some insights. Much of this work follows from the advent of strategic communication models (see e.g. Spence 1974, Crawford & Sobel 1982). Scholars use these models to clarify how a speaker's characteristics affect the persuasiveness of what she says. The value of the models lies in their ability to generate precise and general insights about preference formation.

In the last two decades, political scientists have introduced strategic communication models that provide precise insights about persuasion and preference formation in important political contexts (see Banks 1991 for a review).[4] Calvert (1985), for example, offers one of the earliest signs of the influence of strategic

---

[4] Most formal modelers rely on the maxim that preferences are fixed and exogenous. However, the preferences treated as such are used in a model to define an actor's goals at the outset of a game. When such models involve the possibility of belief change, they involve the possibility that some actors will come to hold different rankings over the options before them later in the game. If such a change is caused by new information, as opposed to a change in the choice set, then rankings changes are preference changes.

communication models. He integrates Bayes' rule—which plays an important role in many strategic communication models—into a decision-theoretic model of information processing. Calvert uses the framework to derive conditions under which a rational actor will engage in "selective exposure"—a behavior in which people pay greater attention to speakers with known biases. This work is important because many scholars use concepts such as selective exposure as assumptions in models of bounded rationality, many of which are presented as an alternative to rational actor models. Calvert, by contrast, derives selective exposure from a rational actor model (see Gerber & Green 1998 for a different view). His work is important, in the context of preference formation research because it shows how belief change is derivable from first principles about actor objectives and clarifies the incentives facing political information seekers—incentives that will affect what information they receive and which preferences they come to hold.

Gilligan & Krehbiel (1987, 1989) were among the first political scientists to use a strategic communication model explicitly to explain an aspect of politics relevant to preference formation. Their efforts clarify how amendment rules on the floor of the US House of Representatives affect the incentives of committee specialists to seek out and provide detailed information about complex legislative proposals. They derive conditions under which closed rules, which prevent the floor from amending committee bills, are beneficial to the median floor member. This beneficial effect arises because the closed rule, which appears to reduce the power of the floor median, gives committee specialists who disagree with the floor median an incentive to find and provide information that reduces everyone's uncertainty. The closed rule works in this way because it allows powerful members on the floor of the House to pre-commit to not overturn certain committee proposals. This pre-committal, in turn, gives the specialists a reward for providing information that makes everyone better off.

This research not only reveals why powerful members of Congress may rationally relinquish their ability to amend committee proposals, it also tells us about the effects of legislative rules and institutions on legislative preferences. It shows that a simple institutional change, such as one that prevents floor amendments to committee bills, changes the quantity and character of the information available to legislators. As a result, this work provides a stirring example of how institutional choices affect the informational foundations from which legislators' preferences can change.

Lupia & McCubbins (1998) use models and experiments to show how political institutions affect preference formation by altering a receiver's perceptions of a speaker's knowledge and interests. They reveal conditions under which a speaker is more likely to reveal what he knows when a third party acts as a potential verifier or when the speaker faces a penalty for lying. This kind of research unites insights from the study of persuasion with the logic of the new institutionalism to provide precise statements about how the context in which political decision-makers interact will affect the information they receive. As a result, this kind of research clarifies the effects of particular institutional choices on the preferences that people are likely to hold.

CONCLUSION

Political scientists are active contributors to the effort to understand why people want what they want. The way forward in this effort for political science is to integrate new knowledge about human cognition and the strategic requirements of political life into existing research programs (for parallel arguments, see Denzau & North 1994, Sniderman 2000). To better understand the formation of political preferences, we must pay closer attention to extant knowledge about basic cognitive tendencies. But this is not enough, because politics is not about individual choices made in isolation; it is collective decision-making in circumstances where individual objectives cannot be achieved simultaneously. It presupposes disagreement and necessitates the possibility of strategic action. The possibility of strategic action affects the quality of information that people receive as well as their incentives for information processing. This fact leads political actors to form preferences differently than they would in many nonpolitical settings. Because the success of many policies and political endeavors (e.g. a presidential campaign, changes in the tax code, or an affirmative action policy) depends on often untested assumptions about how preferences form, substantial public value can be derived from learning more about the unique aspects of political preference formation.

ACKNOWLEDGMENT

We thank Samuel L Popkin for helpful advice.

Visit the Annual Reviews home page at www.AnnualReviews.org

LITERATURE CITED

Aldrich JH, Sullivan JL, Borgida E. 1989. Foreign affairs and issue voting: do presidential candidates waltz before a blind audience? *Am. Polit. Sci. Rev.* 83:123–41

Ansolabehere S, Iyengar S. 1995. *Going Negative: How Political Advertisements Shrink & Polarize the Electorate.* New York: Free

Arrow KJ. 1951. *Social Choice and Individual Values.* New York: Wiley

Banks JS. 1991. *Signaling Games in Political Science.* Chur, Switzerland: Harwood Acad.

Bartels LM. 1993. Messages received: the po-

litical impact of media exposure. *Am. Polit. Sci. Rev.* 87:267–85

Bartels LM. 1998. *Democracy With Attitudes.* Presented at Annu. Meet. Am. Polit. Sci. Assoc., Boston, MA

Bassili JN, ed. 1989. *On-Line Cognition in Person Perception.* Hillsdale, NJ: Lawrence Erlbaum

Bishop GF, Oldendick RW, Tuchfarber AJ. 1982. Political information processing: question order and context effects. *Polit. Behav.* 4:177–200

Brady HE, Ansolabehere S. 1989. The nature of

utility functions in mass politics. *Am. Polit. Sci. Rev.* 83:143–63

Brady HE, Sniderman PM. 1985. Attitude attribution: a group basis for political reasoning. *Am. Polit. Sci. Rev.* 79:1061–78

Bruner JS. 1957. On perceptual readiness. *Psychol. Rev.* 64:123–52

Calvert RL. 1985. The value of biased information: a rational choice model of political advice. *J. Polit.* 47:530–55

Cappella JN, Jamieson KH. 1997. *Spiral of Cynicism: The Press and the Public Good.* New York: Oxford Univ. Press

Carmines EG, Kuklinski JH. 1990. Incentives, opportunities, and the logic of public opinion in American political representation. In *Information and Democratic Processes*, ed. JA Ferejohn, JH Kuklinski. Urbana: Univ. Ill. Press

Chong D. 1993. How people think, reason, and feel about rights and liberties. *Am. J. Polit. Sci.* 37:867–99

Churchland PS, Sejnowski TJ. 1992. *The Computational Brain.* Cambridge, MA: MIT Press

Clark A. 1993. *Associative Engines: Connectionism, Concepts, and Representational Change.* Cambridge, MA: MIT Press

Clark A. 1997. *Being There: Putting Brain, Body, and World Together Again.* Cambridge, MA: MIT Press

Cobb MD, Kuklinski JH. 1997. Changing minds: political arguments and political persuasion. *Am. J. Polit. Sci.* 41:88–121

Crawford V, Sobel J. 1982. Strategic information transmission. *Econometrica* 50:1431–51

Delli Carpini MX, Keeter S. 1996. *What Americans Know About Politics and Why it Matters.* New Haven, CT: Yale Univ. Press

Denzau AT, North DC. 1994. Shared mental models: ideologies and institutions. *Kyklos* 47:3–31

Downs A. 1957. *An Economic Theory of Democracy.* New York: HarperCollins

Eagly AH, Chaiken S. 1993. *The Psychology of Attitudes.* Fort Worth, TX: Harcourt Brace College

Enelow JM, Hinich MJ. 1984. *The Spatial Theory of Voting: An Introduction.* New York: Cambridge Univ. Press

Fazio RH. 1990. Multiple processes by which attitudes guide behavior: the MODE model as an integrative framework. In *Advances in Experimental Social Psychology* Vol. 23, ed. MP Zanna, pp. 75–109. San Diego, CA: Academic

Fazio RH. 1995. Attitudes as object-evaluation associations: determinants, consequences, and correlates of attitude accessibility. In *Attitude Strength: Antecedents and Consequences*, ed. RE Petty, JA Krosnick, pp. 247–82. Mahwah, NJ: Lawrence Erlbaum

Fishbein M. 1963. An investigation of the relationships between beliefs about an object and the attitude toward that object. *Hum. Relat.* 16:233–40

Fishbein M. Ajzen I. 1975. *Belief, Attitude, Intention, and Behavior: An Introduction to Theory and Research. Reading,* MA: Addison-Wesley

Gerber A, Green DP. 1998. Rational learning and partisan attitudes. *Am. J. Polit. Sci.* 42:794–818

Gibson JL. 1998. A sober second thought: an experiment in persuading Russians to tolerate. *Am. J. Polit. Sci.* 42:819–50

Gilbert DT, Fiske ST, Lindzey G, eds. 1998. *Handbook of Social Psychology.* Boston: McGraw-Hill. 4th ed.

Gilligan TW, Krehbiel K. 1987. Collective decision-making and standing committees: an informational rationale for restrictive amendment procedures. *J. Law Econ. Organ.* 3:287–335

Gilligan TW, Krehbiel K. 1989. Asymmetric information and legislative rules with a heterogeneous committee. *Am. J. Polit. Sci.* 33: 459–90

Grether DM, Plott CR. 1979. Economic theory of choice and the preference reversal phenomenon. *Am. Econ. Rev.* 69:623–38

Hastie R, Park B. 1986. The relationship between memory and judgment depends on whether the judgment task is memory-based or on-line. *Psychol. Rev.* 93:258–68

Hastie R, Pennington N. 1989. Notes on the distinction between memory-based versus on-line judgments. See Bassili 1989, pp. 1–17

Higgins ET, King G. 1981. Social constructs: information-processing consequences of individual and contextual variability. In *Personality, Cognition, and Social Interaction*, ed. N Cantor, JF Kihlstrom, pp. 69–121. Hillsdale, NJ: Lawrence Erlbaum

Holland JH, Holyoak KJ, Nisbett RE, Thagard PR. 1986. *Induction: Processes of Inference, Learning, and Discovery.* Cambridge, MA: MIT Press

Hovland CI, Janis IL, Kelley HH. 1953. *Communication and Persuasion: Psychological Studies of Opinion Change.* Westport, CT: Greenwood

Hovland CI, Weiss W. 1951–1952. The influence of source credibility on communication effectiveness. *Public Opin. Q.* 15:635–50

Huckfeldt R, Levine J, Morgan W, Sprague J. 1999. Accessibility and the political utility of partisan and ideological orientations. *Am. J. Polit. Sci.* 43:888–911

Iyengar S. 1990. The accessibility bias in politics: television news and public opinion. *Int. J. Public Opin. Res.* 2:1–15

Iyengar S. 1991. *Is Anyone Responsible? How Television Frames Political Issues.* Chicago: Univ. Chicago Press

Iyengar S. Kinder DR. 1985. Psychological accounts of agenda-setting. In *Mass Media and Political Thought: An Information-Processing Approach*, ed. S Kraus, RM Perloff, pp. 117–40. Beverly Hills, CA: Sage

Iyengar S. Kinder DR. 1987. *News That Matters: Television and American Opinion.* Chicago: Univ. Chicago Press

Iyengar S. Valentino N. 2000. Who says what? Source credibility as a mediator of campaign advertising. In *Elements of Reason: Cognition, Choice, and the Bounds of Rationality*, ed. A Lupia, MD McCubbins, SL Popkin. New York: Cambridge Univ. Press. In press

Jacobs LR, Shapiro RY. 1994. Issues, candidate image, and priming: the use of private polls in Kennedy's 1960 presidential campaign. *Am. Polit. Sci. Rev.* 88:527–40

James W. 1890. *The Principles of Psychology.* New York: Dover

Jarvis WBG, Petty RE. 1996. The need to evaluate. *J. Pers. Soc. Psychol.* 70:172–94

Johnston R, Blais A, Brady HE, Crete J. 1992. *Letting the People Decide: Dynamics of a Canadian Election.* Stanford, CA: Stanford Univ. Press

Kahneman D, Tversky A. 1979. Prospect theory: an analysis of decision under risk. *Econometrica* 47:263–91

Kandel ER, Schwartz JH, Jessell TM. 1995. *Essentials of Neural Science and Behavior.* Norwalk, CT: Appleton & Lange

Kelley S Jr. 1983. *Interpreting Elections.* Princeton, NJ: Princeton Univ. Press

Kelley S Jr, Mirer TW. 1974. The simple act of voting. *Am. Polit. Sci. Rev.* 68:572–91

Kinder DR. 1993. Coming to grips with the holy ghost. In *Experimental Foundations of Political Science*, ed. DR Kinder, TR Palfrey, pp. 43–51. Ann Arbor: Univ. Mich. Press

Kinder DR. 1998a. Communication and opinion. *Annu. Rev. Polit. Sci.* 1:167–97

Kinder DR. 1998b. Opinion and action in the realm of politics. See Gilbert et al 1998, pp. 778–867

Kreps DM. 1990. *A Course in Microeconomic Theory.* Princeton, NJ: Princeton Univ. Press

Krosnick JA. 1988. The role of attitude importance in social evaluation: a study of policy preferences, presidential candidate evaluations, and voting behavior. *J. Pers. Soc. Psychol.* 55:196–210

Krosnick JA. ed. 1990. *Thinking About Politics: Comparisons of Experts and Novices. Soc. Cogn.* 8:1–158 (Spec. issue)

Krosnick JA. Brannon LA. 1993. The impact of the Gulf War on the ingredients of presidential evaluations: multidimensional effects of political involvement. *Am. Polit. Sci. Rev.* 87:963–75

Kuklinski JH, Hurley NL. 1994. On hearing and interpreting political messages: a cautionary tale of citizen cue-taking. *J. Polit.* 56:729–51

Kuklinski JH, Hurley NL. 1996. It's a matter of interpretation. See Mutz et al 1996b, pp. 125–44

Lacy D. 1997. *A theory of nonseparable preferences in survey responses.* Presented at Annu. Meet. Polit. Methodol. Soc., Columbus, OH

Lakoff G. 1987. *Women, Fire, and Dangerous Things: What Categories Reveal about the Mind.* Chicago: Univ. Chicago Press

Lakoff G. Johnson M. 1999. *Philosophy in the Flesh: The Embodied Mind and Its Challenge to Western Thought.* New York: Basic Books

Lasswell HD. 1948. The structure and function of communication in society. In *The Communication of Ideas: Religion and Civilization Series,* ed. L Bryson. New York: Harper & Row

Lau RR. 1982. Negativity in political perception. *Polit. Behav.* 4:353–77

Lau RR. 1985. Two explanations for negativity effects in political behavior. *Am. J. Polit. Sci.* 29:119–38

Lau RR. 1989. Construct accessibility and electoral choice. *Polit. Behav.* 11:5–32

Lichtenstein S, Slovic P. 1971. Reversals of preference between bids and choices in gambling decisions. *J. Exp. Psychol.* 89:46–55

Lodge M. 1995. Toward a procedural model of candidate evaluation. In *Political Judgment: Structure and Process,* ed. M Lodge, KM McGraw, pp. 111–39. Ann Arbor: Univ. Mich. Press

Lodge M, McGraw KM, eds. 1995. *Political Judgment: Structure and Process.* Ann Arbor: Univ. Mich. Press

Lodge M, McGraw KM, Stroh P. 1989. An impression-driven model of candidate evaluation. *Am. Polit. Sci. Rev.* 83:399–419

Lodge M, Steenbergen MR, Brau S. 1995. The responsive voter: campaign information and the dynamics of candidate evaluation. *Am. Polit. Sci. Rev.* 89:309–26

Lodge M, Stroh P. 1993. Inside the mental voting booth: an impression-driven process model of candidate evaluation. In *Explo-*

rations in Political Psychology, ed. S Iyengar, WJ McGuire, pp. 225–63. Durham, NC: Duke Univ. Press

Lodge M, Stroh P, Wahlke J. 1990. Black-box models of candidate evaluation. *Polit. Behav.* 12:5–18

Lupia A. 1994. Shortcuts versus encyclopedias: information and voting behavior in California insurance reform elections. *Am. Polit. Sci. Rev.* 88:63–76

Lupia A, McCubbins MD. 1998. *The Democratic Dilemma: Can Citizens Learn What They Need To Know?* New York: Cambridge Univ. Press

Luskin RC. 1987. Measuring political sophistication. *Am. J. Polit. Sci.* 31:856–99

McCauley RN, ed. 1996. *The Churchlands and Their Critics.* Cambridge, MA: Blackwell

McGraw KM, Hubbard C. 1996. Some of the people some of the time: individual differences in acceptance of political accounts. See Mutz et al 1996, pp. 145–70

McGraw KM, Lodge M, Stroh P. 1990. On-line processing in candidate evaluation: the effects of issue order, issue importance, and sophistication. *Polit. Behav.* 12:41–58

McGraw KM, Pinney N. 1990. The effects of general and domain-specific expertise on political memory and judgment. *Soc. Cogn.* 8:9–30

McGuire WJ. 1968. Personality and susceptibility to social influence. In *Handbook of Personality Theory and Research,* ed. EF Borgatta, WW Lambert, pp. 1130–87. Chicago: Rand-McNally

McGuire WJ. 1985. Attitudes and attitude change. In *Handbook of Social Psychology,* ed. G Lindzey, E Aronson, pp. 233–346. New York: Random House

Mondak JJ. 1993. Source cues and policy approval. *Am. J. Polit. Sci.* 37:186–212

Morrow JD. 1994. *Game Theory for Political Scientists.* Princeton, NJ: Princeton Univ. Press

Mueller JE. 1973. *War, Presidents, and Public Opinion.* New York: Wiley

Mutz DC, Sniderman PM, Brody RA. 1996a. Political persuasion: the birth of a field of study. See Mutz et al 1996b, pp. 1–14

Mutz DC, Sniderman PM, Brody RA, eds. 1996b. *Political Persuasion and Attitude Change.* Ann Arbor: Univ. Mich. Press

Nelson TE, Clawson RA, Oxley ZM. 1997a. Media framing of a civil liberties conflict and its effect on tolerance. *Am. Polit. Sci. Rev.* 91:567–83

Nelson TE, Oxley ZM, Clawson RA. 1997b. Toward a psychology of framing effects. *Polit. Behav.* 19:221–46

Newell A. 1990. *Unified Theories of Cognition.* Cambridge, MA: Harvard Univ. Press

O'Keefe DJ. 1990. *Persuasion: Theory and Research.* Newbury Park, CA: Sage

Ottati VC, Riggle EJ, Wyer RS Jr, Schwarz N, Kuklinski J. 1989. Cognitive and affective bases of opinion survey responses. *J. Pers. Soc. Psychol.* 57:404–15

Page BI, Shapiro RY, Dempsey GR. 1987. What moves public opinion? *Am. Polit. Sci. Rev.* 81:23–43

Petty RE, Cacioppo JT. 1986. *Communication and Persuasion: Central and Peripheral Routes to Attitude Change.* New York: Springer-Verlag

Petty RE, Wegener DT. 1998. Attitude change: multiple roles for persuasion variables. See Gilbert et al 1998, pp. 323–90

Pinker S. 1997. *How the Mind Works.* New York: Norton

Popkin SL. 1994. *The Reasoning Voter: Communication and Persuasion in Presidential Campaigns.* Chicago: Univ. Chicago Press. 2nd ed.

Popkin SL, Dimock MA. 2000. Knowledge, trust, and international reasoning. In *Elements of Reason: Cognition, Choice, and the Bounds of Rationality,* ed. A Lupia, MD McCubbins, SL Popkin. New York: Cambridge Univ. Press. In press

Price V, Tewksbury D. 1997. News values and public opinion: a theoretical account of media priming and framing. In *Progress in Communication Sciences: Advances in Persua-*

sion, ed. GA Barnett, FJ Boster, 13:173–212. Greenwich, CT: Ablex

Quattrone G, Tversky A. 1988. Contrasting rational and psychological analyses of political choice. *Am. Polit. Sci. Rev.* 82:719–36

Rabin M. 1998. Psychology and economics. *J. Econ. Lit.* 36:11–46

Rahn WM, Aldrich JH, Borgida E. 1994a. Individual and contextual variations in political candidate appraisal. *Am. Polit. Sci. Rev.* 88:193–99

Rahn WM, Krosnick JA, Breuning M. 1994b. Rationalization and derivation processes in survey studies of political candidate evaluation. *Am. J. Polit. Sci.* 38:582–600

Riker WH, Ordeshook PC. 1973. *An Introduction to Positive Political Theory.* Englewood Cliffs, NJ: Prentice-Hall

Samuelson W, Zeckhauser R. 1988. Status quo bias in decision making. *J. Risk Uncertainty* 1:7–59

Schuman H, Presser S. 1981. *Questions and Answers in Attitude Surveys: Experiments in Question Form, Wording, and Context.* New York: Academic

Sears DO, Lau RR. 1983. Inducing apparently self-interested political preferences. *Am. J. Polit. Sci.* 27:223–52

Sherman SJ, Mackie DM, Driscoll DM. 1990. Priming and the differential use of dimensions in evaluation. *Pers. Soc. Psychol. Bull.* 16:405–18

Simon HA. 1979. *Models of Thought.* New Haven, CT: Yale Univ. Press

Simon HA. 1985. Human nature in politics: the dialogue of psychology with political science. *Am. Polit. Sci. Rev.* 79:293–304

Simons HW. 1976. *Persuasion: Understanding, Practice, and Analysis.* Reading, MA: Addison-Wesley

Sniderman PM. 2000. Taking sides: a fixed choice theory of political reasoning. In *Elements of Reason: Cognition, Choice, and the Bounds of Rationality,* ed. A Lupia, MD McCubbins, SL Popkin. New York: Cambridge Univ. Press. In press

Sniderman PM, Brody RA, Tetlock PE. 1991.

Reasoning and Choice: Explorations in Political Psychology. New York: Cambridge Univ. Press

Sniderman PM, Glaser JM, Griffin R. 1990. Information and electoral choice. In *Information and Democratic Processes,* ed. JA Ferejohn, JH Kuklinski, pp. 160–85. Urbana: Univ. Ill. Press

Spence AM. 1974. *Market Signaling: Informational Transfer in Hiring and Related Screening Processes.* Cambridge, MA: Harvard Univ. Press

Sullivan JL, Piereson JE, Marcus GE. 1978. Ideological constraint in the mass public: a methodological critique and some new findings. *Am. J. Polit. Sci.* 22:233–49

Tourangeau R, Rasinski KA, Bradburn N, D'Andrade R. 1989. Belief accessibility and context effects in attitude measurement. *J. Exp. Soc. Psychol.* 25:401–21

Tversky A. 1969. Intransitivity of preferences. *Psychol. Rev.* 76:31–48

Tversky A, Kahneman D. 1973. Availability: a heuristic for judging frequency and probability. *Cogn. Psychol.* 4:207–32

Tversky A, Kahneman D. 1981. The framing of decisions and the psychology of choice. *Science* 211:453–58

Tversky A, Kahneman D. 1987. Rational choice and the framing of decisions. In *Rational Choice: The Contrast Between Economics and Psychology,* ed. RM Hogarth, MW Reder. Chicago: Univ. Chicago Press

Tversky A, Thaler RH. 1990. Preference reversals. *J. Econ. Persp.* 4:201–11

van der Pligt J, Eiser JR. 1984. Dimensional salience, judgment, and attitudes. In *Attitudinal Judgment,* ed. JR Eiser, pp. 161–77. New York: Spinger-Verlag

Wilson TD, Hodges SD. 1992. Attitudes as temporary constructions. In *The Construction of Social Judgments,* ed. LL Martin, A Tesser, pp. 37–65. Hillsdale, NJ: Lawrence Erlbaum

Wyer RS Jr, Srull TK. 1989. *Memory and Cognition in Their Social Context.* Hillsdale, NJ: Lawrence Erlbaum

Zaller J. 1992. *The Nature and Origins of Mass Opinion.* New York: Cambridge Univ. Press

Zaller J. 1996. The myth of massive media impact revived: new support for a discredited idea. See Mutz et al 1996b, pp. 17–78

Zaller J, Feldman S. 1992. A simple theory of the survey response: answering questions versus revealing preferences. *Am. J. Polit. Sci.* 36:579–616

Annu. Rev. Polit. Sci. 2000. 3:25–42

CONSTRUCTING EFFECTIVE ENVIRONMENTAL REGIMES

George W. Downs

Department of Politics, New York University, 715 Broadway, New York, New York 10003; e-mail: George.Downs@nyu.edu

Key Words environmental agreements, effectiveness, multilateral institutions, political economy, constructivism

■ **Abstract**   In the environmental literature, accounts of cooperative progress commonly emphasize the activity and leadership of nongovernmental organizations, as well as the constitutive roles that environmental regimes play by legitimizing, by promoting reflectivist discourse, and by redefining roles. This essay lays out the differences between the constructivist and political-economic theories of environmental regime effectiveness and examines the extent to which the constructivist emphasis is empirically justified by three recent collections of case studies. Of the surprisingly modest effects that environmental regimes have had, most appear to have come through the use of mechanisms that already play a prominent role in the political economy literature. Constructivist processes, despite the attention they have received, appear to have had only a marginal impact.

INTRODUCTION

The political science literature on environmental cooperation differs from the literatures of security and trade regimes in at least three ways. One difference is that the environmental literature emphasizes the impact of organizational and institutional strategies on cooperation far more than the effects of socioeconomic and political variables. For every article describing the role of per capita income, type of government, or relative price changes, there are ten that describe the role of nongovernmental organizations (NGOs). A second difference is that both formal and statistical models are far more scarce in the environmental literature; one sees the occasional flowchart or table but equations of any sort are exceedingly rare. Finally, the literature on environmental regulation is far more self-consciously prescriptive; recommendations about how to best promote cooperation are the rule rather than the exception.

Part of the explanation for these differences is undoubtedly that the vast majority of individuals who do research on environmental cooperation are active environmentalists who want to increase the effectiveness of both existing and future regimes. They focus on institutions because institutions promise policy leverage and are amenable to influence. An equally important part of the explanation appears to be that environmental researchers typically view state preferences as being far more malleable than do political economists.

In addition to sharing with political economists the belief that institutions make coordination easier by lowering transaction costs and influence state policy strategies by altering payoffs, environmental researchers also believe that institutions can reconstruct states' identities and their underlying value structures by relying on the transforming power of a variety of social processes. This belief helps explain the nature of the methodology that dominates the field and its institutional focus. The extreme malleability of preferences makes the coefficients and equilibria that might emerge from conventional statistical and formal models seem irrelevant—reflecting, at best, interesting snapshots of an as-yet-undefined historical process. The malleability of state preferences also suggests that social scientists have an unprecedented opportunity to influence environmental outcomes by influencing the institutions that are in a position to reconstruct state preferences, notably regulatory institutions and NGOs.

This essay questions the extent to which this belief in the ability of social processes to alter states' utility functions is substantiated in the growing literature on environmental effectiveness and considers the implications of the answer for estimating the relative explanatory power of constructivist and political economic theories about the role of institutions in the evolution of cooperation. First, however, it is necessary to outline the two theories, highlighting their differences and their effects on empirical expectations about the impact of institutions on the evolution of environmental cooperation.

THE CONSTRUCTIVIST PERSPECTIVE AND EFFECTIVENESS

Constructivism is a notoriously slippery concept that has had many different theoretical representations in connection with institutions (Ruggie 1998, Young 1999, Kingsbury 1997). This essay focuses exclusively on those constructivist processes that are argued to lead to the reconstruction of state identities and the transformation of states' underlying value structures. This focus eliminates processes such as the diffusion of information and the development of new knowledge, neither of which usually leads to a reconstruction of a state's underlying preference structure and both of which have long been integral to the political economy and utilitarian perspectives. Specifically, constructivism is represented here by three processes that play virtually no role in any rival paradigm: legitimation, role definition, and reflectivist appraisal.

Legitimation

Young & Levy (1999:24) argue that those who regard the rules and provisions of regimes as legitimate or authoritative will often comply with their requirements without engaging in detailed calculations of the benefits and costs of doing so. In the case of individuals, this behavior results from socialization. At the institutional level, it occurs through internalization or routinization; bureaucrats charged with implementing a given regime do so without extensive calculations and, if questioned, justify their actions by referring to their mandate.

Constructivists expect the legitimacy of a regime's rules to be a function of the process by which the regime was created and by which the rules were made and of how long the regime has been in place. Frequently mentioned as determinants of legitimacy are democratic decision-making, high consensus standards, and the degree of distributive fairness embodied in standards. The length of time a regime has existed is important because the socialization of individuals grows deeper over time and because a bureaucracy's procedures multiply over time and also become progressively more routinized. Less often mentioned but probably also important is the set of states that support a particular regime standard. Developing countries are characteristically wary of rules that they view as having been designed and backed primarily by developed states.

Role Redefinition

Although regimes rarely create new actors, they do shape the identities and preferences of extant ones by defining roles and assigning them to the various actors. These new roles gradually generate new identities for the states that occupy them, and with these new identities come new interests (Wendt 1992:396–99). For example, the United Nations helped foster the creation of a host of new identities and leadership roles such "permanent member of the Security Council," "friend of the Secretary General," and "nonaligned state." To the extent that this redefinition of roles is driven by a nonutilitarian social process and is not simply an outcome of calculated bargaining, it can be considered a constitutive process.

The literature is not clear about the conditions that lead to significant role redefinition, but the examples given imply that it is related to the size of a regime and the complexity of its goals. Thus, we would expect relatively little role redefinition to emerge from a bilateral water management regime or even the Agreement for the Conservation of Polar Bears compared with the Climate Change Agreement or Convention of International Trade in Endangered Treaties.

Reflection

Reflectivist appraisal processes are more complicated and operate more subtly than legitimation or role redefinition. They generate cooperation by transforming underlying interests as states interact with each other. Wendt (1994) describes two such processes and another that is closely related. In the two processes that he groups together as strictly reflectivist, actors adopt identities by learning through interaction to see themselves as others see them. The more materially or psychologically dependent an actor is on others, the greater will be the impact of the perception of these external actors.

The first reflectivist process emphasizes the impact that cooperative interaction will have on the "other": "By showing others through cooperative acts that one expects them to be cooperators too, one changes the intersubjective knowledge in terms of which their identity is defined" (Wendt 1994:390). The second reflectivist process is a reflective variant of the first. By engaging in cooperative interaction, a state projects something about itself that redefines the intersubjective environment from which it derives its self-conception. Another state absorbs this new presentation of the cooperator, projects this new identity back, and resocializes the cooperator to a new conception of itself. Thus, an actor's self-concept will gradually change and the new identity (e.g. that of a cooperator) will be internalized (Wendt 1994:391). These two processes not only generate a level of cooperation greater than that predicted by a strategic, game-theoretic model, they also produce a convergence of identity such that actors learn to see themselves as "we" and are bound by certain norms.

The third reflectivist process involves the more self-conscious dimension of rhetorical practice, which takes the forms of discussion, dialogue, persuasion, and political argument. Although there is some overlap, this process is more fundamentally transformational and less information-based than that described in the literature of deliberative democracy (Habermas 1987; Elster 1998). According to Wendt (1994:391), "The goal of rhetorical practices in collective action is to create solidarity; thus they may have an important expressive function independent of their instrumental value in realizing collective goals." Acts of cooperation create a language of cooperation that then frames actors' responses to new events. In this way, cooperating engenders further cooperation. Wendt offers the examples of European statesmen talking about a "European identity" and of Gorbachev trying to end the Cold War with a rhetoric of "New Thinking" and a "common European home."

Constructivists and their sympathizers believe that over time these processes together can produce a far higher level of compliance and a far deeper level of cooperation than might be achieved if states were driven by utilitarian calculations alone.

The Transformational Design and Its Assumptions

Although legitimation, role redefinition, and reflectivist appraisal are always operating, their ability to achieve their full cooperative potential depends to some extent on how the regime is designed. Four widely prescribed design recommendations are incorporated into what is sometimes known as the transformational model. This design calls for a policy of inclusive, universal membership, modest initial obligations, consensual decision making, and a preference for conflict resolution techniques over enforcement mechanisms.

Each of the design principles represents an empirical expectation that is tied to the operation of one or more of the three constructivist processes.

1. The more inclusive a regime, the greater the level of cooperation it will produce. Political economists are wary about admitting into a regime states

that are likely to undermine its cooperative evolution out of self-interest (e.g. incorporating the more environmentally regressive oil-producing states into the Climate Change Regime). With their high level of confidence in the ability of institutions to mold state preferences, constructivists are comfortable absorbing the initial cost of incorporating recalcitrant states, anticipating that their goals will become more progressive after legitimation, role redefinition, and reflective appraisal have kicked in. Further, a large membership itself promotes socialization because as state policy makers come to view an environmental problem as a common concern, they will begin to see fulfillment of their state's obligations as intimately linked to its standing in the wider community of states (Chayes & Chayes 1995:27). Thus, activist states and regime officials can apply community pressure to cajole laggard states into increasing their commitment to addressing an environmental problem.

2. Weak rules lead to more effective regimes and more cooperation in the long run than do demanding obligations. Initially, commitments and obligations should consist of few, if any, specific performance targets or timetables. This maximizes participation. Soft law is preferable to hard law because weak standards effectively reduce the price of admission to the regime, thus enticing even the least committed members to join. Once the states are members, the three constructivist processes can transform their preferences toward embracing more ambitious binding commitments. As Levy (1993:76) says of the convention on long-range transboundary air pollution (LRTAP), initially a weak institution oriented only toward scientific research and ambiguous goals, "Weak rules permitted strong consensus-building powers, whereas strong rules would have generated hostility on the part of governments...." Generality and vagueness also promote the ongoing dialogue that transforms and socializes the member states toward more progressive normative development.

3. Consensual decision making produces greater effectiveness than do less demanding, more majoritarian rules. Even if they choose to abide by the wishes of the majority, states that vote against an obligation are likely to feel alienated from the regime and are therefore less likely to actively participate in subsequent discussions connected with it. This interferes with the operation of all three constructivist processes. Moreover, an institution that requires consensus signals that it and the rules it promulgates are legitimate.

4. Coercive enforcement mechanisms operate to sabotage the evolution of effective regimes. The transformational design begins from the assumption that states have a "propensity to comply" with their treaty obligations. Noncompliance with environmental treaties is caused primarily by ambiguous and vague rules, unavoidable time lags between fundamental reform and performance, and the lack of technical or administrative capacity to implement complex environmental regulation. Sanctions not only are inappropriate, it

is argued, but often do more harm than good. By alienating states, the regime reduces the extent to which they view its rules as legitimate and distances them from reflectivist processes. Both tendencies are exacerbated by the fact that only the most powerful states can organize a multilateral sanctioning response.

It is important to note that the transformational design is no mere academic exercise. Fourteen of the 50 multilateral environmental agreements of which the United States is a member, including the Climate Change Convention, possess at least three of its four design prescriptions, and its underlying logic plays a prominent role in policy discussions (Downs 1998:342).

THE POLITICAL ECONOMY PERSPECTIVE

Let us now turn to the political economy literature's expectations about the determinants of environmental regime effectiveness. Political economists make no attempt to explain the nature of utility rankings or underlying tastes but assume that they are exogenous. As such, political economists are agnostic about the role of the processes of legitimation, role redefinition, and reflection in shaping the underlying preferences of states (except insofar as they believe that the evidence suggests that such underlying preferences are relatively stable). Political economists are, however, interested in (a) how an actor's preference for one good as opposed to another is affected by relative prices and (b) how relative prices are determined by technology, information, and the changes in incentives that are brought about by the policies of institutions.

The operation of relative price changes can be quite subtle, and economists have evidenced considerable creativity in devising theoretical arguments and presenting data to show that apparent changes in an actor's underlying utility function are, in fact, effects of relative price changes (North 1990). Becker (1996) has even attempted to explain changes in behavior in addiction or after developing a taste for classical music as the result of an accumulation of what he calls consumption capital.

Even if relative price changes are not the predominant source of state preference changes in the area of environmental regulation, they are certainly important. Some of the relative price changes with the greatest impacts stem directly from the effects of environmentally hazardous processes such as deforestation, acid raid, and ozone depletion. Others are closely tied to technological innovations. For example, the success of the Paris Commission at controlling land-based sources of Northeast Atlantic pollution appears to have more to do with the availability of water-based "muds" than with a sudden willingness of states to embrace more stringent and costly measures. Technology was also the driving force behind the cessation of virtually all offshore dumping and incineration under the Oslo Convention for the Prevention of Marine Pollution by Dumping from Ships and Aircraft. Specifically, the cessation resulted from advances in land-based incineration that reduced the cost of hazardous waste incineration, not from the normative transformation of Britain's environmental policy. Finally, Dupont's development of an alternative to fluorocarbons played a key role in overcoming industry objections to the Montreal Protocol in the US (Benedick 1988).

Because political economists do not believe that state tastes can easily be reconstructed, their predictions and implicit design recommendations are quite different from those of constructivist-oriented scholars. On the predictive side, Barrett (1997) suggests that the incentive for states to remain outside an environmental agreement and "free ride" means that only small multilaterals, and large ones that are very shallow, can be totally self-enforcing in the sense that they are sustained solely by reciprocity rather than by a linkage relationship to an agreement in another area such as trade. Political economists also argue that the prospects for an effective agreement are improved by the active leadership of at least one and probably more than one of the world's great powers because of their economic and military leverage over smaller states. Conversely, they expect an agreement's prospects for effectiveness to be reduced insofar as it depends on the participation of nondemocratic states, because an absence of democratic institutions increases the chances that producer interests, rather than consumer interests, will predominate.

The Transformational Design from a Political Economy Perspective

Political economists express concern about the consequences of combining universal membership with a high consensus norm. If the preferences of more regressive states are not changed or are changed only very slowly, these states will be able to block any progress that might have been possible with a smaller membership. These opportunity costs can be substantial. If Britain had been admitted to the original Coal and Steel Agreement and had maintained the position that it did in fact hold for the next 20 years, the evolution of the European Union would have been far slower. Similarly, India and China would have been able to block the writing of an effective Nonproliferation Treaty (Downs et al 1998).

Political economists are also skeptical of the claim that enforcement hinders cooperation rather than being sometimes necessary to facilitate it. Although enforcement plays a small role in coordination regimes, such as those establishing rules for handling emergencies at sea or delineating the notification procedures to be used for nuclear accidents—where there is little incentive for a state to unilaterally defect—some form of enforcement often plays an important role in Prisoners' Dilemma–type agreements, such as a fishing agreement or the Climate Change Agreement, in which defection can be quite profitable (Downs 1998).

Constructivist theorists who believe that state preferences are most frequently changed by social forces would doubtless respond that the results of models with different assumptions and evidence about the historical importance of relative price changes are hardly conclusive. Even some economists, after all, acknowledge that there is evidence that purely constructivist forces can have an impact; for instance, the abolitionist movement succeeded in changing public opinion in Britain during the 1830s and in the northern states prior to the Civil War (North 1990:85). Is it not possible, the constructivists could ask, that more such examples might be uncovered if those searching for them were less negatively disposed to finding them than are most economists?

Constructivist theorists could further point out that the appearance of NGOs and the evolution of a more closely integrated global society are relatively new phenomena that may have dramatically increased the influence of outside forces on public opinion and state policy making. To the extent that today's world differs from the world of even only 30 years ago, is it unreasonable to believe that new rules hold sway? For better and worse, American culture has transformed the tastes of consumers all over the world. Is it not possible that a concerted campaign on the part of multinational institutions and NGOs or a pattern of continuous interaction between laggard states and more environmentally progressive states might be able to do the same?

Questions about the degree to which a state's underlying value structure can be reconstructed by social forces and about the relative importance of constructivist processes and political economic factors in shaping state preferences concerning the environment are unlikely to be resolved in the near future. However, new insights into these questions should be possible as we sift through the analyses of what has become an impressive number of environmental agreements. The following section considers the evidence contained in three recent collections of essays on effectiveness edited by Weiss & Jacobson (1998), Young (1999), and Victor et al (1998).

ASSESSING THE IMPACT OF CONSTRUCTIVIST PROCESSES

Compliance and Effectiveness

One way to assess the importance of constructivist processes is to examine their impact on compliance rates. Historically, international lawyers in particular have tended to tie compliance closely to effectiveness on the grounds that understanding the former is a prerequisite for predicting the latter. There are, however, numerous conceptual problems associated with using compliance as a surrogate for effectiveness. Because treaty standards are endogenous in the sense that they represent a joint strategy of the states that set them, and because states and the politicians who run them are motivated to appear successful, actors have an incentive to tie the terms of agreements to what they expect to be able to achieve. As a consequence, most compliance rates are likely to be high, especially when the political costs associated with failure are likely to be significant.

It follows that the compliance rate associated with a given treaty may have no relationship whatsoever to effectiveness. States that cannot summon the political will or financial resources to solve a challenging environmental problem but wish to make a nominal gesture will set weak standards and then comply with them because they demand very little. Such standards, however, will rarely be effective. To further confuse matters, it is possible that partial compliance with a treaty that contains ambitious standards could be far more effective.

Beyond the problems posed by endogeneity, compliance studies tend to suffer from other methodological problems common to all areas of effectiveness research, especially those based on case studies. Particularly rare, for example, are careful counterfactual estimates of what would have happened in the absence of a given intervention. Most commonly, an analyst interested in the effect of NGO activity simply studies a case in which such activity was present and assigns any progress in compliance or effectiveness to NGO activity, even though some of that progress might have occurred because of a technological breakthrough, the political efforts of a major state, or any number of other causes. Similarly, the analyst interested in state capacity will compare the compliance rates of high-capacity states with those of low-capacity states and assume that the difference between them represents the impact of capacity instead of other systematic differences in the two types of states (e.g. differences in per capita income or technology).

Engaging Countries: Strengthening Compliance with International Environmental Accords (Weiss & Jacobson 1998), the first of the three books this essay examines, recognizes many of the limitations just discussed, especially the problematic relationship between compliance and effectiveness. The authors' attention to both cross-national and longitudinal variation in compliance rates makes it a rich source of information on the relative importance of structural and social forces, both of which are emphasized.

In many ways this book appears to attest to the relevance of the constructivist vision. Of the four sets of factors the authors believe are responsible for trends toward improved compliance in the late 1980s and the early 1990s, they deem the international environment to be the most important. This is the set that contains the greatest proportion of elements connected with reflectivist processes (e.g. international conferences, public and media opinion, and international NGOs).

Consistent with constructivist theory, Weiss & Jacobson (1998) find that states are highly sensitive to their position relative to other states—not so much because they fear material consequences in the form of formal or informal sanctions as because they fear the social and psychological consequences of being seen as a laggard. Reputation is especially important in areas that are highly visible because of such massive, well-publicized events as the Rio Conference or the concerted efforts of prominent NGOs.

Another process with a strong social dimension that Weiss & Jacobson emphasize is leadership, both by individuals inside a given state and by particular states operating in the international system. Indeed, leadership may be the most important factor of all. The authors note that the history of environmental progress in particular areas suggests that "what might be termed a leader is crucial to the negotiation of environmental accords and to the promotion of compliance with them. In fact, in the cases studied here, it is hard to see how effective progress would have been made without the efforts of leader countries" (Weiss & Jacobson 1998:537).

Without denying that these and other social forces played some role, one may question both how important they were relative to political-economic factors and the degree to which their effect was independent of those factors. The authors offer little evidence about the importance of international factors relative to the other areas, especially the characteristics of the problem area, including what they call the activity involved (i.e. the number of actors involved, the concentration of actors in major countries, and the effect of economic incentives). Yet, the broad features of Weiss & Jacobson's compliance histories coincide strikingly with the expectations of political economists—expectations based on variables very different from those at the foundation of the constructivist program. Thus, just as Barrett (1997) predicts, widespread cooperation in any meaningful sense is extraordinarily rare, and in cases where real progress has occurred, it can almost invariably be explained by the actions of a relatively small number of states whose per capita income is relatively high.

There are also issues concerning the independence of social forces from other aspects of the environment. For example, most of the international environment variables described above are endogenous to the extent that they are a function of the problem area. Major international conferences and NGO activity are a response to the severity of an environmental problem and its resultant damage. Because problem severity and estimated damage are inextricably tied to a problem's economic consequences, it is not easy to determine to what degree states are responding to economic costs versus responding to conferences or NGO activity. Doubtless the latter do have some independent or mediating effect on the outcome, but it is almost certainly less than it appears to be.

It is just as difficult to parse out the constructivist versus political-economic dimensions of leadership. However, the fact that the leadership role is always played by an economically powerful country suggests that the material component, rather than the normative one, is the critical factor. (If it were not, we would expect to see a more conspicuous role played by activist states such as Canada and Sweden, both of which have progressive environmental values and tend to be more trusted by Third World states than are the major powers.) Weiss & Jacobson apparently believe so, noting, "Because of their economic strength, three political units [the United States, the European Union, and Japan] were in a position to play a key role in the formation of environmental accords and in promoting compliance with them" (1998:537). In addition, the central leadership role of these powerful states again brings into question the independent power of NGOs, world conferences, and other dimensions of the international environment to effect change. At a minimum, it suggests that the impact of the latter forces is determined by their ability to activate a powerful state.

Problem Solving Success as Effectiveness

For the reasons outlined above, researchers in political science and economics are paying more attention to the effectiveness of environmental regimes and less attention to compliance rates. Among recent effectiveness studies, *The Effectiveness of International Environmental Agreements* (Young 1999) contains perhaps the most systematic examination of constructivist processes. The authors of each of the book's three detailed case studies were asked to highlight the importance of six different regime functions. Two of these functions are primarily constructivist (legitimation and role definition) and several others contain constructivist elements (learning facilitation and internal realignment).

Mitchell et al (1998), the authors of the case on vessel-born oil pollution at sea, do not attribute any of the regime's success to its impact on role definition. However, they contend that the extrautilitarian impact that regimes had by virtue of the legitimacy or authority of the organizations that implemented portions of the regime were significant. The fact that the International Convention for the Prevention of Pollution from Ships' (MARPOL) equipment provisions had been developed inside the International Maritime Organization (IMO) gave them a legitimacy within the shipping community that they might not have had otherwise. There are at least two reasons for this. First, the shipping industry knew and trusted the IMO, and shipbuilders were used to implementing its regulatory standards in areas such as safety. Second, the transaction costs associated with implementation were reduced because regional organizations in Latin America, Asia, and elsewhere already had memos of understanding in which they agreed to inspect ships for violations of IMO standards.

In assessing the independent contribution of legitimation processes and understanding exactly what the nested cooperation between MARPOL and IMO signifies, it is worth noting that Mitchell et al do not claim that participating in a regime connected with the IMO led states to agree to deeper cooperation, only that implementation was better because the regime was able to exploit the IMO's reputation. The underlying utilities of the actors were never altered. There is also the issue of whether the process represents legitimation or something else. The line between enmeshing a state in a community of discourse and exploiting extant linkages for purely strategic reasons is a very fine one. It seems possible, for example, that policy makers in this case were motivated by purely utilitarian considerations—to take advantage of the reputation and administrative capacity of an existing organization. Reputation may have a normative component, but it may also be nothing more than a simple behavioral history that actors believe tells them something about future reliability.

Stokke et al (1999), the authors of the Barents Sea Fisheries case, assign some importance to role redefinition. However, the role redefinition they describe did not occur because of the fisheries regime. It was brought about by the Law of the Sea, which created 200-mile exclusive economic zones. These zones dramatically increased the power of coastal states to control key fishing areas and reduced the access of third parties to key harvest areas.

Moreover, it is not clear that this calculated redistribution of power was the outcome of a nonutilitarian process. The increased power of coastal states that resulted from the Law of the Sea was a consequence of its establishment of exclusive economic zones. These were the agreement's most distinguishing feature and were the outgrowth of tireless and careful negotiations.

Munton et al (1998), the authors of the case on the control of acid rain, believe (like Mitchell et al) that their case contains evidence of legitimation. The authors argue that although Great Britain had no economic or scientific reason to reduce its sulfur emissions in 1980 beyond a projected 25–29%, it increased that figure to 30% because that figure had been accorded special legitimacy by the regime. This contention is corroborated by the importance of a similar abstract benchmark achieved in 1993 and by roughly comparable events in Russia and Eastern Europe.

This evidence is less ambiguous than that in the cases discussed above. The 30% target does indeed appear to have had the kind, if not the magnitude, of impact that constructivists contend often determines the effectiveness of regimes. The only difficulty, as the authors readily admit, is that the magnitude of the effect described in the case is very modest.

In addition to the two primarily constructivist functions of legitimation and role redefinition, constructivist forces can influence state policies through what Young (1999) calls internal realignment; that is, reshaping the constellation of domestic interests and altering the balance of power among them. Young believes that one of the major contributions of *The Effectiveness of International Environmental Agreements* is to advance our understanding of the centrality of what regimes accomplish by precipitating internal realignments. "One of the most important processes at work here centers on the role of regimes in empowering and legitimizing various interest groups—some would call them communities—seeking to influence the behavior of governments on issues that regimes address" (Young 1999:264). Political economists typically incorporate internal realignment effects into their theories by considering the long-term impact of incentive changes on the political strength of various domestic actors and the coalitions of which they are members (see Gilligan 1997, Downs 1998:339). The constructivist dimension of internal realignment lies primarily in the symbolic significance of agreements and their constitutive effects.

Internal realignment played a small role in the oil pollution and fisheries cases but a larger role in the acid rain case, in which environmental forces seemed able to exploit the regime as a means of building political coalitions and exerting pressure on opposition groups. As a result, according to the case authors, the LRTAP regime played a "modest role" in realigning domestic politics in some countries (Munton et al 1998). Especially in Britain, LRTAP appears to have both inspired interest groups to mobilize and supplied them with a symbol that considerably increases their effectiveness. Internal realignment also seems to have had an effect—though a somewhat smaller one—in Germany.

Despite this evidence, Young's cases reinforce the standard political economy vision of regimes far more than they challenge it. Exogenous changes in relative prices in the form of deteriorating environmental conditions invariably constitute the principal motivation for the creation of the regime, and the country-specific consequences of these price changes interacting with country-specific economic conditions determine most of the differences in the policy positions of individual states. Regimes affect state preferences primarily by restructuring incentives and reducing transaction costs.

The Implementation and Effectiveness of International Environmental Agreements (Victor et al 1998), unlike Young's book, makes no explicit attempt to evaluate the relative importance of nonutilitarian motivations and constructivist processes. Its cases do, however, devote considerable attention to evaluating the impact of "breadth of participation," which the literature argues is central to reflectivist processes. The cases suggest that, consistent with constructivist expectations, greater NGO participation leads to the formulation of more demanding environmental policies. Yet, curiously, this stringency of declared policies does not appear to have much impact on actual state behavior. In the case of NO_x regulation, for example, the United Kingdom, the Netherlands, and Norway all had different levels of NGO participation and correspondingly different policies; yet the three countries all achieved roughly the same level of emissions. More important in accounting for actual outcomes were factors related to the role of relative prices, exactly as economists would have predicted (Raustiala & Victor 1998). In the United Kingdom, emissions became easier to control because of an apparently unrelated restructuring of the power sector and an increase in the natural gas supply. A similar increase in supply was important in the case of the Netherlands. In Norway, emissions went up because of an unanticipated increase in the effluents from ships.

At the international level, the impact of widespread state participation was similar to that of NGO participation within states. Thus, there is no indication that a high level of interaction leads to reflectivist resocialization and more progressive values, especially in the case of nonliberal states, which consistently have the least progressive stance toward the environment. Raustiala & Victor (1998) conclude that however beneficial universal participation may be for establishing the legitimacy of a given regulatory agreement, the reluctance of nonliberal states to vote for demanding standards may condemn widely participative multilaterals to a lifetime of shallow cooperation.

In addition to the participation results, *The Implementation and Effectiveness of International Environmental Agreements* contains some provocative findings about the impact of nonbinding agreements. These findings are potentially relevant to the contructivism–political economy debate because, according to some authors, they perform an explicitly reflectivist function. Kingsbury (1997) suggests that the fact that nonbinding agreements allow states to make more ambitious commitments is by itself an explanation of their effectiveness because such commitments push states toward what they imagine themselves capable of. According to this argument, transparency and extensive implementation reviews are important components of nonbinding agreements not so much because of the social or material sanctions that they threaten but because of the additional opportunity they provide for reflectivist forces to operate. In short, they deepen the constitutive process.

Raustiala & Victor (1998) suggest that under conditions of uncertainty, nonbinding agreements facilitate but do not directly cause more effective cooperation by permitting states to make more ambitious commitments than they would other-wise make. The ambitious goals then inspire them to make more intensive efforts to change the behavior of target groups than they would otherwise. Binding agreements cannot fulfill the same function because states are reluctant to commit themselves to a standard that they could be punished for failing to achieve. Fur-ther, nonbinding agreements facilitate learning by doing and allow states to move forward faster with lower transaction costs. Raustiala & Victor believe that these benefits support taking a new approach to international environmental governance.

Currently, there is great enthusiasm for the power of nonbinding agreements to promote cooperation. Contesting the common assumption that states would be more likely to comply with binding commitments, Weiss (1997) notes that expe-rience reveals little or no difference in compliance. The findings are similar in effectiveness research. According to Raustiala & Victor (1998:685), their cases "point to many instances where nonbinding commitments have had a greater influ-ence on behavior, especially when states have sought the benefits of international cooperation but have been uncertain of their ability to implement commitments." Defection, so feared by advocates of binding agreements, is avoided through the use of transparency and extensive implementation reviews. Since these are not tied to the application of material sanctions in nonbinding agreements, they appear to promote compliance by virtue of the social approbation or diminished status within the community of states that follows from a violation of its normative structure. Thus, in connection with North Sea pollution, Britain was progressively isolated as the "Dirty Man of Europe" and faced high-level pressure at the North Sea Ministe-rial Conference. Raustiala & Victor (1998:688) note that nonbinding agreements not only take advantage of states' concern about losing face and suffering reputa-tional damage but also allow reflectivist processes to operate on individuals who have the most power to influence policy making in their states.

There are several objections to this assessment of the relative effectiveness of nonbinding versus binding agreements and to the constructivist account of how they operate. With respect to estimating the relative effects of the two types of agreements, this conclusion is insensitive to the effects of endogenous selection that plagued earlier work on compliance. Given the obvious differences between binding and nonbinding agreements, it seems extremely unlikely that states employ the two under the same conditions. It may therefore be inappropriate to make di-rect comparisons of their respective compliance rates or levels of effectiveness and to argue consequently that because they are roughly equivalent, they are also inter-changeable. Such comparisons might be like comparing the success rates of United Nations operations in which force is used with operations in which UN activity is restricted to mediation. Perhaps the higher success rate of mediation means that that it works better than force, but perhaps not; it may mean that force tends to be used when officials have good reason to believe that mediation will not be success-ful (e.g. in Korea). At the very least, if one believes that such data shows that there is no reason to use force anymore, one must bear the usually substantial burden of demonstrating either that force and mediation have been employed in similar contexts or that the differences in context do not effect the relative success rates.

There is also a political economy account of how nonbinding agreements operate that must be disposed of before the constructivist account can be embraced wholesale. Indeed, a substantial literature in political science and economics deals with agreements that are nonbinding in the legal sense but are enforced by exogenous relative price changes and the regime-based manipulation of incentives. These include tacit arms control agreements, unofficial cease-fires, price fixing, the recognition of spheres of influence by nation-states, oligarchy, and so forth. This literature is complementary to the literature of international law in its contention that such nonbinding agreements are often motivated by a need for flexibility and a desire to avoid the high transaction costs of more formal agreements. However, the political economy literature differs dramatically in the role that it assigns to normative and material forces in sustaining compliance. According to the political economy literature, tacit arms agreements between rival states and price fixing agreements among oil producers are not held together by a common normative framework so much as by the unspoken knowledge that one party's violation will lead to a comparable relaxation of the agreed-upon standards by the other party.

To support this position, political economists (e.g. Barrett 1997) would point out that their theory predicts that since nonbinding accords exploit the power of reciprocity, relatively few states will be involved, at least in that subset of cases in which such accords lead to deep cooperation. Significantly, this prediction appears accurate in Victor et al's (1998) most prominent examples, e.g. the North Sea case.

CONCLUSION

Unlike the literatures dealing with trade and security cooperation, the literature on environmental cooperation tends to emphasize constructivist explanations of change, as opposed to more traditional political and economic explanations. Explanations for cooperative progress commonly refer to the importance of NGO activity and leadership, and to the socializing and constitutive influence that regimes exert by their capacity to legitimize, promote reflectivist discourse, and redefine roles. This essay has evaluated this constructivist orientation by examining the extensive case evidence contained in three recent volumes dealing with different dimensions of regulatory effectiveness in environmental regimes.

Despite the variation across the twenty-odd cases described in the three books, the empirical picture of environmental cooperation and the role of environmental regimes in changing state preferences differs remarkably little—at least qualitatively—from that which has emerged in the security and trade literatures and from the expectations established by the political economy literature. Relative price changes, usually in the form of costly deterioration of environmental conditions and the development of improved environmental technologies, have been by far the most important determinants of changes in state preferences. Although these exogenous relative price changes may not be sufficient conditions for the establishment of effective regulation, it appears that without them, nothing is likely to happen. Their primacy suggests that they set an important limit on the malleability of state preferences by institutions.

One of the most interesting and well-established findings in the area of multilateral environmental regulation is that cooperation per se has played a very modest role in achieving this progress. A great deal of evidence (Downs et al 1996, Murdoch & Sandler 1997, Sandler 1997, Victor et al 1998) indicates that most cooperative agreements are relatively shallow in the sense that they do not require states to do much more than they would have done in the absence of the agreements. This is not to deny that states have made progress in ameliorating environmental problems such as acid rain, wetland depletion, and water pollution. But such progress has generally occurred relatively independently of regimes. This leads one to conclude that relatively little cooperative progress can be explained by anything that regimes have done, whether by reconstructing preferences along constructivist lines or by manipulating incentives.

This absence of cooperative progress poses a greater challenge for constructivists than for political economists, because it is the constructivists who most strongly emphasize the ability of institutions to reconstruct the underlying value structures of states by promoting identity convergence. However, the three recent books on effectiveness discussed here provide little evidence that such value reconstruction regularly takes place or that it is systematically linked to the design characteristics embodied in the transformational model.

Of the modest contribution that regimes have made, most has come through the use of mechanisms that already play a prominent role in the political economy literature. These include commitment to reciprocal action that is likely to be withdrawn if massive noncompliance is found during implementation review, the creation of modest sanctions and financial incentives, the imposition of political and economic pressure by powerful developed states, and the diffusion of improved information about the costs and trajectory of environmental destruction. Because several of these mechanisms are typically present in the same regime, it is difficult to evaluate their relative importance.

Constructivist processes, at least as they are described in the three books reviewed here, appear to have played a minor role. The most important constructivist processes tend to be reflectivist. A number of cases suggest that developed democratic states and states eager to be accepted into trade organizations such as the European Union are concerned enough about their reputations as environmentally progressive states to adopt policies that they otherwise might not. However, the impact of this reputational incentive is never very great. It inspires states to perform slightly better than a narrower conception of their self-interest would predict, but this small difference does not indicate that these processes are powerful enough to reconstruct the preferences of environmentally unprogressive states.

Evidence of the advocacy effectiveness of NGOs and NGO participation—a constant preoccupation in the environmental literature—is present, but it is more modest and more ambiguous than the literature suggests (Wapner 1996, Princen & Finger 1994, Hurrell & Kingsbury 1992). NGO participation leads to more demanding environmental policies but does not necessarily affect the level of state implementation (Victor et al 1998). This finding suggests that just as relative price changes set limits on the ability of social processes to reconstruct state preferences, government bureaucracy may impose other limits. It also may indicate that NGOs have greater capacity to mobilize opinion than to monitor government activity or environmental outcomes.

The research on effectiveness reported here does, however, point to two potentially interesting areas where constructivist forces interact with political economy processes. One subject for future research is the importance of constructivist processes in animating the regulatory potential that is established by relative price changes and income effects. If one could control for the potential net economic benefits of regulation, would one find a large variance in the effectiveness of regimes and states receiving high scores that could be accounted for by constructivist variables? Beyond controlling for net economic benefits of regulation—no small matter in itself—answering this question would require both further refinement in the infant craft of developing constructivist process indicators and the conscious inclusion of cases where exogenous price changes have occurred but where there has been little or no environmental progress.

A second synthetic area worth exploring is the process Young (1999) calls internal realignment, or the capacity of regimes to empower and legitimize interest groups. Here, it might be relative price thresholds that play the animating role. That is, the impact of realignment—like the impact of regimes themselves—might well be contingent on the achievement of a certain relative price threshold. This would explain why, even though Germany has some of the most radical environmental groups in Europe, neither of Germany's major political parties did much about acid rain until problems began appearing in German forests (Munton et al 1999).

Whatever happens next, environmental researchers in the political science and international-law traditions should temper their faith in the power of social processes to reconstruct state preferences and the feasibility of environmental change strategies based on this alleged power. While neither should be dismissed out of hand, there is no indication that either holds the potential that their proponents claim. If anything, recent effectiveness studies—and the extremely modest levels of multilateral cooperation that have been achieved to date—argue precisely the opposite.

Visit the Annual Reviews home page at www.AnnualReviews.org

LITERATURE CITED

Barrett S. 1997. Towards a theory of international environmental cooperation. In *New Directions in the Economic Theory of the Environment*, ed. C Carlo, D Sinisalco, pp. 239–80. Cambridge, UK: Cambridge Univ. Press

Becker GS. 1996. *Accounting for Tastes.* Cambridge, MA: Harvard Univ. Press. 268 pp.

Benedick RE. 1988. Ozone diplomacy: new directions in safeguarding the planet. Cambridge, MA: Harvard University Press. 512 pp.

Chayes A, Chayes AH. 1995. *The New Sovereignty: Compliance with International Regulatory Agreements.* Cambridge, MA: Harvard Univ. Press. 404 pp.

Downs GD. 1998. Enforcement and the evolution of cooperation. *Mich. J. Int. Law.* 19: 319–44

Downs GD, Rocke DM, Barsoom PN. 1996. Is the good news about compliance good news about cooperation? *Int. Org.* 50:379–407

Downs GD, Rocke DM, Barsoom PN. 1998. Managing the evolution of multilateralism. *Int. Org.* 52:397–418

Elster J, ed. 1998. *Deliberative Democracy.* New York: Cambridge Univ. Press. 282 pp.

Gilligan M. 1997. *Empowering Exporters.* Ann Arbor: Univ. Mich. Press. 186 pp.

Habermas J. 1987. *The Theory of Communicative Action,* Vol. 1. Boston: Beacon. 399 pp.

Hurrell AH, Kingsbury B, eds. 1992. *International Politics of the Environment.* New York: Oxford Univ. Press. 512 pp.

Kingsbury B. 1997. The concept of compliance as a function of competing conceptions of international law. In *Engaging Countries: Strengthening Compliance with International Environmental Accords,* ed. EB Weiss, pp. 49–80. Washington, DC: Am. Soc. Int. Law

Levy M. 1993. European acid rain: the Power of tote-board diplomacy. In *Institutions for the Earth,* ed. PM Haas, RO Keohane, MA Levy, pp. 75–132. Cambridge, MA: MIT Press

Mitchell R, et al. 1999. International vessel-source oil pollution. See Young 1999, pp. 33–90

Munton D, et al. 1999. Acid rain in Europe and North America. See Young 1999, pp. 155–248

Murdoch JC, Sandler T. 1997. The voluntary provision of a pure public good: the case of reduced CFC emissions and the Montreal protocol. *J. Pub. Econ.* 63:331–49

North DC. 1990. *Institutions, Institutional Change, and Economic Performance.* New York: Cambridge Univ. Press. 152 pp.

Princen T, Finger M. 1994. *Environmental NGOs in World Politics.* London: Routledge. 272 pp.

Raustiala K, Victor DG. 1998. Conclusions. In *The Implementation and Effectiveness of International Environmental Agreements,* ed. DG Victor, K Raustiala, EB Skolnikoff, pp. 659–707. Cambridge, MA: MIT Press

Ruggie JG. 1998. *Constructing the World Polity.* London: Routledge. 312 pp.

Sandler T. 1997. *Global Challenges: An Approach to Environmental, Political, and Economic Problems.* Cambridge: Cambridge University Press, 234 pp.

Victor DG, Raustiala K, Skolnikoff EB, eds. 1998. *The Implementation and Effectiveness of International Environmental Agreements.* Cambridge, MA: MIT Press. 737 pp.

Wapner P. 1996. *Environmental Activism and World Civil Politics.* Albany, NY: State Univ. NY Press. 238 pp.

Weiss EB, ed. 1997. *International Compliance with Nonbinding Accords.* Washington, DC: Am. Soc. Int. Law. 264 pp.

Weiss EB, Jacobson HK, eds. 1998. *Engaging Countries: Strengthening Compliance with International Environmental Accords.* Cambridge, MA: MIT Press. 615 pp.

Wendt A. 1992. Anarchy is what states make of it: the social construction of power politics. *Int. Org.* 46:391–425

Wendt A. 1994. Collective identity formation and the international state. *Am. Polit. Sci. Rev.* 88:394–98

Young OR, ed. 1999. *The Effectiveness of International Environmental Agreements.* Cambridge, MA: MIT Press. 326 pp.

Young OR, Levy MA. 1998. The effectiveness of international environmental regimes. In *The Effectiveness of International Environmental Agreements,* ed. O Young, pp. 1–32. Cambridge, MA: MIT Press

Annu. Rev. Polit. Sci. 2000. 3:43–62

GLOBALIZATION AND POLITICS

Suzanne Berger

Department of Political Science, Massachusetts Institute of Technology, Cambridge, Massachusetts 02139; e-mail: szberger@mit.edu

Key Words   internationalization, neoliberalism, trade opening, social dumping, states and markets

■ **Abstract**   This chapter reviews the issues at stake in current public and scholarly debates over the impact of changes in the international economy on domestic politics and society. Over the past two decades, there have been dramatic increases in the flow of portfolio capital, foreign direct investment, and foreign exchange trading across borders at the same time as barriers to trade in goods and services have come down. These changes raise many new questions about the effects of trade and capital mobility on the autonomy of nation-states and the relative power in society of various groups. The first signs of realignments within and between political parties of both the left and the right over issues of national independence and trade openness suggest a rich new terrain for political inquiry.

INTRODUCTION

The rise of public and scholarly interest in globalization and politics is a new phenomenon. Over the past decade, the liberalization of trade, finance, and investment across the world has opened vast new territories to dynamic economic actors. The rise of incomes in developing countries has created large new consumer markets. Producing across national boundaries has shifted research, development, and manufacturing activities involving higher and higher degrees of skill and value into other societies. At the same time, economic institutions are also changing. Corporations that were once vertically integrated are shrinking their boundaries and focusing on core specializations. New partnerships, commodity chains, alliances, and mergers link producers, suppliers, and customers. How do we understand the impact of these complex transformations on our societies as risks, rewards, and security are redistributed in a global economy? How do we understand the impact of these changes on politics?

Before World War I, it was only the rare observer of the international economy who wondered about the effects on domestic politics of soaring levels of cross-border capital movements, migration, foreign direct investment, and the new transportation and communication technologies that accelerated movement of

1094-2939/00/0623-0043$14.00   **43**

information and goods among countries. But the idea that globalization undermines the autonomy and leverage of the nation-state appears in writings from this earlier period of internationalization. Angell (1913:54–55), reflecting on this theme on the eve of the war, had already identified the very same factors that today are imagined to be the motors of globalization.

> This vital interdependence ... cutting athwart frontiers is largely the work of the last forty years. ...[It is] the result of daily use of those contrivances of civilization which date from yesterday—the rapid post, the instantaneous dissemination of financial and commercial information by means of tele-graphy, and generally the incredible increase in the rapidity of communica-tion which has put the half-dozen chief capitals of Christendom in closer contact financially, and has rendered them more dependent the one upon the other than were the chief cities of Great Britain less than a hundred years ago.

From this financial interdependence, Angell deduced the irrationality, indeed the unlikelihood, of war, for he thought it had become too costly to the fabric of international economic exchange to be a conceivable option. This line of theorizing about the politics of open economies was cut off in its infancy by the disastrous failure of predictions such as Angell's and by the fact that national economies closed up at the time of the war. Between World War I and the 1980s, cross-border economic exchanges remained at far lower levels than they had reached at the turn of the century. As the magnitudes of trade, foreign direct investment, and short-term capital flows across national boundaries have skyrocketed since the 1970s, social scientists have returned to Angell's questions.

In this new literature of the 1990s, there is a common understanding of glob-alization as a set of changes in the international economy that tend to produce a single world market for goods, services, capital, and labor. In a formulation that recurs across the spectrum of views on globalization, Glyn & Sutcliffe define it as "the idea that the world is now really a single economy in the macroeconomic sense. That means that the main determinants of income and employment can now only be understood at a global and no longer a national level" (Glyn & Sutcliffe 1992:77). But beyond the definition, there is little agreement. Researchers dis-agree even on the basic characteristics of the globalization process. This review lays out some of the issues that divide them, then focuses on unresolved debates over the political consequences of globalization.

First, if the rise in cross-border economic flows as a proportion of the world's economy is uncontestable, should this be interpreted as the advent of globalization or as an extension and deepening of patterns of internationalization and regional-ization? The case for globalization as a new and irreversible phenomenon is made most strikingly in works written for a large public readership. The pioneer in this territory was Ohmae (1990), who argued that the "interlinked economy" has wiped out national borders. "On a political map, the boundaries between coun-tries are as clear as ever. But on a competitive map, a map showing the real flows of financial and industrial activity, those boundaries have largely disappeared" (Ohmae 1990:18). Or, as a British commentator put it, "[The state's] powers over the price of money ... tax rates, industrial policy, the rate of unemployment, have been blown away" (*Economist* 1995).

Globalization undermines the national state, these observers claim, not only by shrinking the resources under national control for shaping economic and social outcomes, but also by reducing government's legitimacy and authority in the eyes of the public. Across virtually all advanced industrial countries over the past two decades, there has been an erosion of public confidence in central governments. Even when analysts mention the role of specific national causes in this loss of trust, still they tend to emphasize the universality of the shifts—how everywhere globalization destroys national control of information flows, hence weakens a government's ability to influence its public. The effects of the internationalization of the media, the marketing and export of American popular culture, and the deregulation of information all combine to weaken national values and traditions, and in so doing, they dry up the springs of support for national action. The effects of changes in the international economy are experienced through the national political leaders' diminished control both over the material determinants of a country's prosperity and over the vehicles for reaching common public understandings of national well-being. In this widely held view of the coming political order, the eclipse of the national state is the central fact.

This view of globalization appears not only in the writings of those who are optimistic about the effects of these developments on societal well-being, like Ohmae and Friedman (Friedman 1999), but also in the analyses of those who find these changes threatening (Grieder 1997). *L'Horreur Economique*, which warns of the dire consequences of globalization for employment and for national existence, became a best-seller in France (Forrester 1996).

In describing globalization as a full-blown reality, these popular works accept as fact what many scholars more prudently identify as a strong and virtually irreversible trend. These analysts diverge in the weights they assign to various factors in explaining the breakdown of national controls over economies and the acceleration of trade and capital flows across borders. Some find that the key drivers of the process are new information technologies (Castells 1996); others emphasize more heavily the role of financial liberalization and deregulation, as well as the politics of interest and ideology that brought these policy shifts to fruition in all the major advanced countries (Scharpf 1991, Helleiner 1994, Wade 1996, Strange 1997). Yet others focus on a politics of interests set in motion by an "exogenous easing of trade"—changes in rules, technologies, or prices that reduce barriers to international exchange or increase the gains associated with such trade, thus creating new opportunities for some groups within society to gain from buying and selling across national boundaries (Frieden & Rogowski 1996). In this perspective, no matter what initiates liberalization, the process gains momentum as some economic actors realize the possibilities for using their assets more profitably in more open markets.

Indeed, from this point of view, the effects of globalization can be achieved without moving factors of production across borders. To lower wages in the United States, for example, the industrialist need not import labor from Mexico nor move his factories to Mexico. He simply needs to be able (to threaten) to do so. The potential of substituting foreign workers and production for domestic workers and production reduces labor's bargaining power by making the demand for domestic labor more elastic (Rodrik 1997:16–27, Slaughter 1997). In an opening international economy, then, increases in trade and foreign direct investment that are small relative to the size of the domestic economy may trigger large effects on factor and product prices, as Wood (1994) and Rodrik have argued. (Feenstra 1998). Globalization may then come to have major effects on domestic economies and politics even where most investment is national and where goods and services made and sold in the domestic market dominate imports and exports. Despite their different weightings of the factors that produce the globalized economy, all of these accounts of globalization share a common core, namely the declining relevance of national economic units.

In contrast to those who see evolution to a global economy as the determining process of economic life, there are scholars who interpret the changes of the past 20 years as internationalization or as regionalization. Hirst & Thompson (1996) distinguish between an international economy, in which the basic units remain national societies and actors, and a globalized economy, in which "national economies are subsumed and rearticulated into the system by international processes and transactions" (1996:7–13). In their view, the increases in capital mobility, trade, and foreign direct investment over the past two decades should be understood as intensified interaction among entities that remain distinctively national. Even the largest companies, free to invest their funds and develop their activities virtually anywhere in the world, in fact continue to concentrate a large proportion of their employment, investment, research and development, production, and sales in their own home countries, and thus are multinational rather than transnational corporations (Hirst & Thompson 1996:76–98) . Most economic activities are not traded across borders, and production for the domestic market and nontraded services dominate in all but a few small city-states, such as Singapore and Hong Kong (Krugman 1994).

Analysts who see change in the world economy as extension and deepening of older patterns of internationalization, rather than as globalization, also question whether any fundamentally new developments are occurring. If we consider the period from the mid-nineteenth century to the present, what can we learn about variations over time in the levels of mobility of goods, information, capital, and labor across national borders? If the levels of flow of resources across frontiers do have historical precedents, what can we learn from them about the ability of national states to regulate these economic transfers, and, more broadly, about the survival of national politics in an internationalizing economy?

Research on the international economy in the first two decades of the twentieth century has seriously challenged the new conventional wisdom about the globalized economy by pointing to significant internationalization in the past. By 1913, in the most advanced countries, levels of capital and labor mobility across national boundaries were quite comparable to today's levels (Zevin 1992, Strikwerda 1993, Bairoch 1996, Wade 1996, Williamson 1998, Wade 2000). Cable (1995:24,29) points out that it was only in the 1970s and 1980s that the share of trade in gross domestic product (GDP) for countries in the Organization for Economic Cooperation and Development returned to levels that had already been reached in 1913. Foreign direct investment has been estimated at 9% of global GDP in 1913; subsequently it declined to less than half that amount, and by 1990 it had not yet returned to the 1913 level. An *Economist* survey on states and the international economy noted that capital flows were as mobile before World War I as they are today and that net capital transfers were significantly greater (*Economist* 1995:5,9).

It would be a mistake, of course, to expect exact parallels between the situation obtaining in the international economic and political system linking the advanced countries of 1913 and today's international system. There have been real changes in global capital markets, relative even to the degree of integration achieved before the collapse during the two world wars and the Depression. The velocity and gross volume of capital movements today are on a scale that dwarfs those of the turn of the century. New financial instruments, new technologies of communication, and a greater concentration of assetholders with the growth of institutional investors have created a different environment.

Krugman (1995) points to several important differences between contemporary patterns of trade and those of the period of high internationalization before World War I. Today's exchanges include significant proportions of intra-industry trade. The growing capabilities of developing countries have led to the rise in exports from low-wage to high-wage societies as well as to new possibilities for foreign direct investment and outsourcing from high-wage to low-wage economies. This fragmentation of production, enabled by new information and transportation technologies, is transforming industrial organizations in the advanced countries. Finally, in the contemporary global economy, in contrast to that of the earlier period, a number of trading states have emerged with very high ratios of trade to GDP (Krugman 1995:331–37). Despite the differences, the view from the longer perspective does not show an irreversible progression toward ever greater and unprecedented levels of internationalization. Rather, the picture is of high levels of trade at the onset of World War I followed by a devastating shattering of the links of interdependence among the advanced countries, then by a gradual reweaving of the networks of the international economy, and finally a return (by the turn of the twenty-first century) to an international world with national constraints and opportunities that some of our more prescient great-grandparents had already glimpsed.

If there is something radically new in the world economy, some argue that it is not globalization but regionalization (Zysman & Schwartz 1998). The growth of trade and investment within each of the four major economic blocs—the European

Union (EU), North America, Mercosur (Latin America), and East Asia—is far greater than the growth of exchanges among the blocs or between them and the rest of the world (Lawrence 1996). If the phenomena to be explained are interpreted as regionalization and not globalization, then it makes sense to focus on the role of politics in building regional trade pacts (e.g. the EU and the North American Free Trade Agreement) rather than on changes in communication and transportation technologies or on economic theories of comparative advantage, whether in Heckscher-Ohlin or in Ricardo-Viner variants.

Others looking at the domestic economies of the major advanced countries argue that the most striking change over the past twenty years is not the increase in the proportion of the economy that is traded internationally (imports plus exports) but the rise of employment in services relative to manufacturing (Iversen & Wren 1998). Technological changes would explain far more of this transformation of domestic economic and social structures than would internationalization.

In sum, although scholars have a common idea of what globalization is or would be, they do not agree on whether the current changes in the international economic environment are caused by globalization or by something else. Among the candidate theories for something else, internationalization, regionalization, and the rise of a service economy are the main alternatives.

DOES GLOBALIZATION RESHAPE DOMESTIC POLITICS?

The Second Image Reversed

Research on the impact of globalization on domestic politics builds on a paradigm in political science that Gourevitch (1978) has aptly called "the second image reversed," a reference to Waltz's (1959) models of international relations theories. Waltz sought to identify studies that analyze how changes in international factors are transmitted into domestic life. How do changes in the international economy affect domestic actors? Do the same changes produce the same results in national politics everywhere? According to Gourevitch's (1986) research on national responses to common international crises, the mechanism by which changes in the world market are brought into national politics is a process of transmission through changes in the prices domestic producer groups pay and receive. Gourevitch emphasizes the possibilities of politicians' building different domestic coalitions of interests out of the groups mobilized by upheavals in their livelihood deriving from the international economy. In the countries Gourevitch discusses during the crises of 1873–1896, 1929–1949, and the 1970s, the basic "societal actors" or interests are the same: farmers, finance, labor, industrialists. Yet the patterns of accommodation these interests reached, under pressure from external events, and the economic policies these coalitions supported varied greatly from country to country. Party politics, state structures, intermediate associations, and politicians built different alliances among (the same) social groups.

If Gourevitch's map of societal interests reveals a determinacy in the presence and importance of groups in societies at the same level of economic development, his conception of their politics is far more open. Swedish and German farmers in the 1930s may have had similar preferences for protection from the market, but the Swedes ended up supporting a Social-Democratic alliance with workers, whereas the Germans ended up with Nazism (Gourevitch 1986:124–81). In the same research tradition, Katzenstein's (1985) work on neocorporatism in small open economies also focuses on variation in the responses of social groups under comparable pressures from the international economy, depending on political structures and policies (Katzenstein 1985). However similar the maps of social and economic interests in societies at comparable stages of economic advance, political reactions to shifts and shocks from the international economy are essentially indeterminate because they are mediated by political parties, ideologies, strategies, and contingent acts of leadership.

International Trade Theory

Whereas the "second image reversed" literature built on a proto-Marxist historical conception of social actors and a rather wide range of possible political outcomes under world economic pressures, the research inspired by international trade theory suggests both a simpler map of interests and a sharper set of predictions about groups' responses to change in the world economy. Standard theorems of international trade—Heckscher-Ohlin, Stolper-Samuelson, Ricardo-Viner—elaborate Ricardo's original insight about relative comparative advantage as the reason that nations find benefit in exchange. These theorems predict patterns of trade based on different national distributions of the factors of production, and they suggest that social groups, as defined by their stakes in the factors of production, will have their fortunes altered in predictable ways by trade opening or protectionism (Jones 1971, Magee 1978). If interests are distributed in patterns determined by the ownership of factors of production (land, labor, or capital), and these factors are mobile across borders, according to a Heckscher-Ohlin formulation, or as incorporated in traded goods and services, according to the Stolper-Samuelson model, then clear predictions follow about which groups will support and which groups will oppose economic openness. In societies that have relatively abundant capital, hence a comparative advantage in exporting capital or in exporting capital-intensive products, capitalists will support trade opening and labor will oppose it (Rogowski 1987, 1989; Scheve & Slaughter 1998).

How to conceptualize factors of production, and hence social actors, is a major question for this research agenda. For example, should we think of labor as a single factor of production, and characterize societies as more or less endowed with it, or should we distinguish between more skilled and less skilled workers (as defined by education and training) and characterize the relative advantages of societies in terms of the abundance of skilled labor? If we conceive factors of production as scarce assets, should our analysis also include other assets that may create differential stakes in trade opening or closure? Scheve & Slaughter (1998) have tested the effects of homeownership in counties with trade-exposed industries on attitudes toward trade.

There is a clear division among scholars who ground politics in the responses of different interests to the international economy. On one side are the analysts, including Rogowski and Scheve & Slaughter, whose characterization of factors is independent of the sector in which they are employed, and who assume relatively easy mobility of factors among industries. On the other side are those who see factors as specific to a particular industry and not so easily moved from one sector to another, as in Ricardo-Viner formulations of trade theory (Frieden 1991, Frieden & Rogowski 1996). For scholars in the latter camp, the critical variable for political responses to trade opening is the sector in which capitalists have invested or in which workers are employed, so that, for example, both shoe manufacturers and shoe-industry workers would oppose removing barriers to the entry of shoes from lower-cost producers. The shoe manufacturers could not quickly or profitably sell off their shoe factories and reinvest in new sectors; the workers have acquired particular skills in making shoes that may not be transferable to other jobs. In this research agenda, a critical issue is how specific particular assets are (see Alt et al 1996, a review of the research based on Heckscher-Ohlin and Ricardo-Viner models). If the Heckscher-Ohlin predictions based on factor type (labor, capital, or land) are too broad-gauge to capture the logic of economic interest, how much detail about the industry would we need to analyze the dynamic of political responses? Even in one industry, looking at one factor, there are multiple potentially important specificities. We might distinguish capitalists who held shares of footwear companies from those who owned physical plants, or we might distinguish shoe manufacturers in niche markets (high-fashion shoes, orthopedic shoes, work-protective shoes) from standard mass product makers (athletic shoes and the like).

These two approaches from trade theory lead to two distinct predictions about political preferences and behavior. In a test of the two models, Scheve & Slaughter (1998) ask whether individual trade-policy preferences are better accounted for by factor type (which they define by worker skill levels) or by industry of employment (which they characterize by degrees of exposure to trade). They find that the skill level of workers is a better predictor of individual support for restrictions on trade than is employment in a trade-exposed industry. This result is consistent with a Heckscher-Ohlin factor-type model. Other empirical research, however, supports a Ricardo-Viner model (Irwin 1996, Magee 1978). Frieden (1991) argues that in the short run, the specific-factors model better explains responses to trade, although over the long term Heckscher-Ohlin may prevail. Increasing integration of world markets would bring homogenization of interests within factor types, so that eventually, political struggles over globalization would become conflicts between labor and capital rather than between one industry's workers/employers and another's.

Structural Constraints on Government in a Global Economy

If public policy is considered the result of the vector of interest group pressures, then the political models derived from trade theory suggest some simple predictions about the future of the state in a global economy. The growing mobility of capital and the relative immobility of labor would make governments increasingly responsive to the interests of capital. If taxes, industrial policy, environmental regulation, or industrial relations in any society are too costly or constraining, investors will pull up stakes and transfer them elsewhere; workers cannot move so easily. Therefore, the expected results of limiting taxation of capital are that labor will have to shoulder a greater part of the tax burden and that society's ability to fund social welfare expenditures will decline.

The shift in the domestic balance of power between capital and labor that globalization promotes by rewarding mobile factors thus translates into a shift in domestic politics. Social democracy becomes less likely because capital's incentives for cross-class compromise are lowered by its growing power. Even when socialists win electoral majorities, as Mitterrand did in France in 1981, an open economy (in the case of France, the European economy) offers the holders of mobile assets the opportunity to enforce their preferences by threatening to exit. Although capital flight is hardly a new problem for the governments of the left, the range of policy instruments for dealing with it is far narrower than at any time since the beginning of the century.

Globalization shrinks the state by reinforcing the political resources of those groups in society who desire limitation of the use of state powers to redress outcomes in the market. It also ties the hands of even those political forces whose ideological traditions support state intervention in production and redistribution. In this view, it hardly matters whether the left or the right wins elections; the constraints of the internationalized economy will oblige either party to follow the same monetary and fiscal policies or else face a loss of national competitiveness and investment.

Globalization and Neoliberalism

One need not view the world through the lens of international trade theory to see links between globalization and the shrinking of the nation-state. Whereas political economists who have developed political models out of theories of comparative advantage see openness linked to the power of the state by the dynamic of domestic interest struggles, others see globalization as the result of ideological changes that have transformed national governments. The global spread of neoliberal doctrines has everywhere reduced the legitimacy of broad state involvement in the economy and reduced governments' ability to shape or to protect against market outcomes (Evans 1997). The waves of deregulation that have swept away governmental powers virtually across the world over the past two decades have their origin in deep and complex value shifts. These changes first captured the parties of the right, but the Thatcher and Reagan "revolutions" were reenacted in even more far-reaching renunciations on the left (Scharpf 1991, Kitschelt 1994, Gray 1996, Vandenbroucke 1998).

At the same time, the end of the Cold War and the collapse of state socialism opened new terrain for economic liberalism. According to Wes, in 1978 one third of the world's work force lived in centrally planned economies (cited in Vandenbroucke 1998:13). During the past decade, these economies became integrated into world markets. Even in China, the sole remaining major socialist country, capitalism and liberal market principles made major advances. Although it was possible to argue for more or less rapid "transition" to market economies, plausible alternatives to the market economy no longer seemed to exist. Both in liberal democracies and in the former state-socialist countries, the political appeal of socialist or left doctrines that would enlarge the state's mandate to regulate the economy evaporated. Where Communist parties have reemerged, they function mainly as vehicles of populist protest.

The spread of neoliberal norms was propelled not only by the failures of socialism but also by the advocacy of the United States. In a position of unchallenged dominance in global financial and trade institutions, the United States pushed for a rapid end to capital controls across the world and for making International Monetary Fund and World Bank assistance contingent on recipient countries' acceptance of sharp limitations on the role of government in the economy (Wade 2000). From this perspective, globalization, far from reflecting the spontaneous spread of world markets and the toppling of barriers by economic actors eager for new opportunities, is a story driven by politics: ideological change, the contingencies of the collapse of the socialist economy, and US power in the world.

EVALUATING THE CONSTRAINTS ON NATIONAL GOVERNMENTS

Although important differences exist among scholars who emphasize the role of US policy, new technologies, financial markets, or new political values in the irresistible rise of globalization, most accounts advance some mixture of causes and feedbacks. The real divide in the literature lies between those who argue that globalization, however it has come about, has eroded the autonomy and authority of national governments, and those who argue that however much globalization may have occurred, national states still retain their basic powers. Empirical research intended to confirm or refute theory-driven predictions of the erosion of national government's capabilities has focused on four big questions. Has the state lost the levers that enabled it to make macroeconomic policy? Has the state lost the tools of industrial policy and other supply-side policies that played a major role in the postwar growth strategies of newly industrializing economies? Has the state lost the ability to raise the resources to finance extensive welfare and redistributional policies? More generally, have states lost the ability to sustain distinctive forms of capitalism within their societies—distinctive configurations of market and nonmarket institutions that reflect societal preferences and national traditions in the particular ways they build productive institutions and networks to connect economic organizations?

Macroeconomic Sovereignty

In the international economy of the post–World War II era, with capital controls and trade barriers, states were able to use interest rates, the exchange rate, and the supply of money as levers of control in their economies. When rapid economic growth was accompanied by inflation, governments could limit the consequences by obstructing the entry of foreign goods that might compete with more expensive domestic products and by blocking domestic capital from exiting in search of higher returns. When economic growth slowed, governments could devalue the currency to cheapen exports, lower interest rates to stimulate investment, and increase government spending to increase employment. When currencies came under speculative attack, countries responded with currency and investment controls. In a world of free-moving financial capital, once policy-makers renounce the use of capital and trade restrictions, the menu of macroeconomic options is shortened. (For clear expositions of the impact of the integration of financial markets on macroeconomic policy-making that draw different conclusions, see Frieden 1991:430–33; Garrett 1998a:26–50, 1998b; Glyn 1997–1998:4–8.) At best, governments may choose between the value of the currency and the interest rate. The instruments of macroeconomic policy are even more limited in countries that have pegged their currency to the US dollar, as Hong Kong has, and in countries that link their currencies, as the Western Europeans have (first in the European Monetary System and then in a single currency, the euro). As demonstrated by the experience of the states that were hardest hit by the Asian financial crisis (e.g. Thailand), if a country is to stem the outflow of investors and keep the support of international financial institutions, then borders have to be kept open, even when interest rates soar and the currency collapses.

Is this loss of maneuvering room in monetary policy paralleled by a loss of autonomy in fiscal policy? Views divide widely on this point. Rodrik (1997:62–64), among others, concludes that globalization makes it hard to raise the tax burden in general. Globalization reduces the taxation of capital, which is mobile, and shifts the tax burden onto labor, which is less mobile (Przeworski & Wallerstein 1988, Scharpf 1991, Kurzer 1993, Steinmo 1993). Eichengreen (1997:3) explains that the "most basic principle of the theory of tax incidence is that elastically supplied inputs into production escape the burden of taxes; try to tax them and they vanish. ...It is not surprising that capital's share of taxes paid in the leading industrial countries that make up the Organization for Economic Cooperation and Development (OECD) has shifted steadily downward in recent years."

Other research, however, contradicts these findings. Swank (1988a:679) examines corporate tax burden (as a percentage of operating income) in the 1990s for the 17 largest and richest OECD countries and finds little change since the 1970s. He analyzes the impact of international capital mobility on corporate profits taxation for the period 1966–1993 and discovers that "if anything, direct effects of globalization of capital markets are associated with slightly higher business taxes and, to a degree, the diminution of tax policy responsiveness to the conditions that underpin investment" (Swank 1998a:690–91; see also Steinmo & Swank 1999). With respect to trade, however, Swank reports a small positive effect of trade openness on the fall of business-profits taxation (1998a:686). Garrett (1998b:85–89), exploring the prospects for left-labor policies in the 1990s, concludes that trade openness and capital mobility do not diminish government's capacity to tax, nor even its options for increasing the progressivity of the tax system. Social democratic governments based on left-labor coalitions are associated with bigger government and higher corporate taxation than the Anglo-American liberal market systems, but the end of capital controls need not spell the end of redistributive politics. Garrett argues that business obtains many benefits from the state's role in economy and society, especially from public investments in human and physical resources and from redistributive expenditures that reduce social tensions arising from economic dislocation. Therefore, even mobile asset holders will remain in relatively high-tax societies when these environments provide valuable public goods, such as a well-educated workforce, social stability, and proximity to cutting-edge research institutions (Garrett 1996, 1998a, 1998b; Thelen 1999).

Industrial Policy

How does globalization affect the government's capacity to promote a particular set of economic activities within national territory? Both in advanced industrial countries and in developing countries, governments have used a variety of policies to encourage specific industries: preferential credit, export subsidies, research and development grants, military procurement, export subsidies, protection of the domestic market for domestic producers, and others. (For examples from Western Europe, see Shonfield 1969, Levy 1999b; for Japan, see Johnson 1982, Samuels 1987; for industrial policy in the newly industrializing economies, see Wade 1990, World Bank 1993, MacIntyre 1994, Chiu et al 1997, Rodrik 1999.) If government intervention was intended to attenuate a domestic shortage of capital for promising new activities, then globalization should alleviate the problem, since domestic firms can now draw on world capital markets (not only on domestic savings) to finance new investments. But in most other respects, globalization makes it more difficult or even impossible to use such policies as Japan, Korea, Singapore, and Taiwan developed in the postwar decades to build modern industries. Capital mobility makes it very difficult for governments to constrain local investors to provide funds for industry at lower rates of return than they would receive abroad. The extension across national borders of commodity chains that coordinate production functions distributed across multiple countries (Gereffi 1996) weakens the links of interdependence among domestic producers and retailers. The emergence of global suppliers capable of providing services and subassemblies for multinational corporations wherever they locate production may crowd out local suppliers and reduce the multinational corporations' need to cooperate with local producers and to transfer technology and know-how to them (Hatch & Yamamura 1996, Sturgeon 1997).

Most constraining, the rules of the new international trading order limit the kinds of help that governments can provide to domestic industries without violating the antidumping or anticompetition provisions. The mutual charges of protectionism and hidden subsidy that the United States and the European Union have pressed against each other in the World Trade Organization (WTO) over the past year regarding bananas, beef hormones, and the tax advantages that US corporations derive from offshore Foreign Sales Corporations are only the latest examples of the capacity of internationally accepted trade sanctions to restrain government support of particular industries. OECD debated an international treaty on the rights of foreign investors, the Multilateral Agreement on Investment, which is even more far-reaching in its implications for clipping the wings of governments. This accord would have obliged its signatories to treat foreign investment like domestic investment and would have constrained the regulatory options of governments at all levels. Negotiated in secret, the proposed treaty was stopped by a wave of attacks from nongovernmental organizations and social movements that orchestrated a campaign against the Multilateral Accord on Investment on the grounds that it protected the rights of capital but not labor and that it constrained democratic decision-making.

End of the Welfare State?

Does globalization destroy the welfare state? One of the deepest sources of anxiety about international openness is the fear that welfare-state institutions that have buffered the workings of market capitalism will no longer be sustainable (Pierson 1994, Esping-Andersen 1996, Jessop 1996, Rhodes 1996, Rodrik 1997, Stephens et al 1999). In part, the debate revolves around the issue of whether a race to the bottom in wages, social provision, and labor-market regulation is inevitable because of financial market liberalization and because of capital's new opportunities of relocation in low-cost, low-regulation countries. The arguments run along the same lines as those discussed in the section on macroeconomic policy: that government's fiscal policy is constrained by capital mobility, since taxes cannot be raised without reducing the competitive advantage of domestic producers, and that large budgetary deficits, without the possibility of exchange-rate adjustments, raise prospects of inflation and higher interest rates. The likely outcomes are higher unemployment (as government renounces the use of demand stimulation) and cuts in social welfare expenditure (as government tries to contain and lower the deficit). Indeed, the argument is not only that these constraints will over time undermine the welfare state, but that they are already the principal source of pressures that have led to cuts in social spending across the advanced industrial countries.

The empirical evidence suggests far greater resilience and capacity for adaptation within the format of universal social provision than these pessimistic readings of the new distribution of power within advanced societies suggest. First, as discussed above, corporate taxation as a share of tax revenues or as a share of gross domestic product has been quite stable, challenging the notion that states are engaged in a competitive downward spiral to reduce corporate taxes (Garrett 1998b,

C Pierson 1998, Swank 1998a,b). Second, patterns of change in social expenditures vary significantly across countries. Pierson shows that these patterns do not correspond to the predictions that might be derived from assumptions about the vulnerability of social expenditure to pressures from mobile asset holders with increased openness (P Pierson 1998). Swank (1998b:44) analyzed the impact of increasing capital mobility on total social spending in 15 advanced countries and concludes:

> Where institutions of collective interest representation—social corporatism and inclusive electoral institutions—are strong, where authority is concentrated and where the welfare state is based on the principle of universalism, the effects of international capital mobility are absent, or they are positive in the sense that they suggest economic and political interests opposed to neoliberal reforms, or adversely affected by globalization, have been successful in defending the welfare state.

In contrast, where such institutions are weak, capital mobility has had a more dampening effect on social expenditure.

Is globalization really the main explanation for the pressures on welfare state expenditure that are evident across developed countries? Domestic factors—e.g. the aging of the population, a productivity slowdown in service-based postindustrial economies, the maturation of welfare programs—may be at least as important as new developments in the international economy (Iversen & Wren 1998, P Pierson 1998, Stephens et al 1999, Iversen 1999). The welfare state may be in for hard times, but globalization matters only in conjunction with domestic variables that vary from state to state. Its effects on policy are not direct. Rather, where governments have been committed to preserving the basic features of the welfare state (as in the Netherlands), a range of reforms and accommodations have maintained the essential distributive elements of the old social compact (Levy 1999a, Visser & Hemerijck 1997).

National Varieties of Capitalism

Beyond the constraints that globalization may exercise in economic policy-making, there remains the question of its impact on the institutional constellation of different national systems. Albert's *Capitalism vs. Capitalism* (1993) launched a debate over the societal foundations of economic performance. This book, which sketched "Anglo-American" and "Nippo-Rhenish" models, was followed by a wave of research on the specificities of German, Japanese, Italian, French, and other "models" (Albert 1993; Soskice 1991, 1999; Streeck 1992, 1997; Hall 1997).[1] The common

---

[1] Earlier contributions that provided an empirical foundation for this debate about various national capitalisms (Dore 1973, Maurice et al 1986) demonstrated that firms operating in the same industries in different societies had very different organizations that were about equally efficient and productive over time. They showed that organizational differences reflected broad societal characteristics.

intuition underlying all of these contributions is that economic performance is a characteristic of firms understood not as autonomous actors but as social creations, highly dependent on societal resources that they do not themselves create. In Streeck's words (1997:37), firms are "social institutions, not just networks of private contracts or the property of their shareholders. Their internal order is a matter of public interest and is subject to extensive social regulation, by law and industrial agreement." Streeck describes the similarly social and organized character of capital and capital markets. Even firms in the same sector, with the same technologies and products, will differ systematically across societies according to the kinds of resources and frameworks those societies provide.

What kinds of resources and frameworks? Are there as many different national models of capitalism as there are nations? Although these theorists argue for the diversity and pluralism of social types, the diversity is constrained. The basic grid of analysis is institutional configuration or production regime (Soskice 1999:19), defined by the sets of rules and institutions regulating the industrial-relations system, the educational and training system, the relations among companies, and the system of corporate governance and finance. Those four patterns together form a production regime, and the production regimes of the advanced industrial countries fall into regular patterns. In Soskice's categories, there are two broad types: business-coordinated market economies (e.g. Germany, Sweden, Japan, Korea) and liberal market economies (e.g. the United States and Britain).

Contributors to the varieties-of-capitalism literature, then, see more than one kind of industrial society and believe that the different institutional configurations, or production regimes, generate systematically different microbehaviors. From institutional configurations and differences in microbehaviors, these scholars deduce a theory of comparative institutional advantage (Hall 1997). In this perspective, different production regimes, or different capitalisms, should be good at solving different kinds of coordination and production problems, and hence over time should come to specialize in and excel in those activities.

Are these varieties of capitalism, each with its distinctive assets and weaknesses, equally resilient in an open international economy? Within this question are two different issues. First, one may ask whether the characteristics of the new economy—however conceptualized—play to the strengths of some models of capitalism more than others. The American economy, with flexible labor markets, arms-length relations between investors and industry, research and development systems that favor radical change rather than incremental process improvements, well-developed financial markets, and so forth, might be better able to respond to global competition than, for example, German or Japanese capitalism. There are many claims made along these lines, but the evidence is far from clear. It is true that the German and Japanese economies have experienced major difficulties over the past few years, but if one compares the economic growth, employment, and productivity growth of these countries with that of the United States over a 10-year period that corresponds to the same phases of the business cycle, their performance is roughly equivalent. Although one variety of capitalism might do better at particular economic conjunctures, or at solving particular kinds of problems in innovation, production, or distribution, there is no compelling evidence that any of these constellations has a clear economic superiority across the board over time.

The second issue is as follows. If one believes that economic institutions depend on specific societal resources, then globalization might differentially affect models of capitalism by undermining a society's ability to reproduce those resources (Streeck 1997). Capital mobility, for example, might have different effects in a country whose economic system relied heavily on labor-capital negotiation and cooperation in the workplace than in a country where skills are formed outside the workplace and acquired in markets.

GLOBALIZATION AND THE NEW AGENDA OF POLITICS

The case for a decline of national power and sovereignty in an age of globalization stands on two legs. One is the notion that the magnitude and velocity of international economic exchanges have eroded the state's capabilities. The other is the argument that the extension of market relations across national borders diminishes the citizen's attachment to national authority, leading to a decline in the legitimacy of central governments. Contemporary politics in advanced industrial countries provides much evidence of a growing distrust of elected politicians. But there are no signs that the electorate's disillusionment about their representatives reflects a deeper detachment from national loyalties, let alone a transfer of political allegiance and identification to regional or international bodies.

As pressures from the international economy intrude on domestic societies, citizens turn ever more urgently to their own governments for help. What many of them mean by help is protection from the unregulated flow of capital, labor, and information from outside national territory. In their view, domestic problems— e.g. unemployment, delocalization of industry, immigrants, pornography on the internet—are carried into the community by this unregulated flow across unguarded national boundaries. Far from understanding the new relationships induced by internationalization as the product of impersonal and inevitable market forces, many of these citizens see the new situation as one created by their own government's actions in opening the frontiers, in negotiating new trade treaties, and in legislating about immigration. Because the problems appear to have political origins, they appear reversible by government action. Thus, one paradoxical outcome of globalization may be to refocus political attention on the role of the state on the boundaries of national territory (Berger 1995, Kitschelt 1995, Della Porta 1998). Citizens are mobilizing along new lines of cleavage, and in many advanced countries, a new political camp has emerged, organized around a program of reinforcing national controls at the frontiers. Supporters of these views can be found across the political spectrum.

A twenty-first century of nation-states—an expansive, intrusive, and unregulated global economy—these are the future parameters of our opportunities and our dangers. Citizens increasingly understand the relative economic strengths and weaknesses of their societies as products of specific national political arrangements and of different national cultures, not as the result of diverse natural advantages. The combination of these elements makes it likely that the new age of globalization will be one of international conflicts over the economy. We can already glimpse the character of these contests: a mix of conflicting visions of right and interest. The struggles between the United States and Japan in the Structural Impediments Initiative negotiations (1989–1990), between the United States and Europe over the "cultural exception" in the Uruguay Round, between the United States and Europe over beef hormones and genetically modified substances in foods, between Japan and China on the linkages between trade, aid, and nuclear weapons; in the conflicts heating up on internet content, on child labor, on "social clauses," environment, and trade—all reflect different national conceptions both of interest and of the basic norms of social life. Energized partly by interests, partly by ideals, these confrontations do not align one ideological camp against another nor one civilization against another. They do not pit "Asian values" against "Anglo-American" values. Often they mobilize multiple and conflicting traditions within pluralistic national societies. In this way, the conflicts between societies that are induced by globalization threaten to reopen old lines of domestic discord.

Visit the Annual Reviews home page at www.AnnualReviews.org

LITERATURE CITED

Albert M. 1993. *Capitalism vs. Capitalism.* New York: Four Walls Eight Windows

Alt JE, Frieden J, Gilligan MJ, Rodrik D, Rogowski R. 1996. The political economy of international trade: enduring puzzles and an agenda for inquiry. *Comp. Polit. Stud.* 29(6):689–717

Angell N. 1913. *The Great Illusion.* New York: GP Putnam's Sons

Bairoch P. 1996. Globalisation myths and realities: one century of external trade and foreign investment. In *States against Markets: The Limits of Globalisation,* ed. R Boyer, D Drache, pp. 173–92. London: Routledge

Berger S. 1995. Trade and identity: the coming protectionism. In *Remaking the Hexagon: The New France in the New Europe,* ed. G Flynn, pp. 195–210. Boulder, CO: Westview

Cable V. 1995. The diminished nation-state; a study in the loss of economic power. *Daedalus* 129(2):23–51

Castells M. 1996. *The Rise of the Network Society.* Oxford: Blackwell

Chiu SW, Ho KC, Lui TL. 1997. *City-States in the Global Economy. Industrial Restructuring in Hong Kong and Singapore.* Boulder, CO: Westview

Della Porta D, Kriesi H. 1998. Movimenti sociali e globalizzazione. *Riv. Ital. Sci. Polit.* 28(3):451–82

Dore R. 1973. *British Factory—Japanese Factory: The Origins of National Diversity in Industrial Relations.* Berkeley: Univ. Calif. Press

Economist. 1995. October 7, p. 15

Eichengreen B. 1997. The tyranny of the financial markets. *Curr. Hist.* November: 377–82

Esping-Andersen G, ed. 1996. *Welfare States in Transition: National Adaptations in Global Economies.* Thousand Oaks, CA: Sage

Evans P. 1997. The eclipse of the state?

Reflections on stateness in an era of globalization. *World Polit.* 50(1):62–87

Feenstra RC. 1998. Integration of trade and disintegration of production in the global economy. *J. Econ. Perspect.* 12(4):31–50

Forrester V. 1996. *L'Horreur économique.* Paris: Fayard

Friedman T. 1999. *The Lexus and the Olive Tree.* New York: Farrar Straus Giroux

Frieden JA. 1991. Invested interests: the politics of national economic policies in a world of global finance. *Int. Organ.* 45(4):425–51

Frieden JA, Rogowski R. 1996. The impact of the international economy on national policies: an analytical overview. In *Internationalization and Domestic Politics*, ed. R Keohane, H Milner, pp. 25–47. New York: Cambridge Univ. Press

Garrett G. 1996. Trade, capital mobility and the domestic politics of economic policy. In *Internationalization and Domestic Politics*, ed. R Keohane, H Milner, pp. 79–107. New York: Cambridge Univ. Press

Garrett G. 1998a. Global markets and national politics: collision course or virtuous circle? *Int. Organ.* 52(4):787–824

Garrett G. 1998b. *Partisan Politics in the Global Economy.* New York: Cambridge Univ. Press

Gereffi G. 1996. Commodity chains and regional divisions of labor in East Asia. *J. Asian Bus.*

Glyn A. 1997–1998. Egalitarianism in a global economy. *Boston Rev.* 22(6):4–8

Glyn A, Sutcliffe B. 1992. Global but leaderless: the new capitalist order. In *The Socialist Register 1992*, ed. R Miliband, pp. 76–95. London: Merlin

Gourevitch P. 1978. The second image reversed. *Int. Organ.* 32:881–912

Gourevitch P. 1986. *Politics in Hard Times.* Ithaca, NY: Cornell Univ. Press

Gray J. 1996. *After Social Democracy: Politics, Capitalism, and the Common Life.* London: Demos

Grieder W. 1997. *One World, Ready or Not.* New York: Simon & Schuster

Hall PA. 1997. The political economy of adjustment in Germany. In *Oekonomische Leistungsfaehigkeit und institutionelle Innovation*, pp. 293–315. Berlin: WZB-Jahrbuch

Hatch W, Yamamura K. 1996. *Asia in Japan's Embrace. Building a Regional Production Alliance.* Cambridge, UK: Cambridge Univ. Press

Helleiner E. 1994. *States and the Reemergence of Global Finance.* Ithaca, NY: Cornell Univ. Press

Hirst P, Thompson G. 1996. *Globalization in Question.* Cambridge, MA: Blackwell

Irwin DA. 1996. Industry or class cleavages over trade policy? Evidence from the British general election of 1923. In *The Political Economy of Trade Policy: Papers in Honor of Jagdish Bhagwati*, ed. R Feenstra, GM Grossman, DA Irwin, pp. 53–75. Cambridge, MA: MIT Press

Iversen T. 1999. The end of solidarity? Decentralization, monetarism and the social democratic welfare state in the 1980s and 1990s. In *Unions, Employers and Central Banks*, ed. T Iversen, J Pontusson, D Soskice. New York: Cambridge Univ. Press

Iversen T, Wren A. 1998. Equality, employment, and budgetary restraint: the trilemma of the service economy. *World Polit.* 50:507–46

Jessop B. 1996. Post-Fordism and the state. In *Comparative Welfare Systems: The Scandinavia Model in a Period of Change*, ed. B Greve. New York: St. Martin's

Johnson C. 1982. *MITI and the Japanese Miracle.* Stanford, CA: Stanford Univ. Press

Jones RJ. 1971. A three-factor model in theory, trade, and history. In *Trade, Balance of Payments, and Growth*, ed. J Bhagwati et al, pp. 3–21. Amsterdam: North-Holland

Katzenstein P. 1985. *Small States in World Markets: Industrial Policy in Europe.* Ithaca, NY: Cornell Univ. Press

Kitschelt H. 1994. *The Transformation of European Social Democracy.* New York: Cambridge Univ. Press

Kitschelt H. 1995. *The Radical Right in Western Europe.* Ann Arbor: Univ. Mich. Press

Krugman P. 1994. Competitiveness: a dangerous obsession. *Foreign Aff.* 73(2):28–44

Krugman P. 1995. Growing world trade: causes and consequences. *Brookings Pap. Econ. Act.* 1:327–77

Kurzer P. 1993. *Business and Banking.* Ithaca, NY: Cornell Univ. Press

Lawrence RZ. 1996. *Regionalism, Multilateralism and Deeper Integration.* Washington, DC: Brookings Inst.

Levy J. 1999a. Vice into virtue? Progressive politics and welfare reform in continental Europe. *Polit. Soc.* 27(2):239–73

Levy J. 1999b. *Tocqueville's Revenge: The Decline of Dirigisme and the Evolution of France's Political Economy.* Cambridge, MA: Harvard Univ. Press

MacIntyre A, ed. 1994. *Business and Government in Industrialising Asia.* Ithaca, NY: Cornell Univ. Press

Magee S. 1978. Three simple tests of the Stolper-Samuelson theorem. In *Issues in International Economics*, pp. 138–53. London: Oriel

Maurice M, Sellier F, Silvestre J-J. 1986. *The Social Foundations of Industrial Power.* Cambridge, MA: MIT Press

Ohmae K. 1990. *The Borderless World.* New York: Harper Collins

Pierson C. 1998. Contemporary challenges to welfare state development. *Polit. Stud.* 46(4):777–94

Pierson P. 1994. *Dismantling the Welfare State: Reagan, Thatcher and the Politics of Retrenchment in Britain and the United States.* New York: Cambridge Univ. Press

Pierson P. 1998. Irresistible forces, immovable objects: post-industrial welfare states confront permanent austerity. *J. Eur. Public Policy* 5(4):539–60

Przeworski A, Wallerstein M. 1988. Structural dependence of the state on capital. *Am. Polit. Sci. Rev.* 91(3):11–30

Rhodes M. 1996. Globalization and West European welfare states: a critical review of recent debates. *J. Eur. Soc. Policy* 6(4):305–27

Rodrik D. 1997. *Has Globalization Gone Too Far?* Washington, DC: Inst. Int. Econ.

Rodrik D. 1999. *The New Global Economy and Developing Countries: Making Openness Work.* Washington, DC: Overseas Dev. Council

Rogowski R. 1987. Political cleavages and changing exposure to trade. *Am. Polit. Sci. Rev.* 81(4):1121–37

Rogowski R. 1989. *Commerce and Coalitions.* Princeton, NJ: Princeton Univ. Press

Samuels R. 1987. *The Business of the Japanese State.* Ithaca, NY: Cornell Univ. Press

Scharpf F. 1991. *Crisis and Choice in European Social Democracy.* Ithaca, NY: Cornell Univ. Press

Scheve K, Slaughter MJ. 1998. What determines individual trade policy preferences. *Natl. Bur. Econ. Res. Work. Pap. Ser.*, No. 6531

Shonfield A. 1969. *Modern Capitalism.* Oxford, UK: Oxford Univ. Press

Slaughter MJ. 1997. International trade and labor demand elasticities. *NBER Disc. Pap.* No. 6262

Soskice D. 1991. The institutional infrastructure for international competitiveness: a comparative analysis of the UK and Germany. In *The Economics of the New Europe*, ed. AB Atkinson, R Brunetta, pp. 45–66. London: Macmillan

Soskice D. 1999. Divergent production regimes: coordinated and uncoordinated market economies in the 1980s and 1990s. In *Continuity and Changes in Contemporary Capitalism*, ed. H Kitschelt, P Lange, G Marks, JD Stephens, pp. 101–34. Cambridge, UK: Cambridge Univ. Press

Steinmo S. 1993. *Democracy and Taxation.* New Haven, CT: Yale Univ. Press

Steinmo S, Swank D. 1999. *The new political economy of taxation.* Presented at Annu. Meet. Am. Polit. Sci. Assoc., Atlanta, GA

Stephens JD, Huber E, Ray L. 1999. The welfare state in hard times. In *Continuity and Change in Contemporary Capitalism.*, ed. H Kitschelt, P Lange, G Marks, JD Stephens, pp. 164–93. New York: Cambridge Univ. Press

Strange S. 1997. *Casino Capitalism*. Manchester, UK: Manchester Univ. Press

Streeck W. 1992. *Social Institutions and Economic Performance*. Beverly Hills, CA: Sage

Streeck W. 1997. German capitalism: does it exist? Can it survive? In *Modern Capitalism or Modern Capitalisms?* ed. C Crouch, W Streeck, pp. 33–54. London: Sage

Strikwerda C. 1993. The troubled origins of European economic integration: international iron and steel and labor migration in the era of World War I. *Am. Hist. Rev.* 98(4):1106–42

Sturgeon T. 1997. Turn-key production networks: a new American model of industrial organization? Berkeley Roundtable on Int. Econ. Work. Pap. #92A, Univ. Calif., Berkeley

Swank D. 1998a. Funding the welfare state and the taxation of business in advanced market economies. *Polit. Stud.* 46(4):671–91

Swank D. 1998b. Global capital, democracy, and the welfare state: why political institutions are so important in shaping the domestic response to internationalization. Cent. German and Eur. Stud. Work. Pap. No. 1.66, Univ. Calif., Berkeley

Thelen K. 1999. Why German employers cannot bring themselves to dismantle the German model. In *Unions, Employers, and Central Banks*, ed. J Pontusson, DW Soskice, T Iversen, pp. 138–69. New York: Cambridge Univ. Press

Vandenbroucke F. 1998. *Globalisation, Inequality, and Social Democracy*. London: Inst. Public Policy Res.

Visser J, Hemerijck A. 1997. '*A Dutch Miracle.*' Amsterdam: Amsterdam Univ. Press

Wade R. 1990. *Governing the Market: Economic Theory and the Role of Government in East Asian Industrialization*. Princeton, NJ: Princeton Univ. Press

Wade R. 1996. Globalization and its limits: reports of the death of the national economy are greatly exaggerated. In *National Diversity and Global Capitalism*, ed. S Berger, R Dore, pp. 60–88. Ithaca, NY: Cornell Univ. Press

Wade R. 2000. National power, coercive liberalism and "global" finance. In *International Politics: Enduring Concepts and Contemporary Issues*, ed. R Art, R Jervis, pp. 482–89. New York: Addison Wesley Longman. 5th ed.

Waltz K. 1959. *Man, the State, and War*. New York: Columbia Univ. Press

Williamson JG. 1998. Globalization, labor markets and policy backlash in the past. *J. Econ. Perspect.* 12(4):51–72

Wood A. 1994. *North-South Trade, Employment, and Inequality: Changing Fortunes in a Skill-Driven World*. Oxford, UK: Oxford Univ. Press

World Bank. 1993. *The East Asian Miracle: Economic Growth and Public Policy*. New York: Oxford Univ. Press

Zevin R. 1992. Are world financial markets more open? If so, why and with what effects? In *Financial Openness and National Autonomy*, ed. T Banuri, JB Schor. Oxford, UK: Oxford Univ. Press

Zysman J, Schwartz A, eds. 1998. *Enlarging Europe: The Industrial Foundations of a New Political Reality*. Berkeley: Univ. Calif. Int. and Area Stud.

Annu. Rev. Polit. Sci. 2000. 3:63–83

ALLIANCES: Why Write Them Down?

James D. Morrow

Hoover Institution, Stanford University, Stanford, California 94305-6010;
e-mail: morrow@hoover.stanford.edu

Key Words   commitment, intervention in war, neorealism, security, signaling

■ **Abstract**   States formalize some relations into military alliances. A formal commitment could increase credibility by signaling an intention to come to the aid of another state or by creating commitment by altering the costs and benefits of such intervention. In this review, I lay out three considerations in a decision to intervene in a war. Signals require some costs to trasmit information, and I examine some possible costs in alliances. A state's willingness to intervene could be enhanced by audience costs for failure to honor a commitment. Neorealist arguments about alliances are flawed in asserting that security is a public good and in failing to realize that all states have both status quo and revisionist interests. This review surveys a number of smaller topics in alliances—the tradeoff between arms and allies, burden sharing, alliance management and duration, nonsecurity benefits, and domestic politics.

INTRODUCTION

Two or more states form an alliance when they conclude a treaty that obliges them both to take certain actions in the event of war. Commonly, the study of alliances focuses on defense pacts—mutual commitments by states to come to one another's aid if one is attacked—over lesser degrees of commitment, such as ententes. Nevertheless, all formal military agreements share a similar logic with different degrees of expected action in the event of war, and this chapter explores that logic.

Alliances operate in the shadow of war. They are explicit records of the allies' expectations of action in the case of war, and they specify the conditions under which the obligations are activated. However, states cannot be made to live up to their obligations to their allies. Obligations must be self-enforcing to be effective in international politics. Other states must believe that a state will live up to its alliance commitments, and when tested, a state will do so only if it is in its interest at that time. This first point of the necessity of self-enforcement is well understood in the literature on alliances and more generally in international politics. Alliances are not sufficient for the effective assistance of other states.

What is not generally appreciated is the converse of this point—anything that an alliance allows during wartime can also be accomplished without a prewar alliance. States do not need an alliance to intervene on the side of another in a war. Often, effective wartime coalitions have been assembled only after the fighting began. Foreign policy statements short of a formal treaty of alliance may be sufficient to convince prospective attackers of the credible intention to intervene against an attack. Alliances are not necessary for the effective assistance of other states (Stein 1990).

These two points lead to the central question this essay addresses: Why write it down? If alliances are neither necessary nor sufficient for effective intervention in wars on behalf of states with shared interests, and thus for credible deterrence before war, then why do states formally state their military obligations to one another? As we shall see, alliances can have real effects on decisions to intervene in wars, and thus can increase both the deterrence of threats and defense in case of war.

I begin by considering some preliminary issues in defining alliances. The credibility of an alliance is tied to whether a nation comes to the aid of its ally when the latter is under attack, and consequently, decisions whether to intervene in a war are closely related to the considerations involved in forming, maintaining, and breaking alliances. The simple decision calculus presented here produces three considerations in a decision to intervene in a war. It illustrates different arguments about the effects and credibility of alliances. The three considerations lead directly to a discussion of what factors can make an alliance credible and what factors threaten credibility. This calculus also places balance-of-power analyses of alliances, particularly neorealism, into perspective. Actions taken to retain the credibility of an alliance commitment lead to an analysis of intra-alliance politics and the resulting duration of alliances. Motivations for alliances, other than security, arise at this point in the argument. I examine the role of domestic politics in alliances and conclude by discussing open issues in alliances.

PRELIMINARY ISSUES

Alliances should be differentiated from alignments (Dingman 1979). Alignments are not written down by states because the common interest is obvious to all. Some alignments, such as the United States and Israel, support close relations over a long period of time, whereas others, such as the United States and Syria during the Gulf War, pass with the immediate issue. The key difference is that an alignment does not carry the expectation of a continuing relationship; the shared interest carries the entire relationship, and therefore that relationship need not be negotiated formally. An alliance entails a formal commitment between the parties wherein certain specific obligations are written out. Alliances require specification because the allies need to clarify their degree of shared interests, both to each other and to others outside the alliance (Niou & Ordeshook 1994).

From alignment to alliance is a significant step up in formalization of commitment, and further steps are possible that entail greater degrees of commitment. Alliances can be thought of as part of a continuum of security relationship from alignment through federation (Lake 1996, 1999; Weber 1997). Alliances allow their members to retain final freedom of action in foreign policy; tighter forms of relations cede some control over foreign policy to another state. Historically, few sovereign states have voluntarily formed tighter relationships than alliances.

Alliances impose costs on their members. Otherwise, states would form alliances freely. One way to think about these costs is as a tradeoff between security and autonomy (Altfeld 1984; Morrow 1987, 1991), with security defined as the ability to preserve the status quo and autonomy defined as the freedom to pursue changes in the status quo. Commonly, states seek additional security through an alliance at the cost of some of their freedom of action. Lalman & Newman (1991) produce evidence that most states that have formed an alliance have increased their security. If alliances produce credible commitments, then it is more likely that an ally will come to a state's aid, increasing the state's security at the cost of some of its ally's autonomy. Alliances are mutual, so each may gain security at the autonomy cost of its commitment to the other. The following section addresses the logic of decisions to intervene in war as a prelude to a consideration of how alliances could produce credible commitments.

DECISIONS TO INTERVENE IN WAR

A state chooses to intervene in an ongoing war when the benefits it expects to realize from its intervention exceed the expected costs of joining the war (Altfeld & Bueno de Mesquita 1979). There is some chance that the combatant it favors will win even if the state does not intervene. Suppose that states A and B are at war, and third-party state C would prefer that A win. A simple expected utility calculation shows that C's expected utility (u_C) for a war between A and B if C does not intervene is as follows:

$$p(\text{A wins alone})u_C(\text{A wins alone})$$
$$+ [1 - p(\text{A wins alone})]u_C(\text{B defeats A alone}),$$

The probability (p) that B wins the war is 1 minus the probability that A wins. If C intervenes on A's behalf in the war between A and B, the probability of victory for A (with C) may change, as may C's utilities for the outcomes. State C suffers costs of war as follows:

$$p(\text{A and C win})u_C(\text{A and C win})$$
$$+ [1 - p(\text{A and C win})]u_C(\text{B defeats A and C}) - c(\text{C})$$

The final term, $c(\text{C})$, gives C's costs of fighting. State C will intervene in the war when the second expected utility exceeds the first. [I simplify the problem by ignoring the possibility that C's intervention could trigger the intervention of a state D on B's behalf; see Kim (1991) and Siverson & Starr (1991) on such conditional probabilities of intervention.] Comparing the expected utilities above and rearranging terms, I calculate that C will intervene when the following is true:

$$[p(\text{A and C win}) - p(\text{A wins alone})] \times [u_C(\text{A wins alone}) - u_C(\text{B defeats A alone})] +$$

$$p(\text{A and C win}) \times [u_C(\text{A and C win}) - u_C(\text{A wins alone})] +$$

$$[1 - p(\text{A and C win})] \times [u_C(\text{B defeats A and C}) - u_C(\text{B defeats A alone})] > c(\text{C}). \quad 1.$$

The left side of the inequality (Equation 1) breaks into three expressions presented on the three separate lines above, each of which reflects a specific consideration in C's decision whether to intervene. The first expression gives C's marginal effect on state A's chance of defeating B—the increase in probability that A and C together would defeat B over the probability that A would defeat B by itself. This marginal impact is weighted by C's relative preference that A defeat B—the utility difference in the expression. Thus, C is more likely to intervene (all else equal) as its military capabilities relative to A and B increase, because its effect on A's chance of winning will increase. State C also becomes more likely to intervene the more it favors A over B, because the stakes of the war become more important in C's view.

The second expression in Equation 1 gives any possible individual gains that C could earn for its intervention—the increase in C's utility for A winning when C fights alongside A rather than remaining neutral. Such benefits could include explicit side payments that A offers C for its intervention, as when the Allies promised that Italy would receive Trieste and the Trentino if it joined them in World War I. The gains expressed by the second line of Equation 1 could also include other benefits, such as territory or concessions in the peace treaty, that C could secure on its own because of its role in the war. For example, the Soviet Union intervened against Japan in World War II by invading Manchuria, and as a consequence, it extended military control over Manchuria after the war ended in Asia. These gains are weighted by the chance that they can be realized—the probability that A and C together can defeat B.

The third expression gives the losses that C incurs if it intervenes to support A but B wins the war. Beyond the costs of fighting the war, states that join an ongoing war can suffer losses of territory or even be eliminated should their side lose. Turkey joined the Central Powers in World War I and lost its territories outside Anatolia in the peace settlement. As in the second expression, this term is weighted by the chance that it occurs—the probability that B defeats A and C in the war.

All of the terms in these three considerations vary from case to case. The value that a state places on its ally winning $[u_C(\text{A wins alone}) - u_C(\text{B defeats A alone})]$ depends on the issues in the crisis at hand. The willingness of France to intervene on behalf of Russia was greater in crises in the Balkans in 1908 and 1914 than in crises in Asia from 1895 to 1905, and so France played a larger role as a third party in the former crises than in the latter. Further, the exact values of all the terms, the values attached to winning and losing the war, possible side payments if a state should intervene, and the costs of war, are known only to the third party that is deciding whether to intervene. Other states must judge the likely actions of a third party during a crisis. Will it intervene on behalf of its ally if war occurs, and if so, under what conditions?

Recent research provides clear evidence that alliances do increase the probability of intervention and that states consider the credibility of their target's alliances before attacking (Gartner & Siverson 1996, Smith 1996). Although Sabrosky (1980) has observed that only slightly more than a quarter of allies intervene in wars in support of their allies, this raw figure is misleading.[1] A state considering war is more likely to attack when it expects that its target will not receive aid. When the target does receive aid, it is much more likely to win than when it fights alone (Gartner & Siverson 1996). Further, both initiators and targets consider the credibility of the target's alliances, making initiators less likely to initiate a crisis and targets more likely to resist as the credibility of the target's allies rises (Smith 1996). These selection effects make the raw intervention frequencies misleading because we are more likely to observe a war when an alliance is not credible.

We can use these three considerations to think about alliances and theories of alliances by asking how an alliance can change an intervention decision. Because the promise of aid in an alliance is not binding, the alliance has a real effect only if it alters this calculation in the event of war and in the perceptions of key actors before war. This essay now turns to two ways that alliances could have real effects and then considers some specific theories of alliances and their politics.

SIGNALING VERSUS COMMITMENT

An alliance matters only under two conditions: (*a*) if the alliance affects the decision of the allies to intervene on one another's behalf in the event of war, and (*b*) if it allows states outside the alliance to determine that the allies will intervene to support one another. The first condition requires the alliance to change one or more of the considerations above (Equation 1) to make intervention more likely than it would be without the alliance. The second condition entails making a state's considerations in favor of its ally, which are presumably known only to itself, apparent to states considering war with its ally. The first condition relates to

---

[1]Leeds et al (1999) show that states honor their commitments, as written in their alliances, in crises three quarters of the time. Some of the "defections" that Sabrosky counts involve nonaggression pacts or ententes in which the parties are not legally obligated to come to one another's defense. Others are cases where the mutual defense clauses of the alliance are not triggered by the actions in the crisis even though one ally went to war. Still, a noticeable number of formal defense commitments are not honored by states.

defense, the second to deterrence. Both matter even if war does not occur because the expectations about the credibility of the alliance commitment in the event of war will determine the efficacy of the alliance in producing a bargaining advantage in a crisis.

These two conditions, which I call commitment and signaling, define two ways to produce an effective alliance (Morrow 1999). Commitment mechanisms change a state's decision to intervene by altering one or more of the considerations in its decision. Signals render an alliance credible by allowing others to judge correctly how the allies see those considerations, and thus to judge in advance their willingness to come to one another's aid. In practice, alliances work both to signal intentions and to create commitments; however, I separate these two effects for analytic clarity (Fearon 1997, Morrow 1994).

Signaling

If states could predict one another's actions, then alliances could only serve as devices for prewar military coordination. However, the existence of credibility as an issue implies that states cannot predict one another's actions. States considering the use of force cannot know whether their target's allies will come to its aid. The value that a state places on each of the variables in Equation 1, and the costs of war it anticipates, are known only to the state itself. Other states must judge whether it will intervene. Those other states will use the evidence available in the state's foreign policy to judge the depth of its interest in a particular situation. The question in signaling is how a state's foreign policy actions can allow other states to draw clear inferences about its interests and, thus, its likely future actions. Alliances are one of the strongest types of signals available in the panoply of foreign policy acts.

Effective signaling poses an immediate problem. If there were a signal that would always deter others by convincing them of the willingness of allies to come to one another's aid, then even states that had no intention of aiding their allies would wish to send that signal. Other states are uncertain about the interests that a third party holds in a dispute. Suppose that there are several different types of the third-party state, where each type has different values and hence may make different decisions about whether to intervene. For instance, types could differ in their costs for fighting; those with high costs are less likely to intervene than those with low costs. The third party knows its own type. However, other states know only the range of possible types of the third-party state. Their problem is to infer the type of the third party from its actions. Further, a state's type alone does not dictate its actions; the likely effect of actions also determines what actions it takes. All the types of the third-party state, even those that have no intention of coming to the aid of their allies, would like to form a universal deterrent alliance if it existed.

Signals convey information when different types take different actions. Observers can then distinguish types by their actions. The perfect deterrent alliance cannot convey information about third-party type because all types wish to form such an alliance. Separation of types requires that sending the signal entails a cost, something that will discourage some types from sending the signal and thus differentiate types. It could be that the third party pays the cost up front when it forms the alliance, or the costs could follow as a consequence of its commitment; this is a costly signal. It could be that sending the signal bears no direct costs (a situation often called "cheap talk") but leads to actions by other actors that impose costs on the signaling state. The key point is that forming the alliance must have different costs for different types if it is to signal the third party's intentions.

In the case of alliances, the costs could arise out of a greater risk of war. If an ally is more likely than other states to intervene, an alliance could cause a state to join a war that it would not otherwise enter. Snyder (1984, 1997) calls this possibility entrapment. A state with a high cost for war might choose to avoid an alliance out of the fear that it could be impelled to join a costly war in order to save its ally. The formation of the alliance in this case signals that the third party has low costs for fighting and thus is likely to intervene on behalf of its ally in a war. States considering using force against the ally might then be deterred by their increased confidence that the third party would fight as well.

Snyder (1984, 1997) also discusses costs of abandonment, when a state's ally refuses to come to its aid in a crisis. Abandonment occurs when a state acts aggressively—refuses to make concessions in a crisis or even initiates a crisis itself—because it anticipates the support of its ally, which then fails to come to its aid. It is hard to see how the fear of abandonment could make an alliance into a signal that a state would want to send. Only the most aggressive types, those with low costs of war relative to the value of the stakes, are likely to take the actions that trigger abandonment. By incurring the high costs of abandonment, a state sends the wrong signal to both the prospective ally and states outside the alliance—that the state is to be watched but can be taken advantage of.

There is no explanation of how these costs arise, however. These costly signaling arguments assume that alliances have an effect on the commitment of the allies to one another and thus produce these costs. If states treated alliances as meaningless, these costs would disappear, and the signaling qualities of alliances would go with them. This point does not imply that these costs do not exist; it implies only that there must be some other source of costs for alliances to signal interests or that commitment mechanisms make alliances credible, and thus produce these costs and the information they convey.

Alliances can be effective signals by imposing costs on the allies even if the alliance is never tested in a crisis. First, other states judge the commitment of the allies to one another by the similarity of their foreign policies (Altfeld & Bueno de Mesquita 1979). A decision to intervene in a crisis will be determined in part by the specific interests of the state in the issues of that crisis. Differences in perceived interests between the allies can lead to doubts about the reliability of the alliance in the eyes of others; they may think that the allies can be divided on this issue. Alliances thus gain credibility as the allies indicate a broad range of shared interests through their foreign policies. Such coordination of policy imposes costs on the allies because it forces them to adopt some policies that they would not otherwise adopt and to abandon other positions that they would otherwise pursue. The effort to coordinate policy on issues in which the allies are not in clear agreement reduces the likelihood that others will see differences in the allies' interests, making the alliance more credible. These costs of policy alignment occur even if the alliance is never tested and thus can signal the allies' commitment to one another (Morrow 1991, 1994).

Second, military coordination in an alliance can impose costs if it increases the vulnerability of an ally fighting alone. Alliances with extensive coordination of military forces and plans can make it difficult for a state to fight on its own. For example, reduction in British naval forces under NATO made mounting the expeditionary force to the South Atlantic during the Falklands/Malvinas War in 1982 difficult for Britain. Britain might have kept larger naval forces of its own if the US Navy did not have the formal obligation to defend the North Atlantic under NATO. Such costs arise only if the state has to fight without its ally's complementary forces. In the extreme, the allies could overspend on their militaries to convince one another and states outside the alliance of their commitment to one another. O'Neill (1990) argues that NATO theater nuclear forces deployed in the early 1980s played exactly that role. They demonstrated that the European members of NATO were willing to face the domestic political opposition to deploying those missiles to show their commitment to NATO.

In both policy coordination and military coordination, the costs of the alliance occur whether or not the alliance is tested. Those states that are less committed to the alliance and the interests it advances should be less likely to suffer these costs in order to form the alliance. Thus, the alliance is credible because the only states that would be willing to form an alliance would be those that share enough interests to be likely to help one another. In this way, the alliance signals the shared interests of the allies.

Signaling could also occur within alliances. Secret alliances pose a particular problem for this argument; how can something private signal information (Ritter 2000)? Often, there may be a problem of uncertainty between possible allies. They may not know the extent of one another's commitment. Private talks that limit the applicability of the alliance address some of the problems of entrapment and abandonment by allowing each ally to declare what interests it is willing to fight for, allowing the other to adjust its actions accordingly. Secrecy would be a benefit because the allies might not wish to communicate the limits of their commitment to states outside the alliance. This concern could lead to secret provisions appended to a public treaty.

Offensive alliances pose a problem. Each party needs to know that the other is willing to accept the changes in the status quo that it seeks. In terms of the three considerations given in Equation 1, the allies focus on the side payments each will receive from a war—the second consideration. Each needs reassurance that the other will not object to its war aims. Such a private communication could be informative because if state X does not want its ally Y to achieve its war aims, then

X is setting itself up for an additional war to reverse Y's gains from their offensive war. Obviously, the parties wish to keep an offensive alliance secret from their intended targets.

Finally, states might form an alliance to control or reassure one another (Schroeder 1976, Kydd 1998). Here the effect of the alliance is solely on its members, so there is no need to publicize it to states outside the alliance.

Commitment

Signaling works before a crisis by indicating the interests of the parties; commitment works during a crisis by changing the willingness of a state to intervene on behalf of its ally (Fearon 1997). The effects of commitment are thus more direct than those of signaling and produce advantages in both deterrence and defense over the absence of an alliance. If an alliance can alter any of the three considerations (Equation 1) in an intervention decision, then it could create a credible commitment.

There are two main ways that an alliance could create a credible commitment by altering the considerations (Morrow 1994). First, alliances with military coordination improve the ability of the allies to fight together. NATO is the extreme example of this effect; its multinational command structure, common equipment, and extensive cross-national military exercises helped to forge the many national contingents of NATO into a unified fighting force. By raising the chance that the allies will win a war if they fight together, prewar military coordination makes the allies more likely to come to one another's aid. The first consideration focuses on the marginal military impact of intervention; intervention becomes more likely as p(A and C win) $- p$(A wins alone) increases. Such prewar coordination may also inadvertently create the costs of military specialization discussed in the "Signaling" section above.

Second, audience costs—costs imposed by an actor who is not part of the crisis—can create commitment when a state pays such costs if it fails to honor its alliance. A party outside the governments of the allies could impose punishment on the government of a state defecting from its commitment. Such costs are not directly included in the three considerations, but they can be thought of as reducing the marginal costs of fighting the war. The costs of intervention are reduced by creating costs that are suffered if a state fails to fight. As intervention costs decrease, intervention become more likely.

The relevant audience, the group that imposes costs on the unreliable government, has been generally assumed to be other states. A state that fails to live up to its alliance commitments will be deemed unreliable, so other states will be reluctant to ally with it in the future. This reputation cost could convince states to honor their promises in order to be able to make alliances when their security is threatened in the future; the long-term benefit in reputation more than compensates for the short-term cost of fighting.

This external audience argument has some problems. Every decision to intervene is unique, and the interests and values that drive decisions to intervene vary from case to case. Making judgments about future cases from past cases introduces a difficult problem of inference. Did the unwillingness of the United States to come to the aid of South Vietnam in 1975 announce that the United States would not honor its commitment to NATO? Probably not. There are too many differences between the two cases—differences in interests, in ability to affect the outcome of a war, in the likely costs of war—to justify that simple inference. Not all of these differences made the NATO commitment more credible; the likely costs of intervention were certainly much higher in a war in Europe than in countering the North Vietnamese invasion of South Vietnam. The external audience story, then, requires a clear idea about what remains constant from case to case that allows the reputational inference from one case to another. Further, there may not even be a case in the near future against which to test the credibility of other commitments. Although this reputational argument often asserts that the lack of credibility will provoke additional challenges, this need not be the case. Future challenges are unknown at the time the commitment must be honored, so the cost imposed by the external audience may be negligible (Downs et al 1999).

The other possibility is that domestic political audiences impose costs on their leader if she fails to honor her international commitments (Fearon 1994, Smith 1998). The relevant domestic audience in a state, whether it be the mass electorate of a modern democracy or a small clique of military officers supporting a dictator, cares about how its state fares in international politics (Bueno de Mesquita et al 1999). Those with the power to remove the current leader, either through constitutional or other means, may choose to exercise that power if they are displeased with the results of the leader's foreign policy. Alternatively, they may seek only to restrict the power of the leader. Both such restrictions and the threat of removal from office are costs that domestic audiences can impose on leaders whose foreign policy fails. Clear evidence exists that defeat in war leads to a greater chance of removal from office (Bueno de Mesquita et al 1992, Bueno de Mesquita & Siverson 1995). Although no formal study of the evidence has been conducted, it is plausible that leaders who fail to live up to their commitments will face domestic pressure, especially those who face large constituencies. Prime Minister Chamberlain, for instance, was forced to live up to Britain's guarantee to Poland in 1939 through pressure from the House of Commons (Watt 1989).

Whether external or internal audiences impose costs on leaders who fail to honor their states' commitments, audience costs can operate as a commitment device. Because of these costs, the likelihood for a state to intervene on behalf of an ally is greater than it would have been for the same state to intervene in the same crisis without the alliance. The formal alliance thus serves as a commitment device. Without it, the relevant audience would not hold the leader or state responsible for its failure to intervene on behalf of the state whose interests it shares. With it, a state's leader knows that she may face serious consequences if she backs out of her commitment. States and their leaders thus make alliance commitments only to those states whose interests they share and only if they are confident that they will live up to their commitment to their allies in the event of war. Because the precise issues of a crisis and the positions of the contending sides cannot be predicted, it is possible that a state may choose not to intervene despite an alliance and its commitment effects.

The entrapment problem that Snyder (1984, 1997) discusses looms large if alliances operate as commitment devices. If alliances make intervention more attractive to a state, its ally is more confident of its support in a crisis. This confidence can lead the ally to act more aggressively in a crisis or initiate disputes that it would not initiate in the absence of the alliance, leading to entrapment of the state. States can attempt to control entrapment by limiting the terms under which the alliance operates. Defense pacts typically do not bind when one of the allies begins the war itself. A state can claim that it has not violated its alliance when the conditions of the alliance have not been activated.

Thus, one might think that states would seek to make their alliance commitments as explicit as possible, to spell out every possible detail and contingency. However, they rarely do. Instead, alliances detail certain signal contingencies and leave other areas vague, creating the possibility of entrapment in those areas. One drawback of specifying an alliance commitment completely is that states outside the alliance can determine the issues on which the allies will not aid one another, undermining deterrence on those issues. Threatening states will know to challenge the alliance only on the issues it leaves out. By leaving the commitment not fully specified, other states will have to make judgments about when the "halo" of the alliance will operate (Snyder 1997). The allied states may thus gain some advantage of deterrence even on issues on which they would not come to one another's aid. Explicit commitments may also encourage entrapment if one of the allies becomes certain of the support of the other on an issue. We should expect then that states make an explicit commitment on an issue only if they are certain they will come to one another's aid on that issue, leaving the precise nature of their shared interests on other issues unclear.

Signaling and commitment are the two main mechanisms underlying the credibility of alliances. Typically, any alliance exerts both effects. An alliance signals that the allies have shared or complementary interests on a broad enough range of issues that they are likely to come to one another's aid. It also enhances the allies' commitment on specific issues through military coordination or audience costs, be they internal or external. Alliance can improve both deterrence and defense, both by signaling the allies' shared interests to other states (including each other) and by shaping the allies' interest in supporting one another through commitment. Having explained how alliances can have real effects, I now turn to specific theories of alliances in the light of this argument.

NEOREALISM AND THE BALANCE OF POWER

The balance of power is the best-known theory of alliances, and neorealism is the version of that theory currently in the literature (Waltz 1979, Walt 1987, Snyder 1997). In its purest form, balance of power theory examines the strategic incentives for states to come to one another's aid against a state that seeks global domination.

Most states are content with the international status quo and seek only their own security; these may be termed status quo states. Some states, called revisionist states, aspire to overthrow the existing system and replace it with a system of their own design. The paradigmatic example of a revisionist state is Nazi Germany. The key question in balance of power theory is whether the status quo states will coalesce to stop a revisionist state

Neorealists see the deterrence or defeat of a revisionist state as a public good in the sense that the security of all status quo states is improved if a revisionist state is thwarted (Waltz 1979). Neorealists worry that states may not balance—that is, actively join a coalition—against a revisionist state in order to avoid the costs of war, an avoidance they call buckpassing. In neorealist terms, a state may instead bandwagon with a threatening state—join it in the hope of either deflecting the threat to another state or satisfying its demands (Walt 1987). Both buckpassing and bandwagoning are seen as reasons why a balance of power would not form.

The security dilemma compounds the problem of balancing. The security dilemma arises when one status quo state's steps to increase its security, such as arming itself or forming an alliance, decrease the security of another status quo state (Jervis 1978). Two status quo states could find themselves in a spiral of competition even though neither wishes to challenge the other (Jervis 1976). Combined with the problem of entrapment, such a spiral could lead to a general war that no one sought; what Christensen and Snyder call chain-ganging (Christensen & Snyder 1990, Christensen 1997). Successful balancing thus requires striking a balance to avoid both buckpassing and chain-ganging. [Christensen & Snyder (1990) argue that the balance between offense and defense is critical to the relative importance of buckpassing and chain-ganging.]

Both the balancing argument and the security dilemma require that both status quo and revisionist states are possible (Schweller 1994, 1998; also see Glaser 1992, 1994/1995; Kydd 1997). Although the security dilemma assumes only status quo states, there is no dilemma if each state knows the others do not have revisionist designs. If the status quo states knew that they faced a revisionist state bent on conquering them all, then balancing should be much easier because the consequence of the revisionist state winning any war is elimination for all others. The real problem appears to be how states can tell whether other states are revisionist or not.

However, there is an even deeper problem in this argument. All states have both status quo and revisionist interests (Wolfers 1962). For instance, the United States is often considered a status quo state during the Cold War. However, when the Soviet Union collapsed in 1991, the United States did not work to put it back together again; the United States was happy to see that change in the status quo even though it had not taken actions to pursue that revisionist end during the Cold War. Lack of action to bring about change does not imply no desire for change. On some issues, a state works to bring about change, whereas on others, it acts to preserve the status quo. Whether a state challenges the status quo on an issue is determined by the value of the change, the likelihood of achieving the change, and the likely cost of the challenge, including any threat to its other interests (Morrow 1987). Thus, not only do states have both status quo and revisionist interests, but they may act in different ways on the same issue at different times, sometimes challenging the status quo, at other times protecting it, depending on the current situation.

The fact that all states have both status quo and revisionist interests challenges the neorealist logic of balancing. In the terms of the three considerations in a decision to intervene, balancing concerns only the first term in Equation 1. If security against a revisionist state is a public good and is the only motivation for intervening in a war, then the second and third considerations drop out of the decision to intervene. There is no difference for third party C between revisionist state B winning when C passes the buck [u_c(B defeats A alone) in Equation 1] or when it joins state A against B [u_c(B defeats A and C) in Equation 1]. Revisionist state B will conquer C in either case, either at the same time as it conquers A (if C joins A) or later (if A fights alone). Similarly, it makes no difference to C whether B is defeated by A alone or by A and C together; B has been stopped in either case. The decision to intervene, in a purely neorealist world, is simply a question of marginal effect on the outcome compared to the cost of fighting. A state will pass the buck when its marginal effect on stopping the revisionist state, weighted by the value it places on its own existence, is smaller than its expected costs for fighting. However, the diversity of state goals means that states generally expect to gain side payments from joining a war. Side payments mitigate the problem of buckpassing because they provide an additional motivation for uniting against a revisionist state. States can use their intervention as an opportunity to gain other desirable changes in the status quo. These "private goods" render the provision of the public good of security less problematic.

Similarly, the pure security dilemma does not exist because all states understand that others have revisionist as well as status quo aims. Instead, the question is whether two states with conflicting interests might be willing to use force to change the status quo. States must make judgments about the strength of each other's motivations. Such judgments are difficult because the two types of state with a revisionist aim—those willing to use force and those unwilling to do so—wish to imitate one another. The former wishes not to alarm possible opponents of its challenge, whereas the latter would like to see change even though it is unwilling to force the issue. These incentives make separation of the types, and hence accurate judgments about future actions, difficult (Fearon 1995).

The dilemmas lie in these questions of signaling of intentions and discerning motivations from those signals. How extensive are the demands of a revisionist state? The problem facing Britain and France in the late 1930s was not a lack of willingness to fight a Germany seeking global domination; rather, the problem was correctly divining the extent of Hitler's ambitions. If the Sudetenland really had been his last territorial demand, that price of peace would have been well worth paying. In advance of Hitler's actions in 1939, the leaders of Britain and France could not be certain that Hitler was lying at Munich. After the fact, of course, it was clear that Hitler had grander ambitions. The spiral and deterrence models of Jervis (1976) thus reflect the problem of inferring intentions from actions and matching responses to the types of opponents. These models are not general theories of conflict; rather, they form a matched pair of problems, with each looming larger in some cases than in others.

Alliances can help address the inferential problem to the extent that they clarify commitments and intentions. However, the balance of power is not truly a theory of alliances; it is a theory of strategic interests and the alignments that should result from those interests. The question of which coalitions form looms over the question of why nations choose to formalize some relations but not others. Neorealists generally study alliances and alignments as essentially equivalent (e.g. Walt 1987, Snyder 1997). To be sure, both express shared or complementary interests, but there is a further question as to why some sets of interests are formalized and others are not. My discussion of alliances as signals and commitment devices is relevant to the issues that concern neorealists, such as the formation of a coalition against a revisionist state.

Formal models of alignments in balance of power situations do not produce the conclusions of the neorealists. Niou & Ordeshook (1990, 1994; Niou et al 1989) do not find that bipolar systems are particularly stable; they do find that multipolar systems are often stable in the sense that no actors are eliminated. Their model attempts to look at balance of power dynamics explicitly. Smith (1995) and Powell (1999) use more detailed three-actor models to look at incentives to balance versus incentives to bandwagon and find that bandwagoning is far more common in the models than in neorealist theory. Other actors choose not to be involved at all when neorealist theory says they should balance. None of these models demonstrates that the logic of neorealism is wrong; multipolar systems are difficult to model because of the complexity of the possible interactions. The models of Smith and Powell may fail to capture all the relevant concerns. Nevertheless, it is troubling that some simple attempts to formalize neorealist logic lead to results so different from the informal arguments. Because these strategic problems are complex, models should be most useful for refining our intuition.

OTHER ISSUES

Arms Versus Allies

A state can enhance its security either by seeking allies or by building up its own military (Altfeld 1984). Arms and allies are both costly and bring security with different consequences. Alliances add security immediately with the costs of commitment to the ally, the possibility of entrapment, and the need to align policy with the ally to render the alliance credible. A state can count on its own military during a war, but expansion of the military requires additional resources in money and manpower. Therefore, states face a tradeoff between arms and allies; both produce the same end result—greater security—with different costs. We should expect that states substitute arms and allies for each other in their security policies

(Altfeld 1984, Morrow 1993, Sorokin 1994). Building up arms lowers the need to seek new allies or tighten existing alliances and vice versa.

Conybeare (1992, 1994) portrays the arms-allies problem as a question of investing in security, where each method carries different types of risks. States seek to increase their security and reduce their risk by diversifying their sources of security. Conybeare portrays risk in terms of fluctuations in military capabilities. It might be more useful to consider the riskiness of an alliance in terms of entrapment and abandonment.

Although this tradeoff between arms and allies seems apparent, direct evidence of it is limited. Few studies have attempted to assess this tradeoff directly, and the evidence is mixed (e.g. Most & Siverson 1987). The problem may be that the tradeoff works at the margin, yet we can only observe aggregate changes in security policy, such as military expenditures and a complete alliance portfolio. Over time, a state's security policy adjusts slowly to evolving conditions. Only shocks in a state's security position, such as the emergence of a new rival or a dramatic outcome of a war, lead to large changes in a state's security, calling for a substantial response. Even with the tradeoff, substantial responses in security policy are likely to increase arms and allies simultaneously. The parallel is an income effect in consumer choice theory in economics; if a consumer's income rises, she is likely to buy more of two goods, even if they are substitutes for each other. Therefore, attempts to assess the tradeoff between arms and allies using aggregate data are likely to find that arms and allies rise and fall together, rather than in opposition to one another. The tradeoff is obscured by outside determinants that lead a state to seek greater security.

The proper way to test the tradeoff between arms and allies lies in hypotheses drawn from explicit theory of security policy, including the tradeoff. This task is difficult because it requires a three-actor model to incorporate endogenous alliances, and the tradeoff of each actor must be modeled separately. Sorokin (1994) has made the best effort to date. Morrow (1993) presents suggestive case descriptions of the tradeoff's effects on security policy at the margins in the 1860s and before the World Wars. This tradeoff is an open question in the alliance literature.

Burden Sharing

Burden sharing is closely related to the arms-allies tradeoff. If the goal of an alliance is deterrence of a threat, then successful deterrence does operate as a public good in that all of the allies are protected from the threatening power. That deterrence depends on the collective military power of the alliance, so each ally has an incentive to reduce its own military because it bears the full cost while all the allies share the benefit in deterrence. The impetus to "free ride" on alliance partners is stronger for smaller allies because the aggregate military power of the alliance depends mainly on the contributions of the larger members. The conclusion is that the military burden is shared unequally in alliances, with the largest members bearing more than their share (Olson & Zeckhauser 1966, Sandler 1993).

NATO is the most commonly studied case of burden sharing. The usual hypothesis is that the United States, being the largest ally, bears a disproportionately large share of the military burden of the alliance. Because NATO is an unusually large alliance with a wide range of sizes of members, the conditions for burden sharing are dramatic. Extensive data on military expenditures and other contributions to alliance security are easy to obtain, which makes the NATO case additionally attractive to study. The usual conclusion is that NATO does exhibit the "free riding" problem of burden sharing in that the smaller members' share of the burden is smaller than their relative size in the alliance would predict.

The generality of the burden sharing problem is not clear, however. NATO is a very unusual alliance on many grounds, e.g. number of members, duration, and degree of formalization of institutions. Studies of other alliances from earlier periods reveal that burden sharing does not seem to occur (Thies 1987, Conybeare & Sandler 1990). Furthermore, burden sharing in NATO has changed over time (Oneal 1990). Part of the problem may be the distinction between deterrence and defense (Murdoch & Sandler 1982). Defense, as argued above, produces private benefits, so allies that expect to have to fight may build larger militaries in the interest of self-protection in wartime. Allies may also hold different ideas of their interests, and as each builds a military to suit its own interests, the question of what sort of forces to build is more important than burden sharing. For example, during the Cold War, the United States built a military not only to defend Western Europe but also to address American global interests. Its NATO allies might have preferred that the United States build a military more suited to the defense of Europe, with a larger army and less carrier airpower.

Management and Duration of Alliances

Once formed, an alliance relationship must be managed. The duration of an alliance is an indicator of successful alliance management. There are two views of alliance management. Morrow (1991) discusses how changes in capabilities and interests drive the willingness of states to retain or exit an alliance. A state's comparison of its security and autonomy with and without an alliance drives its decision of whether to break that alliance (Berkowitz 1983). Changes in the capabilities of the state and its ally alter its security in and out of the alliance. Any such change makes an alliance more likely to break; increases in a state's capabilities improve its own security outside the alliance, decreases in its ally's capabilities reduce its security in the alliance, and either ally can break the alliance. Morrow (1991) provides a test that supports this argument. A large change in interests could also cause an alliance to break by shifting what the state sees as its security and autonomy interests. Berkowitz (1983) finds that shifting interests undermine commitments to multilateral alliances. Siverson & Starr (1994) show that a change in a state's regime is likely to cause one or more of its alliances to end. Because a state's understanding of its interests often changes when its current regime falls, the authors provide some evidence that changes in interests increase the chance that an alliance will terminate.

Snyder (1997) views alliance management as a balancing act between abandonment and entrapment. States use their foreign policy to reassure their allies and warn off prospective enemies when their allies fear abandonment. When their allies become adventuresome, states use their foreign policy to reduce their commitment and the possibility of entrapment. The conditions under which these considerations lead a state to break an alliance are unclear, and so are the conclusions of the argument about alliance duration.

Symmetric Versus Asymmetric Alliances

The argument so far assumes that allies seek security at some cost of autonomy, that is, that the allies have the common goal of security (Altfeld 1984). An alternative pattern, in which one ally offers security while obtaining other desired ends, is also possible (Morrow 1991). Such alliances with asymmetry of ends also show asymmetry of capabilities; the smaller ally receives security and makes concessions that its larger defender desires. These concessions could include some degree of control over the smaller ally's foreign and domestic policy or means that allow the larger ally to project power to advance other interests in changing the status quo. Such asymmetric alliances last longer than their symmetric counterparts for two reasons. First, changes in the smaller ally's capabilities are not likely to convince either ally to leave the alliance; the smaller will still depend on the larger for its security, and the benefits the larger receives from the alliance do not depend on the smaller's capabilities. Second, the asymmetric alliance produces a more even mix of complementary goals for the parties, and thus is likely to be more stable. Statistical evidence shows that asymmetric alliances are more common than symmetric ones (Morrow 1991) and last longer (Bennett 1997).

An alternative explanation for asymmetric alliances and their increased duration arises from the need of the smaller ally to reassure its larger protector by providing it with control over key dimensions of its policy (Lake 1996, 1999). The problem of entrapment looms large in an asymmetric alliance. The smaller ally, being unable to advance a desire for change on its own, may attempt to create a crisis that will force its larger ally to come to its aid. Before the larger protector is willing to extend that commitment, it demands some control over the behavior of the smaller state to reduce the possibility of entrapment. Consequently, asymmetric alliances last longer because they are difficult to form. An asymmetric alliance forms only when the parties solve the entrapment problem. Once this is solved, the resulting alliance is quite stable because the smaller ally is protected from abandonment and the larger is protected from entrapment. However, this argument does not explain why asymmetric alliances are more common than symmetric ones.

Domestic Politics and Alliances

This essay has only touched on the role of domestic politics; here I discuss it directly. Snyder (1997:143) describes the influence of domestic politics on interests and judging strategies as follows:

Much more common are cases in which the systemic constraints leave considerable room for choice, and domestic constraints then determine actual choices, or at least narrow the range of choice. In such cases, it is often hard to say whether external or internal causation is predominant. For example, the British ententes [that created the Triple Entente before World War I] were responses to both increasing external demands on resources and domestic economic-political limits on available resources. Since constraints, either external or internal, are rarely absolute, Britain faced a choice between satisfying external constraints at some domestic cost—that is, increasing or maintaining armaments—or sacrificing some external goals to meet domestic constraints. Its actual choice was a combination of the two.

States view international politics through a lens of domestic politics. All states have both status quo and revisionist interests. The definition of a state's interests and when it should pursue change instead of working to keep the status quo lie in the hands of a state's leader and government. Leaders understandably care about the views of those who keep them in office, their support coalition (Bueno de Mesquita et al 1999). Judgments about foreign policy—which international interests to pursue, when, and how—are made with an eye on their domestic consequences. Because members of a leader's support coalition care about how their state fares internationally, the actual results of foreign policy do matter to leaders concerned about their own future in power. Still, the support coalition and its view of the nation's role in international politics shape the way leaders act internationally.

The type of domestic regime determines the magnitude and membership of the support coalition. Modern mass democracies require broad coalitions across society, quite unlike those found in an ancient monarchy. These shifts in coalitions do alter alliances. A prime minister who survives in office solely on the assent of his king depends primarily on his personal reputation in his foreign policy. Democracies face the problem that their leaders' hold on office is more tenuous than in other types of systems, so prospective allies of a democracy project a greater chance of change in leader and possibly policy. In response, democracies have checks, such as formal ratification of treaties, and visible mechanisms that reassure their allies that they will not break their commitments (Cowhey 1993). Because the hurdle of making a treaty among democracies is higher, the resulting alliances last longer (Gaubatz 1996, Bennett 1997). Further, democracies are more likely to ally with each other than with other types of states, even though they make fewer alliances than other types of regimes (Siverson & Emmons 1991). Finally, democracies support their allies more often than authoritarian states do (Rapp 1996).

WHERE DO WE GO FROM HERE?

In future research on alliances, both theoretical and empirical, more detailed understandings of signaling and commitment would be a major advance. Does prewar military coordination impose a cost on allies, and can we measure those costs even crudely? The dynamics of audience costs on alliances are not fully understood, whether those costs are imposed by an internal or external audience. Audience costs must be endogenized in a model to be understood. For instance, is it possible for one state to infer another state's present degree of resolve from a past case, and is there a plausible model that incorporates this foreign reputation argument? Theoretical developments should lead directly to more detailed empirical studies of these processes across a wide spectrum of cases.

Entrapment has not been explored fully. Existing models of alliance commitments do not consider the possibility of entrapment because they assume the identity of a threatening state. Entrapment requires that the ally be able to provoke conflict on its own. Formal models of entrapment should also help explain why states do not completely state their obligations to one another. Although alliances often include some specific provisions, much is left unspecified. Although specificity controls entrapment, it also limits the deterrence effect across all issues, especially those that may arise in the future. An empirical study of the conditions under which entrapment is likely, and of its consequences, would be interesting.

The tradeoff between arms and allies poses a puzzle. We do not know what the arms-allies tradeoff theory predicts in equilibrium. Such a prediction is difficult because modeling the tradeoff for just one state is difficult, and three states appear to be the minimum for a model of alliances. Empirical work in this area must wait for the models to be worked out in order to provide hypotheses to be tested. As noted above, the tradeoff would not be observed directly.

Finally, further work on how domestic politics shapes security strategies would be welcome. Different regime types have different alliance behavior; can we trace those differences directly back to important features of those regimes? Changes in leaders may lead to important changes in alliance policy or to little change. Specific characteristics of different systems, such as the form of ratification, should be examined for their effects on alliance reliability and duration. Tying domestic politics to signaling and commitment strategies will help resolve key problems in understanding why states write down some commitments but not others.

Visit the Annual Reviews home page at www.AnnualReviews.org

LITERATURE CITED

Altfeld MA. 1984. The decision to ally. *West. Polit. Q.* 37:523–44

Altfeld MA, Bueno de Mesquita B. 1979. Choosing sides in war. *Int. Stud. Q.* 23:87–112

Bennett DS. 1997. Testing models of alliance duration, 1816–1984. *Am. J. Polit. Sci.* 41:846–78

Berkowitz BD. 1983. Realignment in international treaty organizations. *Int. Stud. Q.* 27:77–96

Bueno de Mesquita B, Morrow JD, Siverson RM, Smith A. 1999. Policy failure and political survival. *J. Confl. Resolut.* 43:147–61

Bueno de Mesquita B, Siverson RM. 1995.

War and the survival of political leaders. *Am. Polit. Sci. Rev.* 89:841–55

Bueno de Mesquita B, Siverson RM, Woller G. 1992. War and the fate of regimes. *Am. Polit. Sci. Rev.* 86:638–46

Christensen TJ. 1997. Perceptions and alliances in Europe, 1865–1940. *Int. Organ.* 51:65–98

Christensen TJ, Snyder J. 1990. Chain gangs and passed bucks. *Int. Organ.* 44:137–68

Conybeare JAC. 1992. A portfolio diversification model of alliances. *J. Confl. Resolut.* 36:53–85

Conybeare JAC. 1994. Arms versus alliances. *J. Confl. Resolut.* 38:215–35

Conybeare JAC, Sandler T. 1990. The Triple Entente and the Triple Alliance 1880–1914. *Am. Polit. Sci. Rev.* 84:1197–206

Cowhey PF. 1993. Domestic institutions and the credibility of international commitments. *Int. Organ.* 47:299–326

Dingman RV. 1979. Theories of, and approaches to, alliance politics. In *Diplomacy,* ed. PG Lauren, pp. 245–66. New York: Free. 286 pp.

Downs GW, Gilligan MJ, Rocke DM. 1999. *Reputation and cooperation.* Presented at Annu. Meet. Am. Polit. Sci. Assoc., 95th, Atlanta, GA

Fearon JD. 1994. Domestic political audiences and the escalation of international disputes. *Am. Polit. Sci. Rev.* 88:577–92

Fearon JD. 1995. Rationalist explanations for war. *Int. Organ.* 39:379–414

Fearon JD. 1997. Signaling foreign policy interests. *J. Confl. Resolut.* 41:68–90

Gartner SS, Siverson RM. 1996. War expansion and war outcome. *J. Confl. Resolut.* 40:4–15

Gaubatz KT. 1996. Democratic states and commitment in international relations. *Int. Organ.* 50:109–39

Glaser CL. 1992. Political consequences of military strategy. *World Polit.* 44:497–538

Glaser CL. 1994/1995. Realist as optimists. *Int. Secur.* 19:50–90

Jervis R. 1976. *Perception and Misperception in International Politics.* Princeton, NJ: Princeton Univ. Press. 445 pp.

Jervis R. 1978. Cooperation under the security dilemma. *World Polit.* 30:167–214

Kim CH. 1991. Third-party participation in wars. *J. Confl. Resolut.* 35:659–77

Kydd A. 1997. Game theory and the spiral model. *World Polit.* 49:371–400

Kydd A. 1998. *Rational security institutions.* Presented at Annu. Meet. Am. Polit. Sci. Assoc., 94th, Boston

Lake DA. 1996. Anarchy, hierarchy, and the variety of international relations. *Int. Organ.* 50:1–33

Lake DA. 1999. *Entangling Relations.* Princeton, NJ: Princeton Univ. Press. 332 pp.

Lalman D, Newman D. 1991. Alliance formation and national security. *Int. Interact.* 16:239–53

Leeds BA, Long AG, Mitchell SM. 1999. *Reevaluating alliance reliability: specific threats, specific promises.* Presented at N. Am. Meet. Peace Sci. Soc., 33rd, Ann Arbor, MI

Morrow JD. 1987. On the theoretical basis of a measure of national risk attitudes. *Int. Stud. Q.* 31:423–38

Morrow JD. 1991. Alliances and asymmetry. *Am. J. Polit. Sci.* 35:904–33

Morrow JD. 1993. Arms versus allies. *Int. Organ.* 47:207–33

Morrow JD. 1994. Alliances, credibility and peacetime costs. *J. Confl. Resolut.* 38:270–97

Morrow JD. 1999. The strategic setting of choices. In *Strategic Choice and International Relations,* ed. DA Lake, R Powell, pp. 77–114. Princeton, NJ: Princeton Univ. Press. 271 pp.

Most BA, Siverson RM. 1987. Substituting arms and alliances, 1870–1914. In *New Directions in the Study of Foreign Policy,* ed. CF Herrmann, CW Kegley, JN Rosenau, pp. 131–57. Boston: Allen & Unwin. 538 pp.

Murdoch J, Sandler T. 1982. A theoretical and empirical analysis of NATO. *J. Confl. Resolut.* 26:237–65

Niou EMS, Ordeshook PC. 1990. Stability in anarchic international systems. *Am. Polit. Sci. Rev.* 84:1207–34

Niou EMS, Ordeshook PC. 1994. Alliances in anarchic international systems. *Int. Stud. Q.* 38:167–92

Niou EMS, Ordeshook PC, Rose GF. 1989. *The Balance of Power.* Cambridge, UK: Cambridge Univ. Press. 359 pp.

Olson M, Zeckhauser R. 1966. An economic theory of alliances. *Rev. Econ. Stat.* 48:266–79

Oneal JR. 1990. The theory of collective action and burden sharing in NATO. *Int. Organ.* 44:379–402

O'Neill B. 1990. The intermediate nuclear force missiles. *Int. Interact.* 15:345–63

Powell R. 1999. *In the Shadow of Power.* Princeton, NJ: Princeton Univ. Press. 310 pp.

Rapp WE. 1996. *Theory of democratic alliance reliability.* PhD thesis, Stanford Univ. 276 pp.

Ritter JM. 2000. *Silent partners: secret alliances in international politics.* PhD thesis, Harvard Univ.

Sabrosky AN. 1980. Interstate alliances. In *The Correlates of War,* Vol. II, ed. JD Singer, pp. 161–98. New York: Free. 328 pp.

Sandler T. 1993. The economic theory of alliances. *J. Confl. Resolut.* 37:446–83

Schroeder PW. 1976. Alliances, 1815–1945. In *Historical Dimensions of National Security Problems,* ed. K Knorr, pp. 227–62. Lawrence: Univ. Press Kansas. 387 pp.

Schweller RL. 1994. Bandwagoning for profit. *Int. Secur.* 19:72–107

Schweller RL. 1998. *Deadly Imbalances.* New York: Columbia Univ. Press. 267 pp.

Siverson RM, Emmons J. 1991. Birds of a feather. *J. Confl. Resolut.* 35:285–306

Siverson RM, Starr H. 1991. *The Diffusion of War.* Ann Arbor: Univ. Mich. Press. 141 pp.

Siverson RM, Starr H. 1994. Regime change and the restructuring of alliances. *Am. J. Polit. Sci.* 38:145–61

Smith A. 1995. Alliance formation and war. *Int. Stud. Q.* 39:405–25

Smith A. 1996. To intervene or not to intervene. *J. Confl. Resolut.* 40:16–40

Smith A. 1998. International crises and domestic politics. *Am. Polit. Sci. Rev.* 92:623–38

Snyder GH. 1984. The security dilemma in alliance politics. *World Polit.* 36:461–95

Snyder GH. 1997. *Alliance Politics.* Ithaca, NY: Cornell Univ. Press. 414 pp.

Sorokin GL. 1994. Arms, alliances, and security tradeoffs in enduring rivalries. *Int. Stud. Q.* 38:421–46

Stein AA. 1990. *Why Nations Cooperate.* Ithaca, NY: Cornell Univ. Press. 219 pp.

Thies WJ. 1987. Alliances and collective goods. *J. Confl. Resolut.* 31:298–332

Walt SM. 1987. *The Origin of Alliances.* Ithaca, NY: Cornell Univ. Press. 321 pp.

Waltz KN. 1979. *Theory of International Politics.* New York: Random House. 251 pp.

Watt DC. 1989. *How War Came.* New York: Pantheon. 736 pp.

Weber K. 1997. Hierarchy amidst anarchy. *Int. Stud. Q.* 41:321–40

Wolfers A. 1962. *Discord and Collaboration.* Baltimore, MD: Johns Hopkins Univ. Press. 283 pp.

Annu. Rev. Polit. Sci. 2000. 3:85–115

WHEELS WITHIN WHEELS: Rethinking the Asian Crisis and the Asian Model

Robert Wade

Watson Institute for International Studies, Brown University, Providence, Rhode Island 02912, and London School of Economics, London WC2A 2AE, United Kingdom; e-mail: R.Wade@LSE.ac.uk

Key Words   finance, international, East Asia, globalization, economic governance, capital controls

■ **Abstract**   The East Asian economic crisis of 1997–1999 had its causes not mainly in the "East Asian model" nor even in departures from the model, but in international capital markets and the governments of the core economies, especially the United States and Japan. The post–Bretton Woods system, without any link between the dollar and gold, allowed the United States to finance persistent external deficits by creating US government bonds. These bonds raised the foreign reserves of the surplus countries, notably Japan and East Asia. The rise in reserves triggered credit booms that generated asset inflation and industrial overcapacity. The booms gave way to crisis. The East Asian variant differed from the earlier Japanese one by being fueled by very large capital inflows in the early to mid 1990s from recession-hit Japan and Europe, as well as from the United States. This perspective, which highlights causes outside of East Asia, suggests that emerging market economies will remain vulnerable to such crises in the absence of capital controls, a different system of international payments, and a more equal world income distribution. It also suggests unexpected directions for political science research.

> To its credit [Korea] has acknowledged its faults with remarkable candour. It has not tried to blame foreigners for its troubles, nor has it hid behind tariff barriers or currency controls. Instead, it has pledged to abandon the economic system that took it from poverty to prosperity in a generation. (*Economist* 1999)

> The Korean economy is another kind of leftover Cold War artifact, good for an era of security threats and close bilateral relations with Washington but of questionable use in the global "world without borders" of the 1990s.... It is a highly leveraged, highly political, manifestly corrupt nexus between the state and big business.... [It] has always been intrinsically unstable and therefore vulnerable to exactly the sort of financial calamity that has now befallen it. (Woo-Cumings 1997)

1094–2939/00/0623–0085$14.00

INTRODUCTION

During the year following mid 1997, several East Asian economies—especially South Korea, Thailand, Malaysia, and Indonesia, combined population nearly 350 million—went haywire. Their currencies and stock markets plunged, banks failed, real interest rates shot up, exports fell, imports fell by even more, firms shut down, people who had worked at regular jobs for 10 or 20 years suddenly found themselves on the street, and anxiety took hold. It became not merely a crisis but a collapse, perhaps the world's steepest and deepest since the Great Depression (apart from natural disasters, famines, wars, and transitions from communism).

Yet these same economies had until then constituted "the East Asian miracle" (World Bank 1993). By the 1990s, their fast economic growth was one of the certainties of our age. They had been growing at 5–10% a year for decades. Korea had not had a year of significantly less than 5% real growth in its gross domestic product (GDP) since 1980, Thailand not since 1972. Add in China growing at over 9% a year since the mid 1980s, and nearly 30% of the world's population experienced a doubling of GDP every decade or so—unprecedented in human history. Add in Japan, and by the early 1990s, the region accounted for a quarter of world output, half of world growth, and almost two thirds of world fixed capital investment. In 1990–1996, residents of Taiwan, South Korea, Singapore, and Hong Kong (combined population 73 million) took out almost 19,000 patents in the United States, compared with 1100 for the top four Latin American countries, 1300 for the whole of east and central Europe, 20,000 for France, and 17,500 for Britain (both with populations of 58 million).

Through the 1980s, Asia, led by Japan, seemed set to become an equal leg of a tripolar world with North America and Europe. The United States seemed a diminished giant—the world's biggest debtor nation, dependent on a continually depreciating dollar to sell its exports and on Asian savings to fund its deficits, constrained militarily by the "Vietnam syndrome," and unable to sustain political coalitions of support in the United Nations and other multilateral organizations. Latin America after 1982 hardly counted except as a place from which to collect debts. The whole of the western hemisphere was being eclipsed. On the other side of the Atlantic, Europe appeared introspective, enfeebled by low growth and high unemployment and dependent on the Americans even for its defense. To many commentators, both western and Asian, it was increasingly unclear how the West could claim superiority for its neoliberal model when the results in terms of economic growth, income distribution, education, and social cohesion looked manifestly inferior to Asia's (Foot & Walter 1999).

By the late 1980s, commentators began to ring the arrival of the "Pacific Century" and the premature close of the "American Century," whose beginning had been proclaimed as recently as 1945. Books appeared with titles like *Pacific Century, Pacific Rising, Pacific Destiny, Megatrends Asia,* and *Asia Pacific*. The audacity of it all was symbolized by sleepy Kuala Lumpur launching a bid for world city status by planning not just the tallest building in the world but the two tallest buildings in the world, the 88-story twin towers of Petronas, the state oil company.

The crisis shocked the world not only because it happened in the context of sustained success but also because it did not result from the things that are thought to be the normal causes of economic crisis in developing countries—bad "fundamentals," meaning fiscal deficits, trade deficits, and inflation. It was unanticipated in both onset and severity. Even worse, unlike earlier crises of developing countries, it seemed to threaten the stability of the international financial system itself. As a result, the Asian crisis has spawned more discussion of the redesign of the rules of global finance and of domestic financial systems than any crisis since the Depression. Some commentators dubbed it the first twenty-first century crisis.

The "official-academic" consensus on the crisis was that, although its causes were not the standard ones, they were, nevertheless, still mostly "homegrown" (Fischer 1998). Deputy US Treasury Secretary Lawrence Summers explained, "[This crisis] is profoundly different because it has its roots not in improvidence but in economic structures. The problems that must be fixed are much more microeconomic than macroeconomic, and involve the private sector more and the public sector less." Most of the political science literature on the crisis accepts the idea of mostly homegrown causes. (Collections on the crisis include *Cambridge Journal of Economics* 1998, Jomo 1998, *World Development* 1998, *IDS Bulletin* 1999, and Pempel 1999. See also Cumings 1998; Lim 1998; Doner 1999; Henderson 1999; Putzel 2000; Weiss 1999, 2000; Yoshitomi & Ohno 1999.) This literature concentrates on identifying the political causes in each country and sometimes goes on to compare why events happened one way in one country, another way in another. Like the broader official-academic consensus, its leitmotif is failure of Asian governance. The Asian model, it says, worked for a time but then stopped working; hence the crisis.

In this essay I explain the weaknesses of the "failure of Asian governance" theory. I then outline an alternative, the "failure of international financial markets" theory, which says that the Asian crisis is only one in a series of financial crises that have rotated around the zone of countries closely integrated into world capital markets during the late 1980s and 1990s, especially in weakly institutionalized "emerging market" economies (developing countries of interest to international investors). The crises tend to be associated with an open capital account and large foreign capital inflows, producing a credit bubble, which sometimes ends in crisis. Regional and national factors have some influence over where and when the credit boom blows out and the form that the blowout takes; but the dynamics of core economies and international capital markets are deeply implicated in the phenomenon itself.

Think of the metaphor of wheels within wheels. The Asian crisis can be explained partly by the motion of the inner wheels, the trends in national and regional variables. But the overall result was driven more by the motion of the outer wheels and the tighter integration between inner and outer wheels made in the 1990s. At the end of the essay I outline some issues for political science research highlighted by this metaphor.

THE "FAILURE OF ASIAN GOVERNANCE" THEORY

The trigger of the crisis, everyone agrees, was the sharp reversal of private capital flows starting in mid 1997. Net private inflows of about $93 billion in 1996 to Korea, Thailand, Malaysia, Indonesia, and the Philippines became net outflows of about $12 billion in 1997, the $105 billion turnaround amounting to 11% of combined GDP. No economy can withstand such a whiplash withdrawal of capital without severe disruption.

The key question is why the private capital inflows were so "excessive" (as defined after the event). According to the official-academic consensus, the reasons were (*a*) "lack of transparency" in company and bank accounts, which meant that institutional investors could not know the truth about the position of their borrowers; (*b*) "weak prudential regulation" by the monetary authorities, which allowed banks to lend to heavily indebted companies; (*c*) "poor" exchange rate management, meaning commitment to a fixed exchange rate, which seemed to rule out foreign exchange risk, making foreign borrowing too cheap; and (*d*) "moral hazard," meaning that investors expected that the banks and firms they were lending to would be bailed out by the Asian governments ("implicit guarantees"). These causes are themselves the consequences of East Asia's "cronyistic"—or less pejoratively, "relationship"—system of economic governance. In this system, (*a*) banks rather than capital markets intermediate finance, (*b*) banks, big firms and governments have close and long-term relations, and (*c*) agreements are made behind the scenes, unmonitored by independent parties and unenforced by courts, and the government has a direct influence on who gets credit and other support. This system resulted in inefficient investments that could not repay the foreign financial claims piling up against them.

In the words of Federal Reserve Chairman Alan Greenspan, crisis-afflicted Asia suffered from "a free market veneer over a state-managed economic structure," which has "inevitably led to the investment excesses and errors to which all similar [state-influenced] endeavors seem prone" (Sanger 1998). In the echoing words of the managing director of the International Monetary Fund (IMF), Michel Camdessus, "countries must take great care to ensure that their affairs are conducted in an irreproachable and transparent manner and that all forms of corruption, nepotism, and favoritism are shunned; yet, over time in Asia, these afflictions took hold and overpowered systems that were otherwise remarkably successful" (Camdessus 1998).

The consensus within each crisis-affected country has tended to focus on the country's crisis as a singular event with country-specific causes. Indonesians and foreign Indonesian experts talked of "the Indonesian crisis" and found its causes in, for instance, the Suharto family's cronyism. Koreans and foreign Korean experts talked of "the Korean crisis" and found its causes in the misdeeds of the Kim Young Sam government and its corrupt relations with some of the conglomerates, or in more structural and long-lasting problems. "The cause of the crisis was our disrespect for the rule of law," declared the governor of North Cholla province (You 1999). "The Korean economic system has always been intrinsically unstable, and therefore vulnerable to exactly the sort of financial calamity that has now befallen it," claimed the US-based Korean political scientist Meredith Jung-en Woo-Cumings (1997).

The nearly unanimous conclusion among both US and Asian policy elites was that the national model (for those with a national focus) or the "East Asian" model (for those with a regional focus) had outlived its usefulness. Korea, Indonesia, and the others had become too complex, or too corrupt, for the economy to be "intervened" in as in the past. Moreover, internal evolution aside, such intervention could no longer work in the new realities of global capital markets. The crisis was merely the messenger delivering the wake-up call to effect radical structural reforms and establish "sound" institutions and policies in banking, capital markets, corporate governance, labor markets, and the like. "Sound" is code for "consistent with the prescriptions of the Washington Consensus," that is, consistent with the Anglo-American model of a free market economy with (*a*) arms-length relations between banks, firms and government, (*b*) regulation by formal contracts enforced in courts of law, and (*c*) capital market as the basis of the financial system. "Sound" further implies consistency with a policy configuration of small government, low taxes, low budget deficits, low welfare spending, and very low inflation.

But interpreting the Asian crisis is not merely an academic debate. For many American commentators, the crisis was cause for celebration. First communism had been defeated, and now the Asian alternative too. The Pacific Century was dead; the American Century was back. "The sudden collapse of Asia's house of cards," said one journalist, "is beginning to be seen as the end of an outdated economic and political system based largely on the mercantilist, government-run Japanese model—much as the fall of the Berlin Wall symbolized the demise of communism" (Dale 1998). Henry Kissinger, former US Secretary of State, warned, "Even [Asian] friends I respect for their moderate views argue that Asia is confronting an American campaign to stifle Asian competititon. It is critical that at the end of this crisis, when Asia will reemerge as a dynamic part of the world, America be perceived as a friend that gave constructive advice and assistance in the common interest, not as a bully determined to impose bitter social and economic medicine to serve largely American interests" (1998).

Many of the proponents of the failure-of-Asian-governance theory had earlier championed the idea that Asia was successful because of free markets and good economic management, and they were none too careful to reconcile their discovery of basic flaws in Asian capitalism with their earlier explanation of success. But the theory served western interests well. For all their devotion to the principles of free trade and the division of labor, many in the West regarded Asia's rise as a threat. As the Cold War wound down, they saw economic issues becoming more important determinants of a country's overall power status than the traditional military ones, and it appeared easier for economic superpowers such as Japan to gain leverage over security issues than for military superpowers such as the United States to gain leverage over economic issues. These observers worried about Japan's growing economic dominance in fast-growing Asia, dominance that seemed to be related to the ability of its government and businesses to operate in the "cronyistic" or "relationship" system better than the shorter-term and formal-contract-oriented western governments and businesses could. The West needed to find ways to encourage Asia to make its economic institutions more congenial to western firms and governments.

Moreover, the failure-of-Asian-governance theory implies that western and Japanese investors acted responsibly—rationally—in lending as much as they did. Since only irresponsible investors deserve not be repaid, the theory underwrote the moral obligation on Asian debtors to repay foreign investors. And since international capital markets had no more than a secondary role in the crisis, not much had to be done by the governments of developed countries or by international organizations to change the regime under which their banks and institutional investors worked internationally. The theory implies that more transparency is needed in corporate and governmental accounts, certainly, and that the IMF should exercise closer surveillance of developing countries (though not of the major industrial countries).[1] But such expensive innovations as an international lender of last resort are not needed, nor restrictions on western institutional investors, nor capital controls in developing countries. Small changes at the international level and in the source countries are enough to protect the tendency of capital markets toward benign equilibrium. In the words of Michel Camdessus, "A lack of transparency has been found at the origin of the recurring crises in the emerging markets, and it has been a pernicious feature of the 'crony capitalism' that has plagued most of the crisis countries and many more besides." Therefore, "[t]here is a strong consensus for making transparency the 'golden rule' of the new international financial system" (Camdessus 1999). With this golden rule in place, capital markets will be stable and deliver big net benefits to developing countries open to them. This is a key assumption of the failure-of-Asian-governance theory.

EVIDENCE FOR THE "FAILURE OF ASIAN GOVERNANCE" THEORY

Those who advance the failure-of-Asian-governance theory, including many Asians, find it attractive because it justifies strong market-liberalizing changes ("reforms") in Asia and exonerates foreign investors, foreign governments, and

---

[1]In August 1999 the IMF Board was considering a report that urges strengthened IMF surveillance of developing countries. The report suggests that the developed countries are already well enough covered by other bodies.

the international financial regime (Woods 1995). This is why it became the standard explanation even though it meets the normal criteria of evidence not much better than its epistemological cousin, the theory of witchcraft.

A key argument of the theory is that "lack of transparency" (including lax government enforcement of disclosure laws) was an important cause of the crisis. To accept this argument, we need evidence supporting the following assertions:

1. Information was lacking on variables that are strongly associated with impending crisis.

2. Had investors known this information—and registered it as indicating a rising probability of crisis—they would have invested significantly less money.

3. The crisis-affected countries had become significantly less transparent over the 1990s.

4. The crisis-affected countries were less transparent than non-crisis-affected comparator countries.

5. In the set of financial crises from the late 1970s onwards, a low level of transparency is associated with crisis and a high level of transparency is associated with non-crisis.

The IMF, the US Treasury, and other proponents of the argument provide no evidence. With reference to Asia, plenty of information about relevant macro variables was publicly available. There is no evidence of systematic misreporting of macro variables relevant to crisis. Most of the relevant data about Thailand's foreign debt was easily available in the two years before the crisis. Everyone knew about the real estate bubble and its financing out of short-term foreign debt. Everyone knew about Indonesian corruption. Everyone knew about Korea's high corporate debt-to-equity ratios (Furman & Stiglitz 1998).

All that we know about capital markets suggests that even had investors been sure of an eventual crisis they would not have lent less today if profits looked good and exit looked open; they would have waited until the last week.

Data on trends in transparency over the 1990s hardly exists. But evidence on people's assessments of corruption—which can be seen as a subset of lack of transparency—shows no increase in perceived corruption in Asian countries in the run-up to the crisis; indeed the corruption score went down in Indonesia and Korea during the 1990s (see Figure 7 in Furman & Stiglitz 1998).

Even if actual transparency did not deteriorate, crisis could still be caused by lack of transparency if international investors began to attach more importance to transparency and therefore weighted the constant level more negatively. But if they gave a more negative weighting, one would expect risk premiums to rise. In fact, risk premiums fell right up to the onset of the crisis.

Within Asia, lack of transparency does not begin to differentiate between the crisis countries and the non-crisis countries. The crisis countries—Korea, Thailand, Malaysia, and Indonesia—all had strongly negative GDP growth in 1998.

The non-crisis countries—Taiwan, China, India, Sri Lanka, and Bangladesh—had significantly positive growth in 1998. One would be hard put to argue that China and India had greater transparency than Korea and Malaysia. Lack of transparency is clearly not a sufficient condition of crisis. Neither is it a necessary condition. Two paragons of transparency have had serious financial crises, namely the United States' Savings and Loan crisis of 1984–1991 and Scandinavia's much bigger currency-cum-banking crisis in the late 1980s to early 1990s.

The transparency argument occludes the information failures of capital markets. Investors were ignorant not mainly because information was falsified or unavailable but because they were not paying attention to what was available. They were not paying attention because their incentives to gather and process information on individual countries in order rationally to assess risks and returns are quite low. The incentives are low because it is easier and cheaper for investors to see what others are doing and herd along—especially if the countries have open capital accounts that allow them to get their money in and out very quickly. "It is very hard to find people who think independently about how to invest in Asia. They are terrified about underperforming the benchmark," said a former Asian fund manager to explain why regional stock indexes, supposed indicators of investor behavior, drive investor behavior (Landler 1999).

The managing director of the IMF calls for transparency as the centerpiece of a reform strategy for the world financial architecture. But the evidence is simply not there. This is not to deny that poor-quality information, especially in the accounts of companies and banks, may have worsened the crisis by making it difficult for investors to distinguish between more and less sound entities, thereby contributing to a panicky rush for the exits; or to deny that countries that seek to integrate fully into world capital markets do need to improve the quality of their macro- and firm-level financial information in order to discourage "excessive" inflows and to check the magnitude of panic once a pullout begins. Institutionalizing robust transparency, however, takes years, perhaps decades. If so, the logic of Camdessus' own argument about transparency implies that countries that fall short on the transparency dimension should go very slowly in their integration into world capital markets. Camdessus, however, is one of the strongest advocates of fast financial integration. He assumes that robust transparency can be quickly achieved.

Similarly unsupported is the argument that "weak prudential regulation of Asian banks" was a major cause of the crisis—meaning that basic prudential rules limiting lending to affiliated companies were regularly broken, banks were under-capitalized, and the share of nonperforming loans in total loans was high or else concealed. If weak prudential regulation was a major cause, we should find that the banking systems of the crisis countries were in worse shape than those of non-crisis countries and became worse during the 1990s. Moody's Investor Services ranked banks on a quality index in 1996. The ranking shows little to distinguish the quality of banks in the Asian crisis economies from those in non-crisis emerging markets [B Bosworth (unpublished) cited in S Radelet, J Sachs (unpublished)]. According to data from the Bank for International Settlements (1997), banks in Malaysia and Indonesia were stronger in 1997 than they had been a few years earlier (as indicated, for example, by the falling share of nonperforming loans). Furthermore, if weak prudential regulation was a major cause of the crisis, it should also be the case that the strength of prudential regulation is largely independent of the volume of capital inflows. But in fact, as explained below, the strength of prudential regulation is partly a function of the volume of capital inflows.

The underlying argument about the relationship model of capital allocation implies a large and general deterioration in investment quality in East Asia in the years leading up to the crisis. One measure of investment quality is the incremental capital-to-output ratio (ICOR). ICORs for the four main crisis countries did indeed all rise starting around 1991, indicating some decline in returns to capital (see Figure 2.7 in World Bank 1999). But in longer perspective, the ICORs moved cyclically and synchronously between the East Asian countries from the early 1970s onward. By 1996, they had not exceeded the upper end of their range over the previous 25 years.

Moreover, the deterioration of investment in the crisis countries during the 1990s might plausibly be attributed to an investment boom. Their ratios of gross domestic investment to GDP in 1991–1996 were 5–10 percentage points higher than in the preceding 15 years. All economies tend to experience some deterioration in investment quality during an investment boom, whether they have a relationship model of capital allocation or an "efficient," arms-length, formal-contract model. The fact that the Asian economies experienced some deterioration in investment efficiency does not necessarily indict the relationship model itself.

The accounting rate of return on assets of non-financial corporations is another measure of investment efficiency. By this measure, too, the results conflict with the official-academic consensus. Average returns in most East Asian countries over the period from 1988 to 1994 had run at a relatively high rate of ~5–8%, compared with ~1–3% in the advanced industrial countries. Japan and Korea were the exceptions among the East Asian economies, with a rate of ~2%. The corresponding US rate was 2.3% (Claessens et al 1998, Chang 1998).

Rates of return in most of the crisis countries did fall sharply between 1995 and 1996. The fall was probably due to the slowdown in economic growth that most East Asian countries experienced at this time (part of the world-wide slowdown of 1996) and to the normal build-up of vulnerabilities in the late stages of an investment boom. The fall in rates of return might well have had an important role in triggering the panic of 1997. But it is difficult to argue that the fall in rates of return in 1995–1996 was the result of long-standing structural distortions attributable to the relationship model of capital allocation.

If space permitted, the same kind of exercise would show that the popular "moral hazard" argument about the crisis has no more empirical support than its cousins.

THE "FAILURE OF INTERNATIONAL FINANCIAL MARKETS" THEORY

A plausible explanation of the Asian financial crisis has to accommodate several big facts. First, currency and/or banking crises have become much more frequent since 1980 than they were in the period after World War II. From the late 1970s to 1996, at least 69 countries had at least one major banking crisis (the net worth of the banking system sank to zero or less). The inclusion of countries of the former Soviet Union and some other cases where the data are not fully satisfactory would raise the figure to nearly 90. Between 1975 and 1995, at least 87 countries had at least one major currency crisis (depreciation by more than 25% in one year). In at least 10 of these cases (excluding the Asian cases of 1997–1998), banking and currency crises occurred together, causing very large falls in GDP [5–12% in the first year and negative or only slightly positive growth for several years thereafter (Caprio & Klingebiel 1998, Furman & Stiglitz 1998)]. A second crucial fact is that crises have commonly occurred in response to "success"—the Wall Street crash of 1929 being the most dramatic example. So we should not assume, as the usual story does, that if Asia had a crisis there must be flaws in the basic structures of Asian capitalism. Third, the Asian crisis was regional, with several countries falling into a pile at about the same time. Fourth, as noted above, the crisis was unanticipated by those whose job it is to anticipate such things (with the partial exception of Thailand, where by 1996 there was more of a consensus of recession ahead). To develop an explanation of the Asian crisis that accomodates these facts, we need to move away from Asian specifics.

A General Story of Financial Fragility

Start with the general tendency in capitalist economies for economic activity to move in cycles, with financial crisis as part of the cycle. A plausible reason for this tendency is as follows (Minsky 1982, Veneroso 1999). In the upswing (which might be started by large capital inflows), the financial system tends to become more fragile, for reasons inherent in the upswing process itself rather than in relationship governance or other political variables. Investment relative to GDP tends to rise above trend, and the proportion of investment financed by debt (rather than retained earnings or sale of equity) tends to rise. Higher corporate debt-to-equity ratios make for more financial fragility than do lower ones, because debt must be repaid as a proportion of the debt irrespective of the level of profits (or ability to repay), whereas equity must be repaid as a share of whatever profits happen to be.

Other factors amplify the tendencies towards financial fragility. When fiscal policy is countercyclical, the boom lowers the government's fiscal deficit, so the government borrows less; more of household savings are therefore intermediated through banks to firms, ending up boosting corporate debt-to-equity ratios. The expectations of business managers, investors, and consumers tend to become extrapolative (everyone expects the boom to continue indefinitely) and then eu-phoric, so economic agents reduce their cushion of reserves with which to counter a downturn. Under these conditions, a standard policy response—raising interest rates to slow demand—may cause debt-to-equity ratios to rise even further as higher interest rates reduce retained earnings and as firms, wishing to continue to invest at above-trend rates, borrow more to offset the fall in retained earnings. Where the equity market is significant, more equity finance reduces financial fragility, other things being equal; but in the presence of extrapolative expectations, equity price bubbles easily develop, people borrow more against rising equity values, investment goes up, and financial fragility is compounded. If corporate managers are compensated in stock options, they have an incentive to boost the stock price, which may lead them to buy in equity in order to make it scarcer and substitute the equity with borrowed funds, resulting in higher debt-to-equity ratios (as in the United States during the 1990s).

All this concerns a closed economy. When the economy is relatively small and open to imports (as are most of the emerging market economies), the boom causes imports to rise, causes the current account deficit to rise, causes rest-of-world savings to flow in to finance the deficit, causes the real exchange rate to appreciate, and causes the profits of companies in the tradeable goods sectors to fall. When, in addition, the capital account is open and domestic interest rates are much higher than interest rates in capital-surplus economies, the boom sucks in much more capital than is needed to finance the current account deficit, as foreign investors rush to diversify their portfolios and follow the herd. Euphoric expectations take hold.

When the private capital inflows rise above what is needed to finance the current account deficit, the central bank's foreign exchange reserves rise too (assuming that the exchange rate is not left to float). Or, if the country is running large current account surpluses and does not reexport sufficient capital (e.g. Japan after 1986), the surpluses translate directly into higher reserves. Whatever the cause of the higher reserves, the domestic financial system, especially in developing countries, will probably be unable to offset or neutralize ("sterilize") the increase, that is, unable to prevent the increased foreign exchange reserves from feeding through into an increase in the domestic money supply. When a foreign investor takes his currency (US dollars) to the central bank in order to buy domestic currency (baht), he receives baht. This makes a net increase in the supply of baht in circulation. To offset or sterilize this increase in the money supply, the central bank or treasury could undertake "open market operations"—sell government baht bonds in the market, receive baht in return, and take that baht out of circulation.

However, sterilization has at least three big problems. First, it is typically expensive, because the interest the central bank or treasury has to pay on the baht bonds is higher than the interest it earns from the foreign bonds it buys with the US dollars (typically low-interest US Treasury bills), whereas without sterilization, the central bank gets interest income on its US bonds with no interest expense at all. Second, in a developing country, sterilization may not be feasible because the market for government bonds and bills in the domestic currency is small and the range of other financial instruments is also small. (Indeed, to the extent that the government sells the baht bonds to banks rather than to other investors, the bonds become part of the banks' money base, along with cash, and can be used to support bank credit creation. So even sale of sufficient government baht bonds to absorb all the extra baht released by the conversion of the original US dollars into baht may still not prevent a capital inflow from increasing the domestic money supply.) Third, to the extent that sterilization does succeed in lowering the money supply relative to the unsterilized level, it raises interest rates—which perpetuates the inflows. In short, sterilization is anything but a straightforward solution to the problems of capital inflows.

The capital inflows therefore tend to generate excess liquidity in the form of a domestic credit boom: The money supply increases faster than the output of goods and services. The credit boom may "vent" itself through (*a*) a surge in consumer goods imports, which widens the current account deficit; (*b*) inflation in consumer goods prices (CPI inflation); (*c*) a surge in "investment" in asset markets, notably real estate and stocks, causing asset price inflation; and/or (*d*) a surge in industrial investment, reflecting an assumption that the resulting increase in production can be exported if not sold at home. The surge in industrial investment also manifests itself as a widening of the current account deficit through higher capital goods imports.

In relatively open economies, there are limits to the inflationary response, because as domestic prices rise and the real exchange rate appreciates, imports will be sucked in. Where consumption propensities are high, a credit boom is likely to manifest itself as a surge of imported consumer goods. This causes a sharp deterioration in the current account that is not matched by prospects of additional foreign exchange earnings in the future. Where savings propensities are high, on the other hand, a credit boom is likely to vent itself in some combination of (*a*) increased capital goods imports, justified initially on the grounds that the imports are sustainable because the borrowing country will be able to repay the capital inflow from the increased output; (*b*) asset price inflation, e.g. property and stock market bubbles; and (*c*) increasingly speculative expansion of industrial capacity fueled by too-cheap foreign borrowing and export optimism.

Such an economy is now primed with multiple sources of endogenously generated financial fragility, including some or all of the following:

1. a rate of increase of productive capacity above trend (above labor force growth and productivity growth), perhaps amounting to an industrial capacity bubble;
2. a relatively high and rising ratio of corporate debt to equity;
3. an asset price bubble;
4. a smaller cushion of safety held by all economic agents in the grip of extrapolative expectations;

5. a high and rising current account deficit;

6. relatively high and rising external debt (which must be repaid out of foreign exchange earnings).

Under these conditions, devaluation, increases in interest rates, and decreases in demand can tip whole swathes of the corporate sector into illiquidity. Quite small shocks—e.g. rumors of increases in Japanese or US interest rates or sudden downturns of export earnings—can now precipitate financial crisis in the form of a forced devaluation or a cascade of credit contraction and debt defaults. Foreigners begin to repatriate their investments, residents begin to shift their savings overseas, speculators sell the currency forward, all helping to trigger the crisis.

The East Asian Model

In this general story of how a successful capitalist economy can become financially fragile and then financially unstable, the next step is to show how East Asia managed to avoid these crisis dynamics until the 1990s, while growing very fast. Begin with the formulation of the model given above: (*a*) Banks, rather than capital markets, are the central financial entities; (*b*) banks, big firms, and governments have close and long-term relations; and (*c*) agreements are made behind the scenes, unmonitored by independent parties and unenforced by courts, and the government has a role in determining who gets credit and other support. This could be called alliance capitalism or relationship-based economic governance, distinct from formal-contract-based or rule-based governance. The model applies more fully to northeast Asia than to southeast Asia.

Relationship-based governance has some economic development advantages over a formal-contract–based system. Agreements can be enforced outside of a formal legal system, allowing the economy to avoid the social costs of the elaborate institutional arrangements of rule-based governance; hence the economy has lower average transactions costs when the number of major players is small (S Li, "The Benefits and Costs of Relation-Based Governance: an Explanation of the East Asian Miracle and Crisis," unpublished).

But at this level of generality many other emerging market economies have broadly similar institutional arrangements. How could relationship-based governance go with sustained fast growth in East Asia as compared to, say, Latin America? The fast growth resulted from the coming together of this institutional structure with rates of saving and investment much higher than in other regions. Most of the saving is done by households, which deposit most of their savings in (low-risk) banks. The banks are treated as akin to public utilities, serving a public purpose even when privately owned, and are regulated to secure that purpose; their collective performance is judged less by their profitability than by their service to other sectors. Corporations finance their investments in large part by borrowing from banks. The thinness of securities markets means that banks need to develop close relations with their big borrowers, because if a borrower goes into difficulties, the bank does not have the option of selling the loan on a securities market. Corporations' ability to borrow multiples of their equity and not be constrained by retained earnings or by the risk preferences of equity buyers partly explains the extraordinarily high levels of investment and the massive change in the composition of manufacturing output toward the fastest growing sectors, electronics and machinery.

The institutional arrangements of the relationship model help to counter the tendency toward financial instability inherent in an economy experiencing high (above-trend) levels of investment and high corporate debt-to-equity ratios. The long-term relations between banks and firms provide a buffer so that banks do not call their loans and pitch firms into bankruptcy when they run into liquidity difficulties, as they might in a more short-term, formal-contract-based model. Also, the government stands ready to support both firms and banks in the event of shocks that affect swathes of the economy at once (such as sharp rises in interest rates or sharp falls in demand)—but not unconditionally. The government steers its support by an industrial policy that seeks to promote certain investments ahead of others and to overcome the "coordination failures" endemic to free markets when the physical capital endowment is not already large.[2] On the other hand, firms' and banks' dependence on the government's support gives it capacity to implement the industrial policy. (See Rodrik 1995, the single best explanation of "getting interventions right" in East Asia. Other important references on the role of the state in East Asian development include Evans 1995, Kohli 1994, Weiss 1998, Woo-Cumings 1999, Lall 1998, and others cited in Wade 1992.) The exposure of many firms to export markets and the overarching importance given to exporting helps to discipline the government, the banks, and the firms so that relationship-based governance, with only weak (impersonal) mechanisms of monitoring and enforcement, does not necessarily (*pace* Greenspan, Camdessus and others) degenerate into inefficiencies and cozy rental havens to the point of outweighing the economy-wide savings on average transactions costs. The export orientation is a necessary condition of the continued high rates of investment, given less than continental-sized economies.

In sum, close and long-term relations between banks, firms, and governments help to prevent one of the strengths of the East Asian model—high investment sustained by high corporate debt-to-equity ratios—from becoming a source of financial instability. These relations help the government to overcome otherwise endemic coordination failures. The emphasis on exporting helps to discipline those close and long-term relations in line with a national interest test, and allows continued high rates of investment to be validated in sales.

Another important stability condition of the model is a restricted movement of financial capital across the national borders. Foreign exchange can be bought and

---

[2]A coordination failure occurs when an investor fails to invest because he cannot be sure that other, uncoordinated investors will undertake the complementary investments needed for his investment to succeed.

sold for purposes related to trade or direct investment in plant and equipment but not for such other purposes as buying shares on the secondary market or short-term foreign borrowing. Domestic savings are already so high that the increment of foreign finance is unlikely to be invested as productively. A partly closed capital account helps to prevent the structure of long-term relations from being disrupted by short-term-oriented entities playing by different rules, such as those of a formal-contract-based system. Such disruption would be especially damaging if free capital mobility were allowed before the development of impersonal mechanisms of monitoring and enforcement.

With this model, East Asia was able to grow fast through the 1980s and into the 1990s, reaping the gains of high debt-to-equity ratios, coordinated investments, and low average transactions costs, without falling into more than occasional short-term crises. The internal structure was complemented by two external conditions: western markets open enough to absorb rapidly increasing Asian exports (validating the high level of investment), and abundant foreign direct investment from Japan, especially after yen appreciation in the mid-1980s raised production costs there.

The Surge in World Capital Markets and the Emerging Markets' Boom and Bust

Finance began to surge on a world scale in the early 1990s, reflected in fast-rising ratios of financial stocks and flows to world GDP. The surge had its roots in the US fiscal and current account deficits that began to grow in the early 1980s. The United States financed its external deficits by attracting capital inflows, mostly in the form of foreign purchases of US government debt (especially Treasury bills), denominated in US dollars. At the other end of the US deficits, the surplus countries accumulated US dollars. Their businesses changed their dollar earnings into local currency at their domestic commercial banks, and their commercial banks deposited the dollars with the central bank. The central bank, rather than sit on the dollars and earn no interest, used them to purchase income-earning US assets, notably Treasury bills (or invested them in a third country, which in turn invested in US Treasuries or other assets). This is the process by which the United States was able to sustain its external deficits by creating debt (or credit) without short-run limits, as long as the US dollar was accepted as the main international reserve currency.

In the surplus countries, the accumulation of US assets, particularly Treasuries, boosted the central banks' foreign exchange reserves. Between 1982 and 1996 the world's central bank reserves rose by well over 200%. This provided the foundation for a surge in world liquidity. With sterilization difficult for the reasons given above, the increase in reserves permitted the commercial banks to expand their lending, generating a boom. The process of rising reserves in surplus countries then led, in some cases, to excessive credit creation, overheating, excess capacity, and asset inflation, followed by crisis. East Asia has experienced two rounds of this process during the late 1980s and 1990s, first in Japan, then in Korea and southeast Asia.

Japan ran large current account surpluses through the 1980s, especially with the United States. By 1986, the surpluses had become so large—matching the excess of Japanese savings over investment—that Japan could not export enough capital to the United States and Asia to prevent the surpluses from boosting reserves by 200% in two years (1986 to 1987). The reserve expansion swelled the Japanese bubble—a surge of investment, share prices, and property values up to 1990, accompanied by an outpouring of capital in the forms of foreign direct investment, portfolio investment, and bank lending, much of it to East Asia. By 1990, the credit boom had led to overcapacity throughout the economy. Overcapacity put downward pressure on prices and profits. Compared to prospective declining earnings, stock market and property valuations looked wildly inflated. Wholesale prices began to fall, raising the real burden of debt. The economy entered a slump from which it had not recovered 10 years later.

This whole sequence of events would have been unlikely under the Bretton Woods regime (from the postwar years to 1971–1973). Had the dollar remained linked to gold, such that holders of dollars could exchange them at a fixed rate for gold, US external deficits would have caused a fall in US gold reserves as foreign central banks exchanged dollars for gold. The fall in gold reserves would have caused a contraction of bank lending in the United States. The fall in bank lending would have squeezed domestic demand, reducing the demand for imports and increasing the supply of exports, reestablishing current account balance. Meanwhile, Japan's external surpluses would have boosted domestic lending and domestic demand, raising the demand for imports and decreasing the supply of exports, also reestablishing external balance. Hence, the rise in Japan's reserves would have been matched by a fall in US reserves, and the resulting price level and aggregate demand changes would have produced a reverse flow of reserves and an elimination of persistent imbalances. In the post–Bretton Woods world, however, where reserves are created by US government debt that other countries allow as legal reserves, there was no such discipline on the US government. It went on financing its external deficits by selling US government debt almost indefinitely. The expansion of reserves in Japan due to Japan's external surpluses was therefore not matched by a fall in US reserves. Consequently, the world base for credit expansion rose (R Duncan, "The Origin of Economic Bubbles," unpublished).

By the early 1990s, the United States was still running large external deficits financed by capital inflows, but the domestic economy was in recession, unable to use the sizable inflows domestically. Hence, the United States became not only the biggest recipient of capital inflows but also a major source of capital outflows as US investors bought foreign assets, especially stocks. It became the world's great savings entrepot. Meanwhile, the Japanese economy was still running large external surpluses and accumulating reserves, but because Japan's recession was much more severe than the United States', its banks were under great pressure to lend abroad. Europe suffered from low growth and high unemployment, and the

Nordic countries experienced a serious banking crisis, all of which encouraged European banks to diversify outside Europe. All three components of the core, therefore, were engaged in a process of outward investment chiefly financed by credit creation on the basis of rising world reserves, itself based largely on rising US external debt.

With recession throughout the OECD world,[3] international banks and fund managers came to regard emerging markets as the place to make high rates of return on investment and lending. Many emerging market countries carried out far-reaching financial liberalization in the late 1980s and 1990s, including opening the economy to inflows of foreign loans and portfolio capital. Propelled by the dynamics described above, foreign capital flooded in. The capitalization of stock markets of emerging market countries nearly doubled as a proportion of world capitalization between 1990 and 1993 (Aitken 1998).

The inflow of foreign funds would bring greater stock market price stability in emerging markets, said the experts, because stock prices would be more firmly based on economic fundamentals, thanks to the longer time horizons of institutional investors. What resulted, however, was a boom in emerging market stock prices followed by a series of collapses. The money managers herded into emerging markets in the name of diversifying their portfolios, which raised asset prices, which strengthened the argument for more investment and more diversification. Concurrently, these countries were privatizing and liberalizing in accord with the Washington Consensus. Investors interpreted the rise in asset prices as a vindication of those policies, reinforcing the herding of policy makers around the Washington Consensus. Stock market bubbles and policy-making bubbles reinforced each other (Krugman 1995).

The result was a strong correlation between the capital inflows to different emerging market countries, despite the diversity of policies pursued by those countries and the differences in the soundness of their economic fundamentals. The correlation became more pronounced as the volume of flows increased in the 1990s (Aitken 1998; Pettis 1996, 1998).

The Build-up to Crisis in East Asia

Financial Opening   In the late 1980s and 1990s several East Asian governments, with Thailand in the lead, lifted most restrictions on capital mobility. (In a longer treatment, the Indonesian case would receive separate attention.) They allowed free inflow and outflow of foreign capital, eased restrictions on the entry of foreign banks and investment houses, and accelerated domestic financial liberalization as well. This happened in the space of a few years. Little attention was given to strengthening impersonal or arms-length methods of bank regulation and supervision—which had previously been achieved through relationship ties. Suddenly, established Asian banks that had been protected from competition and

---

[3]Organisation for Economic Co-operation and Development.

had limited experience of foreign financial markets found themselves able to borrow in those markets. New banks, often managed by people with no banking experience at all, rushed to reap the profits of foreign borrowing. Restrictions were lifted on the neoliberal assumption that if the foreign borrowing was private-to-private it could be presumed to be safe and productive.

Capital Inflow   As East Asian governments liberalized and opened the financial system, foreign capital flooded in during the 1990s, attracted by fast growth, high interest rates relative to the cost of borrowing in the core economies, and stable exchange rates with the US dollar (which eliminated the risks of a devaluation loss on investment). It surged after the Mexico crisis of 1994–1995, when the whole of Latin America looked shaky. Private inflows to Korea, Thailand, Malaysia, Indonesia, and the Philippines amounted to $40 billion in 1994 and over $100 billion in 1996, twice as high as the consolidated current account deficit. Some of the capital went into direct investment in manufacturing as core country firms, especially Japanese firms, responded to intensifying worldwide competition by acquiring lower-cost Asian manufacturing sites for simpler products. But most of the capital inflow took the form of bank loans and portfolio investments with short-term maturities, especially from Japanese banks anxious to compensate for their limited domestic lending possibilities. And more and more of it was invested in assets prone to bubbles, notably stocks and real estate.

Financial Fragility   With a relationship-based system of governance and surging short-term inflows during the 1990s, East Asian countries were in the position described by an Indonesian economist: "It's as if the Government had gotten rid of the policeman at every corner, but didn't bother to put up stop signs or lights. The traffic moved faster, but was prone to accidents" (quoted in Passell 1998).

The inflow of foreign funds increased the reserve assets of the domestic financial systems. Thailand's reserves increased at 15–25% per year in 1984–1986, 40–55% in 1987–1990, and 15–25% in 1991–1995. The domestic financial systems were not able to offset or sterilize the increased foreign exchange reserves. The leveraging of unsterilized foreign capital inflows resulted in the dramatic investment surge in East Asia through the 1990s, with investment-to-GDP ratios 5–10% higher than in the preceeding 15 years. Thailand in 1993–1995 was the extreme case, with gross domestic investment at 45% of GDP; Korea's was 37%, still extraordinarily high.

By the mid 1990s, East Asia had three major sources of financial fragility. One was fragile corporate finances, because of above-trend investment and the high share of debt finance (Wade 1990, Haggard & Lee 1995, Wade & Veneroso 1998). The second source was banks that were fragile because of lending against bubble-driven asset values. The third source was a balance of payments that was fragile because of excessive short-term foreign claims relative to liquid foreign assets, or excessive short-term debt relative to foreign exchange reserves. "Excessive" means anything near or over 100% of foreign exchange reserves, because at that point foreign short-term creditors know that if they are last to call their loans and convert back into US dollars or yen, the reserves may not be sufficient for them to be repaid (Rodrik & Velasco 1999). This is the condition for a panicky pullout and a forced devaluation. Korea's external debt, the majority of it short-term, ballooned from very little in 1990 to around $150 billion in 1996, justified in the name of the great slogans of 1990s Korean politics, "let the free market work!" and "globalize or die!" By 1996, Korea's short-term debt to foreign exchange reserves was over 200%, Indonesia's over 150%, and Thailand's just under 150%.

In short, East Asia's continued high growth rates during the 1990s concealed a change in the source. By the mid 1990s, an appreciable part of the total was bubble growth rather than real growth, in the sense that company profits and debt repayment came to depend increasingly on rising asset prices. Conjunctural shocks then kicked in.

Conjunctural Shocks   In the mid 1990s, returns on investment in the United States rose, making emerging markets less attractive. And in 1996 East Asian exports suddenly faltered. Slowing world growth was partly to blame. World manufactured export growth fell from nearly 9% a year in 1990–1995 to 2% in 1995–1996. Also, Japan and China, which together constitute four fifths of the East Asian GDP, suddenly slowed in 1996 and 1997, dimming prospects of exporting to them and intensifying competitition against their exports in third markets. The recent devaluations in China and Mexico put downward pressure on East Asian export prices. The appreciation of the dollar against the yen in 1995, and therefore of East Asian currencies linked to the dollar, was a major blow to exports. For example, Thailand's manufactured export growth fell from 21% a year in 1990–1995 to −1.6% a year in 1995–1996. Underneath the conjunctural events were longer-term problems of (*a*) sustaining the growth of leading sectors in the face of growing excess manufacturing capacity worldwide and (b) catching up as East Asian countries approached the technological frontier.

Maintaining the Peg   Why did Thailand, for one, not devalue by 1996 (since Thailand had been running substantial current account deficits, bigger than the others', since the early 1990s)? In the Thai case, the answer involves the finance ministry's losing its earlier technocratic independence and becoming obligated to those who could bring down the government. Hence the finance ministry did not accept a confidential World Bank urging for a small, orderly devaluation in 1996. Even a small devaluation would have hurt those in the political elite to whom the Thai finance ministry was obligated because they had borrowed abroad without taking out protection against a devaluation (i.e. without hedging). But politicization of the finance ministry was probably secondary to the worry that a so-called small and orderly devaluation would turn out to be neither.

International investors commonly respond to a 10% devaluation (or widening of the band) in an emerging market not by saying, "This devaluation looks about right because the currency was 10% overvalued, so we'll keep our money in," but by saying, "This shows the government has lost credibility, so we'll pull our money out." More generally, breaking the currency peg might disrupt the inflow of (short-term) capital, and the Thai economy, like the Korean and the Indonesian economies, had by this time become heavily dependent on these inflows even for refinancing debt. So the peg was maintained, at great expense to exports. This is a key link between the real economy and the financial determinants of the crisis.

Indeed, it might be argued that by the mid 1990s, a new but largely implicit development strategy had emerged in some of the East Asian countries. Whereas the old strategy had been based on a highly competitive export sector, for which a degree of undervaluation of the currency was helpful, the new one, as the currencies rose with the dollar against the Japanese yen and German mark after 1995, focused on continuing to attract foreign capital as the principal motor of development. The debt was by then so large that its refinancing became a central objective of government policy, which meant avoiding anything that would undermine the confidence of foreign investors—including devaluation (Putzel 2000).

More Financial Fragility   For a time the governments' assurances about maintaining the currencies, along with the gestalt of "miracle Asia" and worries about Latin America, kept the disturbing trends in corporate balance sheets beyond foreign investors' attention. Indeed, private foreign inflows continued to rise, and at decreasing risk premiums, up to mid 1997. By then the degree of financial fragility was such that quite small shocks could trigger a gestalt shift from "miracle Asia" to "meltdown Asia" (Wade 1998a).

The Costs of Overinvestment   The Asian crisis was a crisis of overinvestment—in real estate and stocks relative to sustainable valuations ("asset bubble"), as well as in manufacturing relative mainly to conjuncturally falling demand growth and secondarily to long-term worldwide overcapacity in manufacturing. The Mexican crisis of 1994–1995 had a similar root—a domestic credit boom generated by unsterilized foreign capital inflows, which were attracted by proximity to the United States and by anticipated economic success. But the credit boom in Mexico vented itself in a surge of imported consumer goods, reflecting high consumption propensities, whereas the Asian credit boom vented itself more in excess investment, reflecting high savings propensities. Of the two types of crises—one driven by excess consumption, the other by excess investment—an excess consumption crisis is generally easier and quicker to recover from, because it entails less debt and excess capacity to be worked out of. And indeed Mexico after

1994 did recover more quickly than Asia after 1997.[4] The severity of Asia's crisis was the other side of two of its great developmental strengths relative to Latin America: its huge savings and its high debt-to-equity ratios. They financed high investment, which caused fast growth, which attracted excess foreign capital in the form of debt, which financed excess investment. Once the crash began, the external crisis (the forced devaluation) and the internal crisis (the contraction of credit and the resulting debt default) ricocheted around each big firm's balance sheet, interacting in a vicious circle, to yield not merely crisis but collapse. The contractionary policy response imposed by the IMF only made matters worse.

Recovery   The only recovery solution was some combination of debt reduction and increased foreign exchange earnings. In principle, the debt burden could be reduced by default, rescheduling, faster growth, or inflation; and foreign exchange earnings could be increased by a lucky increase in export prices or by squeezing the domestic economy to reduce imports and shift more resources into export production. In practice, the squeeze solution dominated. It solved the external crisis sometime in 1998, as foreign exchange reserves ballooned and exchange rates stabilized at, in most cases, around 70% of the pre-crisis level. But it worsened the internal credit contraction crisis, which continued into 1999. By mid 1999, two years after the onset, the recovery of production and incomes looked fragile and uneven, more like a W than a V.

---

[4]If recovery from an excess-consumption crisis is easier than recovery from an excess-investment crisis, how do we explain the Latin American crisis of the 1980s? That was an excess-consumption crisis, yet recovery took most of a decade. Latin America's per capita GDP growth in 1980–1989 was -0.5%, whereas East Asia's was over 6%. The contrast between Latin America in the 1980s and Mexico/Latin America in 1994–1995 depends on the additional variable of world liquidity. The 1982 crisis came at a time of sharp contraction in world liquidity. The hike in interest rates and the slowdown in export markets meant that Latin America's debt burdens kept growing faster than the countries' ability to repay, and the countries paid more in debt servicing than they brought in (negative net resource transfers). Due to the drying up of world excess liquidity, no new private capital came in voluntarily as bridging finance. Rather, the governments screwed down the domestic economy to release resources for debt repayment, and the IMF and World Bank/Interamerican Development Bank provided official finance. This combination allowed enough debt servicing to avoid a formal default. It was seven years before voluntary private flows resumed in response to a combination of expanding world liquidity and Brady Plan rescheduling and conversion of loans into tradable securities. The Mexican crisis of 1994–1995 occurred at a time of expanding world liquidity, so United States/IMF bridging finance and some debt forgiveness were quickly arranged and voluntary private finance flowed back within a year. Also, the United States had a more direct interest in a speedy Mexican recovery in 1994–1995 than it had had in a speedy Latin American recovery in the 1980s.

Causality

How do we know that the culprit is private capital inflow surges blowing out a credit boom, and not bad bankers or the other villains of the Asian cronyism story? The first part of the answer lies in the striking correlation, mentioned above, between capital flows across emerging markets. During the 1990s, private capital inflows to developing countries typically grew at 10–20% a year. But they surged twice, in 1993 and in 1996, both times doubling the inflow of the previous year. Each surge was followed the next year by major financial crisis in emerging markets, the first time in Mexico and Latin America, the second time in Asia (Howell 1999).

Second, it is well known that bank regulation and enforcement of prudential limits becomes very difficult in the face of a capital inflow surge, even in a sophisticated, rule-based (not relationship-based) financial system with skilled financial managers. As former Federal Reserve Chairman Paul Volcker (1999) explained, "In benign periods ... banking supervision and banking regulations have very little political support and strong industry opposition. That's true in developed countries as well as developing countries which by the nature of things are bound to be behind the curve of market developments, best practice and strong institutions." There is no need to resort to Asian specifics to explain why, given the inflows, Asian bank regulators were less than effective. The inflow process itself undercuts the ability of regulators to regulate (Blecker 1999, UNCTAD 1998).[5]

Third, the entire financial system of the typical emerging market economy is no bigger than an average American regional bank. Tiny changes in the share of world capital flows going into a particular country can swamp the system, however skilled and uncronyistic the bankers and monetary authorities.

If private capital inflows were the main culprit, how do we know that opening the financial system was the crucial factor behind the inflows? How do we know the crucial factor was not lack of transparency, weak prudential regulation, moral hazard, or those other faults that, according to the usual story, led responsible, rational foreign bankers and investors to lend more than they would have lent had they known the truth, and had they not had grounds to believe the loans were implicitly guaranteed? As shown above, the usual story falls down at the first nudge, above all because these factors do not differentiate the countries that had a crisis from those that did not. The most affected countries (Korea, Thailand, Malaysia, and Indonesia, which all had negative growth in 1998) were not worse in these respects than the least affected countries (China, Taiwan, India, and the rest of South Asia, which had positive growth in 1998). What does differentiate

---

[5]Volcker's argument about the generic difficulties of bank regulation, even in sophisticated and transparent systems, is borne out by the behavior of US Savings and Loan banks in the 1980s. They had been restricted to housing finance, the safest and least innovative form of banking, but suddenly the restrictions on both their deposit taking ("Regulation Q") and their lending were lifted. They went wild, producing the fiasco of bad banking known as the Savings and Loan crisis. The recapitalization of the banks took over 3% of the US GDP.

the most and the least affected countries is capital mobility. All of the most affected countries opened the financial system to capital flows more or less fully by the mid 1990s. The least affected have in common restricted capital mobility, with capital transactions more limited to trade and direct investment. During the 1990s, the countries with restricted capital flows did not experience anything like the capital inflows of those with open capital accounts; their short-term debt to foreign exchange reserves remained much lower, and their corporate sectors were less vulnerable to exchange rate, interest rate, and investment shocks (Gray 1999), so they experienced less outflow.

If this evidence is not sufficient, try a thought experiment. Would Korea have been better off with short-term debt to foreign exchange reserves in mid 1997 at, say, 50% than above 200%? Yes. Would it have lost much in terms of social profit by cutting back its short-term inflows? No, because by the mid 1990s, most of the inflows were fueling a speculative industrial capacity bubble. But putting a ceiling on the ratio would have required the government to limit the inflows produced by uncoordinated decisions of private entities that did not have to take account of the social risks to which their private decisions exposed the rest of the society.

In short, Asian governments are deeply implicated in the crisis for opening the financial system quickly in the 1990s without linking the pace of the opening to the build-up of effective rule-based (rather than relationship-based) governance of financial markets, including institutions of accounting, auditing, rating, and legal cases and codes, in the false belief that if the capital was moving private-to-private it must be safe. Certainly company performance was deteriorating by the mid 1990s across the region. But the major problem was domestic financial structures not robust enough to handle the heavy shocks to which they were exposed by precipitous financial opening in conditions of surging world capital markets. Had the governments not abandoned some basic principles of the East Asian model— above all, the principle of strategic rather than open-ended integration into world financial markets—the economies would probably not have experienced a serious crisis, although they would also have grown more slowly.

On the other hand, the deeper causes of the Asian crisis lie in the core economies and their governments, especially that of the United States, and in the kind of international financial system they have created. The US decision to break the link between the dollar and gold (rather than cut expenditure for the Vietnam War and the Great Society) allowed persistent imbalances to build up in the world economy because increases in surplus countries' reserves were no longer matched by falls in reserves of the United States, the main deficit country. The United States' reluctance to rein in its external deficits, and its preference to finance them by creating debt that other countries accumulated as foreign exchange reserves, then produced (given the post–Bretton Woods payments system) a surge in world liquidity that eventually produced excess capacity and financial fragility worldwide. Both Japan's boom and bust and the later Asian miracle and bust were manifestations of the same systemic process. Explanations that locate the causes within the crisis countries occlude this basic point.

A POLITICAL SCIENCE AGENDA

Why did the governments of the crisis-affected countries open the financial system in the 1990s, and why did the governments of the less affected countries [notably Taiwan (Chu 1999)] do so less? Why did the governments of the crisis-affected countries sit on their hands as the debt built up, why did they allow domestic and foreign bankers to blow up asset and industrial capacity bubbles, why did they give up coordinating investments—why did they depart from the East Asian model? Some of the explanation can be found in the inner wheels of national politics and class (see Gills 1996, Woo 1991, and the works on the crisis cited above). The power balance between manufacturing, finance, and the state was changing during the 1990s in favor of private finance; parts of the state itself became increasingly beholden to financial interests and private (Thai, Korean) financiers saw their interests as aligned with those of foreign financiers, all wanting unrestricted cross-border financial transactions.

This makes an important research agenda for comparative politics. Especially interesting is the politics between those whose interests remain rooted in the national territory (and therefore related to the success of the national economy), the growing number of those whose interests lie in maximum mobility of assets and who have less stake in the success of the national economy, and those (including some powerful manufacturers, domestic and foreign) whose interests are in between. The crisis has led the manufacturers, notably in Thailand, to press for more state help for industrial upgrading—not only state backing for higher quality standards but also a more active promotional role, even as the governments talk the neoliberal language of reducing state involvement in industry.

But more than the power balance is changing. There is also a longer-term trend for average transaction costs to rise as the economies become more complex and open and the number of transaction partners rises (Li 1999). Relationship-based systems become less effective as average transaction costs rise, and the spread of neoliberal ideas erodes their legitimacy. This may generate a movement away from a relationship-based system, including abrupt removal of restrictions such as capital controls that had helped to stabilize the system. Such a movement could cause the sort of governance vacuum in financial markets that emerged in Asia during the 1990s.

For international political economy, the issue is the credit bubble that is rotating around the developed and emerging market countries, blowing out periodically at high cost to people's lives. The bubble is driven by excess world liquidity generated in the core economies. With higher excess comes higher volatility of financial flows within and between regions. The control of this liquidity is increasingly concentrated in a small number of investing institutions. Small changes in their portfolios between regions, countries, and sectors can trigger enormous volatility in any one country, swamping its regulatory rules and institutions. It is quite misleading to say, with the US Treasury and the IMF, that the solution to the volatility is "sound" financial institutions in emerging markets, because the inflows themselves can easily undermine the capacity to maintain soundness. The solution is to curb the inflows.

This is exactly what the great configuration of financial interests in the west, whose power to shape national policies and international regimes has grown as excess liquidity has grown, does not want. Here the international political economy agenda merges into an American political agenda. The configuration is led by what could be called the Wall Street–Treasury complex, analogous to the military-industrial complex (Bhagwati 1998, Kristof with Sanger 1999). It connects Wall Street, the US Treasury, the US Congress, the IMF, the World Bank, and the US economics profession (Frey et al 1984, Kolm 1988), with the City of London and the UK Treasury as an offshore adjunct. This complex is the seat of the great campaign of the late 1980s and 1990s to open up emerging markets to free capital mobility, with the US Treasury at the helm (Wade 1996a, 2000).

The campaign has been played out partly in hardball bilateral negotiations, such as the Financial Services Talks between the US Treasury and the Korean Finance Ministry during 1990–1992. These began with specific issues (such as raising or eliminating Korea's 5% limit on foreign ownership of Korean firms) and evolved into demands for fundamental structural reform because, in the words of a US negotiator, "it became apparent that many of the difficulties faced by foreign institutions in Korea were connected to structural distortions in the financial sector resulting from the highly regulated nature of the system and the government's heavy-handed intervention" (Fall 1995).

The campaign has also been played out in multilateral forums such as the IMF, the GATT/WTO, the Multilateral Agreement on Investment, and the Asia Pacific Economic Council (APEC; Wade 1998b). This campaign demonstrates US "unilateral internationalism" in full force. The Clinton administrations of 1993–2000 and the post-1994 Congress have used international organizations such as the IMF and APEC as tools to advance US foreign policy objectives insofar as they cloak the objectives with multilateral legitimacy and spread the costs over other states—but not insofar as the United States has to compromise its own margin of maneuver by honoring obligations of membership that run against its immediate interests.

The US Treasury virtually dictated the conditions attached to the emergency IMF financing arranged for Thailand, Indonesia, and Korea. Those conditions were meant to force the crisis countries, which by then had no bargaining room, to undertake structural changes intended to create institutions and rules closer to those of Anglo-American capitalism and more acceptable to US business. Small, elite groups within the crisis countries had wanted to move in this direction anyway, as noted above, but even the Korean negotiators were pushed much farther than they wanted to go. The disbursements of the emergency financing were tranched against compliance with the conditions. The US General Accounting Office established a task force of 31 people in 1998 to investigate Korea's and other beneficiaries' compliance with IMF conditions.

In the Mexican bailout of 1994, by contrast, the US Treasury and IMF assembled a massive and credible international rescue package of $50 billion to stabilize the peso at once, and the government did not promulgate an attached reform program (privatization and faster liberalization of the telecommunications sector and financial services) until several months after the credit line became available.

As a result, the forced devaluation did not interact with domestic credit contraction nearly as much it did in Asia. Why the difference in policy response? Mexico had already done much of what the United States wanted Asia to do. Also, the United States had a strong national interest in seeing a quick recovery on its southern border, whereas its national interest in Asia was not in quick recovery but in opening markets, so that American firms could operate in East Asia as easily as Japanese firms did.

The United States–led campaign for free capital mobility worldwide is not just a reflex of sectoral financial and business interests. Wall Street's ascendancy in US politics during the 1980s and 1990s has accompanied fundamental shifts in values. Above all, the Depression/Bretton Woods idea that society should shelter the individual from certain risks was supplanted by the idea that social arrangements should allow the citizen-investor-gambler to profit from risk. This means that all citizens should provide for their income in old age by building wealth in the stock market, in contrast to the Depression-to-the-1970s view that the government should provide a minimum income to be financed from taxes collected from the current generation of workers, whether those workers wished later to enjoy the same protection or not. The shift in the principle of pensions—which has gone much farther in the United States than in continental Europe or Japan—is driving a basic realignment of interests in the United States away from the protection of labor income (from which are paid the taxes that finance a pay-as-you-go pension scheme) toward the protection of capital income (from which stock market investors benefit).

Wall Street's dominance is related to this realignment. Wall Street has been able to shape the Treasury's agenda especially decisively during the (Democratic) Clinton administrations, for reasons partly related to the funding base of the Democratic Party (Ferguson 1995). But, funding of the Clinton presidency aside, the US Treasury sees free capital mobility worldwide as a matter of vital US national interest, for when so many US citizen-investor-gamblers depend on the stock market and stock-market-invested pension and mutual funds, US money managers must be able to move finance without let or hindrance wherever returns are highest. On the other hand, opening other countries' financial sectors causes no harm to US domestic interests (Wade 1998–1999). Perhaps, in addition, it has occurred to the Treasury, the State Department, and the security apparatus that the debt trap can be operated to US advantage: As countries build up their private debt, they become more and more subject to the threat of capital pullout, and the US government can influence the likelihood of pullout and use its influence to advance US foreign policy objectives, such as boosting the position of US firms in Asia. That question cannot be answered yet. We do know, however, that the Treasury said virtually nothing about the dangers of financial opening in its dealings with Asian countries (Kristof with Sanger 1999).

By some measures, controlling for skill levels in the population at large, the US federal government is among the least competent in the world. The interesting question is how the United States nevertheless manages to articulate a substantive definition of its national foreign economic interest, to keep the definition stable, and to implement it to a degree that makes the German and Japanese governments look feeble. In the Asian crisis, the Treasury managed largely to exclude all the other agencies (State, Commerce, CIA) from the table; but how (Gopinath 1999)?

In terms of solutions, one element, as noted, is capital controls. But larger scale changes are needed to dampen the tendencies toward booms and busts. The world needs a new system of international payments, such that each country could pay for cross-border transactions in its own currency rather than having to earn a foreign currency (mainly US dollars) in order to pay for goods or repay borrowings. This could be achieved by an international clearing agency that would clear payments between countries internally, between one account and another, without the payments having to go through an open foreign exchange market (Wade 1999). The world also needs a substantial rise in wages in the large developing economies in order to reduce the amount of world excess capacity. China, Vietnam, Indonesia, and Mexico—the countries that account for the largest part of foreign direct investment in low-wage countries—ought to reach a collective agreement to impose on incoming foreign firms a minimum wage of, say, $10 per day instead of the current $3 or less. These countries could justify their action to hostile foreign investors with the argument Henry Ford used to justify his decision to raise the wages of his workers—so that they could afford to buy his cars. Western governments and multilateral organizations such as the World Bank should encourage unionization and democratization for the same reason—to encourage the growth of global wages in line with global output and limit the tendency toward excess capacity. Environmental protection would have to be stepped up at the same time.

The events described in this essay are one episode in a bigger pattern stretching back to the birth of global capitalism in the 1840s. Since then, there have been several periods of surges in world liquidity, cross-border capital flows, and trade (Wade 1996b). Each period has created a justifying ideology similar to our current "globalization." It claims that the world has moved permanently into a new and more promising era; that the growing density of market relations allows more stable as well as faster growth; that a single set of policies—liberalization of markets for goods and finance, small government, and fiscal discipline—is best for capturing the benefits of globalization. According to the new ideology, countries that adopt these policies and accompanying free market institutions can expect reliable inflows of foreign capital; countries that plunge into crisis or fall behind do so because of their own mismanagement. Angell proclaimed some of these ideas in *The Grand Illusion* (1911). The world economy had become so interdependent, thanks to science, technology, and economics, as to make national independence an anachronism (the grand illusion), and wars between modern nations "an impossibility," he said (three years before World War I). The *Economist* said about Japan shortly before the crash in early 1990, "What Japanese investors have become aware of is the dramatic way Japan's blue-chip companies have changed the sources of their earnings through restructuring. This has made their profits too erratic to give any meaning to rigid measures such as a p/e ratio. Instead investors have started to assess a company's future stream of earnings by looking at the total value of a firm's assets.... The implication is that shares may be underpriced." Today, the IMF promulgates globalization ideas constantly.

> Countries that align themselves with the forces of globalization and embrace the reforms needed to do so, liberalizing markets and pursuing disciplined macroeconomic policies, are likely to put themselves on a path of convergence with the advanced economies, following the successful Asian newly industrialized economies. These countries may expect to benefit from trade, gain global market share, and be increasingly rewarded with larger private capital flows. Countries that do not adopt such policies are likely to face declining shares of world trade and private capital flows, and find themselves falling behind in relative terms. (IMF 1997:72)

According to Weber (1997), globalization has made for "a more flexible and adaptive economy that adjusts to shocks more easily and with less propensity for sparking a new cycle." On the other hand, "The ... argument that complex markets might act in synergy and come crashing down together is simply not supported by a compelling logic or empirical evidence." This was published 10 years after stock markets around the world had crashed together, and just as the Asian crisis began, to be followed by the Russian crisis, the Brazilian crisis, and the sharp falls in core economy stock markets in the latter part of 1998. The globalization champions underplay the tendency for the globalization process itself to generate instabilities that bring the surge in liquidity, capital flows, and trade to a temporary end.

Political scientists living in the core economies have a special responsibility to examine the role of core economy governments, banks, institutional investors, and economics professions in generating these instabilities, and to challenge those institutions' explanations of crisis that place the causes far away within the crisis-affected countries.

ACKNOWLEDGMENTS

I thank Kenneth Shadlen, Richard Duncan, Dietrich Rueschemeyer, Michael Pettis, James Putzel, Pravin Krishna, Timothy Besley, Robert Brenner and Richard Doner for comments on the first version of this paper. I thank the Russell Sage Foundation for financial support.

Visit the Annual Reviews home page at www.AnnualReviews.org

LITERATURE CITED

Aitken B. 1998. Have institutional investors destabilized emerging markets? *Contemp. Econ. Policy* 16:173–84

Bank for International Settlements. 1997.

Annual Report. Basel: Bank Int. Settlements

Bhagwati J. 1998. The capital myth: the difference between trade in widgets and dollars. *Foreign Aff.* May

Blecker R. 1999. *Taming Global Finance: A Better Architecture for Growth and Equity.* Washington, DC: Econ. Policy Inst.

Cambridge Journal of Economics. 1998. *Special Issue on the Asian Crisis.* 22 (6)

Camdessus M. 1999. *Governments and economic development in a globalized world.* Remarks at Int. Gen. Meet. Pacific Basin Econ. Counc, 32nd, Hong Kong, May 17

Camdessus M. 1998. *From the Asian crisis towards a new global architecture.* Address by the managing director of the International Monetary Fund to the Parliamentary Assembly of the Council of Europe, Strasbourg, France, June 23

Caprio G, Klingebiel D. 1998. *Bank insolvencies: cross-country experience. Policy Res. Work. Pap. 1620*, World Bank

Chang H-J. 1998. Interpreting the Korean crisis. *Cambridge J. Econ.* 22:735–46

Chu Y-H. 1999. Surviving the East Asian financial storm: the political foundation of Taiwan's economic resilience. See Pempel 1999

Claessens S, Djankov S, Lang L. 1998. *East Asian corporates: growth, financing and risks over the last decade. Policy Res. Work. Pap. 2017.* Washington, DC: World Bank

Cumings B. 1998. The Korean crisis and the end of "late" development. *New Left Rev.* 231: 43–72

Dale R. 1998. Asia crisis will bolster U.S. presence. *Int. Herald Trib.,* Jan. 20

Doner R. 1999. *Towards an activist approach to industrial upgrading in post-crisis Thailand? Work. Pap.,* Polit. Sci. Dept., Emory Univ.

Economist. 1989. April 15

Economist. 1999.The Koreas: survey. July 10, p. 4

Evans P. 1995. *Embedded Autonomy: States and Industrial Transformation.* Princeton, NJ: Princeton Univ. Press

Fall J. 1995. The US-Korea financial dialogue. In *US-Korea Economic Partnership*, ed. Y-S Kim, Oh K-S. Avebury

Ferguson T. 1995. *Golden Rule: The Investment Theory of Party Competition and the Logic of Money-Driven Political Systems.* Chicago: Univ. Chicago Press

Fischer S. 1998. In defense of the IMF. *Foreign Aff.* 77(4):103–6

Foot R, Walter A. 1999.Whatever happened to the Pacific Century? *Rev. Int. Stud.* 25:245–69

Frey B, et al. 1984. Consensus and dissensus among economists: an empirical enquiry. *Am. Econ. Rev.* 74(5):986–94

Furman J, Stiglitz J. 1998. Economic crises: evidence and insights from East Asia. *Brookings Papers in Economic Activity*, 2

Gills B. 1996. Economic liberalisation and reform in South Korea in the 1990s: a 'coming of age' or a case of 'graduation blues'? *Third World Q.* 17(4):667ff

Gopinath D. 1999. Who's the boss? *Inst. Investor* Sept:89–94

Gray D. 1999. *Assessment of corporate sector value and vulnerability. Tech. Pap. 455.* Washington, DC: World Bank

Haggard S, Lee CH. 1995. *Financial Systems and Economic Policy in Developing Countries.* Ithaca, NY: Cornell Univ. Press

Henderson J. 1999. Uneven crises: institutional foundations of East Asian economic turmoil. *Econ. Soc.* 28(3):327–68

Howell M. 1999. Asia's "Victorian" financial crisis. *IDS Bull.* 30(1)

IDS Bulletin. 1999. East Asia: What happened to the development miracle? 30(1). Spec. issue

IMF. 1997. *World Economic Outlook* (May). Washington, DC: Int. Monetary Fund

Jomo KS, ed. 1998. *Tigers in Trouble: Financial Governance, Liberalisation and Crises and East Asia.* Hong Kong: Hong Kong Univ. Press

Kissinger H. 1998. The Asian collapse: one size does not fit all economies [editorial]. *Washington Post.*, Feb. 9, p. A19

Kohli A. 1994. Where do high growth political economies come from? The Japanese lineage of Korea's developmental state. *World Dev.* Sept:1269–94

Kolm S-C. 1988. Economics in Europe and in the US. *Eur. Econ. Rev.* 32(1):207–12

Kristof N with Sanger D. 1999. How U.S. wooed Asia to let cash flow in. *New York Times*, Feb. 16, p. A10

Krugman P. 1995. Dutch tulips and emerging markets. *Foreign Aff.* 74(4):28–44

Lall S. 1998. Technological capabilities in emerging Asia. *Oxford Dev. Stud.* 26(2):213–43

Landler M. 1999. Market place. *New York Times*, Aug. 20, p. C5

Lim L. 1998. Whose "model" failed? Implications of the Asian economic crisis. *Washington Q.* 21(3):25ff

Minsky H. 1982. *Can "It" Happen Again? Essays on Instability and Finance*: Sharpe

Passell P. 1998. Experts say Indonesia can boom, long-term. *New York Times*, May 22, p. A10

Pempel TJ, ed. 1999. *The Politics of the Asian Economic Crisis*. Ithaca, NY: Cornell Univ. Press

Pettis M. 1996. The liquidity trap: Latin America's free market past. *Foreign Aff.* 75(6):2–7

Pettis M. 1998. The new dance of the millions: liability management and the next debt crisis. *Challenge* 41(4):90–100

Putzel J. 2000. The Asian crisis: developmental states and crony capitalists. In *Rethinking Development in East Asia: From the Miracle Mythology to the Economic Crisis*, ed. P Massina. Richmond, UK: Curzon. In press

Rodrik D. 1995. Getting interventions right: how South Korea and Taiwan grew rich. *Econ. Policy* Apr.:55–107

Rodrik D, Velasco A. 1999. *Short-term capital flows*. Presented at ABCDE Conf., World Bank, Washington, DC, Apr. 28–30

Sanger D. 1998. Greenspan sees Asian crisis moving world to western capitalism. *NY Times*, Feb. 13, D1

Summers L, Summers V. 1989. When financial markets work too well: a cautious case for a securities transactions tax. *J. Financ. Serv. Res.* 3

UNCTAD. 1998. International financial instability and the world economy. In *Trade and Development Report 1998*. New York/Geneva: United Nations

Veneroso F. 1999. *Towards a theory of financial instability*. Presented at conf. on Structure, Instability, and the World Economy: Reflections on the Economics of Hyman P. Minsky, Jerome Levy Inst., Bard College, April 21–23, Annandale-on-Hudson, NY

Volcker P. 1999. *Making globalization work*. Luncheon address, Overseas Dev. Counc., March 18

Wade R. 1990. *Governing the Market*. Princeton, NJ: Princeton Univ. Press

Wade R. 1992. East Asia's economic success. *World Polit.* 44:270–320

Wade R. 1996a. Japan, the World Bank, and the art of paradigm maintenance: *The East Asian Miracle* in political perspective. *New Left Rev.* 217:3–36

Wade R. 1996b. Globalization and its limits: reports of the death of the national economy are greatly exaggerated. In *National Diversity and Global Capitalism*, ed. S Berger, R Dore. Ithaca, NY: Cornell Univ. Press

Wade R. 1998a. From 'miracle' to 'cronyism': explaining the Great Asian Slump. *Cambridge J. Econ.* 22(6):693–706

Wade R. 1998b. The Asian debt-and-development crisis of 1997–? Causes and consequences. *World Dev.* 26(8):1535–53

Wade R. 1998–1999. The fight over capital flows. *Foreign Policy* 113:41–54

Wade R. 1999. Out of the box: rethinking the governance of international financial markets. Unpubl. pap., Watson Inst., Brown Univ.

Wade R. 2000. National power, coercive liberalism and "global" finance. In *International Politics: Enduring Concepts and Contemporary Issues*, ed. R Art, R Jervis, pp. 482–89. New York: Addison Wesley Longman. 5th ed.

Wade R, Veneroso F. 1998. The Asian crisis: the high debt model versus the Wall

Street–Treasury–IMF complex. *New Left Rev.* 228:3–23

Weber S. 1997. The end of the business cycle? *Foreign Aff.* July/August:65–82

Weiss L. 1998. *The Myth of the Powerless State: Governing the Economy in a Global Era.* Cambridge, UK: Polity

Weiss L. 1999. State power and the Asian Crisis. *New Polit. Econ.* 4(3):317–42

Weiss L. 2000. Developmental states in transition: adapting, dismantling, innovating, not "normalizing." *Pacific Rev.* 13(1):1–30

Woo Jung-En. 1991. *Race to the Swift: State and Finance in Korean Industrialization.* New York: Columbia Univ. Press

Woo-Cumings M. 1997. *Bailing out or sinking in? The IMF and the Korean financial crisis.* Presented at Econ, Strategy Inst. Conf., Washington, DC, Dec. 2

Woo-Cumings M, ed. 1999. *The Developmental State.* Ithaca, NY: Cornell Univ. Press

Woods N. 1995. Economic ideas and international relations: beyond rational neglect. *Int. Stud. Q.* 39:161–80

World Bank. 1999. *Global Economic Prospects and the Developing Countries, 1998/99.* Washington, DC: World Bank

World Bank. 1993. *The East Asian Miracle: Economic Growth and Public Policy.* Washington, DC: World Bank

World Development. 1998. Special section: viewpoints on the Asian financial crisis. 26(8)

You J-K. 1999. Cause and effect. *Far East. Econ. Rev.* 1 July, p. 38

Yoshitomi M, Ohno K. 1999. *Capital-account crisis and credit contraction. Work. Pap., Asian Dev. Bank Inst., Tokyo*

Annu. Rev. Polit. Sci. 2000. 3:117–48

POST-SOVIET POLITICS

David D. Laitin
*Department of Political Science, Stanford University, Stanford, California 94305;
e-mail: dlaitin@stanford.edu*

Key Words Russia, area studies, federal, democratization, economic growth

■ **Abstract** Since the collapse of the Soviet Union in 1991, the area specialty of Soviet Politics has been transformed. Research on six themes is reviewed: state and revolution, democratization, federalism, economic growth, international relations, and institutional legacies reflecting the communist past. The review finds that post-Soviet research speaks directly to current trends in political science, and the findings of this research should impel generalists to re-specify their theories. A recommendation is offered that the study of post-Soviet politics should push political science away from a notion of institutionalization and in the direction of identifying institutional equilibria.

INTRODUCTION

This review summarizes political science research on the states of the former Soviet Union (FSU), with special emphasis on the Russian Federation. In an intellectual milieu in which area studies is under attack, it is important to ask what contributions have been made to our general understanding of politics by scholars who have specialized knowledge of the post-Soviet republics. In this review, I show the continued relevance of area expertise to a discipline with pretensions to scientific method. Area specialists in the post-Soviet field are re-examining current theories very much in line with our disciplinary standards. But I also argue that there has been insufficient boldness for area students in "thinking of our task as *changing the mainstream, creating a new intellectual agenda*" (McAuley 1997:7, italics in original). In this regard, I suggest two themes—one having to do with the relationship of state and democracy, the other having to do with modeling institutions—in which post-Soviet political science can play a crucial role in recasting current theory.

POST-SOVIET POLITICAL SCIENCE

The post-Soviet field has been in dynamic interaction with recent theoretical developments in political science. Unlike in the Cold War era (see Fleron & Hoffmann's 1993 review), post-Sovietologists have clear incentives to speak directly to their disciplines, and generally they do.

1094-2939/00/0623-0117$14.00

State and Revolution

Post-Soviet research has been consumed by the Soviet collapse and the halting moves toward state reconstitution. First, the deinstitutionalization that began in the late Gorbachev period is a phenomenon that demands explanation. The super-federation [that is, the federation of the union republics of the Soviet Union, not the Autonomous Soviet Socialist Republics (ASSRs) of the union republics] broke up into its constituent parts, and all-Union authority disappeared. The Communist Party's unchallenged right to monitor state practice dissipated. Many of the prized institutions of the state—the armed forces, the health care system, the houses of culture, the academies of science—ceased providing public goods. (Other institutions, such as the metros, have maintained excellent service.) Because Huntington (1968) had persuasively argued that Leninist institutions were adaptable and strong, finding an explanation for the causes of the Soviet institutional collapse has been of compelling concern to Sovietologists. Second, as the leaders of the post-Soviet states have attempted to construct new institutions—functioning markets, property rights, electoral systems, political parties, legislatures—political scientists have had a golden opportunity to examine the formation of institutional rules and the effects of rules on individual or group behavior. Thus, the Soviet collapse has fostered research on the demise of (once thought to be) impregnable institutions and on the dynamics of institutional reconstruction.

On the issue of how to code the collapse, a debate rages among specialists as to whether events in Russia and the Soviet Union from 1989 to 1991 constitute a revolution. McAuley (1997) argues that there was no revolution, McFaul (1996:170) holds that it was a revolution of a special kind (a peaceful one), and Hough (1997) contends that it was one of the great modern revolutions. None of the area experts in this debate has coded the Soviet collapse using the eight-element Boolean scheme to characterize revolutions that was developed by Goldstone (1991). But since Goldstone does not present a theory of the processes unleashed by the different combinations of elements (of which there are 128), using his scheme—even if we got the definitions right—would not help explain the consequences of the particular form of state breakdown for Russia's political future. Ultimately, the resoution of this debate as to whether the Soviet Union experienced a revolution depends all too much upon one's definition of a revolution and one's subjective evaluation as to the scope of changes that actually took place. However, in light of Skocpol's (1979) finding that all social revolutions lead to the strengthening of the state, it is important to ask, as McFaul (1996) does: To the extent to which there was a revolution in the Soviet Union in 1991, why did it lead to the apparent emasculation of the state? An answer to this question would broaden our understanding of the paths of revolutionary development, and this would require a comparative framework that goes far beyond post-Soviet studies.

On the causes of institutional collapse, scholars divide. Suny (1993) sees collapse as caused by the emergence of national consciousnesses, seeded by the Soviet state, that could not be contained by that state; Roeder (1993) sees it as inherent in the sclerotic institutional arrangement of Leninist states; Hough (1997) sees it as caused by the loss of will by the Soviet intelligentsia (and incredibly self-destructive policies by Gorbachev) to lead what was sure to be an extremely difficult political and economic transition; and Solnick (1998) sees it as the loss of confidence by agents of the state in the ability and will of the Soviet leadership to exert domination over government and society. The studies by Roeder (1993) (in analyzing agency problems for "selected" officials) and Solnick (1998) (in seeing the collapse in terms of a cascade) engage directly neo-institutionalist models within political science and provide clues to more general issues of institutional collapse. In fact, all of these studies merit close scrutiny by the new institutionalists in political science, as the findings should compel them to include in all models of institutional growth the possibility of rather rapid collapse.

At least as important as the questions of institutional collapse are the questions of post-Soviet reinstitutionalization of state functions. The post-Soviet Russian state (consistent with McFaul's 1996 claim on the postrevolutionary weakening of the state) is immensely weak in the provision of property rights, the substitution of public over private enforcement of contracts, the provision of public health, the fulfillment of military missions, the control of smuggling through its borders, and macroeconomic management. To be sure, there are functions, such as the incorporation of all but one of the federal units into the organizational structure of the state, that the Russian Federation has performed well. Moreover, as the studies of Wegren (1998) and Hough (2000) illustrate, it may be an error to code the impoverishment of rural life or the nonpayment of taxes as signs of state weakness. It may well be the case that the state is pursuing its own interests (e.g. the provision of cheap food for urban areas, the maintenance of low unemployment) successfully. Analysts who disagree with these policies (or take the government's word as to what its goals are) may see outcomes as evidence of a weak state rather than a strong state serving a particular coalition. Since state strength is partly a function of issue area and partly a function of government goals, a general scale of state strength is probably not possible.

The more interesting questions revolve around attempts to construct new state institutions, the degree of success, and the unintended consequences of such attempts. Papers are beginning to appear that give details on newly formed institutions. Adams (1996) has provided details on the workings of the Russian National Security Council. Hendley (1997) has published new material on the arbitrage courts. Woodruff (1999) has examined the "struggle for sovereignty over money" (a losing battle so far) in post-Soviet Russia, with the notion of a national currency as a key element of a strong state. The institutions of the post-Soviet state are just beginning to command careful study. Because their future is unknown, they should provide valuable data to develop theories not only of the mechanics of institutions (the degree to which they structure incentives), which is part of the political science mainstream, but in their dynamics (the degree to which they get undermined or transformed) as well, which would be far more innovative.

Democracy

Post-soviet research on the supposed transitions to democracy has focused on five questions: (*a*) Are the FSU states experiencing transitions to democracy at all? (*b*) Is there any connection between successful democratization and the existence of civil society? (*c*) To the extent that there is democratization, what particular democratic institutions have been selected and why? (*d*) What are the characteristics of the post-Soviet voter? (*e*) What sort of party systems are in the making?

Have There Been Transitions to Democracy?   The so-called transitologists entered the post-Soviet field with gusto, sparking a vigorous debate as to whether the experience of Russia or other FSU states was comparable to that of Latin America and southern Europe in the 1970s and 1980s (Schmitter & Karl 1994). Bunce (1995) countered Schmitter & Karl by pointing to the disanalogy between democratization and communist collapse. McFaul (1996) entered the fray as well; he argues that a peaceful revolution has a different dynamic from the elite bargaining model that the transitologists so heavily relied upon, and discounts their predictions. Roeder (1994) is among those who refuse to specify a path with only a democratic outcome, and models the possibility of an autocratic and an oligarchic outcome. Democracy in some post-Soviet republics could emerge, he reasons, but more because of a deadlock between autocratic and oligarchic elements than an elite bargain posited by transitologists. On this question of a democratic outcome for Russia, Hough (2000) wisely reminds his readers that in the United States, Great Britain, and other contemporary democracies, the period from initial constitutional design to the institutionalization of democracy was quite long. From the American success in the Revolution, after eight years (the period since the collapse of the Soviet Union at the time Hough was writing), there was mostly turmoil between the states and no federal constitution. Hough suggests that it would be unreasonable to expect Russia in the late 1990s, even if it were on a path of democracy, to look very democratic. What is occurring now may be democratization or it may be a short interregnum before another period of authoritarian rule; the question remains open.

Is There a Connection Between Democratization and Civil Society?   Heavily influenced by Putnam's neo-Tocquevillian approach (1993), post-Soviet researchers have asked to what extent the existence or reemergence of civil society, despite all attempts by Soviet rule to eliminate it, facilitates democracy. Hosking (1990) sounded a journalistic clarion call awakening scholars to the realities of civil society in the Gorbachev period. Stoner-Weiss's (1997) work is attentive to the role of business networks for the effectiveness of local governments in the early post-Soviet period. Hahn (1993) has published data on changes in Russian political culture in Yaroslavl, suggesting the existence of a civic culture. As yet, however, there is no clear measurement instrument for the development of a civil society applied to post-Soviet Russia that would provide a benchmark to assess the foundations for efficient democratic institutions. Petro (1999) examines the growth of civic associations in Novgorod since 1991. He finds, as Putnam's work on Italy would suggest, a clear relationship between vigorous civic associations and efficient local government. In contrast to Putnam, however, his data show (as do many reexaminations of the Putnam argument in Italy and elsewhere) that efficient government preceded the existence of these associations, and in fact played a role in their emergence. This case is in line with many critiques of Putnam's thesis, and its evidence will stimulate a more general reformulation.

What Democratic Institutions Have Been Selected? A vibrant normative and empirical literature in political science compares democratic institutions based on such criteria as fairness and efficiency. Voting rules capture much attention, but the relationship of executive and legislative branches (usually portrayed as presidentialism versus parliamentarism) gets pride of place (Linz & Stepan 1996). Easter (1996), in comparing the countries in the FSU with those in Eastern Europe, finds some empirical confirmation of the Linz/Stepan thesis that parliamentarism brings more secure democratic transitions. But he detects a flaw in the normative implications that are drawn, as the factors that lead countries to "choose" parliamentarism are also factors that make democracy more stable. Easter focuses on the structure of old regime elites. To the extent that they are consolidated (and were therefore able to secure through decree property rights in the new regime) or reformed (they were weakened, but had considerable resources to reform and then marginalize new actors, as was the case with Russia), the new elites invariably chose presidentialism. To the extent that they were dispersed and internally fragmented, the new elites divided power among themselves by choosing parliamentarism. The same factor (dispersion of power) should also explain the success of democracy. If so, it is not parliamentarism but dispersion of elite power that causes success.

In a similar vein, Geddes (1996) assumes that politicians choose institutions that best maximize their hold on power. Although her focus is on Eastern Europe, her hypothesis should apply to the FSU states as well. It explains why the communists in the early period of chaos (around 1989), feeling that the opposition was disunited, pushed for strong presidentialism. Later on, when communists were ousted and the parties controlling the legislatures were unsure of their own long-term power, there was an interest among them in parliamentarism. Unlike the arguments of Shugart & Carey (1992), Geddes' work shows that a strong presidency did not result from a cooperative solution of actors to a shared problem of uncertainty; rather, it resulted from the inability of weak parties to curtail the independent power of the presidency. Scholars who examined the democratizing processes in the FSU and Eastern Europe were less impressed with the collective search for institutions that work and more impressed with the choice of institutions as a short-term power-maximizing strategy with long-term effects.

What Are the Characteristics of the Post-Soviet Voter? Studies of the post-Soviet voter have become a small industry. On the one hand, scholars with experience in analyzing elections elsewhere have brought new standards to interviewing and polling (e.g. Brady & Kaplan 1998) and to the analysis of electoral data in overcoming in part the ecological problems of making inferences about voter strategies from aggregate data (Myagkov et al 1997). Bringing new standards to surveys goes well beyond electoral concerns. The longitudinal studies associated with the "paths of a generation" project (see e.g. Titma et al 1998), conducted in Estonia, are an invaluable source of data on the generation that came of age when the Soviet Union collapsed.

On the other hand, extensive surveys have been conducted to capture the reasoning and motivations of the post-Soviet voter. Hough et al (1996), relying on an extensive network of interviewers in all the republics, have found intriguing variations in voting behavior across the federation. One finding, namely that small-town Russia votes vastly more with the communists than would be predicted by any linear function (Hough et al 1996:5), reveals previously unknown political orientations in rural Russia. Bahry & Way (1994) have found that unlike their Western counterparts, Russians with high socioeconomic status (SES) are less likely to vote than those with low SES (but those with high SES tend to engage in other forms of electoral activity at a higher rate than their lower status neighbors). Gibson's surveys (1997) show some antiliberal propensities in the Russian population, which make them more open to antidemocratic appeals than are Western voters. This issue is by no means settled, as the debate rages on how best to interpret survey data on the democratic tendencies of Russian citizens (Finifter & Mickiewicz 1992; Miller et al 1994, 1996; Finifter 1996). Rose & Tikhomirov (1996) rely on their New Russia Barometer to isolate the characteristics of the Russian voter. Using discriminant function analysis, they identify four types of voters: "reds blamed," "confident authoritarians," "lumpen traditionalists" (the younger, less educated group that trusts traditional institutions but not the state), and "aspiring nationalists." How these categories map onto a spectrum of issue space has not received attention. TJ Colton (unpublished manuscript) provides a comprehensive analysis of the Russian voter based on data from a decade of elections, and this work promises to make electoral data from Russia comparable with similar studies in other democracies.

Is There an Emergent Party System?   Modern democracies rely on parties to screen, recruit, and process candidates for public office. The set of parties in any democracy forms a party system, which itself has implications for the mechanics of any democratic polity. Democratic theorists have therefore put much effort into the description of Russian parties and into the analysis of the emerging party system. The essays in the volume edited by Colton & Hough (1998) on the parties competing both at the center and in the regions provide an ethnographically based description of the early organizational standing of most Russian parties.

As for the party system, Fish (1994) has shown that Russian parties in the transition had been ridden by factions and defections; that they did not develop mass memberships and loyal followings; that they overlapped in ideology, without programmatic differentiation; that parties with identical goals failed to consolidate, seriously compromising their chances of maximizing seats for representatives who shared those goals; and that those representatives who got elected failed to enact legislation along the lines of their manifestos. The result was a party system composed of a large number of weakly institutionalized parties that were not organized to capture the voters whose ideal issue points were close to their party line. Fish suggests that because of this "syndrome of ineffectiveness," Russia did not have a party system but rather a "movement society."

To explain the early noninstitutionalization of Russian parties, several theories have been offered. Fish suggests that the timing of the "founding election" was too sudden and did not allow parties to nominate candidates. Furthermore, the Soviet and post-Soviet states did not process demands by organizations, first because of intransigence and later because of decay, and thus there was no pay-off for organization by interested associations. Parties could not therefore aggregate the interests of well-organized groups. Moser (1999) suggests that the reason for noninstitutionalization may be that Russian elites, not connected to any clear social base, found it rational to run as independents, with no constraints coming from well-institutionalized parties that could strategically nominate candidates. Another possible explanation is that there were no enforcers among the parties that shared issue space, creating a collective-action dilemma as to how to fulfill a "power sharing contract" (J Zielinski, manuscript in preparation). Meanwhile, Smyth (1998) attributes the lack of institutionalization of the Russian party system to candidate incentives inherent in a mixed plurality and proportional representation electoral system.

There may well be some truth to all of these claims, but the value on the dependent variable is hardly stable. In 1995 Fish reported an emergent, albeit inchoate, multiparty system. McFaul earlier observed (1993) that there was indeed an emergent bipolar system of parties (reform and antireform) that had still not fully consolidated. This is consistent with Sobyanin's (1994:Appendix 8.1) complex accounting system of 14 factions underlying two broad coalitions. Yet, even controlling for whether the country had democratic institutions in the pre-Soviet period, it may still be necessary to explain why the consolidation of a party system in the Russian Federation and most of the post-Soviet states has been so much slower than in Eastern Europe and the Baltics.

Overall, despite the new information about the voters, the electoral institutions, and the party systems, the literature on post-Soviet democratization lacks engagement with current trends concerning democracy in the wider discipline and lacks boldness to set new agendas for political science. The weak party system in Russia should allow area specialists to assess the importance of parties in conveying voter preferences to legislators. Until now, such evaluations have been difficult because virtually all the democracies examined in the standard literature have coherent party systems. Different values on key parameters, as in the Russian case today, allow for tests of robustness of new theoretical claims.

On the question of boldness, area specialists might take advantage of two opportunities. First, following Roeder (1994), the paths toward institutional breakdown should be included in studies of the mechanics of democracy. For example, models ought to include actors with an interest in subverting the democratic process. If substantial resources of the state are being used to help fragment the party system as a strategy to enhance state power, or even to lay the groundwork for a preemptive coup, studies linking electoral rules to party fragmentation would be missing the fundamental political game driving state authorities to a new authoritarian system. Perhaps it would be more useful to think of democratization and authoritarianism as alternative equilibria, with Russia not yet tipped into either camp. Thinking this way would give a more dynamic quality to standard institutional approaches to democracy that were built from the American experience.

Second, democratic theorists of the post-Soviet experience might link their work more tightly with the literature on the state, since the fundamental question that troubles post-Soviet democracy is not the absence of rights but the absence of institutions to protect those rights (Holmes 1997). Whereas the literature in American political science focuses on legislative oversight of state agencies, post-Soviet political science has a comparative advantage in building theory on an assumption of legislative interest in the creation of autonomous state agencies.

The Nation

The uprisings of the Soviet republican nationalities in the 1980s raised a set of interlinked questions for area specialists and, more generally, for comparativists. First, did these movements significantly help undermine the Soviet system, and if so, how did they successfully confront a leviathan state? Second, what was the sequencing of the uprisings, and what does it tell us about the causes of national movements? Third, what kind of nationalism is emerging in the post-Soviet world, and will it be a threat to liberalism? Fourth, under what conditions will nationalist movements take a violent hue?

National Uprisings and the Soviet Collapse   It may well be part of popular wisdom that the nationalist movements in the Baltics (the "singing revolution," in which popular song festivals mobilized nationalist sentiments) and related defiances of Soviet power that spread to other union republics caused the Soviet collapse. Suny (1993) certainly suggests that the Soviet nurturing of nationalities backfired on the empire, as imperial subjects mobilized as national freedom fighters. Brubaker (1996:Ch. 2) too sees in Soviet nationality policy the seeds of organized rebellion against it. But few political scientists have attributed much causal weight to nationalism and nationalist movements in accounting for the Soviet collapse.

Most political scientists realized that singing revolutions succeed only if the state elites lose the will to rule, a point that Breuilly (1994) emphasizes in his comparative work on nationalism. Motyl (1987) argues correctly that Ukrainian rebellion in the late Soviet period was impossible because the Soviet state maintained the reputation of putting down national rebellions with such fortitude that it would be irrational for any nationality to confront the state directly. It took a Soviet leader who was unwilling to use force to maintain the reputation of the state, and a divided Russian central elite, to undermine Soviet state coherence. In line with this approach, but turning popular wisdom on its head, Snyder portrays the modern nation-state as an effective "instrument" in promoting economic and military security. Nation-states attracted loyalty due to their effectiveness, but "where they lagged in effectiveness, they stimulated an even more urgent form of nationalism, spurred by the demand to create a more effective state" (Snyder 1993:9). He therefore generalizes that "nationalism reflects a need to establish an effective state to achieve a group's economic and security goals. The most aggressive nationalist movements arise when states fail to carry out those tasks, spurring people to create more effective states" (Snyder 1993:5). It was the failure of the Soviet state to govern effectively that enabled and encouraged the national revivals. If there is a conclusion on the relationship of nationalism to state collapse, it is that state collapse promotes nationalism.

The Significance of Sequencing   Research on the sequencing of the national revivals has helped bury the idea that they were generated by feelings of cultural distance from the Moscow center. Treisman (1997) compares the constituent units of the Russian Federation on the degree to which they exhibited political-legal separatism in the period of 1990–1994. He finds that higher levels of institutional status, advanced economic development, industrial wealth, export capacity, and natural resources are significant predictors of separatism. In addition, ethnic separatism does not vary with concentration of the titular nationality (i.e. the nationality after which the republic was named), ethnic language usage, or ethnic language schooling. Gorenburg (1999) compares a set of Turkic republics inside the Russian Federation, finding that the best predictor of national mobilization is the level of institutional resources in the Soviet political structure. In a study of Ukraine, Wilson (1997) finds similarly that nationalism succeeds to the extent that there had been a "state" experience for the national cadre seeking political independence.

This research has shown that under conditions of state collapse the key to a powerful and successful national revival is the availability of a state apparatus to give reality to the national goal. This finding is not fully commensurate with studies of nationalism with a third-world focus (e.g. Horowitz 1985). It will be the task of the next generation of political scientists, when the Soviet dust has settled, to sort out the intervening variables and explain the sequences of national revival movements in different political contexts. But it is clear already that scholars such as Treisman and Gorenburg, in emphasizing the institutional basis of national revivals, have built a strong foundation for their successors.

Post-Soviet Nationalisms   Much research has gone into the question of whether the content of post-Soviet nationalisms will be civic or ethnic. Snyder (1993:12) sees ethnic nationalism arising "spontaneously when an institutional vacuum occurs." Increasingly, however (see Brubaker 1998), the ethnic/civic dichotomy has fallen into disrepute. Consider Estonia: Its nationalism is powerful, but its state is built on the rule of law. How should one interpret its rules that effectively denied Russians (who made up about 40% of the late-Soviet population) the right to vote in its founding election? On the one hand (the civic argument), Russians did not meet residency requirements in the Estonian Republic (because Estonia had been an occupied state since 1944, and Russian migration into it was therefore illegal). On the other hand (the ethnic argument), Estonians wanted to nationalize their state so that it would be purely Estonian, and any legal argument that allowed this would suffice. All nationalism is a mix of ethnic and civil strands (Yack 1996), and a researcher's political ideology can all too easily determine the coding of particular cases.

Instead of coding nationalism based on a rather blunt set of categories, a few political scientists have employed discourse analysis to capture trends in the content of the emerging nationalisms. Urban (1994) portrays Russian nationalism as facing a different challenge from the nationalisms of Eastern Europe. In contrast to Eastern European nationalism, in which identity could be built on a common knowledge that communism was never really "theirs," Russia, Urban suggests, does not enjoy this luxury. "There, a discourse of identity forfeits from the outset the possibility of constructing some *other nation* onto which might be loaded the negative moment in the recreation of a national community" (1994:733, italics in original). Communists call their enemies fascists or lumpens; democrats suggest their enemies are not civil or normal. The nationalist card has ominous implications for Russia, Urban argues, as it would necessarily entail targeting internal enemies, those who should be excluded from public life. Thus, Eastern European nationalists can be liberals, whereas in Russia this combination is not easily sustained. Brudny (1998), however, finds a longer tradition of locating internal enemies within Russian nationalist discourse and uses a different political logic to explain its post-Soviet resurgence.

Breslauer & Dale (1997), through a search on a computerized data base of newspaper accounts, examined national discourse in Russia from the late Gorbachev period. They find that throughout this period, up through the first war in Chechnya, Yeltsin's notion of nation-building was "de-ethnicized." He often spoke of *Rossiyanye* (the citizens of the state), not *Russkiye* (Russian ethnics). He referred to the *narod* (the people), but not the *natsiya* (the nation). Breslauer & Dale's data show that in Yeltsin's political battles with a variety of opponents, he resisted ethnicization of the rhetoric and resisted terms such as spirituality, organic unity, and uniqueness, which were used by his right-wing rivals. In fact, he resisted all nationally loaded terminology and opposed a new national ideology, which he feared would be grandiose in failure like communism or fascism. Yet Yeltsin eventually called for such an ideology, and Breslauer & Dale show how the changes in the political opposition (the nationalists and communists had purged their own radicals, and were seeking support from the median voter) pushed Yeltsin toward the articulation of a new tradition that entailed the invention of a glorified Russian state history.

Laitin (1998) examined the content of the national ideology of the Russians living in the near abroad. Laitin's content analysis of their self-references and others' references to them indicated that a new identity group was forming, namely the Russian-speaking population. It emerged in part because people from a variety of nontitular nationalities (Russians, Belarusans, Ukrainians, and Jews) were all thrown into the same boat when the republican language laws were passed in 1989, giving them a common cultural basis for antititular opposition. It emerged as well because Russians living in the near abroad were strong believers in the defunct Soviet identity, which itself was built on a belief that national identities were historically backward. These Russians thus felt comfortable as part of a population rather than mobilizing as a nation. In a similar vein, Skinner (1994) examines the re-creation of a Cossack (quasinational) identity in post-Soviet states.

Distinct from the literature on Russian nationalism, the literature on nationalism in the non-Russian union republics during the Soviet period was largely written by scholars with an interest in the historical fulfillment of "their" nation. With rare exceptions (Suny 1993, Motyl 1992), there was little effort to see how a particular national experience was distinct from, or similar to, other national experiences (Laitin 1991). Hough's *Journal of Soviet Nationalities* was exemplary in its attempt to apply social science theory to the question of nationalism while including comparative data. Of especial interest was the issue devoted to Olson's paper (1990) and Hough's (1990) response applying his free-rider model to the question of national movements in the Soviet period. Also important was Arel's (1990) paper comparing regional and national identities in Ukraine.

The Association for the Study of Nationalities, founded in Soviet times, has grown into a major scholarly society in the post-Soviet era, and its journal *Nationalities Papers* is lively. A few books have appeared on post-Soviet nationalism in the republics (e.g. Wilson 1997, Taagepera 1992). There is as yet no agenda-setting paper comparing the implications of nationalism of the non-Russian union republics, although Haas (1997) promises to address this area.

The key to future work will be to track nationalist ideology as it is being produced rather than classifying it along some preconceived macro set of categories. Political scientists will need to identify the mechanisms linking national ideologies as they form and political action that can be explained by differential national discourses and identities.

Violence in Post-Soviet Nationalist Movements   Concerning inter-nationality violence in the post-Soviet period, several area experts have offered new explanations. Beissinger (1998:410), looking closely at the post-Soviet cases, asks an insightful question: "Why did those who challenged the borders of the USSR contest them nonviolently, while those who challenged the borders of republics contest them violently?" His answer rests on resources and opportunities that allow groups to contest state power. Beissinger melds work in social movement theory with that of nationalist arousals, a marriage that has long been seeking its matchmaker. Bunce (1999) compares the dismemberment of the Soviet Union, Yugoslavia, and Czechoslovakia, also with the goal of differentiating the violent case (Yugoslavia) from those that split apart with minimal violence. She identifies two factors of importance: the interests of the military and whether the dominant national group had its own institutions under the ancien régime. Since there were no unique Russian or Czech institutions in the communist period, post-communist leaders of these republics were compelled to minimize tensions between them and those republics that had their own institutional apparatuses. This minimized the level of violence. Laitin (1998:ch. 12) compares four post-Soviet republics to show why processes such as assimilation, consociation, and emigration set patterns of large-scale inter-nationality violence that are distinct from processes of interstate violence.

Explaining the horrid scale of violence in the post-Soviet world while at the same time accounting for its rarity remains a key test for all students of ethnic violence. Fearon & Laitin (1996), Posen (1993), and Fearon (1998) have offered theoretical suggestions for why this is so. But the careful case work made possible by the large number of ethnically mixed post-Soviet cases, with great variation in levels of nationalism and degrees of inter-nationality violence, allows students of post-Soviet politics to test standard theories and propose new theoretical alternatives.

The Political Preconditions for Economic Growth

A group of bright, powerful, and remorseless neoliberal economists has provided political science real (rather than straw) men in order to think through the political preconditions for economic growth in the post-Soviet context. Anders Åslund, Andrei Shleiffer, Maxim Boycko, Jeffrey Sachs, David Lipton, and Robert Vishny were all part of a group, most associated with the Macroeconomic and Finance Unit, that allied with young Russian economists such as Yegor Gaidar and Boris Fedorov with the goal of radically transforming the Russian economy. They wrote extensively of their goals and strategies (see Boycko et al 1995, Åslund 1995 for the iconic texts). Their tripartite program involved liberalization, stabilization, and privatization, but it self-consciously ignored the goal of production because the stimulation of production could all too easily work against stabilization. A focus on production, they feared, would give industrialists license to feed resources to favored state enterprises.

By 1998, with production (as expected) in decline but stabilization in tatters, the continued optimism of Åslund and a few of his collaborators appeared farcical and made them splendid targets for political science fire (e.g. YM Herrera, unpublished paper). But it took a fellow economist (Stiglitz 1999) to drop acid rain on them. Stiglitz accused these "market Bolsheviks" of ignoring the preexisting situation of the Russian polity—the set of institutions that was supposedly responsible for administering reforms—but building into their models the improvement of those institutions that would result from the proposed reforms. They could then blame the polity for not properly carrying out the reforms when in fact their model should have endogenized that probability. Their accusations concerning *kto vinovat?* (who is guilty?) were thus, according to Stiglitz, self-servingly naive.

This opens the question of the state's role in fostering economic growth, a concern left largely unattended by economists (but see Popov 1998). Political scientists quickly moved into this quasi-vacuum. Przeworski and collaborators (1995) pressed for a vision of the state that enables markets to flourish and invests in human capital to insure future economic growth. But they did not specify the institutional package that, under post-communist conditions, would maximize economic growth.

It was foolhardy, as most analysts recognized by the mid-1990s, to pose the question as one of market-led shock therapy versus gradualist state-led growth. The more useful approach asks what the implications of various government/economy mixes for post-socialist economic growth are. Hellman (1998), a pioneer of this approach, has demonstrated decisively that the most successful economic reforms among the FSU states were those run by governments that were most constrained by the presence in their parliaments of representatives whose constituents would lose out if the proposed reforms were enacted.

This finding is a challenge to the authoritarian dreams of the neoliberals (in which a reform-oriented government would administer shock therapy on the country and then disappear, as the economy would then be self-regulating). It is also a challenge to many strong-state advocates, as Hellman shows that post-socialist citizenries did not vote against neoliberal reforms. Political scientists now have an opportunity to expand on Hellman's findings, and, relying on data accumulated by Popov (1998), to bring China and other post-communist Asian states into the equation. The institutional mixes for successful reform may well be more varied than Hellman's work suggests.

Frye (1997) introduces into the discussion of economic transformation institutions that stand somewhere in between state and economy, and his work suggests that effective regulation can be fostered at this level. He examines the growth and workings of the self-governing institution regulating the Russian equities market, demonstrating the need for quasi-state, quasi-private self-governing organizations as a foundation for economic growth. The Russian government has tended to set levels of taxation for market transactions that drive all trades underground; yet stock and commodities markets without any form of regulation would discourage risk-averse investors. Frye therefore suggests that self-governing organizations are a market-inducing level for regulation in the Russian context. The systematic investigation of the institutional foundations for modern economic growth is already one of the burgeoning areas of political science, and as Hellman's and Frye's work shows, data from the FSU (and, it is hoped, other post-communist states) will play an important role in sorting out the institutional requisites for such growth.

The Federation

Federal theory in political science was rejuvenated by Riker's classic treatise in 1964, but the wind went out of its sails for a long period when few pressing empirical issues involving federalism were on area students' agendas. Developments in neo-institutional theory in political science (Montinola et al 1995) and the unraveling of the Soviet federation (Roeder 1991) changed that. Federalism became a major concern both in political theory and in area studies. In regard to Russia, the guiding question was whether it would tear apart as did its predecessor, the Soviet Union. The issue has three components: the stability of federations whose constituent parts are "owned" by nationalities, the stability of federations depending on the way power is shared, and the economic implications of federal as opposed to unitary institutions.

On the issue of ethnically based federations, Riker's analysis suggested that ethnically based constituent units would be more likely to have their own political parties and would therefore better be able to subvert a federal bargain. Bednar and colleagues (J Bednar, WW Eskridge, JA Ferejohn, unpublished observations) make a somewhat different argument. They hypothesize that in decentralized power arrangements, there will inevitably be numerous opportunities for passing the buck, trying to induce other jurisdictions to pay for public goods useful to one's own constituency. This form of cheating will invariably create tensions, as constituent governments will engage in defensive activities to protect their semi-sovereign rights. However, if the constituent units are ethnic ones, the dangers of heightened tensions are ever-present because the cheating could easily be interpreted as ethnic slights.

The logic of federal collapse with ethnically based units was certainly apparent in 1991, when the newly formed republican parties of the titular-led republics all abandoned their federal relations with the Moscow center once the opportunity presented itself. As Bednar et al (J Bednar, WW Eskridge, JA Ferejohn, unpublished observations) suggest, nearly all republics complained that they were especially slighted by the federal bargain. But anomalies such as India were always in the scopes of political scientists interested in federalism. In India, the ethnically based federation is not always stable nor its members content, but it persists. In Nigeria, after a bloody civil war in 1967–1970, in which one federal unit sought to secede, the country is immensely unstable, but the federal structure remains reasonably intact.

Since 1991, the federalism that exists within Russia, though hardly stable, has not broken apart at its seams. Two observations are in order. First, the constellation of interests is different in Russia than it was in the Soviet Union, giving decisive elites in nationally based republics an interest in the federation. Gorenburg (1999) and Giuliano (2000), for example, show that in the Turkic-speaking titular republics there is a powerful set of interests that wants to remain part of the Russian Federation. According to Gorenburg, it is largely the bilingual elites (speaking the titular language and Russian) in the major cities who have the greatest interest in maintaining political ties with Moscow; according to Giuliano, it is largely the economic elites who have left the command economy and who see commercial possibilities in the wider Russia who have the greatest interest in maintaining the Russian Federation. In either case, the internal politics of the titular republics are not uniformly pushing for greater levels of autonomy toward some new breaking point. Divisions within the federal units mean that united fronts against federal power are not forming. Meanwhile, Hanson (1998) suggests that without a dominating ideology dictating to them, the Russian republics have no big issue to catalyze them into separatist action. A second observation is based on Herrera's findings (1999) that the dynamics in at least one ethnically Russian federation member (Sverdlovsk) produce powerful incentives for separation. So the distinction between stable (not ethnically based) oblasts and unstable (ethnically based) republics ought not be set as starkly as theory now has it.

As for federal stability under various constitutional arrangements, Ordeshook (1996), a one-time student of Riker, issues a compelling challenge. Based on a comparative examination of the United States, Germany, Canada, Australia, and Czechoslovakia, Ordeshook finds that standard bargaining theory fails to explain federal success. Considering a federal center and its constituent units as an $N + 1$ bargaining game, Ordeshook claims that historical experience demonstrates that no bargain can remain stable, and there will always be "leave" threats by the units as part of bargaining strategy. Success, he recognizes (drawing not on Riker but on Madison and Hamilton), requires that the units of the federation be "constituent parts" of the national state and not merely separate bargaining units. For this to occur, there must be a somewhat ambiguous sharing of authority between levels and a situation in which national and regional politicians find their careers furthered by competing in elections at both the regional and national levels. Under these (and other) conditions, Ordeshook finds that "leave" threats are minimized. In his examination of Russian federalism, he notes that federal treaties reduce the ambiguity of shared authority, and that careers tend to be made at either the national or regional levels. He is therefore not sanguine about the long-term stability of the Russian Federation.

But one may question Ordeshook's (1996) assumption that the Russian Federation is so similar to other federations that similar electoral rules could be predicted to have similar consequences. He ignores the fact that most regional representatives serve only at the mercy of the Russian president, a fact that calls into question whether Russia is a federation at all. Also, the Russian Federation's asymmetry gives it a particular political dynamic, as emphasized by Solnick (1995). Solnick argues that federal authorities in Russia fear that they would fail in enacting any general rules that would work for all regions, and if they tried, they would lose credibility. The center therefore has preferred bilateral negotioations, more or less in the $N + 1$ design that Ordeshook fears. Lapidus (1999) takes this same factor of asymmetry, as does Solnick, but sees this as a more divisive force. Nonetheless, the results to date have been stable (with Chechnya the glaring counterexample). As a result of separate deals, the republics and the oblasts do not coordinate with each other, and the center has therefore been able to coopt regions with those separate deals (e.g. Tatarstan and Bashkortostan did not organize against the invasion of Chechnya, in part because each had its separate deal.) Thus, Moscow's separate deals not only weakened coordination among the regions and oblasts but also brought satisfaction to restive regions. Solnick is not willing to call the federal experiment a success. The next problem Moscow will face, he admitted, "will be avoiding a competitive frenzy of deal-making in the wake of the coming regional elections" (Solnick 1995:58). Solnick relies mostly on a rather soft bargaining model, but his rich understanding of the nature of the strategic situation (competitive bargaining reducing coordination among the regions) calls out for theorists to model the federal game as it is actually being played in today's Russian Federation. Treisman's (1999) findings, i.e. that Moscow's fiscal appeasement of recalcitrant regions enhanced both the asymmetry and the stability of the federation, provide yet another empirical critique of Ordeshook's (1996) prognosis.

As for the economic-growth consequences of federalism, a model in positive theory (Montinola et al 1995), using contemporary China as its example, deduces that under certain conditions, the competition by constituent units for growth-promoting industries would deter the imposition of unreasonable rents on investments. Thus, to the extent that federalism promotes competition among constituent federal units for investments, it should induce faster economic growth than a unitary state with a national set of industrial regulations. In a cogent analysis of the Russian case, relying on the Montinola et al model, Slider finds a "market-distorting federalism," in which "bargaining with the center over special privileges and access to funds ... allows regional officials to avoid taking steps that might encourage market development at the price of eroding their own power" (1997:457). Slider's study confirms the model in that certain conditions must be met for a federation to be market-preserving. But still to be addressed is the question of endogeneity, i.e. whether, for example, social groups favoring economic expansion created the conditions for Chinese regional policies, and social groups intent on collecting rents (the reformed *nomenklatura*) blocked those conditions in Russia. If so, the supportive federal institutions would be more the consequence than the cause of market expansion. The relationship of federal institutions to market growth is now a well-formulated research question, and Slider's contribution shows the healthy relationship between theory and area studies that should be cultivated across the discipline.

International Relations

Perhaps more than any of the subfields of post-Soviet studies, that of international relations (IR) has been in flux. Post-Soviet IR scholars are, like Russia itself, in search of a new identity. This is largely because of the fluidity of the political context, with no stable value on a dependent variable demanding explanation. As Holloway explains (1995:270), in the post-Soviet period "there is no longer a Soviet foreign policy but a whole cluster of states seeking to consolidate their statehood and to define their interests and their policies." Under these conditions, "the things that international relations theory tends to take for granted—states and interests, for example—are themselves problematic" (Holloway 1995:282–83). The instability in foreign policy in the early years of the Russian Federation as sovereign state is illuminated by Malcolm (1996:105–6), who notes how difficult it was to start a foreign policy from scratch, especially one centered on relations with other states also starting from scratch. What requires explanation is therefore not clear. To add to the field's problems, studies of post-Soviet foreign policy lost their luster, perhaps because Russia ceased to be a great power locked in bipolar conflict with the United States. An excellent new beginning was attempted by Wallander (1996). This volume is the result of a Harvard Russian Research Center seminar that brought together young scholars experimenting with new approaches to Russian security.

Without a stable value on any dependent variable, but consistent with general practice in the IR field, the subfield of post-Soviet foreign policy has focused mainly on the sources of policy. Having an interest in discounting the force of the international system, area specialists have sought to highlight the importance of ideas, interests, identities, and institutions. In focusing on ideas during the late Soviet period, Herman (1996), Mendelson (1998), and Checkel (1993) traced changes in thinking of a new breed of Soviet leaders (associated with the "new thinking" that was propagated by specialist networks) during the 1980s. These authors carefully construct case studies that show the particular political contexts in which ideas influence foreign policy. These case studies show how underdetermining were international pressures. In fact, Mendelson (1998) shows that the new thinking under Gorbachev succeeded in getting the leadership to reverse course in Afghanistan despite US pressures on the Soviet Union, which worked domestically in the opposite direction.

Zisk (1996) has tried to link interests of defense industrialists to Russian policy. No clear linkage has been established. In fact, sectors in Russia during the 1990s were insufficiently organized to exert a discernible effect on policy (see also Evangelista 1996). Nonetheless, this research provides valuable data on early manifestations of domestic pressures on Russian foreign policy makers.

Domestic Institutions   Some attention has been given to domestic sources of foreign policy (Zimmerman 1996, Menon 1995, McFaul 1997/1998, Gow 1992, Malcolm et al 1996, Bouchkin 1995). Zimmerman argues that as Russia democratizes, we should expect greater influence of the attitudes of the attentive public in foreign policy outcomes, and he has therefore begun collecting data on these attitudes. No links between domestic attitudes and foreign policy strategies are yet apparent. On the question of whether democratic institutions have an impact on foreign policy behavior, Snyder (1996) examined early foreign policy returns and found anomalies in the literature on the democratic peace. Although he takes no firm position on democracies, he argues that democratizing states such as the post-Soviet ones are less likely to be peaceful toward one another than solidly authoritarian states would be. Menon (1995) makes a similar claim in an examination of Russia and five Central Asian states. He details how domestic instability having to do with ethnic and economic tensions could breed radical movements that imperil these regimes, which in turn could "trigger external intervention" (Menon 1995:167). Meanwhile, survey data analyzed by Braumoeller (1997) show in Ukraine, but not in Russia, a significant association between liberalism (in terms of support of positive and negative freedoms and competition in government) and nationalism, with the attendant willingness to use force to protect fellow nationals. This is a limitation of the democratic peace literature, and suggests that liberalism is not monolithic but is subject to different emphases in different contexts. With foreign policy still in flux, all these studies on the domestic sources of foreign policy are necessarily speculative and preliminary.

International Institutions   Wallander (1999) shows the power of international institutions in making possible the peaceful withdrawal of Russian troops from Central Europe after the demise of the Soviet state. Her study demolishes a certain brand of realist thinking that would expect a resurgence of autonomist behavior by European states in the post–Cold War environment. These realists do not consider the possibility that states could use preconstructed international institutions as resources to fulfill national interests at lower costs than through self-help. The willingness of Russian and German foreign policy makers to employ such a strategy did not always lead to success, but it was a strategy often pursued in addressing a plethora of sticky security issues. However, international institutions are not always pareto-improving. Stone (1996) examines negotiations among the member states of the Council for Mutual Economic Assistance, established in 1949 to promote the integration of socialist economies. His work provides both theory and data showing the conditions under which international cooperative institutions lead to pareto-deficient outcomes. Mendelson & Glenn (personal communication) have conducted a series of studies on the impact of Western nongovernmental organizations on political parties, the media, environmental policy, and conflict resolution in post-Soviet states. Wallender (1999) may be correct that some international institutions can foster cooperation that would not have been possible if they did not exist. Yet other international institutions can constrain states or their citizens from exploring new policy alternatives. Still others can put pressures on states for reform in a way that might backfire. Further work on the impact of international institutions on FSU states has the potential of sorting out these effects and thereby enriching the literature on the impact of international institutions on state behavior.

Identity   Prior to any discussion of ideas and interests, or even institutions, we need to know how the new Russian state identifies itself. In seeking to explain foreign policy trends, and riding the wave of the new constructivist approach to international relations (Katzenstein 1996), several scholars have emphasized the uncertain identity of Russia, with implications for its role on the international stage—Great Power, Eurasian leader, or Western state. The politics of identity, as suggested by Timmerman (1992), Hopf (1998), and Light (1996), necessarily precedes the choice of strategy. The question of how closely to ally and integrate with the West arose concurrently with the question of who the Russians were, absent their Soviet identity, and who they wanted to be (Light 1996:35–41). Still lacking in this emergent literature is any refinement of constructivist or identity theories that would explain outcomes not only in the cases under study but also in out-of-sample (and out-of-region) cases.

Foreign Policy   Parallel to the work focusing on the potential force of a variety of independent variables, there have been explanations accounting for the overall course of Russian foreign policy. Upon taking power in the fluid time immediately following the Soviet collapse, Boris Yeltsin and Foreign Minister Andrei Kozyrev pursued a liberal, Atlanticist policy of security cooperation and economic integration with the West. But in the months preceding Kozyrev's resignation, pro-Western liberals were on the defensive, both on the home and foreign fronts. Why?

To give some structure to this discussion, Dawisha & Parrott (1994) categorize five possible Russian foreign policy orientations. Checkel (1995) suggests a number of factors that are all are pressing toward the more "right-shifting" Russian foreign policy. MacFarlane (1994) suggests that there has been a rightward trend from liberalism to realism, but that it hasn't gone toward a fully right-wing nationalist foreign policy orientation. "Liberal internationalism," he explains, "essentially ignored or skipped over the question of identity-formation, focusing instead on world order. For a variety of reasons, this was impossible to justify for long.... But radical nationalist messianism was not a viable substitute. Its aspirations far outstripped the state's capacities.... The solution attempted by Russian leaders is a middle ground" (MacFarlane 1994:265). He therefore sees Russia pulled more and more into a realist peacekeeping role on its borders as a principal component of its foreign policy repertoire (MacFarlane & Schnabel 1995). Alternatively, Beissinger (1995) traces the right-moving foreign policy to persistent images of "empire" embedded in the consciousnesses of the Russian foreign policy elites and the elites of the former subjugated (within the Soviet Union) republics.

McFaul's (1997/1998) explanandum is the nonbelligerent foreign policy of Russia—more liberal than the consensus holds—which also contradicts the theoretical expectations of Snyder (1996) that weak and transitional democracies are quite war-prone. McFaul argues that "the political and economic winners in Russia's transition are the very groups that would not benefit from war" (McFaul 1997/1998:21). The exception, McFaul acknowledges, is Chechnya, in which the so-called losers dominated; the resulting fiasco only served, at least in the short term, to discredit them. McFaul pushes adherents of Snyder's position to explain away this anomaly within their theory or to state parameters in which their theory is likely not to hold.

The Future of International Relations Research in Russia   The enduring contribution of IR research in the post-Soviet period is in the hard-won data from interviews and field observations. Descriptions of the policy environment in this turbulent period will surely outlast the theoretical debates that frame those descriptions. Moreover, this body of work illustrates the limits of the application of seemingly general theories. For example, Evangelista (1996) sought to apply models of international political economy to the post-Soviet energy sector. He found that Rogowski's model (1989) would predict a political cleavage of communists and farmers against the owners of capital, but found it impossible to identify the latter class in terms of real political actors. Similarly, in applying Frieden's (1991) model of asset specificity, Evangelista (1996) was unable to measure the bargaining power of labor in different sectors, since wages are a weak indicator of what workers seek to maximize. He therefore concludes that regional specialists are needed to address specific historical contexts, even in the testing of general theory. The works discussed in this section are therefore of importance to general IR theorists, as the details set limits to the applicability of several theories.

Nonetheless, the post-Soviet IR field may be too constrained by its engagement with standard IR theory, paying insufficient attention to the wider political science discipline. For example, consider Wallander's (1999) exemplary study of Russian/German bargaining. It is true, but trivial, that states with available resources (in this case, access to international institutions) will employ those resources in their foreign policy strategies. Only in a field consumed by a war of paradigms (what matters most: institutions or structures?) would such a finding be important. A more analytically interesting finding, however, is that in the dismantling of a particular type of nuclear reactor, the parties involved were unable to agree on a risk-sharing strategy, if, for example, the reactor blew up and caused damages and lawsuits worldwide. Without a risk-sharing strategy, the dangerous acceptance of the status quo results. Wallander's analysis speaks directly to a general theoretical issue, namely the conditions under which institutions can work out risk-sharing agreements. The ease of movement to superior equilibria on some issues and the near impossibility on others, with small differences in institutional framework, are outcomes that demand a positive theory of international institutions and equilibrium selection. Wallander provides suggestive reasons for the variation, and future research could specify those reasons so that they could be applied to out-of-sample cases. The post-Soviet IR field, in sum, has engaged productively with questions driving the wider IR field, but less than optimally with parallel analyses in other subfields within political science.

Institutional Legacies

Path dependency is intuitively obvious yet extremely difficult to nail down in a precise way. Area specialists are especially attuned to legacies, as Meyer (1994) points out, and scholars with area expertise are in an excellent position to give substance to a rather abstract notion. Jowitt has been the principal theorist of such legacies. He insisted at the moment of the transition, "Whatever the results of the current turmoil in Eastern Europe, one thing is clear: the new institutional patterns will be shaped by the 'inheritance' and legacy of forty years of Leninist rule" (1992:285). Leninist rule, according to Jowitt, reinforced salient features of traditional culture, such as the rigid dichotomization of the official (seen negatively) and the private (seen insularly) realms, leading to a political culture dominated by dissimulation and rumor-mongering. It also created autarchic collectives that fragmented rather than integrated society, such that the members of each collective have no regard for the life situation of members of other collectives—thus, there is no cultural support for sympathy with others' plights. These Leninist legacies are likely, Jowitt contends, to confront the Civic Forums and other democratic and liberal organizations in Eastern Europe with "anti-civic, anti-secular, anti-individual forces" (Jowitt 1992:304).

Hanson (1997), following a related idea of Jowitt's concerning the Leninist "charismatic-rational conception of time," seeks to explain the waste of resources, shoddiness of goods, and lack of incentives that undermined the socialist experiment. There was a "final-exam economy—since an endless summer vacation (communism) was always held to be just around the corner, the most rational thing to do was to 'cram'. Under Brezhnev this sense began to dissipate. But Gorbachev attempted, unsuccessfully, at least at first through 'acceleration' (*uskorenie*) to reestablish charismatic-rational time" (Hanson 1997:ix). This legacy, the reader surmises, must have influenced the current attempts to rationalize the post-Soviet economy.

Other political scientists have stipulated the effects of historical legacies in a less grandiose way. Hendley (1997) shows how legacies of Soviet law, in which top-down regulations were invariably decreed to fulfill the interests of those in the center, made shareholders of post-Soviet firms skeptical that the cumulative voting mechanisms required by the joint-stock law of 1995 were written to serve their interests. More broadly, Hendley finds that enterprise directors appeal to personal networks in Moscow rather than the courts for support when they face conflicts with outside firms, largely because this was their mode of operation in the Soviet period. Yet the courts have not been thoroughly ignored by business, suggesting that the Soviet legal legacies have half-lives.

Crowley (1997:187) has examined the strategic moves of Soviet and post-Soviet miners in both the Donbass and Kuzbass. Although in many arenas material interest was determinative of action, Crowley still found ideological legacies that structured choice. Seeking to explain miners' flip-flop from an embrace of the market (even when, especially for the Donbass miners, a move toward the market was a step toward redundancy) to an embrace of the Communist Party in the mid-1990s, Crowley reexamines Soviet rhetoric. This rhetorical legacy, he argues, left the miners not only lacking an alternative to capitalism (other than communism, which they supported), but also lacking an alternative within capitalism (such as social democracy). The miners, he concludes, had "no institutional channel to express their grievances in the political realm" other than as communists. The Manichean world-view, capitalism or communism, was for the miners the whole choice set. "While miners everywhere are given to radicalism," Crowley concludes, "the direction their radicalism takes is underdetermined" (1997:189).

Bahry & Way examine participation among the Russian electorate, and controlling for a variety of factors, they show that the old and poor are far more likely to vote than the well-to-do. They attribute this in part to the Soviet electoral legacy because "The residues of Soviet mobilization ... have an impact on all forms of conventional activity; but they seem to be especially pronounced for voting, the most ritualized form of Soviet participation. Soviet elections may have been designed as vehicles for legitimating the status quo, but they appear ultimately to have given older citizens a habit that has become a powerful political weapon" (1994:352).

Other examples of legacies abound in the literature. Beissinger (1995) suggests that the legacy of "empire" continues to drive foreign policy thinking both in Russia and in the now independent but once union republics of the USSR. Motyl (1997) argues that the legacy of an emasculated-by-totalitarianism civil society greatly weakens either the will (in Russia) or the capacity (in Ukraine) of the elites in post-Soviet states (with the Baltics being the exception) to fashion and execute radical reform measures. Luong (1996) points to differential political cleavages (ethnic versus regional) in post-Soviet Central Asia that are traced to Soviet strategies of rule. Burawoy & Krotov, based on observations of the Soviet wood industry in summer 1991 (Polar Furniture), argued that most economists were "underestimat[ing] the capacity of the Soviet economy to reproduce itself and resist transformation" (1992:17). With the opening to the market, a regional conglomerate of firms partly owned by the state, the Northern Territories' Wood Association, emerged with the goal of connecting firms that had supply networks with each other. In a sense, Burawoy & Krotov report, it replaced the party state as the mechanism to reduce anarchy in the relations of production. The real profit within the system, however, is in controlling the barter and other intra-industry trade networks, and in having a monopoly over those networks, a clear legacy of the Soviet period.

McAuley (1997) has a keen eye for Soviet legacies and a strategy for finding them. She reports that outside of Moscow, where elites have little incentive to hide their ingrained Soviet practices, they are easy to detect. In Naberezhnye Chelny, home of KamAZ auto plant in Tatarstan, McAuley examined a by-election to the Supreme Soviet and saw the electoral material as almost a satire on Soviet-style electioneering, except that the authors of these tracts were serious. "New constitutional rules on the separation of powers and democratic electoral procedures," she concludes, "not only failed to dislodge the incumbents but also allowed them to secure their position as patrons" (McAuley 1997:91–108). In fact, the old elite in the republics created an executive presence even stronger than before, marginalizing the legislature and the nationalists. Elsewhere (1997:Ch. 4), McCauley studied electoral dynamics in Krasnodar krai and finds the old division of reds and experts dividing the elite, as the grounds of political battle hardly changed from the Soviet period. These legacies—at least for some period—constrain the workings of newly created institutional incentives.

Despite this abundant literature pointing to Soviet legacies, the magnitude of their effects is difficult to determine. Institutions and interests weigh in to diminish the impact of such legacies. For example, a student of Jowitt (Geddes 1996) found the Leninist legacy to have little explanatory power on questions of party strategy. To take another example, the principal theme in what will become the standard source for voting in post-Soviet Russia (TJ Colton, unpublished manuscript) shows that "variables in reasonably clear-cut categories—electors' social traits, their appraisals of the health of the economy and polity ... leadership evaluations, and assessments of the performance and promise of incumbents and opposition ... all have a significant bearing on how post-Soviet Russians vote." This does not sound as if the Russian voter were mired in Leninist categories; rather, democratic institutions set new incentives, to which Russian voters responded as any voting citizens would. In fact, in the decade following the Soviet collapse, what Jowitt considered "clear" has not yet been confirmed with any cross-sectional data that includes non-Leninist states.

Perhaps one should think of legacies as historical features that work to block or divert political processes from the directions predicted by general theory or influence equilibrium selection under conditions of multiple equilibria. Political science cannot ignore the extended period of transition before the values on outcome variables are commensurate with the predictions on the effects of institutional change. The institutional legacies diverting outcomes from their predicted directions need to be accounted for, and the information in area scholarship is crucial for such analysis. This would call for studies that measure the magnitude and persistence of legacies, as Kitschelt & Smyth (1997) have done in regard to comparative Russian and East European blockages to programmatic party competition, rather than just pointing to their existence. The apparently gigantic legacy of Leninism—with varying levels of impact across Soviet, Warsaw Pact, and Asian space—and the creation of democratic-like institutions in that space allow for some path-breaking research in political science, led by post-Soviet experts, on the constraints of path dependency.

AN ASSESSMENT

This review has summarized political science research on the states of the former Soviet Union with special emphasis on the Russian Federation. I have ignored much of the literature on the non-Russian republics in the post-Soviet period, and on the Soviet period itself (written by post-Soviet scholars, taking advantage of opened archives).

But the field of post-Soviet political science has been cultivated, and the early yield has been impressive. A new generation of scholars has combined field work with new theoretical concerns. Political scientists who have been credentialed in other fields have moved into Soviet studies, bringing new methods and perspectives. Senior scholars whose careers were forged during the Soviet period have played an important role in adapting new methods while speaking to theory in their countries of specialty. Whereas the field of comparative politics is portrayed as a battlefield between area studies and theory, in the post-Soviet field the tensions (combining modern methods with field observations) are usually within the framework of each particular study (and therefore productive) rather than in wars of maneuver between groups of scholars representing opposing camps (and therefore destructive). This excursion into a terrain that is territorially defined demonstrates that portraits of the comparative field are too often caricatures. Similarly, in IR, post-Soviet scholars without great difficulty have placed their studies at the core of subfield debates.

Contributions to General Theory

The contributions of post-Soviet studies to political science are substantial. For one, as should be clear from the discussion on path dependency, deviations from expected actions as predicted by theory can sometimes be accounted for by institutional legacies that require an understanding of history to specify correctly.

Second, post-Soviet scholars have provided iconic narratives of general political processes that have been more globally theorized. This work not only gives flesh to skeletal theories but provides information on the mechanisms that translate values on independent variables to values on dependent variables. Breslauer & Dale's (1997) assessment of how Yeltsin moved to a new nationalist discourse, as discussed above, contributed a compelling narrative to the Hobsbawm & Ranger (1983) corpus showing how traditions are invented.

Third, scholars with area expertise have often undermined the foundations of comparative analyses by showing that the structure of situations, the principal actors, or the goals of these actors are not as postulated by the generalists. For example, the notion that the Russian party system is fragmented because of the early calling of the founding election, or because of a coordination problem faced by party entrepreneurs living in the same Downsian neighborhood, may make for sharp theory. But these explanations, according to Hough (2000), are misguided. He provides evidence that Yeltsin paid for minor parties, enriching their entrepreneurs, in order to siphon off votes from any united opposition. Hough similarly seeks to discredit theories that seek reasons why Members of Parliament (MPs) in the Duma do not win elections based on the resource situation of parties, which is presumably so weak that they are unable to produce coherent candidate lists. Rather, Hough argues, MPs seek not to maximize reelection [as political scientists educated by Mayhew's (1974) work automatically assume], but to maximize the chances of getting a job in the presidential administration, where they can sell licenses or reap benefits from graft.

Hendley (1997) too examines Russian strategic logic from the ground. General directors of enterprises often rely on privately retained "contract enforcers" rather than courts to settle interfirm conflicts, even if the latter will allow for a wider range of contracts with low transactions costs. However, reliance on the law would require the general director to cede internal authority to the firm's legal division, whereas reliance on contract enforcers assures the director of uncompromised control over the firm. The strategic game here is not between firms seeking to lower transactions costs (as in the new institutionalism, which Hendley calls in this context the development argument), but within firms whose general directors seek to marginalize their newly created legal departments.

Woodruff (1999) has also attacked premature modeling of post-Soviet politics. In the literature on reform, Woodruff argues, analysts rely on a "rational expectations" model in which a reformist government seeks to commit to austerity, so that private actors condition their behavior on the expectation of noninflation. In actuality, Woodruff asserts, the central government is too weak to block local creation of alternative means of payment. To fill a vacuum, local governments in Russia promoted nonmonetary exchange (barter) to protect industry and maintain critical services. The central government was strategically fighting a battle for the monopoly rights to issue money, but American political scientists were interpreting that behavior as if policy makers were seeking to commit the government to austerity.

Work of this nature is crucial to keep theorists modeling what is actually going on rather than what would be theoretically interesting if it were going on. Area specialists have an eye for detail, and that, as Darwin has taught us, is where truth lies. To be sure, area specialists are sometimes too lost in detail. McAuley's (1997) descriptions of the difficulty for Shaimiev, the governor of Tatarstan, to sleep one particular night may be excessive in detail. But without a commitment to the details of political life, our models are too easily unhooked from political reality.

Finally, data collected from the FSU have provided important amendments to partially established theory. Institutions do not spontaneously arise to protect property once traders are permitted to flourish. People who are more highly educated are not always more likely to vote than those who are less educated. The constituent units of federations that are based on nationality do not inexorably seek greater autonomy from the center until the center collapses. Revolutions do not always yield strengthened states. These findings are not so weighty as to knock established theory out of the water (but no findings, however strong, seem to have that effect on any social science theory). Rather, these findings compel students of markets, voting, federations, and revolution to narrow the parameter values in which their theories have explanatory value. Setting the limiting conditions in which relationships will hold is an important part of science, and post-Soviet area studies has performed that task well.

Opportunities for a New Agenda

The post-Soviet field could be a bit more ambitious still. Observation of the basic trends of the Soviet collapse should compel us to reorder the questions that have long stood on political science agendas. This has always been the case in political theory, as our substantive agendas reflect the world we study. What questions should the collapse of communism and the subsequent rise of ill-defined quasi-states compel us to rethink? Observing the detritus of the Soviet Union in the 1990s—in which our entire political landscape has been altered—should inspire us to pose big questions that set the agenda for the wider field of political science.

I have two conjectures. The first has to do with liberalism and rights. Holmes & Sunstein (1999) have suggested that whereas in the Cold War period Western theorists considered mostly the benefits of rights, the Soviet and Russian collapse compel us to consider the costs of rights. If in the Soviet period citizens could not hope to be treated fairly by the law because they lacked constitutional protections, in the Russian period (as Solomon 1995:98 details) citizens may not get justice because courts lack heating oil. The institutional provision of the most basic public goods, merely a theoretic fantasy of the new institutionalists in the 1980s, has become a dominant theme in post-Soviet comparative politics. So, when the dominant other for the United States is Soviet totalitarianism, liberalism for American social scientists is equated with the benefits of rights to all citizens; but when the dominant other is Russian anarchy, liberalism becomes equated with the capacity to provide rights. The dominant other sets the agenda for the very framing of research on liberalism. As suggested at the end of the section on democracy, it would be exciting if post-Soviet political science incorporated this idea and therefore linked theoretically the literature on the state and that on democracy. Under what conditions, this literature could ask (to take just one example), will legislators vote to insulate state agencies not only from successor legislatures but from themselves?

A second paradigm-shifting perspective that has emerged from the collapse of Soviet communism challenges social science to explain both the emergence of islands of order under conditions of turbulence and a continent of chaos under conditions of stability. In the Soviet period, it was common to describe Leninist organizations as highly institutionalized and therefore stable (Huntington 1968); yet the late 1980s showed that they could disappear almost as if they had never existed (Solnick 1998). Meanwhile, under conditions of state chaos, reports from Hendley (1997), Frye (1997), and Wallander (1999) reveal islands of institutional stability. The trick will be to explain political and economic collapse without overexplaining them (thinking of comparisons to other post-communist cases such as Poland and China). Both the possibility of cascades undermining stability and the imposition of stable expectations (only in some realms) under conditions of chaos are core elements of the post-Soviet experience, opening opportunities for a richer understanding of coordination dynamics.

The ideas that institutionalized social outcomes are subject to cascades and that new patterns of coordination can rather quickly be established are not well understood in American political science. Students of Schelling (1978) applied these ideas to local processes, for example, whether ice hockey players would wear helmets, but research in cultural identification and societal institutions did not make use of them. The notion of an equilibrium suggests—and this is quite different from what is suggested in 1960s notions of institutionalization—that things are stable only because no person has an incentive to deviate from normal practice. However, under conditions in which a few people have an incentive to deviate, and others see the possibility of a better individual existence if a critical mass of their fellow citizens were to deviate, cascades to a radically different equilibrium are possible. To be sure, equilibrium analysis is not yet attuned to issues of selection under conditions of multiple equilibria or of shift from one equilibrium to another. In fact, theoretical work by Schofield (1999) suggests that the recognition of cascades in certain kinds of markets should induce us to give up the assumption of equilibrium. But in the Soviet context, some work has already been done along these lines. Sachs (1995) has done preliminary thinking on cascades, and Allio et al (1997) have analyzed equilibrium selection on modes of privatization in post-communist societies. Equilibrium theory, far more than institutionalization, sensitizes researchers to the ever-present yet low likelihood of institutional collapse, as well as the mechanisms of coordination under conditions of uncertainty (Laitin 1999).

The collapse of the Soviet Union should help push social science away from seeking explanations for values on dependent variables thought of as institutionalized outcomes; rather, they should seek to describe equilibria in such a way that both stability and radical shift can be explained. As suggested in the reviews of the literature on the state and of the literature on democracy, not only the mechanics but the dynamics of institutional space need to be examined. Furthermore, the post-Soviet world is the ideal arena for modeling not only incentives toward equilibria but shifts across equilibria through cascades. Although it would have been folly to demand that social science predict the Soviet collapse (Remington 1995, Kuran 1991), it would be equally imprudent to continue working with a methodology of social science that does not see the fragility of coordination in political life. The brittleness of our institutions, even when they successfully condition behavior for long periods, is a major lesson of the Soviet collapse. It should help foster in social science the study of institutional equilibria rather than institutionalized outcomes.

This is not a call for economistic hegemony. Equilibrium selection is largely determined by expectations of what fellow citizens will do under new conditions, and these expectations are in part determined by cultural beliefs (Greif 1994) and historical legacies. A positive theory of historical legacies and cultural beliefs is in the offing once action is plotted on equilibrium paths. The rich combinations of legacies versus new material incentives, and of turbulence versus new institutional orders, both of which are characteristic of post-Soviet politics, make post-Soviet politics an excellent arena for theoretical agenda setting.

Visit the Annual Reviews home page at www.AnnualReviews.org

LITERATURE CITED

Adams JS. 1996. The Russian National Security Council. *Probl. Post-Communism* 43(1):35–42

Allio L, Dobek MM, Mikhailov N, Weimer DL. 1997. Post-communist privatization as a test of theories of institutional change. In *The Political Economy of Property Rights*, ed. DL Weimer, pp. 319–48. Cambridge, UK: Cambridge Univ. Press

Arel D. 1990. The parliamentary blocs in the Ukrainian Supreme Soviet. *J. Sov. Nationalities* 1(4):108–54

Åslund A. 1995. *How Russia Became a Market Economy.* Washington, DC: Brookings Inst.

Bahry D, Way L. 1994. Citizen activism in the Russian transition. *Post-Sov. Aff.* 10(4):330–66

Beissinger MR. 1995. The persisting ambiguity

of empire. *Post-Sov. Aff.* 11(2):149–84

Beissinger MR. 1998. Nationalist violence and the state: political authority and contentious repertoires in the former USSR. *Comp. Polit.* 30(4):401–22

Bouchkin AA. 1995. Russia's far eastern policy in the 1990s: priorities and prospects. See Dawisha & Dawisha 1995, pp. 66–83

Boycko M, Shleifer A, Vishny R. 1995. *Privatizing Russia.* Cambridge, MA: MIT Press

Brady HE, Kaplan C. 1998. *The development of electoral participation and party attachment in Estonia from 1988 to 1993.* Poster presented at Annu. Meet. Am. Polit. Sci. Assoc., Boston

Braumoeller BF. 1997. Deadly doves: liberal nationalism and the democratic peace in the Soviet successor states. *Int. Stud. Q.* 41(3):375–402

Breslauer GW, Dale C. 1997. Boris Yel'tsin and the invention of a Russian nation-state. *Post-Sov. Aff.* 13(4):303–32

Breuilly J. 1994. *Nationalism and the State.* Chicago: Univ. Chicago Press. 2nd ed.

Brubaker R. 1996. *Nationalism Reframed.* Cambridge, UK: Cambridge Univ. Press

Brubaker R. 1998. Myths and misconceptions in the study of nationalism. In *The State of the Nation: Ernest Gellner and the Theory of Nationalism,* ed. JA Hall, pp. 272–306. New York: Cambridge Univ. Press

Brudny YM. 1998. *Reinventing Russia.* Cambridge, MA: Harvard Univ. Press

Bunce V. 1995. Should transitologists be grounded? *Slavic Rev.* 54(1):111–27

Bunce V. 1999. *Subversive Institutions: the Design and the Destruction of Socialism and the State.* Cambridge, UK: Cambridge Univ. Press

Burawoy M, Krotov P. 1992. The Soviet transition from socialism to capitalism. *Am. Sociol. Rev.* 57(1):16–38

Checkel J. 1993. Ideas, institutions, and the Gorbachev foreign policy revolution. *World Polit.* 45(2):271–300

Checkel J. 1995. Structure, institutions, process: Russia's changing foreign policy. See Dawisha & Dawisha 1995, pp. 42–65

Colton TJ, Hough JF, eds. 1998. *Growing Pains: Russian Democracy and the Election of 1993.* Washington, DC: Brookings Inst.

Crowley S. 1997. *Hot Coal, Cold Steel: Russian and Ukrainian Workers from the End of the Soviet Union to the Post-Communist Transformation.* Ann Arbor: Univ. Mich. Press

Dawisha A, Dawisha K, eds. 1995. *The International Politics of Eurasia,* Volume 4. *The Making of Foreign Policy in Russia and the New States of Eurasia.* Armonk, NY: Sharpe

Dawisha K, Parrott B. 1994. *Russia and the New States of Eurasia.* Cambridge, UK: Cambridge Univ. Press

Easter GM. 1996. Personal networks and post-revolutionary state building: post-Soviet Russia reexamined. *World Polit.* 48(4):551–78

Evangelista M. 1996. From each according to its abilities: competing theoretical approaches to the post-Soviet energy sector. See Wallander 1996, pp. 173–205

Fearon JD. 1998. Commitment problems and the spread of ethnic conflict. In *The International Spread of Ethnic Conflict,* ed. D Lake, D Rothchild, pp. 107–26. Princeton, NJ: Princeton Univ. Press

Fearon JD, Laitin DD. 1996. Explaining interethnic cooperation. *Am. Polit. Sci. Rev.* 90(4):715–35

Finifter AW. 1996. Attitudes toward individual responsibility and political reform in the former Soviet Union. *Am. Polit. Sci. Rev.* 90(1):138–52

Finifter AW, Mickiewicz E. 1992. Redefining the political system of the USSR: mass support for political change. *Am. Polit. Sci. Rev.* 86(4):857–74

Fish MS. 1994. *Democracy from Scratch.* Princeton, NJ: Princeton Univ. Press

Fish MS. 1995. The advent of multipartism in Russia. *Post-Sov. Aff.* 11(4):340–83

Fleron FJ, Hoffmann EP. 1993. Communist studies and political science: cold war and peaceful coexistence. In *Post-Communist*

Studies & Political Science, ed. FJ Fleron, EP Hoffmann, pp. 3–23. Boulder, CO: Westview

Frieden JA. 1991. *Debt, Development, and Democracy*. Princeton, NJ: Princeton Univ. Press

Frye T. 1997. Governing the Russian equities market. *Post-Sov. Aff.* 13(4):366–95

Geddes B. 1996. Initiation of new democratic institutions in Eastern Europe and Latin America. In *Institutional Design in New Democracies*, ed. A Lijphart, C Waisman, pp. 15–41. Boulder, CO: Westview

Gibson JL. 1997. The struggle between order and liberty in contemporary Russian political culture. *Aust. J. Polit. Sci.* 32(2):271–90

Giuliano E. 2000. *Paths to the decline of nationalism: ethnic politics in Russia*. PhD thesis, Univ. Chicago

Goldstone JA. 1991. *Revolution and Rebellion in the Early Modern World*. Berkeley: Univ. Calif. Press

Gorenburg D. 1999. *Nationalism for the masses: minority ethnic mobilization in the Russian Federation*. PhD thesis, Harvard Univ.

Gow J. 1992. Independent Ukraine: the politics of security. *Int. Relations* 11(3):253–67

Greif A. 1994. Cultural beliefs and the organization of society. *J. Econ. Hist.* 102(5):912–50

Haas EB. 1997. *Nationalism, Liberalism and Progress*. Ithaca, NY: Cornell Univ. Press

Hahn J. 1993. Continuity and change in Russian political culture. In *Post-Communist Studies and Political Science: Methodology and Empirical Theory in Sovietology*, ed. FJ Fleron, EP Hoffmann, pp. 299–330. Boulder, CO: Westview

Hanson SE. 1997. *Time and Revolution: Marxism and the Design of Soviet Institutions*. Chapel Hill: Univ. NC Press

Hanson SE. 1998. *Ideology, interests, and identity: comparing secession crises in the USSR and Russia. Program on New Approaches to Russian Security, Work. Pap. No. 10*. Davis Center, Harvard Univ.

Hellman JS. 1998. Winners take all: the politics of partial reform in postcommunist transitions. *World Polit.* 50(2):203

Hendley K. 1997. Legal development in post-Soviet Russia. *Post-Sov. Aff.* 13(3):228–51

Herman RG. 1996. Identity and national security. See Katzenstein 1996, pp. 271–316

Herrera YM. 1999. *Imagined economies: regionalism in the Russian Federation*. PhD thesis, Univ. Chicago

Hobsbawm EJ, Ranger T, eds. 1983. *The Invention of Tradition*. Cambridge, UK: Cambridge Univ. Press

Holloway D. 1995. The state of the field: Soviet foreign policy. In *Beyond Soviet Studies*, ed. D Orlovsky, pp. 269–86. Washington, DC: Johns Hopkins Univ. Press

Holloway D, Naimark N, eds. 1996. *Reexamining the Soviet Experience*. Boulder, CO: Westview

Holmes S. 1997. What Russia teaches us now. *Am. Prospect July/Aug.*:30–39

Holmes S, Sunstein C. 1999. *The Cost of Rights: Why Liberty Depends on Taxes*. New York: Norton

Hopf T. 1998. The promise of constructivism in international relations theory. *Int. Secur.* 23(1):171–200

Horowitz DL. 1985. *Ethnic Groups in Conflict*. Berkeley: Univ. Calif. Press

Hosking G. 1990. *The Awakening of the Soviet Union*. Cambridge, MA: Harvard Univ. Press

Hough JF. 1990. The logic of collective action and the pattern of revolutionary behavior. *J. Sov. Nationalities.* 1(2):34–65

Hough JF. 1997. *Democratization and Revolution in the USSR 1985–1991*. Washington, DC: Brookings Inst.

Hough JF. 2000. *The Logic of Economic Reform in Russia*. Washington, DC: Brookings Inst.

Hough JF, Davidheiser E, Lehmann SG. 1996. *The 1996 Russian Presidential Election*. Washington DC: Brookings Inst.

Huntington SP. 1968. *Political Order in Changing Societies*. New Haven: Yale Univ. Press

Jowitt K. 1992. *New World Disorder: The Leninist Extinction*. Berkeley: Univ. Calif. Press

Katzenstein PJ, ed. 1996. *The Culture of National Security.* New York: Columbia Univ. Press

Kitschelt H, Smyth R. 1997. *Issues, identities, and programmatic parties. The emerging Russian party system in comparative perspective.* Presented at Am. Polit. Sci. Assoc., Washington, DC

Kuran T. 1991. Now out of never: the element of surprise in the East European revolution of 1989. *World Polit.* 44(1):7–48

Laitin DD. 1991. The national uprisings in the Soviet Union. *World Polit.* 44(1):139–77

Laitin DD. 1998. *Identity in Formation: The Russian-Speaking Populations in the Near Abroad.* Ithaca, NY: Cornell Univ. Press

Laitin DD. 1999. Identity choice under conditions of uncertainty. In *Competition and Cooperation,* ed. JE Alt, M Levi, E Ostrom, pp. 273–302. New York: Sage

Lapidus GW. 1999. Asymmetrical federalism and state breakdown in Russia. *Post-Sov. Aff.* 15(1):74–82

Light M. 1996. Foreign policy thinking. See Malcolm et al 1996, pp. 33–100

Linz JJ, Stepan A. 1996. *Problems of Democratic Transition and Consolidation.* Baltimore, MD: Johns Hopkins Univ. Press

Luong PJ. 1996. *The Soviet legacy in central Asia: creating and institutionalizing regional political identities, capacities, and loyalties.* Presented at Am. Assoc. Advance. Slavic Stud.

MacFarlane SN. 1994. Russian conceptions of Europe. *Post-Sov. Aff.* 10(3):234–69

MacFarlane SN, Schnabel A. 1995. Russia's approach to peacekeeping. *Int. J.* 50(2):294–324

Malcolm N. 1996. Foreign policy making. See Malcolm et al 1996, pp. 101–68

Malcolm N, Pravda A, Allison R, Light M. 1996. *Internal Factors in Russian Foreign Policy.* Oxford, UK: Oxford Univ. Press

Mayhew DR. 1974. *Congress: the Electoral Connection.* New Haven, CT: Yale Univ. Press

McAuley M. 1997. *Russia's Politics of Uncertainty.* Cambridge, UK: Cambridge Univ. Press

McFaul M. 1993. Party formation after revolutionary transitions: the Russian case. In *Political Parties in Russia,* ed. A Dallin, pp. 7–28. Berkeley: Univ. Calif., Berkeley, Int. and Area Studies

McFaul M. 1996. Revolutionary transformation in comparative perspective: defining a postcommunist research agenda. See Holloway & Naimark 1996, pp. 167–96

McFaul M. 1997/98. A precarious peace: domestic politics in the making of Russian foreign policy. *Int. Secur.* 22(3):5–35

Mendelson SE. 1998. *Changing Course: Ideas, Politics, and the Soviet Withdrawal from Afghanistan.* Princeton, NJ: Princeton Univ. Press

Menon R. 1995. In the shadow of the bear: security in post-Soviet Central Asia. *Int. Secur.* 20(1):149–81

Meyer AG. 1994. Observations on the travails of Sovietology. *Post-Sov. Aff.* 10(2):191–95

Miller AH, Reisinger WM, Hesli VL. 1994. Reassessing mass support for political and economic change in the former USSR. *Am. Polit. Sci. Rev.* 88(2):399–411

Miller AH, Reisinger WM, Hesli VL. 1996. Understanding political change in post-Soviet societies: a further commentary on Finifter and Mickiewicz. *Am. Polit. Sci. Rev.* 90(1):153–66

Montinola G, Qian Y, Weingast B. 1995. Federalism, Chinese style: the political basis for economic success in China. *World Polit.* 48(1):50–81

Moser RG. 1999. Independents and party formation: elite partisanship as an intervening variable in Russian politics. *Comp. Polit.* 31(2):147–65

Motyl AJ. 1987. *Will the Non-Russians Rebel?* Ithaca, NY: Cornell Univ. Press

Motyl AJ, ed. 1992. *Thinking Theoretically about Soviet Nationalities.* New York: Columbia Univ. Press

Motyl AJ. 1997. Structural constraints and starting points: the logic of systemic change in

POST-SOVIET POLITICS **147**

Ukraine and Russia. *Comp. Polit.* 29(4):433–47

Myagkov M, Ordeshook P, Sobyanin A. 1997. The Russian electorate: 1991–1996. *Post-Sov. Aff.* 13(2):134–66

Olson M. 1990. The logic of collective action in Soviet-type societies. *J. Sov. Nationalities* 1(2):8–27

Ordeshook PC. 1996. Russia's party system: Is Russian federalism viable? *Post-Sov. Aff.* 12(3):195–217

Petro NN. 1999. The Novgorod region: a Russian success story. *Post-Sov. Aff.* 15(3):235–61

Popov V. 1998. Institutions count more than liberalization speed. *Transition* Oct.:25–26

Posen B. 1993. The security dilemma and ethnic conflict. *Survival* 35(1):27–47

Przeworski A, ed. 1995. *Sustainable Democracy.* Cambridge, UK: Cambridge Univ. Press

Putnam R. 1993. *Making Democracy Work.* Princeton, NJ: Princeton Univ. Press

Remington TF. 1995. Common knowledge: Soviet political studies and the problem of system stability. In *Beyond Soviet Studies*, ed. D Orlovsky, pp. 159–92. Washington, DC: Woodrow Wilson Cent.

Riker WH. 1964. *Federalism.* Boston, MA: Little, Brown

Roeder PG. 1991. Soviet federalism and ethnic mobilisation. *World Polit.* 43(2):196–232

Roeder PG. 1993. *Red Sunset.* Princeton, NJ: Princeton Univ. Press

Roeder PG. 1994. *Post-Soviet institutions and ethnopolitics.* Presented at Annu. Meet. Am. Polit. Sci. Assoc., New York

Rogowski R. 1989. *Commerce and Coalitions.* Princeton, NJ: Princeton Univ. Press

Rose R, Tikhomirov E. 1996. Russia's forced-choice presidential election. *Post-Sov. Aff.* 12(4):351–79

Sachs JD. 1995. Russia's struggle with stabilization: conceptual issues and evidence. *Proc. World Bank Ann. Conf. Dev. Econ., 1994.* ed. M Bruno, B Pleskovic

Schelling T. 1978. *Micromotives and Macrobehavior.* New York: Norton

Schmitter PC, Karl TL. 1994. The conceptual travels of transitologists and consolidologists: How far to the east should they attempt to go? *Slavic Rev.* 53(1):173–85

Schofield N. 1999. The heart of the Atlantic Constitution: international economic stability, 1919–1998. *Polit. Soc.* 27(2):173–215

Shugart MS, Carey JM. 1992. *Presidents and Assemblies.* Cambridge, UK: Cambridge Univ. Press

Skinner B. 1994. Identity formation in the Russian Cossack revival. *Eur.-Asia Stud.* 46(6):1017–37

Skocpol T. 1979. *States and Social Revolution.* Cambridge, UK: Cambridge Univ. Press

Slider D. 1997. Russia's market distorting federalism. *Post-Sov. Geog. Econ.* 38(8):445–60

Smyth R. 1998. *The political implications of mixed electoral systems: explaining the evolution of Russian parties.* Presented at Midwest Polit. Sci. Assoc., Chicago

Snyder J. 1993. Nationalism and the crisis of the post-Soviet state. *Survival* 35(1):5–26

Snyder J. 1996. Democratization, war, and nationalism in the post-communist states. In *The Sources of Russian Foreign Policy After the Cold War*, ed. C Wallander, pp. 21–40. Boulder, CO: Westview

Sobyanin A. 1994. Political cleavages among the Russian deputies. In *Parliaments in Transition: The New Legislative Politics in the Former USSR and Eastern Europe*, ed. TF Remington, pp. 181–215. Boulder, CO: Westview

Solnick SL. 1995. Federal bargaining in Russia. *E. Eur. Const. Rev.* 4(4):52–58

Solnick SL. 1998. *Stealing the State.* Cambridge, MA: Harvard Univ. Press

Solomon PH Jr. 1995. The limits of legal order in post-Soviet Russia. *Post-Sov. Aff.* 11(2):89–114

Stiglitz JE. 1999. *Whither reform? Ten years of the transition.* Keynote Address, World Bank, Annu. Bank Conf. Dev. Econ., Washington, DC, Apr. 28–30

Stone RW. 1996. *Satellites and Commissars.* Princeton, NJ: Princeton Univ. Press

Stoner-Weiss K. 1997. *Local Heroes.* Princeton, NJ: Princeton Univ. Press

Suny RG. 1993. *The Revenge of the Past.* Stanford, CA: Stanford Univ. Press

Taagepera R. 1992. *Estonia: Return to Independence.* Boulder, CO: Westview

Timmerman H. 1992. Russian foreign policy under Yeltsin: priority for integration into the "Community of Civilized States." *J. Communist Stud.* 8(4):163–85

Titma M, Tuma NB, Silver BD. 1998. Winners and losers in the postcommunist transition: new evidence from Estonia. *Post-Sov. Aff.* 14(2):114–36

Treisman DS. 1997. Russia's ethnic revival: the separatist activism of regional leaders in a post-communist order. *World Polit.* 49(2):212–49

Treisman DS. 1999. *After the Deluge: Regional Crises and Political Consolidation in Russia.* Ann Arbor: Univ. Mich. Press

Urban M. 1994. The politics of identity in Russia's postcommunist transition: the nation against itself. *Slavic Rev.* 53(3):733–65

Wallander C. 1996. *The Sources of Russian Foreign Policy after the Cold War.* Boulder, CO: Westview

Wallander CA. 1999. *Mortal Friends, Best Enemies.* Ithaca, NY: Cornell Univ. Press

Wegren SK. 1998. *Agriculture and the State in Soviet and Post-Soviet Russia.* Pittsburgh, PA: Univ. Pittsburgh Press

Wilson A. 1997. *Ukrainian Nationalism in the 1990s: A Minority Faith.* Cambridge, UK: Cambridge Univ. Press

Woodruff D. 1999. *Money Unmade.* Ithaca, NY: Cornell Univ. Press

Yack B. 1996. The myth of the civic nation. *Crit. Rev.* 10(2):193–211

Zimmerman W. 1996. Soviet and post-Soviet foreign policy processes: a preliminary assessment. See Holloway & Naimark 1996, pp. 197–216

Zisk KM. 1996. The foreign policy preferences of Russian defense industrialists: integration or isolation? See Wallander 1996, pp. 95–120

Annu. Rev. Polit. Sci. 2000. 3:149–66

INTERNATIONAL INSTITUTIONS AND SYSTEM TRANSFORMATION

Harold K. Jacobson

*Center for Political Studies, Institute for Social Research, University of Michigan,
Ann Arbor, Michigan 48106-1248; e-mail: hkj@umich.edu*

Key Words accountability, economic integration, nongovernmental organizations, norms, scientists

■ **Abstract** Starting in the 1990s, scholarship has produced interesting, new, nu-anced ideas about the potential role of international institutions in transforming the global political system. Political scientists have achieved a new understanding of how the Westphalian system came into being, and this understanding has provided a rudimentary model of the dynamics of system transformation. The new institutional-ism has provided insights into the possible role of institutions. Scholars have developed new understandings of secondary consequences of conducting interactions among nation-states through international institutions. The study of a particular institution, the European Union, has been revitalized and important knowledge has emerged about its dynamics and trajectory. Finally, scholars have begun to raise questions about the properties of a non-Westphalian system, especially about how democratic account-ability could be established. This chapter examines each of these developments in turn.

STYLIZED TRADITIONAL VIEWS OF THE CONTRIBUTION OF INTERNATIONAL INSTITUTIONS

International institutions that bring nation-states together in formal organizational structures are a prominent feature of the contemporary global political system. They did not exist when the Wesphalian system was created in the seventeenth century. They first came into being in the nineteenth century. With some interruptions, their number has grown steadily, though with variation in form and type. At the close of the twentieth century, there are more than 250 conventional international governmental organizations (IGOs), more than 1500 other international bodies, and roughly 3700 other institutions of special types, making a total of almost 5500 (Union of International Associations 1997).

What is the role of these international institutions? Are they simply instruments that facilitate interactions among territorially defined sovereign states, or will they

149

contribute to the transformation of the Westphalian system? If the latter is the case, what is the nature of their contribution, and toward what ultimate condition will the transformation move?

Political scientists specializing in international relations have generally shunned these questions. We have explored the nature of the Westphalian system and its operation (Waltz 1979), and we have developed theories about the dynamics of change within the system (Organski & Kugler 1980), but we have seldom considered the possibility that the Wesphalian system could be transformed into some other type of system with different properties. Political scientists, particularly the realists and neorealists, have generally assumed the permanence of the Westphalian system.

Based on this assumption, the most prevalent position among scholars of international politics has been to follow Morgenthau's lead. Although Morgenthau acknowledged that a substantial number of IGOs had been created, he summarized their function in the system as places "in which most nations have co-operated for the furtherance of their common interests" (1949:211). Morgenthau stated that the United Nations had been intended at its inception to be the instrument of the permanent members of the Security Council for maintaining the status quo that was established at the end of World War II. Other nations, however, appropriated the language of the United Nations Charter. "All nations appear as the champions of the United Nations and quote its charter in support of the particular policies they are pursuing" (Morgenthau 1949:68). In short, according to Morgenthau, IGOs were tools that nation-states used as they desired and could, sometimes for cooperative purposes and sometimes for contestation. Pursuing policies through IGOs might amplify or diminish the power of particular states, but this would not affect the basic character of the system.

Various scholars developed much more sophisticated versions of the view that international institutions are basically instruments of nation-states. Regime theory, as developed by Keohane and Krasner and their associates, provided persuasive explanations of why states should turn to and stick with international institutions and what the effects of pursuing policies through international institutions might be (Keohane 1984, Krasner 1983); however, in regime theory, international institutions modify rather than transform the Westphalian system. Neoliberal institutionalism has similarly disregarded system transformation (Ruggie 1998:874).

Despite this lack of explicit attention in mainstream contemporary scholarship, advocates, commentators, and even some governmental officials have long held a vision of the system transformation that they believe should and could occur. The tapestries that hang in the *Palais des Nations*, the European headquarters of the United Nations and formerly the headquarters of the League of Nations, dramatize this vision. These tapestries portray the evolution and growth of human associations, starting with the family in the first tapestry and moving in subsequent tapestries to the clan or tribe, the nation-state, the League of Nations, and ultimately world government. In this perspective, international institutions are an intermediate step on the road to world government. Few scholars have openly subscribed to this vision, but many have implicitly accepted it and based their policy recommendations on it. The literature of the post–World War II period is filled with proposals for strengthening international institutions by giving them greater autonomy from nation-states, including independent access to financial resources and an independent military capability (Falk 1975). These proposals directly attack key aspects of sovereignty, the monopoly that nation-states have on taxing their citizens and on legitimately raising and using military forces.

In the 1990s, these stylized traditional views—that the Westphalian system will endure or that world government will eventually supplant it—have increasingly been supplemented by interesting, new, nuanced ideas. A fresh understanding has emerged of how the Westphalian system originated, and this understanding has provided a rudimentary model of the dynamics of system transformation. The new institutionalism has provided insights into the potential role of institutions. The secondary consequences of conducting interactions among nation-states through international institutions are better understood. The study of a particular institution, the European Union (EU), has been revitalized and important knowledge has been gained about its dynamics and trajectory. Finally, scholars have begun to ask what properties a different system might have, and especially how democratic accountability could be established. This essay examines each of these developments in scholarship about international politics and institutions.

THE DYNAMICS OF SYSTEM TRANSFORMATION

Spruyt (1994a,b) analyzed the formation of the Westphalian system, set out an important new interpretation of that process, directed attention to the importance of understanding processes, and outlined a model of system transformation. Earlier analyses of the formation of sovereign states and the emergence of the state system had emphasized the superior abilities of sovereign states to mobilize and deploy military forces, and the process of the transition from the feudal to the state system seemed linear (Tilly 1975). Spruyt presented a more complex analysis.

Spruyt (1994a,b) argued that population growth and technological developments put pressures on the feudal order and created new possibilities for economic growth and trade. The increase in trade led to the formation of towns and strengthened the power of some political groups and leaders. New political alliances formed. These alliances built on and were shaped by those already in existence. Different ways of organizing political authority emerged. In Capetian France, the sovereign, territorially defined state was built. Among the German states, city leagues were created, the most important of which was the Hanseatic League. In Italy, city-states became the new form of political authority.

Over a period of centuries, the sovereign state triumphed in the competition among these varying ways of organizing political authority because it was the most successful at providing the standardization and certitude with respect to weights and measures and monetary matters that were essential to the expansion of commerce. Greater commerce enabled the sovereign state to provide for the needs of a larger population and to improve standards of living. The success of sovereign states inspired emulation in areas where political authority was organized differently; actors were motivated to centralize political authority in a territorially defined unit. Sovereign states found it easier to deal with other sovereign states and created frameworks in which such entities could interact, resulting in mutual empowerment. Other political entities were excluded. In Spruyt's account (1994a,b), the superior war-fighting capacity of the sovereign state was only one of many factors explaining the emergence of the Westphalian system, and it came into play rather late.

The model that emerges from Spruyt's historical account can be summarized as follows. Challenges to existing arrangements for the allocation of political authority arise from exogenous sources, such as population growth and technological developments. Groups and individuals respond, acting from self-interest and from their existing political bases and structures. New forms for organizing political authority are developed. These forms reflect the political power of relevant actors and build on existing institutions. There is competition among them, and one form ultimately triumphs because its responses to the challenges are more successful than those of the other forms.

This model provides a useful perspective from which to consider the possibilities of system transformation in the contemporary period and the role that international institutions might play. At the dawn of the twenty-first century, there are powerful exogenous forces challenging the Westphalian system, including population growth, the development and spread of information technology, the internationalization of production and financial flows, and global environmental change, especially climate change. International institutions can be seen as new forms for organizing political authority. The increase in their total number raises questions about their role.

INSIGHTS FROM THE NEW INSTITUTIONALISM

After a period of neglect, social scientists have rediscovered institutions. A substantial and interesting literature exploring the consequences of institutions has developed. This new literature defines institutions in broad terms as "the humanly devised constraints that shape human interactions" (North 1990:3). International institutions fit clearly within this definition. Spruyt's work is informed by the new institutionalism.

March & Olsen are leading contributors to the new institutionalism literature (e.g. 1989). In a 1998 article they explicitly explore possible applications of institutionalism to the study of the dynamics of international political orders (March & Olsen 1998). They contrast two interpretations of human behavior: the logic of consequential calculation and the logic of appropriateness. The consequentialist interpretation sees "an international system of interacting autonomous, egoistic, self-interested maximizers." The appropriateness interpretation sees "political actors as acting in accordance with rules and practices that are socially constructed, publicly known, anticipated, and accepted" (March & Olsen 1998:953) These authors do not believe that the two logics are mutually exclusive. Any action probably involves elements of both. Because action is based on conformity with rules as well as calculations of self-interest, institutions matter.

The new institutionalism discourages hopes of predicting the broad course of international relations and thus of predicting system transformation. "Historical interpretations of the development of international orders are made difficult by the necessity of learning from small samples of uncontrolled conditions" (March & Olsen 1998:969). Many propositions that can be derived from the new institutionalism literature help to identify the direction and nature of system change. Drawing from theories of biological evolution, the new institutionalism emphasizes both path dependence and competition among institutional forms leading to the elimination of the less efficient. As North put it, "Once a development path is set on a particular course, the network externalities, the learning process of organizations, and the historically derived subjective modeling of the issues reinforce the course" (1990:99). He continued, "Path dependence means that history matters. We cannot understand today's choices ... without tracing the incremental evolution of institutions" (North 1990:100).

Institutional adaptation is likely to lag behind changes in the environment (March & Olsen 1989). Institutional changes, when they do occur, are likely to involve marginal adjustments to existing practices and structures. Over time, some institutions become less and less efficient in dealing with problems, leading to abrupt changes when their constituents perceive them to fail. "Social, economic, and political systems are all prone ... to at least moderate jerkiness in fundamental transformations" (March & Olsen 1998:965).

March & Olsen (1998) explore two specific ways in which institutions affect the dynamics of system transformation. The first concerns the formation of identities, the second the development of competence and capability. The authors acknowledge the great force of nation-states in molding identities, but they also maintain that this could change gradually and without much conscious intention. They argue that international identities may "evolve from a 'spillover' of domestic democratic orientations and identities into international politics" (March & Olsen 1998:962). They speculate that democracies may import democratic practices into their international relations, especially those with other democracies. They also maintain that democratic norms are contagious, spreading from democracies to less democratic nation-states. March & Olsen also see international identities evolving "from the practice of expert cooperation around specific tasks" (1998:963).

Institutions structure relations among political actors and affect their potential influence. Political actors develop competencies and capabilities in working within the framework of institutions. "Having the capability of doing new things leads, in turn, to seeing their desirability. Capabilities stimulate recognition of the salience of problems to which they can provide solutions. By transforming capabilities, therefore, competence transforms agendas and goals" (March & Olsen 1998:966).

Although relatively few of the scholars who analyze international institutions refer directly to the new institutionalism, the insights of this literature have had a marked effect on the research agenda for the field. This effect is apparent in the emerging literature on the secondary consequences of conducting international relations through international institutions.

SECONDARY CONSEQUENCES OF INTERNATIONAL INSTITUTIONS

The primary consequences of using international institutions to conduct international relations involve the institutions' direct effects on those relations. To what extent have United Nations peacekeeping operations contributed to limiting interstate violence? To what extent have the General Agreement on Tariffs and Trade, and more recently the World Trade Organization, reduced barriers to trade? What has been the impact on gender equality of the Convention on the Elimination of All Forms of Discrimination against Women? A great deal of research on international institutions has been devoted to attempting to answer such questions and to developing theoretical explanations about the conditions under which conducting international relations through international institutions would produce particular effects. These effects would be primary consequences.

March & Olsen's (1998) propositions about the potential consequences for system transformation involve secondary consequences. Less research has been devoted to this approach, but the quantity and sophistication of that research has increased during the 1990s.

Political scientists have long been interested in March's & Olsen's proposition that international institutions affect the relative power of various actors. Their interest, however, focused primarily on effects on the relative power of states (Keohane & Nye 1977). In other words, they examined how international institutions affected the conduct of international politics within the Westphalian system, not how they might be transforming the Westphalian system.

Some research asked in addition whether international institutions might be introducing new actors onto the world stage. This research concluded that executive heads of IGOs and the secretariats that they direct could have an independent impact on international relations (Cox 1969, Cox & Jacobson 1974).

In the 1990s, this strand of research has confirmed that executive heads of IGOs and the officials who staff secretariats do influence international negotiations (Hampson 1995), and it has begun to delineate the extent of such influence and the conditions under which it can be exercised (Moravcsik 1999). It has also shown how conducting international relations through international institutions has empowered national and international nongovernmental organizations (NNGOs and INGOs) and transnational advocacy networks. Scholars have described the characteristics of these actors and analyzed how they exercise influence and the consequences of their influence.

New Actors: Nongovernmental Organizations

Many observers have asserted that non-state actors and especially NGOs are playing a greater role than before in international politics (Mathews 1997). The increase in their numbers is notable. In the first decade of the twentieth century there were fewer than 200 INGOs; by middle of the 1990s, there were more than 20,000 (UIA 1997). Their growth reflects rising educational levels, new and improved communications possibilities (especially the internet, e-mail, and facsimile transmissions), and the global spread of democracy, among other factors. NNGOs and INGOs flourish in democracies but often cannot even be formed in nondemocratic states.

International institutions have also contributed to their growth. International institutions gave NGOs a place in global political processes. Article 71 of the United Nations Charter allows the Economic and Social Council (ECOSOC) to "make suitable arrangements for consultation with nongovernmental organizations which are concerned with matters within its competence." This article was inserted into the Charter at the insistence of NGOs, which were present at the discussions in San Francisco. No such provision had been included in the Dumbarton Oaks Proposals, which had been prepared by China, the Soviet Union, the United Kingdom, and the United States, and which were the basis for the San Francisco negotiations. Prior to the end of World War II, except for including representatives of labor and employers in national delegations to the International Labor Organization, NGOs had largely been excluded from international negotiations and conferences.

The arrangements for consultation that have been developed under Article 71 allow NGOs to be represented at ECOSOC and other United Nations meetings, to submit written communications, and in some instances to propose agenda items and to make oral presentations. The extent of the privileges depends on the category in which NGOs are placed (United Nations 1996).

Article 71 provided a formal structure that recognized NGOs and gave them legitimacy in international politics. It also gave them voice. By 1998, slightly more than 100 NGOs had general consultative status with the United Nations, and almost 1500 had a more limited status. This number was significantly higher than it had been at the beginning of the decade (Weiss & Gordenker 1996). Other IGOs have adopted similar practices, and over time, NNGOs and INGOs have gained a variety of other privileges and have inserted themselves in many international proceedings.

Beginning in the 1960s, NGOs have attended major thematic conferences organized by the United Nations on such topics as the environment, human rights, population, and women. In addition, at the Stockholm Conference on the Human Environment in 1972, NGOs began holding a forum at the same time and in the same place as the intergovernmental conference. These forums, which have become an important feature of international politics, have given NGOs unprecedented visibility and access to media.

NGO participation in the conferences and in the related forums has gained momentum. No more than 500 NGOs participated in the forum at the Stockholm Conference; some 1400 registered at the United Nations Conference on Environment and Development in Rio de Janeiro in 1992 (Brenton 1994) and 18,000 participated in the parallel forum (Clark et al 1998).

The growth in NGO participation in the meetings of IGOs and the thematic conferences organized by these bodies is indisputable. Assessing the significance of this development is difficult, but research in the 1990s has made a significant start in doing this. Researchers have produced several case studies, many of which have been included in edited volumes (Thakur 1994, Risse-Kappen 1995, Weiss & Gordenker 1996, Willetts 1996, Dorsey 1997, Keck & Sikkink 1998). Explicit or implicit conceptual frameworks have shaped some of the studies. All provide rich narratives that allow the tracing of political processes.

One broad conclusion is that NGOs beget NGOs and transnational advocacy networks. Transnational advocacy networks are "networks of activists, distinguishable largely by the centrality of principled ideas or values in motivating their formation" (Keck & Sikkink:1).

INGOs and NNGOs facilitate the development of national affiliates or NNGOs even when governments are less than enthusiastic about their formation and existence (Willetts 1996). INGOs give legitimacy to NGOs. By utilizing the forums that IGOs provide, INGOs can protect NNGOs to some extent. In addition, they sometimes provide financial resources collected by or from affiliates or members in richer industrialized states. Members of INGOs train and coach members of NNGOs. Transnational advocacy networks have been formed and strengthened by the possibilities for communications and personal contacts that IGO thematic conferences and related forums provide. NGOs provide havens for members of transnational advocacy networks. The increased ease of communications generally has facilitated these developments.

In the early years following World War II, NGOs and the members of INGOs were concentrated in the industrialized states of North America, Western Europe, and Australasia. As a consequence of the developments described above, the number of NGOs in other states has increased. By the late 1990s, although NGOs continued to be more prevalent in Western states, they could no longer be seen as an almost exclusively Western phenomenon.

AGENDA SETTING

There is broad agreement among international relations scholars that NGOs perform agenda-setting functions. The mechanisms developed under Article 71 of the United Nations Charter and other similar institutional arrangements formally provide opportunities for NGO agenda setting in international institutions. These formal provisions do not necessarily ensure, however, that attention is given to NGOs' proposals and ideas. The case studies demonstrate that NGOs have become masters at framing issues so that they command widespread public attention and thus get onto national and international agendas.

On the basis of their case studies, Keck & Sikkink (1998) argue that transnational advocacy networks have greatest success in commanding attention when they frame the debate so that the issues involve bodily harm to individuals and legal equality of opportunity. This framing, they argue, addresses "aspects of belief systems or life experiences that transcend a specific cultural or political context" (1998:204).

Keck & Sikkink (1998) have developed a model that they call the boomerang pattern, in which NGOs can raise issues at the national level even when the national government initially refuses to pay attention. In this model, the NNGO whose government has disregarded its requests activates a transnational advocacy network that would include INGOs and NNGOs in other states. These NNGOs would pressure their states, and the INGOs and NGOs would pressure IGOs, and the other states and the IGOs would bring pressure on the state that initially refused to pay attention to its NNGOs' requests.

MONITORING

Beyond agenda setting, NGOs have gained an increasingly important role in monitoring the performance of other actors in the global political system. They are involved in checking on states, especially the extent to which states fulfill commitments they accepted when they acceded to conventions and treaties. They also check on IGOs, monitoring the extent to which they adhere to the policies they have accepted.

According to its Statute, Amnesty International's basic objective is "to contribute to the observance throughout the world of the Universal Declaration of Human Rights" (Cook 1996). Amnesty International has used its consultative status at the United Nations and other IGOs to raise a variety of human rights issues, including complaints against the practices of specific states. Although Amnesty International is particularly visible and received the Nobel Prize for its activities, many other NGOs perform similar functions in monitoring the human rights performance of states.

NGOs are also active in monitoring the performance of states with respect to environmental issues (Princen 1994). In some cases, NGOs have even been given formal roles in the processes to ensure compliance with international environmental accords (Raustiala 1997).

The case studies of Keck & Sikkink (1998) show that states have modified their policies and practices in response to complaints by NGOs in international forums. The authors conclude that transnational advocacy networks are more likely to be successful when they are dense and strong and the targets are vulnerable to material and moral leverage. Not surprisingly, small, vulnerable states are more likely to modify their policies than larger, stronger states.

In the 1980s, NGOs launched the multilateral development bank (MDB) campaign, which raised questions about the environmental and social impact of MDB funded projects. In response, the World Bank created procedures so that NGOs and grassroots movements could be involved in its projects. Case studies in a volume edited by Fox & Brown (1998) demonstrate that NGO/grassroots protests have resulted in the modification of World Bank policies and projects. Prospective loans have been blocked before they received formal bank approval, ongoing project loans have been cancelled, loan disbursements have been temporarily suspended, subprojects within projects have been blocked, steps have been taken to mitigate social and environmental impacts, new projects have been designed in response to past protests, and there has been a spillover of project campaigns on World Bank policies and projects.

Fox & Brown develop an interactive model that shows how NGOs and grassroots movements affect policy (1998:498,535–39). The model can be used to generate hypotheses about the conditions under which NGOs and grassroots movements will be successful in promoting sustainable development practices. Success depends on pro–sustainable development advocacy groups in bank donor countries and pro–sustainable development advocacy groups and grassroots movements in borrowing countries working with pro–sustainable development personnel within the World Bank and the governments of the donor and borrowing countries.

Fox & Brown distinguish between organizational adaptation and learning. Adaptation involves behavior changes in response to pressures without adjustments in an organization's overall goals and procedures. Learning, "in contrast, involves disseminating new conceptual frameworks and institutional changes throughout an organization, thus leading to qualitatively new goals and priorities, as well as changes in behavior" (Fox & Brown 1998:10). For learning to occur, NGOs and grassroots movements must have allies within governments and IGOs. NGOs and grassroots movements reinforce and help channel pressures for change within organizations.

OPERATIONAL ACTIVITIES

In the 1990s, NGOs have become increasingly involved in operational activities, particularly in providing humanitarian relief and development assistance. Some NGOs, such as CARE, the International Committee of the Red Cross, and Médicins sans Frontières, were created to perform operational activities and have always done so. What is different in the 1990s is that NGOs have frequently been called on to perform operational activities in collaboration with, or sometimes on behalf of, states and IGOs.

This operational role is perhaps the most problematic of those that NGOs have assumed. Case studies point particularly to problems of coordination and cooptation (Weiss & Gordenker 1996). When NGOs become substantially financially dependent on governments or IGOs, they risk losing the strength and legitimacy that come in part from their independence from governments.

ISSUE AREAS: Security Too

Most of the case studies on NGOs have dealt with their activities in environmental, human rights, and population issues. Price (1998) has demonstrated that NGOs have also been active and effective in dealing with a security issue. His case study recounts the success of NGOs and other non-state actors in the International Campaign to Ban Land Mines (ICBL). The ICBL succeeded in getting states to negotiate, sign, and ratify the Convention on the Prohibition of the Use, Stockpiling, Production, and Transfer of Anti-Personnel Mines and their Destruction, commonly known at the Ottawa treaty.

Price (1998) shows how several states changed their policies from opposing a ban to supporting the treaty as a result of the ICBL's efforts. He also argues that an international norm against the use of anti-personnel land mines has been created, which has affected the policies of even those states that are not parties to the Ottawa treaty. In support of this argument, he notes that even states that have announced that they will not sign or accede to the Ottawa treaty have modified their policies. Other case studies have confirmed Price's analysis and conclusions (Thakur & Maley 1999).

These studies focus particularly on democratic states. Evangelista (1995, 1999) has shown that transnational networks and organizations can even have an effect on the security policies of an authoritarian government. He demonstrates that transnational networks and organizations, particularly the Pugwash movement, played an important role in bringing about the changes in Soviet policies that made arms control possible. The route to effectiveness in the cases he examines was introducing new ideas to the leadership and convincing the leadership that these ideas were meritorious. When the centralized Soviet state collapsed and was replaced by the less centralized Russian Federation, the effectiveness of transnational networks and organizations diminished. Although many of the processes that Evangelista traces resemble those in other cases, the networks and organizations placed less emphasis on public pressure within the Soviet Union. It is striking that many of the same techniques that NGOs have used in other areas were effective in the security area.

GLOBAL CIVIL SOCIETY

Some observers, including the Commission on Global Governance (1995), have interpreted the increase in the number of NGOs and their activities as a principal element in the emergence of a global civil society. The academic literature, in contrast, is cautious. Clark et al (1998:33), in the one analysis that addresses the question specifically, conclude that "it is too soon to declare that a global civil society has definitely emerged." Although generally they do not address this question directly, none of the case studies discussed here contains evidence to the contrary.

Clark and her colleagues analyze the activities of NGOs at United Nations thematic conferences on the environment, human rights, and women. They trace changes in these activities between the time when the conferences began in the 1960s and their most recent iterations in the 1990s. They argue that although differences among NGOs have narrowed, they are still large. NGOs frequently split along North/South lines, and these divisions overlap with the differences between small grassroots organizations and the larger, more established organizations. Clark et al (1998:34) argue, "Governments are standing firm in their claims to ultimate sovereignty over the issues that seem to most affect their ability to control the distribution of power and resources."

Assessing the significance of NGOs goes to the heart of the issue of system transformation. Even if it is an exaggeration to claim that civil society has emerged, it is uncontestable that in the second half of the twentieth century, NGOs have gained a place in world politics that they did not have before. They have gained status and influence. They affect outcomes in a variety of fields, including security. Sovereign, territorially defined nation-states are no longer the only actors in world politics, if ever they were.

As they have gained influence, however, several questions have been raised about NGOs. Perhaps the most important involves accountability. As NGOs have gained influence, observers and scholars have increasingly asked whom NGOs represent and how they make decisions.

Molding Identities

The first proposition of March & Olsen (1998), that international institutions could contribute to system transformation by shaping identities, has inspired less research than the proposition that international institutions affect the relative power of actors. Nevertheless, the question has been explored. March & Olsen (1998) refer to Peter Haas' well-known work on epistemic communities (Haas 1990, 1992).

In his study of international environmental cooperation with respect to the Mediterranean Sea, Haas argued that epistemic communities played a vital role in the cooperation that was achieved. Epistemic communities are knowledge-based communities that have a common approach to understanding, and on that basis give common policy advice (Haas 1990:55). Haas argued that in its efforts to improve the environmental condition of the Mediterranean Sea, the United Nations Environment Programme helped create and shape an epistemic community. This epistemic community then played a major role in shaping a plan and bringing governments of states to approve and implement the plan.

Haas subsequently (1992) led a group that investigated the roles of epistemic communities in other areas. The case studies covered a wide range of issues including nuclear arms control, trade, finance, natural resource management, and pollution. Haas concluded that the increasingly complex and technical nature of issues under negotiation created a "hospitable environment for epistemic communities" (1992:387). He called for a research program on epistemic communities.

Although scholars routinely refer to epistemic communities, relatively few subsequent studies have systematically explored their role. Considerable research, however, has continued the broad themes that Haas developed.

Haas reported that conducting international relations through international institutions empowers new non-state actors, a finding that has been repeated and is widely accepted. (The way in which NGOs and transnational advocacy networks have been empowered was discussed above.) Other studies have reaffirmed Haas's finding about the expanded role of scientists (Benedick 1991, Brenton 1994), and still others have shown that other groups, such as central bankers, have also gained an expanded role (Risse-Kappen 1995).

There is less agreement on the extent to which the new actors develop a common approach to problem solving and are able to use it to facilitate agreements. Keck & Sikkink (1998) show the intricate interplay between the goals of transnational advocacy networks and legitimization of norms by international institutions. Transnational advocacy networks seek this legitimization. In turn the legitimization reinforces the determination of the networks to achieve their goals. Of course, self-selection plays a major role in the constitution of such networks.

Jervis (1999) has broadened this point to suggest that international institutions, by working through domestic political processes, can be a force for changing preferences and for increasing the value attached to international cooperation. He argues that traditional international relations scholarship has underestimated these dynamic effects of institutions. Agreement among scientists has been more problematic than among other nongovernmental actors (Hampson 1995). In some areas, new information has led to the disintegration of consensus. Moreover, in negotiations in arms control, trade, and the environment, lawyers and national bureaucrats have increasingly displaced outside experts (Hampson 1995), and lawyers and national bureaucrats are more likely than scientists to be concerned with issues of sovereignty and national interests. Another related issue is the linkage between knowledge, power, and interests. Litfin has argued that even when consensual knowledge exists, it does not lead in a linear fashion to agreement (Litfin 1994).

March & Olsen (1998) also mention the potential spillover of democratic practices, which Slaughter (1997) demonstrates. Slaughter's essay is about the increasing importance of transgovernmental cooperation. National officials meet within and outside the framework of international institutions with increasing frequency. The result of their meetings is not the proclamation of new international regulations, but rather the harmonization of national regulations. These officials act independently within their national institutions to make their national regulations similar and compatible. Transgovernmental cooperation is most dense among democracies, but officials from nondemocratic states are increasingly involved. Involvement in transgovernmental networks pushes these individuals toward adopting democratic practices. International institutions are important because they sometimes stimulate this transgovernmental networking and cooperation and frequently provide a cover for it.

STUDIES OF THE EUROPEAN UNION

For many years, the study in the United States of the European Community was dominated by the neofunctionalist paradigm of Haas (1958) and Monnet (1978). The basic dynamic of this paradigm was that sectoral integration would produce pressures for further integration, leading ultimately to the creation of a federal state. Once sectoral integration began, private parties would find that progress toward greater integration would facilitate the pursuit of their own goals. These private actors would pressure their governments to take further steps toward integration. The additional steps would in turn stimulate further pressure for more steps, and the process would continue. The paradigm was vague as to when a federal state would be created and what its features would be.

When the pace of integration flagged in the 1970s and early 1980s, US scholars lost interest in the paradigm. A lively discussion flourished, however, among political actors and scholars in Europe about whether or not the European Community should be seen and promoted as a nascent nation-state (Murray & Rich 1996). Some forcefully argued the federalist position (Sidjanski 1992), whereas others took a more reserved position (Welsh 1996).

In more recent US scholarship on the EU, a debate has developed between those who argue that the process of integration has been driven by the national governments involved in the project (Moravcsik 1998) and those who argue that supranational actors, especially the European Commission and the Court of Justice, have been the driving forces (Sweet & Brunnell 1998). Each side has made persuasive arguments using particular cases to illustrate their points. Because the cases are almost always different, the debate has not been fully engaged.

As a result of these discussions and debates, there is broad agreement that although the institutions of the EU have gained greater authority and capacity in the 1980s and 1990s, national governments are not fading away. National governments remain powerful forces within the EU (Moravcsik 1998). These simultaneous developments have led scholars to explore more deeply the future of the EU.

An emerging view is that the EU may be unique—that because it is treaty-based yet involves a pooling of sovereignty, it may not resemble any existing form of organizing political authority (Keohane & Hoffmann 1991). Sbragia's study of policy making in the EU concludes, "The political system they are constructing...will be an original one. The insistence on the representation of territorially defined governments, in fact, will lead to a reconceptualization of federalism, representation, and the functions of government" (1992:291). As a new way of organizing political authority emerged in Europe in the seventeenth century, another new form may have emerged in Europe in the twentieth.

SYSTEM TRANSFORMATION AND DEMOCRATIC ACCOUNTABILITY

A strong case can be made that the global political system is in some process of system transformation and that international institutions are deeply engaged in that process, both as contributors and as new forms of organizing political authority. Just as the system of concentrating political authority in sovereign, territorially defined states emerged in Europe in the seventeenth century and then was diffused to the entire globe during the following three centuries, a new system is now emerging in Europe that may ultimately be diffused to the world.

If this were the case, at least for the imaginable future it would negate the simple linear model of system transformation portrayed in the tapestries in the *Palais des Nations*. In Europe and elsewhere, nation-states retain their appeal and vitality. Despite a profusion of new actors, the world does not appear to be slipping into a neomedievalism, a confused situation with multiple overlapping and conflicting forms of authority. The current transformation is more orderly and structured.

Yet, precisely because new forms of organizing political authority have emerged, basic normative questions have arisen. Dahl has posed them most sharply. After noting the trend toward having more and more decisions be made in international governmental organizations, Dahl asks whether democratic controls could be established for these decisions, and he specifically considered the European Union. He finds that "[b]argaining, hierarchy, and markets determine the outcomes. Except to ratify the results, democratic processes hardly play a role" (Dahl 1998:115).

The democratic deficit in the EU has been widely noted, and steps have been taken to correct it, such as strengthening the power of the parliament and trying to make the commission's processes more transparent. Dahl doubts the effectiveness of these steps, and he is even more skeptical that democratic control could be established in IGOs that have more members than the EU has.

Slaughter (1997) argues that when policies are changed as a consequence of the efforts of transgovernmental networks to harmonize national policies, national procedures for maintaining democratic accountability are maintained and can be effective. Whether these procedures would meet the criteria that Dahl uses to evaluate democratic accountability may be questionable.

Keohane has argued that scholars must pay greater attention to issues concerning the democratic deficit in international institutions. His survey of scholarship on international institutions concludes, "Combining global governance with effective democratic accountability will be a major challenge for scholars and policymakers alike in the years ahead" (1998:94). It is likely to be the most important issue in system transformation.

Visit the Annual Reviews home page at www.AnnualReviews.org

LITERATURE CITED

Benedick RE. 1991. *Ozone Diplomacy: New Directions in Safeguarding the Planet.* Cambridge, MA: Harvard Univ. Press. 300 pp.

Brenton T. 1994. *The Greening of Machiavelli: The Evolution of International Environmental Politics.* London: Earthscan. 282 pp.

Clark AM, Friedman, EJ, Hochstetler K. 1998. The sovereign limits of global society: a comparison of NGO participation in UN world conferences on the environment, human rights, and women. *World Polit.* 51(1):1–35

Commission on Global Governance. 1995. *Our Global Neighborhood: The Report of the Commission on Global Governance.* Oxford, UK: Oxford Univ. Press. 410 pp.

Cook H. 1996. Amnesty International at the United Nations. In *"The Conscience of the World": The Influence of Non-Governmental Organizations in the UN System,* ed. P Willetts, pp. 181–213. Washington, DC: Brookings Inst. 333 pp.

Cox RW. 1969. The executive head: an essay on leadership in international organization. *Int. Org.* 23(2):205–30

Cox RW, Jacobson HK. 1974. *The Anatomy of Influence: Decision Making in International Organization.* New Haven, CT: Yale Univ. Press. 497 pp.

Dahl R. 1998. *On Democracy.* New Haven, CT: Yale Univ. Press. 217 pp.

Dorsey E. 1997. The global women's movement: articulating a new vision of global governance. In *The Politics of Global Governance: International Organizations in an Interdependent World,* ed. PF Diehl, pp. 335–59. Boulder, CO: Lynne Reiner. 421 pp.

Evangelista M. 1995. The paradox of state strength: transnational relations, domestic structures, and security policy in Russia and the Soviet Union. *Int. Organ.* 49(1):1–38

Evangelista M. 1999. *Unarmed Forces: the Transnational Movement to End the Cold War.* Ithaca, NY:Cornell Univ. Press. 406 pp.

Falk RA. 1975. *A Study of Future Worlds.* New York: Free. 495 pp.

Fox JA, Brown LD, eds. 1998. *The Struggle for Accountability: The World Bank, NGOs, and Grassroots Movements.* Cambridge, MA: MIT Press. 570 pp.

Haas EB. 1958. *The Uniting of Europe: Political, Social, and Economic Forces 1950–1957.* Stanford, CA: Stanford Univ. Press. 552 pp.

Haas P. 1990. *Saving the Mediterranean: The Politics of Environmental Cooperation.* New York: Columbia Univ. Press. 303 pp.

Haas P, ed. 1992. Knowledge, power and international policy coordination. *Int. Org.* 46(1):1–390 (spec. issue)

Hampson FO. 1995. *Multilateral Negotiations: Lessons from Arms Control, Trade, and the Environment.* Baltimore, MD: Johns Hopkins Univ. Press. 421 pp.

Jervis R. 1999. Realism, neoliberalism, and cooperation: understanding the debate. *Int. Secur.* 24(1):42–63

Keck ME, Sikkink K. 1998. *Activists Beyond Borders: Advocacy Networks in International Politics.* Ithaca, NY: Cornell Univ. Press. 227 pp.

Keohane RO. 1984. *After Hegemony: Cooperation and Discord in the World Political Economy.* Princeton, NJ: Princeton Univ. Press. 290 pp.

Keohane RO. 1998. International institutions: can interdependence work? *Foreign Policy* 110:82–97

Keohane RO, Hoffmann S. 1991. *The New European Community: Decisionmaking and Institutional Change.* Boulder, CO: Westview. 208 pp.

Keohane RO, Nye JS. 1977. *Power and Interdependence: World Politics in Transition.* Boston: Little, Brown. 273 pp.

Krasner SD, ed. 1983. *International Regimes.* Ithaca, NY: Cornell Univ. Press. 372 pp.

Litfin K. 1994. *Ozone Discourses: Science and Politics in Global Environmental Cooperation.* New York: Columbia Univ. Press. 257 pp.

March JG, Olsen JP. 1989. *Rediscovering Institutions: The Organizational Basis of Politics.* New York: Free. 211 pp.

March JG, Olsen JP. 1998. The institutional dynamics of international orders. *Int. Organ.* 52(4):943–69

Mathews JT. 1997. Power shift. *Foreign Aff.* 76(1):51–66

Monnet J. 1978. *Memoirs.* Garden City, NY: Doubleday. 544.

Moravcsik A. 1998. *The Choice for Europe: Social Purpose and State Power From Messina to Maastricht.* Ithaca, NY: Cornell Univ. Press. 514 pp.

Moravcsik A. 1999. A new statecraft? Supranational entrepreneurs and international cooperation. *Int. Organ.* 53(2):267–306

Morgenthau H. 1949. *Politics Among Nations: The Struggle for Power and Peace.* New York: Knopf. 489 pp.

Murray P, Rich R, eds. 1996. *Visions of European Unity.* Boulder, CO: Westview. 232 pp.

North DC. 1990. *Institutions, Institutional Change and Economic Performance.* Cambridge, UK: Cambridge Univ. Press. 152 pp.

Organski AFK, Kugler J. 1980. *The War Ledger.* Chicago: Univ. Chicago Press. 292 pp.

Price R. 1998. Reversing gun sights: transnational civil society targets land mines. *Int. Organ.* 52(3):613–44

Princen T, Finger M. 1994. *Environmental NGOs in World Politics: Linking the Local and the Global.* London: Routledge. 262 pp.

Raustiala K. 1997. States, NGOs, and international environmental institutions. *Int. Stud. Q.* 41(4):719–40

Risse-Kappen T, ed. 1995. *Bringing Transnational Relations Back In: Non-State Actors, Domestic Structures, and International Institutions.* Cambridge, UK: Cambridge Univ. Press. 323 pp.

Ruggie JG. 1998. What makes the world hang together. *Int. Organ.* 52(4):855–85

Sbragia AM, ed. 1992. *Euro-Politics: Institutions and Policymaking in the "New" European Community.* Washington, DC: Brookings Inst. 303 pp.

Sidjanski D. 1992. *L'avenir Federaliste de l'Europe: la Communaute Europeenne, des Origines au Traite de Maastricht.* Paris: Presses Univ. France. 440 pp.

Slaughter AM. 1997. The real new world order. *Foreign Aff.* 76(5):183–97

Spruyt H. 1994a. Institutional selection in international relations. *Int. Organ.* 48(4):527–57

Spruyt H. 1994b. *The Sovereign State and its Competitors.* Princeton, NJ: Princeton Univ. Press. 288 pp.

Sweet AS, Brunell TL. 1998. Constructing a supranational constitution: dispute resolution and governance in the European Community. *Am. Polit. Sci. Rev.* 92(1):63–81

Thakur R. 1994. Human rights: Amnesty International and the United Nations. *J. Peace Res.* 31(2):143–60

Thakur R, Maley W. 1999. The Ottawa convention on landmines: a landmark humanitarian treaty in arms control? *Global Governance* 5(3):273–302

Tilly C, ed. 1975. *The Formation of National States in Western Europe.* Princeton, NJ: Princeton Univ. Press. 711 pp.

Union of International Associations. 1997. *Yearbook of International Organizations. 1996/1997.* Brussels: UIA

United Nations. 1996. Documents on the formal arrangements for consultative status. In *Conscience of the World: the Influence of Nongovernmental Organizations in the*

UN System, ed. P Willetts, pp. 290–309. Washington, DC: Brookings Inst. 333 pp.

Waltz K. 1979. *Theory of International Politics*. Reading, MA: Addison-Wesley. 251 pp.

Weiss TG, Gordenker L, eds. 1996. *NGOs, the UN, and Global Governance*. Boulder, CO: Lynne Reiner. 249 pp.

Welsh M. 1996. *Europe United? The European Union and the Retreat from Federalism*. New York: St. Martins. 196 pp.

Willetts P, ed. 1996. *"The Conscience of the World": The Influence of Non-Governmental Organizations in the UN System*. Washington, DC: Brookings Inst. 333 pp.

Annu. Rev. Polit. Sci. 2000. 3:167–82

SUCCESS AND FAILURE IN FOREIGN POLICY

David A. Baldwin

Institute of War & Peace Studies, Columbia University, New York, New York 10027; email: dab12@columbia.edu

Key Words   evaluation, sanctions, force, effectiveness, utility, costs, statecraft, victory

■ **Abstract**   The field of foreign policy analysis needs a common set of concepts and analytical frameworks to facilitate comparison of alternative policy options. Not only is general agreement lacking, there is not even a common understanding of what is meant by success. In order to build policy-relevant knowledge concerning success and failure in foreign policy, the following questions must be addressed: How effective is a policy instrument likely to be, with respect to which goals and targets, at what cost, and in comparison with what other policy instruments? Failure to address each question may lead to serious policy mistakes.

INTRODUCTION

Foreign policy is usually viewed as purposive behavior. Specifying the conditions for success or failure of such behavior is arguably one of the most, if not the most, important topic to be studied. Scholarly attention to this topic, however, is not commensurate with its importance. The field of foreign policy studies is preoccupied with the processes of foreign policy making and has tended to neglect the outputs of such processes. In 1975, the *Handbook of Political Science* identified "the concentration on policy process and the neglect of policy output" as "one of the major deficiencies in the study of foreign policy" (Cohen & Scott 1975: 382–83). The situation is not much different today. Most discussions of foreign policy success and failure are left to journalistic pundits or to scholars writing for such journals as *National Interest, Foreign Affairs, Foreign Policy, or The New York Review of Books.*

Although such journals make an important contribution, there is also a need for the kind of rigorous, systematic analysis usually found in more academic journals, such as *World Politics, International Organization*, or *American Political Science Review*. Although the research published in such journals is high quality, it is often lacking in policy relevance (Lepgold 1998). The purpose of this article is to formulate an analytical framework for rigorous, systematic, policy-relevant foreign policy evaluation. (For a similar attempt at setting forth a framework for

1094-2939/00/0623-0167$14.00   **167**

systematic analysis of foreign policy outputs, see George & Simons 1994 and Baldwin 1985.) Although examples are drawn mostly from the literature on economic sanctions[1] and military force, the approach is intended to be applicable not only to techniques of statecraft, but also to influence attempts of any kind by any actor.

After a brief overview of the state of the field, the article addresses the nature of policy-relevant knowledge and outlines an approach to evaluating foreign policy success. The article also examines the policy context of success and the case of military force. The central purpose is to facilitate scholarly discussion by focusing attention on important concepts and criteria relevant to assessing the success of foreign policy instruments.

FOREIGN POLICY EVALUATION: The State of the Field

The Persian Gulf War in 1991 was preceded by a spirited discussion of the techniques of statecraft most appropriate for dealing with Iraq's invasion of Kuwait (Freedman & Karsh 1993). Some analysts favored exploring every last diplomatic possibility, some advocated reliance on economic sanctions, and others argued that only military force would do the job. Clearly, what was needed was an analytical framework for comparing the utility of various types of statecraft. However, to the extent that scholarly literature on the utility of techniques of statecraft existed, it was compartmentalized into various "islands" of literature. There was a literature on economic sanctions that (endlessly) debated the question of whether such measures work (for references, see Baldwin 1985 and Hufbauer et al 1990) but had little to say about the utility of sanctions in comparison with other techniques of statecraft. There was a literature on military force that discussed its pros and cons but rarely discussed nonmilitary alternatives to force (for references, see Art & Waltz 1999, Shultz et al 1993, Baldwin 1995). The literature on diplomacy was diffuse in focus and rarely attempted to evaluate its utility relative to other policy instruments (e.g. Watson 1983). And the literature on propaganda barely existed in 1990 (for references, see Jowett & O'Donnell 1992 and Lasswell et al 1979/1980).

---

[1]For reasons explained elsewhere (Baldwin 1985), I prefer "economic statecraft" (both the term and the concept) to "economic sanctions." The term economic sanctions is used here for two reasons: (*a*) the literature on economic sanctions is more easily identifiable than that on economic statecraft, which is a broader concept; and (*b*) the term economic sanctions is often used loosely to refer to a large part of economic statecraft. By using the term economic sanctions, I reluctantly acquiesce to (sloppy) common usage. Since this grudging acquiescence has recently been confused with advocacy (e.g. Pape 1997, 1998), I wish to make it clear that I neither approve of nor advocate use of the term economic sanctions. The fact that one sins does not mean that one approves of sin, much less that one advocates it.

The conventional wisdom is that economic sanctions do not work, i.e. they have a low rate of success (e.g. Tsebelis 1990, Kunz 1997, Morgan & Schwebach 1997, Pape 1997, Preeg 1999). One quantitative study estimates that they have a success rate of 35% (Hufbauer et al 1990). To describe this success rate as low, however, implies some criterion of judgment, a criterion that is rarely specified. Is 0.350 a low batting average for a baseball player? Only those who know nothing about the game of baseball would agree. The problem is that we know more about the game of baseball than we do about the "game" of foreign policy. Is 0.350 a low "batting average" for a foreign policy instrument? Such knowledge does not exist. It is often implied, however, that competent and knowledgeable policy makers should achieve a much higher success rate when using economic sanctions (e.g. Tsebelis 1990).

Although many studies address the question of whether economic sanctions work, very few address such questions as the following: Does military force work? Does diplomacy work? Does propaganda work? Despite the paucity of such studies, conventional wisdom holds that military force usually works. Pape (1997:90) asserts that "military instruments are often thought to be the only effective means for achieving ambitious foreign policy goals like taking or defending territory."[2] Art (1996:10) contends that force is "central to statecraft." Even works that downplay the importance of force in international affairs view it as more effective than other means if costs are ignored (Keohane & Nye 1989:16–17; see also Baldwin 1989:151–55).

The literature on foreign policy evaluation is also characterized by analytical and conceptual anarchy. Analytical approaches and conceptual definitions abound. Authors not only disagree as to whether various techniques of statecraft work; they disagree on the very definition of "work."

The chaotic state of the field is illustrated by a recent debate about the success of international peacekeeping operations (Druckman & Stern 1997). Five scholars disagreed with respect to numerous issues, including (*a*) the meaning of the terms success and failure; (*b*) the relevance of counterfactuals;[3] (*c*) the relevance of costs; (*d*) actor designation (e.g. national government, international organization, or humankind); and (*e*) whether to judge success in terms of actor goals or in terms of higher values, such as global peace and justice. Noting that "the difficulties in evaluating peacekeeping missions are both conceptual and methodological," the monitors of the debate are pessimistic about future progress. "Even though further progress depends on developing a broad conceptual framework that can guide evaluation, given the differences in perspectives evident from the remarks of the experts consulted here, we are unlikely to see research in the near future guided by a single analytical framework" (Druckman & Stern 1997:163–64).

---

[2] The Louisiana Purchase (1804) apparently does not qualify as "taking territory."

[3] The "positivist" scholars expressed the most reservations about counterfactual analysis. Given the importance of causal analysis to most positivists, this is, to say the least, surprising.

Despite such pessimism, the purpose of this article is to propose an analytical framework applicable to judging the success of peacekeeping operations, economic sanctions, military undertakings, and other types of influence attempts.

WHAT IS POLICY-RELEVANT KNOWLEDGE?

Policy-relevant knowledge is what policy makers need to know in order to choose among alternative courses of action. It refers to the rational adaptation of means to ends. Ultimately, policy-relevant knowledge is not a substitute for wisdom, since it is concerned only with intermediate goals, i.e. those that are means to higher ends. Policy analysis, therefore, focuses on the efficient pursuit of given ends.

Wildavsky (1979) has suggested a seemingly contrary view that "creativity" in policy analysis consists of formulating problems that have solutions. He illustrates the point with the following story:

> Mike Teitz tells about a soldier in New Zealand who was ordered to build a bridge across a river without enough men or material. He stared along the bank looking glum when a Maori woman came along asking, "Why so sad, soldier?" He explained that he had been given a problem for which there was no solution. Immediately she brightened, saying, "Cheer up! No solution, no problem." (Wildavsky 1979:3)

Creativity, however, is not necessarily the same as rational problem solving. It may be true that such an approach stimulates creative thinking, but it is not a substitute for rational adaptation of means to ends. A country with an unexpected budget surplus of $10 billion will have no trouble finding problems to solve. The difficulty lies in choosing among them. Which problems should be solved and which should be addressed at a later time? Of the many alternative ways to spend the money, which will maximize the utility (i.e. welfare) of the country? Problems do not disappear just because solutions are not available or cannot be readily identified. The soldier in the story may have been cheered by the woman's admonition, but it did not make his problem go away.

A better way to characterize policy analysis is, "No scarcity, no problem!" Policy choice involves choosing among alternative courses of action under conditions of resource scarcity. If everyone can have his cake and eat it too, there are no choices to be made and no need for policy on this issue. Policy problems arise because there are not enough resources available to cope with all of the problems facing policy makers. Under such conditions, policy makers need ways to compare alternative courses of action, i.e. alternative ways of using scarce resources.

Knowledge about the likely utility of a technique of statecraft, therefore, is policy-relevant only insofar as it is helpful in deciding whether or not to use one technique rather than another. Is it helpful to know that economic sanctions only work 35% of the time or that they have a 0.35 probability of working in a particular case? Without comparable knowledge about the likely utility of alternative policy instruments, such knowledge has no policy relevance whatsoever.

ESTIMATING POLICY SUCCESS

Estimating the success or failure of policy instruments is difficult because the concept of success is slippery, recipes for success can be misleading, the dimensions of success are multiple, and clear-cut victories or defeats are few.

The Concept of Success

Success is a slippery concept. Unlike power or wealth, success is not just one of many goals that people may choose to pursue. To the extent that human behavior is purposeful, everyone may be said to pursue success. This is because success is defined in terms of favorable or desired outcomes. Both the definition of success and the implicit rules used in applying the term suggest that costs are an important part of the concept. Successful undertakings are those without excessive costs. Winning a nuclear war by destroying life as we know it or imposing economic sanctions that secure compliance of the target state only by bankrupting the country that imposed them are unlikely to be described as instances of success. "The operation was a success, but the patient died" does not mean what it seems to say. It is a sardonic expression implying that the term success is being misused. If success is defined in terms of favorable policy outcomes, it is necessary to consider both costs and benefits in assessing the success of an undertaking. The concept of a Pyrrhic victory implies a difference between real and apparent victory, and it is as relevant to nonmilitary as to military statecraft.

Recipes for Success

Some recipes for success in foreign policy making are difficult to reconcile with the above concept of success. One such recipe is the advice to pursue modest goals (e.g. Leyton-Brown 1987:309, Druckman & Stern 1997:157, 163). The poet's admonition that "a man's reach should exceed his grasp" is described by one author as "a fine philosophy of life, but a poor prescription for economic sanctions" (Leyton-Brown 1987:309). Such recipes have more to do with creating the illusion of success than with achieving it.

Logically, the specification of a standard of achievement precedes specification of the determinants of, or conditions for, the success of an undertaking. Any statement that purports to specify the determinants or conditions of success presupposes a concept of success. Take, for example, the following recipe for success: "If you want to get to the other side of this river, you will have to swim or find a bridge." In this example, getting to the other side of the river is the operational definition of success, and swimming or finding a bridge are alternative means for accomplishing this goal. The advice to change your goal from crossing the river to the more modest one of staying on this side of the river is not a recipe for success; it is a redefinition of success. This bit of semantic sleight-of-hand should not be misconstrued as advice on how to succeed. It makes little sense to describe someone as pursuing success without specifying success in doing what. If a prospective student asks for advice on how to succeed in college, one must first ascertain whether the goal is to get good grades or to get a sound education. "Take easy courses" may be good advice with respect to the first goal, but "take challenging courses" may be more appropriate advice with respect to the second. Likewise, when advising foreign policy makers on how to make economic sanctions successful, one must first ascertain the goals in terms of which success is to be defined. Advising them to pursue modest goals or not to "bite off more than they can chew" violates this basic precept of prior goal specification. Those who never run a race will never lose a race, but they will never win one either. Economic sanctions that are never used will never fail, but they will never succeed either. "Stick to easy things" may be a recipe for avoiding failure, but it is hardly a recipe for success.

Another so-called recipe for success is the "more is better" approach that characterized military planning for the Persian Gulf War. The idea that massive and overwhelming military force is always preferable to graduated escalation was one of the lessons that some military thinkers derived from the Vietnam War (Gacek 1994, Summers 1981). The problem with this recipe is that it fails to provide guidelines for determining how much is enough. More always seems to be better. This perspective is likely to appeal to those who conceive of national security in terms of "interests that are pursued notwithstanding the costs incurred" (Leffler 1990:145). From the standpoint of a rational policy maker, however, there are no such interests.

A more defensible, but less glamorous, recipe is the marginal utility approach, which prescribes using a technique of statecraft until the marginal benefits of doing so equal the marginal costs of doing so. Instead of "never bite off more than you can chew," the marginal utility approach would counsel foreign policy makers to take successively larger bites until the bites became unchewable, then back off a little. Those who never bite off more than they can chew may seldom choke, but they are unlikely to make maximum use of their chewing ability either. "Take small bites" is hardly a recipe for great accomplishments. It also begs the question of how much smaller than the chewable maximum the bite should be.

Dimensions of Success

In business, as in foreign policy making, success is multidimensional. In business, the costs of advertising, marketing, and production must be considered along with the revenues produced by sales in assessing the overall success of a firm. In foreign policy, the effects on allies, the trade-offs among national interests, and the effects on adversaries must all be considered in assessing the overall success of a technique of statecraft. The difference is that business firms have the common denominator of money; they can add up the consequences of their various activities in monetary terms in order to calculate a "bottom line," i.e. profits. Foreign policy makers have no such standard of value and must confine themselves to rough judgments in estimating the overall success of an undertaking. It is nevertheless helpful to identify some dimensions of success with respect to which such judgments may be made.[4]

Effectiveness

Since (most) foreign policy is goal-oriented,[5] evaluating effectiveness in accomplishing goals is a necessary but not sufficient ingredient in estimating success. If there are concepts of success that do not include goal attainment, they have not yet come to the attention of this writer. This is not to say that estimating effectiveness is simple or easy. Consider the following propositions:

1. Foreign policy makers usually pursue multiple goals with respect to multiple targets. During the Persian Gulf crisis, the goal of US foreign policy makers was not solely to force Saddam Hussein to withdraw from Kuwait. Additional goals included restoring the government of Kuwait, minimizing damage to Kuwait, discouraging Israeli intervention, encouraging United Nations support, reassuring potential allies that the United States was determined but not trigger-happy, discouraging other potential aggressors from trying to emulate Iraq's behavior, and so on. These various goals and targets were not equally important, but neither were they trivial enough to justify ignoring them. "Winning the war" is an oversimplification of the goals of any war, and "achieving the primary goal" is an equally misleading way to define the success of economic sanctions. Despite the widespread acknowledgment that the goals and targets of foreign policy tend to be multiple, success is often measured solely in terms of primary goals and targets (see Baldwin 1985).

2. Policy change and behavior are not the same thing. When President Reagan authorized the exchange of weapons for hostages, it was the policy of the United States not to negotiate with terrorists on such matters. Even "behavior" is more complex than a narrow behavioristic focus on overt actions would suggest (on narrow behaviorism, see Oppenheim 1981:191). Dimensions of behavior that are of potential interest to foreign policy makers include not only easily observable policy changes, but also changes in beliefs, attitudes, opinions, expectations, emotions, and/or predispositions to act.

3. Goal attainment is a matter of degree (Simon 1976:177). Art (1996:24) has applied this insight to foreign policy by observing that "a given instrument

---

[4]Although the dimensions of success discussed here are not arbitrary, neither are they definitive. There are many ways to divide success.

[5]Even those who view foreign policy as expressive rather than instrumental do not dispute that it is usually instrumental.

can carry a state part of the way to a given goal, even though it cannot carry the state all the way there. At one and the same time, an instrument of statecraft can usefully contribute to attaining many goals and yet by itself be insufficient to attain any one of them." Some writers, however, ignore gradations in effectiveness and classify policy outcomes in terms of either success or failure (e.g. Pape 1997).[6] Levy (1969:95) labels this classification the fallacy of misplaced dichotomies. "To set up a distinction in binary form when the things referred to vary by degree or in some other fashion is not only the classic misuse of the law of the excluded middle, it also guarantees the begging of important questions" (Levy 1969:95). Dahl (1976:26) labels the same phenomenon "the lump-of-power fallacy" (see also Baldwin 1985:130–31).

The spectrum of degrees of goal attainment should not be confined to positive numbers. The possibility of negative goal attainment should be considered. For example, an attempt to undermine the stability of a regime (e.g. Castro or Saddam) might trigger a rally-round-the-flag effect that strengthens the regime. The possibility of such "negative power" was recognized long ago by Dahl (1957).

Costs to the User

Evaluating the success of a foreign policy instrument solely in terms of effective goal attainment is akin to evaluating the success of a business firm solely on the basis of sales. A firm that sells a million widgets but loses money is less successful than a firm that sells only two widgets but makes money. Dahl & Lindblom (1953:38–39) long ago explained why costs must be considered in estimating success:

> An action is rational to the extent that it is "correctly" designed to maximize goal achievement.... Given more than one goal (the usual human situation), an action is rational to the extent that it is correctly designed to maximize net goal achievement.... The more rational action is also the more efficient action. The two terms can be used interchangeably.... An action is "correctly" designed to maximize goal satisfaction to the extent that it is efficient, or in other words to the extent that goal satisfaction exceeds goal cost.[7]

In judging the success of instruments of statecraft, as in judging the success of a business firm, costs should be an important part of the calculation. Unfortunately, the success of economic and military statecraft is often estimated solely on the basis of goal achievement without reference to the costs incurred (e.g. Blechman & Kaplan 1978; Leyton-Brown 1987; Tsebelis 1990; Art 1996; Pape 1996, 1997;

---

[6]Pape (1996) also ignores degrees of success in assessing the effectiveness of coercion by military means (cf Mueller 1998:204–5).
[7]On success as net value, see also Simon (1976) and Knorr (1966).

Morgan & Schwebach 1997). The following passage provides a typical view of "successful" sanctions:

> What does it mean for sanctions to be successful? In general, we are interested in determining the conditions (if any) under which economic sanctions produce an intended (on the part of the sanctioner) change in policy by the target state.... The focus of the debate regarding the effectiveness of sanctions is on whether they can enable the sanctioner to achieve its goals of altering the behavior of the target. (Morgan & Schwebach 1997:29)

Clearly, costs are not part of this conception of success; effectiveness is everything.

Costs to the Target

Inflicting costs for noncompliance on the target of an influence attempt is often used as a measure of success (Dahl 1968, Harsanyi 1962). Other things being equal, the higher the costs for noncompliance that an instrument of statecraft inflicts on the target, the more successful it is. Imposing costs for noncompliance is sometimes confused with failure. Pape (1998:197), for example, objects to treating the costs inflicted for noncompliance as a measure of success: "The fact that a target that refuses to concede may suffer substantial costs does not turn failure into success." Schelling responds to such reasoning in a brilliant essay entitled "The Strategy of Inflicting Costs." Is it worthwhile for one's adversary to spend money on a bullet if one can protect oneself with the purchase of a bulletproof vest? Schelling concludes, "He has wasted his money if the vest is cheap, made a splendid investment if my vest is expensive, and if asked what he accomplished by buying his bullet should have the good sense to say that he imposed a cost on me, not that he hoped to kill me and was frustrated" (1984:274).

Bueno de Mesquita (1981:90) uses logic similar to Schelling's to explain why even countries that expect to lose a war may find it worthwhile to fight:

> What, then, can a victim who expects to lose gain from fighting? Presumably such a victim can hope to impose a sufficient cost on the opponent to reduce the concessions that have to be made at the time of surrender. It may hope, for instance, to impose enough costs to prevent the need for a total, unconditional surrender.

To classify such a situation as total failure would be misleading.

Stakes for the User

Not all foreign policy goals are equally important. Winning World War II and winning the release of a political prisoner in another country are not equivalent accomplishments. To weight such achievements equally in judging the overall success rate of a technique of statecraft would be misleading. Other things being equal, the bigger the stakes, the more valuable is the degree of achievement and the more successful is the influence attempt.

Stakes for the Target

The more the target has at stake, the more difficult the undertaking is likely to be. [Among the few to recognize this point are Morgan & Schwebach (1995: 259–60) and Kirshner (1997:34); see also Baldwin (1985:133).] In competitive diving, the points awarded for execution are weighted for the difficulty of the dive. A similar scheme is appropriate for judging the success of a foreign policy instrument. Thus, a small degree of goal achievement in a difficult task might constitute a greater success than a higher degree of achievement in an easy task. Deterring the Soviet Union from launching nuclear missiles at the United States was probably a relatively easy task, although the stakes were very high for the United States. By comparison, getting South Africa or Rhodesia to change the way their societies were governed was relatively difficult, even though the stakes were lower for the United States. Other things being equal, the more difficult the undertaking, the more valuable is the achievement.

Other Criteria

Although the criteria specified above seem relevant to any foreign policy undertaking, other criteria may be applicable as well (for discussion, see Dunn 1994:282–89, Dahl & Lindblom 1953). For example, the equity with which the costs and benefits of the undertaking are distributed may be an important consideration in some situations. Economists often use Pareto optimality as a criterion for judging the success of trade negotiations. Some might want to use the criterion of adequacy, the extent to which the influence attempt solves the problem at hand. One could plausibly argue, for example, that the use of military statecraft with respect to Iraq in 1991 produced an adequate solution to the problem even though it did not achieve all of its goals completely.

SUCCESS IN A POLICY CONTEXT

The temptation to infer policy implications from estimates of past or future success of a policy instrument seems irresistible. Consider the following example: "If policy makers are aware that sanctions can rarely have an impact (and they should be) then sanctions should occur only in those instances in which there is a fair chance that they would 'work'" (Morgan & Schwebach 1997:45–46).

The question of whether a technique of statecraft is likely to work is different from the question of whether it should be used (George & Simons 1994:268–69). Knowledge about the likely success of a foreign policy instrument provides no useful guidance to policy makers as to whether it should be used. Only comparative analysis of the prospective success of alternative instruments provides policy-relevant knowledge. Even if the expected utility of using a technique of statecraft is low, the expected utility of alternative techniques may be even lower. Before one can agree with Nossal (1994:xv) that "sanctions are a notoriously poor tool of statecraft," it is necessary to consider alternative policy options. No matter how much one detests swimming, it may seem quite appealing if the only alternative is sinking.

The need for comparative evaluation of both the costs and benefits of policy alternatives is demonstrated by Simon (1976) and Bueno de Mesquita (1981).

> An administrative choice is incorrectly posed, then, when it is posed as a choice between possibility A, with low costs and small results, and possibility B, with high costs and large results. For A should be substituted a third possibility C, which would include A plus the alternative activities made possible by the cost difference between A and B. If this is done, the choice resolves itself into a comparison of the results obtainable by the application of fixed resources to the alternative activities B and C. (Simon 1976:179)

Bueno de Mesquita (1981:183) employs similar logic with respect to the alternatives of force and diplomacy:

> Leaders expecting a larger net gain through diplomacy than through war ... should rationally elect to pursue their goals through diplomatic bargaining and negotiating. This is true even if the expected gross gain from war is larger than the gross gain from diplomacy, provided that the cost differential is large enough (as it frequently is) to make the net effect of diplomacy preferable to war.

The implication of such reasoning is that one technique of statecraft may be preferable to another even when the former is more likely to achieve a given set of goals, provided the cost differential is big enough.

The purpose of evaluating the success of policy instruments is to judge the wisdom of past or future use of such instruments. In order to make such judgments, one must ask whether some other instrument would have worked (or will work) better. The existence of policy options is sometimes denied. For example, it is often said that in August 1990, at the beginning of the Persian Gulf crisis, the United States had no military options (e.g. Freedman & Karsh 1993:67). Likewise, policy makers sometimes justify past decisions by asserting that they had no alternative. It is the responsibility of policy analysts, however, to point out that policy makers always have options. A policy maker can legitimately claim that he did the best he could in a difficult situation, but he cannot claim there was no other option. "I did the best I could" is a legitimate plea for understanding; "I had no alternative but to do what I did" is an attempt to absolve the policy maker from responsibility for his or her decisions.

Foreign policy instruments are used in situations characterized by strategic interaction. The targets of such influence attempts are not passive or inert objects; they are likely to react. Tsebelis (1990) suggests that both policy analysts and policy makers commit what he calls the Robinson Crusoe fallacy by failing to take account of strategic interaction. Although it is true that the intended effects of a foreign policy instrument are often offset or nullified by reactions of the target state, the only implication for policy is to counsel foreign policy makers against expecting too much. Because all techniques of statecraft are employed in the context of strategic interaction, one must assume that all are equally affected by such interaction unless there is evidence to the contrary. And if strategic interaction affects all techniques equally, it has no relevance to the policy maker trying to choose among them. Policy makers are only interested in the differences among policy instruments, not in the similarities. Strategic interaction may lower the probability that a given policy instrument will be successful, but as long as some techniques have more probability of success than others, the rational policy maker will continue to use them. Sometimes foreign policy makers are faced with a dismal set of alternatives.

MILITARY FORCE

Military force remains an important instrument of statecraft. Given the potential damage that military statecraft can produce, especially in the nuclear age, it is important to estimate its utility accurately and in ways that facilitate comparison with nonmilitary techniques of statecraft. Unfortunately, neither the costs nor the benefits of military statecraft have received the scholarly attention they deserve.

The outcomes of wars tend to be characterized in dichotomous terms as victory or defeat. Considering the importance of assessing war outcomes, one might expect to find a large literature on the nature of military success. Indeed, one could argue that the central point of the most famous book ever written on war (i.e. Clausewitz 1976) concerned the criteria appropriate for determining success in war. Nevertheless, the literature on military force contains few discussions of the meaning of success (for exceptions, see Jervis 1989:16–19 and Hobbs 1979). Even quantitative studies that are rigorous in many respects rely on "the consensus among acknowledged specialists" (Small & Singer 1982:182; Wang & Ray 1994) in assessing war outcomes. One is left to wonder who these specialists are, how they arrived at their conclusions, and how their consensus was determined.

Although Clausewitz wrote before the invention of game theory, he clearly laid the groundwork for thinking about war in nonzero-sum terms. Despite Clausewitz and despite Schelling's (1984:269) contention that war itself is "a dramatically nonzero-sum activity," the tendency to treat war as a zero-sum conflict persists in the literature on military statecraft. War outcomes are usually coded in terms of "win," "lose," or "draw," which are consistent with zero-sum games, rather than in terms of the degree to which each participant was able to achieve its multiple goals (see Art 1996:9, Bueno de Mesquita 1981, Small & Singer 1982, Wang & Ray 1994, Stam 1996). Indeed, in nonzero-sum games, it is conceivable that all participants may be winners or all may be losers. A global nuclear war would make this point painfully obvious.

Military statecraft tends to be the most costly means of pursuing foreign policy goals. Annual defense spending by the United States approaches $300 billion, while spending on nonmilitary statecraft (State Department, United Nations, etc) is less than $10 billion. Of course, not all of the costs of statecraft are measurable in terms of government spending. Building nuclear weapons, for example, creates some probability of nuclear war. The costs of such a war, discounted for its likelihood, should be part of the calculus of costs. To argue otherwise would be akin to the contention that playing Russian roulette is not costly if the player wins. If he is using a six-shooter, the correct cost calculation would include the probability of one in six that he will die.

Economic sanctions also have costs that are not measurable in budgetary terms. For example, when trade is suspended, the costs of business foregone should be part of the cost calculus of sanctions, as business groups are continually pointing out. Even so, estimates of the value of business foregone as a result of US economic sanctions do not begin to approach the annual defense budget. Military force is not always more expensive than other policy instruments, but it usually is.

If military force is so expensive, one might expect those who study it to be especially concerned with its costs. This is not necessarily the case. Of course, it is not difficult to identify students of military statecraft who give serious attention to the costs of using it, e.g. Jervis, Stam, Knorr, Schelling, Brodie, George, and Bueno de Mesquita. It is equally easy, however, to find works that purport to say something about the utility of military statecraft but devote little or no attention to the costs of using it (Art & Waltz 1999, Pape 1996, Blechman & Kaplan 1978, Art 1996). And although nuclear weapons have been an important ingredient in military statecraft for the last half century, a recent study by the Brookings Institution (Schwartz 1998) argues that the costs of such weaponry have received woefully inadequate attention.

Cost is an intrinsic part of the concept of utility, and utility calculations are what estimates of success are all about. The concept of a Pyrrhic victory implies that appearances can be deceiving with respect to war outcomes. Costs matter. A Pyrrhic victory is no victory at all. To evaluate the success of a war outcome without reference to the costs incurred by the participants is seriously misleading. Although Small & Singer (1982:182) ignore costs in coding winners and losers of wars, they at least admit that this is a possible weakness in their approach. Other writers (e.g. Wang & Ray 1994) include no such admission.

Clausewitz's (1976:87) description of war as "the continuation of policy by other means" implies that success or failure in war should be assessed in the same way that the success or failure of other policy means are assessed. It implies that military force is simply an alternative instrument available to policy makers for the pursuit of particular ends. If policy makers are to choose between military force and alternative means, they must have an analytical framework that facilitates comparing the likely utility of one instrument with that of others. In assessing war outcomes, as in estimating the success of other instruments, success is best considered a matter of degree; zero-sum assumptions are misleading; and cost considerations are essential.

CONCLUSION

Foreign policy decisions often have momentous consequences. Providing foreign policy makers with the kind of knowledge that would help them to choose more rationally among various instruments of statecraft deserves higher priority among scholars than it has received. The emergence of such knowledge has two requisites.

First, the nature of policy-relevant knowledge must be understood. In order to make rational policy decisions, policy makers need to ask how effective a policy instrument is likely to be, with respect to which goals and targets, at what cost, and in comparison with what other policy instruments. Some have suggested that partial knowledge has policy value. Pape, for example, maintains that "learning that one of the instruments is rarely effective is in itself a finding of ... policy value" (1998:198). But a little knowledge can be a dangerous thing. Failure to ask all of the questions above can lead to serious policy mistakes. This is not to suggest that every scholar must address all of these questions. Any study of the utility of techniques of statecraft that fails to address all of the above questions, however, should carry a disclaimer similar to that on cigarette packages, e.g. "Warning: the knowledge contained in this study omits some of the important questions essential to rational policy making; any attempt to formulate policy based on this study could be hazardous to the health of that policy."

Second, the development of concepts and analytical criteria that permit the comparison of alternative techniques of statecraft is both possible and desirable. In order to compare military force and economic sanctions, for example, a conception of success common to both and a set of criteria applicable to both are necessary. Any approach that fails to allow for degrees of success (or failure) or fails to account for both the expected costs and benefits of each technique can seriously mislead policy makers.

Before criticizing foreign policy failures, one should ponder the meaning of success and failure in foreign policy. Before reiterating the Vietnam-era slogan of "Why not victory?" one should ask, "What does victory mean, and how would we know it when we see it?"

Visit the Annual Reviews home page at www.AnnualReviews.org

LITERATURE CITED

Art RJ. 1996. American foreign policy and the fungibility of force. *Secur. Stud.* 5:7–42

Art RJ, Waltz KN, eds. 1999. *The Use of Force: Military Power and International Politics.* New York: Rowman & Littlefield. 5th ed.

Baldwin DA. 1985. *Economic Statecraft.* Princeton, NJ: Princeton Univ. Press

Baldwin DA. 1989. *Paradoxes of Power.* New York: Basil Blackwell

Baldwin DA. 1995. Security studies and the end of the cold war. *World Polit.* 48:117–41

Blechman BM, Kaplan SS. 1978. *Force Without War: U.S. Armed Forces as a Political Instrument.* Washington, DC: Brookings Inst.

Bueno de Mesquita B. 1981. *The War Trap.* New Haven, CT: Yale Univ. Press

Clausewitz C. 1976. *On War*, ed./transl. MH Howard, P Paret. Princeton, NJ: Princeton Univ. Press

Cohen BC, Scott HA. 1975. Foreign policy. In *Handbook of Political Science*, Vol. 6. *Policies and Policymaking*, ed. FI Greenstein, NW Polsby. Reading, MA: Addison-Wesley

Dahl RA. 1957. The concept of power. *Behav. Sci.* 2:201–15

Dahl RA. 1968. Power. *International Encyclopedia of the Social Sciences,* Vol. 12. New York: Free

Dahl RA. 1976. *Modern Political Analysis.* Englewood Cliffs, NJ: Prentice-Hall. 3rd ed.

Dahl RA, Lindblom CE. 1953. *Politics, Economics, and Welfare: Planning and Politico-Economic Systems Resolved into Basic Social Processes.* New York: Harper & Row

Druckman D, Stern PC. 1997. Evaluating peacekeeping missions. *Mershon Int. Stud. Rev.* 41:151–65

Dunn WN. 1994. *Public Policy Analysis: An Introduction.* Englewood Cliffs, NJ: Prentice-Hall

Freedman L, Karsh E. 1993. *The Gulf Conflict: 1990–1991.* Princeton, NJ: Princeton Univ. Press

Gacek CM. 1994. *The Logic of Force: The Dilemma of Limited War in American Foreign Policy.* New York: Columbia Univ. Press

George AL, Simons WE, eds. 1994. *The Limits of Coercive Diplomacy.* Boulder, CO: Westview. 2nd ed.

Harsanyi JC. 1962. Measurement of social power, opportunity costs, and the theory of two-person bargaining games. *Behav. Sci.* 7:67–80

Hobbs R. 1979. *The Myth of Victory: What is Victory in War?* Boulder, CO: Westview

Hufbauer GC, Schott JJ, Elliott KA. 1990. *Economic Sanctions Reconsidered.* Washington, DC: Inst. Int. Econ. 2nd ed.

Jervis R. 1989. *On the Meaning of the Nuclear Revolution: Statecraft and the Prospect of Armageddon.* Ithaca, NY: Cornell Univ. Press

Jowett G, O'Donnell V. 1992. *Propaganda and Persuasion.* London: Sage. 2nd ed.

Keohane RO, Nye JS. 1989. *Power and Interdependence.* Boston: Scott, Foresman. 2nd ed.

Kirshner J. 1997. The microfoundations of economic sanctions. *Secur. Stud.* 6:32–64

Knorr K. 1966. *On the Uses of Military Power in the Nuclear Age.* Princeton, NJ: Princeton Univ. Press

Kunz DB. 1997. *Butter and Guns: America's Cold War Economic Diplomacy.* New York: Free

Lasswell HD, Lerner D, Spier H, eds. 1979/1980. *Propaganda and Communication in World History.* 3 vols. Honolulu: Univ. Hawaii Press

Leffler MP. 1990. National security. *J. Am. Hist.* 77:143–65

Lepgold J. 1998. Is anyone listening? International relations theory and the problem of policy relevance. *Polit. Sci. Q.* 113:43–62

Levy MJ. 1969. "Does it matter that he's naked" bawled the child. In *Contending Approaches to International Politics*, ed. K Knorr, JN Rosenau, pp. 87–109. Princeton, NJ: Princeton Univ. Press

Leyton-Brown D, ed. 1987. *The Utility of International Economic Sanctions.* New York: St. Martin's

Morgan TC, Schwebach VL. 1995. Economic sanctions as an instrument of foreign policy. *Int. Int.* 21:247–63

Morgan TC, Schwebach VL. 1997. Fools suffer gladly: the use of economic sanctions in international crises. *Int. Stud. Q.* 41:27–50

Mueller K. 1998. Strategies of coercion: denial, punishment, and the future of air power. *Secur. Stud.* 7:182–228

Nossal KR. 1994. *Rain Dancing: Sanctions in Canadian and Australian Foreign Policy.* Toronto: Univ. Toronto Press

Oppenheim FE. 1981. *Political Concepts: A Reconstruction.* Chicago: Univ. Chicago Press

Pape RA. 1996. *Bombing to Win: Air Power and Coercion in War.* Ithaca, NY: Cornell Univ. Press

Pape RA. 1997. Why economic sanctions do not work. *Int. Secur.* 22:90–136

Pape RA. 1998. Reply to evaluating economic sanctions. *Int. Secur.* 23:195–98

Preeg EH. 1999. *Feeling Good or Doing Good with Sanctions: Unilateral Economic Sanctions and the U.S. National Interest.* Washington, DC: CSIS

Schelling TC. 1984. *Choice and Consequence: Perspectives of an Errant Economist.* Cambridge, MA: Harvard Univ. Press

Schwartz SI, ed. 1998. *Atomic Audit: The Costs and Consequences of U.S. Nuclear Weapons Since 1940.* Washington, DC: Brookings Inst.

Shultz R, Godson R, Greenwood T, eds. 1993. *Security Studies for the 1990s.* Washington, DC: Brassey's

Simon HA. 1976. *Administrative Behavior: A Study of Decision-Making Processes in Ad-ministrative Organization.* New York: Free

Small M, Singer JD. 1982. *Resort to Arms: International and Civil Wars.* London: Sage

Stam AC. 1996. *Win, Lose, or Draw.* Ann Arbor: Univ. Mich. Press

Summers HG. 1981. *On Strategy: A Critical Analysis of the Vietnam War.* Washington, DC: GPO

Tsebelis G. 1990. Are sanctions effective? A game-theoretic analysis. *J. Confl. Resolut.* 34:3–28

Wang K, Ray JL. 1994. Beginners and winners: the fate of initiators of interstate wars involving great powers since 1495. *Int. Stud. Q.* 38:139–54

Watson A. 1983. *Diplomacy.* New York: McGraw-Hill

Wildavsky A. 1979. *Speaking Truth to Power: The Art and Craft of Policy Analysis.* Boston: Little, Brown

Annu. Rev. Polit. Sci. 2000. 3:183–219

Economic Determinants
of Electoral Outcomes

Michael S. Lewis-Beck

Dept. of Political Science, University of Iowa, Iowa City, Iowa 52242;
e-mail: michael-lewis-beck@uiowa.edu

Mary Stegmaier

Dept. of Government and Foreign Affairs, University of Virginia, Charlottesville,
Virginia 22901; e-mail: ms2bu@virginia.edu

■ **Abstract**   Economic conditions shape election outcomes in the world's democracies. Good times keep parties in office, bad times cast them out. This proposition is robust, as the voluminous body of research reviewed here demonstrates. The strong findings at the macro level are founded on the economic voter, who holds the government responsible for economic performance, rewarding or punishing it at the ballot box. Although voters do not look exclusively at economic issues, they generally weigh those more heavily than any others, regardless of the democracy they vote in.

INTRODUCTION

In his pivotal book, *Political Control of the Economy*, Tufte (1978:65) articulated what he called a basic principle:

> When you think economics, think elections;
> When you think elections, think economics.

More than 20 years have passed since this axiom was articulated. Is it true? In particular, is economics the driving force behind electoral outcomes in democracies? And, if so, how does it work? These are the leading questions this essay attempts to answer by distilling the research literature. [For earlier literature reviews, see Monroe (1984), Kiewiet & Rivers (1985), Lewis-Beck (1988:chs. 2 and 3), Schneider & Frey (1988), Nannestad & Paldam (1994), Anderson (1995:ch. 3), Norpoth (1996a).] The task is not simple. The flow of scholarly papers on the topic has changed from a trickle to a torrent of over 300 articles and books on economics and elections. What holds this disparate collection of publications together is their tests of the economic voter hypothesis. In its elementary reward-punishment version, that hypothesis may be stated as follows: The citizen votes for the government if the economy is doing all right; otherwise, the vote is against. The inspiration for the hypothesis, now widespread in the scholarly literature, comes from Key

1094-2939/00/0623-0183$14.00   **183**

(1964:568). In the press, economic voting is routinely used as a sweeping explanation of electoral outcomes. For example, *New York Times* journalists concluded that in the 1992 US presidential race, "More than any other issue, the economy was Bill Clinton's ticket to the presidency" (Rosenbaum & Lohr 1996).

The research at hand tests this claim from every possible angle. Fortunately, economics and elections is a subfield of political science (and economics) where much has been learned. Increasingly refined tools of theory and method have been successfully applied to ever richer data bases.

We divide this presentation into four sections. The first section considers United States elections, since they have been the most extensively investigated. Presidential support is examined first, then congressional. Methodological issues are discussed at appropriate points and, ultimately, generalizations are offered about the impact of economics on the American voter. The second section explores a comparative example, the French presidential and National Assembly elections. The comparison is especially useful because French elections exhibit institutional differences that highlight the conditional aspects of economic voting. The third section reviews the findings of selected other nations that have been fairly heavily researched, Britain and Denmark in particular. The fourth section is truly comparative, evaluating the studies that have examined economic voting in a sample of nations, rather than in one nation alone. Finally, we draw conclusions about the place of economics in democratic voting models.

THE MOST STUDIED NATION: The United States

By far, there are more economic voting studies on the United States than on any other country. Therefore, we begin with that case, which in some ways defines the lines of debate for work elsewhere. We look first at presidential popularity and vote functions, then examine individual-level survey data on presidential voting. After that, we turn to congressional vote functions and survey data on House of Representative elections.

US Presidential Popularity Functions

There are two streams of work treating economic influences on US presidential elections, vote functions and popularity functions. [Nannestad & Paldam (1994:213) call these "VP-functions."] In popularity functions, the dependent variable is job approval rating from a public opinion poll, and in vote functions it is vote choice itself.

The earliest research on popularity functions was by Mueller (1970, 1973), and, at least conceptually, it continues to shape current efforts. Data are aggregate time series gathered over the post–World War II period. The percentage of the public approving of how the president is handling his job, according to a Gallup poll, is the variable to be explained. The independent variables, besides the economy, are war, political scandal, international crisis, and term cycles. Examples of such a model in appear in Table 1. These efforts by Norpoth (1985:179) and Beck

TABLE 1   Earlier examples of US popularity functions

Variable	(1)[a]	(2)[b]	(3)[c]
Popularity lagged		0.84*	0.89*
Food inflation		−0.49*	−0.26*
Inflation	−139.33		
Inflation lagged	−306.42*		
Unemployment	0.93		
Unemployment change		−2.76*	−1.65*
Vietnam	0.97*	−0.41	−1.12
Watergate	−2.96*	−2.64	−1.85
Rally around the flag	2.54*		
Inauguration	19.95*		
Term dummies			
Kennedy		14.46*	13.86*
Johnson		18.43*	20.93*
Nixon		18.46*	15.07*
Ford		33.86*	22.90*
Carter		18.15*	17.41*
Reagan		22.17*	15.93*
Constant	−1.32*	10.07*	7.02*
Random MA(2)	0.37*		
R-squared		0.88	0.90
Adjusted R-squared	0.69		
Degrees of freedom		121	388
N	80		

* = Statistical significance at 0.05 one-tail, or better.

[a](1) Quarterly presidential popularity, 1961:1–1980:4 (from the monthly Gallup Poll percentage who approve of how the current president is handling his job), differenced and predicted from differenced economic variables (inflation, inflation lagged one quarter, unemployment) and dummies for the Vietnam War, Watergate, the rally-around-the-flag effect, inauguration, and presidential term, with ARIMA (autoregressive integrated moving averages) transfer function estimation (Norpoth 1985:179).

[b](2) Quarterly presidential popularity, 1953:2–1986:2 (from the monthly Gallup Poll), predicted from its lagged value, contemporaneous economic variables (inflation of food prices, change in the unemployment rate), a Vietnam variable (number of soldiers killed), and dummies for Watergate and each new administration, with OLS (ordinary least squares) estimation (Beck 1991:94).

[c](3) Monthly presidential popularity, 1953:3–1986:6, with the same independent variables and OLS estimation as in column 2 (Beck 1991:94).

(1991:94) are representative of the first wave of US popularity function estimation (Frey & Schneider 1978a, Kernell 1978, Monroe 1978, Golden & Poterba 1977, Kenski 1980, Hibbs et al 1982). Fairly long time series (monthly or quarterly) on presidential approval (invariably Gallup ratings) were predicted from a few macroeconomic indicators (unemployment, income, gross national product, inflation) and several political variables (almost always measured with dummies). An important conclusion of these studies was summed up by Norpoth (1985:180) as follows: "There can be little doubt that the economy matters for presidential popularity." However, beyond that generalization, much remained unsettled. What economic variables count? What is the lag structure? The estimates of Table 1 illustrate these concerns. In column 1, unemployment has no statistically significant effect, whereas in column 2 it does. In column 1, inflation has no statistically significant contemporaneous effect, only a significant lagged effect. But in column 2, the statistically significant inflation effect is lagged. In column 3, the specification is the same as in column 2, but the analysis is on monthly rather than quarterly data. The inflation and unemployment effects are again significant and the magnitudes are naturally reduced (although by about one half rather than one third, which raises the interesting question of the proper level of aggregation).

Despite the lack of resolution, the search for the preferred macroeconomic indicators, and their lagged effects pattern, has been largely abandoned. In the second wave of popularity function work, objective economic measures have been replaced with subjective ones. The models now contain aggregate perceptual evaluations of general economic performance instead of hard data on unemployment, inflation, income, or growth. A summary of responses from two types of questions, such as these posed by the Michigan Survey of Consumer Attitudes and Behavior since the 1960s, are most often used.

Q1. Would you say that at the present time business conditions are better or worse than a year ago?

Q2. [H]ow about a year from now, do you expect that in the country as a whole business conditions will be better, or worse than they are at present, or just about the same?

The first item is retrospective, asking the respondent to assess the performance of the national economy over the past year. The second item again asks for a national economic assessment, but over the forthcoming year, so it is prospective. The items have certain advantages. First, their responses appear to combine and weigh all the objective macroeconomic measures. For example, if 60% of respondents say business conditions are better and only 20% say they are worse, then on balance the overall economy looks good that year ($60 - 20 = +40$). Second, assuming that voters respond to their interpretation of the economy rather than to its objective condition, the economic effects on the vote might be more strongly and more accurately recorded (but see Kramer 1983). Third, the presence of a prospective as well as a retrospective measure facilitates the testing of whether economic voters are sophisticated or naive. Chappell & Keech (1985, 1991) have argued that voters

TABLE 2 Later examples of US popularity functions (figures in parentheses are standard errors)

Variable	(1)[a]	(2)[b]	(3)[c]
Political variables	†	‡	‡
Popularity lagged		0.81*	0.79*
		(0.04)	(0.04)
Retrospective business	0.10*	0.03	
	(0.03)	(0.02)	
Prospective business	−0.007		0.08*
	(0.065)		(0.03)
Retrospective personal		0.10	
		(0.07)	
Prospective personal			0.11
			(0.09)
Adjusted R-squared	0.84	0.90	0.91
N	136	141	147

* = Statistical significance at 0.05 one-tail, or better.

† = Coefficients for political variables in the model not shown: presidential change scored 1 for each quarter a fresh president assumes office, 0 otherwise; dummies for the Watergate and Iran-Contra scandals and the Gulf War; a Vietnam variable scored as percentage public approval of the war.

‡ = Coefficients for political variables in the model not shown: dummies for every administration, Watergate, the Iran hostage incident, and the Gulf War; Vietnam War deaths; counter variables for important events.

[a](1) Quarterly presidential popularity (Gallup approval percentage), 1960:1—1993:4, predicted from the political variables (†), retrospective business (scored percentage who call business conditions "better" over the last year − percentage who say "worse"), and prospective business (scored percentage who say business conditions will be "better" next year − percentage who say "worse"), estimated with conditional least squares and an AR(1) (first order autoreprssive) correction (Norpoth 1996b:783).

[b](2) Quarterly presidential popularity (Gallup percentage approval), 1954—1996, predicted from the political variables (‡), popularity lagged, retrospective business (the same item as in column 1, scored on a 200-point scale as a net measure of positive and negative evaluation), and retrospective personal (a net measure of those who reported family finances "better" − those who said "worse"), estimated from OLS. (Erikson et al 2000).

[c](3) The same variables as in column 2 except for the economic variables, which here are prospective business (a net measure of those who said business conditions in the next 12 months would be "good" − those who said "bad") and prospective personal (a net measure of those who said a year from now family finances would be "better" − those who said "worse").

rate the president according to the economic future his policies will deliver. In contrast to this sophisticated prospective voter is the naive retrospective voter, who merely judges the president according to the economic performance of the immediate past. In the terms of MacKuen et al (1992), prospective voters behave more as bankers, retrospective voters as peasants.

A central controversy in popularity function research today is whether economic voters are retrospective or prospective. Table 2 reports some illustrative results on this issue. In column 1 are estimates for a Norpoth (1996b:783) model, supporting his consistent finding of "a substantial influence of retrospective views of the economy, but not with any [influence] for economic expectations." Columns 2 and 3, by contrast, show Erikson et al's (2000) dominant result: "Voters respond in terms of their expectation of the future level of prosperity." Thus, two leading scholars, looking at essentially the same data, and following model specifications that are conceptually similar, arrive at estimates that yield opposite conclusions. One discovers an exclusively retrospective economic voter, the other an exclusively prospective economic voter. To complicate matters further, the middle position— the economic voter is retrospective and prospective in more or less equal amounts— is advocated by Clarke & Stewart (1994), in their own careful analysis of the presidential approval data.

Why these conflicting results? It is worth recalling the phrase, "God is in the details." Although on the surface the models of Table 2 appear similar, there are differences. First, the time series cover different periods, 1960–1993 versus 1954–1996. Second, the political variables, though conceptually alike, are not measured the same way. In column 1, a general dummy stands for an adminstration change, the Vietnam War is tracked in terms of public approval, and there is no "events" or "rally" variable. By way of contrast, column 2 uses specific dummies for each administration, tracks the Vietnam War in terms of soldiers killed, and includes a variable for tracking special "events." Third, column 1 is estimated with Box-Tiao intervention analysis and an AR(1) error correction, whereas column 2 uses a lagged dependent variable on the right-hand side as a control, after which ordinary least squares (OLS) is applied. Fourth, multicollinearity may be rendering coefficients unstable, subject to serious change from one specification to the next. For example, the retrospective item correlates 0.84 with the prospective item "good-bad times next 12 months" (Norpoth 1996b:785). Once these points are considered, it is less surprising that differences are observed.

US Presidential Vote Functions

Although scholars have enthusiastically pursued the study of presidential popularity functions, some of that enthusiasm seems misplaced, since they fail to measure the variable of ultimate interest—presidential vote. The plentiful work on vote functions looks directly at macroeconomic effects on election outcomes, usually measured as the incumbent party share of the two-party popular vote, in an annual post–World War II time series. Table 3 summarizes the model specifications from most of the major studies. All are single-equation regression models with no more than four independent variables. There is invariably an economic measure, usually gross national product (GNP) or gross domestic product (GDP), with a lag structure that is seldom the same from model to model. Most models contain a candidate evaluation measure, usually presidential popularity itself.

Vote function research has experienced two waves, the first stressing explanation, the second stressing forecasting. The first began with Tufte (1978) and

TABLE 3   Model specifications for leading US presidential vote function studies*

Author	Independent variables
Tufte (1978:122)	Income, candidate evaluation
Fair (1978:168)	GNP, time, incumbency
Hibbs (1982:394)	Personal income
Lewis-Beck & Rice (1984)	Presidential popularity, GNP
Abramowitz (1988)	Presidential popularity, GNP, incumbency
Erikson (1989)	Income, candidate evaluation
Campbell & Wink (1990)	Presidential trial-heat, GNP
Lewis-Beck & Rice (1992)	Popularity, GNP, House vote, primaries
Campbell (1996)	Presidential trial-heat, GDP
Abramowitz (1996)	Popularity, GDP, time in office
Norpoth (1996c)	Past votes, GNP, inflation, primary
Lewis-Beck & Tien (1996)	Popularity, GNP, peace and prosperity
Wlezien & Erikson (1996)	Leading indicators, presidential popularity
Holbrook (1996b)	Presidential popularity, personal finances

*To appreciate fully these models, it is of course necessary to consult the work directly.

essentially ended with Erikson (1989). The second wave, somewhat overlapping the first, began with Lewis-Beck & Rice (1984), gathered momentum after the Lewis-Beck & Rice (1992) forecasting book, and continues still. The multiple forecasting papers published in 1996 (see Table 3) were revised for 2000 (Campbell & Garand 2000). The equations in Table 4 illustrate results from the two waves. Column 1 offers an explanatory model from Erikson (1989), while column 2 offers a forecasting model from Lewis-Beck & Tien (1996).

Some of the explanatory models in Table 3 view presidential vote as essentially economically determined (Fair 1978, 1982, 1988, 1996; Hibbs 1982, 1987). However, the Erikson (1989) equation in column 1, Table 4, which derives theoretically from Tufte's (1978) referendum model, sees presidential voters as responding to a mix of economic and noneconomic issues. In particular, the incumbent party vote share rises when its candidate is more likeable and income growth steepens. These two variables together account for almost 90% of the variance, a greater portion than the economically determined models, which yield R-squared between 0.63 and 0.70 (see, respectively, Hibbs 1982 and Fair 1978). Clearly, the explanatory vote functions establish that economic predictors rival, if not surpass, the political predictors in importance. In column 1, for example, the t-ratio of the Income variable exceeds that of the Candidate variable.

The Lewis-Beck & Tien (1996) equation of column 2 in Table 4 also starts with political economy notions. Voters respond to the national economic performance

TABLE 4 Examples of presidential vote function models
(figures in parentheses are *t*-ratios)

Variable	(1)[a]	(2)[b]
Cumulative income	2.77* (5.28)	
Candidate evaluation	6.50* (4.31)	
Presidential popularity		0.16* (2.11)
GNP change		1.83* (3.33)
Peace/prosperity		0.14* (2.35)
Constant	44.64	27.34
Adjusted R-squared	0.89	0.88
SEE[†]	2.21	2.26
N	10	11
D-W[†]	2.10	1.87

* = Statistically significant at 0.05 or better.

[†]SEE, standard error of estimate; D-W, Durbin-Watson statistic.

[a](1) Dependent variable = percentage of the popular two-party vote (1948–1984); weighted income = percentage change in disposable income per capita, weighted over the 15 pre-election quarters; candidate evaluation = "like" responses over "dislike" responses about candidate characteristics in the American National Election Surveys (Erikson 1989).

[b](2) Dependent variable = percentage of the popular two-party vote (1952–1992); presidential popularity = the Gallup Poll approval rating in July; GNP change = percentage change (nonannualized) in GNP (constant dollars) from the fourth quarter of the year before the election to the second quarter of the election year; peace and prosperity = sum of the percentage of two-party respondents who favored the president's party on keeping the US out of war and the country prosperous (Gallup Poll questions) (Lewis-Beck & Tien 1996).

as measured by GNP growth, and they respond to the national political performance as measured by presidential popularity. These assessments are retrospective, as is standard with all vote function models. Because their primary purpose is forecasting, the measures have a lead time of several months, i.e. the indicators for making the November forecast are available in the summer. Measuring the predictor variables with lead time is the principal characteristic distinguishing forecasting vote functions from explanatory ones. The forecasting models of Table 3 (the 1996 citations) all fit well, generating *R*-squared of ∼0.90 or better, and economics always looms large. For example, in column 2, the *t*-ratio of the GNP variable is greater than that of the popularity variable.

The model of column 2, in addition, uses both prospective (prosperity assessment) and retrospective (GNP) economic factors. Uniquely, it gives evidence that presidential voters look to the future—which party is more likely to bring prosperity—as well as the economic past. This finding bears on a developing strand of work concerning the "rationality" of economic voting in presidential elections. Are presidential voters naively retrospective, evaluating election-year economic growth, or do they prospectively "focus only on that portion of growth likely to persist after the election" (Alesina et al 1993:14)? From their own analysis, these researchers rejected the rational choice idea, concluding that "the effects of the economy on voting are consistent with naive retrospective voting" (Alesina et al 1993:26). However, Suzuki & Chappell (1996:235), on the basis of their vote function, could not reject the rational voter view. They claimed that presidential voting behavior reveals "marginal voters' awareness of economic constraints and the implications of vote choices for their long-term economic well-being."

US Presidential Election Surveys

Although virtually all the vote function investigations suggest strong economic voting effects, this is merely an inference from aggregates to individuals. Until voters themselves are examined directly, and economic evaluations linked to choice, the impressive time series results are open to the charge of ecological fallacy. In terms of theory, how might American voters translate the economy into a vote? The pioneering work of Key (1966:61) provides a guiding perspective: "The patterns of flow of the major streams of shifting voters graphically reflect the electorate in its great, and perhaps principal, role as an appraiser of past events, past performance, and past actions. It judges retrospectively." Applying the Key argument, Fiorina (1978, 1981:26) came up with the retrospective economic voter hypothesis of "an electorate that treats elections ... as referenda on the incumbent administration's handling of the economy."

Do voters actually think this way? Simple survey evidence suggests they do. Table 5 shows poll results on national economic evaluation and vote intention just before the 1996 presidential contest. Of those who saw the economy as good, 57% said they would back incumbent Clinton, whereas among those who saw it as bad, only 31% would. This bivariate table, from one election survey, provides little more than anecdotal information, but it points to the questions that need answering. What dimensions of the economy does the presidential voter evaluate? How important are these evaluations, once other variables are controlled for?

Three dimensions of economic evaluation dominate the literature: target, time, and context. The target is the object of evaluation, essentially either a person or a nation. A voter evaluating his or her personal finances is called a pocketbook voter or an egotropic voter. A voter judging national economic conditions is called a collective or sociotropic voter (Kinder & Kiewiet 1981). The American National Election Studies (ANES) poses these two items, the first pocketbook, the second collective:

TABLE 5   National economic assessment and vote
intention, September 1996*

Candidate Preference	National economy good (%)	National economy bad (%)
Clinton	57	31
Dole	30	50
Perot	5	8
Other response	8	11
Column percent	100	100

*Total $N = 1281$. Respondents were asked to evaluate the national economy as "good" or "bad" and to state their candidate preference. These data are assembled from the *New York Times/CBS News Poll* taken September 2–4, 1996 (*New York Times* 1996).

During the last few years has your financial situation been getting better, getting worse, or has it stayed the same?

Would you say that at present business conditions are better or worse than they were a year ago?

The time dimension refers to whether the voter is looking at the economic past or the economic future. The above items point the respondent to "the last few years" or "a year ago." Therefore, they are backward looking, or retrospective. If instead they asked about the next few years or the coming year, they would be forward looking, or prospective. The third dimension, context, considers whether the economic target is explicitly linked to policy (Lewis-Beck 1988:39; see also Fiorina 1981:8081). For example, the second item changes from a simple to a complex context with the addition of the parenthetical phrase: "Would you say that at present [government policy is making] business conditions better or worse than they were a year ago?"

There are other dimensions, but these three—target, time, and context—have produced the biggest yield, almost exclusively from the ANES data. Therefore, we focus on these findings. In the first phase of this work, the central issue concerned pocketbook versus sociotropic effects. In Table 6 are illustrative equations estimated for the 1976 presidential election. The model of column 1 explores, in a preliminary way, the effect of central retrospective economic evaluations (Fiorina 1981:40). The model of column 2, by Kiewiet (1983:98), offers a more extensive specification, including controls on party identification and a host of economic issues (most of which are not shown because they failed to achieve statistical significance). The pocketbook variable, "financial situation," consistently fails to reach a conventional level of statistical significance. The only significant personal

TABLE 6 Pocketbook vs sociotropic economic voting in the 1976 election

	(1)[a]	(2)[b]
Financial situation		
same	−0.03	
better	−0.06	−0.02
worse		−0.19
Head of household not unemployed	0.21[†]	
Business conditions		
same	−0.08	
better	0.35[‡]	0.53[‡]
worse		−0.15
Government inflation policy		
fair	0.07	
good	0.42[‡]	
Government unemployment policy		
fair	0.21[†]	
good	0.21	
Approve of Ford	1.39[‡]	
Approve Nixon pardon	0.85[‡]	
Civil rights		
too fast	0.19[†]	
too slow	−0.43[†]	
Republican		0.67[‡]
Democrat		−0.73[‡]
Percent correctly predicted	80.1	
Pseudo-R-squared		0.40
N	1379	923

[†]$p < 0.05$.

[‡]$p < 0.01$.

[a](1) The dependent variable is dichtomous (1 = Ford, 0 = Carter). The coding of the independent variables, all from the 1976 ANES, is described in Fiorina (1981:36–40). The estimation procedure is probit.

[b](2) The dependent variable, the data source, and the estimation procedure are the same as in column 1. The coding of the independent variables is described by Kiewiet (1983:95–99). The following independent variables were included in the analysis but are not in the table because they failed to reach statistical significance: the "personal economic experiences" variables of inflation, declining income, unemployment, taxes, and general economic problems; the "national economic assessments" variables of inflation, taxes, more government programs, less government spending, and general economic problems.

economic effect depends on whether the head of the respondent's household is employed ("head not unemployed" in column 2).

These results typify the literature, which concludes that in US presidential elections, there is little pocketbook voting. Kiewiet (1983:35) concluded that, in general, the probability of a presidential incumbent vote shifts only 13% even if all economic opinion moves from "worse than a year ago" to "better than a year ago." A pooled survey analysis arrived at a comparable estimate of rather faint pocketbook effects (Markus 1988). By contrast, sociotropic voting is relatively strong. According to column 1 of Table 6, favorable judgments of government policies on unemployment and inflation heightened the likelihood of a vote for the incumbent president. Furthermore, as shown in both columns 1 and 2, when voters see that general business conditions have improved, they are more likely to support the incumbent. In conclusion, Kiewiet (1983:99) remarked that sociotropic factors seem to have had an impressive effect on voting decisions.

Generally speaking, in US presidential elections, sociotropic evaluations are found, and they are unambiguously stronger than the pocketbook evaluations (Kinder & Kiewiet 1979, 1981). In his seminal book, Kiewiet (1983) reinforced this judgment, based on his analyses of presidential elections from 1960 to 1980. Subsequent studies of more recent contests continue to show strong collective effects and weak to nonexistent personal economic effects. [On the 1984 election, see Kinder et al (1989); on 1984 and 1988, see Lanoue (1994); on 1956–1988, see Markus (1992); on 1992 and 1996, see Alvarez & Nagler (1995, 1998).]

Look at results from the 1992 and 1996 presidential elections. In a multinomial probit estimation, Alvarez & Nagler(1995) found that, in 1992, family financial situation did not have a statistically significant impact on presidential choice, whereas the assessment of the national economy was very influential. Similarly, from their analysis of the 1996 ANES data, they concluded that "the national economy had a strong effect in returning Clinton to office in 1996.... The overwhelming impact of the economy in 1992 was not just a fluke" (Alvarez & Nagler 1998:1360–62). They observed that economic perceptions had a much greater impact on choice than perceptions about other issues. If a group of voters shifted their national economic assessment from "worse" to "better," the probability of their voting for Clinton rose by 0.38. This rise was much smaller for other issue shifts. When a group's opinion on Social Security shifted from wanting it increased (0.56) to wanting it cut (0.42), their likelihood of voting for Clinton shifted by 0.14; when their opinion on welfare shifted from "increase" (0.57) to "cut" (0.49), the likelihood of a Clinton vote shifted by 0.08; when their opinion on abortion shifted from pro-choice (0.59) to pro-life (0.29), the likelihood of a Clinton vote shifted by 0.30. Economics has a greater effect than all these other issues, including abortion.

The research reviewed thus far has focused on retrospective economic voting, which forms the bulk of the empirical evidence. However, there is some investigation of prospective effects. Its theoretical impetus comes from Downs, rather than Key. According to Downs (1957:39), "When a man votes, he is helping to select the government which will govern him during the coming election period....

He makes his decision by comparing future performances he expects from the competing parties." Fiorina (1981:139) explored the impact of 1976 ANES items on future economic expectations that asked whether the problems of inflation and unemployment "would be handled better by the Democrats, by the Republicans, or about the same by both." He found that they outperformed complex collective retrospective items (Fiorina 1981:170). Lewis-Beck (1988:121), examining a special battery of Michigan Consumer Survey questions, showed that prospective personal finances (a year from now you will be better off) were a statistically significant predictor of 1984 presidential vote intention, whereas retrospective personal finances items were not. In contrast, Lanoue (1994) found significant prospective effects operating in the 1988 presidential election but not in the 1984 election. Conducting an extensive investigation of the ANES presidential election surveys 1956–1988, Lockerbie (1992) learned that prospective economic voting effects were pervasive and were much stronger than retrospective effects. He calculated that, overall, prospective items had 43% of the impact of party identification. Although this is an impressive conclusion, it is undercut by the author's admitted difficulties with item consistency across the surveys.

In sum, the survey evidence shows that economic voting is a regular feature of US presidential elections, always representing an important, not to say the most important, issue in the campaign. Still, arguments persist in the research literature about the nature of its presence. Are the apparent economic effects a psychological artifact of placing the economic questions too close to the vote questions in the survey instrument, as Sears & Lau (1983) contended, at least for the pocketbook items? A proximity analysis of ANES economic evaluation and voting items by Lewis-Beck (1985) indicated that this hypothesized effect was not occurring. However, he did go on to agree with Sears & Lau that these contextual effects could take place in certain surveys, such as exit polls (Lewis-Beck 1988:50). As a general rule, prudence requires that key economic and political survey items be placed at a distance from each other, in order to avoid a reactivity bias.

Working with a special question battery in the Michigan Consumer Surveys prior to the 1984 presidential contest, Lewis-Beck (1988:121) separated the economic and political items by about 70 questions to forestall this contextual bias. Besides the expected impact of collective economic evaluations, he found significant pocketbook effects, but only of a prospective type (Lewis-Beck 1988:121). The finding is of special interest because it employed panel data, to better control for party identification (i.e. July vote intention was predicted from January party identification). Panel data have seldom been used in the economic voting literature, and then only for the purpose of getting less endogenous measures of party identification (see especially Fiorina 1981:98).

Utilizing panel data to explore the temporal dynamic of individual economic voting seems the next frontier in US presidential survey studies. When individuals are surveyed at two or more points in time, their evaluations can record real economic change; the variation observed is more likely to be causal. Positive results would help rule out Kramer's (1983) standing dissent that in a survey cross section there can be no "real" variance because there is only one economy being measured at one point in time. Further, the particular pattern of reported economic change observed in panel data would tap into regional variations in economic conditions, which have been largely neglected. Finally, the panel approach promises to overcome the biases that may persist even when cross sections and time series are pooled (Kiewiet & Rivers 1985:225).

US Congressional Voting

One might argue that economic voting research in the United States really began in the congressional arena, with a seminal paper by Kramer. His thesis was that when congressional voters judged economic performance to be satisfactory, they voted for the party of the president; otherwise, they did not (Kramer 1971:131). To test this proposition, he examined the effects of the macroeconomic indicators of inflation, unemployment, and income on House election outcomes in aggregate time series models (1896–1964, excluding 1912, 1918, 1942, and 1944). Income was found to have a statistically significant impact; a 1% decline in real per capita personal income produced a 0.5% fall in the House vote share of the incumbent party (Kramer 1971:140–41). Leading economists quickly attacked this finding, chiefly on the grounds that it made little sense for voters to think about the economy this way (Stigler 1973, Arcelus & Meltzer 1975). In response, Kramer carried out further analysis and arrived at the even stronger conclusion that "all three economic variables do influence congressional elections" (Goodman & Kramer 1975:1264).

Writing at about the same time, Tufte (1975, 1978) also uncovered potent economic effects on the congressional vote. He theorized that House elections held between presidential terms were referenda on the economic and political performance of the president. This straightfoward notion, coupled with powerful empirical results, helped spark numerous aggregate time series models featuring economic conditions and congressional elections. Table 7 gives three examples. In column 1 is Tufte's (1978:112) original midterm equation for a standardized House vote change, in which two highly significant independent variables, presidential approval and change in per capita disposable income, explain most of the variance. In column 2 is the Hibbs (1982:410) midterm equation, where roughly three quarters of the variance in incumbent House vote is attributable to income change (geometrically weighted). In column 3 is a preliminary Lewis-Beck & Rice (1992:63) extension, which modifies the dependent variable to examine directly incumbent-party seat change and which incorporates presidential-year elections. According to the model in column 3, economic effects remain strong, with a 1% rise in the growth rate of real disposable income generating a six-seat gain for the president's party. All three models, in sum, show important economic effects.

The results of Table 7 give some idea of the contours of political economy models for House elections. A few examples for the Senate could be trotted out, and they do show the importance of economic conditions in that arena (Abramowitz & Segal 1986, Lewis-Beck & Rice 1992:ch. 5). The Senate still seems to be the

TABLE 7 Selected models of congressional election outcomes (figures in parentheses are standard errors; * = statistically significant at 0.05 or better)

Variable	(1)[a]	(2)[b]	(3)[c]
Income	0.62*	0.93*	6.20*
	(0.17)	(0.21)	(1.93)
Popularity	0.13*		0.60*
	(0.04)		(0.30)
Midterm			29.08*
			(7.90)
Constant	−10.74	−3.15	−63.75
R-squared	0.825	0.76	0.66
N	8	9	22

[a](1) The dependent variable = standardized vote loss of president's party (percentage share corrected for average over eight previous elections); independent variables = income (the election-year change in real disposable income per capita) and popularity (Gallup presidential approval rating just before the election); N = midterm elections 1946–1974 (Tufte 1978:108–13).

[b](2) The dependent variable = standardized vote loss; independent variable = geometrically weighted average income (values closer to the election are weighted more heavily); N = midterm elections 1946–1978 (Hibbs 1982:410).

[c](3) The dependent variable = seat change for president's party; independent variables = income (growth rate of real disposable income six months prior to the election) and popularity (presidential job approval in the June Gallup). Midterm = a dummy for whether it is a midterm or on-year election; N = House elections 1948–1990 (Lewis-Beck & Rice 1992:60–66).

"forgotten side" of the economics and congressional elections debate (Hibbing & Alford 1982). But for the House, many aggregate time series models have been developed. Table 8 shows ten such House models and their explanatory variables. Some models focus only on midterm elections, whereas others include presidential election years as well. Further, the dependent variable is sometimes vote share and sometimes seat share. Regardless of these distinctions, or of the different independent variables over different time series, all produce good statistical fits, usually with R-squared values of ~0.8 or more.

Economics is almost always measured with a version of income. In some models, economics shows a significant effect, but in others it does not. In a few cases, the lack of economic effect is because economic variables are absent from the equation (Campbell 1986, Oppenheimer et al 1986). But in other cases, economics fails to register significance despite its presence in the specification (Jacobson 1989, Marra & Ostrom 1989, Erikson 1990, Alesina et al 1993). To resolve these contradictory findings, it is important to look at individual voters. Kiewiet (1983: 102–7) sequentially analyzed the House election surveys from the ANES, 1958–1980, estimating a series of probit equations containing a battery of economic

TABLE 8   Specification of leading congressional election models*

Author	Independent variables
Kramer (1971:140–141)	Election year per capita personal income (V)
Tufte (1978:112)	Election year income, fall Gallup Poll (V, M)
Hibbs (1982:410)	Geometric average of past income (V, M)
Campbell (1986)	Presidential vote, presidential popularity (M)
Oppenheimer et al (1986)	Seats exposed
Jacobson (1989:786)	Challenger quality, past seats, challenger quality times presidential popularity
Marra & Ostrom (1989:556)	Presidential popularity, popularity change, party identification, seats at risk, events
Erikson (1990:384–91)	Past House vote (V, M)
Lewis-Beck & Rice (1992:69)	Income, presidential popularity, seats exposed, incumbent tenure
Alesina et al (1993)	Republican incumbent, past vote, military mobilization, growth (V)

*V = dependent variable of vote share, otherwise it was seat share; M = only midterm elections were studied, otherwise it was midterm and on-year elections together. In order to appreciate fully the models, the reader should consult the original studies.

items, with a control on party identification. After finding that the "national business conditions" variable produced a statistically significant effect in five of the seven elections, he concluded, "Voters who believe that conditions in the nation's economy have improved over the previous year are much more likely to cast their ballots for congressional candidates of the incumbent president's party than are voters who believe that national economic conditions have deteriorated" (Kiewiet 1983:107).

Later work on congressional election surveys sustains the conclusion of individual level economic effects. Brown & Woods (1991) developed a structural equation model to compare the effects of local forces (party image, challenger quality, incumbency, and candidate evaluations) and national forces (party identification, issue proximity, and retrospective evaluations) on vote in the 1978 House elections. They reported significant pocketbook effects, as well as significant national retrospective economic effects, even after extensive controlling. This result was corroborated in a pooled analysis of ANES congressional surveys, 1980–1990, which found that personal and sociotropic retrospective economic variables moved voters to reward or punish House candidates of the incumbent party (Romero & Stambough 1996). Finally, Lockerbie (1991), examining the most extensive data set—the 14 ANES House surveys from 1956 through 1988—uncovered significant retrospective and, especially, prospective economic effects. (Unfortunately, consistent items on these two dimensions were not available across the surveys.) All told, the survey work on economic voting at the congressional level seems to establish the proposition that in House elections, voters do punish the president's party for economic bad times and reward it for good times.

The aggregate time series models that fail to show the connection between economics and elections appear to suffer from faulty measurement, specification, or analysis. This assessment is reinforced by Kiewiet & Udell's (1998) thorough reexamination of the original Kramer (1971) model. Using a longer time series (1892–1992) and improved measures, they showed that "regardless of the construction of alternative data series for GNP and unemployment, and regardless of the particular specification that was employed, a century of economic and political data uphold Kramer's basic findings: electoral support for congressional candidates of the incumbent party increases along with income and job growth, and decreases with higher rates of inflation" (Kiewiet & Udell 1998).

A MUCH-STUDIED NATION: France

Economic voting theory is transnational (Eulau & Lewis-Beck 1985:1) and merits testing in any democracy. Thus far, we have examined only the US case because by far the most research has been done on that case. The American work, however, encouraging as it is, can do no more than suggest that economics is a strong force in other electoral systems. Indeed, it may be that the US case is unique and holds no generalizations about economic voting. Therefore, a comparative look is important. We begin with a simple comparison to one other democracy— France. The theoretical argument for the comparison rests on the common claim that, among the advanced democracies, the US and France are exceptional (see Hoffman 1992:25). A Franco-American comparison, then, offers a tough test. If economic voting is vigorous in France, the notion that it is a powerful cross-national model receives support. Furthermore, because many French electoral institutions are different, the comparison allows signficant refinements of the conditions under which economic effects may vary. As with the US case, we first look at popularity functions, then vote functions, and finally individual-level survey data.

French Popularity Functions

Popularity functions for the French executive—the president or the prime minister—are plentiful. Typically, the dependent variable is the percentage who respond positively to the Institut Français d'Opinion Publique (IFOP) national survey sample question, "Are you satisfied with X as President (Prime Minister)?" The usual economic independent variables are income, inflation, and unemployment, controlled on a series of political dummies. The leader in this research, working since the late 1970s, has been Lafay. In Table 9 are two of his popularity functions, the first for the president, the second for the prime minister. Essentially, as in the

TABLE 9 Two French popularity functions (figures in parentheses are *t*-ratios)

	(1)[a]	(2)[b]
Inflation	−0.028* (3.4)	
Perceived inflation		0.30* (2.7)
Unemployment	−0.103* (6.6)	
Perceived unemployment		−0.26* (1.8)
Income	0.029* (3.1)	
Collective prospective		0.16 (1.4)
Exchange rate	−0.253* (6.8)	
Barre Plan	−0.310* (4.7)	
PM dummies		
Mauroy	0.707* (7.0)	37.25* (9.7)
Fabius		28.89* (9.1)
Chirac		19.40* (4.4)
R-squared	0.77	0.93
Degrees of freedom	104	91

*Statistical significance at 0.05 one-tail, or better.

[a](1) The dependent variable = logit of the proportion "satisfied" with the president in a monthly IFOP (Institut Français d'Opinion Publique) poll, measured monthly 1974–1983; the independent variables = inflation (rate over 6 months, lagged one month), unemployment (rate lagged one month), income (real disposable growth over 15 months, lagged one month), exchange rate (francs per dollar, lagged one month). The Barre Plan = a dummy for that prime minister's economic plan, PM dummy for the Socialists in government in and after June 1981; the estimation is weighted least squares (Lafay 1985:92–93).

[b](2) The dependent variable = popularity of the prime minister (percentage of respondents finding the prime minister "reliable" in a Societé Française d'enquêtes par sondage poll), monthly data from December 1978 to April 1987; independent variables = perceived inflation (percentage who think government is doing a good job against inflation), perceived unemployment (percentage who think government is doing a good job against unemployment), collective prospective evaluation (percentage who think conditions will improve in the near future); Mauroy, Fabius, Chirac = dummy variables for each new prime minister; other independent variables (not shown) are lagged values of perceived inflation, perceived unemployment, and the dependent variable. Estimation is with OLS (Lafay 1991:131).

US models, popularity is seen as a function of macroeconomic indicators (real or perceived)—income, inflation, and unemployment—plus dummies for political events and adminstrations.

These results are typical of the French case in that they show statistically significant economic effects and snug model fits. Numerous French popularity functions have been estimated by various scholars, and all but one (i.e. Lecaillon 1981) demonstrate an economic impact (see reviews in Lafay 1985, 1991). What is not clear is which of the three leading indicators—unemployment, income, or inflation—is most important. Nor is the lag structure clear. For example, the presidential popularity model of column 1 has long-distributed lagged economic effects of up to 15 months, whereas the model of Lewis-Beck (1980) has short, simple lagged effects from two months prior. Another underdeveloped issue is retrospective versus prospective economic impacts on popularity. (The coefficient of the collective prospective variable in column 1, Table 9, is the only empirical test of this idea. The result is suggestive, but falls short of statistical significance at the 0.05 level.)

French National Voting

In France, popularity function work has been largely set aside in favor of vote function work, where popularity is sometimes an independent variable. Lafay & Servais (1995:xv) found that popularity (of the parties) before an election was highly predictive of the result, and they made a very accurate forecast of the 1995 Chirac presidential victory. Presidential popularity itself (i.e. percent of respondents satisfied with the president) is highly correlated with presidential vote on the second round ($r = 0.77$), and it generates a comparable prediction (Lewis-Beck 1995). However, the macroeconomy alone is also very predictive. Table 10 shows selected vote function models for French elections.

In column 1, a measure of the economic growth rate accounts for almost all the variation in presidential election outcomes across the Fifth Republic. This effect holds only if the president is the "political economic incumbent," i.e. the chief public manager of the economy (Lewis-Beck 1997:321). If the president commands a ruling coalition in the National Assembly, then he has been responsible for shaping the economic policy of the nation. Under cohabitation, however, where the president and the prime minister are of rival coalitions, then the political economic incumbent becomes the prime minister. (This explains why, in the equation of column 1, the GNP variable is scored 0 for 1995. No economic performance was attributed to the Socialist President Mitterrand, since the prime minister was the Gaullist Balladur). French voters, then, are assumed to be rather sophisticated, appropriately shifting the target of economic responsibility (more on this below).

Vote function work on the French case actually began with legislative, rather than presidential, elections. The pathbreaking research of Rosa & Amson (1976) examined National Assembly contests from 1920 to 1973. They found that the vote share of leftist parties was heavily determined by fluctuations in inflation,

TABLE 10   Selected French vote functions (figures in parentheses are *t*-ratios)

Variable	(1)[a]	(2)[b]	(3)[c]
Popularity		−0.38*	
		(3.69)	
GNP	1.27*	−0.13	
	(7.48)	(0.05)	
Presidential vote			0.71*
			(7.69)
Unemployment			−4.73*
			(4.93)
Ideology			3.76*
			(4.27)
Instability			−1.31*
			(1.90)
Constant	47.26*	68.28*	11.39*
	(59.79)	(14.73)	(2.43)
R-squared	0.93	0.73	
Adjusted R-squared	0.92	0.65	0.71
SEE[†]	1.14	3.40	3.22
D-W[†]	2.47	1.82	
N	6	10	110

*Statistical significance at 0.05 one-tail, or better.

[†]SEE, standard error of estimate; D-W, Durbin-Watson statistic.

[a](1) The dependent variable = the percentage of second round presidential votes received by the candidate of incumbent party coalition, 1965–1995; independent variable = GNP (growth rate for the election year, except 1995 is coded 0); estimation = OLS (Lewis-Beck 1997:322).

[b](2) The dependent variable = percentage of first round National Assembly votes going to the opposition, 1958–1993; independent variables = presidential popularity six months before in an IFOP poll and GNP (the growth rate in the quarter six months before the election). Estimation = OLS (Lewis-Beck 1995:40).

[c](3) The dependent variable = percent of first round National Assembly vote going to the ruling coalition, by region (1978, 1981, 1986, 1988, 1993); independent variables = presidential vote [percentage of the last presidential vote (first round) going to candidates of the current ruling coalition], unemployment (change in the rate the year prior to the election), ideology [dummy to indicate whether since 1973 the region is ideologically (left versus right) voting consistently with the incumbent], instability (a dummy to indicate whether the legislative majority has switched ideologically at least twice since 1973). Estimation = OLS (Jérôme et al 1999).

unemployment, and income. In column 2 of Table 10 is a legislative vote function for Fifth Republic elections. It is similar in cast to many post–World War II US congressional election models. Opposition vote share is largely accounted for by presidential popularity and economic growth. (In contrast to the US case, collinearity plagues such models. For the variables of column 2, growth and popularity are correlated at 0.98.) This model, applied ex ante to forecast the 1997 National Assembly elections, surprised conventional wisdom by accurately predicting the defeat of the Right (Fauvelle-Aymar & Lewis-Beck 1997). Column 3 displays a somewhat different vote function, using a pooled time series design first pursued in France by Lafay (1993). Legislative election results from the 22 official regions of France are pooled across the 1978–1993 contests, yielding a much larger sample than the traditional vote functions allowed. The strategy permits detailed modeling of the region's political history and ideological tendencies, in addition to establishing strong economic effects. Specifically, the unemployment coefficient indicates that a one-percentage-point increase in the rate costs the ruling party coalition about 5% of the first-round vote (Jérôme et al 1999).

One limitation of the VP function literature is that it says nothing directly about how individual voters actually perceive and act on the economy. Several survey investigations, however, do point to the mental processes of the French economic voter. Table 11 provides selected vote equations estimated on individual survey respondents. The first, in column 1, is an idealized model in which legislative vote intention is held to be determined strictly by economic evaluations. The R-squared indicates that the economy, by itself, is capable of explaining a fair amount of variance in support for the ruling parliamentary coalition. There are no personal retrospective effects, a typical French finding. But collective effects, both retrospective and prospective, appear strong. For example, considered as a linear probability model, the equation says that, if the voter sees the economic future as likely to be improved, as opposed to made worse, the probability of an incumbent vote rises by 42% (Lewis-Beck 1988:56). Economic effects in presidential elections are assessed in column 2. This more fully specified model, estimated on second-ballot voters of the second and final ballot in the 1995 contest, demonstrates a similar pattern: no significant personal effects, but significant collective effects, especially prospective. Indeed, "the belief that Chirac would bring a better economy seems a decisive factor in his victory" (Lewis-Beck 1997:261).

The French electoral system has institutional features that allow the testing of economic voting under different rules. The influence of the two-ballot system is an example. On the first ballot of the 1995 presidential contest, there were eight leading candidates. With this wide array of choices, subtleties of economic voting can be explored. Lewis-Beck (1997:251–61) found support for a number of intriguing hypotheses. First, the closer the candidate was to the center of power, the more prevalent economic voting became. For instance, economic effects were highly visible in voting for the major party candidates—Gaullist, Socialist, Communist, National Front—but scarcely noticeable for minor party candidates. A second discovery was that voters were sophisticated, able under cohabitation to

TABLE 11   Selected survey models of the individual French vote

	(1)[a]	(2)[b]	(3)[c]
Personal Retrospective	0.00	0.02	
Collective Retrospective	0.06***	−0.09*	0.43*
Personal Prospective		−0.09*	
Collective Prospective	0.21***	−0.40**	
Personal Complex	−0.03		
Collective Complex	0.03		
Anger	0.08***		
Religion		−0.34**	−0.24***
Class		0.70**	0.14**
Ideology		1.82**	2.46***
Cohabitation			0.22***
Cohabitation × Economics			−0.24***
R-squared/percent correct	0.28	88.3%	74.9%
N	642	2321	5684

*Statistical significance at 0.10.

**Statistical significance at 0.05.

***Statistical significance at 0.01.

[a](1) The dependent variable = vote intention based on the question, "If there were a General Election tomorrow which party would you support"; ruling coalition (Socialist, Communist, MRG, PSU = 1); opposition (Gaullists, Radical UDF, CDS/UDF, PR/UDF, Ecologist, National Front = 0). Independent variables are personal retrospective (personal finances scored from 5 = "a lot better" to 1 = "worse"); collective retrospective (national economy, scored from 5 = "a lot better" to 1 = "worse"); collective prospective [a year from now government policies will have "improved" (= 1) the economy, "not made much difference" = 2, "made worse" = 3]; personal complex [the impact of government policies on personal finances was "good" (= 3) to "bad" (= 1)]; collective complex [the impact of government policies on the economy has been "good" (= 3) to "bad" (= 1)]; anger (feel angry over government economic policies, from "never" = 5 to "always" = 1. All the variables were measured in 1984 in Euro-Barometer No. 21, and estimation is OLS (Lewis-Beck 1988:56).

[b](2) The dependent variable = second ballot 1995 presidential vote (1 = Chirac, 0 = Jospin). Economic independent variables are personal retrospective, personal prospective, collective retrospective, and collective prospective economic evalutions (better = 1 to worse = 5); religion, i.e attendance at Mass (from 1 = "several times a week" to 6 = "never" or not Catholic); class, i.e. self-employed (1 = farmers, business, artisans, liberal professionals, 0 = other) and white-collar (1 = salaried, not blue-collar, 0 = other), which was not shown because it was not significant ; ideology [right-left self-placement from 7 (extreme right) to 1 (extreme left)]. The data are from the 1995 French National Election Survey; estimation is logit (Lewis-Beck 1997).

[c](3) The dependent variable is a dichotomy, vote intention for incumbent party scored 1 (Socialists if the prime minister is Socialist, RPR-UDF if the prime minister is RPR-UDF), 0 = otherwise. The independent variable of economics is the collective retrospective evaluation of the national economy (1 = better to −1 = worse). The remaining independent variables are ideology (left to right, from −1 to +1); religion = 1 for regular Mass attenders, 0 for irregular Mass attenders, −1 = otherwise. Class = 1 for blue collar workers, = −1 for self-employed, and 0 = other; cohabitation = 1 for a cohabitation period (1986–1988, 1993–1995); cohabitation × Economics = an interaction term, the estimation is logit. The data are from a Euro-Barometer pool, 1984–1994 (Lewis-Beck & Nadeau 2000).

place economic responsibility with the prime minister and his party rather than the president. That is, a perception of economic downturn took first-ballot votes from Prime Minister Balladur, a Gaullist candidate, but gave first-ballot votes to Jospin, the Socialist candidate. Third, cohabitation, another institutional feature of the French system, has its own effects on economic voting, as the equation in column 3 shows. In National Assembly elections, the impact of collective retrospective voting is cut in half if the contest occurs during a cohabitation period. Apparently, voters recognize that a prime minister who must work with a president from a rival coalition is inevitably a less effective economic manager; therefore, they mete out less praise or blame at the legislative ballot box (Lewis-Beck & Nadeau 2000).

OTHER SINGLE-NATION STUDIES: Britain, Denmark, and the Rest

The economic voting hypothesis has been pursued in other country studies. After the United States and France, the most commonly studied countries are Britain and Denmark. Economic voting effects, sometimes rather strong ones, have been uncovered in virtually all these studies.

BRITAIN

Popularity functions characterize the research on Britain (but for a thoughtful exception, see Hibbing 1987). This emphasis is no surprise; the first popularity function paper ever published (Goodhart & Bhansali 1970) was on the British case. This pathbreaking article posed the question that has now been repeated worldwide: "[H]ow far were swings in political popularity affected by economic circumstances?" (Goodhart & Bhansali 1970:45). The authors sought to model government popularity, measured from a public opinion time series on vote intention in the now familiar way, as a function of key macroeconomic indicators and electoral trends. According to their results, government support was strongly responsive to the inflation rate and the unemployment level. Their bold confirmation of the political-economy idea sparked other papers, some of which supported the idea (Frey & Schneider 1978b, Pissarides 1980, Whiteley 1986) and some of which did not (Miller & Mackie 1973, Mosley 1978, Chrystal & Alt 1981).

The apparent impasse over the modeling of British popularity functions was broken with the introduction of Falklands (Malvinas) War variables. Some researchers found that Falklands effects dwarfed economic effects (Dunleavy & Husbands 1985, Clarke et al 1986, Norpoth 1987). Others found massive economic effects and trivial Falklands effects (Sanders et al 1987). The economic variables they identified were personal economic expectations, the unemployment rate, the exchange rate, and the public sector borrowing requirement.

Since the Falklands War, British popularity function work has evolved in focus, examining the more general question of the dimensions of economic voting—retrospective or prospective, personal or collective (Clarke & Stewart 1995, Price & Sanders 1995, Clarke et al 1997). In the models, objective macroeconomic indicators are giving way to aggregated economic perceptions based on monthly surveys. For example, in the Sanders et al (1991:166) study, the personal expectations index was built from the monthly Gallup item, "How do you think the financial situation of your household will change over the next twelve months?" Besides this aggregated personal prospective measure, there are personal retrospective, collective prospective, and national retrospective measures. In Britain, Sanders (1991, 1993) has championed the determining role of the personal prospective dimension for government popularity.

Sanders (2000) has summarized many of the findings–and much of the controversy—surrounding economic voting in the United Kingdom today. Monthly popularity is modeled in an extended time series, 1974–1997, with controls imposed for the Falklands War and the Thatcher removal. He found that the macroeconomic indicators of inflation and unemployment have no effect. However, subjective economic assessments—personal expectations, inflation perceptions, and unemployment perceptions—have significant, predictable effects. (It is worth noting that whereas the personal assessment is prospective, the collective assessments of inflation and the economy are retrospective). He concluded that "voters reward government with their support if their economic prospects look good and if they perceive that unemployment and inflation are falling; they inflict punishment by withdrawing their support if expectations are falling or if they perceive that unemployment or inflation are rising" (Sanders 2000).

Denmark

Denmark provides a useful European contrast to the British case. Economic voting research on this small, continental, multiparty democracy has yielded different results. The first Danish popularity function paper, which in standard fashion linked objective macroeconomics with government support, showed that that link snapped in the 1970s (Paldam & Schneider 1980). In a recent effort by Nannestad & Paldam (2000), the dependent variable was government support (as a monthly average of different polls between 1986 and 1997), where the government was four times a Conservative-Liberal–led coalition and once a Social Democratic–led coalition (1993–1997). The focus has switched to the effects of perceptual measures of the economy, aggregated from the monthly government Consumer Confidence Index—sociotropic retrospective, sociotropic prospective, egotropic retrospective, and egotropic prospective. After an extensive series of tests, the authors concluded that during 1986–1997, "the level of government support in Denmark is not influenced by the level of the variables measuring economic evaluation" and that, based on their data, "there simply was no economic voting in Denmark during this period" (Nannestad & Paldam 2000).

Nevertheless, cross-sectional survey research by these and other investigators has found substantial economic voting in this period. Nannestad & Paldam (1995) examined multiple surveys from 1990 to 1993, containing a battery of 13 economic evaluation questions and vote intention questions. They found pervasive economic voting, but it took an unusual form—egotropic effects dominated sociotropic effects, which were extremely weak. Thus, they presented the strongest case for pocketbook voting in the entire economics and elections survey literature. Their explanation for the result is the "cultural hypothesis. In a welfare state the government *is* responsible for the economy of the individual, so it is only reasonable that he hold it responsible in his voting" (Nannestad & Paldam 1995:57, italics in original). Furthermore, they have replicated the result in an elaborate, pooled, cross-sectional time series design, described in "From the Pocketbook of the Welfare Man" (Nannestad & Paldam 1997).

Despite the allure of the unique claim, the Danish "pocketbook voter" has not been discovered by other researchers. Hibbs (1993) strongly argued against its existence, saying that collective societies foster sociotropic, not egotropic, voters. Borre (1997), employing surveys of the 1987, 1990, and 1994 general elections, estimated economic voting models for each. The dependent variable was dichotomous (vote for a government party or not), the control variables were social class and left-right ideology, and the economic variables were a personal retrospective item (on family economic situation) and a collective retrospective item (on the economic situation of the country). He found that there were never significant pocketbook effects, but there were always significant collective effects (Borre 1997:357). He concluded that evaluation of the national economy "exerts a considerable effect on the vote ... those who believe the economy has improved a lot give the government on the average a 28 percent higher vote than those who believe the economy has deteriorated a lot" (Borre 1997:359).

In sum, Borre's conclusions are essentially the opposite of Nannestad & Paldam's. Why the differences? Hibbs (1993:21) asserted that the unusual results of Nannestad & Paldam stem, at least in part, from their failure to use a standard simple retrospective item on the national economy. But Nannestad & Paldam (1994) claimed that they examined such an item, along with four other sociotropic measures, and still came to the same conclusion. The puzzle of the Danish case has yet to be solved.

Other Single-Nation Studies

Besides Denmark and Britain, economic voting studies have been carried out in many other democracies. At least one paper can be cited for virtually every established democracy, and work is under way on at least some of the new democracies. However, to take the risk of characterization, the relevant research in most of these remaining nations tends to be represented by one investigator, one approach, or even one article. This characterization implies nothing about the quality of the work, but it does mean that these single-country findings are short on the dynamic needed to sustain a review narrative. Therefore, we simply list economic and elections publications from selected other democracies: Canada (Clarke & Kornberg 1992, Nadeau & Blais 1993); Germany (Feld & Kirchgässner 2000); Italy (Bellucci 1991); Japan (Anderson & Ishii 1997); Mexico (Brophy-Baermann 1994); the Netherlands (Irwin & Van Holsteyn 1997); Poland (Powers & Cox 1997); Russia (Colton 1996); Spain (Lancaster & Lewis-Beck 1989). Consulting these works or their authors will give the reader a good start on the relevant data and issues for modeling the economic vote in the country of interest. The list is limited to English language publications, as we assume that area specialists versed in the language of the country can more effectively pursue an in-depth search.

MULTIPLE-NATION STUDIES

So far, we have looked at how economic voting theory stands up in individual democracies. On the basis of that research review, it is safe to say that economic forces impose a heavy and variegated rule on elections in the United States, France, Britain, and Demark. These countries are certainly not identical. The steady stream of positive results issuing from them increases our confidence and knowledge about the generalizability of political economic effects. But what of other nations? Are these positive results peculiar to these four? As a check against this small-sample problem ($N = 4$), we need studies that examine many nations. Fortunately, there are several such studies. Most sample the high-income democracies, such as the nations of Western Europe. But there is a growing body of comparative economic voting research on the low-income democracies, and some relevant research even samples from the world's population of democracies.

The High-Income Democracies

Paldam (1991) was the first to look at a pooled vote function. He considered 17 high-income democracies (Australia, Belgium, Canada, Denmark, Ireland, Finland, France, Germany, the Netherlands, Italy, Japan, New Zealand, Norway, Austria, Sweden, the United Kingdom, and the United States), which yielded an aggregated data base of 197 elections, over the time period 1948–1985. The dependent variable was percentage point vote change for the government from one election to the next, the economic independent variables were inflation, growth, and unemployment (at different lags), and the controls were a series of institutional variables (country size, number of parties, left-right rule, years in power, and majority-minority government). Paldam (1991:25) commented that the economic results "are either insignificant or explain very little indeed." By contrast, another pooled vote function analysis of similar design, but limited to five nations (Britain, France, Germany, Italy, and Spain) and 27 elections (1967–1987), found that rising unemployment and inflation significantly lowered the number of seats won by the ruling coalition (Lewis-Beck & Mitchell 1990).

Following these two studies, Powell & Whitten (1993) conducted an economic voting analysis on ~100 aggregated elections, 1969–1988, from a cross section of 19 industrialized nations. They reported that economic voting depends on political context, defined as voting cohesion in government, nature of the committee system, strength of the bicameral opposition, minority government status, and coalition government status. These conditions determine whether responsibility for economic policy is clear. In countries with clear lines of responsibility, GDP growth and unemployment (directly and interactively) significantly affected the government vote; however, in countries where policy responsibility is unclear, none of these variables were significant. Chappell & Veiga (2000) have examined the responsibility hypothesis in their own pooled analysis of 136 elections from 13 Western European countries (Austria, Belgium, Denmark, Finland, France, Germany, Ireland, Italy, the Netherlands, Portugal, Spain, Sweden, and the United Kingdom). Responsibility variables—main party, coalition government, minority government, and openness—do not significantly influence change in government support. However, the inflation rate does. "Our strongest finding is that voters punish increases in inflation" (Chappell & Veiga 2000).

These aggregate, essentially Western European, pooled studies are contradictory. Some show economic effects, some do not. Among the studies that show an effect, there is dispute about whether the effect depends on political context. These disagreements can be partly resolved by looking at individual voters in these countries. Lewis-Beck (1988) estimated the same individual economic voting model on election survey data from five Western European nations. Although he uncovered no pocketbook effects, he found sharp collective retrospective and prospective effects. Further, "Changing economic conditions exert a force on Western European voters that approaches and sometimes exceeds the force of more traditional factors" (Lewis-Beck 1988:85). He discovered that economic voting varied in strength by country; it was strongest in Britain, followed by Spain, Germany, France, and Italy in that order (Lewis-Beck 1988:105). The key variable accounting for this pattern was "coalitional complexity," i.e. the number of parties in the ruling coalition (Lewis-Beck 1988:108). At one extreme was Britain, with one ruling party, and at the other extreme was Italy, with five parties in the ruling coalition. An economically disgruntled voter may have difficulty deciding which party to blame when several parties govern (Anderson 1995). With a multiparty ruling coalition, there is a "diffusion of government responsibility" and incumbent alternatives for dissent (Lewis-Beck 1986:341).

These particular individual-level survey findings by Lewis-Beck reinforce the aggregate findings of Powell & Whitten on the conditioning role of "clarity of responsibility." Anderson (2000) further developed this line of argument, in a convincing, pooled cross-sectional examination of 1994 Eurobarometer surveys from 13 European countries: Belgium, Denmark, France, Germany, Greece, Ireland, Italy, Luxembourg, the Netherlands, Norway, Portugal, Spain, and the United Kingdom. For example, he found statistically significant retrospective sociotropic effects in countries with either low or high clarity of responsibility (using the

Powell & Whitten measure). However, the effect was 1.5 times greater in the high-clarity group than in the low-clarity group. Overall, Anderson concluded that "voters' ability to express discontent with economic performance is enhanced when accountablity is simple. Voters' economic assessments have stronger effects on government support when it is clear who the target is, when the target is sizable, and when voters have only a limited number of viable alternatives to throw their support to" (Anderson 2000).

The Low-Income Democracies

The low-income democracies have been the subject of much less economic voting research than the United States and Western Europe. Nevertheless, important work has begun. Pacek (1994) provided the first comparative look at macroeconomic conditions and electoral outcomes in Eastern Europe. Examining 1990–1992 district-level data for Poland, Czechoslovakia, and Bulgaria, he found that rising unemployment lowered the vote support for reformist incumbent administrations. A more recent Eastern European analysis (Fidrmuc 2000) examined a pooled county-level data set on 1992–1998 elections from the Czech Republic, Hungary, Poland, and Slovakia ($N = 442$). Fidrmuc found that change in the vote share of the government was significantly influenced, in the expected direction, by unemployment change and wage growth. According to Fidrmuc (2000), "there is indeed a strong relationship between economic developments and voting behavior in the post-communist societies." Survey research results to underpin these macro-level findings are scarce. But Anderson et al (2000) have compared political economy models of the vote for Nicaragua and Hungary, using election survey data. According to their analysis of the 1994 Hungarian parliamentary election (and the 1990 Nicaraguan election), incumbent vote was significantly influenced by collective retrospective and collective prospective economic evaluations.

Remmer (1991:785) analyzed 21 presidential elections in 12 Latin American countries and claimed that her "results provide some support for the view that incumbents pay the price for short-term economic setbacks." Moreover, she reported that her results provide a Latin American extension of the political economy connection found in US and Western European elections. Pacek & Radcliff (1995) conducted a more general analysis of economics and elections in the developing world. They studied observations on 52 elections in eight nations: Botswana, Costa Rica, India, Jamaica, Sri Lanka, Trinidad and Tobago, Uruguay, and Venezuela. The dependent variable was incumbent vote share in presidential elections, regressed on the economic independent variable of change in real per capita GNP, plus controls (including a lagged dependent variable and country dummies). They found strong economic effects: "[E]ach percentage point decline in real per capita Gross Domestic Product [costs] the incumbent governments about 1.1% of the vote" (Pacek & Radcliff 1995:735). They concluded "that economic conditions may be far more important determinants of the vote in developing countries than in the West, at least when times are bad."

Finally, Wilkin et al (1997) sampled from the world's list of democracies, developing and developed ($N = 38$ elections, 1998–1994). They reported that for "every percentage point of GDP growth in the election year, [the major incumbent] party stands to gain 1.4 per cent of the vote" (Wilkin et al 1997:307). Their fitting conclusion was that "regardless of the complexities of the political context—whether it is fragmented party systems, coalition governments, divided control, or lack of party cohesion—voters around the world find a way of translating economic demands into partisan support" (Wilkin et al 1997:314).

SUMMARY AND CONCLUSION

Economics and elections form a tight weave. When anchoring economic threads snag, governments can fall. We have reviewed these interlacings at the macro and micro levels, in the electorate and in the elector. Electorates, the "nation as voter," are strongly affected by global economic fluctuations, real and perceived. For all democratic nations that have received a reasonable amount of study, plausible economic indicators, objective or subjective, can be shown to account for much of the variance in government support. In multivariate competition, controlling for other aggregate issue measures, the economic indicators hold their own. Indeed, the savvy modeler, given the choice of only one predictor, would do well to select an economic measure. Which one? The answer varies from country to country. It could be unemployment, inflation, or growth, perhaps measured perceptively, perhaps at a lag. That measurement variability is not a theoretical weakness. Rather, it incorporates, as it should, the institutional history of economic performance and statistical reporting in that particular country. Also, it is in harmony with the value of specifying political context, as is done in the positive cross-national studies. Electoral institutions, which shape the distribution of political economic responsibility in a nation, can affect much. Where government is led by one party, rather than several in coalition, the economy-polity link is especially firm.

The powerful relationship between the economy and the electorate in democracies the world over comes from the economic responsiveness of the electors, the individual voters. Among the issues on the typical voter's agenda, none is more consistently present, nor generally has a stronger impact, than the economy. Citizen dissatisfaction with economic performance substantially increases the probability of a vote against the incumbent. In a sense, it is even more important than long-term factors such as partisan identification, because of its greater volatility. Opinion on economic performance—satisfied versus dissatisfied—can alter dramatically from one election to the next, whereas party identification and other long-term forces change little. Thus, the fall of a government is more likely to come from a shift in economic evaluations than from a shift in party attachments.

What is the psychology of the economic vote? The classic reward-punishment model appears sound. Voters, regardless of the democracy in which they live, assess national economic conditions and reward or punish the politicians responsible for those conditions. When judging the economy, they tend to look at multiple indicators rather than a single one (e.g. only unemployment) and arrive finally at a summary view. That view is subjective; it comes from an internal calculus that may use unique weights, and it is based on impressions from various sources, as well as on hard numbers from statistical reports. For example, a voter may decide that the economy has done badly over the last year. This collective retrospective judgment will tend to produce a vote against a party in government. Moreover, economic voters are not naive. They discern when a party is more clearly responsible for economic policy, and adjust the likelihood of their sanction accordingly. Further, they are capable of prospective judgments on party promises, in conjunction with retrospective judgments of party performance.

We have evaluated the evidence from economics and elections research, drawn conclusions about the state of our knowledge, and provided a depiction of the economic voter. We have covered much, but space limitations prevented us from covering everything. This review has focused on national (i.e. presidential, legislative) elections, to the exclusion of gubernatorial, state, primary, or local elections (Simon et al 1991, Lewis-Beck & Rice 1992:ch. 7, Bowler & Donovan 1994, Mondardi 1994, Partin 1995, Jérôme & Lewis-Beck 1999). The dependent variable of vote was always about party or candidate share, never vote turnout (Rosenstone 1982, Pacek & Radcliff 1995, Southwell 1996). The overarching hypothesis tested was the symmetric reward or punishment of the incumbent. The idea that economic voting is asymmetric, with mostly punishment and little reward (or vice versa), was not pursued (Bloom & Price 1975, Lewis-Beck 1988:ch. 5, Radcliff 1994). Nor was the policy-oriented hypothesis pursued. It stresses that the economic voter favors a different party for different problems, e.g. Democrats are considered better at dealing with unemployment, regardless of incumbency status (Weatherford 1978, Kiewiet 1983:99, Parker 1986, Hibbs 1992). This missing literature is not huge, but it does exist.

What should the agenda for future research be? Since economic voters act largely on their perceptions of the national economy, it is important to know what they actually know about the economy. Data on the economic information of the average voter are being gathered, but more work should be done (Holbrook & Garand 1996, Blendon et al 1997, Paldam & Nannestad 2000). Because a good deal of the average voter's economic information must come from the media, establishing these media connections is in order (Behr & Iyengar 1985, Mutz 1994, Goidel & Langley 1995, Hetherington 1996, Holbrook 1996a, Haller & Norpoth 1997). This work, and actually almost all extant economic voting research, assumes the most relevant evaluation dimension is global economic output, i.e. "How is the nation's economy doing?" But economic distribution may be an emerging relevant dimension. That is, what are the electoral effects of rising income inequality and insecurity? We can cite no published scientific paper on that exciting question. Another area where little research has been done is the impact of electoral institutions on economic voting within single countries. The French research is suggestive and signals possibilities for work in other countries. Within Europe generally, there is also the question of the effects of the European Union on economic voting nationally and for the European Parliament. Finally, little is known about economic voting in Third World countries (although this is changing, as the papers reviewed here attest). One imagines that the reward-punishment paradigm can be extended to transitional democracies in Africa, for example. However, different dimensions, such as economic globalization, may emerge as more important. In fact, in the long run, increasing globalization may change the character of economic voting in western nations as well.

Visit the Annual Reviews home page at www.AnnualReviews.org

LITERATURE CITED

Abramowitz A. 1988. An improved model for predicting presidential election outcomes. *PS* 21:843–47

Abramowitz A. 1996. Bill and Al's excellent adventure: forecasting the 1996 presidential election. *Am. Polit. Q.* 24:434–42

Abramowitz A, Segal J. 1986. Determinants of the outcomes of Senate elections. *J. Polit.* 48:433–40

Alesina A, Londregan J, Rosenthal H. 1993. A model of the political economy of the United States. *Am. Polit. Sci. Rev.* 87:12–33

Alvarez RM, Nagler J. 1995. Economics, issues and the Perot candidacy: voter choice in the 1992 presidential elections. *Am. J. Polit. Sci.* 39:714–44

Alvarez RM, Nagler J. 1998. Economics, entitlements, and social issues: voter choice in the 1996 presidential election. *Am. J. Polit. Sci.* 42:1349–63

Anderson CJ. 1995. *Blaming the Government: Citizens and the Economy in Five European Democracies.* Armonk, NY: Sharpe

Anderson CJ. 2000. Economic voting and political context: a comparative perspective. *Electoral Stud.* In press

Anderson CJ, Ishii J. 1997. The political economy of election outcomes in Japan. *Br. J. Polit. Sci.* 27:619–30

Anderson L, Lewis-Beck MS, Stegmaier M.

2000. Post-socialist democratization: a comparative political economy model of the vote for Hungary and Nicaragua. *Studiji Politolohichnoho Tsentru Geneza.* Lviv, Ukraine: In press

Arcelus F, Meltzer AH. 1975. The effects of aggregate economic variables on congressional elections. *Am. Polit. Sci. Rev.* 69:1232–40

Beck N. 1991. The economy and presidential approval: an information theoretic perspective. See Norpoth et al 1991, pp. 85–102

Behr R, Iyengar S. 1985. Television news, real-world cues, and changes in the public agenda. *Public Opin. Q.* 49:38–57

Bellucci P. 1991. Italian economic voting: a deviant case or making a case for a better theory?, 1953–1979. See Norpoth et al 1991, pp. 63–84

Blendon RJ, Benson JM, Brodie M, Morin R, Altman DE, et al. 1997. Bridging the gap between the public's and economists' views of the economy. *J. Polit. Econ. Persp.* 11(3): 105–18

Bloom H, Price D. 1975. Voter response to short-run economic conditions: the asymmetric effect of prosperity and recession. *Am. Polit. Sci. Rev.* 69:124–54

Borre O. 1997. Economic voting in Danish electoral surveys 1987–1994. *Scand. Polit. Stud.* 20(4):347–65

Bowler S, Donovan T. 1994. Economic conditions and voting on ballot propositions. *Am. Polit. Q.* 22:27–40

Brophy-Baermann M. 1994. Economics and elections: the Mexican case. *Soc. Sci. Q.* 75: 125–35

Brown RD, Woods JA. 1991. Toward a model of congressional elections. *J. Polit.* 53:454–73

Campbell J. 1986. Forecasting the 1986 midterm elections to the House of Representatives. *PS:* 83–87

Campbell J. 1996. Polls and votes: the trial-heat presidential election forecasting model, certainty, and political campaigns. *Am. Polit. Q.* 24:408–33

Campbell J, Garand J, eds. 2000. *Before the Vote: Forecasting American National Elections.* Thousand Oaks, CA: Sage

Campbell J, Wink K. 1990. Trial-heat forecasts of the presidential vote. *Am. Polit. Q.* 18: 251–69

Chappell H, Keech W. 1985. A new view of political accountability of economic performance. *Am. Polit. Sci. Rev.* 79:10–27

Chappell H, Keech W. 1991. Explaining aggregate evaluations of economic performance. See Norpoth et al 1991, pp. 207–20

Chappell H, Veiga LG. 2000. Economics and elections in Western Europe: 1960–1997. *Electoral Stud.* 19: In press

Chrystal KA, Alt JE. 1981. Some problems in formulating and testing a politico-economic model of the United Kingdom. *Econ. J.* 91: 730–36

Clarke H, Kornberg A. 1992. Support for the Canadian Federal Progressive Conservative Party since 1988: the impact of economic evaluations and economic issues. *Can. J. Polit. Sci.* 25:29–53

Clarke H, Stewart M. 1994. Prospections, retrospections, and rationality: the "bankers" model of presidential approval. *Am. J. Polit. Sci.* 38:104–23

Clarke H, Stewart M. 1995. Economic evaluations, prime ministerial approval and governing party support: rival models considered. *Br. J. Polit. Sci.* 25:145–70

Clarke H, Stewart M, Whiteley P. 1997. Tory trends: party identification and the dynamics of conservative support since 1992. *Br. J. Polit. Sci.* 27:299–319

Clarke H, Stewart M, Zuk G. 1986. Politics, economics and party popularity in Britain, 1979–1983. *Electoral Stud.* 5:123–41

Colton TJ. 1996. Economics and voting in Russia. *Post-Soviet Aff.* 12(4):289–317

Downs A. 1957. *An Economic Theory of Democracy.* New York: Harper & Row

Dunleavy P, Husbands CT. 1985. *British Democracy at the Crossroads: Voting and Party Competition in the 1980s.* London: Allen & Unwin

Erikson RS. 1989. Economic conditions and the presidential vote. *Am. Polit. Sci. Rev.* 83(2): 568–73

Erikson RS. 1990. Economic conditions and the congressional vote: a review of the macrolevel evidence. *Am. J. Polit. Sci.* 34: 373–99

Erikson RS, MacKuen MB, Stimson JA. 2000. Bankers or peasants revisited: economic expectations and presidential approval. *Electoral Stud.* 19: In press

Eulau H, Lewis-Beck MS, eds. 1985. *Economic Conditions and Electoral Outcomes: The United States and Western Europe.* New York: Agathon

Fair R. 1978. The effect of economic events on votes for president. *Rev. Econ. Stat.* 60:159–73

Fair R. 1982. The effect of economic events on votes for president: 1980 results. *Rev. Econ. Stat.* 63:322–25

Fair R. 1988. The effect of economic events on votes for president: 1984 update. *Polit. Behav.* 10:168–77

Fair R. 1996. Econometrics and presidential elections. *J. Polit. Econ. Persp.* 10:89–102

Fauvelle-Aymar C, Lewis-Beck MS. 1997. L'Iowa donne l'opposition gagnante. *Libération* 4978(23 mai):15

Feld LP, Kirchgässner G. 2000. Official and hidden unemployment and the popularity of government: an econometric analysis of the Kohl government. *Electoral Stud.* 19: In press

Fidrmuc J. 2000. Economics of voting in post-communist countries. *Electoral Stud.* In press

Fiorina M. 1978. Economic retrospective voting in American national elections: a micro-analysis. *Am. J. Polit. Sci.* 22:426–43

Fiorina M. 1981. *Retrospective Voting in American National Elections.* New Haven, CT: Yale Univ. Press

Frey BS, Schneider F. 1978a. An empirical study of politico-economic interaction in the U.S. *Rev. Econ. Stat.* 60:174–83

Frey BS, Schneider F. 1978b. A politico-break economic model of the United Kingdom. *Econ. J.* 88:243–53

Goidel RK, Langley RE. 1995. Media coverage of the economy and aggregate economic evaluations: uncovering evidence of indirect media effects. *Polit. Res. Q.* 48:313–28

Golden D, Poterba J. 1980. The price of popularity: the political business cycle reexamined. *Am. J. Polit. Sci.* 24:696–714

Goodhart CAE, Bhansali RJ. 1970. Political economy. *Polit. Stud.* 18:43–106

Goodman S, Kramer G. 1975. Comment on Arcelus and Meltzer, the effect of aggregate economic conditions on congressional elections. *Am. Polit. Sci. Rev.* 69:1255–65

Haller HB, Norpoth H. 1997. Reality bites: news exposure and economic opinion. *Public Opin. Q.* 61:555–75

Hetherington M. 1996. The media's role in forming voters' national economic evaluations in 1992. *Am. J. Polit. Sci.* 40:372–95

Hibbing J. 1987. On the issues surrounding economic voting: looking to the British case for answers. *Comp. Polit. Stud.* 20:3–33

Hibbing J, Alford J. 1982. Economic conditions and the forgotten side of congress: a foray in U.S. Senate elections. *Br. J. Polit. Sci.* 12:505–13

Hibbs DA. 1982. President Reagan's mandate from the 1980 elections: a shift to the right? *Am. Polit. Q.* 10:387–420

Hibbs DA. 1987. *The American Political Economy: Macroeconomics and Electoral Poli-*tics. Cambridge, MA: Harvard Univ. Press

Hibbs DA. 1992. Partisan theory after fifteen years. *Eur. J. Polit. Economy* 8:361–73

Hibbs DA. 1993. *Solidarity or Egoism?* Aarhus, Denmark: Aarhus Univ. Press

Hibbs D, Rivers D, Vasilatos N. 1982. On the demand for economic outcomes: macroeconomic performance and mass political support in the United States, Great Britain, and Germany. *J. Polit.* 43:426–62

Hoffman S. 1992. Delusions of world order. *NY Rev. Books* 39(7):37–43

Holbrook T. 1996a. *Do Campaigns Matter?* Thousand Oaks, CA: Sage

Holbrook T. 1996b. Reading the political tea leaves: a forecasting model of contemporary presidential elections. *Am. Polit. Q.* 24:506–19

Holbrook T, Garand J. 1996. Homo economus? Economic information and economic voting. *Polit. Res. Q.* 49:351–75

Irwin G, Van Holsteyn J. 1997. Where to go from here? Revamping electoral politics in the Netherlands. *West Eur. Polit.* 20(2):93–118

Jacobson GC. 1989. Strategic politicians and the dynamics of U.S. House elections, 1946–86. *Am. Polit. Sci. Rev.* 83:773–93

Jérôme B, Jérôme V, Lewis-Beck MS. 1999. Polls fail in France: forecasts of the 1997 legislative election. *Int. J. Polit. Forecasting* 15:175–84

Jérôme B, Lewis-Beck MS. 1999. Is local politics local? French evidence. *Eur. J. Polit. Res.* 35(March):181–97

Kenski H. 1977. The impact of economic conditions on presidential popularity. *J. Polit.* 39:764–73

Kernell S. 1978. Explaining presidential popularity. *Am. Polit. Sci. Rev.* 71:44–66

Key VO. 1964. *Politics, Parties, and Pressure Groups.* New York: Crowell. 5th ed.

Key VO. 1966. *The Responsible Electorate.* New York: Vintage

Kiewiet DR. 1983. *Macroeconomics and Micropolitics: The Electoral Effects of Economic Issues.* Chicago: Univ. Chicago Press

Kiewiet DR, Rivers D. 1985. A retrospective on retrospective voting. In *Economic Conditions and Electoral Outcomes: The United States and Western Europe*, ed. H Eulau, MS Lewis-Beck, pp. 207–31

Kiewiet DR, Udell M. 1998. Twenty-five years after Kramer: an assessment of economic retrospective voting based upon improved estimates of income and unemployment. *Econ. Polit.* 10:219–48

Kinder D, Adams G, Gronke PW. 1989. Economics and politics in the 1984 American presidential election. *Am. J. Polit. Sci.* 33:491–515

Kinder D, Kiewiet DR. 1979. Economic discontent and political behavior: the role of personal grievances and collective economic judgements in congressional voting. *Am. J. Polit. Sci.* 23:495–527

Kinder D, Kiewiet DR. 1981. Sociotropic politics: the American case. *Br. J. Polit. Sci.* 11(April):129–41

Kramer G. 1971. Short-term fluctuations in U.S. voting behavior, 1896–1964. *Am. Polit. Sci. Rev.* 65:131–43

Kramer G. 1983. The ecological fallacy revisited: aggregate- versus individual-level findings on economics and elections, and sociotropic voting. *Am. Polit. Sci. Rev.* 77:92–111

Lafay JD. 1985. Important political change and the stability of the popularity function: before and after the French general election of 1981. In *Economic Conditions and Electoral Outcomes: The United States and Western Europe*. ed. H Eulau, MS Lewis-Beck, pp. 78–97. New York: Agathon

Lafay JD. 1991. Political dyarchy and popularity functions: lessons from the 1986 French experience. See Norpoth et al 1991, pp. 123–39

Lafay. JD 1993. Les prévisions des modèles politico-économiques. *Figaro* (19 mars):IX

Lafay JD, Servais M. 1995. Des sondages préélectoraux aux modèles politico-économétriques. *Figaro*(4 mai):XV

Lancaster T, Lewis-Beck MS. 1989. Regional vote support: the Spanish case. *Int. Stud. Q.* 33:29–43

Lanoue DJ. 1994. Retrospective and prospective voting in presidential-year elections. *Polit. Res. Q.* 47:193–205

Lecaillon J. 1981. Popularité des gouvernements et popularité économique. *Consummation* 3:17–50

Lewis-Beck MS. 1980. Economic conditions and executive popularity: the French experience. *Am. J. Polit. Sci.* 24:306–23

Lewis-Beck MS. 1986. Comparative economic voting: Britain, France, Germany, Italy. *Am. J. Polit. Sci.* 30:315–46

Lewis-Beck MS. 1985. Pocketbook voting in US national election studies: fact or artifact? *Am. J. Polit. Sci.* 29:348–56

Lewis-Beck MS. 1988. *Economics and Elections: The Major Western Democracies*. Ann Arbor: Univ. Michigan Press

Lewis-Beck MS. 1995. Comparaison de prévision des élections présidentielles en France et aux États-Unis. *J. Société Stat. Paris* 136(1): 29–45

Lewis-Beck MS. 1997. Who's the chief? Economic voting under a dual executive. *Eur. J. Polit. Res.* 31(3):315–25

Lewis-Beck MS, Mitchell G. 1990. Modelos transnacionales de voto economico: estudio de un conjunto de paises europeos. *Revista Inst. Estud. Econ.* 4:65–81

Lewis-Beck MS, Nadeau R. 2000. French electoral institutions and the economic vote. *Electoral Stud.* 19: In press

Lewis-Beck MS, Rice T. 1984. Forecasting U.S. House elections. *Legis. Stud. Q.* 9:475–86

Lewis-Beck MS, Rice T. 1992. *Forecasting Elections*. Washington, DC: Congressional Quarterly Press

Lewis-Beck MS, Tien C. 1996. The future in forecasting: prospective presidential models. *Am. Polit. Q.* 24:468–91

Lockerbie B. 1991. Prospective economic voting in U.S. House elections, 1956–1988. *Legis. Stud. Q.* 16:239–61

Lockerbie B. 1992. Prospective voting in presidential elections, 1956–1988. *Am. Polit. Q.* 20:308–25

MacKuen M, Erikson R, Stimson J. 1992. Peasants or bankers? The American electorate and the U.S. economy. *Am. Polit. Sci. Rev.* 86:597–611

Markus G. 1988. The impact of personal and national economic conditions on the presidential vote: a pooled cross-sectional analysis. *Am. J. Polit. Sci.* 32:137–54

Markus G. 1992. The impact of personal and national economic conditions on presidential voting, 1956– 1988. *Am. J. Polit. Sci.* 36: 829–34

Marra RF, Ostrom CW. 1989. Explaining seat change in the U.S. House of Representatives, 1950–1986. *Am. J. Polit. Sci.* 33:541–69

Miller WL, Mackie M. 1973. The electoral cycle and the asymmetry of government and the opposition popularity: an alternative model of the relationship between economic conditions and political popularity. *Polit. Stud.* 621:263–79

Mondardi F. 1994. Primary voters as retrospective voters. *Am. Polit. Q.* 22:88–103

Monroe KR. 1978. Economic influences on presidential popularity. *Public Opin. Q.* 42: 360–69

Monroe KR. 1984. *Presidential Popularity and the Economy.* New York: Praeger

Mosley P. 1978. Images of the "floating voter": or the "political business cycle" revisited. *Polit. Stud.* 26:375–94

Mueller J. 1970. Presidential popularity from Truman to Johnson. *Am. Polit. Sci. Rev.* 64: 18–34

Mueller J. 1973. *War, Presidents, and Public Opinion.* New York: Wiley

Mutz D. 1994. Contextualizing personal experience: the role of the mass media. *J. Polit.* 56:689–715

Nadeau R, Blais A. 1993. Explaining elections outcomes in Canada: economy and politics. *Can. J. Polit. Sci.* 26:775–90

Nannestad P, Paldam M. 1994. The VP function: a survey of the literature on vote and

popularity functions after 25 years. *Public Choice* 79:213–45

Nannestad P, Paldam M. 1995. It's the government's fault! A cross-section study of economic voting in Denmark, 1990/93. *Eur. J. Polit. Res.* 28:33–62

Nannestad P, Paldam M. 1997. From the pocketbook of the welfare man: a pooled cross-section study of economic voting in Denmark, 1986–1992. *Br. J. Polit. Sci.* 27:119–37

Nannestad P, Paldam M. 2000. Into Pandora's box of economic evaluations. A study of the Danish macro VP-function 1986–1997. *Electoral Stud.* 19: In press

Norpoth H. 1985. Politics, economics and the cycle of presidential popularity. In *Economics and Electoral Outcomes*, ed. H Eulau, MS Lewis-Beck, pp. 167–86. New York: Agathon

Norpoth H. 1987. Guns and butter and government popularity in Great Britain. *Am. Polit. Sci. Rev.* 81:949–60

Norpoth H. 1996a. The economy. In *Comparing Democracies: Elections and Voting in Global Perspective*, ed. L LeDuc, RG Niemi, P Norris, pp. 299–318. Thousand Oaks, CA: Sage

Norpoth H. 1996b. Presidents and the prospective voter. *J. Polit.* 58:776–92

Norpoth H. 1996c. Of time and candidates: a forecast for 1996. *Am. Polit. Q.* 24:443–67

Norpoth H, Lewis-Beck MS, Lafay JD. 1991. *Economics and Politics: The Calculus of Support.* Ann Arbor: Univ. Michigan Press

Oppenheimer B, Stimson J, Waterman R. 1986. Interpreting U.S. congressional elections: the exposure thesis. *Legis. Stud. Q.* 11:227–47

Pacek AC. 1994. Macroeconomic conditions and electoral politics in East Central Europe. *Am. J. Polit. Sci.* 38:723–44

Pacek AC, Radcliff B. 1995. Economic voting and the welfare state: a cross-national analysis. *J. Polit.* 57:44–61

Paldam M. 1991. How robust is the vote function? A study of seventeen nations over four decades. See Norpoth et al 1991, pp. 9–32

Paldam M, Nannestad P. 2000. What do voters know about the economy? A study of Danish data, 1990–1993. *Electoral Stud.* 19: In press

Paldam M, Schneider F. 1980. The macroeconomic aspects of government and opposition popularity in Denmark 1957–1978. *Natl. Økonomisk Tidsskrift* 118:149–70

Parker G. 1986. Economic partisan advantages in congressional contests: 1938–1978. *Public Opin. Q.* 50:387–401

Partin R. 1995. Economic conditions and gubernatorial elections: is the state executive held accountable? *Am. Polit. Q.* 23:81–95

Pissarides CA. 1980. British government popularity and economic performance. *Econ. J.* 90:569–81

Powell GB, Whitten GD. 1993. A cross-national analysis of economic voting: taking account of the political context. *Am. J. Polit. Sci.* 37:391–414

Powers DV, Cox JH. 1997. Echoes from the past: the relationship between satisfaction with economic reforms and voting behavior in Poland. *Am. Polit. Sci. Rev.* 91:617–33

Price S, Sanders D. 1995. Economic expectations and voting intentions in the UK, 1979–1987: a pooled cross-section approach. *Polit. Stud.* 43:451–71

Radcliff B. 1994. Reward without punishment: economic conditions and the vote. *Polit. Res. Q.* 47(3):721–31

Remmer KL. 1991. The political impact of economic crisis in Latin America in the 1980s. *Am. Polit. Sci. Rev.* 85:777–800

Romero DW, Stambough SJ. 1996. Personal economic well-being and the individual vote for congress: a pooled analysis, 1980–1990. *Polit. Res. Q.* 49:607–16

Rosa JJ, Amson D. 1976. Conditions économiques et elections: une analyse politico-économetrique (1920–1973). *Rev. Française Sci. Polit.* 26:1101–24

Rosenbaum DE, Lohr S. 1996. *NY Times.* Aug 3

Rosenstone S. 1982. Economic adversity and voter turnout. *Am. J. Polit. Sci.* 26:25–46

Sanders D. 1991. Government popularity and the next general election. *Polit. Q.* 62:235–61

Sanders D. 2000. The real economy and the perceived economy in popularity functions: how much do the voters need to know? *Electoral Stud.* 19: In press

Sanders D, Marsh D, Ward H. 1991. Macroeconomics, the Falklands War and the popularity of the Thatcher government: a contrary view. *Br. J. Polit. Sci.* 20:161–84

Sanders D, Ward H, Marsh D, Fletcher T. 1987. Government popularity and the Falklands War: a reassessment. *Br. J. Polit. Sci.* 17:281–313

Sears DO Lau RR. 1983. Inducing apparently self-interested political preferences. *Am. J. Polit. Sci.* 27:223–52

Schneider F, Frey BS. 1988. Politico-economic models of macroeconomic policy: a review of empirical evidence. In *Political Business Cycles*, ed. T Willett. Durham, NC: Duke Univ. Press

Simon DM, Ostrom CW, Marra RF. 1991. The president, referendum voting, and subnational elections in the United States. *Am. Polit. Sci. Rev.* 85:1175–92

Southwell PL. 1996. Economic salience and differential abstention in presidential elections. *Am. Polit. Q.* 24:221–36

Stigler G. 1973. General economic conditions and national elections. *Am. Econ. Rev. Pap. Proc.* 63:160–67

Suzuki M, Chappell HW. 1996. The rationality of economic voting revisited. *J. Polit.* 58:224–36

Tufte ER. 1975. Determinants of the outcomes of midterm congressional elections. *Am. Polit. Sci. Rev.* 69:812–26

Tufte ER. 1978. *Political Control of the Economy.* Princeton, NJ: Princeton Univ. Press

Weatherford MS. 1978. Economic conditions and electoral outcomes: class differences in the political response to recession. *Am. J. Polit. Sci.* 22:917–38

Whiteley PF. 1986. Macroeconomic performance and government popularity in Britain: the short-run dynamics. *Eur. J. Polit. Res.* 14: 45–61

Wilkin S, Haller B, Norporth H. 1997. From Argentina to Zambia: a world-wide test of economic voting. *Electoral Stud.* 16:301–16

Wlezien C, Erikson R. 1996. Temporal horizons and presidential election forecasts. *Am. Polit. Q.* 24:492–505

Annu. Rev. Polit. Sci. 2000. 3:221–50

EMOTIONS IN POLITICS

G. E. Marcus

*Department of Political Science, Williams College, Williamstown, Massachusetts 01267;
e-mail: George.E.Marcus@Williams.edu*

Key Words   affect, mood, cognition, judgment, memory

■ **Abstract**   The study of emotion in politics has been active, especially as it relates
to the personality of political leaders and as an explanation for how people evaluate significant features around them. Researchers have been divided into two groups—those
who study leaders and those who study publics. The research programs have also been
divided between those who use emotion to explain reliance on early experience that
dominates contemporary judgment and those who use emotion to explain why people
respond to the immediate contemporary circumstances around them. More recently,
theory and research have attempted to reconcile these two seemingly contradictory
roles by integrating them. Emotion's role in politics is pervasive both because emotion
enables past experience to be encoded with its evaluative history and because emotion
enables contemporary circumstances to be quickly evaluated. More recently still, theoretical models and supporting evidence suggest that there are multiple channels of
emotional evaluations.

INTRODUCTION

It would be hard to identify a single political thinker of note in the Western tradition who did not give emotion substantial attention. Aristotle (1954, 1983), Plato
(1974), Hobbes (1968), Descartes (1989 [1649]), and the Scottish enlightenment
thinkers, especially Hume (1739–1940) and Smith (1959), among many others,
all thought it necessary to understand emotion in order to explore human nature
and our capacities for politics. How these thinkers understood emotion remains
a valuable question (Elster 1999, Rorty 1996). Yet a longstanding bias toward
cognitive accounts has dominated the study of political judgment (Hilgard 1980).

Perhaps the mysterious character of emotion has been largely to blame for the
difficulty of executing scientific studies of emotion in politics. Also perhaps responsible is the dominant view in political theory that progress and democratic
politics require less emotion and more reason (Arkes 1993). It has been common,
at least since Madison (1961 [1787]), to treat emotion as an unavoidable factor in
politics that should be constrained and minimized so that reason dictates judgment
with minimal distraction (Callan 1997, Holmes 1995). Notwithstanding this view,
political scientists have actively explored a broad array of roles that emotion plays

in motivation and judgment. But although political science's recent attention to emotion in politics reflects considerable variety in theoretical direction and application, a consensus on the effects of emotion in politics remains to be achieved.

To provide some order to the proliferation of research on emotion in politics, I now broadly (and somewhat unjustly) characterize the overall pattern of interest and theoretical strategies common in political science. The use of emotion generally fits into one of two approaches. First, it has long been theorized that an account of the stable and particular characteristics of any person, especially his or her characteristic way of approaching decisions and actions, must include emotion as a facet of personality. Lasswell (1930, 1948) long ago held that politics is the expression of personal emotions. More generally, attention to political leaders and their decision-making styles has focused on their characteristic emotional inclinations. Among the most popular applications of this approach have been case studies of important political leaders (Rogow 1963; Langer 1972; Greenstein & Destler 1983; Volkan & Itkowitz 1984; Barber 1985; Greenstein 1987, 1994; Volkan et al 1997; George & George 1998). A variant of this approach is to explore the role of emotion in the specific instance of important political decisions made by political leaders (Janis 1982, Blight 1990, Steinberg 1996). In each of these projects, emotional dispositions secured early in life are used to account for the stable orientations political leaders display in dealing with the recurring situations, crises, and decisions they confront.

The second common application explores how people experience different emotional reactions to contemporary circumstances. Here the focus shifts from the emotion inherent in the personality of the individual to the emotion that is attached to external events, symbols, situations, individuals, or groups, in order to provoke a reaction in the audience. Emotion is used to explain why people deviate from their characteristic dispositions. The presumption is that although people may have characteristic ways of resolving pressing issues, they may do something out of the ordinary because of some provocative stimulus, as when someone says, "I just lost it, he made me so angry!"

Aristotle's *Rhetoric* (1954) offers counsel on how a leader should use emotion to gain influence over the audience he hopes to lead. A modern example can be found in Sears & Citrin's (1982) study of the emotional grounds for the public support that led to passage of Proposition 13 in California. They summarize, as follows, what led to the success of this tax-limiting proposition (Sears & Citrin 1982:222–23):

> [A] surge of recklessness, a period of nearly blind emotion, [surrounded] the passage of Proposition 13, when anger at the government seemed to dominate the public's thinking. The usual explanations for the voters' choices still held sway, but this added hostility proved a potent weapon for the tax revolt. At this point, the tide of anti-government emotion eroded stable attitudes about what government should do. The public's desire for maintaining the status quo of services plummeted, their perceptions of

government inefficiency rose considerably, and their anger focused on the "bureaucrats."

In this passage, Sears & Citrin (1982) use emotion to explain people's departure from their normal behavior, not to explain the normal behavior itself. These two perspectives have long coexisted. On the one hand, emotions enable people to steadfastly remain true to their most deeply held values and attitudes (Sears 1993). On the other hand, emotions are capable of stirring people up, causing them to abandon their habitual commitments. Although these two perspectives seem difficult to reconcile, they do agree on the central importance of emotion in memory, evaluation, judgment, and action.

Recent Reviews

Elster (1999) provides an excellent, if not comprehensive, account of how emotion has been historically understood in the Western tradition. The scientific study of emotion began with Darwin (1998 [1872]) and James (1883, 1894). Cornelius (1996) provides an excellent history of the scientific treatment of emotion in psychology beginning with James.

Several recent reviews in psychology offer overviews of current work on emotion, and some of these touch on emotion in politics. Excellent overviews include those by Zajonc (1998) and Cacioppo & Gardner (1999). More specific review topics have included feelings as subjective experience (Schwarz & Clore 1996); the interrelationship of emotion and memory (Blaney 1986); the relationship between emotion and motivation (Bradley 2000); the roles of emotion in evaluation (Tesser & Martin 1996), political judgment (Ottati 2000), and electoral politics (Glaser & Salovey 1998); and the neuroscience of emotion (Damasio 1994, LeDoux 1996, Rolls 1999). In addition, there are two collections of important papers on emotion, one published some 20 years ago (Rorty 1980) and one more recent (Ekman & Davidson 1994).

ORGANIZING SCHEMA

This chapter identifies recurring themes, such as those mentioned above, as well as key definitions and common strategies in the study of emotions in politics. It offers a review of current findings, a review of the available theoretical models, and a consideration of measurement issues. Let us begin with definitions.

Definitions

In the past, political scientists thought of emotion as the expression of underlying personality drives (Lasswell 1930), largely in psychoanalytic terms (Davies 1980), or as the result of cognitive processes (Abelson et al 1982). Since then, without denying the role of cognitive processes in assigning semantic terms to emotional experience, more political scientists have seen emotional expression as resulting from distinct affective processes (Marcus 1991). This shift argues that evaluations arising from emotional processes, independent of prior or concurrent cognitive processes, can influence not only emotional expression but also thoughts, decisions, and political behavior.

This claim requires special attention to such key terms as emotion and mood, cognition and affect, evaluation and perception. Each of the reviews cited above uses some or all of these key terms. There is some consensus that, for example, moods can be differentiated from emotions because emotions have an explicit source (i.e. a reason why we feel as we do), whereas moods do not have a subjectively self-identifiable referent (Clore et al 1994). For instance, Wood et al (1990) define mood as "a general and pervasive feeling state that is not directed toward a specific target." Batson et al (1992) draw the more idiosyncratic distinction that emotions reflect past experience, whereas moods are anticipations of future experience.

The field of emotion is rife with basic disagreements about crucial conceptual definitions. The term cognition has been applied in a variety of ways. It is often used as a synonym for information processing (Lazarus 1984), a concept so all-inclusive that it would be hard to exclude any neurological action as evidence of cognition. More typically, cognition is used as a synonym for thinking (Ottati & Wyer 1993). Cognitive processes, which generate the perceptual features of an object, are often contrasted with affective reactions, which constitute evaluations. This follows the long tradition of equating cognition with thinking and affect with feeling, paralleling an even older tradition that contrasts the purported features of rationality with the purported features of emotionality (Elster 1999).

Recent work in neuroscience established the independence of these two processes and further established that affective evaluations generally arise before conscious perceptions (Rolls 1999). In the 1980s, a major controversy arose between those who claimed that emotional expression depends on cognitive attributions (Wiener et al 1978, Roseman 1984, Weiner & Graham 1984, Roseman et al 1986, Russell & McAuley 1986, Sacks & Bugental 1987, Smith et al 1993, Quigley & Tedeschi 1996, Roseman et al 1996) and those who claimed that emotional response arises from affective processes that are largely independent of cognitive processes (Moreland & Zajonc 1979; Kunst-Wilson & Zajonc 1980; Zajonc 1980, 1982; Granberg & Brown 1989; Bornstein & D'Agostino 1992; Murphy & Zajonc 1993; Murphy et al 1995). Much of this controversy depended on definitions. If cognition is a scientific synonym for conscious awareness, generally, or thinking in semantic terms, more specifically, then the empirical findings that emotional processes produce emotional responses outside of consciousness are less controversial. A good deal of work in political science has addressed the independent contributions of effective and cognitive assessment in politics.

A currently unresolved issue involves the structure or taxonomic character of emotion. There have been, broadly speaking, three theoretical approaches to the structure of emotion: the valence view, the discrete or basic view, and at least two two-dimensional models. Substantive conclusions about the role of emotion depend on the relative scientific merit of these views. A recent controversy concerned measurement error in self-reported emotional response. Although attention to the measurement of emotion has been greater in psychology than in political science, the contribution of political scientists to resolving the measurement problem may prove of equal consequence (Green et al 1993, Green & Citrin 1994, Marcus & MacKuen 1996, Marcus et al 2000).

Strategies

Some researchers focus on the personalities and decision making of political leaders. Others focus on mass publics, exploring the role of emotion in political judgment or in securing enduring disposition. As a result of this division of labor, and the attendant differences in research programs (the former more reliant on case studies, the latter more reliant on experiments and survey research), it is hard to integrate the research literature into a comprehensive account. In addition to research on leaders versus research on followers, there is a conflict between two theoretical accounts. One faction uses emotional attachments to explain how people are shaped by the enduring influence of earlier experience, via personality formation. The other uses emotion to explain how the impact of some contemporary individuals, groups, crises, or events is much magnified by their emotional content. Thus, the strategies fall into a fourfold typology, with two different domains of study crossed by the two contradictory premises.

This organization of strategies, though at times forced, supplies some taxonomic structure to my review of the research and theoretical literature. In the first section, I review the literature that addresses the capacity of emotion to secure previous experience and its lessons against the complex variety of contemporary experience. In the second section, I review the literature that addresses the ability of emotion to enhance the impact of some contemporary experience.

EMOTIONS ANCHOR BEHAVIOR AND ATTITUDES

Personality and Affect

Perhaps the oldest view of emotion in political science is emotion as personality. Its best-known advocate was Lasswell (1930, 1948). The most common application of this approach has been case studies of political leaders, which find in leaders' early, formative experiences the sources for their characteristic manner of responding to the contemporary political challenges they confront (e.g. Greenstein & Destler 1983, 1994; Volkan & Itkowitz 1984; Volkan et al 1997; George & George 1998). The primary theoretical approach has been psychoanalytic and focused on character (Renshon 1998). Other ways of addressing personality are considered by Greenstein (1987, 1992).

Barber (1985) takes a somewhat different tack. He defines presidential personality as being anchored by two basic dispositions: a characteristic inclination to action (active) or inaction (passive), and a characteristic inclination to anticipate rewards (positive) or punishments (negative). Barber's personality theory, a two-factor model, anticipates one of the two variants of such models. His dimensions of personality, active-passive and positive-negative, parallel the models of affect advanced by psychologists Russell (1980, Russell & Barrett 1999, Russell & Carroll 1999) and Diener (1995). As shown below (where the various structure-of-emotion models are reviewed), Barber's characterization of presidents as active or passive and as positive or negative can be readily transformed by rotation to the alternative model. The alternative model depicts people as characteristically calm or anxious and characteristically extraverted or introverted. The primary claim is that early experiences, and the emotional reactions they generate, shape adult behavior.

A variant in the treatment of affect as personality has been to focus on some particular recurring syndrome. A syndrome of particular note is the capacity to form an emotional bond with the public, treated as either a "charismatic" bond (Madsen & Snow 1991) or as a form of "narcissism," either benign or malevolent (Volkan & Itkowitz 1984, Post 1993, Steinberg 1996, Volkan et al 1997). In general, these approaches consider the embedding of past experience in emotional tendencies to be a danger to the rational assessment of contemporary challenges. If a leader's actions are driven by needs rooted in his past, his emotions become the basis of "motivated errors" (Stein 1988) resulting from systematic misperceptions and delusions that can lead to systematic under- or overestimation of threat (Janis & Mann 1977, Janis 1982). For example, Steinberg (1996) finds President Johnson's decisions on the war in Vietnam to be heavily influenced by his emotional needs. On the other hand, Blight (1990) argues that the introduction of emotion, notably fear, into the Cuban Missile Crisis was largely responsible for minimizing distractions by nonrational considerations into Kennedy's decision making, and for its success. Blight's research presages a growing interest in the possible adaptive benefits of emotion (de Sousa 1987, Frank 1988, Gibbard 1990, Tooby & Cosmides 1990, Marcus 1991).

Two more approaches to the role of emotion in personality are worth noting. The role of emotion in the execution of evil has been considered by Baumeister (1997), Lifton (1986), and Arendt (1963). Each explains the willingness to engage in evil acts by the capacity to inhibit emotional response, i.e. the absence of empathy. Monroe (1996) finds that people who display a disposition to empathy are most likely to undertake heroic acts of altruism in moments of need. Greenstein (1969) and Masters and Sullivan (McHugo et al 1985, Sullivan & Masters 1988, Masters & Sullivan 1993) explore the emotional linkages between political leaders and the public.

Apart from the preponderant reliance on psychoanalytic approaches to personality, political scientists have not made much use of current attention to personality and affect in academic psychology (Rusting & Larsen 1998, Zuckerman 1991) and especially recent work on "big three" or "big five" models of personality (Digman 1989, Goldberg 1990, John 1990, McCrae & John 1992, Saucier 1992, Zuckerman et al 1993, Costa & McCrae 1995). This lacunae offers a rich opportunity for new research.

Evaluation Is Affect

The theoretical construction of affect as personality in leaders—their embedded response to the present by reference to the lessons of the past and to the inner needs of personality—has a parallel in the study of the role of affect in citizens. Emotion is conceived as an affective "glue" to ensure reliance on longstanding dispositions (Sears 1993), which Sears calls "symbolic politics" (Sears et al 1979, 1980). Affective responses to early experience become life-long lessons that ensure a measure of stability and continuity in the manner and substance of people's response to the recurring challenges they face (Sears & Valentino 1997, Sears & Funk 1999). The conception of partisan identification as an "affective orientation to an important group object" (Campbell et al 1960:121) reflects a similar view of affect as a mechanism by which the experience of the past guides the actions of the present.

The conception of affect as evaluation—whether a historical evaluation that shapes responses to the present, or a contemporaneous evaluation that shapes responses to current events (as in communications or persuasion research)—has certainly been a central focus of affect research. But the dominance of affect as evaluation has had two detrimental effects. First, the structure of evaluation is generally conceived as a valence conception of liking–disliking (Osgood et al 1957). The consensus has been that approach–avoidance is the singular evaluative task performed by emotion. As a result, researchers adopting this approach have largely ignored the important alternative that multiple and varied evaluations may be performed by multiple affective systems. Hence the nature of the structure of affective response has been tied to a theoretical and methodological presumption that the structure of evaluation is adequately accounted for by a single bipolar dimension.

Second, researchers who study symbols (Edelman 1964, Elder & Cobb 1983, Edelman 1988) have identified the affective component of symbols as the key to their capacity to persuade and motivate action. Without emotional response, stimuli have no capacity to engage. Not surprisingly, this raises a normative concern that emotions can generate irrational responses (Sears & Citrin 1982, Jamieson 1992). The widespread presumption that the impact of emotions, via symbolic manipulation, is a major source of irrationality has delayed (until recently) attention to the possibility that emotions, in at least some instances, can motivate cooperative behavior. For example, Scholz & Lubell (1998) have shown that compliance with tax obligations is partly related to the emotional responses that attend a behavioral disposition toward compliance. Monroe and Carlson have found that emotional empathic response to people in need is an important causal factor in initiating helping behavior (Carlson et al 1988, Monroe 1996).

Summary Judgment Is Affective

A popular conception of emotional response conceives it as a passive repository of cognitive inputs (Hastie 1986, Lodge & Hamill 1986, Lodge et al 1989, Rahn et al

1990, Glaser & Salovey 1998). Therefore, it is not surprising that the affective component of attitudes has predictive power in matters of interest to political science, such as voting (Kenney & Rice 1988, Rahn et al 1990). The on-line model of judgment (Hastie & Park 1986, Lodge & Taber 1998) identifies two roles for emotion: affect as a summary judgment stored in memory, typically defined as a valence "tag" (Fiske & Pavelchak 1986), and affect as a contemporary response to current circumstances.

The treatment of emotional responses as a summary repository results from efforts to provide a cognitive account of emotion. It is presumed that emotional responses arise from prior information processing (Ortony et al 1989, Ottati & Wyer 1991). This approach generally precludes treating affective evaluations as arising from distinct and independent processes, even though it has long been recognized that attitudes, with their three components of feelings, thoughts, and behavior (Rosenberg & Hovland 1960), are only weakly interrelated (Breckler 1984, Breckler & Wiggins 1989).

Emotional evaluation also plays a role in "framing" and "priming" studies. Emotional reactions to contemporary cues (frames or primes) seem to facilitate recall of prior, similarly valenced events (Edwards 1990, Krosnick & Kinder 1990, Tulving & Schacter 1990, Derryberry 1991, Bargh et al 1992, Krosnick & Brannon 1993, May et al 1995, Nelson et al 1997). The ability of contemporary moods to facilitate memory is important in the work of Forgas (1992, 1995). See also Bargh (1992) for an argument that prior emotional tagging of stimuli can elicit the emotional cue as an evaluation on even subliminal presentation of those stimuli. The general hypothesis predicts assimilation, or contagion, effects. This approach is discussed in more detail later in this review.

The power of affective evaluations in predicting, for example, the vote (Kelley 1983) naturally led to considerable research on people's emotional reactions to a wide range of political stimuli. Describing the characteristic emotional responses of political leaders has been one area of research on affect (Marcus 1988). The influence of attractiveness on candidate evaluation was the focus of Rosenberg's research (Rosenberg et al 1986). Klein (1991) has found that overall feelings about presidential candidates display a negativity bias, such that a voter weights negative personality traits more heavily than positive ones to arrive at an overall feeling toward a candidate. Masters and Sullivan have shown that politicians characteristically provoke two independent emotional responses, one "hedonic" and one "agnostic" (McHugo et al 1985; Sullivan & Masters 1988; Masters & Sullivan 1989a,b, 1993; Masters 1991; Masters et al 1991).

Emotional reactions are generated by political institutions, such as Congress (Hibbing & Theiss-Morse 1995); by political issues and positions (Conover & Feldman 1986; Kinder & Sanders 1990, 1996); and by one's nation, conceptualized as public mood (Rahn et al 1996, Rahn 2000) or conceptualized as patriotism (Schatz & Staub 1997, Staub 1997, Schatz et al 1999). Given the importance of morality in political judgment, especially in democratic societies, it is surprising that the role of emotion in moral socialization has not received more attention (but see Dienstbier 1984). Mikula et al (1998) find that perceptions of injustice characteristically elicit a feeling most commonly described as anger. Feelings of cooperation and antagonism are central to perceptions of allies and enemies (Volkan 1988).

Emotional reactions to groups, particularly in identifying targets for intolerance, have been a major topic of research on political tolerance judgments (Gibson & Bingham 1982, Sullivan et al 1982, Gibson 1992, Marcus et al 1995). Research on emotional reactions to groups more generally (Wilcox et al 1989) and on affect toward groups and the issue of affirmative action (Kinder & Sanders 1996), in addition to work on affirmative action and group biases (Nelson 1998), reveal the emotional character of dispositions (Cooper 1959). Emotional reactions to major events such as war (Kinder 1994), to campaign events (Brader 1999) and campaign advertising (Kern 1989), and to the state of the economy (Conover & Feldman 1986) show that affective reactions are a ubiquitous aspect of human perception and judgment.

The conclusion that emotional response is deeply implicated in evaluation and judgment creates a dilemma. The measurement of emotional response remains a contentious area; different claims are advanced about the structure of emotional response and the appropriate means of obtaining valid and reliable measures. The merit of the substantive findings cited above depends on how the researchers resolved measurement issues in each instance.

EMOTIONS ENABLE CONTEMPORARY RESPONSIVENESS

Although much of the research literature cited above treats emotional response as a primary supporting mechanism of memory, not all political science research has limited the impact of emotion to that role. The literature reviewed below explores another understanding of emotional response. Rather than presuming that emotional responses derive from cognitive perceptions, researchers increasingly see evaluation as a distinct, independent mental operation. Rolls (1999) reports on the neuroscience of independent emotional appraisal. He finds that perception (i.e. awareness of the descriptive features of stimuli) arises separately from the emotional neural pathways that execute evaluation. Hence, emotional responses can support contemporaneous evaluation independent of conscious perception.

Affect Is Information

The principal theoretical statement of affect as information is that of psychologists Schwarz (1990) and Schwarz & Clore (1996). Another theoretical statement is offered by political psychologists Lodge & Tabor (1998) in their version of the on-line model of political judgment. In both theories, emotion serves as an immediate evaluation of contemporary circumstances. Some studies suggest that, for most people, the default condition is reliance on these affective evaluations (Kuklinski et al 1991, Marcus et al 1995).

Both theories rely on two presumptions. First, they presume that evaluations are simple, defined by the need for swift approach–avoidance assessment (i.e. a valence assessment). This claim has been regularly challenged, initially by Abelson et al (1982), Plutchik (1980a), and Russell (1980) and more recently by a considerable literature on the structure of affective responses, all of which finds that at least two dimensions are needed to account for the variation in people's emotional response (Watson & Tellegen 1985; Plutchik & Kellerman 1989; Marcus 1991; Marcus et al 1998; Watson & Clark 1992; Cacioppo & Berntson 1994; Marcus et al 1996; Cacioppo et al 1997; Russell & Barrett 1999; Russell & Carroll 1999; Tellegen et al 1999b; Watson et al 1999). Below, I discuss more fully the issues related to the structure of emotional response.

The second presumption is that the primary substantive impact of evaluative assessments is one of assimilation. That is, positive moods induce more positive judgments and negative moods induce more negative judgments. A variant is the presumption that moods perceived in others will have assimilation effects on subjects (Hatfield et al 1992, Hatfield et al 1994). A number of studies report results confirming this pattern (Hsee et al 1990, Sullins 1991, Gump & Kulik 1997). However, some studies suggest that contemporary mood may yield counterassimilation effects. In one study (Isbell & Wyer 1999), subjects whose moods had been manipulated (happy or sad) read an article about political candidates that included information about issue positions. The authors found that mood had a contagion or assimilation effect (i.e. happy subjects rated candidates more positively and sad subjects rated candidates more negatively) if the subjects were unmotivated. However, motivated subjects—those who showed greater partisan intensity or had been told they were going to vote on the candidates—displayed a counterassimilation effect. That is, happy subjects "over-corrected" by rating politicians lower, and sad subjects rated them higher (see Ottati & Isbell 1996 for other experimental evidence that assimilation effects of mood are not necessarily the general pattern in political judgments).

One common application of affect as information has been the linkage between social category and affective information. If someone is a member of group A, a group I like (or dislike), then I can quickly assess him by applying to him the affective tag of group A (Fiske & Pavelchak 1986). Thus, group affect becomes a reliable heuristic of wide political application (Brady & Sniderman 1985). Individuals need not work to obtain details about the target individual. They need only refer to the group affect tag.

Thus, contemporary political judgments are likely to be influenced by contemporaneous emotions, enabling affect to be a channel for persuasion. Roseman et al (1986) argue for an assimilation effect, explaining that an angry speaker will be most effective if his audience is similarly angry. [See also Agres et al (1990) and Chadhuri & Buck (1995) for related work on emotion in persuasion. For a consideration of the role of affect in persuasion in psychology, see Petty et al (1991) and Millar & Tesser (1986a, 1989).] The affective content of a target, such as a facial display, is important. Interpretations of facial expressions as reassuring or threatening (Aronoff et al 1992), and more generally how subjects perceive facial expressions and decipher their emotional content (Ekman & Rosenberg 1997), have been studied. Affective content is also likely to be an essential facet of evaluation of political leaders (McHugo et al 1985, Sullivan & Masters 1988, Masters 1989, Warnecke et al 1992, Masters & Sullivan 1993, Way & Masters 1996a). A contemporaneous emotional reaction to a political situation thus offers an important insight into how people understand their circumstances. Miller & Krosnick (1999) provide evidence that a sense of threat, aroused by the anticipation of policies that one opposes, can motivate action. These studies are consistent with a long tradition in psychology that views affect as intimately engaged with memory, enabling us to recall prior experiences based on their emotional valence and strategic significance (Titchener 1895).

Affect versus Cognition

Affective processing became more prominent in psychology beginning with the seminal work of Zajonc (1980, 1982), a psychologist. The idea that emotional processes occur outside of conscious awareness, which was initially treated with skepticism (Lazarus 1982, 1984), is no longer much disputed. Moreover, the weight of opinion in psychology has shifted to a view that these unconscious evaluations are far more active, and hence far more important, than conscious cognitive processing (Bargh & Chartrand 1999). Indeed, one study found that people attending to emotionally rich stimuli can extract more information from those stimuli than can people in emotionally impoverished circumstances (Halberstadt & Niedenthal 1997), which suggests that emotional evaluations are of greater strategic significance than cognitive ones.

In political science, a popular tradition of research has explored the contrasts between reliance on affective cues and reliance on cognitive or descriptive cues. Affective cues have been found to have considerable influence on voter judgment (Christ 1985, Marcus 1988, Ragsdale 1991). More generally, studies in psychology (Millar & Tesser 1986a,b) have explored how people make judgments when instructed to attend to different states of mind, either affective cues (feelings) or cognitive cues (thoughts). Political tolerance judgments have been shown to be influenced by such "state of mind" manipulation (Ottati et al 1989, Kuklinski et al 1991, Marcus et al 1995). Thus, attitudes may have either an affective base or a cognitive base. Earlier studies came to different conclusions about whether persuasion is best achieved by matching persuasive focus with attitude foundation (Edwards 1990) or by mismatching (Millar & Millar 1990). More recent work suggests that affect-based persuasions are more influential than cognition-based persuasions in changing affect-based attitudes, but this matching effect does not hold when cognitive persuasion is directed at cognition-based attitudes (Fabrigar & Petty 1999). Additionally, Erdley & D'Agostino (1988) have shown that that affective information can prime through noncognitive channels. Thus, affect-based persuasive messages have an advantage over cognitive appeals, a finding that is especially pertinent during political campaigns.

In the contentious arena of politics, the identification of threat is crucial. Marcus and colleagues find that threat is experienced largely through affective channels rather than through explicit cognitive perceptions (Marcus et al 1995, Marcus et al 1998). Lavine et al (1999) find that authoritarians are more responsive to threat messages than to reward-based messages, indicating that some personality types are especially attuned to threat signals (Feldman & Stenner 1997).

In political science, Greene (1998, 2000) has shown that partisan identification can be established by either affective or cognitive identification (see also Granberg & Brown 1989). Patriotism may also have affective and cognitive orientations (Schatz & Staub 1997, Staub 1997, Schatz et al 1999), as may empathy (Hoffman 1984) and prejudice (Jackson & Sullivan 1990, Stangor et al 1991). Similarly, people may be more attentive to either affective or cognitive cues in their evaluations of leaders (Jones & Iacobucci 1989). Resistance to persuasive messages may be either affective or cognitive (Zuwerink & Devine 1996). Gunther & Thorson (1992) found more "emotional" messages, i.e. those bearing more positive emotion, to be more persuasive, but this finding may result from a relationship between emotionality and greater attention to emotionally encoded information (Halberstadt & Niedenthal 1997). This conclusion is supported by research (Hibbing & Theiss-Morse 1998) showing that cognitive appraisals of Congress are rather stable and impervious to media modification, whereas emotional reactions are more responsive (the effect is strongest among political novices).

Reliable measures of the affective and cognitive properties of evaluation have been created (Crites et al 1994). The phrase "affective and cognitive" may give the impression that one or the other must dominate. It is more likely, however, that instead of a contrast between cognitive and affective evaluations, there is a contrast between affective-only and cognitive-plus-affective evaluations. It is highly unlikely that any target of consideration is devoid of emotional content or influence.

Affect Reactions Mediate Judgment

The research reviewed above presumes that people rely on either cognitive or affective channels of information. However, there is an additional role for affect. Affective state of mind, contemporary mood, may mediate how judgments are made in addition to providing information about the target stimulus. That is, the subject's affective state of mind may shape which factors are judged and how they are weighed (Rusting 1998).

Thus, affective reactions to groups change how subjects respond to policy options (Sniderman & Piazza 1993, Kinder & Sanders 1996). In political campaigning, so-called negative campaigning may induce people to pay more attention to the campaign, as research suggests that negative information is attended to more than positive information (Derryberry 1991, Pratto & John 1991, Taylor 1991, Ito et al 1998b). Thus, affect may influence the manner of information processing (Way &

Masters 1996a,b) with subliminal threat cues gaining more attention. But affective subliminal effects are apparently most robust when subjects are unaware, i.e. not attending to the target of affective stimulation (Bornstein & D'Agostino 1992).

With the added attention to the role of emotion in the formation of judgment, the normative view of that role has begun to shift. The conventional view has been that the intrusion of affect into decision making undermines what would otherwise be a clearer and more rational consideration (Janis & Mann 1977). Jervis et al advanced the common view that emotion undermines sound judgment (1985:4).

> Motivated biases arise from the emotions generated by conflicts that personal needs and severe situational dilemmas pose. These biases serve important psychological functions, primarily minimizing ... discomfort.... The individual will pay a high price in the future as reality inescapably shapes and defeats the policy, but in the interim he or she avoids intolerable psychological stress and conflict.

This view is confirmed by work on the effects of anger (Lerner et al 1998). The inducement of anger yielded simpler cognitive processing, less attention to available information, and greater reliance on heuristics. However, these effects were reversed if subjects were told they would be held responsible for their views (i.e. if they anticipated having to justify their reactions). Thus, the intrusion of emotion, in and of itself, is not necessarily detrimental to the quality of decision making. Work on emotion and stereotypical thinking (Bodenhausen 1993, Bodenhausen et al 1994a,b) also suggests a more complex set of relationships, with different emotional states having different effects. Isbell & Wyer (2000) found that the effect of mood manipulation on subjects judging political candidates was counterassimilated when subjects were motivated and assimilated when they were not, indicating that the motivational status is highly relevant to the role of emotion in decision making. But although there are many studies on the role of emotion in politics, much more work will be necessary to achieve a sound theoretical and empirical understanding.

THEORETICAL MODELS

The task of theory building is twofold. First, a theory must provide a measurement model enabling researchers to define and measure the phenomenon of interest. Second, a theory must explain why emotional responses occur as well as how and when variations in emotional response influence judgment and behavior. How much do we now know about these two facets of a theory of emotions in politics?

Structure of Emotion

In the case studies of leadership, the descriptive component is largely drawn from psychodynamic sources. In psychoanalytic formulations, the subjective experience of emotions takes the form of discrete, sometimes termed basic, emotions. In discrete-emotion formulations, distinct and specified circumstances are associated with a limited number of intense but differentiated manifestations of discrete emotion states, such as anger or love (Tomkins 1962, 1963, 1981, 1984). Thus, a common theme is that a subject's specific emotional response to a situation depends on the underlying attribution of the subject and the subject's prior experiences (Davies 1980). Discrete emotions are, in general, held to arise from attribution of the self (for example, a characterization of the self as weak or strong) and the circumstances (Frijda et al 1989). These discrete emotions constitute an important element of personality (Diener et al 1995). A more recent view holds that emotional responses are evolutionary adaptations to the need to encode environmental information (Tooby & Cosmides 1990). Discrete-emotion theories are found mainly in leadership studies, but Kinder (1994) has applied this approach to account for people's responses to leaders, issues, and salient events.

Among researchers treating emotion as a summary judgment, the more common descriptive measurement approach draws on the social-psychological school rather than the psychodynamic. Summary evaluative judgments are commonly treated as a simple singular valence assessment, i.e. positive or negative, like or dislike (McGraw et al 1991). However, other models have also been suggested. Dual-channel measurement theories argue that at least two dimensions are needed to adequately characterize emotional experience. Unlike discrete-emotion theories (Roseman 1984), which hold that each of the basic emotions is distinct, dual-channel theories hold that all subjective experiences arise from more than one underlying affective process. These multiple processes combine to form the subjective experiences that are then semantically differentiated into the many terms we ascribe to the rich variety thus produced (Storm & Storm 1987).

Two dual-channel models have been in the psychological literature for about 20 years. The earlier of the two has been advanced primarily by Russell (1980, 1983; Russell & Bullock 1985; Russell et al 1989a; Russell & Barrett 1999; Russell & Carroll 1999), a psychologist. In this view, one channel determines the valence of emotional experience while the other determines the degree of arousal. A measurement literature is available (Mehrabian 1995, 1996; Russell et al 1989b). Also in this vein is work by other psychologists, most notably Plutchik (1980a,b), Diener & Emmons (1985), Plutchik & Kellerman (1989), and Larsen & Diener (1992). This approach has been applied to personality (Apter 1989).

The second of the two-channel theories argues that each channel performs a distinct strategic evaluation. One channel evaluates the degree of threat or novelty in the environment. The other channel evaluates the success or failure of familiar actions, routines, or practices. This approach has been advanced mainly by psychologists Tellegen and Watson (Zevon & Tellegen 1982, Tellegen 1985, Watson & Tellegen 1985, Watson et al 1999) and Cacioppo (Berntson et al 1993; Cacioppo & Berntson 1994; Cacioppo et al 1997, 1999), and by political scientist Marcus (1988, 1991). There is a measurement literature for this theory as well (Watson 1988; Bagozzi 1993; Watson & Clark 1994, 1997; Marcus & MacKuen 1996;

Watson & Walker 1996; Cacioppo et al 1997). Personality applications are also evident in this model of emotion (Boddy et al 1986, Gray 1987a,b, Broadbent & Broadbent 1988, Malatesta 1990, Watson et al 1992, Carver & White 1994, Corr et al 1995, Berry & Hansen 1996, Watson & Walker 1996).

Methodological Quandaries

The psychology literature has arrived at a consensus that the structure of emotion is two-dimensional (Zajonc 1998). However, this consensus was charged with failing to consider measurement error (Green et al 1993). This challenge led to special issues in the *Journal of Personality and Social Psychology* (Cacioppo et al 1999b, Diener 1999, Green et al 1999, Russell & Barrett 1999, Watson et al 1999) and *Psychological Science* (Green & Salovey 1999, Tellegen et al 1999a,b; for additional citations that bear on the issue, see Russell & Carroll 1999, Watson & Tellegen 1999). Some authors (Nelson 1998; Rahn 1998, 2000) have understood Green et al (1993) to mean that a single bipolar dimension is sufficient to describe the structure of emotion. However, even when measurement error is taken into account, a single dimension is not sufficient to account for the full variance in emotional response (Nelson 1998). This attention to measurement is surely appropriate.

Recently, Green and Salovey (personal communication) have clarified that their original work (Green et al 1993) was meant only to claim that happy and sad mood terms reside on the same dimension and not to claim that only one bipolar dimension suffices to describe emotional response, The measurement problem is not primarily a measurement theory problem but a theoretical underspecification problem. Moreover, the controversy has largely been confined to measures of self-report, ignoring the studies that use electromyographic measures of facial muscles (Cacioppo et al 1986) or techniques that allow mapping of brain activity (Tomarken et al 1990; Tomarken et al 1992; Wheeler et al 1993; Davidson & Tomarken 1994; Davidson 1993, 1995; Robinson 1995; Sutton & Davidson 1997). Still other measurement approaches use the startle reflex as a method of ascertaining emotional response (Bradley et al 1990; Lang et al 1990, 1993; McNeil et al 1993; Lang 1994, 1995; Ito et al 1998a). All of these studies conclude that at least two dimensions are required to explain the variance in emotional response. Hence, a substantial array of results from a variety of methodologies points to the need for a two-channel model of emotion, a point on which Green and Salovey now agree with Russell, Cacioppo, Watson, Tellegen, and Marcus. Such controversy as remains turns on whether the description of emotion is better described by valence and arousal dimensions or by enthusiasm and anxiety dimensions (somewhat mislabeled as "positive" and "negative" psychology). Determining which of these two alternatives is more useful requires research that weighs the evidence for the substantive claims of the competing accounts.

Some other methodological contributions merit notice. Reliable measures of the affective or cognitive foundation of attitudes toward stimuli have been developed

(Crites et al 1994). There is a useful literature on using self-report to measure emotional responses (Bagozzi 1993; Watson & Clark 1994; Mehrabian 1995, 1996; Ottati 1997; Watson et al 1988; also see Watson & Tellegen 1999). The measurement of emotional responses to a target stimulus must take into account whether the focus is on the global character of the target or on some specific properties thereof (Ottati 1997).

An additional implication of dual-channel models of emotion is that ambivalence will be an important element in the experience of emotion. A literature on the measurement of emotional ambivalence is available (Hass et al 1992, Breckler 1994, Thompson et al 1995, Cacioppo et al 1997). There is also a substantial literature of psychophysiological measurement (Cacioppo et al 1986, 1988, 1993; Fridlund & Cacioppo 1986; Harmon-Jones & Allen 1996), although it is uncommon for political scientists to use such measures.

Functional Models

Relative to the dominant tradition, functional models of emotion take a more neutral stance toward the role of emotion. Rather than presuming that emotions detract from the rationality or efficiency of thought or action, functional models of emotion consider whether and how emotional processes provide adaptive benefits. Thus, at least some contemporary theories reflect a change in normative orientation away from the earlier concern with affect-introduced bias and misperception, toward a view of emotions as helpful heuristic devices that offer context-contingent judgment strategies (Forgas 1995). A second development has been increasing reliance on neuroscience to better understand how the brain uses emotional processing. The neuroscience approach makes emotion less mysterious and readily comparable to cognitive processing (Armony & LeDoux 1997).

Personality Theories   As noted above, personality and emotion are closely linked. Theories of personality, or at least some dimensions of personality, have increasingly been interpreted as set points, or baseline and reactive dispositions, for individual differences in emotional expression and emotional reactivity. Consequently, just as personality is expected to depict the stable, enduring qualities of an individual (Conley 1984), so too the functional continuity of emotional dispositions can be in part accounted for by stable emotional dispositions (Zuckerman et al 1993, Watson & Walker 1996, Cacioppo et al 1999a).

Voters seem to look for reliable personality cues that signal the likelihood of a candidate's success. Zullow and colleagues have found that candidates who convey pessimism are more likely to be defeated (Zullow et al 1988, Zullow & Seligman 1990). More generally, emotional dispositions may explain stable inclinations in responding to salient threats (Mogg et al 1990), the possibility of national separation (Flett et al 1999), or a general sense of national threat of various kinds (Feldman & Stenner 1997). In addition, emotional dispositions have been found to account partially for the role of threat in political tolerance judgments (by Marcus et al 1995) and judgments more generally (by Broadbent & Broadbent 1988). Thus, trait and state aspects of emotion are interconnected (Gross et al 1998).

Single-Channel Theories   As noted, valence accounts fail to adequately account for emotional response, but a considerable literature continues to thrive, in part driven by continued reliance on "feeling thermometers" and the like in various communal data-gathering programs. It is hoped that multiple-channel theories of emotion will guide future research.

Multiple-Channel Theories   Multiple-channel theories of emotion presume that affective reactions derive from multiple evaluative processes resulting in multiple affective dimensions. Although work in the 1950s seemed to establish that evaluation was global and formed a single dimension (Osgood et al 1957), in fact this conclusion derived from the reliance on paired oppositions, the semantic differential, which imposes a single-valence structure on the data. Once data gathering enables subjects to disaggregate their emotional responses, then it becomes clear that salient stimuli often evoke multiple, simultaneous emotional reactions (Lang et al 1993, Lang 1994, Ito et al 1998b).

Multiple-channel theories, such as those of psychologist John Cacioppo (Cacioppo & Bernston 1994; Cacioppo et al 1997, 1999b), neuroscientists C Robert Cloninger (1986), Jeffrey Gray (1987a,b, 1990; Gray & McNaughton 1996), and Jaak Panksepp (1989, 1998), or political scientist George E Marcus (1991; Marcus et al 1995, 2000), each argue that more than one evaluative process is ongoing and subserved by emotional processes at any given time.

There is evidence of multiple-channel responses to groups (see Hass et al 1992, Nelson 1998). More generally, if there are multiple channels of evaluation, then there should be evidence of multiple motivational consequences. Evidence supporting multiple-channel theories of evaluation can be shown by differential effects of each channel on learning and political judgment (Marcus & MacKuen 1993, Brader 1999). Psychology has been primarily focused on differential responsiveness to each channel, as in Cacioppo's bivariate model (Cacioppo & Berntson 1994, Cacioppo et al 1997), whereas political science is likely to be more interested in the differential effects of each channel (Marcus et al 2000). Evidence of the asymmetric effects of the two channels in politics has been reported (Marcus & MacKuen 1993).

CONCLUSION

Although a full understanding of emotion is not yet realized, there has been a general shift from presumption of disruption and distortion to a more functional and less normatively biased view. Such a shift in normative orientation was recommended more than 50 years ago in psychology (Leeper 1948). That recommendation is something else political science could borrow from psychology.

LITERATURE CITED

Abelson RP, Kinder DR, Peters MD, Fiske ST. 1982. Affective and semantic components in political personal perception. *J. Pers. Soc. Psychol.* 42:619–30

Agres SJ, Edell JA, Dubitsky TM, eds. 1990. *Emotion in Advertising*. Westport, CT: Quorum Books. 383 pp.

Apter MJ. 1989. *Reversal Theory: Motivation, Emotion and Personality*. London: Routledge. 208 pp.

Arendt H. 1963. *Eichmann in Jerusalem: A Report on the Banality of Evil*. New York: Viking. 275 pp.

Aristotle. 1954. *Rhetoric*. Transl. W Rhys Roberts. New York: Modern Library. 289 pp.

Aristotle. 1983. *The Politics*. Transl. TA Sinclair. New York: Penguin Books. 586 pp. Rev. ed.

Arkes H. 1993. Can emotion supply the place of reason? In *Reconsidering the Democratic Public*, ed. GE Marcus, RL Hanson, pp. 287–305. University Park, PA: Penn. State Univ. Press

Armony JL, LeDoux JE. 1997. How the brain processes emotional information. *Ann. NY Acad. Sci.* 821:259–70

Aronoff J, Woike BA, Hyman LM. 1992. Which are the stimuli in facial displays of anger and happiness? Configurational bases of emotion recognition. *J. Pers. Soc. Psychol.* 62:1050–66

Bagozzi RP. 1993. An examination of the psychometric properties of measures of negative affect in the PANAS–X scales. *J. Pers. Soc. Psychol.* 65:836–51

Barber JD. 1985. *The Presidential Character: Predicting Performance in the White House*. Englewood Cliffs, NJ: Prentice-Hall. 582 pp. 3rd ed.

Bargh JA, Chaiken S, Govender R, Pratto F. 1992. The generality of the automatic attitude activation effect. *J. Pers. Soc. Psychol.* 62:893–912

Bargh JA, Chartrand TL. 1999. The unbearable automaticity of being. *Am. Psychol.* 54:462–79

Batson CD, Shaw LL, Oleson KC. 1992. Differentiating affect, mood, and emotion: toward functionally based conceptual distinctions. In *Emotion*, ed. MS Clark, pp. 294–326. Newbury Park, CA: Sage

Baumeister RF. 1997. *Evil: Inside Human Violence and Cruelty*. New York: Freeman. 431 pp.

Berntson GG, Boysen ST, Cacioppo JT. 1993. Neurobehavioral organization and the cardinal principle of evaluative ambivalence. *Ann. NY Acad. Sci.* 702:75–102

Berry DS, Hansen JS. 1996. Positive affect, negative affect, and social interaction. *J. Pers. Soc. Psychol.* 71:796–809

Blaney PH. 1986. Affect and memory: a review. *Psychol. Bull.* 99:229–46

Blight JG. 1990. *The Shattered Crystal Ball: Fear and Learning in the Cuban Missile Crisis*. Savage, MD: Rowman & Littlefield. 199 pp.

Boddy J, Carver A, Rowley K. 1986. Effect of positive and negative reinforcers on performance as a function of extraversion-introversion: some tests of Gray's theory. *Pers. Indiv. Differ.* 7:81–88

Bodenhausen GV. 1993. Emotion, arousal, and stereotypic judgments: a heuristic model of affect and stereotyping. In *Affect, Cognition, and Stereotyping: Interactive Processes in Group Perception*, ed. D Mackie, D Hamilton, pp. 13–37. San Diego: Academic

Bodenhausen G, Sheppard LA, Kramer GP. 1994a. Negative affect and social judgment: the differential impact of anger and sadness. *Eur. J. Soc. Psychol.* 24:45–62

Bodenhausen GV, Kramer GP, Süsser K. 1994b. Happiness and stereotypic thinking in social judgment. *J. Pers. Soc. Psychol.* 66:621–32

Bornstein RF, D'Agostino PR. 1992. Stimulus recognition and the mere exposure effect. *J. Pers. Soc. Psychol.* 63:545–52

Brader T. 1999. *Campaigning for hearts and minds: how campaign ads use emotion and information to sway the electorate.* PhD thesis, Harvard Univ., Cambridge, MA

Bradley MM. 2000. Motivation and emotion. In *Handbook of Psychophysiology*, ed. JT Cacioppo, LG Tassinary, GG Berntson. New York: Cambridge Univ. Press

Bradley MM, Cuthbert BN, Lang PJ. 1990. Startle reflex modification: emotion or attention? *Psychophysiology* 27:513–22

Brady H, Sniderman P. 1985. Attitude attribution: a group basis for political reasoning. *Am. Polit. Sci. Rev.* 79:1061–78

Breckler SJ. 1984. Empirical validation of affect, behavior, and cognition as distinct components of attitude. *J. Pers. Soc. Psychol.* 47:1191–1205

Breckler SJ. 1994. A comparison of numerical indexes for measuring attitude ambivalence. *Educ. Psychol. Measur.* 54:350–65

Breckler SJ, Wiggins EC. 1989. Affect versus evaluations in the structure of attitudes. *J. Exp. Soc. Psychol.* 25:253–71

Broadbent D, Broadbent M. 1988. Anxiety and attentional bias: state and trait. *Cogn. Emot.* 2:165–83

Cacioppo JT, Berntson GG. 1994. Relationship between attitudes and evaluative space: a critical review, with emphasis on the separability of positive and negative substrates. *Psychol. Bull.* 115:401–43

Cacioppo JT, Berntson GG, Klein DJ, Poehlmann KM. 1999a. The psychophysiology of emotion across the lifespan. *Ann. Rev. Gerontol. Ger.* 17:27–74

Cacioppo JT, Petty RE, Loseh ME, Kim HS. 1986. Electromyographic activity over facial muscle regions can differentiate the valence and intensity of affective reactions. *J. Pers. Soc. Psychol.* 50:260–68

Cacioppo JT, Gardner WL. 1999. Emotion. *Annu. Rev. Psychol.* 50:191–214

Cacioppo JT, Gardner WL, Berntson GG. 1997. Beyond bipolar conceptualizations and measures: the case of attitudes and evaluative space. *Person. Soc. Psychol. Rev.* 1:3–25

Cacioppo JT, Gardner WL, Berntson GG. 1999b. The affect system has parallel and integrative processing components: Form follows function. *J. Pers. Soc. Psychol.* 76:839–55

Cacioppo JT, Klein DJ, Berntson GG, Hatfield E. 1993. The psychophysiology of emotion. In *The Handbook of Emotion*, ed. R Lewis, JM Haviland, pp. 119–42. New York: Guilford

Cacioppo JT, Martzke JS, Petty RE, Tassinary LG. 1988. Specific forms of facial EMG response index emotions during an interview: from darwin to the continuous flow hypothesis of affect-laden information processing. *J. Pers. Soc. Psychol.* 54:592–604

Callan E. 1997. *Creating Citizens: Political Education and Liberal Democracy. Oxford Political Theory*, ed. D Miller, A Ryan. Oxford, UK: Clarendon. 262 pp.

Campbell A, Converse PE, Miller WE, Stokes DE. 1960. *The American Voter.* New York: Wiley & Sons

Carlson M, Charlin V, Miller N. 1988. Positive mood and helping behavior: a test of six hypotheses. *J. Pers. Soc. Psychol.* 55:211–29

Carver CS, White TL. 1994. Behavioral inhibition, behavioral activation, and affective response to impending reward and punishment: the BIS/BAS scales. *J. Pers. Soc. Psychol.* 67:319–33

Chadhuri A, Buck R. 1995. Affect, reason, and persuasion: advertising strategies that predict affective and analytic-cognitive responses. *Hum. Commun. Res.* 21:422–41

Christ WG. 1985. Voter preference and emotion: using emotional response to classify decided and undecided voters. *J. Appl. Soc. Psychol.* 15:237–54

Cloninger CR. 1986. A unified biosocial theory of personality and its role in the development of anxiety states. *Psychiatr. Dev.* 3:167–226

Clore GL, Schwarz N, Conway M. 1994. Affective causes and consequences of social information processing. In *Handbook of Social Cognition*, 1:323–417. ed. RS Wyer Jr, TK Srull. Hillsdale, NJ: Erlbaum. 2 vols. 2nd ed.

Conley JJ. 1984. Longitudinal consistency of adult personality: self-reported psychological characteristics across 45 years. *J. Pers. Soc. Psychol.* 47:1325–33

Conover P, Feldman S. 1986. Emotional reactions to the economy: I'm mad as hell and I'm not going to take it any more. *Am. J. Polit. Sci.* 30:30–78

Cooper JB. 1959. Emotion in prejudice. *Science* 130:314–18

Cornelius RR. 1996. *The Science of Emotion: Research and Tradition in the Psychology of Emotions*. Upper Saddle River, NJ: Prentice Hall. 260 pp.

Corr PJ, Wilson GD, Fotiadou M, Kumari V, Gray NS, et al. 1995. Personality and affective modulation of the startle reflex. *Pers. Individ. Differ.* 19:543–53

Costa PT, McCrae RR. 1995. Primary traits of Eysenck's P-E-N system: three- and five-factor solutions. *J. Pers. Soc. Psychol.* 69: 308–17

Crites SL, Fabrigar LR, Petty RE. 1994. Measuring the affective and cognitive properties of attitudes: conceptual and methodological issues. *Pers. Soc. Psychol. Bull.* 20:619–34

Damasio AR. 1994. *Descartes' Error: Emotion, Reason and the Human Brain*. New York: Putnam's Sons. 312 pp.

Darwin C. 1998 (1872). *The Expression of the Emotions in Man and Animals*. New York: Oxford Univ. Press. 3rd ed. 472 pp.

Davidson R, Tomarken A. 1994. Frontal brain activation in repressors and nonrepressors. *J. Abnorm. Psychol.* 103:339–49

Davidson RJ. 1995. Cerebral asymmetry, emotion and affective style. In *Brain Asymmetry*, ed. RJ Davidson, K Hugdahl, pp. 361–87. Cambridge, MA: MIT Press

Davidson RJ. 1993. Parsing affective space: perspectives from neuropsychology and psychophysiology. *Neuropsychology.* 7:464–75

Davies AF. 1980. *Skills, Outlooks and Passions: A Psychoanalytic Contribution to the Study of Politics*. Cambridge, UK: Cambridge Univ. Press. 522 pp.

de Sousa R. 1987. *The Rationality of Emotion*. Cambridge, MA: MIT Press. 373 pp.

Derryberry D. 1991. The immediate effects of positive and negative feedback signals. *J. Pers. Soc. Psychol.* 61:267–78

Descartes R. 1989 (1649). *The Passions of the Soul*. Transl. SH Voss. Indianapolis, IN: Hackett. 165 pp.

Diener E. 1999. Introduction to the special issue on the structure of emotion. *J. Pers. Soc. Psychol.* 76:803–4

Diener E, Emmons RA. 1985. The independence of positive and negative affect. *J. Pers. Soc. Psychol.* 47:1105–17

Diener E, Smith H, Fujita F. 1995. The personality structure of affect. *J. Pers. Soc. Psychol.* 69:130–41

Dienstbier RA. 1984. The role of emotion in moral socialization. In *Emotion, Cognition, and Behavior*, ed. C Izard, J Kagan, R Zajonc, pp. 484–514. New York: Cambridge Univ. Press

Digman JM. 1989. Five robust trait dimensions: development, stability and utility. *J. Pers.* 57:195–214

Edelman M. 1964. *The Symbolic Uses of Politics*. Urbana: Univ. Ill. Press. 201 pp.

Edelman M. 1988. *Constructing the Political Spectacle*. Chicago: Univ. Chicago Press. 137 pp.

Edwards K. 1990. The interplay of affect and cognition in attitude formation and change. *J. Pers. Soc. Psychol.* 59:202–16

Ekman P, Davidson RJ, eds. 1994. *The Nature of Emotion*. New York: Oxford Univ. Press. 496 pp.

Ekman P, Rosenberg E, eds. 1997. *What the Face Reveals: Basic and Applied Studies of Spontaneous Expression Using the Facial Action Coding Systems (FACS)*. Ser. Affect. Sci., ed. RJ Davidson, P Ekman, K Scherer. New York: Oxford Univ. Press. 495 pp.

Elder CD, Cobb RW. 1983. *The Political Uses*

of Symbols. Longman Prof. Stud. Polit. Commun. Policy, ed. JB Mannheim. New York: Longman. 173 pp.

Elster J. 1999. *Alchemies of the Mind: Rationality and the Emotions.* Cambridge, UK/New York: Cambridge Univ. Press. xi, 450 pp.

Erdley CA, D'Agostino PR. 1988. Cognitive and affective components of automatic priming effects. *J. Pers. Soc. Psychol.* 54:741–47

Fabrigar LR, Petty RE. 1999. The role of affective and cognitive bases of attitudes in susceptibility to affectively and cognitively based persuasion. *Pers. Soc. Psychol. Bull.* 25:363–81

Feldman S, Stenner K. 1997. Perceived threat and authoritarianism. *Polit. Psychol.* 18:741–70

Fiske ST, Pavelchak M. 1986. Category-based versus piecemeal-based affective responses: developments in schema-triggered affect. In *The Handbook of Motivation and Cognition: Foundations of Social Behavior*, ed. R Sorrentino, E Higgins, pp. 167–203. New York: Guilford

Flett GL, Endler NS, Fairlie P. 1999. The interaction model of anxiety and threat of Quebec's separation from Canada. *J. Pers. Soc. Psychol.* 76:143–50

Forgas JP. 1992. On mood and peculiar people: affect and person typicality in impression formation. *J. Pers. Soc. Psychol.* 62:863–75

Forgas JP. 1995. Mood and judgment: the affect infusion model (AIM). *Psychol. Bull.* 117:39–66

Frank R. 1988. *Passions Within Reason.* New York: Norton. 304 pp.

Fridlund AJ, Cacioppo JT. 1986. Guidelines for human electromyographic research. *Psychophysiology* 23:567–89

Frijda NH, Kuipers P, Schure E. 1989. Relations among emotion, appraisal, and emotional action readiness. *J. Pers. Soc. Psychol.* 57:212–28

George AL, George JL. 1998. *Presidential Personality and Performance.* Boulder, CO: Westview. 287 pp.

Gibbard A. 1990. *Wise Choices, Apt Feelings.* Cambridge, MA: Harvard Univ. Press. 346 pp.

Gibson JL. 1992. Alternative measures of political tolerance: must tolerance be "least-liked"? *Am. J. Polit. Sci.* 36:560–77

Gibson JL, Bingham RD. 1982. On the conceptualization and measurement of political tolerance. *Am. Polit. Sci. Rev.* 76:603–20

Glaser J, Salovey P. 1998. Affect in electoral politics. *Person. Soc. Psychol. Rev.* 2:156–72

Goldberg LR. 1990. An alternative "description of personality": The Big-Five Factor structure. *J. Pers. Soc. Psychol.* 59:1216–29

Granberg D, Brown TA. 1989. On affect and cognition in politics. *Soc. Psychol. Q.* 52: 171–82

Gray JA. 1987a. The neuropsychology of emotion and personality. In *Cognitive Neurochemistry*, ed. SM Stahl, SD Iversen, EC Goodman, pp. 171–90. Oxford, UK: Oxford Univ. Press

Gray JA. 1987b. *The Psychology of Fear and Stress.* Cambridge: Cambridge Univ. Press. 2nd ed. 422 pp.

Gray JA. 1990. Brain systems that mediate both emotion and cognition. *Cogn. Emot.* 4:269–88

Gray JA, McNaughton N. 1996. The neuropsychology of anxiety: reprise. In *Perspectives on Anxiety, Panic and Fear*, ed. DA Hope, 43:61–134. Lincoln: Univ. Nebr. Press

Green DP, Citrin J. 1994. Measurement error and the structure of attitudes: are positive and negative judgments opposites? *Am. J. Polit. Sci.* 38:256–81

Green DP, Goldman SL, Salovey P. 1993. Measurement error masks bipolarity in affect ratings. *J. Pers. Soc. Psychol.* 64:1029–41

Green DP, Salovey P. 1999. In what sense are positive and negative affect independent? *Psychol. Sci.* 10:304–6

Green DP, Salovey P, Truax KM. 1999. Static, dynamic, and causative bipolarity of affect. *J. Pers. Soc. Psychol.* 76:856–67

Greene S. 1998. *Affective and cognitive components of partisanship: a new approach.*

Presented at Annu. Meet. Midwest Polit. Sci. Assoc., Chicago

Greene S. 2000. Race, gender, and the psychological structure of partisanship. *Women Polit.* In press

Greenstein F. 1969. The benevolent leader: children's images of political authority. *Am. Polit. Sci. Rev.* 54:934–43

Greenstein FI. 1987. *Personality and Politics: Problems of Evidence, Inference and Conceptualization.* Princeton, NJ: Princeton Univ. Press. 200 pp.

Greenstein FI. 1992. Can personality and politics be studied systematically? *Polit. Psychol.* 13:105–28

Greenstein FI. 1994. *The Hidden-Hand Presidency: Eisenhower as Leader.* Baltimore, MD: Johns Hopkins Univ. Press. xxii, 286 pp.

Greenstein FI, Destler IM. 1983. *The Reagan Presidency: An Early Assessment.* Garfield Found. Public Aff. Study. Baltimore, MD: Johns Hopkins Univ. Press. vii, 197 pp.

Gross JJ, Sutton SK, Ketelaar T. 1998. Relations between affect and personality: support for affect-level and affective reactivity views. *Pers. Soc. Psychol. Bull.* 24:279–88

Gump BB, Kulik JA. 1997. Stress, affiliation, and emotional contagion. *J. Pers. Soc. Psychol.* 72:305–19

Gunther AC, Thorson E. 1992. Perceived persuasive effects of product commercials and public service announcements. *Commun. Res.* 19:574–96

Halberstadt JB, Niedenthal PM. 1997. Emotional state and the use of stimulus dimensions in judgment. *J. Pers. Soc. Psychol.* 72:1017–33

Harmon-Jones E, Allen JJB. 1996. Anterior EEG asymmetry and facial EMG as evidence that affect is involved in the mere exposure effect. *Psychophysiology* 33:544

Hass RG, Katz I, Rizzo N, Bailey J, Moore L. 1992. When racial ambivalence evokes negative affect, using a disguised measure of mood. *Pers. Soc. Psychol. Bull.* 18:786–97

Hastie R. 1986. A primer of information-processing theory for the political scientist. In *Political Cognition*, ed. R Lau, D Sears, pp. 11–39. Hillsdale, NJ: Erlbaum

Hastie R, Park B. 1986. The relationship between memory and judgment depends on whether the task is memory-based or on-line. *Psychol. Rev.* 93:258–68

Hatfield E, Cacioppo JT, Rapson R. 1992. The logic of emotion: emotional contagion. In *Review of Personality and Social Psychology*, ed. MS Clark, 14:151–77. Newbury Park, CA: Sage

Hatfield E, Cacioppo JT, Rapson RL. 1994. *Emotional Contagion. Studies in Emotion & Social Interaction*, ed. P Ekman, KR Scherer. Cambridge, UK: Cambridge Univ. Press. 240 pp.

Hibbing JR, Theiss-Morse E. 1995. *Congress as Public Enemy: Public Attitudes Toward American Political Institutions.* Cambridge Univ. Press Ser. Polit. Psychol., ed. J Kuklinski. New York: Cambridge Univ. Press. 186 pp.

Hibbing JR, Theiss-Morse E. 1998. The media's role in public negativity toward congress: distinguishing emotional reactions and cognitive reactions. *Am. J. Polit. Sci.* 42:475–98

Hilgard ER. 1980. The trilogy of the mind: cognition, affection, and conation. *J. Hist. Behav. Sci.* 16:107–17

Hobbes T. 1968. *Leviathan.* ed. CB Macpherson. London: Penguin. 729 pp.

Hoffman M. 1984. Interaction of affect and cognition in empathy. In *Emotion, Cognition, and Behavior*, ed. C Izard, J Kagan, R Zajonc, pp. 103–31. New York: Cambridge Univ. Press

Holmes S. 1995. *Passions and Constraint: On the Theory of Liberal Democracy.* Chicago: Univ. Chicago Press. 337 pp.

Hsee CK, Hatfield E, Carlson JG. 1990. The effect of power on susceptibility to emotional contagion. *Cogn. Emot.* 4:327–40

Hume D. 1739–40. *A Treatise of Human Nature.* London: Penguin. 678 pp.

Isbell LM, Wyer RS Jr. 1999. Correcting for mood-induced bias in the evaluation of political candidates: the role of intrinsic and extrinsic motivation. *Pers. Soc. Psychol. Bull.* 25:237–49

Ito TA, Cacioppo JT, Lang PJ. 1998a. Eliciting affect using the international affective picture system: trajectories through evaluative space. *Pers. Soc. Psychol. Bul.* 24:855–79

Ito TA, Larsen JT, Smith NK, Cacioppo JT. 1998b. Negative information weighs more heavily on the brain: the negativity bias in evaluative categorizations. *J. Pers. Soc. Psychol.* 75:887–900

Jackson LA, Sullivan LA. 1990. Cognition and affect in evaluations of stereotyped group members. *J. Soc. Psychol.* 129:659–72

James W. 1883. What is emotion? *Mind* 9:188–204

James W. 1894. The physical basis of emotion. *Psychol. Rev.* 1:516–29

Jamieson KH. 1992. *Dirty Politics: Deception, Distraction, and Democracy.* New York: Oxford Univ. Press. 335 pp.

Janis IL. 1982. *Groupthink.* Boston: Houghton Mifflin. 2nd ed. 349 pp.

Janis IL, Mann L. 1977. *Decision Making.* New York: Free. 488 pp.

Jervis R, Lebow RN, Stein JG. 1985. *Psychology and Deterrence.* Baltimore, MD: John Hopkins Univ. Press. 270 pp.

John OP. 1990. The "big five" factor taxonomy: dimensions of personality in the natural language and in questionnaires. In *Handbook of Personality Theory and Research*, ed. LA Pervin, pp. 66–100. New York: Guilford

Jones LE, Iacobucci D. 1989. The structure of affect and trait judgments of political figures. *Multivariate Behav. Res.* 24:457–76

Kelley S. 1983. *Interpreting Elections.* Princeton, NJ: Princeton Univ. Press. 267 pp.

Kenney P, Rice TR. 1988. Presidential prenomination preferences and candidate evaluations. *Am. Polit. Sci. Rev.* 82:1309–19

Kern M. 1989. *30-Second Politics: Political Advertising in the Eighties.* New York: Westport. 237 pp.

Kinder D, Sanders LM. 1996. *Divided by Color: Racial Politics and Democratic Ideals.* Chicago: Univ. Chicago Press. 391 pp.

Kinder DR. 1994. Reason and emotion in American political life. In *Beliefs, Reasoning, & Decision-Making: Psycho-Logic in Honor of Bob Abelson*, ed. R Schank, E Langer, pp. 277–314. Hillsdale, NJ: Erlbaum

Kinder DR, Sanders LM. 1990. Mimicking political debate with survey questions: the case of white opinion on affirmative action for blacks. *Soc. Cogn.* 8:73–103

Klein JG. 1991. Negativity effects in impression formation: a test in the political arena. *Pers. Soc. Psychol. Bul.* 17:412–18

Krosnick JA, Brannon LA. 1993. The impact of the Gulf War on the ingredients of presidential evaluations: multidimensional effects of political involvement. *Am. Polit. Sci. Rev.* 87:963–75

Krosnick JA, Kinder DR. 1990. Altering the foundations of support for the president through priming. *Am. Polit. Sci. Rev.* 84:497–512

Kuklinski JH, Riggle E, Ottati V, Schwarz N, Wyer RS Jr. 1991. The cognitive and affective bases of political tolerance judgments. *Am. J. Polit. Sci.* 35:1–27

Kunst-Wilson WR, Zajonc RB. 1980. Affect discrimination of stimuli cannot be recognized. *Science* 207:557–58

Lang A, ed. 1994. *Measuring Psychological Responses to Media.* Hillsdale, NJ: Erlbaum. 244 pp.

Lang PJ. 1995. The emotion probe: studies of motivation and attention. *Am. Psychol.* 50:372–85

Lang PJ, Bradley MM, Cuthbert BN. 1990. Emotion, attention, and the startle reflect. *Psychol. Rev.* 97:377–95

Lang PJ, Greenwald MK, Bradley MM, Hamm AO. 1993. Looking at pictures: affective, facial, visceral and behavioral reactions. *Psychophysiology* 30:261–73

Langer W. 1972. *The Mind of Adolf Hitler.* New York: Basic Books. 286 pp.

Larsen RJ, Diener E. 1992. Promises and

problems with the circumplex model of emotion. In *Emotion*, ed. MS Clark, pp. 25–59. Newbury Park, CA: Sage

Lasswell H. 1930. *Psychopathology and Politics*. Chicago: Univ. Chicago Press. 319 pp.

Lasswell H. 1948. *Power and Personality*. New York: Norton. 250 pp.

Lavine H, Burgess D, Snyder M, Transue J, Sullivan JL, et al. 1999. Threat, authoritarianism, and voting: an investigation of personality and persuasion. *Pers. Soc. Psychol. Bull.* 25:337–47

Lazarus R. 1982. Thoughts on the relations of emotion and cognition. *Am. Psychol.* 37:1019–24

Lazarus R. 1984. On the primacy of cognition. *Am. Psychol.* 39:124–29

LeDoux J. 1996. *The Emotional Brain: The Mysterious Underpinnings of Emotional Life*. New York: Simon & Schuster

Leeper R. 1948. A motivational theory of emotion to replace 'emotion as disorganized response.' *Psychol. Rev.* 55:5–21

Lerner JS, Goldberg JH, Tetlock PE. 1998. Sober second thought: the effects of accountability, anger, and authoritarianism on attributions of responsibility. *Pers. Soc. Psychol. Bull.* 24:563–74

Lifton RJ. 1986. *The Nazi Doctors: Medical Killing and the Psychology of Genocide*. New York: Basic Books. 561 pp.

Lodge M, Hamill R. 1986. A partisan schema for political information processing. *Am. Polit. Sci. Rev.* 80:505–20

Lodge M, Taber C. 1998. Three steps toward a theory of motivated political reasoning. In *Elements of Political Reason: Understanding and Expanding the Limits of Rationality*, ed. A Lupia, M McCubbins, S Popkin. New York: Cambridge Univ. Press

Lodge MG, McGraw KM, Stroh P. 1989. An impression-driven model of candidate evaluation. *Am. Polit. Sci. Rev.* 83:399–420

Madison J, Hamilton A, Jay J. 1961 (1787). *The Federalist Papers*, ed. J Cooke. Cleveland: World. 672 pp.

Madsen D, Snow PG. 1991. *The Charismatic Bond: Political Behavior in Time of Crisis*. Cambridge, MA: Harvard Univ. Press. 187 pp.

Malatesta CZ. 1990. The role of emotions in the development and organization of personality. In *Nebraska Symposium on Motivation*, ed. RA Thompson, 36:1–56. Lincoln: Univ. Nebr. Press

Marcus GE. 1988. The structure of emotional response: 1984 presidential candidates. *Am. Polit. Sci. Rev.* 82:735–61

Marcus GE. 1991. Emotions and politics: hot cognitions and the rediscovery of passion. *Soc. Sci. Inf.* 30:195–232

Marcus GE, MacKuen M. 1993. Anxiety, enthusiasm and the vote: the emotional underpinnings of learning and involvement during presidential campaigns. *Am. Polit. Sci. Rev.* 87:688–701

Marcus GE, MacKuen M. 1996. *Measuring Mood in the 1995 NES Pilot Study. Tech. Rep. Natl. Election Stud. Natl. Board Overseers*. Univ. Michigan, Ann Arbor

Marcus GE, Neuman WR, MacKuen M. 2000. *Affective Intelligence and Political Judgment*. Chicago: Univ. Chicago Press. In press

Marcus GE, Neuman WR, MacKuen M, Sullivan JL. 1996. Dynamic models of emotional response: the multiple role of affect in politics. In *Research In Micropolitics*, ed. M Delli Carpini, L Huddy, RY Shapiro, 5:33–59. Greenwich, CT: JAI

Marcus GE, Sullivan JL, Theiss-Morse E, Wood S. 1995. *With Malice Toward Some: How People Make Civil Liberties Judgments. Political Psychology*, ed. J Kuklinski. New York: Cambridge Univ. Press. 288 pp.

Marcus GE, Wood SL, Theiss-Morse E. 1998. Linking neuroscience to political intolerance and political judgment. *Polit. Life Sci.* 17:165–78

Masters R, Sullivan D. 1993. Nonverbal behavior and leadership: emotion and cognition in political attitudes. In *Explorations in Political Psychology*, ed. S Iyengar, W McGuire, pp. 150–82. Durham, NC: Duke Univ. Press

Masters RD. 1989. *The Nature of Politics*. New

Haven, CT: Yale Univ. Press. 298 pp.

Masters RD. 1991. Individual and cultural differences in response to leaders' nonverbal displays. *J. Soc. Issue* 47:151–65

Masters RD, Frey S, Bente G. 1991. Dominance & attention: images of leaders in German, French, & American TV news. *Polity* 23:373–94

Masters RD, Sullivan DG. 1989a. Facial displays and political leadership in France. *Behav. Proc.* 19:1–30

Masters RD, Sullivan DG. 1989b. Nonverbal displays and political leadership in France and the United States. *Polit. Behav.* 11:123–56

May CP, Kane MJ, Hasher L. 1995. Determinants of negative priming. *Psychol. Bull.* 118:35–54

McCrae RR, John OP. 1992. An introduction to the five-factor model and its applications. *J. Pers.* 60:175–215

McGraw KM, Pinney N, Neumann D. 1991. Memory for political actors: contrasting the use of semantic and evaluative organizational strategies. *Polit. Behav.* 13:165–89

McHugo GJ, Lanzetta JT, Sullivan DG, Masters RD, Englis B. 1985. Emotional reactions to expressive displays of a political leader. *J. Pers. Soc. Psychol.* 49:1512–29

McNeil DW, Vrana SR, Melamed BG, Cuthbert BN, Lang PJ. 1993. Emotional imagery in simple and social phobia: fear versus anxiety. *J. Abnorm. Psychol.* 102:212–25

Mehrabian A. 1995. Framework for a comprehensive description and measurement of emotional states. *Genet. Soc. Gen. Psychol. Monogr.* 12:339–61

Mehrabian A. 1996. Pleasure-arousal-dominance: a general framework for describing and measuring individual differences in temperament. *Curr. Psychol.* 14:261–92

Mikula G, Scherer KR, Athenstaedt U. 1998. The role of injustice in the elicitation of differential emotional reactions. *Pers. Soc. Psychol. Bull.* 24:769–83

Millar MG, Millar KU. 1990. Attitude change as a function of attitude type and argument

type. *J. Pers. Soc. Psychol.* 59:217–28

Millar MG, Tesser A. 1986a. Effects of affective and cognitive focus on the attitude-behavior relation. *J. Pers. Soc. Psychol.* 51:270–76

Millar MG, Tesser A. 1986b. Thought-induced attitude change: the effects of schema structure and commitment. *J. Pers. Soc. Psychol.* 51:259–69

Millar MG, Tesser A. 1989. The effects of affective-cognitive consistency and thought on the attitude-behavior relationship. *J. Exp. Soc. Psychol.* 25:189–202

Miller JM, Krosnick JA. 1999. *The impact of policy change threat on grassroots activism.* Presented at Annu. Meet. Midwest Polit. Sci. Assoc., Chicago, IL

Mogg K, Mathews A, Bird C, Macgregor-Morris R. 1990. Effects of stress and anxiety on the processing of threat stimuli. *J. Pers. Soc. Psychol.* 59:1230–37

Monroe KR. 1996. *The Heart of Altruism: Perceptions of a Common Humanity.* Princeton, NJ: Princeton Univ. Press. 292 pp.

Moreland RL, Zajonc RB. 1979. Exposure effects may not depend on stimulus recognition. *J. Pers. Soc. Psychol.* 37:1085–89

Murphy ST, Monahan JL, Zajonc RB. 1995. Additivity of nonconscious affect: combined effects of priming and exposure. *J. Pers. Soc. Psychol.* 69:589–602

Murphy ST, Zajonc RB. 1993. Affect, cognition, and awareness: affective priming with optimal and suboptimal stimulus exposures. *J. Pers. Soc. Psychol.* 64:723–39

Nelson TE. 1998. Group affect and attribution in social policy opinion. *J. Polit.* 61:567–84

Nelson TE, Clawson RA, Oxley ZM. 1997. Media framing of a civil liberties conflict and its effect on tolerance. *Am. Polit. Sci. Rev.* 91:567–83

Ortony A, Clore GL, Collins A. 1989. *The Cognitive Structure of Emotions.* New York: Cambridge Univ. Press. 207 pp.

Osgood CE, Suci GJ, Tannenbaum PH. 1957. *The Measurement of Meaning.* Urbana: Univ. Ill. Press. 342 pp.

Ottati V. 2000. The psychological determinants

of political judgment. In *Blackwell Handbook in Social Psychology, Vol 1. Intraindividual Processes*, ed. A Tesser, N Schwarz. Cambridge, MA: Blackwell. In press

Ottati VC. 1997. When the survey question directs retrieval: implications for assessing the cognitive and affective predictors of global evaluations. *Eur. J. Soc. Psychol.* 27:1–21

Ottati VC, Isbell LM. 1996. Effects of mood during exposure to target information on subsequently reported judgments: an on-line model of misattribution and correction. *J. Pers. Soc. Psychol.* 71:39–53

Ottati VC, Riggle EJ, Wyer RS Jr, Schwarz N, Kuklinski J. 1989. Cognitive and affective bases of opinion survey responses. *J. Pers. Soc. Psychol.* 57:404–15

Ottati VC, Wyer RS Jr. 1991. The cognitive mediators of political choice: toward a comprehensive model of political information processing. In *Information and Democratic Processes*, ed. JA Ferejohn, JH Kuklinski, pp. 186–216. Champaign: Univ. Ill. Press

Ottati VC, Wyer RS Jr. 1993. Affect and political judgment. In *Explorations in Political Judgment*, ed. S Iyengar, W McGuire, pp. 296–320. Durham, NC: Duke Univ. Press

Panksepp J. 1989. The neurobiology of emotions: of animal brains and human feelings. In *Handbook of Social Psychophysiology*, ed. H Wagner, A Manstead, pp. 5–26. Chichester, UK: Wiley & Sons

Panksepp J. 1998. *Affective Neuroscience: The Foundations of Human and Animal Emotions*. Ser. Affect. Sci., ed. RJ Davidson, P Ekman, K Scherer. New York: Oxford Univ. Press. 466 pp.

Petty RE, Gleicher F, Baker SM. 1991. Multiple roles for affect in persuasion. In *Emotion and Social Judgments*, ed. JP Forgas, pp. 181–99. Oxford: Pergamon

Plato. 1974. *The Republic*. New York: Penguin. 2nd ed. 464 pp.

Plutchik R. 1980a. *Emotion: A Psychoevolutionary Synthesis*. New York: Harper & Row. 440 pp.

Plutchik R. 1980b. A general psychoevolutionary theory of emotion. In *Emotion: Theory, Research and Experience*, Vol. 1. *Theories of Emotion*, ed. R Plutchik, H Kellerman, pp. 3–34. San Diego: Academic

Plutchik R, Kellerman H, eds. 1989. *Emotion Theory, Research, and Experience*. Vol. 4. *The Measurement of Emotions*, Vol. 4. *Emotion Theory, Research, and Experience*. ed. R Plutchik, H Kellerman. San Diego: Academic

Post JM. 1993. Current concepts of the narcissistic personality: implications for political psychology. *Polit. Psychol.* 14:99–121

Pratto F, John OP. 1991. Automatic vigilance: the attention-grabbing power of negative social information. *J. Pers. Soc. Psychol.* 61:380–91

Quigley BM, Tedeschi JT. 1996. Mediating effects of blame attributions on feelings of anger. *Pers. Soc. Psychol. Bul.* 19:1280–88

Ragsdale L. 1991. Strong feelings: emotional responses to presidents. *Polit. Behav.* 13:33–65

Rahn W. 1998. *Political Campaigns and Public Mood: A Proposal for the 1998 NES Pilot Study*. Ann Arbor, MI: Natl. Election Stud. 15 pp.

Rahn W. 2000. Affect as information: the role of public mood in political reasoning. In *Elements of Reason: Cognition, Choice, and the Bounds of Rationality*, ed. A Lupia, M McCubbins, S Popkin. New York: Cambridge Univ. Press. In press

Rahn WM, Aldrich JH, Borgida E, Sullivan JL. 1990. A social-cognitive model of candidate appraisal. In *Information and Democratic Processes*, ed. J Ferejohn, J Kuklinski, pp. 136–59. Urbana-Champaign: Univ. Ill. Press

Rahn WM, Kroeger B, Kite CM. 1996. A framework for the study of public mood. *Polit. Psychol.* 17:29–58

Renshon SA. 1998. *The Psychological Assessment of Presidential Candidates*. New York: Routledge. 515 pp.

Robinson RG. 1995. Mapping brain activity

associated with emotion. *Am. J. Psychiatry* 152:327–29

Rogow AA. 1963. *James Forrestal, A Study of Personality, Politics, and Policy.* New York: Macmillan. xv, 397 pp.

Rolls ET. 1999. *The Brain and Emotion.* Oxford/New York: Oxford Univ. Press. ix, 367 pp.

Rorty EO, ed. 1980. *Explaining Emotions.* Berkeley: Univ. Calif. Press. 543 pp.

Rorty EO, ed. 1996. *Aristotle's Rhetoric.* Berkeley: Univ. Calif. Press. 440 pp.

Roseman I. 1984. Cognitive determinants of emotions: a structural theory. In *Review of Personality and Social Psychology*, ed. P Shaver, pp. 11–36. Beverly Hills, CA: Sage

Roseman I, Abelson RP, Ewing MF. 1986. Emotions and political cognition: emotional appeals in political communication. In *Political Cognition*, ed. R Lau, DO Sears, pp. 279–94. Hillsdale NJ: Lawrence Erlbaum

Roseman IJ, Antoniou AA, Jose PE. 1996. Appraisal determinants of emotions: constructing a more accurate and comprehensive theory. *Cogn. Emot.* 10:241–77

Rosenberg MJ, Hovland CI. 1960. Cognitive, affective, and behavioral components of attitudes. In *Attitude Organization and Change*, ed. MJ Rosenberg, CI Hovland, pp. 1–14. New Haven, CT: Yale Univ. Press

Rosenberg S, Bohan L, McCafferty P, Harris K. 1986. The image and the vote: effects of candidate presentation on voter preference. *Am. J. Polit. Sci.* 30:108–27

Russell D, McAuley E. 1986. Causal attributions, causal dimensions, and affective reactions to success and failure. *J. Pers. Soc. Psychol.* 50:1174–85

Russell JA. 1980. A circumplex model of affect. *J. Pers. Soc. Psychol.* 39:1161–78

Russell JA. 1983. Pancultural aspects of human conceptual organization of emotions. *J. Pers. Soc. Psychol.* 45:1281–88

Russell JA, Barrett LF. 1999. Core affect, prototypical emotional episodes, and other things called *emotion*: dissecting the elephant. *J. Pers. Soc. Psychol.* 76:805–19

Russell JA, Bullock M. 1985. Multidimensional scaling of facial expressions: similarity from preschoolers to adults. *J. Pers. Soc. Psychol.* 48:1290–98

Russell JA, Carroll JM. 1999. On the bipolarity of positive and negative affect. *Psychol. Bull.* 125:3–30

Russell JA, Lewicka M, Niit T. 1989a. A cross-cultural study of a circumplex model of affect. *J. Pers. Soc. Psychol.* 57:848–56

Russell JA, Weiss A, Mendelsohn GA. 1989b. Affect grid: a single-item scale of pleasure and arousal. *J. Pers. Soc. Psychol.* 57:493–502

Rusting CL. 1998. Personality, mood, and cognitive processing of emotional information: three conceptual frameworks. *Psychol. Bull.* 124:165–96

Rusting CL, Larsen RJ. 1998. Personality and cognitive processing of affective information. *Pers. Soc. Psychol. Bull.* 24:200–13

Sacks CH, Bugental DB. 1987. Attributions as moderators of affective and behavioral responses to social failure. *J. Pers. Soc. Psychol.* 53:939–47

Saucier G. 1992. Benchmarks: integrating affective and interpersonal circles with the big-five personality factors. *J. Pers. Soc. Psychol.* 62:1025–35

Schatz RT, Staub E. 1997. Manifestations of blind and constructive patriotism: personality correlates and individual-group relations. In *Patriotism in the Lives of Individuals and Nations*, ed. D Bar-Tal, E Staub, pp. 229–45. Chicago: Nelson Hall

Schatz RT, Staub E, Levine H. 1999. On the varieties of national attachment: blind versus constructive patriotism. *Polit. Psychol.* 20:151–75

Scholz JT, Lubell M. 1998. Adaptive political attitudes: duty, trust, and fear as monitors of tax policy. *Am. J. Polit. Sci.* 42:903–20

Schwarz N. 1990. Feelings as information: informational and motivational functions of affective states. In *Handbook of Motivation and Cognition: Foundations of Social Behavior,* ed. R Sorrentino, ET Higgins, 2:527–61. New York: Guilford

Schwarz N, Clore GL. 1996. Feelings and phenomenal experiences. In *Social Psychology: Handbook of Basic Principles*, ed. ET Higgins, AW Kruglanski, pp. 433–64. New York: Guilford

Sears DO. 1993. Symbolic politics: a socio-psychological theory. In *Explorations in Political Psychology*, ed. S Iyengar, WJ McGuire, pp. 113–49. Durham, NC: Duke Univ. Press

Sears DO, Citrin J. 1982. *Tax Revolt: Something for Nothing in California*. Cambridge, MA: Harvard Univ. Press. 278 pp.

Sears DO, Funk CL. 1999. Evidence of long-term persistence of adults' political predispositions. *J. Polit.* 61:1–28

Sears DO, Hensler C, Speer L. 1979. Whites' opposition to "busing": self-interest or symbolic politics? *Am. Polit. Sci. Rev.* 73:369–85

Sears DO, Lau RR, Tyler TR, Allen HM Jr. 1980. Self-interest vs. symbolic politics in policy attitudes and presidential voting. *Am. Polit. Sci. Rev.* 74:670–84

Sears DO, Valentino NA. 1997. Politics matters: political events as catalysts for preadult socialization. *Am. Polit. Sci. Rev.* 91:45–65

Smith A. 1959. *The Theory of Moral Sentiments*. Indianapolis, IN: Liberty Fund. 412 pp.

Smith CA, Haynes KN, Lazarus RS, Pope LK. 1993. In search of the "hot" cognitions: attributions, appraisals, and their relation to emotion. *J. Pers. Soc. Psychol.* 65:916–29

Sniderman PM, Piazza TL. 1993. *The Scar of Race*. Cambridge, MA: Harvard Univ. Press. 212 pp.

Stangor C, Sullivan LA, Ford TE. 1991. Affective and cognitive determinants of prejudice. *Soc. Cogn.* 9:359–91

Staub E. 1997. Blind versus constructive patriotism: moving from embeddedness in the group to critical loyalty and action. In *Patriotism in the Lives of Individuals and Nations*, ed. D Bar-Tal, E Staub, pp. 213–29. Chicago: Nelson Hall

Stein JG. 1988. Building politics into psychology: the misperception of threat. *Polit. Psychol.* 9:245–71

Steinberg B. 1996. *Shame and Humiliation: Presidential Decision Making on Vietnam*. Montreal: McGill-Queen's Univ. Press. 397 pp.

Storm C, Storm T. 1987. A taxonomic study of the vocabulary of emotions. *J. Pers. Soc. Psychol.* 53:805–16

Sullins ES. 1991. Emotional contagion revisited: effects of social comparison and expressive style on mood convergence. *Pers. Soc. Psychol. Bull.* 17:166–74

Sullivan D, Masters R. 1988a. Happy warriors: leaders' facial displays, viewers emotions, and political support. *Am. J. Polit. Sci.* 32:345–68

Sullivan JL, Piereson J, Marcus GE. 1982. *Political Tolerance and American Democracy*. Chicago: Univ. Chicago Press. 278 pp.

Sutton SK, Davidson RJ. 1997. Prefrontal brain asymmetry: a biological substrate of the behavioral and inhibition systems. *Psychol. Sci.* 8:204–10

Taylor SE. 1991. Asymmetrical effects of positive and negative events: the mobilization-minimization hypothesis. *Psychol. Bull.* 110:67–85

Tellegen A. 1985. Structures of mood and personality and their relevance to assessing anxiety, with an emphasis on self-report. In *Anxiety and the Anxiety Disorders*, ed. AH Tuma, JD Maser, pp. 681–716. Hillsdale, NJ: Erlbaum

Tellegen A, Watson D, Clark LA. 1999a. Further support for a hierarchical model of affect. *Psychol. Sci.* 10:307–9

Tellegen A, Watson D, Clark LA. 1999b. On the dimensional and hierarchical structure of affect. *Psychol. Sci.* 10:297–303

Tesser A, Martin L. 1996. The psychology of evaluation. In *Social Psychology: Handbook of Basic Principles*, ed. ET Higgins, AW Kruglanski, pp. 400–32. New York: Guilford

Thompson MM, Zanna MP, Griffin DW. 1995. Let's not be indifferent about (attitudinal)

ambivalence. In *Attitude Strength: Antecedents and Consequences*, ed. RE Petty, JA Krosnick, pp. 361–86. Hillsdale, NJ: Erlbaum

Titchener EB. 1895. Affective memory. *Philos. Rev.* 4:65–76

Tomarken AJ, Davidson RJ, Henriques JB. 1990. Resting frontal brain asymmetry predicts affective response to films. *J. Pers. Soc. Psychol.* 59:791–801

Tomarken AJ, Davidson RJ, Wheeler RE, Doss RC. 1992. Individual differences in anterior brain assymetry and fundamental dimensions of emotion. *J. Pers. Soc. Psychol.* 62:676–87

Tomkins SS. 1962. *Affect, Imagery, and Consciousness*. Vol. 1. *The Positive Affects*. New York: Springer

Tomkins SS. 1963. *Affect, Imagery, and Consciousness*. Vol. 2. *The Negative Affects*. New York: Springer

Tomkins SS. 1981. The quest for primary motives: biography and autobiography of an idea. *J. Pers. Soc. Psychol.* 41:306–29

Tomkins SS. 1984. Affect theory. In *Approaches to Emotion*, ed. KR Scherer, P Ekman, pp. 163–95. Hillsdale, NJ: Erlbaum

Tooby J, Cosmides L. 1990. The past explains the present: emotional adaptations and the structure of ancestral environments. *Ethol. Sociobiol.* 11:375–424

Tulving E, Schacter DL. 1990. Priming and human memory systems. *Science* 247:301–6

Volkan VD. 1988. *The Need to Have Enemies and Allies*. Northvale, NJ: Aronson. 298 pp.

Volkan VD, Itkowitz N. 1984. *The Immortal Ataturk: A Psychobiography*. Chicago: Chicago Univ. Press. 374 pp.

Volkan VD, Itkowitz N, Dod AW. 1997. *Richard Nixon: A Psychobiography*. New York: Cambridge Univ. Press. 190 pp.

Warnecke AM, Masters RD, Kempter G. 1992. The roots of nationalism: nonverbal behavior and xenophobia. *Ethol. Sociobiol.* 13:267–82

Watson D. 1988. The vicissitudes of mood measurement: effects of varying descriptors, time frames, and response formats on measures of positive and negative affect. *J. Pers. Soc. Psychol.* 55:128–41

Watson D, Clark LA. 1992. Affects separable and inseparable: on the hierarchical arrangement of the negative affects. *J. Pers. Soc. Psychol.* 62:489–505

Watson D, Clark LA. 1994. *The PANAS-X: Manual for the Positive and Negative Affect Schedule—Expanded Form*, Univ. Iowa, Iowa City. Unpublished manuscript. 35 pp.

Watson D, Clark LA. 1997. Measurement and mismeasurement of mood: recurrent and emergent issues. *J. Pers. Assess.* 68:267–96

Watson D, Clark LA, McIntyre CW, Hamaker S. 1992. Affect, personality and social activity. *J. Pers. Soc. Psychol.* 63:1011–25

Watson D, Clark LA, Tellegen A. 1988. Development and validation of brief measures of positive and negative affect: the PANAS scales. *J. Pers. Soc. Psychol.* 54:1063–70

Watson D, Tellegen A. 1985. Toward a consensual structure of mood. *Psychol. Bull.* 98:219–35

Watson D, Tellegen A. 1999. Issues in the dimensional structure of affect—effects of descriptors, measurement error, and response formats: comment on Russell and Carroll. *Psychol. Bull.* 125:601–10

Watson D, Walker LM. 1996. The long-term stability and predictive validity of trait measures of affect. *J. Pers. Soc. Psychol.* 70:567–77

Watson D, Wiese D, Vaidya J, Tellegen A. 1999. The two general activation systems of affect: structural findings, evolutionary considerations, and psychobiological evidence. *J. Pers. Soc. Psychol.* 76:820–38

Way B, Masters R. 1996a. Emotion and cognition in political-information processing. *J. Commun.* 46:48–65

Way BM, Masters RD. 1996b. Political attitudes: interactions of cognition and affect. *Motiv. Cogn.* 20:205–36

Weiner B, Graham S. 1984. An attributional

approach to emotional development. In *Emotion, Cognition, and Behavior*, ed. C Izard, J Kagan, R Zajonc, pp. 167–91. New York: Cambridge Univ. Press

Wheeler RE, Davidson RJ, Tomarken AJ. 1993. Frontal brain asymmetry and emotional reactivity: a biological substrate of affective style. *Psychophysiology* 30:82–89

Wiener B, Russell D, Lerman D. 1978. Affective consequences of causal ascriptions. In *New Directions in Attribution Research*, ed. JH Harvey, RF Kidd. 2:59–90. Hillsdale, NJ: Erlbaum

Wilcox C, Sigelman L, Cook E. 1989. Some like it hot: individual differences in responses to group feeling thermometers. *Public Opin. Q.* 53:246–57

Wood JV, Saltzberg JA, Goldsamt LA. 1990. Does affect induce self-focused attention? *J. Pers. Soc. Psychol.* 58:899–908

Zajonc RB. 1980. Feeling and thinking: preferences need no inferences. *Am. Psychol.* 39:151–75

Zajonc RB. 1982. On the primacy of affect. *Am. Psychol.* 39:117–23

Zajonc RB. 1998. *Emotions.* In *Handbook of Social Psychology*, ed. D Gilbert, S Fiske, G Lindzey, 1:591–632. New York: McGraw Hill. 4th ed.

Zevon M, Tellegen A. 1982. The structure of mood change: an ideographic/nomothetic analysis. *J. Pers. Soc. Psychol.* 43:111–22

Zuckerman M. 1991. *Psychobiology of Personality. Problems in Behavioral Sciences*, ed. JA Gray. Cambridge, UK: Cambridge Univ. Press. 482 pp.

Zuckerman M, Kuhlman DM, Joireman J, Teta P, Kraft M. 1993. A comparison of three structural models for personality: the big three, the big five, and the alternative five. *J. Pers. Soc. Psychol.* 65:757–68

Zullow H, Oettingen G, Peterson C, Seligman MEP. 1988. Pessimistic explanatory style in the historical record CAVing LBJ, presidential candidates, and East versus West Berlin. *Am. Psychol.* 43:673–82

Zullow HM, Seligman MEP. 1990. Pessimistic rumination predicts defeat of presidential candidates, 1990 to 1984. *Psychol. Inq.* 1:52–61

Zuwerink JR, Devine PG. 1996. Attitude importance and resistance to persuasion: It's not just the thought that counts. *J. Pers. Soc. Psychol.* 70:931–44

Annu. Rev. Polit. Sci. 2000. 3:251–76

THE CAUSES AND CONSEQUENCES OF ARMS RACES

Charles L. Glaser

Harris Graduate School of Public Policy Studies, University of Chicago, Chicago, Illinois 60637; e-mail: c-glaser@uchicago.edu

Key Words   arms races, arms control, structural realism, spiral model, bureaucratic politics

■ **Abstract**   This chapter reviews the literature on causes of arms races, their consequences, and when a state should build up arms and engage in an arms race if necessary. The literature tends to equate external causes with threats; the chapter argues for a broader understanding that includes all causes of rational arming behavior. Internal causes of arms races are then understood to be factors within the state that lead it to adopt suboptimal policies. Although the causes and consequences of arms races are usually dealt with separately, in fact they are closely connected. When a state engages in an arms race because this is its best option, the state is acting rationally, the causes of the arms race are external, and the arms race has no consequences of its own. In contrast, when a state arms because domestic interests have distorted its policy, the arms race produces negative consequences. Research on the consequences of arms races has been hindered by the lack of a fully developed theory of when a state should race; progress on defensive realism is helping to fill this gap.

INTRODUCTION

Arms races have generated a great deal of interest for a variety of reasons. They are widely believed to have significant consequences for states' security, but agreement stops there. In the debate over their consequences, one side holds that arms races increase the probability of war by undermining military stability and straining political relations. The opposing view holds that engaging in an arms race is often a state's best option for avoiding war when faced with an aggressive adversary. Debate over the causes of arms races is just as divided. One school believes that arms races are primarily rational responses to external threats and opportunities, whereas arms race skeptics believe that arms buildups are usually the product of a mixture of internal, domestic interests, including those of the scientists involved in research and development (R&D), the major producers of weapons systems, and the military services that will operate them. The policy implications of these contending views are equally contradictory; critics see arms control as a way to reduce the probability of war and rein in domestic interests that are distorting the state's security policy, and proponents argue that military competition is most likely to protect the state's international interests and preserve peace.

Arms buildups and arms races also play a prominent role in international relations (IR) theory. Building up arms is one of a state's three basic options for acquiring the military capabilities it requires to achieve its international goals; the other two are gaining allies and cooperating with its adversary to reduce threats. In broad terms, choosing between more competitive and more cooperative combinations of these options is among the most basic decisions a state must make, and it is often the most important.

The literature that focuses on arms races is large and diverse. Scholars working on various aspects of arms race questions have analyzed case studies, worked with large-n data sets, and developed many types of formal models. Beyond the literature that focuses specifically on arms races, more general work on IR theory—including structural realism, the security dilemma, defensive realism, and neoclassical realism—addresses the question of when a state should pursue cooperative policies and when it should pursue more competitive ones. This more general work contributes significantly to answering the question of when a state should engage in an arms race.

The following sections of this chapter review the literature on the causes of arms races, on the consequences of arms races, and on when a state should build up arms and race if necessary.[1] The literature divides causes into internal and external causes, and it usually deals with the causes and consequences of arms races as separate topics. This chapter argues that in fact the causes and consequences are closely connected. When a state decides to engage in an arms race because this is its best available option for achieving its international goals, given the constraints imposed by the international system, the state is acting rationally, the causes of the arms race are external, and the race has no consequences of its own. In contrast, when a state builds up arms because domestic interests have distorted its policy, the state is acting suboptimally, the causes of the arms race are internal, and the race itself produces negative consequences. Assessing the consequences of arms races therefore requires a fully developed theory of when a state should build up arms and race if necessary, to which states' actual arming behavior can be compared. The lack of such a theory has hindered research on the consequences of arms races; progress on defensive realism is helping to fill this gap.

---

[1] Whether to build up arms is a decision that a state makes on its own, whereas an arms race results from the interactive decisions of two (or more) states. Therefore, although it is common to refer to a state deciding to engage in a race, it is more precise to say that a state decides whether to build up arms than to say that a state decides to engage in an arms race. The two are closely linked, however; the decision on whether to build up arms will usually require a state to evaluate whether doing so will increase the probability that its adversary will respond with a buildup of its own. States often expect that a buildup will provoke a reaction, and therefore the decision to build up arms is essentially a decision to engage in an arms race.

CAUSES OF ARMS RACES

Many authors have characterized the literature on causes of arms races in terms of external versus internal causes, or equivalent categories (Buzan 1987, Russett 1983, Evangelista 1988, Hammond 1993:59–66, Buzan & Herring 1998; Gleditsch 1990 provides a somewhat different division; also on why states race, see Gray 1971, 1974). Although these categories are useful, the literature has tended to interpret external causes too narrowly, equating "external" with reacting to threats and action-reaction phenomena. Internal causes of arms races are of interest primarily because they help to explain why states have chosen suboptimal policies—building up arms when cooperative policies such as arms control or unilateral restraint would have had better prospects of achieving their goals. It is most useful to envision external causes in contrast to internal ones and, therefore, more broadly to include all factors that would lead a rational state to engage in an arms race.[2]

External Causes: Models of Rational Behavior

The prevailing view in the arms race literature is that external causes explain arms races in which states are reacting to the threat posed by an adversary's arms buildup. Buzan & Herring (1998:83), for example, argue, "The basic proposition of the action-reaction model is that states strengthen their armaments because of the threats the states perceive from other states. The theory implicit in the model explains the arms dynamic as driven primarily by factors external to the state."[3] This action-reaction process can lead to an endless arms race in which each reaction is met by still another reaction.

Action-reaction logic gained prominence in the 1960s as an explanation of the US–Soviet nuclear arms race. Secretary of Defense McNamara argued, "Whatever their intentions or our intentions, actions—or even realistically potential actions— on either side relating to the buildup of nuclear forces necessarily trigger reactions on the other side. It is precisely this action-reaction phenomena that fuels the arms race" (McNamara 1967; see also Freedman 1981). A fuller version of this argument (Rathjens 1969) stressed that uncertainty about Soviet capabilities tended to fuel overreactions, since the United States tended to plan its forces against "greater-than-expected threats," and that the long lead-time required to develop new weapons systems resulted in further overreaction because the United States

---

[2]In fact, it might be better simply to rename the categories, replacing "external causes" with "causes of rational arming behavior" and replacing "internal causes" with "causes of suboptimal arming behavior." These new labels are more accurate, since some causes of rational arming behavior, such as states' goals, are not external to the state. However, to maintain a close correspondence to the arms race literature, this essay continues to use the labels that are currently used in the literature.

[3]However, unlike most of the literature, their chapter on the action-reaction model includes a discussion of factors that goes beyond pure security motives.

had to develop reactions well before Soviet actions actually occurred. As a result, although the basic logic of action-reaction is straightforward, identifying the phenomenon in practice could be more difficult, since the timing and magnitude of reactions might not directly match actions (Allison 1974). Rathjens (1969) argued that the United States overreacted to uncertainty at the time of the "missile gap" by deploying a massive intercontinental ballistic missile (ICBM) force, which fueled Soviet deployments of both ICBMs and defenses against ballistic missiles, which led to US deployment of multiple independently targeted reentry vehicles (MIRV missiles), which was likely to lead to Soviet deployment of mobile missiles.

Although action-reaction, threat-based explanations are certainly important, there is another potentially equally important source of rational arms race behavior. A state might build up arms and race because it wants to expand for reasons other than security, that is, because it is greedy, not because it is threatened. The arming behavior of these states might look as though each is reacting to the other, but the driving force behind this competition is not the security that lies at the core of the action-reaction explanation. The greedy state wants to acquire the military capability necessary to compel its adversary to make concessions or to win a war if its demands cannot be achieved peacefully, whereas the other state reacts to preserve its security in the face of an increased threat. The greedy state will keep building up arms, even if its security-seeking adversary stops.

The consequences of conflating external explanations with security-driven, action-reaction explanations are apparent in descriptions of the Anglo-German naval race. This race is frequently identified as a prominent example of an action-reaction race (Buzan 1987, Hammond 1993), but the German naval buildup can also be interpreted as part of Germany's effort to shift the military balance in the hope of gaining colonial and continental goals (Kennedy 1980). The German decision was not fueled by a British naval buildup. More importantly, a British decision not to respond to the German challenge would not have convinced Germany to cancel its naval program, and the prospects for arms control were poor. Thus, although the British and German buildups were coupled, action-reaction logic—at least when it is understood as reaction to a growing threat—does not capture the true cause of this race. (In addition, many explanations of the German naval buildup emphasize internal, domestic factors; see e.g. Lamborn 1991, Snyder 1991.)

Envisioning external causes broadly to include the full range of factors that influence rational arming behavior is valuable for a number of reasons. First, and most basic, as explained above, since external causes are paired with internal causes to span the full range of explanations for arms races, and since internal causes are of interest primarily for explaining suboptimal behavior, external causes should explain the full range of rational state arming behavior. Second, identifying external causes with the sources of rational behavior emphasizes that in order to understand these causes we need a theory of when (that is, under what conditions) a state should build up arms and when it should pursue more cooperative policies instead. As discussed above, a state's decision should depend on its own goals and its beliefs about its adversary's goals. It could also depend on a variety of other factors, including the state's power, the nature of military technology, the quality of information that each state has about the other's military programs, the speed with which the state can launch a buildup of its own, etc. Therefore, all of these factors could be sources of rational arms racing and provide a much richer explanation of why an arms race occurs than identifying more generally the adversary's buildup. Research that focuses on when a state should engage in an arms race is reviewed in a later section.

Third, and more specific, the inclusion of diverse motives and goals within the category of external causes enables us to better link causes of arms races with a key division in the IR theory literature and the policy recommendations that follow. Interactions between security seekers are described by the security dilemma, the spiral model, and structural realist theories. In contrast, the decisions of greedy states lie in the domain of neoclassical realism, which sees greedy states as the driving force behind competition and war,[4] and in the deterrence model, which focuses on the subset of greedy states that are also secure (Jervis 1976). The most important disagreement during the Cold War over how the United States could best cope with the risks of its arms race with the Soviet Union hinged on beliefs about Soviet motivations. Individuals who saw the Soviet Union motivated primarily by insecurity applied the spiral model and called for cooperative policies—arms control and unilateral restraint—whereas those who believed that the Soviet Union was not threatened by the United States and was motivated entirely by greed applied the deterrence model and called for the most competitive policies. Both of these views, as well as mixed views in the middle, are based on theories of rational international behavior and belong in the category of theories of external sources of arms races.

Before leaving external causes, it is necessary to at least mention Richardson arms race models, since they have generated a huge and influential literature. Richardson (1960) developed a descriptive model of interactive arming, in which changes in a state's military expenditures are influenced by three factors: the military expenditures of the adversary, the economic burden of previous purchases of military forces, and the extent of the state's "grievance" against the adversary. His model is a pair of linked differential equations, with constant coefficients for each of the three factors. In this model, the states do not have an explicit objective, and the model does not include strategic behavior. Rather, the parameters in the model, for example, the intensity of the state's reaction to the adversary's expenditure, determine the course of the arms race. For certain values, the arms race reaches a stable equilibrium; for others, armaments continue to grow at increasing rates. A tremendous amount of effort has gone into developing different versions of the Richardson model and much of the mathematics is quite complex.

---

[4]An important proponent of these arguments is Schweller (1994, 1998); his basic criticism of balance-of-threat theory—that it sees all alliances as reactions to threats—parallels the point here about viewing all arms races as reactions to threats. See Rose (1998) for a recent review.

Extensive reviews have been published by Busch (1970), Russett (1983), Isard (1988), and Etcheson (1989). Empirical tests of the models have produced mixed results, and most found little evidence that the United States and the Soviet Union were involved in an arms race. However, Ward (1984) built a model that included stocks of deployed weapons, as well as defense expenditures, and found that the United States and the Soviet Union did react to the relative balance of deployed forces. Given the expectation that states will act strategically and that states that are reacting to each other will nevertheless sometimes be out of synch due to uncertainty about the other's buildup and the complexity of developing and fielding large modern weapons systems, it is hard to know what to make of these results.

Internal Causes: Models of Suboptimal Behavior

Explanations that focus on internal causes of arms races locate the causes within the activities and operations of states. Whereas explanations that focus on external causes imagine the state as a unitary actor, these explanations focus on how the structure of the state—its political processes, institutions, and interest groups—contributes to arms races. Analysts of arms races have identified a large number of internal causes. Buzan & Herring (1998; see also Buzan 1987) provide a good overview of this literature, which includes the potential impact on a state's arming decisions of the institutionalization of military R&D, the institutionalization of military production, electoral politics, bureaucratic politics, and the military-industrial complex.

Explanations that focus on internal causes of state behavior go beyond external/rational explanations only if they explain deviations from rational behavior (on this general point, see Fearon 1998). If states act rationally, then there is little reason to focus on their internal workings to explain their international behavior.[5] External/rational models therefore usually assume that states are unitary actors, even though they obviously are not. Simply finding organizations and actors with interests that diverge from the state's national interests is insufficient to support an internal explanation; it is necessary to demonstrate that those interests led the state to adopt suboptimal behavior. Although many studies of states' arms-acquisitions decisions are sensitive to this requirement, there is nevertheless some inclination to see activity within the state suggesting support for internal explanations.[6]

---

[5]This somewhat overstates the case, since if external/rational models leave a state's options indeterminate, internal-sources models could be useful for understanding how states choose among the range of rational options.

[6]This discussion glosses over some of the complexities that arise once the state is no longer viewed as a unitary actor. It then becomes possible both that the national interest is not well defined and that the preferred means for pursuing a given interest cannot be determined by assessing the positions of actors who hold divergent preferences. Under these conditions, assessing suboptimal behavior can be problematic (see Downs & Rocke 1995, Bueno de Mesquita 2000).

The available space does not allow in-depth discussion of each of the internal-causes arguments, but a quick look at what they have in common suggests some important points. Most of these arguments hold that when a state organizes itself to meet its military requirements, it creates structures and institutions that have interests of their own and that have the political power to pursue these interests. (The exception is the argument positing electoral politics as a source of arms races.) Suboptimality arising from these sources is therefore not easily eliminated because the state needs these institutions to pursue its international goals. For example, the nature of modern military technology requires states to support an extensive R&D establishment. That establishment also sees its own interests advanced by promoting technological change and can therefore becomes a driving force in an arms race (Brooks 1975; Shapley 1978a,b; Buzan 1987; Evangelista 1988). The close connection between civilian and military technology can also generate a technological imperative. An example of this phenomenon is the increased accuracy of ballistic missiles, which can be explained as largely the result of incremental improvements in a large number of technologies, many of which were not accomplished with improved missile accuracy as a primary goal (but see also Mackenzie 1990).

The case of military production is similar. Producers of weapons systems obviously have an interest in a continuing arms buildup. One way to insure demand is to design more technologically advanced weapons and then convince the military that these weapons systems are best matched to their needs. According to Kaldor (1981), because standards for assessing effectiveness are highly subjective and weapons systems are rarely tested, and because weapons producers make improved systems available, states end up producing increasingly sophisticated, complex, and expensive systems that do not increase military effectiveness, at least not to a degree commensurate with increases in costs. In addition, a state in an ongoing military competition may have to help preserve its military-industrial base to insure its ability to build next-generation weapons systems or large numbers of sophisticated weapons quickly. For example, Kurth (1971) argues that there exists a "follow-on imperative" because "the Defense Department would find it risky and even reckless to allow one of only six or seven [aerospace] production lines to wither and die for lack of a large production contract." Again, the result can be an arms buildup and a continuation of an arms race when it is unnecessary.

Bureaucratic-politics arguments, which were developed partly in reaction to rational-actor, action-reaction arguments, hold that because of the complexity and duration of the weapons-development process, the military services are the key players in shaping the weapons systems that a state buys. This is important because the services' preferences are likely to diverge somewhat from the state's interests. According to Allison & Morris (1975:125), who challenge the action-reaction interpretation of the US ICBM program, anti-ballistic missile decisions, and MIRV deployment, "Service organizational health is seen to depend on maintaining the autonomy of the organization and preserving what its members view to be the 'essence' of the organization, sustaining morale, maintaining or expanding roles and missions, and keeping or increasing budgets."[7] The result could be that states deploy types and numbers of weapons systems that fuel unnecessary competition, or that they simply buy the wrong weapons. For example, Steinbruner & Carter (1975) argue that the Trident submarine was larger and faster than it needed to be, which left it at best no more effective than a smaller, slower, and less expensive version. The authors attribute this outcome largely to a battle for control within the US Navy.

In the years since these bureaucratic-politics arguments were developed in the 1970s, a number of studies of US weapons acquisition have found support for the impact of organizational interests, but others have found little impact. Brown's (1992) study of US strategic bomber programs finds support for both external/strategic and organizational arguments but no support for technological or economic arguments (see also Farrell 1997). In contrast, Rhodes (1994) finds that the composition of US naval forces was not influenced by bureaucratic politics. He argues that this is a critical case for the bureaucratic-politics model because issues of force structure are of central importance to the Navy's essence and to the distribution of resource within the Navy, yet these issues rarely attract the high-level political attention required to counter organizational interests.

More recent theoretical work has extended organizational arguments to questions of military doctrine, finding that military organizations tend to prefer offensive doctrines (Posen 1984, Snyder 1984, Van Evera 1984; but see Kier 1997). Although not usually considered part of the arms race literature, these arguments should be included because they identify additional ways in which military organizations could lead states into unnecessary arms competition.

Once we envision internal causes as sources of suboptimality, we should also add misperceptions—both individual and national-level—to the already long list of internal causes of arms races. Although psychological explanations are well established in the IR literature, they are not usually noted as part of the arms race literature. Jervis's description of the spiral model, which can be used to explain arms races (as well as competition more generally), has a rational foundation, but common cognitive errors can both generate and accelerate suboptimal competition (Jervis 1976; see also Jervis et al 1985). For example, if leaders tend to understand their own arms buildups as demanded by their external situations, while interpreting the adversary's buildup as reflecting its goals, they will overlook the possibility that the adversary is also striving for security and react with a buildup when the more appropriate course might be to propose an arms control agreement. Similarly, militaries are often inclined to inflate the threat posed by adversaries (Van Evera 1984); a state that adopts this view of its international environment will be inclined to build up arms when it should not.

The relative importance of the various internal causes, and the relative importance of internal causes versus external, are likely to vary across countries. Most of the domestic-structure arguments focus on the United States and should not be

---

[7] See also Halperin (1974); for early criticism of these arguments, see Art (1973) and Krasner (1972); for more recent assessments, see Welch (1992) and Bendor & Hammond (1992).

expected to apply equally well to all other states (Buzan & Herring 1998:114–18). For example, most states do not have large military R&D establishments, and many do not produce sophisticated weapons systems. Consequently, these states will be less influenced by R&D and weapons-production establishments than are major powers that are on the cutting edge of military technology.

Evangelista's (1988) study of military innovation found significant differences in the importance and timing of internal and external causes in the United States and the Soviet Union. He found that "the openness and decentralization of U.S. society encourage technological innovations in weaponry, whereas the [former] Soviet Union inhibits innovation with its obsessive secrecy and centralization." As a result, internal causes played a larger and earlier role in the United States, with scientists seeking support for technical innovations from the military. External causes entered the process later, playing an important role in establishing support once the weapons system began to face bureaucratic barriers and to require approval by Congress and the executive branch. In contrast, in the Soviet Union, innovation resulted when civilian and military leaders identified external threats and then endorsed efforts to respond.

Although there is not a full consensus, the literature on internal causes suggests that they often influence states' arms acquisition decisions. Most authors find that both internal and external causes play a role in states' decisions to build up arms,[8] although there is substantial disagreement over the relative importance of these causes. However, whether internal causes regularly play a decisive role in states' decisions to engage in an arms race is less clear. It is one thing to show that various internal causes influence the specific design or production of a weapons system—for example, the size of a submarine or the timing of the deployment of a new aircraft—and quite another to show that the key decisions, the forks in the road, that may be decisive in defining an arms race are the product of internal sources. The case of MIRV, which was a fork in the road, is sufficiently complex that, although organizational interests certainly mattered, strategic rationales also played a powerful role in the outcome (Greenwood 1975). Many assessments of the impact of internal causes can be sharpened by first asking what arms buildup, if any, the state should have engaged in, given its goals and the conditions it faced. Establishing this rational baseline requires a theory for when a state should build up arms. Divergences from this baseline can then be attributed to internal causes.

CONSEQUENCES OF ARMS RACES—DO THEY INCREASE THE PROBABILITY OF WAR?

Much of the interest in arms races is generated by the belief that they are dangerous, specifically, that they increase the probability of war. The consequences of arms races have been studied from a number of angles, including developing

---

[8]There are exceptions, however; for example, Senghaas (1990) argues that domestic causes are overwhelmingly dominant.

propositions inductively by looking at multiple cases, studying the correlation between arms races and war using large data sets, and building formal models of the impact of arms buildups on states' decisions about whether to initiate war.[9] Downs (1991) provides a good assessment of the literature on the consequences of arms races, and of the literature on when a state should engage in an arms race, which is the focus of the following section.

Inductive Hypotheses Based on Multiple Case Studies

Two important articles (Huntington 1958, Kennedy 1983) offer hypotheses and insights based on a detailed knowledge of a number of arms races. These articles do not systematically present and explore cases but instead use examples from the cases to develop and support their insights.

Huntington's 1958 article remains one of the most influential and widely read works on arms races. Based on his analysis of 13 arms races, Huntington identifies two sets of relationships between arms races and war. First, he argues that there is an inverse relationship between the length of an arms race and the probability that it will end in war. This is because a danger point (sometimes two) occurs at the beginning of every race. Once a state initiates a challenge by launching a buildup, the challenged state must decide if it can acquire allies and/or deploy armaments that are sufficient to restore the previous military balance. If the challenged state finds that it cannot, then it may conclude that launching a preventive war is its best option. As examples, Huntington identifies Tirpitz's concern that Britain might attack before Germany's naval buildup was sufficiently far along to deter attack, and interest within the United States in preventive war to stop the Soviet Union from acquiring nuclear weapons. Alternatively, if the challenged state fails to respond for some reason other than a lack of capability, it may then decide to respond once it finds itself in a dangerously weakened position. Recognizing this danger, the initial challenger may launch a preventive war to preserve the military advantages it achieved by launching its buildup. These arguments lead to Huntington's conclusion regarding duration—if war does not occur at either of these danger points, a sustained race is likely to result, and "the regularity of the increases in itself becomes an accepted and anticipated stabilizing factor in the relations between the two countries" (Huntington 1958:63). The preventive-war logic that Huntington uses to link arms races with war finds support in a large body of work on shifts in the distribution of power and preventive war (Levy 1987, Van Evera 1999:ch. 4). Less developed, and more controversial, is Huntington's claim that the reactive arms buildups become accepted and enable political relations to improve. At this level of generality, it seems as likely that a sustained arms race will damage political relations, much as the spiral model describes (Jervis 1976).

---

[9]Space limits prohibit discussion of this latter line of work. Important examples include Intriligator & Brito (1984) and Morrow (1989); Downs (1991:86–90) assesses this type of research.

Second, Huntington argues that quantitative arms races tend to lead to war and that qualitative races do not. In quantitative races, one side is likely to achieve definitive superiority; it is a marathon in which one or both states are likely to become exhausted, or in which the state that is falling behind will opt for war. In contrast, qualitative races start over with each major innovation, thereby always giving the state that is behind in the race a chance to catch up. Huntington notes that qualitative races generate anxiety about technological breakthroughs, but he argues that in fact this fear is misplaced because states tend to achieve major innovations nearly simultaneously. Huntington contends that quantitative races are more dangerous because they impose ever-increasing demands on the countries' resources. Generating popular support for these burdens requires governments to create an increasingly hostile picture of the enemy. "Prolonged sufficiently, a quantitative race must necessarily reach a point where opinion in one country or the other will demand that it end, if not by negotiation, then by war" (Huntington 1958:76). In contrast, qualitative races require the continuous redeployment of resources but not continuous increases.

These arguments about qualitative versus quantitative races are problematic; there is little reason to expect that they will hold in general. It is not clear why the costs of a quantitative race have to increase with time, or why the costs of a qualitative race do not, or why a lead in a quantitative race is more likely to result in preventive war. It also seems unlikely as a general rule that quantitative races are likely to run longer than qualitative ones. Under certain conditions, quantitative races may simply damp out. For example, if two states are interested only in security and if defending is easier than attacking, then parity may be acceptable to both countries. Once both countries have built up to a level at which their forces are adequate to defend and deter, increases in force size could stop. Under these conditions, qualitative improvements could then have the effect of restarting this race and making it more expensive. For example, if qualitative improvements in US and Soviet nuclear forces had stopped with early-generation ballistic missiles, it seems likely that the Cold War nuclear race would have been less intense and less costly. Further, when defense has the advantage, a shift toward offense advantage could make attacking more attractive, reducing both states' security and making war more likely than if the qualitative race had not occurred. I turn to these arguments in a more general framework below.

Kennedy (1983) draws on knowledge of many arms races to conclude that arms races are the product of political differences. "[U]ltimately, this argument is saying that arms increases—and arms races—are the reflection of complex political/ideological/racial/economic/territorial differences, rather than phenomena which exist, as it were of themselves, uncaused causes" (1983:174). In the same spirit, the key reason that arms limitations have often failed is "because an agreement over reducing the number and size of weapons alone, without agreement over the non-military causes of the rivalry, has seemed to one side or the other—usually to the challenging expanding power—to be pointless" (1983:174).

These conclusions bear upon two key issues. First, Kennedy is arguing that arms races have no independent effect on the probability of war, but instead, like war, reflect deep causes. In effect, he claims that arms races are driven by external/rational causes, not internal causes. Although he does not develop this at any length, it is an important argument that can strongly influence how we envision the consequences of arms races.

Second, within the family of rational causes, Kennedy appears to contend that what I have termed greedy states—i.e. states that want to change the status quo for reasons other than security—are the driving force behind arms races. The quotation above gives this impression, and two of his examples support this position. Kennedy points out that Prussia rejected efforts to halt its arms race with France in 1869–1870 because this would have compromised Bismarck's plan to revise the European order. He also notes that France's position at the 1898 Hague Conference was influenced by its desire to keep open the possibility of regaining Alsace-Lorraine.

However, in the end, Kennedy's position on the basic question of what drives arms races is not so clear. Toward the end of his essay, he argues that an arms race will "all too easily contribute to the upward spiral of fears and hatreds and suspicions which were themselves the cause of the original armaments increases" (1983:175). But arguing that fears and suspicions were original causes of the arms race is quite a different argument. Although it too is within the rational-causes family, this argument focuses on the security dilemma, not the desire to revise the status quo for nonsecurity reasons. Moreover, although Kennedy's examples are clear in that they illustrate that arms competition reflected states' interests, they are ambiguous as to whether greed or security (or both) was key. For example, he argues that at the 1898 Hague Conference, Germany and Russia disagreed over proposals for limiting arms, each preferring the proposals that played to its own strengths. Yet, since states can desire improved military capabilities to pursue either greedy or security-driven goals, the example as presented is unclear on this issue. Interesting as Kennedy's analysis is, it leaves unresolved the nature of the fundamental disagreements that drove these arms races and, as a result, whether the states might have had available policies that were preferable to engaging in an arms race.

In addition to these articles, a final study that deserves mention here is Hammond's (1993), which provides useful background and descriptions of most of the arms races that are commonly identified in the literature, some of which Hammond argues do not really qualify as arms races. Hammond characterizes each race along a number of dimensions, including its mode (that is, whether its source is external or internal), medium (land, sea, or air), goals, type (qualitative or quantitative), and intensity. His clearest conclusion, which is consistent with the other multiple-case studies, is that arms races sometimes end in war but often do not. Hammond argues that arms racing should be viewed as a sometimes appropriate means for a state to achieve its goals, but he sheds little light on the conditions under which this is the case and therefore on whether states' decisions to engage in arms races were well matched to the opportunities and challenges they faced.

Overall, these studies leave no doubt that arms races are a complex phenomenon and that it is impossible to predict whether a race is likely to end in war without addressing the states' relative military positions at the beginning of the race, the nature of military technology involved, states' relative abilities to compete, and (perhaps most important) the states' goals. However, valuable as these studies are, they would benefit from being placed in a more general theoretical framework, both to sharpen some of their propositions and to clarify the generality of others.

Large-*n* Studies

Much of the empirical work on whether arms races lead to war has analyzed large data sets built on data from the Correlates of War project (see Sample 1997 and Siverson & Diehl 1989 for reviews). Wallace (1979) launched this line of research with a study of whether serious disputes between nations engaged in an arms race have a significantly greater probability of resulting in war than those between states engaged in more normal military competition. Wallace chose to focus on states that were involved in serious disputes to insure that their arms buildups were directed at each other and not coincidental. He analyzed 99 militarized international disputes and found a strong statistical association between arms races and the escalation of crises to war. Wallace cautioned that "it is conceivable that the result is a spurious effect of ongoing hostility and tension between the powers" but concludes nevertheless that it is difficult to argue that "arms races play no role in the process of leading to the outset of war."

Wallace's article generated a number of significant criticisms. Weede (1980) argued that Wallace's analysis failed to separate out whether wars were resulting from the arms race or instead from one state's failure to arm fast enough to keep up its side of the race. Wallace (1980, 1982) responded to this criticism by exploring whether the "status quo" power declined relative to the "revisionist" power.[10] Although his analysis produced mixed results of the association between the revisionist power winning the race and disputes escalating to war, any relationship that did exist was less strong than that between arms races and war, and Wallace concluded that his original conclusion remained strong.

---

[10]Wallace's terminology of "revisionist" and "status quo" states does not map directly into greedy and security-seeking states, and therefore his terminology is not converted here. His terms categorize states by their actions, whereas the other terms categorize states by their motivations. In Wallace's analysis, one state is the revisionist and the other is the status quo power; in contrast, this is not necessarily the case when states are categorized by motives—for example, both states could be security seekers, even though they are involved in conflict.

Two other basic criticisms have been leveled at Wallace's work. First, a number of scholars (Weede 1980, Altfeld 1983, Diehl 1983) focused on the nature of the cases, arguing that many of them were not independent but instead closely linked to one of the two world wars. As a result, some of the supposed arms races did not reflect countries reacting to each other, and some of the escalations to war probably reflected the impact of alliances on the spread of war and not the impact of the arms race. Second, critics raised doubts about Wallace's measure of when an arms race exists. Altfeld (1983) argued that the threshold was set too low; changing this, however, did not alter Wallace's basic conclusion. Diehl (1983) criticized the construction of Wallace's arms race index, which multiplied the two countries' arms growth rates together, thereby creating the possibility that an intense buildup by only one country could lead to an index that qualified as an arms race. Diehl developed a different arms race index and revised the data set to reduce some of the problems noted above. He then found, contrary to Wallace, that there is little association between arms races and the escalation of militarized disputes to war.

New contributions to this debate have further complicated the picture. Horn (1987) has developed another measure of when two countries are in an arms race, which suggests that arms races are less common than the other studies indicate. His work finds that arms races that occur over shorter periods (6 years) do not significantly correlate with war, but that for arms races over longer periods (12 years) there is a significant relationship, although it is not as strong as the one found by Wallace. Most recently, Sample (1996, 1997, 1998) has determined that the disputes that do not escalate tend to be either Cold War cases involving nuclear weapons, or early disputes in enduring rivalries. She finds that "with the exception of the Cold War, virtually every case in which two countries are both arming at abnormally high levels was at war within five years" (1997:16) and therefore concludes that arms races are more closely associated with the escalation of disputes than the ongoing debate has suggested.

Given the complexity of the issues in studying the correlation between militarized disputes and war, chances are that continuing refinements and advances in this line of study will be possible. Two important issues that have not played a central role so far deserve mention. First, by focusing on the escalation of disputes, this body of work does not address the possibility that arms races could generate disputes, or alternatively deter disputes and in turn war (on a related issue, see Diehl & Kingston 1987). Second, the use of total spending to measure arms racing may sometimes be misleading, especially in a qualitative race, because innovations in military forces may not result in increases in spending, even though they pose a significant challenge to states' abilities to perform their military missions.

However, the bigger question is what can be learned from this line of study, not what is required to improve it. Much of this work is introduced as an effort to resolve a debate between the preparedness model (if you seek peace, prepare for war) and the arms race model, or the armaments-tension dilemma (Singer 1958), or the spiral model (Jervis 1976), all of which hold that if you prepare for war, an arms race is likely to result, which will increase the probability of war. The debate is important because, among other reasons, the two model types are said to prescribe quite different policies; the preparedness model calls for arms buildups and the spiral model for unilateral restraint and arms control. However, a closer look at these models shows that these studies cannot resolve this debate.

A much fuller statement of the preparedness model is found in the deterrence model (which should not be confused with deterrence theory more generally), which assumes that the defending state's adversary is a greedy state that will not be made insecure by the defender's arms buildup. A fuller statement of the arms race model is found in the spiral model, which has two important variants: (*a*) the rational spiral model, which assumes that all states are interested only in security but that they face a security dilemma that can lead them into conflict; and (*b*) the misperceptions spiral model, which adds individual and/or state-level misperceptions to the rational spiral model (Jervis 1976, 1978; Glaser 1992, 1997).

The deterrence and spiral models disagree about the nature of the adversary, not primarily about the nature of interaction in the international system. One model could apply in one situation, the other in another situation, and a mixture of the models would apply in situations in which the adversary was an insecure and greedy state. Consequently, an effort to figure out which model is correct is misguided. Yet, this is the stated aim of the large-*n* studies discussed above, and their implicit assumption that all arms races are essentially the same is consistent with this objective. However, basic IR theories suggest that the implications of arming, and in turn the consequences of arms racing, depend on states' goals and therefore that analyses need to distinguish different types of arms races along this dimension.

A possible rejoinder to this criticism is that these large-*n* studies are helpful in assessing the distribution of types of states over time, since war would correlate with spiral model conditions, and disputes that did not escalate would correlate with deterrence model conditions. This information could be useful, even though it would not provide good guidance for how to deal with any specific future arms race. However, these studies do not provide it. They might seem to, since the preparedness model and deterrence model call for arming to achieve peace, whereas the arms race model and spiral model are said to view arming as a cause of war. However, for three reasons, this is not the case. First, contrary to some descriptions, the dangers created by the security dilemma, and the negative spiral that it can fuel, are not always best handled by arms control and cooperation. Under certain conditions, competition is the state's best option, even though it may not prevent war. Second, arming in a preparedness/deterrence model situation does not guarantee peace. This would be the case, for example, if the adversary would not be deterred by even highly effective military capabilities. Arming may still be the defender's best bet, and the fact that such a competition ends in war does not necessarily discredit the policy. Nor does it necessarily suggest that the adversary was the type identified by the spiral model and not by the deterrence model. Consequently, even assuming that states choose their best options, the fact that some arms races end in war does not tell us which type of adversary they faced.

Third, some arms races may end in war because states chose the right type of policy but made mistakes in implementing it. For example, if a state fails to arm soon enough, and thereby allows its adversary to acquire a militarily significant lead in the arms race, the race may end in war, when better arms racing behavior might have ended in peace. In a preparedness/deterrence model situation, the problem is that the state raced poorly, not that it should have cooperated instead of racing.

In sum, these analyses of large data sets can tell us neither which model provides better guidance nor what the distribution of types of states has been across time. The problem is not with large-n studies per se, as compared to case studies, but instead with the weak connection between IR theory and the design of these studies.

WHEN SHOULD A STATE ENGAGE IN AN ARMS RACE?

Deciding when a state should engage in an arms race requires a rational theory of behavior. In this type of theory, the outcome of a state's behavior is best thought of as resulting from the conditions it faces and not from the behavior itself. More specifically, building up arms and racing if necessary are one type of behavior (or strategy) available to a state. When conditions facing the state make arms racing its best option, we should attribute outcomes, whether peace or war, to the conditions and not to the race. Therefore, although this section reviews work that is usually viewed as addressing the consequences of arms races, I treat it separately here.

There is not yet a fully developed theory of when a state should build up arms and risk generating an arms race, instead of choosing other options, including most obviously cooperation—in the form of arms control or unilateral restraint— and alliance. At a minimum, such a theory should address how a state's decision depends on (*a*) its own goals and its assessment of its potential adversary's goals, (*b*) the probability that its adversary can and will respond to a buildup, (*c*) the impact of a mutual buildup on the state's ability to perform the military missions required to deter, defend and attack, and (*d*) the impact of an arms race on the states' relationship—specifically, whether an arms race would generate strained relations and political fears. In addition, such a theory should include a dynamic dimension, which considers how changes over time in states' abilities to compete should influence their current arming behavior.

Defensive Realism

Structural realism, especially defensive realism, provides a start on such a theory (Waltz 1979 remains the classic statement of structural realism; on defensive realism see Snyder 1991, Glaser 1994/95, Van Evera 1999). Defensive realism focuses on states that are motivated only by security, and it assumes states' knowledge of others' motives is based only on the information communicated by their international policies. The security dilemma plays a central role, explaining how states that have fundamentally compatible goals can still end up in competition

(Jervis 1978). The key variables that influence whether a state can achieve a high level of security, and whether it will have to rely on competitive policies to achieve it, are power and the variables that determine the nature and magnitude of the security dilemma—the offense-defense balance and offense-defense differentiation.

The arguments about the relationship between security-dilemma variables and arms races are the more thoroughly developed. When defense has the advantage, a state can deploy forces that will increase its security more than they decrease the adversary's security. An arms buildup may be necessary to achieve forces that are large enough for deterrence and defense, but the state's security will increase with successive action and reaction cycles, and arms races should peter out (for related analysis, see Hoag 1961). Beyond a certain point, the state should stop its buildup, not only because it will be wasting resources but because, as discussed below, continuing to arm risks signaling malign motives and thereby damaging political relations with its adversary. A lack of arms races is likely to be associated with peace because defense advantage can make both cooperative military policies and peace a state's best options.

The situation is different when offense has the advantage, since states with equal size forces cannot achieve high levels of security. When a state adds forces, its adversary needs to make a larger addition to restore its ability to defend; this dynamic promises to fuel an intense arms race. However, racing may nevertheless be the state's best option because failing to do so risks falling behind its adversary and becoming even more vulnerable to attack. Arms races are likely to be associated with war because offense advantage can make both an arms race and war a state's best option, and because differences in force size, which are likely to be generated by an arms race, create larger incentives for war (Van Evera 1999).[11] Whether a state should enter into an arms control agreement that freezes forces at parity depends on how the risks of falling behind in a race compare to the risks posed by the adversary's ability to cheat on the agreement, which in turn depends on the nature of unilateral and cooperative means of verification.

The implications of a qualitative arms race depend on its impact on the balance. For example, a qualitative change that shifts the balance toward defense will reduce the intensity of the arms race and the probability of war, whereas a change that shifts the balance toward offense will have the opposite effect. Timing, however, will be important—even an innovation that shifts the balance toward defense could provide the state that acquires it first with military capabilities that could be used for offense and possibly incentives for preventive war.

When offense and defense are differentiated, a state has the option of deploying forces that are useful only for protecting its territory. This deployment does not

---

[11]However, the impacts of offense advantage may be more diverse than the argument stated here acknowledges. For example, Fearon (1995) argues that offense-advantage may increase the variance of war outcomes by making both total victory and total defeat more likely. This could increase the willingness of states to make concessions, thereby reducing the probability of war.

reduce its adversary's ability to defend itself and therefore should not provoke a strong reaction. Differentiation also makes possible arms control agreements that ban offense, thereby increasing both states' ability to defend. When offense has the advantage, a state may have to pursue arms control, instead of a unilateral policy of deploying defense, because the adversary's deployment of offensive forces could leave the state unable to afford an effective defensive policy. Much of the literature of classic arms control theory, although it preceded offense-defense theory, emphasizes the value of limiting systems that favor offense (Schelling & Halperin 1961).

In addition to addressing military capabilities, defensive realism also addresses how arming behavior can influence the political relationship between states. The key is that a state's decision can communicate information about its goals, which may increase or decrease the other's insecurity. For example, a state that chooses to build offensive forces when defense has the advantage will signal that it is a greedy state, because under these conditions a state interested only in security would build defensive forces (Glaser 1994/95; on signaling more generally see Jervis 1970). Signaling arguments can also explain how spirals of hostility can develop without misperceptions. For example, when states are uncertain about the size or type of forces required to maintain a given level of security, a security-seeking state that builds larger forces or offensive forces risks convincing others that it is greedy, since all greedy states will choose these force deployments but only some security seekers will (Glaser 1997; Kydd 1997a, which is discussed below, studies another type of rational spiral). As a result, under these conditions of uncertainty, a state has incentives to moderate its arming behavior. The result can be a tradeoff between arming in the hope of improving its military capabilities, and restraint designed to communicate its benign intentions, which increases the adversary's security and in turn its own security.

Within structural-realist analyses of when a state should engage in an arms race, further research is needed on how states should proceed when structural tradeoffs are indeterminate, on how to measure the offense-defense balance (Glaser & Kaufmann 1998), on developing a dynamic theory that includes power and offense-defense variables that change over time (Kim & Morrow 1992, Powell 1999:ch. 4 explore the implications of shifts in the distribution of power), and on how states should choose between arming and gaining allies (Morrow 1993, Sorokin 1994).

Other Levels of Analysis

A full theory of when a state should build up arms and risk an arms race must go beyond the assumptions imposed by structural realism. One obvious extension is to bring greedy states into the theory. The expectation is that greedy states will be more interested in building up arms and more willing to risk an arms race than security-seeking states are under a range of conditions. For example, when offense and defense are distinguishable, greedy states are more likely to opt for offense, because offense is necessary for expansion, even though their adversary's acquisition of offensive forces will reduce their own security. We also expect greedy states to make the tradeoff between acquiring military capabilities and signaling benign intent quite differently, since preserving the adversary's security is less essential to their goals. Development of these arguments would fall into the neoclassical family of theories, which to date has focused on alliance choices and not arming behavior (Schweller 1994, 1998).

A further expansion of the theory would relax structural realism's assumption that a state does not gather useful information about the adversary's motives and intentions by studying the adversary's political system, leadership, and domestic politics. On the one hand, this type of information might help reduce spirals between security seekers. Kydd (1997b), for example, argues that the policy process in modern democracies is sufficiently transparent that, if a democracy is a security seeker, other states will be able to figure this out. This knowledge should have the effect of moderating competition that would be generated by purely structural interactions and reduce, if not eliminate, the need for security-seeking states to engage in arms races. Further, by showing that a state is interested only in security, state-level information about motives reduces the dangers of competitive policies, allowing a security-seeking state to compete vigorously against greedy states without worrying about the need to moderate its policy so as not to generate self-defeating insecurity. This is part of the logic that underlies the deterrence model's claim that an arms buildup will, at worst, result in wasted resources. Research on how states assess others' motives and how much reliable information is available at the unit level (D Edelstein, dissertation in progress) is necessary to support this line of argument on when states should arms race.

Formal Models

Formal modelers have addressed many aspects of the question of when states should engage in arms races. This literature is large, so I have chosen a few pieces that connect especially well with the nonformal theories described above. Downs (1990), Isard (1988:ch. 2) and Intriligator & Brito (1990) offer helpful reviews and assessments of this body of work.

Downs et al (1985) explore the types of 2×2 games that can generate arms races and the relative effectiveness of three different strategies—unilateral restraint, tacit bargaining, and formal arms control negotiations—for generating cooperation. They explain that when states have perfect information, the two key types of games that can generate an arms race are Prisoners' Dilemma and Deadlock—a situation in which a state prefers mutual defection, i.e. an arms race, to mutual cooperation, i.e. both states stop building up arms. Although analysts have usually turned to Prisoners' Dilemma to explain arms races, Downs et al (1985) argue that Deadlock provides a simple explanation for arms races and may therefore be more prevalent than generally assumed. In support of this possibility, they explain that

Deadlock does not require that states have greedy/expansionist objectives, that is, states need not have fundamental conflicts of interest. The payoff orderings in the 2×2 games reflect preferences over means, such as arming versus not arming—not preferences over ends, for example, altering the territorial status quo versus maintaining it. Thus, consistent with structural realism, states that are interested only in security could have Deadlock preferences over arming. For example, a state that has superior technology might prefer a mutual buildup to mutual restraint because this would increase its security.

The second key argument of Downs et al (1985) is that if states have imperfect information, more types of games can lead to arms races. Most important, Stag Hunt—in which states prefer mutual cooperation to unilateral defection—does not lead to an arms race when there is perfect information, but if a state believes incorrectly that its adversary is acquiring a weapons system, then it too will decide to acquire the weapon and the arms race is on. Third, they show that even small amounts of poor information can undermine tacit bargaining strategies that would otherwise be effective in curbing competition (Tit-for-Tat is the prime example). Finally, their article shows that the success of various strategies for curbing an arms race depends on the game that states are in and the quality of information they have. In sum, in broad terms, Downs et al (1985) provide another useful perspective for understanding that whether states should race and the types of policies that may be successful in slowing a race depend on a variety of factors, including states' goals, the nature of military technology, the balance of forces at the beginning of the race, and, as Downs et al emphasize, the quality of information.

Powell (1993, 1999:ch. 2) explores the factors that influence the intensity of arms buildups and whether they will lead to war. He focuses on the tradeoff that a state must make between allocating its resources to domestic ends and to military means (the guns-versus-butter tradeoff).[12] In each period of the game, a state makes this choice and then decides whether to attack the other state. If a state attacks, the probability of victory is assumed to be a function of the relative amounts of the states' military spending. Winning the war enables the state to devote all of its resources to domestic ends in all future periods. The model assumes complete information, so uncertainty about the other's motives, which plays a central role in the security dilemma, is not present, and signaling one's type is not an issue. Two of the key parameters in the model are the offense-defense balance and the extent of the states' willingness to accept risks—which can viewed as a measure of their aggressiveness. Powell finds that states increase their military allocations, which means that arms competition becomes more intense, as the offense-defense balance shifts toward offense and as either state becomes more aggressive. A shift

---

[12]Some interesting models of the guns-versus-butter tradeoff are not discussed here. Brito & Intriligator (1985) explore how asymmetric information and the opportunity to negotiate a redistribution of resources affect the probability of war. Oren (1998) explores how a state's arming behavior is affected by the interaction between the adversary's capabilities and the state's assessment of the adversary's intentions, which is determined exogenously.

toward offense advantage does not necessarily make war more likely, although a large enough shift will lead to war. These findings are essentially consistent with those of defensive realism and arguments that address greedy states. However, by focusing on the tradeoff between consumption and military spending, Powell develops arguments that are precluded by defensive realism's simplifying assumption that states can be envisioned as security seekers. In Powell's model, states value security because it is necessary to ensure future consumption. Increasing military spending, although it increases security, decreases the value of the status quo because the state has less left to consume. Consequently, offense-advantage can increase the probability of war by reducing the value of the status quo because the state must spend more on military forces, in addition to increasing the probability that the attacker will prevail, which is the effect emphasized by defensive realism.

Focusing on how arming can influence political relations, Kydd (1997a) develops a formal model of how arming decisions can provoke fear and provide reassurance. He starts with a puzzle. If a state builds arms to increase its own security, why can it conclude when an adversary matches its buildup that this indicates aggressive/greedy motives? Kydd shows that although psychological biases are often invoked to explain this puzzle, in fact concluding that the adversary is greedy can be rational behavior. Both states in his model are uncertain about the value that the other places on winning a war, and each is also uncertain about how the other state views its motives. A state's belief about how its motives are perceived by an adversary influences how the state interprets the adversary's arms buildup. For example, if state A believes that B perceives it as likely to be a security seeker, then A will rationally interpret B's arms buildup to indicate that B is more likely to be a greedy state. The basis for A's conclusion is that if state A is interested only in security, then it is not a threat to its adversary B, so if B is building up arms, it must be because B is greedy. Kydd shows that, under a wide range of conditions, a rational adversary will find the state's buildup to be provocative, and also that there are conditions under which states can use restraint to reassure adversaries. [See Downs & Rocke (1990:ch. 4) for another model of the potential of unilateral restraint to slow an arms race when states are uncertain of each other's preferences.] Kydd's analysis adds to our understanding of the spiral model—the strategic interactions are sufficiently complex and subtle that they are difficult to fully appreciate without a formal model.

CONCLUSION

A theme of this essay is that the causes and consequences of arms races are more closely linked than the literature recognizes and takes advantage of. In addition, we have seen from a variety of angles that understanding when a state should build arms and risk provoking an arms race is essential to evaluating both the causes and consequences of arms races. This section summarizes the relationships between these three questions and identifies implications for future research.[13]

From the perspective of the causes of arms races, internal and external sources are potentially complementary, and often the difficult question is how much they each explain. However, when we change perspective and ask whether arms races have undesirable consequences, the internal and external factors provide opposite answers. If a state is influenced only by external factors, and it decides to build up arms and race, then the state's behavior is rational; the arms race is its best option, given its goals and the constraints and opportunities it faces. Whatever the outcome of the arms race, the race itself should not be assigned responsibility, since it is essentially only a reflection of exogenous variables. In contrast, when internal factors explain a state's decision to build up arms, the state has available policies that are preferable to arming, and the arms race itself can be understood to be undesirable, increasing the probability and/or the costs of war or at least wasting resources. In other words, arms races only have negative consequences when internal factors cause a state's decision to race.

To assess whether a state's behavior is rational, and therefore to assess whether internal factors are distorting its policy, we often need a theory that explains when a state should race. Certain arms procurement decisions may have sufficiently little impact on a state's overall strategy that they can be assessed in narrow military-technical terms. For example, a case mentioned above—the size and speed of Trident submarines—is probably this type of decision. However, other decisions about whether to acquire new types of weapons systems or to increase force size must be assessed in the context of a state's overall military strategy and therefore must be evaluated in the context of the state's goals, resources, and geopolitical setting. This analysis requires a theory that is built on basic structural variables and that can address choices of military doctrine, force requirements, and cooperative versus competitive arming policies. This type of theory is also required to assess the consequences of an arms race when a state does engage in suboptimal behavior.

The first step, therefore, toward a better understanding of the causes and consequences of arms races is to have a better theory of when states should build up arms and risk an arms race—one that is general enough to capture the essential features of arms races and that is developed enough to be used to assess historical cases. Defensive realism is progressing in this direction. Its integration of offense-defense variables and power enables a more nuanced assessment of states' military options than is possible with power alone, and its identification of the signals sent by states' arming decisions enables assessment of the role of military policy in influencing states' relations. However, defensive realism still requires fuller development, and an adequate theory of when a state should engage in an arms race must be more general than defensive realism, expanded to deal with a

---

[13]The manuscript "When Do Arms Races Make War Unnecessarily Likely?" (C Glaser, unpublished) represents an initial effort in this direction.

wider variety of states and with the impact of information that is available at the unit level. Applied to specific arms races, such a theory can be used to determine whether states should have engaged in the race, and, if they should not have, to assess the consequences.

ACKNOWLEDGMENT

For valuable comments on an earlier draft of this chapter, I wish to thank George Downs.

Visit the Annual Reviews home page at www.AnnualReviews.org

LITERATURE CITED

Allison GT. 1974. Questions about the arms race: who's racing whom? In *Contrasting Approaches to Strategic Arms Control*, ed. R Pfaltzgraff, pp. 31–72. Lexington, MA: Lexington Books

Allison GT, Morris FA. 1975. Exploring the determinants of military weapons. *Daedalus* 104:99–129

Altfeld MF. 1983. Arms races—and escalation: a comment on Wallace. *Int. Stud. Q.* 27:225–31

Art RJ. 1973. Bureaucratic politics and American foreign policy: a critique. *Policy Sci.* 4:467–90

Bendor J, Hammond TH. 1992. Rethinking Allison's models. *Am. Polit. Sci. Rev.* 86:301–22

Brito DL, Intriligator MD. 1985. Conflict, war and redistribution. *Am. Polit. Sci. Rev.* 79:943–57

Brooks H. 1975. The military innovation system and the qualitative arms race. *Daedalus* 104:75–98

Brown M. 1992. *Flying Blind: The Politics of the U.S. Strategic Bomber Program*. Ithaca, NY: Cornell Univ. Press

Bueno de Mesquita B. 2000. *Principles of International Politics: People's Power, Preferences, and Perceptions*. Washington, DC: CQ Press

Busch PA. 1970. Appendix: mathematical models of arms races. In *What Price Vigilance?*

The Burdens of National Defense, ed. B Russett, pp. 193–233. New Haven, CT: Yale Univ. Press

Buzan B. 1987. *An Introduction to Strategic Studies: Military Technology and International Relations*. New York: St. Martin's

Buzan B, Herring E. 1998. *The Arms Dynamic in World Politics*. Boulder, CO: Lynne Rienner

Diehl PF. 1983. Arms races and escalation: a closer look. *J. Peace Res.* 20:205–12

Diehl PF, Kingston J. 1987. Messenger or message? Military buildups and the initiation of conflict. *J. Polit.* 49:801–13

Downs GW. 1991. Arms races and war. In *Behavior, Society, and Nuclear War, Vol. Two*, ed. PE Tetlock, JL Husbands, R Jervis, PC Stern, C Tilly, pp. 73–109. New York: Oxford Univ. Press

Downs GW, Rocke DM. 1990. *Tacit Bargaining, Arms Races, and Arms Control*. Ann Arbor: Univ. Mich. Press

Downs GW, Rocke DM. 1995. *Optimal Imperfection? Domestic Uncertainty and Institutions in International Relations*. Princeton NJ: Princeton Univ. Press

Downs GW, Rocke DM, Siverson RM. 1985. Arms races and cooperation. *World Polit.* 38:118–46; reprinted in *Cooperation Under Anarchy*, ed. KA Oye, pp. 118–46. Princeton, NJ: Princeton Univ. Press

Etcheson C. 1989. *Arms Race Theory: Strategy*

and Structure of Behavior. Westport, CT: Greenwood

Evangelista M. 1988. *Innovation and the Arms Race.* Ithaca, NY: Cornell Univ. Press

Farrell T. 1997. *Weapons Without a Cause: The Politics of Weapons Acquisition in the United States.* New York: St. Martin's

Fearon JD. 1998. Domestic politics, foreign policy, and theories of international relations. *Annu. Rev. Polit. Sci.* 1:289–313

Fearon JD. 1995. Rationalist explanations for war. *Int. Organ.* 49:379–414

Freedman L. 1981. *The Evolution of Nuclear Strategy.* New York: St. Martin's

Glaser CL. 1992. Political consequences of military policy: expanding and refining the spiral and deterrence models. *World Polit.* 44:497–538

Glaser CL. 1994/95. Realists as optimists: cooperation as self-help. *Int. Secur.* 19:50–90

Glaser CL. 1997. The security dilemma revisited. *World Polit.* 50:171–201

Glaser CL, Kaufmann K. 1998. What is the offense-defense balance and can we measure it? *Int. Secur.* 22:44–82

Gleditsch NP. 1990. Research on arms races. See Gleditsch & Njolstad 1990, pp. 1–14

Gleditsch NP, Njolstad O, eds.1990. *Arms Races: Technological and Political Dynamics.* London: Sage

Gray CS. 1971. The arms race phenomenon. *World Polit.* 24:39–79

Gray CS. 1974. The urge to compete: rationales for arms racing. *World Polit.* 26:207–33

Greenwood T. 1975. Making the *MIRV: A Study in Defense Decision Making.* Cambridge, MA: Ballinger

Halperin MH. 1974. *Bureaucratic Politics & Foreign Policy.* Washington, DC: Brookings Inst.

Hammond GT. 1993. *Plowshares into Swords: Arms Races in International Politics, 1840–1991.* Columbia: Univ. South Carolina Press

Hoag M. 1961. On stability in deterrent races. *World Polit.* 13:503–27

Horn MD. 1987. *Arms races and the international system.* PhD thesis. Univ. Rochester

Huntington SP. 1958. Arms races: prerequisites and results. *Public Policy* 8:41–86

Intriligator MD, Brito DL. 1984. Can arms races lead to the outbreak of war? *J. Confl. Resolut.* 28:63–84

Intriligator MD, Brito DL. 1990. Arms race modeling: a reconsideration. See Gleditsch & Njolstad 1990, pp. 58–77

Isard W. 1988. *Arms Races, Arms Control, and Conflict Analysis: Contributions from Peace Science and Peace Economics.* New York: Cambridge Univ. Press

Jervis R. 1970. *The Logic of Images in International Relations.* Princeton, NJ: Princeton Univ. Press

Jervis R. 1976. *Perception and Misperception in International Politics.* Princeton, NJ: Princeton Univ. Press

Jervis R. 1978. Cooperation under the security dilemma. *World Polit.* 30:167–214

Jervis R, Lebow NL, Stein JG, eds. 1985. *Psychology and Deterrence.* Baltimore, MD: Johns Hopkins Univ. Press

Kaldor M. 1981. *The Baroque Arsenal.* New York: Hill & Wang

Kennedy PM. 1980. *The Rise of the Anglo-German Antagonism, 1860–1914.* London: Allen & Unwin

Kennedy P. 1983. Arms-races and the causes of war, 1850–1945. In *Strategy and Diplomacy, 1870–1945,* PM Kennedy, pp. 165–77. London: Allen & Unwin

Kier E. 1997. *Imagining War: French and British Military Doctrine Between the Wars.* Princeton, NJ: Princeton Univ. Press

Kim W, Morrow J. 1992. When do power shifts lead to war? *Am. J. Polit. Sci.* 36:896–922

Krasner SD. 1972. Are bureaucracies important? (Or Allison in Wonderland). *For. Policy* 7:159–79

Kurth JR. 1971. A widening gyre: the logic of American weapons procurement. *Public Policy* 19:373–404

Kydd A. 1997a. Game theory and the spiral model. *World Polit.* 49:371–400

Kydd A. 1997b. Sheep in sheep's clothing: why

security seekers do not fight each other. *Secur. Stud.* 7:114–55

Lamborn AC. 1991. *The Price of Power: Risk and Foreign Policy in Britain, France, and Germany.* Boston: Unwin Hyman

Levy JS. 1987. Declining power and the preventive motivation for war. *World Polit.* 40:82–107

Mackenzie D. 1990. *Inventing Accuracy: A Historical Sociology of Nuclear Missile Guidance.* Cambridge, MA: MIT Press

McNamara RS. 1967. The dynamics of the nuclear strategy. *Dept. State Bull.* 57:Oct. 9

Morrow JD. 1989. A twist of truth. *J. Confl. Resolut.* 33:500–29

Morrow JD. 1993. Arms versus allies: tradeoffs in the search for security. *Int. Organ.* 47:207–33

Oren I. 1998. A theory of armament. *Confl. Manage. Peace Sci.* 16:1–29

Posen BR. 1984. *The Sources of Military Doctrine: France, Britain and Germany Between the Wars.* Ithaca, NY: Cornell Univ. Press

Powell R. 1993. Guns, butter, and anarchy. *Am. Polit. Sci. Rev.* 87:115–32

Powell R. 1999. *In the Shadow of Power: States and Strategies in International Politics.* Princeton, NJ: Princeton Univ. Press

Rathjens GW. 1969. The dynamics of the arms race. *Sci. Am.* 220:15–25;reprinted in *Progress in Arms Control?*, ed. BM Russett, BG Blair, pp. 33–43. San Francisco: Freeman

Rhodes E. 1994. Do bureaucratic politics matter? Some disconfirming findings from the case of the U.S. Navy. *World Polit.* 47:1–41

Richardson LF. 1960. *Arms and Insecurity.* Pittsburgh, PA: Boxwood

Rose G. 1998. Neoclassical realism and theories of foreign policy. *World Polit.* 51:144–72

Russett B. 1983. International interactions and processes: the internal vs. external debate revisited. In *Political Science: The State of the Discipline*, ed. AW Finifter, pp. 541–68. Washington, DC: Am. Polit. Sci. Assoc.

Sample SG. 1996. *Arms races and the escalation of disputes to war.* PhD thesis. Vanderbilt Univ.

Sample SG. 1997. Arms races and dispute escalation: resolving the debate. *J. Peace Res.* 34:7–22

Sample SG. 1998. Military buildups, war and realpolitik. *J. Confl. Resolut.* 42:156–75

Schelling TC, Halperin MH. 1961. *Strategy and Arms Control.* New York: Twentieth Century Fund

Schweller RL. 1994. Bandwagoning for profit: bringing the revisionist state back in. *Int. Secur.* 19:72–107

Schweller RL. 1998. *Deadly Imbalances: Tripolarity and Hitler's Strategy of World Conquest.* New York: Columbia Univ. Press

Senghaas D. 1990. Arms race dynamics and arms control. See Gleditsch & Njolstad, pp. 15–30

Shapley D. 1978a. Technology creep and the arms race: ICBM problem a sleeper. *Science* 201(Sept. 22):1102–05

Shapley D. 1978b. Technology creep and the arms race. *Science* 201(Sept. 29):1192–96

Singer JD. 1958. Threat-perception and the armament-tension dilemma. *J. Confl. Resolut.* 2:90–105

Siverson RM, Diehl PF. 1989. Arms races, the conflict spiral, and the onset of war. In *Handbook of War Studies*, ed. MI Midlarsky, pp. 195–218. Boston: Unwin Hyman

Snyder J. 1984. *The Ideology of the Offensive: Military Decisions and the Disasters of 1914.* Ithaca, NY: Cornell Univ. Press

Snyder J. 1991. *Myths of Empire: Domestic Politics and International Ambition.* Ithaca, NY: Cornell Univ. Press

Sorokin GL. 1994. Arms, allies, and security tradeoffs in enduring rivalries. *Int. Stud. Q.* 38:421–46

Steinbruner J, Carter B. 1975. Organizational and political dimensions of strategic posture: the problems of reform. *Daedalus* 104:131–54

Van Evera S. 1984. *Causes of war.* PhD thesis. Univ. Calif., Berkeley

Van Evera S. 1999. *Causes of War: Power and the Roots of Conflict.* Ithaca, NY: Cornell Univ. Press

Wallace MD. 1979. Arms races and escalation: some new evidence. *J. Confl. Resolut.* 23:3–16

Wallace MD. 1980. Some persisting findings: a reply to Professor Weede. *J. Confl. Resolut.* 24:289–92

Wallace MD. 1982. Armaments and escalation: two competing hypotheses. *Int. Stud. Q.* 26:37–56

Waltz KN. 1979. *Theory of International Politics.* Reading, MA: Addison-Wesley

Ward MD. 1984. Differential paths to parity: a study of the contemporary arms race. *Am. Polit. Sci. Rev.* 78:297–317

Weede E. 1980. Arms races and escalation: some persisting doubts. *J. Confl. Resolut.* 24:285–87

Welch DA. 1992. The organizational process and bureaucratic politics paradigms: retrospect and prospect. *Int. Secur.* 17:112–46

Annu. Rev. Polit. Sci. 2000. 3:277–303

CONSTITUTIONAL POLITICAL ECONOMY: On the Possibility of Combining Rational Choice Theory and Comparative Politics

Norman Schofield

Center in Political Economy Washington University, St. Louis, Missouri 63130; e-mail: schofld@wueconc.wustl.edu

Key Words constitution, institution, core belief, election

■ **Abstract** Rational choice theory has typically used either noncooperative game theory or cooperative, social choice theory to model elections, coalition bargaining, the prisoner's dilemma, and so on. This essay concentrates on the ideas of William Riker and Douglass North, both of whom, in very different ways, studied events of the past in an attempt to understand constitutional or institutional transformations. The key notion presented here is the "belief cascade," a change in the understanding of the members of a society when they face a quandary. This idea is used to critique simple vote-maximizing models of elections, derived from Downs' earlier conception of party competition. Inferences are drawn on the possible applications of rational choice theory to the study of constitutional political economy in order to provide some insight into the differences between democratic polities.

INTRODUCTION

> To the extent that individuals really are individual, each an autonomous end in himself [or herself], to the extent that they must be somewhat mysterious and inaccessible to one another, there cannot be any rule that is completely acceptable to all. (Arrow 1973:262)

Because two earlier contributions to this series (Laver 1998, Austen-Smith & Banks 1998) have dealt with formal models of government formation and positive political theory, I use in this essay a rather general interpretation of rational choice theory. First, it is necessary to emphasize a distinction (made also by these two previous contributions) between noncooperative game theory (NCGT) and cooperative theory (CT). Both theories had their origin, in some sense, in von Neumann's fertile mind (NCGT in von Neumann 1928, CT in von Neumann & Morgenstern 1944). CT, which was concerned initially with questions of simple voting (majority rule, for example, and questions of division) was extended by Arrow 's (1951) original work in social choice theory. NCGT, as it is currently conceived, derives to a considerable degree from Nash's (1950, 1951) equilibrium concept. There has always been a degree of intellectual antagonism between the two theories. This is illustrated by the story that when Nash sought out the great mathematician, von Neumann, at the Institute for Advanced Study at Princeton University, with his notion of (Nash) equilibrium, von Neumann's comment was, "That's trivial you know. That's just a fixed point theorem" (Nasar 1998:94, quoting Harold Kuhn).

In my view, neither CT or NCGT alone can provide a basis for a rational choice theory of social behavior. However, the two theories in combination can help in providing important insights. The combination that I have in mind will lead to a theory of "belief games," which combines the individual focus of NCGT and the collective or coalitional aspect of CT. To illustrate what I mean by a belief game, I offer the following extended example involving the possibility of revolt in a society.

Consider a country with a repressive state apparatus supported by an outside military power. Any action against the state—any demonstration, or expression of desire, for freedom of speech—will be met by harsh countermeasures, certainly jail, possibly death. Whether a single individual would go against the state is a difficult decision to model. What are the individual's subjective or estimated cost functions, and what are the individual's beliefs, or subjective probability estimates that the state intends to carry out this threat of punishment? What are the individual's beliefs that the action against the state would go undetected? What are the individual's fundamental preferences (moral outrage or horror, etc)? A "simple-minded" rational choice theory would pose expected costs against benefits and figure out what action the individual should take. The fundamental preferences can never really be determined, but it is possible to formulate, to some degree at least, estimates of the beliefs of the individual. Moreover, we can perhaps infer the preferences of the individual over acts. I base this distinction between fundamental preferences and preferences over acts on the work of Savage (1954). Modern noncooperative Bayesian game theory does indeed focus on the connection between beliefs and preferences over acts, but if it is to be useful, the fundamental preferences have to be incorporated in some sense. For most individuals, these fundamental preferences are based on some form of self preservation.

In the tyrannical situation described above, one would expect that, in Nash equilibrium, no individual would "rationally" go against the state. More precisely, if we assume each individual is risk-averse (over the punishment of death) and believes that the state is moderately competent at locating troublemakers and intends to punish them, then no individual will contest the state.

Now suppose the outside military support dissipates. Beliefs of individuals about the capacity of the state will change. Let us assume, however, that almost everyone still believes that if one individual contests the state, then punishment will surely follow. Further, let us suppose that if more than a certain percentage contest, then the state will retreat or capitulate. The situation in which nobody contests is clearly a Nash equilibrium. Of course, there may be some highly risk-preferring individuals who would like to contest the state. If it is certain that they will be caught and punished, then we cannot "rationalize" their acts against the state. Suppose, however, that some sufficiently large proportion have agreed to contest simultaneously. This collective act is not a Nash equilibrium, because in this story, it is obvious that everyone else (except perhaps the minions of the state) would like to join the revolution. So the other Nash equilibrium is that everyone (except the minions) contests the state.

The NCGT model is not very interesting. There are two Nash equilibria (at least), but no plausible explanation is offered of how the society goes from one situation to another. [This is not entirely true. Young (1998) proposes a model of crossing the gap between Nash equilibria, which is based on adaptive learning. Learning is obviously involved, but it may occur in fits and starts, as I suggest below.] The CT model is also unpersuasive. A coalition comprising a sufficiently large percentage could be regarded as decisive. If it forms, it can force the state apparatus to capitulate. Therefore CT assumes it does form. But again, the question is how, precisely, does it form?

This story of protestors against a tyrannical regime is taken from Karklins & Petersen (1993). Their framework viewed formally is neither CT nor NCGT. Instead they focus on another component of the belief calculus. Does each individual (to be called ego) in a group of a certain size believe that the other individuals in the group will join with ego in the protest? If this is a credible belief in the group, then they might (given their cost calculations) choose to protest. The first coalition to create such a group-specific belief in solidarity may well be students, since their cost calculations are somewhat different from those of the rest of society. Moreover, they probably know each other well and perhaps feel isolated intellectually, as a group, from the regime. The leaders of the students will attempt to persuade their colleagues that the correct beliefs are those that would sustain the protest. These beliefs can be interpreted as probabilities q (that if the students protest, the regime will still be maintained) and p (if maintained, the regime will effectively punish the protestors). Obviously q and p are decreasing functions of the size of the body of protestors. The costs involved are those pertaining to the maintenance of tyranny and those associated with punishment by the state.

The form of the calculation over whether it is rational for an individual, ego, to protest, is obvious (at least to ego), but the decision depends on ego's belief over how many others will protest. What is in fact crucial to the protest is whether the coalition leader can persuade a sufficiently large majority of the students that they have a valid belief in the rationality of protest. This is a conditional belief; each one must believe both that the others in the group have made the "calculations" and that the others feel the same as ego. This rather complicated arrangement in beliefs we may call "common knowledge." How it is attained is something of a mystery. I have suggested (Schofield 1985) that common knowledge of this kind is at the heart of collective action situations, such as the prisoner's dilemma, but I offered no formal clues as to its attainment.

Arrow, as the quotation at the head of this section suggests, regards the question of common knowledge to be one of the deepest conundrums of social science (see e.g. Arrow 1986). My own view is that empirical work in anthropology and political economy will provide clues to the common knowledge foundations for society. (For work in this direction see Bates 1989 and Ensminger 1992.)

Clearly, common knowledge must be a kind of belief equilibrium, in the sense that no one in the group can reasonably doubt the beliefs of the others. The point of the exhortations of the leader (or leaders) is to maintain the belief equilibrium. It can of course be the case that some aspect of the belief underlying the equilibrium is false.

When the students took over Tiananmen Square, I am sure they believed, and thought the belief reasonable, that the regime would acquiesce. A rational choice explanation is that they felt that q (the probability that the regime would not change) was low, and even if no change occurred, the probability that they would be punished (p) was also low. Because it seems obvious that a significant portion of the students held this belief, I identify this belief (in the justification of protest) as a "core belief" among the students. (The term core is used in voting games and economic theory to denote a stable outcome.) It is plausible that the students hoped to generate a "belief cascade" in the population as a whole, so as to bring about a new core belief for the society.

As in the story from Eastern Europe presented by Karklins & Petersen (1993), once the students have protested successfully against the state, the cost-benefit calculation of other groups, such as workers, could change. If the students are not punished, then Bayesian updating results in lower q and p probabilities. Workers may then protest, and if they are successful, more groups in the society will join the revolution. It is this fairly rapid evolution or transformation in beliefs that has been called a belief cascade (for discussion and application of this idea, see Bikhchandani et al 1992, Denzau & North 1994, Lohmann 1994, Kuran 1995, Petersen 1999; S Parikh, unpublished manuscript).

The state, in such a story of revolt, probably wants to do everything in its power to halt the start of such a belief cascade. However, the regime is very possibly in a state of extreme uncertainty or perplexity—i.e. in a quandary—when the student protests start. If the state does nothing, or acquiesces, then the belief cascade may occur in the fashion described above. It is also possible that if workers are unpersuaded by the demonstration effect intended by the students, the protest will fizzle out. On the other hand, punishing the students may bring out the workers in sympathy. "Uncertainty" describes a situation in which there is no rationalizable way of ascribing probabilities to outcomes resulting from possible acts.[1]

The students considering protest or revolt are also in an "uncertain" quandary. The leaders of a protest try to resolve the student quandary by attempting to persuade their colleagues that the outcomes are not uncertain (by the above definition)

---

[1] Schofield (1999a) describes the importance to John Maynard Keynes of the notion of uncertainty and discusses its evolution in his thought from his early work, including its connection to the philosophical ideas of GE Moore.

but rather can be described only in terms of "risk," i.e. credible probabilities and reasonable costs.

The point of my detailed explication of this story is that both CT and NCGT are rather blunt instruments with which to examine fundamental problems in comparative politics: how political and economic institutions come into being and change through time. Once an institution is in place, the apparatus of NCGT may well prove useful in examining the connection between the rules of the institutional game and the equilibrium in acts of the players within the game. However, as Riker commented 20 years ago,

> the losers [in a constitutional system] are likely to want to change the committees and jurisdictions in the hope of winning on another day. In the end, therefore, institutions are no more than rules and rules themselves are the product of social decisions. Consequently the rules are also not in equilibrium. One can expect that losers on a series of decisions under a particular set of rules will attempt (often successfully) to change institutions and hence the kind of decisions under them. (Riker 1980:444)

This quotation is from a published version of Riker's address to the International Political Science Association, made in Moscow in 1979. It is interesting how apposite it would become for the Soviet Union a decade later. It is doubtful indeed that anyone in Riker's audience in 1979 entertained the thought that almost the entire institutional apparatus of the Soviet Union would collapse within 15 years. As Riker also said in his address (1982a:24), "[T]he most important conclusion of the line of reasoning set forth in this paper is that, in the long run, nearly anything can happen in politics."

In fact, Riker's remarks were directed at the ideas implicit in the work of the neo-institutionalists (e.g. Shepsle 1979) who made use of NCGT to come to determinate solutions on voting in committees, under fixed agendas or jurisdictions. In a sense, the neo-institutionalists were themselves responding to the so-called chaos theorems obtained in the social choice research program carried out by Plott, Kramer, McKelvey, Schofield, Cohen, Matthews, and others over the previous 10 years or so. (See Austen-Smith & Banks 1998 and Laver 1998 for the possible relevance of these results for the study of politics; see Austen-Smith & Banks 1999 for a recent survey of positive political theory.)

Because Riker's formal work was based on CT, he later focused on the possibility of heresthetic maneuvers by leaders to introduce new alternatives into the set of possibilities. For example, if there are initially only two alternatives available (a and b) and a majority prefers a to b, then a heresthetician may be able to introduce a third option c that a majority prefers to both a and b. If the heresthetician also prefers c, then such a maneuver could make sense. Since Riker had also studied American federalism (Riker 1964, 1984), it was an obvious step for him to consider examples from US constitutional history to illustrate this notion of heresthetic. His early examples included voting on the Wilmot Proviso in 1846 (Riker 1982b:223–27), the consequences of the Lincoln-Douglas debates in Illinois in 1858 (Riker 1986), the popular vote in the presidential election of 1860 [won by Lincoln with a plurality of 40% (Riker 1982b:230–31)], and the ratification of the US Constitution in 1787 (Riker 1984, 1993, 1995, 1996a; Fink & Riker 1989). In all of these cases, the result of the heresthetic had profound consequences for the US Constitution. In my own view, Riker was correct to focus on such institutional or constitutional transformations. Indeed, the study of such transformations is extremely important for comparative politics. However, the formal apparatus that Riker utilized, based as it was on preference manipulation within the context of CT, seems inadequate. The reason should be clear from the above example of citizen revolt. Simply introducing a new alternative will not, by itself, permit a heresthetic move or engender an institutional transformation. A key feature, typically, is that the decision facing the society or group involves an uncertain quandary. Riker was certainly aware of this feature of the background to heresthetic acts; witness his lengthy discussion of the rhetoric used by the protagonists during the process of the ratification of the Constitution in 1787 (Riker 1996a).

The following sections set out a framework that develops Riker's earlier intuitions on heresthetic maneuvers. In this way, rational choice theory can be used to approach the question of institutional or constitutional change. In studying such belief games I have been much influenced by Riker, of course, but also by North (1990). Although North writes as an economic historian, and is concerned with those institutional properties that encourage growth, he also concentrates on the reasons for institutional change. Unlike Riker, who devoted most of his attention to voting processes, North has focused on exchange, and thus on the system of property rights and its relationship to economic growth. However, North has also argued that understanding perceptions, or beliefs, is crucial in making sense of the performance of institutions. Indeed, North argued that changes in beliefs may cause institutional change.

In a sense, therefore, both Riker and North wished to adapt rational choice theory in different ways to study constitutional change. In the next two sections I offer my own interpretation of their work and attempt to extend it in an effort to suggest how rational choice theory can be used in comparative political economy.

INTERPRETATIONS OF CONSTITUTIONAL CHANGE IN AMERICA

> Political decisions are almost invariably made by winning coalitions.
> (Riker 1996b)

Scholars of comparative politics supposedly study differing political arrangements in order to deduce laws or causal connections between the institutions and outcomes. It has been argued that to infer any such relationship, it is necessary for the institution to be stable. Although this restriction may provide useful insights, an alternative procedure is to attempt to understand *why* an institution is stable. Following Riker, this means asking why "losers," who persistently fail to reach their goals, do not attempt to change the institution. As the previous section's example of citizen revolt may suggest, changing an institution is no easy matter; it generally can be brought about only by changing the beliefs of a "winning coalition." In other words, to understand institutional stability from a rational choice perspective, it is necessary to conceive of an institution as an equilibrium in some very general "meta-game" (Calvert 1995).

It may prove feasible within such an institutional equilibrium to examine the game, internal to the institution, where the "rules" are fixed, and to use NCGT to study the local equilibria in behavior. Although I do not consider formal NCGT or CT to be equipped, as yet, to study the meta-institutional game, in some situations rational choice theory may provide insight into how these institutional, or constitutional, equilibria may be changed.

The examples that follow are all from US constitutional history and are intended to develop Riker's intuition. Consider first the presidential election of 1860. Lincoln won 40% of the popular vote (and 180 electoral college seats) for the Republican party. Stephen Douglas, the northern Democrat, took about 30% (but only 12 electoral college seats). The eastern Whig, Bell, took about 12% of the vote (39 seats), and the southern Democrat, Breckinridge, took 18% of the vote (and 72 electoral college seats). Details of the election are provided by Holt (1992).

The electoral institution, based on state constituencies, magnified Lincoln's vote (from 40% of the vote to about 60% of the electoral college). As is well understood from Duverger's Electoral Law (Duverger 1954), this "plurality" institution gave Lincoln a majority of the electoral college, and the presidency. Nothing about this is particularly surprising. It is perhaps surprising, however, that the Democratic party split before the election. Had Douglas and Breckinridge maintained a unified Democrat coalition, they would presumably have collected, say, 48% of the popular vote. Even so, it is unlikely that a Douglas-Breckinridge platform would have won the presidency. Riker's point was that the split among the Democrats was induced by Lincoln during the Lincoln-Douglas debate in Freeport, Illinois, in August 1858, during their senate race. Riker (1986) argued that Lincoln's heresthetic was to introduce a second dimension, concerning slavery. The problem of slavery had of course been a deeply contentious quandary since at least the ratification of the Constitution. It had been suppressed either by explicit gag rules in the House of Representatives (Miller 1995) or by an implicit compromise over the balance of northern and southern states (Weingast 1998).

The Whig and Democratic party coalitions had been able to maintain themselves precisely because of this suppression of the slavery issue. We may suppose that competition between the parties was restricted to an east-west dimension, with Whigs to the east and expansionist Democrats to the west. Figure 1 gives a schematic representation of the 1860 election, once the north-south social dimension (representing slavery) was introduced. As the figure suggests, Lincoln simultaneously attacked Douglas in the west and the Whigs to the east.

Riker (1986) gave no clear indication why the social dimension associated with slavery became so important in the 1860 election. To explain why this occurred, I use the framework of a belief game, introduced in the previous section. First,

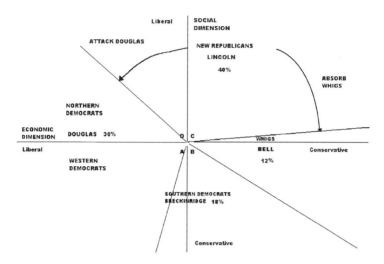

Figure 1 Schematic representation of the 1860 election, once the north-south social dimension (representing slavery) was introduced.

however, it is useful to look at the earlier presidential elections of 1844 and 1848, in order to show just how difficult was Lincoln's transformation of US politics.

In 1844, the Democrats' candidate, James Polk, a slaveholder from Kentucky, had been chosen by the party (but only on the ninth ballot). By invoking a two thirds rule in the Democrat Convention, southern Democrats had managed to veto Martin Van Buren, a Jacksonian who had been elected President back in 1836. In November 1844, Polk beat the Whig candidate, Clay, by only 38,000 votes out of 2.7 million, taking 170 electoral college seats to Clay's 105. The strengths of the Democratic and Whig parties were fairly evenly divided between north and south. Of the ten northern states, six had majorities for Clay, whereas six of the ten southern states chose Polk. Of the five midwestern and western states, only Ohio chose Clay. Although there was a slight preponderance of support in the south for the Democrats, it is fairly clear that it was the appeal of Polk to western expansionism that won the election. Indeed, one of the issues of the election was the annexation of Texas.

The party of abolitionism, the Liberty party, managed to win 62,000 votes in the election with significant support only in Vermont, Massachusetts, and New Hampshire, and with somewhat less support in Maine, Connecticut, New York, and Michigan (see Holt 1999, for full details on this election).

The election did have one important effect. Northern democrats in the House, feeling betrayed by their southern colleagues in the party due to the nomination of Polk, voted with northern Whigs in late 1844 to suspend the gag rule. This permanent rule, put in place in 1840, had prohibited the submission of petitions "praying the abolition of slavery" (Miller 1996).

The slavery issue did become more important in the 1848 election, when Van Buren had his revenge on southern Democrats. As the Free Soil presidential candidate, Van Buren significantly reduced the vote for the Democratic candidate, Cass, in New York and Pennsylvania. As a consequence, the Whig candidate, Zachary Taylor, won pluralities in 14 of the older 25 states. As for the two new states, Iowa and Florida, Cass won a majority in the former and Taylor in the latter. While Van Buren had no chance of election, his candidacy gave Taylor the presidency. Like the election of 1860, this election illustrates Duverger's principle. Although Van Buren received nearly 300,000 votes out of about 2.8 million (~11%), he took no electoral college votes. Taylor, with a plurality (48.5%) but not a majority of the popular vote, took 163 electoral college votes (or 56%) compared with the 127 won by Cass. The issue of slavery could affect the presidential outcome, but it could not by itself prove the basis for a successful candidate.

As mentioned above, Riker (1986) emphasized the split in the Democratic party between northern and southern sections in 1860. However, it is clear that Van Buren could not effect such a split in 1848. Indeed, no Free Soil or Liberty candidate could obtain a plurality of the vote prior to 1860. The idea of a belief cascade helps explain how Lincoln did achieve this.

I have suggested elsewhere (Schofield 1999b) that for a majority of northern voters before 1860, the situation was an uncertain quandary. Slavery was a concern, but the uncertainties associated with trying to curtail its extension into the new states of the West were too great for the majority of northern voters to make any rational choice in this sphere of policy. In his speeches in February and March 1860 in New York and New Haven, Lincoln gave a constitutional justification, in terms of the Founders' earlier decisions, for restricting slavery. He further argued that the *Dred Scott* decision of the Supreme Court in 1857 directly threatened free labor.

In my view, for a majority of voters in the North, Lincoln's interpretation transformed the slavery quandary from a problem of uncertainty into a problem of risk. In choosing Lincoln, the northern majority implicitly accepted the belief (the probability) that the South intended to "impose" slave labor on the North. The expected costs of electing Lincoln, which made war more probable, were less than the expected costs of acquiescing to the South.

I do not contend that a majority of northern voters adopted identical beliefs over the possibilities of the extension of slavery or of civil war. The fact that a majority of the voters in each of 14 northern and midwestern states chose Lincoln (Holt 1992) suggests that this majority accepted the belief that the risks and costs of war were tolerable. In other words, Lincoln created a belief cascade in the northern electorate. The results were a civil war and the eventual total transformation of the US Constitution.

There are clear differences between the presidential elections of 1848 and 1860. The 300,000 voters for the Free Soil party in 1848 may be seen as having had fundamental preferences (moral outrage and so on) that made slavery abhorrent. The rest of the voters in the North saw issues such as expansion and the tariff as much more important. Lincoln's arguments before the election of 1860 focused on persuading the electorate that the expected costs of tyranny (the credible cost of expansion of slavery and the probability that this would occur) exceeded the probable expected cost of war (given the probability, p, that the South would not retreat). The belief cascade that was created led to a core belief in the North (held by a majority there) that Lincoln was justified.

Admittedly this is conjectural. The point is that an explanation based on rational choice theory requires an attempt to "rationalize" or make sense of such belief cascades, in order to understand how the core belief that it created can transform a constitution. (Recent work by Bates et al 1998, Weingast 1997a, and Rutten & Weingast 1998 can be interpreted from this point of view.)

I have suggested (Schofield 1999a) that this process of constitutional transformation frequently passes through four stages:

1. Initially the institution or constitution is in equilibrium. Political competition obeys certain ground rules (such as the implicit conventions governing competition between Democrats and Whigs in the 1840s).

2. A quandary comes into being, but the consequences of action are uncertain. "Prophets of chaos" (Schofield 1999a) attempt to bring the quandary into focus, but uncertainty still persists. (For example, John Quincy Adams fought the gag rule in the House of Representatives in the 1840s, and in so doing, sought to bring the issue of slavery to the center of debate.)

3. An "architect of order" (Schofield 1999a) transforms the uncertain quandary into a question of risk, and in a sense solves the quandary, or at least brings it into sharper focus. The quandary thus becomes a dilemma, over which a choice must be made. The belief cascade, if it is created, generates a number of mutually antagonistic coalitions, but the ground rules of the institution no longer apply.

4. The core belief held by a winning coalition results in a transformation of the ground rules (that frame the Constitution) either through war or by some other form of political upheaval.

The above discussion of the lead-up to the Civil War is not meant to imply that the transformation is always through war. The earlier constitutional ratification of 1787 in the United States certainly was a major transformation that was undertaken in a peaceful, though perhaps contentious, fashion. In my view, the quandary of that time was that the Confederation of States was threatened by imperial powers (Spain, Britain, and possibly France). Different states held different views about Spain's intentions after it had closed the Mississippi to US shipping. (The complicated negotiations after the War of Independence had given Spain control of New Orleans.) Constitutional protagonists such as Jay, Hamilton, and Madison agreed that a stronger Union was necessary to deal with such threats. This itself created a quandary, since it was unclear how factional turbulence in a greater Union could be mitigated. I have suggested elsewhere (Schofield 1998) that Madison's analysis in *Federalist X* (1993[1787]) provided a key to resolving this quandary. Madison argued that a heterogeneous and extensive republic (whose constituencies were themselves heterogeneous) would tend to be governed by representatives, whose choices would be based on their beliefs about the best decision for the public good. In such a constitutional system, the effect of factions would be limited. It is plausible that Madison's argument derived from Condorcet's (1785; see McLean & Hewitt 1994:120–158 for translated extracts) work in France, possibly after discussions with Franklin in May 1786.[2] Madison, being less of an optimist than Condorcet, saw the danger of factions in a unicameral assembly. The proposal of a bicameral assembly of House and Senate, with the cross-veto power of a generally elected president, was a subtle solution to the quandary. Although Federalists and anti-Federalists may have disagreed on the details of the institutional arrangements to be implemented, Madison's proposals seem to have provided a credible solution to the problem of union. The core belief thus created had a significant impact on the process of ratification.

Riker's work on federalism suggests that we can learn much from studying those times when a profound quandary is perceived and perhaps resolved by a rapid transformation of the Constitution. In contrast, when the ground rules of the Constitution are established and stable, then institutions may well evolve, but at a much slower pace.

I suggest that political scientists adopt the notion of punctuated equilibrium, developed in paleobiology to account for the alternation of slow and fast evolution (Eldridge & Gould 1972). As in biology, periods of fast constitutional evolution may be highly contingent, unpredictable, or chaotic. I reject the neo-institutional argument (Fiorina & Shepsle 1982) that a rational choice theory of politics must necessarily be based on some form of stable equilibrium model. The relation of equilibrium theories of slow evolution to contingent explanations of fast evolution has preoccupied North for the last quarter century (see e.g. North 1993, 1994). Whereas Riker concentrated essentially on political change (induced through voting), North has been particularly interested in the fiscal characteristics of the state. These two endeavours are, in a sense, complementary.

In the next section I discuss some of North's work, along with that of other political economists who have utilized a similar perspective in examining the relationship between the state and its citizens.

PERSPECTIVES ON LEVIATHAN

Institutions are the rules of the game in a society or, more formally,... the humanly devised constraints that shape human interaction .... Institutional change shapes the way societies evolve through time .... (North 1990:3)

---

[2] An earlier version of Madison's argument appeared in April 1787 (Madison 1999 [1787]). It is known that Madison visited Philadelphia in 1786, where Franklin was then residing. Given that Franklin founded a Society for Political Enquiry in Philadelphia on his return from France, I conjecture that Madison and Franklin discussed these constitutional issues prior to the Constitutional Convention (Schofield 2000).

North's earlier work emphasized the evolution of the market economy, particularly that of the United States during 1790–1860 (North 1961). He soon turned, however, to the effect of property rights and institutional arrangements on the "capture of the gains of exchange" (Davis & North 1970) and to the relationship between individual incentives in the political economy and economic growth (North & Thomas 1970). In their book, North & Thomas (1973) began an examination of constitutional power in European polities, and in particular on the ability of the Crown to tax or borrow, and thus to engage in war. For example, in comparing England and France, they noted that whereas the English Parliament had been able to wrest control over taxing authority from the monarch, in France "the chaos of the fifteenth century ... had led the Estates General to give up power over taxes to Charles VII" (North & Thomas:1973:98).

In a later book, North (1981) attempted to set up a unified "public choice" theory based on property rights, to account for the first economic revolution (the transition from hunter/gatherer economies to agriculture) as well as the second (industrial) revolution of the eighteenth and nineteenth centuries. To develop the theory, North essentially proposed a "neo-Hobbesian theory of the state," in which the state contracts to set up a system of property rights and taxes. Of course, the Leviathan (Hobbes 1651) may maintain a set of inefficient property rights if these are compatible with wealth maximizing by the sovereign. This inefficiency may cause Leviathan to decline over the long run. These observations by North predate Kennedy's (1987) pessimistic inferences that Leviathan will always be pulled into imperial adventures and eventual decline. North also suggested that structural crises over the control of the state can occur. These may be resolved, and the institutions of the state transformed, by belief cascades of the kind described above. These ideas of North were developed further by Levi (1988), who used the notion of the "predatory state" to examine republican Rome and the introduction of income tax in Britain in 1799, and to compare French and English systems of taxation. One of Levi's interests was in the role of war, both as an incentive and excuse for the state to raise revenue. An important piece of work by North & Weingast (1989) was on the fiscal revolution accompanying the "glorious revolution" of 1688. Setting up the Bank of England, and credibly committing Leviathan (namely the Houses of Parliament) to repay debts, led to an enhanced ability of the British state to engage in war (see also Weingast 1997b).

In my opinion, the background to expelling James II and welcoming William and Mary in 1688 has to be sought in the English Civil War of 1641–1648, in the dictatorship (or "protectorate") of Cromwell and in the wars of the Commonwealth in Ireland and Europe. The notion of belief cascades could, in principle, be used to understand these constitutional changes.

After 1688, British tax revenues rose dramatically (Brewer 1988). Britain was readily able to borrow, and to repay its debts, in order to finance the numerous wars with France in the eighteenth century. By the American Revolutionary War of 1776–1784, British and French debts had each increased to something like 240 million pounds sterling (about 20 years of government revenue). Because it had transformed its fiscal institutions, Britain was able to manage its debt, and indeed successfully prosecute the later wars with Napoleonic France. France, on the other hand, incurred additional debts of at least a billion livres (more than 100 million pounds sterling) because of its provision of aid to the American colonies. Without the initial news of this promised aid in July 1776, it is doubtful that the colonies would have declared independence. Moreover, without the assistance of the French fleet and army at Yorktown in 1781, the colonies would probably never have attained independence (Schofield 1998).

The historian Jonathan Dull has argued that "French participation [in the War of Independence] was an event of incalculable cost to the French participants themselves ... not only the usual costs of war but bankruptcy and the subsequent rending of her entire political and social fabric" (Dull 1981:76–77). The economic historians Hoffman (1994), Root (1994), and Rosenthal (1998) have all studied the reasons why France was unable to follow Britain in devising efficient fiscal institutions prior to 1789. Norberg (1994) has also shown how the French war expenditure of 1776–1783 caused its bankruptcy and led eventually to the French Revolution. The Revolution and Napoleon's ascendency must have in turn created a fiscal revolution within France, which gave her the power to challenge the rest of Europe.

The point is that a fiscal revolution is necessary before a country can successfully fight wars. In addition, a country must develop the institutional capacity to fight. For example, in the Seven Years War between Britain and France (1756–1763), Britain developed the logistic capability of coordinating fleet and army; this enabled her to take Quebec (1759) from the French, and then Havana, Cuba, and Manilla, Philippines, from the Spanish. In the American Revolutionary War, the French were intially deterred from a formal alliance with the American colonies prior to 1778, since they had only 52 ships of war to Britain's 66. By 1782, France had increased its fleet to 73 and was allied with Spain, with 54 men-of-war. Britain meanwhile had increased its fleet to 94 (Dull 1981). Although France had solved the logistic problems of coordinating fleet and army, and was able to assist the colonies in 1781, it was clearly unable at that time to solve the more complex fiscal problems associated with war.

It is ironic that the beliefs in rationality held by Condorcet and the other philosophes of the French Enlightenment took root in America after the American Revolution (Commager 1977). The French philosophes themselves were often, like Condorcet, hunted down, imprisoned, or killed during the Terror of the French Revolution (Schama 1989).

Mention of the French Revolution and the Terror brings us to a major concern of twentieth century social science: the possibility of the irrational or totalitarian state. We may regard this concern as a quandary over the compatibility of individual freedom and security with economic efficiency. Keynes' writings on the matter are still relevant.

> [I]ndividualism, if it can be purged of its defects and its abuses, is the best safeguard of personal liberty ... [and] of the variety of life, which emerges

precisely from this extended field of personal choice, and the loss of which is the greatest of all losses of the homogeneous or totalitarian state.... The authoritarian state systems of to-day seem to solve the problem of unemployment at the expense of efficiency, and of freedom. (Keynes 1936:380–81)

Keynes solved this quandary of liberty and efficiency by distinguishing between commodity and asset markets. The former could be expected to satisfy the Marshallian equilibrium hypothesis, whereas the latter, like stock markets, may be dominated by chaotic speculation. By government intervention to control speculation in asset markets, equilibrium and efficiency could be attained, and the (relatively) decentralized economic system could function in a fashion compatible with political liberty (Schofield 1999a).

Keynes was also aware that the international system could degenerate into the Hobbesian war of competitive devaluations supported by tariff barriers, etc. The international economic system set up under the Bretton Woods Scheme after World War II was not, however, of Keynesian design. Its stability depended on a hegemonic, or dominant, player (namely the United States) to maintain cooperation between states. By 1960, observers such as Triffin (1960) had begun to speculate that international cooperation could break down. The post–World War II monetary system was based both on the maintenance of value in the dollar and on a constant outflow of dollars from the United States. These two requirements seemed incompatible, and indeed the rigid dollar-gold link was broken first by Johnson in 1968 and then by Nixon in 1972.

The extraordinary economic and political problems of the 1970s may well have been induced by governments believing in a Keynesianism that Keynes himself would not have accepted. There seems very little theoretical basis to the notion that, by playing with money aggregates, a government can permanently adjust inflation/unemployment combinations. But it was the case in the early 1970s that the weakening restrictions of the gold standard and the growing international flow of dollars gave governments the opportunity to experiment with inflation/unemployment ratios conducive to reelection. Such an act by government violates the medieval fiduciary relationship between the sovereign and the people, proscribing the debasement of the coinage.

Goodhart & Bhansali (1970) were perhaps the first to note that inducing an electorally optimal short-term combination of inflation and unemployment, along the so-called Phillips curve, would also probably trigger inflationary expectations. As Brittan (1978:172) later observed, "Over a run of political cycles the short-term Phillips curve will drift upwards ... democratic myopia and economic time lags will land the economy with an excessive rate of inflation."

A host of prophets of chaos studied the deleterious economic effects of governmental electoral rationality (Nordhaus 1975, MacRae 1976, Tufte 1978). In one of the most interesting arguments of that time, Beer (1982) postulated that in polities with first-past-the-post (or plurality) electoral systems, such as Britain and the United States, the decline of party identification would permit small groups in the polity to be unconstrained in their "rent-seeking" claims. Because plurality electoral procedures magnify vote swings, relatively small groups could black-mail the government. It was certainly true that, in Britain, competition between labor groups became intense during the 1970s. With inflation approaching 25% on occasion, weakly organized groups, such as nurses and university teachers, lost economic ground rapidly. Olson (1982) also suggested that economies that had been devastated by war (such as Japan and Germany) had transformed their institutions and were less likely to be beset by "economic sclerosis" and by the "stagflationary" effects of the inability to adapt.

Keynes was vilified for providing the theoretical justification (at least in Britain and the US) for this violation of the fiduciary relationship (Buchanan & Wagner 1977).

In arguments somewhat related to those of Olson, the theorists of "consociational" or "corporatist" democracy (Lijphart 1969, Lehmbruch 1979, Crouch 1985) argued that democracies with strong socialist or social democrat parties, and encompassing labor unions, should be able to manage political bargaining more effectively than the liberal market economies (such as Britain and the United States).

Garrett (1998) has examined the recent arguments that such consociational democracies have proved less adept at maintaining economic growth in the so-called global economy of the 1990s. Table 1 adapts information for 1980–1995 taken from his book.

The four consociational/corporatist economies have all quite powerful socialist/social democrat parties that were in office at least at some time during the 1980s. Garrett also includes Finland and Norway in this first category but places France in the second, "mixed" category. In the mixed category, the left controlled, on average, less than one quarter of the cabinet positions during the 1980s. In the four liberal polities, the left was out of power in the 1980s. It is not obvious that the 12 countries can be so readily classified. Nonetheless, Table 1 is suggestive. There does seem to be a tendency for governments of corporatist democracies to absorb a greater share of gross domestic product and to run budget deficits. Unemployment in the 1980s in the Scandinavian democracies tended to be lower than in the Organisation for Economic Co-operation and Development as a whole, whereas growth was somewhat lower and inflation somewhat higher than in, for example, the United States.

The predictions of the prophets of chaos of the 1970s and early 1980s were confounded, particularly in the late 1980s and early 1990s. The liberal polities of the United States and United Kingdom did not fall into a stagflationary trap, forced by their electoral systems to attempt to keep unemployment down and inflationary expectations up. The next section of this essay argues that the trap was avoided by the United States and the United Kingdom because a core political belief was generated in the early 1980s in these two polities about the appropriate relationship between economics and government. Moreover, it was precisely because of the

TABLE 1 Twelve democratic polities: 1980–1995 (adapted from Garrett 1998)

Country[a]	Union[b]	G[c]	B[d]	E[e]	U[f]	I[g]	M[h]
Corporatist							
Sweden	83	67	8.0	1.9	2.2	8.2	10.4
Denmark	74	62	3.0	1.5	8.3	6.5	14.8
Austria	46	52	3.8	2.4	3.2	3.8	7.0
France	10	53	4.6	1.9	9.0	7.0	16.0
Average		*59*	*4.9*	*1.9*	*5.7*	*6.4*	*12.0*
Mixed							
Belgium	55	56	6.0	2.0	10.9	4.8	15.7
Italy	34	54	9.1	2.1	10.3	10.8	21.2
Germany	31	49	3.0	2.1	7.6	2.9	10.5
Netherlands	23	54	3.3	1.6	9.6	2.9	12.5
Average		*53*	*5.4*	*1.95*	*9.6*	*5.4*	*15.0*
Liberal							
UK	38	43	5.6	2.0	9.5	7.6	17.1
Canada	32	48	6.2	2.6	9.2	6.4	15.6
US	15	34	2.9	2.6	7.1	5.5	12.6
Japan	25	34	0.9	4.2	2.5	2.5	5.0
Average (with Japan)		*40*	*3.9*	*2.85*	*7.0*	*5.5*	*12.5*
Average (without Japan)		*42*	*4.9*	*2.4*	*8.6*	*6.5*	*15.1*
Overall Average		51	4.7	2.2	7.4	5.8	13.2

[a] The countries are grouped according to percentage share of left-wing cabinet portfolios over 1980–1990.
[b] Percentage trade union membership in 1990.
[c] Government spending (G), as percent GDP, 1991–1995.
[d] Budget deficit (B), as percent GDP, 1991–1995.
[e] Economic growth (E), per annum average, 1980–1990.
[f] Unemployment (U), average percent, 1980–1990.
[g] Inflation (I), average percent, 1980–1990.
[h] "Misery" (M) index, $U + I$, average, 1980–1990.

plurality nature of the electoral system in the two polities that this core belief could be effectively implemented. For the moment, I emphasize the differences between Table 1, for the 1980s, and Table 2, which presents similar economic data for 1998–1999. Inflation is obviously not a problem for the developed economies at present.

Indeed, deflation (falling prices) has begun to be a serious problem in Japan. Average unemployment has fallen in the three liberal polities (excluding Japan) but is up elsewhere, most notably in Germany, Italy, and France. Budget deficits in the countries in the European Union (EU) were required to be under 3% in 1999, so the budget balance figures for these countries may be distorted. Japan, however, is running a budget deficit of 6%, while the United States, Canada, and Britain appear to be in budget surplus. It is possible that France, Belgium, Germany, and Italy have high unemployment figures because of the EU requirement of low

TABLE 2   Twelve democratic polities: July 1999 (data from *Economist* 1999)

Country	B^a	E	U	I^b	M
Corporatist					
Sweden	−1.9	3.6	5.9	0.3	6.2
Denmark	−1.0	1.0	5.7	2.4	8.1
Austria	+2.1	1.4	4.3	0.4	4.7
France	+2.9	2.3	11.4	0.3	11.7
Average	—	*2.0*	*6.8*	*0.9*	*7.7*
Mixed					
Belgium	+1.3	1.6	10.9	0.7	11.6
Italy	+2.7	0.9	12.0	1.4	13.4
Germany	+2.0	0.7	10.5	0.4	10.9
Netherlands	+0.7	3.0	3.4	2.3	5.7
Average	—	*1.55*	*9.2*	*1.2*	*10.4*
Liberal					
UK	−0.4	0.6	6.2	1.3	7.5
Canada	−1.3	3.2	7.6	1.6	9.2
US	−1.7	4.0	4.3	2.0	6.3
Japan	+6.0	0.1	4.6	−0.4^c	5.0
Average (with Japan)	—	*2.0*	*5.7*	*1.3*	*7.0*
Average (without Japan)	—	*2.6*	*6.0*	*1.6*	*7.6*
Overall average	—	1.85	7.2	1.1	8.3

[a] A negative figure is a *positive* budget balance as percent of GDP.

[b] Consumer price inflation over July 1998–July 1999.

[c] Since the "deflation" of −0.4% is an economic bad, I have interpreted this as 0.4% in computing the misery index.

budget deficits, and the imposition (through the monetary discipline of a single currency) of low inflation. Since their unemployment rates have been high since at least 1994, it is more likely that these figures are due to structural features of the political economy. In line with Garrett's (1998) argument, the three social democratic/corporatist polities (Sweden, Denmark, and Austria) have all managed to maintain low inflation, moderate unemployment, and reasonable growth.

Garrett's (1998) interpretation on the different policy choices, and quite different policy outcomes, of these 12 countries is based on macropolitics, on variations of electoral and political preferences. Any rational choice theory of politics, if it is to give deeper insight into these differences, must build up from individual voter choices to party strategies. The obvious way to attempt this is through an empirical and theoretical study of elections. The next section suggests ways to proceed, through a critique of rational choice, preference-based models of elections derived from the seminal work of Downs (1957). Instead, I suggest that Condorcet's and Madison's understanding of elections, as methods of "belief aggregation," could prove more useful in studying the relationship between constitutions and political behavior.

RATIONAL CHOICE MODELS OF JURIES, COMMITTEES, AND ELECTIONS

> The two great points of difference between a Democracy and a Republic are first, the delegation of the Government, in the latter, to a small number of citizens elected by the rest: secondly, the greater number of citizens, and greater sphere of country, over which the latter may be extended.
>
> The effect of the first difference is ... to refine and enlarge the public views, by passing them through the medium of a chosen body of citizens, where wisdom may best discern the true interest of their country ... Under such a regulation, it may well happen that the public voice pronounced by the representatives ... will be more consonant to the public good, than if pronounced by the people themselves ... On the other hand ... [M]en of factious tempers ... may ... by corruption ... betray the interests of the people. (Madison 1993[1787]:409)

As indicated above, Madison's argument in this passage is compatible with the implications of the "jury theorem" of Condorcet (1785). Condorcet's focus was on the aggregation of beliefs of the members of a jury seeking the truth (*qua* public good) in a situation of risk. Assuming that the average propensity (among the jurors) to choose a true proposition exceeds one half, Condorcet demonstrated that a majority is more likely to find the truth than is the average juror. The theorem depended on the assumption of independence of the jurors' choices. Madison's arguments can be interpreted to mean that the "greater sphere" of the republic implies heterogeneity in beliefs and thus a low average level of statistical dependence in voter choice (see Ladha & Miller 1996 for the argument). Thus Condorcet's theorem could hold for the republic, as envisioned by Madison.

In directing attention to Condorcet's work more than 150 years later, Black (1958:196) saw little relevance in the jury theorem, since he considered voting to be a method of preference aggregation. In contrast, the jury theorem focuses on belief aggregation, on the attempt to ascertain the truth of the matter. The huge formal literature of the 40 years since Black's work on voting in committees or elections has (until recently) followed Black in regarding preference, rather than belief, as the key notion. In my judgment, this focus may have rendered much of this literature irrelevant to the study of comparative politics.

To see the basis for this assertion, consider again the classic framework of Savage (1954). Fundamental preferences, because they are fundamental, can never be observed. In fact, preferences over acts are derived from the beliefs of the individual, but these beliefs are not static objects. Although they may be described as probabilities, they are functions, based on the information available, of the model of knowledge used by the individual, including the model of other individuals' modeling capabilities. This complex structure holding between the members of the society I termed "common knowledge." So at the very least, attempting to model decision making in a jury or committee requires that we consider changes in this structure of knowledge. Whether this is possible is contentious. Some recent attempts at modeling juries, using the apparatus of NCGT, are interesting, but their conclusions seem to be unduly dependent on the theoretical assumption imposed (Austen-Smith & Banks 1996). It certainly seems that belief cascades of the kind discussed above can occur in any decision-making situation.

It may be useful to think of social choice in terms of a continuum, with a "pure" committee at one end and a "pure" jury at the other. In a pure committee, preferences over options are fixed, and acts are strategically chosen to further each voter's goals (as described by preferences). Beliefs are relevant only insofar as they affect strategic choices. A parliament of the republic acting as a pure committee would necessarily exhibit the factional behavior so feared by Madison (and for that matter, Adam Smith). In contrast, the parliament acting as a pure jury would seek the truth of the nature of the public good, would be open to argument, and would attain a consensus, not a compromise.

A typical parliament is neither a pure committee nor a pure jury. However, the institutional and constitutional structures that were adopted in the United States after 1787 were designed, in some sense, to induce jury-like behavior both in the Congress and in the choice of president, and to mitigate the possibility of factional, committee-like behavior.

If elections to a Congress or Parliament are like voting in a pure committee, then the representatives themselves are unlikely to comprise a jury. Thus, any attempt to determine how a democratic polity behaves must first consider the true nature of elections, and in particular, the effect of the electoral system on the way voters choose.

In European-style polities with disciplined parties, party leaders, policy declarations and the like, voters choose from among a small set of discrete things called parties. [Cox (1997) provides an extensive discussion of the strategic, preference-based voter choice under various electoral rules.] In the "spatial" model, these parties are identified with policy points. Voters choose parties that are proximate, and parties choose points that maximize something (votes, seats, or probability of winning). In the Downsian two-party model with a single policy dimension, parties converge (Downs 1957). In the macro political economy models (e.g. Brittan 1978) discussed above, parties offer different inflation-unemployment combinations that appeal to distinct sets of voters. In fact, however, parties neither converge nor necessarily induce economically irrational outcomes for political, or vote maximizing, motives. To see where the various models may have gone wrong, let us compare the plurality electoral systems of Britain and the United States with those of the polities of Europe, typically based on some form of proportional representation.

So-called party identification in Britain and the United States has declined (Clarke & Stewart 1998). It seems that the proportion of the electorate with fixed political preferences has dropped during the last few decades. Possibly this is because parties change policy position. Alternatively, voters may have become more astute at evaluating parties, at determining the credibility of party claims.

After at least a decade of economic woes, the election of 1979 in Britain gave the Conservatives, under Thatcher, about 44% of the vote (and 53% of the seats) to Labour's 37% (and 42% of the seats). The center Liberal Democrats took most of the remaining vote (and very few seats, less than 2%). As expected under Duverger's first law (Duverger 1954), plurality electoral rule leads essentially to a two-party system. However, counter to the inferences of the Downsian model, there was no convergence. Empirical work currently in progress strongly suggests the various parties in Britain did not maximize "expected vote shares." (This inference is made in the context of an empirical model of the response of the electorate to party policy positions; see Quinn et al 1999.) What Brittan (1978) neglected to consider in his analysis was that a party leader, such as Thatcher in 1979, could attract a minority of the electorate with a risky policy that would eventually change Britain's economic prospects. The electoral system gave the Conservatives sufficient political power to bring about the promised changes over the next 15 years or so. During the same period the Labour party elite, with strongly held beliefs over appropriate economic policies, could not attain a parliamentary majority, even with the support of the Liberal Democrats.

It seems a plausible inference that the plurality electoral system in Britain allowed for a risky policy choice (involving, in particular, a transformation of the labor market). The unemployment-inflation figures in Table 2 for Britain suggest that this risky choice paid off. After Thatcher, unwise decisions over the revaluation of sterling and disagreements over European integration within the Conservative Party gave the Labour Party an opportunity to reevaluate its policy manifesto and to choose a somewhat more centrist leader, Tony Blair. Even so, empirical analysis suggests that the Labour Party position, at the election of May 1997, was not chosen simply to maximize the expected popular vote for the party.

This brief discussion is offered in support of the thesis that, under a plurality electoral system, crucial elections can occur that depend on changes in beliefs and lead to policy choices that induce further changes. That is, a deep political or economic quandary is addressed by a risk-taking politician. Enough of the electorate are persuaded by the politician's interpretation of the quandary to change their beliefs over the appropriate policy choice, and the electoral system endows the politician with the power to effect the change. In Britain under Thatcher, and in the United States after the election of Reagan in 1980, political choices brought about high unemployment and, eventually, relatively low inflation. Because inflation derives from economic beliefs about future price changes, we can say that political beliefs eventually transformed economic beliefs. At a theoretical level, a focus on electoral preferences misses the reasons for the transformation.

Under a proportional electoral system, neither Britain nor the United States would have been able to impose such policy changes. In Germany, for example, the large right-of-center party (the Christian Democrats) depended for decades on the small, centrist Free Democrat party for a parliamentary majority. Even after obtaining a plurality under Gerhard Schröder, the Social Democratic Party has been unable to implement policies that would reduce the level of government debt below the current level of over $800 billion. (Under proportional representation, the Social Democratic Party has to rely on the Greens for support.) France's position is similar. Since 1997, the Socialist Party under Jospin, with 25% of the vote (and 43% of the seats), has depended on the support of the smaller Communist Party for support in forming the government.

Duverger (1954:215) made a more general point. "[T]he centre does not exist in politics: there may well be a Centre party, but there is no centre tendency: no centre doctrine.... Every Centre is divided against itself." Duverger's later work (1984) developed this intuition, arguing that plurality electoral systems give voters a clear choice. One way to interpret Duverger's argument is that plurality systems are inherently more competitive and induce behavior by parties that, in difficult situations, may be more risk preferring. Indeed, an extension of his argument is that political economies based on plurality rule may be able to engage in a greater degree of political and economic experimentation. In turn, it is possible that beliefs can change more dramatically in such polities than in those based on proportional representation. (Note that this conjecture is only intended to be relevant for the contemporary period.)

The data presented in Table 2 certainly suggest that France, Germany, Belgium, and Italy were all unable in the recent past to implement risky policy initiatives, designed, for example, to reduce labor-market rigidities. (It does not seem plausible that high unemployment in many of the countries in the European Union is due simply to the risk aversion of the German Central Bank with regard to inflation.) Although it is possible that adopting the euro in 2002 will open up these European markets, it is also possible that economic protection will be seen as the only risk-averse way to deal with budget deficits and unemployment.

Duverger was not quite correct that the political center never exists. Both Italy, until 1992, and Japan (over the last 40 years) have had dominant center parties (the Christian Democrats and the Liberal Democratic Party, respectively). In a sense, competition was internalized and took a factional form. It appears that the lack of real competition in Italy led to intense corruption involving the Mafia (Robb 1996). In Japan, Liberal Democratic Party factions competed in costly multicandidate elections, with funding from large banks, financial institutions, and corporations. The cross-flow of money between the party and these institutions induced a property market boom. The recent crash in Japan has caused a wave of bankruptcies that the polity finds impossible to face. Meanwhile, many of the Asian economies have been infected by the resulting economic disorder, and the true level of political corruption is becoming apparent.

At the same time, the utter and surprising transformation of the Russian political economic institutions (which was so welcomed by western leaders) has continued to surprise. A constitution that endows the president with great power and an electoral system that creates a fragmented Duma have led to astonishing levels of corruption, and to the domination of large sectors of the economy by gangsters or mafiosi. The details of the resignation of Yeltsin at the end of December 1999 suggest the extent of this corruption.

It seems from these observations that when constitutional rules lessen the degree of real political competition, then corruption flourishes. If such an argument is valid, then it creates a constitutional quandary, for example, for the design of the institutions of the European Union. Although great hopes have been raised by the prospect of European Union, two of the principal institutions, the Council of Ministers and the European Commission, are appointed rather than elected. The European Parliament, though elected, is fragmented and lacks any real political power. Recent investigation into corruption in the Commission suggests that the designers of the European institutions were unduly optimistic about the jury-like properties of such powerful committees of appointed delegates.

These issues of competition and representation are at the heart of constitutional political economy. Rational choice theory may provide a tool to study the effects of constitutional details on the motivations of politicians and the beliefs of voters. However, this tool will only prove effective if its practitioners pay close attention to the political world and attempt to address the important substantive issues of political choice.

CONCLUSION

> I like the organization of the government into Legislative, Judiciary and Executive.... I solely approve of the greater House [the Senate] being chosen by the people directly. I am captivated by the compromises of the opposite claims of the great and little states ... I like the negative given to the Executive with a third of either house.
>
> I will now add what I do not like. First, the omission of a bill of rights.... The second feature I dislike ... is the abandonment of the necessity of rotation in ... the case of the President.... An incapacity to be elected a second time would have been the only effective preventative [of disorder]. (Jefferson writing to Madison from Paris on December 20, 1787, quoted in Bailyn 1993:210–12)

Both Madison and Jefferson were, of course, acutely aware of how constitutional details could affect the stability of the polity and mitigate the likelihood of tyranny or factional chaos. In my judgment, the founders hoped to create the political institutions that would balance risk. The very nature of the presidential election suggests that a successful candidate must be a risk taker. As I have already indicated, successful British prime ministers, such as Thatcher, have also been risk takers.

Risk takers may choose war, as Lincoln did, and sometimes such a choice is necessary. However, the leadership of a risk taker without any institutional restriction is likely to lead to disaster. (One has only to think of the regimes of the dictators in mid-century or of recent events in the Balkans.) I suspect that the institutional structures of both the House and Senate lead them to be moderately risk averse or risk neutral. On the whole they are inclined, perhaps, to pull back the president from overly risky choices. It is well known that democracies tend not to go to war. However, it is difficult to judge whether the risk aversion that seems to characterize the European multiparty polities at present is a good thing or not. But probably neither risk aversion nor extreme risk preference is in the long-run interests of citizens in a democratic polity.

Understanding how constitutions actually operate, how they affect the motivations of voters and leaders, of consumers and producers, is the great problem facing students of comparative politics and of political economy. In this task, the kind of rational choice theory that I have in mind can be a useful tool. Holding to a particular kind of formalism, whether NCGT or CT, because it is familiar and gives simple equilibrium answers, will not give much insight. Looking at historical situations or tempering formal models through empirical analysis is the best way to understand ourselves and the world in which we live. The ideas of Riker and North, and their intellectual colleagues in political and economic history, suggest how to use and contribute to a general theory of rational choice.

ACKNOWLEDGMENTS

I gratefully acknowledge financial support provided by the National Science Foundation under Grant SBR-98-18582. William Riker's efforts at combining rational choice theory and political history, and Douglass North's work in economic history, have clearly influenced my own views. Conversations with Iain McLean, Gary Miller, and Andrew Rutten have also helped in my efforts at critique and synthesis. I thank Margaret Levi and Kim Kadota for their editorial suggestions. I also appreciate the permission of Geoff Garrett to present the data given in Table 1, and the comments of seminar participants at Yale University, MIT, and Washington University in St. Louis.

Visit the Annual Reviews home page at www.AnnualReviews.org

LITERATURE CITED

Arrow K. 1951. *Social Choice and Individual Values.* New York: Wiley. 124 pp.

Arrow K. 1973. Some ordinalist-utilitarian notes on Rawls' sense of justice. *J. Phil.* 70:245–63

Arrow K. 1986. Rationality of self and others in an economic system. *J. Bus.* 59:385–99

Austen-Smith D, Banks J. 1996. Information aggregation, rationality and the Condorcet jury theorem. *Am. Polit. Sci. Rev.* 90:34–45

Austen-Smith D, Banks J. 1998. Social choice theory, game theory and positive political theory. *Annu. Rev. Polit. Sci.* 1:259–87

Austen-Smith D, Banks J. 1999. *Positive Political Theory.* Ann Arbor: Michigan Univ. Press. 208 pp.

Bates R. 1983. *Essays on the Political Economy of Rural Africa.* Berkeley: Univ. Calif. Press. 178 pp.

Bates R, de Figueiredo R, Weingast B. 1998. The politics of interpretation: rationality, culture and transition. *Polit. Soc.* 26:603–42

Beer S. 1982. *Britain Against Itself.* London: Faber & Faber. 251 pp.

Bikchandani S, Hirschleifer D, Walsh I. 1992. A theory of fads, fashion, customs and cultural change as information cascades. *J. Polit. Econ.* 100:992–1026

Black D. 1958. *The Theory of Committees and Elections.* Cambridge, UK: Cambridge Univ. Press

Brewer J. 1988. *The Sinews of Power: War, Money and the English State, 1688–1783.* Cambridge, MA: Harvard Univ. Press. 290 pp.

Brittan S. 1978. Inflation and democracy. In *The Political Economy of Inflation,* ed. F Hirsch, J Goldthorpe, pp. 161–85. London: Martin Robertson

Buchanan J, Wagner R. 1977. *Democracy in Deficit: The Political Legacy of Lord Keynes.* New York: Academic. 195 pp.

Calvert R. 1995. Rational actors, equilibrium, and social institutions. In *Explaining Social Institutions,* ed. J Knight, I Sened, pp. 57–93. Ann Arbor: Michigan Univ. Press

Clarke H, Stewart M. 1998. The decline of parties in the minds of citizens. *Annu. Rev. Polit. Sci.* 1:357–78

Commager H. 1977. *The Empire of Reason.* Garden City, NJ: Doubleday. 342 pp.

Condorcet M. 1785. *Essai sur l'application de l'analyse à la probabilité des décisions rendues à la pluralité des voix.* Paris:Imprimerie Royale

Cox G. 1997. *Making Votes Count.* Cambridge, UK: Cambridge Univ. Press. 340 pp.

Crouch D. 1985. Corporatism in industrial relations: a formal model. In *The Political Economy of Corporatism,* ed. W Grant, pp. 63–88. London: Macmillan

Davis L, North DC. 1970. Institutional change and American economic growth: a first step

towards a theory of institutional innovation. *J. Econ. Hist.* 30:131–49

Denzau A, North DC. 1994. Shared mental models: ideologies and institutions. *Kyklos* 47:3–31

Downs A. 1957. *An Economic Theory of Democracy.* New York: Harper & Row. 310 pp.

Dull J. 1981. France and the American Revolution seen as tragedy. In *Diplomacy and Revolution: The Franco-American Alliance of 1778,* ed. R Hoffman, P Albert, pp. 73–106. Charlottesville: Univ. Virginia Press

Duverger M. 1954. *Political Parties: Their Organization and Activity in the Modern State.* London: Methuen. 439 pp.

Duverger M. 1984. Which is the best electoral system? In *Choosing an Electoral System,* ed. A Lijphart, B Grofman, pp. 31–39. New York: Praeger

*Economist.*1999.Vol. 352, No. 8129, July 24

Eldridge N, Gould S. 1972. Punctuated equilibria: an alternative to phyletic gradualism. In *Models in Paleobiology,* ed. T Schopf, pp. 82–115. New York: Norton

Ensminger J. 1992. *Making a Market: The Institutional Transformation of an African Society.* Cambridge, UK: Cambridge Univ. Press. 212 pp.

Fink E, Riker W. 1989. The strategy of ratification. In *The Federalist Papers and the New Institutionalism,* ed. B Grofman, D Wittman, pp. 220–55. New York: Agathon

Fiorina M, Shepsle K. 1982. Equilibrium, disequilibrium, and the general possibility of a science of politics. In *Political Equilibrium,* ed. P Ordeshook, K Shepsle, pp. 49–64. Boston, MA: Kluwer

Garrett G. 1998. *Partisan Politics in the Global Economy.* Cambridge, UK: Cambridge Univ. Press. 185 pp.

Goodhart C, Bhansali R. 1970. Political economy. *Polit. Stud.* 18:43–106

Hobbes T. 1968 (1651). *Leviathan; or the Matter, Forme and Power of a Common-Wealth, Ecclesiastical and Civill,* ed. C MacPherson. Harmondsworth, UK: Penguin

Hoffman P. 1994. Early modern France: 1450–1700. In *Fiscal Crises, Liberty and Representative Government, 1450–1789*, ed. P Hoffman, K Norberg, pp. 226–52. Stanford, CA: Stanford Univ. Press

Holt M. 1992. Abraham Lincoln and the politics of union. In *Political Parties and American Political Development from the Age of Jackson to the Age of Lincoln*, ed. M Holt, pp. 323–53. Baton Rouge: Louisiana State Univ. Press

Holt M. 1999. *The Rise and Fall of the American Whig Party*. Oxford, UK: Oxford Univ. Press. 1248 pp.

Jefferson T. 1993 (1787). Letter to Madison, Dec. 20, 1787. In *Debate on the Constitution*, ed. B Bailyn, I:209–13. New York: Library Classics US

Karklins R, Petersen R. 1993. Decision calculus of protesters and regimes: eastern Europe 1989. *J. Polit.* 55:588–614

Kennedy P. 1987. *The Rise and Fall of the Great Powers*. New York: Random House. 677 pp.

Keynes J. 1936. *The General Theory of Employment, Interest and Money*. London: Macmillan. 428 pp.

Kuran T. 1995. *Private Truths, Public Lies*. Cambridge, MA: Harvard Univ. Press. 423 pp.

Ladha K, Miller G. 1996. Political discourse, factions and the general will: correlated voting and Condorcet's jury theorem. In *Collective Decision Making*, ed. N Schofield, pp. 393–410. Boston: Kluwer

Laver M. 1998. Models of government formation. *Annu. Rev. Polit. Sci.* 1:1–25

Lehmbruch G. 1979. Consociational democracy, class conflict and the new corporatism. In *Trends Towards Corporatist Intermediation*, ed. G Lehmbruch, P Schmitter, pp. 1–28. London: Sage

Levi M. 1988. *Of Rule and Revenue*. Berkeley: Univ. Calif. Press. 253 pp.

Lijphart A. 1969. Consociational democracy. *World Polit.* 21:207–25

Lohmann S. 1994. The dynamics of informational cascades: The Monday demonstra-tions in Leipzig, East Germany, 1989–91. *World Polit.* 47:42–101

MacRae C. 1976. A political model of the business cycle. *J. Polit. Econ.* 85:239–63

Madison J. 1993 (1787). Federalist X. In *Debate on the Constitution*, ed. B Bailyn, I:404–11. New York: Library Classics US

Madison J. 1999 (1787). Vices of the political system of the United States. In *Madison: Writings*, ed. J Rakove, pp. 69–80. New York: Library Classics US

McCracken P. 1977. *Towards Full Employment and Price Stability*. Paris: OECD. 340 pp.

McLean I, Hewitt F. 1994. *Condorcet: Foundations of Social Choice and Political Theory*. Aldershot, UK: Elgar

Miller W. 1996. *Arguing about Slavery*. New York: Knopf. 577 pp.

Nasar S. 1998. *A Beautiful Mind*. New York: Simon & Schuster. 459 pp.

Nash J. 1950. Equilibrium points in N-person games. *Proc. Nat. Acad. Sci. USA* 36:48–49

Nash J. 1951. Non-cooperative games. *Ann. Math.* 54:286–95

Norberg K. 1994. The French fiscal crisis of 1788 and the financial origins of the revolution of 1789. In *Fiscal Crises, Liberty and Representative Government, 1450–1789*, ed. P Hoffman, K Norberg, pp. 252–98. Stanford, CA: Stanford Univ. Press

Nordhaus W. 1975. The political business cycle. *Rev. Econ. Stud.* 42:167–90

North DC. 1961. *The Economic Growth of the United States, 1790–1860*, New York: Prentice Hall. 304 pp.

North DC. 1981. *Structure and Change in Economic History*. New York: Norton. 228 pp.

North DC. 1990. *Institutions, Institutional Change and Economic Performance*. Cambridge, UK: Cambridge Univ. Press. 152 pp.

North DC. 1993. Institutions and credible commitment. *J. Inst. Theor. Econ.* 149:11–23

North DC. 1994. Economic performance through time. *Am. Econ. Rev.* 84:359–68

North DC, Thomas R. 1970. An economic theory of the growth of the western world. *Econ. Hist. Rev.* 23:1–17

North DC, Thomas R. 1973. *The Rise of the Western World: A New Economic History.* Cambridge, UK: Cambridge Univ. Press. 170 pp.

North DC, Weingast B. 1989. Constitutions and commitment: the evolution of institutions governing public choice in 17th century England. *J. Econ. Hist.* 49:803–32

Olson M. 1982. The political economy of comparative growth rates. In *The Political Economy of Growth*, ed. D Mueller, pp. 7–52. New Haven, CT: Yale Univ. Press

Petersen R. 1999. *Resistance and Rebellion.* Cambridge, UK: Cambridge Univ. Press. In press

Pocock T. 1998. *Battle for Empire, 1756–1763.* London: O'Mara Books. 272 pp.

Quinn K, Martin A, Whitford A. 1999. Voter choice in multiparty democracies: a test of competing theories. *Am. J. Polit. Sci.* 43:1231–47

Riker W. 1964. *Federalism: Origin, Operation, Significance.* Boston: Little Brown. 169 pp.

Riker W. 1980. Implications from the disequilibrium of majority rule for the study of institutions. *Am. Polit. Sci. Rev.* 74:432–46

Riker W. 1982a. Implications from the disequilibrium of majority rule for the study of institutions. In *Political Equilibrium*, ed. P Ordeshook, K Shepsle, pp. 3–24. Boston, MA: Kluwer (reprinted with addendum)

Riker W. 1982b. *Liberalism against Populism.* San Francisco: Freeman. 310 pp.

Riker W. 1984. *The Development of American Federalism.* Boston, MA: Kluwer. 233 pp.

Riker W. 1986. *The Art of Political Manipulation.* New Haven, CT: Yale Univ. Press. 152 pp.

Riker W. 1993. Rhetorical interaction in the ratification campaign. In *Agenda Formation*, ed. W Riker, pp. 81–123. Ann Arbor: Michigan Univ. Press

Riker W. 1995. The experience of creating institutions: the framing of the U.S. Constitution. In *Explaining Social Institutions*, ed. J Knight, I Sened, pp. 121–44. Ann Arbor: Michigan Univ. Press

Riker W. 1996a. *The Strategy of Rhetoric: Campaigning for the Ratification of the Constitution.* New Haven, CT: Yale Univ. Press. 283 pp.

Riker W. 1996b. Foreword. In *Collective Decision-Making*, ed. N Schofield, p. xv. Boston, MA: Kluwer

Robb P. 1996. *Midnight in Sicily.* London: Harvil. 323 pp.

Root H. 1994. *The Fountain of Privilege.* Berkely: Univ. Calif. Press. 280 pp.

Rosenthal J-L. 1998. The political economy of absolutism reconsidered. In *Analytical Narratives*, ed. R Bates, A Greif, M Levi, J-L Rosenthal, B Weingast, pp. 64–108. Princeton, NJ: Princeton Univ. Press

Rutten A, Weingast B. 1998. *Ideas, interests and credible commitment in the American Revolution.* Discuss. Pap., Dept. Polit. Sci., Stanford Univ., Stanford, CA

Savage L. 1954. *The Foundations of Statistics.* New York: Dover. 310 pp.

Schama S. 1989. *Citizens: A Chronicle of the French Revolution.* New York: Knopf. 948 pp.

Schofield N. 1985. Anarchy, altruism and cooperation: a review. *Soc. Choice Welfare* 2:207–19

Schofield N. 1998. *America, Britain, France and Spain, 1763–1804: core beliefs in America at the War of Independence and at the ratification of the Constitution.* Discuss. Pap. 201, Cent. Polit. Econ., Washington Univ., St. Louis, MO

Schofield N. 1999a. The heart of the Atlantic constitution. *Polit. Soc.* 27:173–215

Schofield N. 1999b. The Amistad and Dred Scott affairs: heresthetics and beliefs in antebellum America, 1837–1860. *Homo Oeconomicus* 16:49–67

Schofield N. 2000. The evolution of the American constitution. *Brit. J. Polit. Sci.* In press

Shepsle K. 1979. Institutional arrangements and equilibrium in multidimensional voting bodies. *Am. J. Polit. Sci.* 23:27–60

Triffin R. 1960. *Gold and the Dollar Crisis.* New Haven, CT: Yale Univ. Press. 320 pp.

Tufte E. 1978. *Political Control of the Economy*. Princeton, NJ: Princeton Univ. Press. 168 pp.

von Neumann J. 1928. Zur theorie der Gesselschaftsspiele. *Math. Ann.* 100:295–320

von Neumann J, Morgenstern O. 1944. *Theory of Games and Economic Behavior*. Princeton, NJ: Princeton Univ. Press. 641 pp.

Weingast B. 1997a. The political foundations of democracy and the rule of law. *Am. Polit. Sci. Rev.* 91:245–63

Weingast B. 1997b. The political foundations of limited government: parliament and sovereign debt in 17th and 18th century England. In *The Frontiers of the New Institutional Economics*, ed. J Drobak, J Nye, pp. 213–46. New York: Academic

Weingast B. 1998. Political stability and civil war. In *Analytical Narratives*, ed. R Bates, A Greif, M Levi, J-L Rosenthal, B Weingast, pp. 148–93. Princeton, NJ: Princeton Univ. Press

Young P. 1998. *Individual Strategy and Social Structure: An Evolutionary Theory of Institutions*. Princeton, NJ: Princeton Univ. Press. 189 pp.

Annu. Rev. Polit. Sci. 2000. 3:305–30

FOUCAULT STEALS POLITICAL SCIENCE

Paul R. Brass

1905 East Blaine Street, Seattle, Washington 98112-2916;
e-mail: brass@u.washington.edu

Key Words   power, knowledge, governing, discipline, normalization

■ **Abstract**   The subject matter of what has been traditionally considered central to political science, namely, power and government, has been stolen by Foucault while central trends in the discipline as a whole have departed markedly from serious engagement with those topics. Yet Foucault's discussions and analyses of power and government are so original, so striking in their import not only for the way we do political science, but for our lives, thought, and practices as scholars, that his work ought by now to have become a focal point for the resurrection of these topics and their restoration to centrality in the discipline.

INTRODUCTION

The title suggested for this article was "The Foucauldian Turn in Political Science." Regrettably, however, I do not think that such a turn has occurred in the discipline. On the contrary, the subject matter of what has been traditionally considered central to the discipline, namely, power and government, has been stolen by Foucault while central trends in the discipline as a whole have departed markedly from serious engagement with those topics. Yet Foucault's discussions and analyses of power and government are so original, so striking in their import not only for the way we do political science, but for our lives, thought, and practices as scholars, that his work ought by now to have become a focal point for the resurrection of these topics and their restoration to centrality in the discipline. Indeed, I would have preferred, mimicking Veyne (1997), to title this article "Foucault Revolutionizes Political Science," but that revolution is still far distant. It is my purpose here to demonstrate the importance of Foucault's insights into the nature of power and governance for a discipline that calls itself political science. I also provide several illustrations from recent political science writing that has been influenced by Foucault to indicate directions that a few scholars have taken in the hope that many will soon follow. In selecting the topics of power and governance, I have left out a considerable array of other themes that recur in Foucault's writings that are also of relevance to political science, including

1094-2939/00/0623-0305$14.00   **305**

political practices, freedom (Dumm 1996), justice, ideology, political resistance, revolution, and gender studies (Butler 1999), all of which merit serious analysis and reflection within the discipline, but which cannot all be covered in the space provided here.

POWER AND KNOWLEDGE

The Power/Knowledge Relationship

Foucault's clearest statements on the relationship between power and knowledge are found in a collection of his essays, *Power/Knowledge* (Foucault 1980a). In those essays, Foucault undermined the entire basis for the traditional distinction between power and knowledge, embodied in the phrase of resistance to the unjust use of power: "speak truth to power." In Foucault's thought, the phrase reveals that those who speak it do not know the relations among power, truth, and knowledge. Indeed, the phrase is self-contradicting. There is neither knowledge nor truth that can be separated from power—not only the power in politics that political scientists have traditionally studied, but the power that reveals itself in systems of knowledge and practices in disciplines such as medicine (Foucault 1980c), psychiatry, criminology, and the institutions associated with them: the hospital, the asylum, and the prison. It reveals itself also in talk and practice in the domain of sexuality. Nor is the exercise of power confined to these institutions and practices; they are only the ones Foucault himself studied.

Power, in fact, exists alongside knowledge and the "regimes of truth" embedded in all knowledge systems, practices, and institutions in society, from the family to the school to the factory to the army to the agencies of the state. It is not only alongside knowledge but dependent on it. "Nothing," wrote Foucault, "can function as a mechanism of power if it is not deployed according to procedures, instruments, means, and objectives which can be validated in more or less coherent systems of knowledge" (1997a:52–53). But the obverse is also true, namely, that power cannot function without knowledge. Power produces knowledge (Foucault 1980b:59) in order to rule, regulate, control, and discipline. The power to confine persons to asylums, hospitals, and prisons, for example, made them accessible for study and observation, which produced modern psychiatric, medical, and criminological knowledge. This knowledge in turn was put to the service of the administrative state and became itself a part of "the machinery of power" (Foucault 1980c:176) by which, for example, in the case of medical knowledge, society as a whole was regulated through standards established for the maintenance of public health and healthy conditions of life, which in turn required mechanisms of observation and surveillance extending throughout the population.

This relationship between knowledge and power means that existing bodies of knowledge contain no vantage point for a critique of power relations.[1] On the contrary, "we have an entirely interwoven network," (Foucault 1997a:66) in which knowledge cannot function without power nor power without knowledge. Every statement within a framework of knowledge "exerts a certain power and it creates, at the same time, a possibility," and every "exercise of power ... implies at least a *savoir-faire*" (Foucault 1997a:66–67). But it is not just a question of *savoir-faire*, which is an elementary form of practice. Foucault was most concerned with the disciplinary practices associated with systems of knowledge emerging from and applied within societal institutions. As Clegg has put it (1989:153), the "disciplinary practices" associated with all modern institutions are also "'discursive practices,' knowledge reproduced through practices made possible by the framing assumptions of that knowledge." In order to exercise another form of power, that of critique, one must first step outside the very frameworks of knowledge that produce the power relations themselves.[2]

Why are knowledge and power so intimately connected in modern societies? It is because all the disciplinary practices that pervade such societies, radiating out from institutions and the systems of knowledge that support them, have one central focus: knowledge of man. It is the focus on man that is central in all these institutions and in modern life in general. What is man? What are his inner motivations? What are his needs, wants, aspirations? What are the different types of man? Among those types, which are normal, which pathological? Which are to progress through the normal institutions of society, from birth to school to work to marriage to hospital to cemetery? Which are to deviate from the normal path for a temporary or permanent detour in a prison or asylum (or nowadays in a homeless shelter)?

This modern knowledge of man itself originates in institutions that focus on man, such as the hospital, the asylum, and the prison. In those institutions, the answers to the questions about man are "discovered" and techniques of power are devised to intervene in an attempt to normalize the patient, make him well, sane, or otherwise fit to return to society. These techniques of power derived from the knowledge base discovered in such institutions work on the inner being as well as the outer frame of the person (see e.g. Foucault 1979:23–26).

One of the earliest and most powerful of the techniques invented in the modern age that exemplifies the integral relationship between power and knowledge

---

[1]"There is no power relation without the correlative constitution of a field of knowledge, nor any knowledge that does not presuppose and constitute at the same time power relations" (Foucault 1979:27). There is, therefore, no place from which intellectuals, for example, can "speak truth to power," since they "are themselves agents of [a] system of power" (Foucault 1977:207).
[2]Clegg has again stated the position well; there is, he notes, no "transcendent position which can be constituted outside of discursive practices" from which to analyze power. It is "the knowledge/power relation" itself that must become "the object of analysis" (1989:152).

is the examination (Foucault 1979:185–87). The medical examination defines the disease and at the same time provides the knowledge necessary to prescribe its treatment; the academic examination certifies that knowledge has been success- fully transmitted from teacher to student, thus qualifying the latter to move to the next stage in his training or to embark on the career for which he has been trained and examined; the psychological examination certifies not only competence but normality. In all these cases, types of power are exercised, some more awesome than others. Most are not usually considered part of the field of study of power re- lations in political science. Certainly, you may say, a doctor must have the power to examine his patient, prescribe for his cure, and determine when he has recovered. What has this to do with politics? Perhaps nothing in the conventional sense, but the power exercised may be one of life or death in which the knowledge used may be faulty, the patient's means to determine its efficacy may be lacking, and the only means of redress may lie in another arena of power, the law courts. This power exercised through the examination technique is, however, in some ways even more awesome when it is exercised to define a person's place in society in relation to a scheme of knowledge that claims to know the difference between the normal and the pathological, the neurotic and the psychotic, the antisocial being and the civil being. Political science has recognized such techniques as aspects of the exercise of power only in totalitarian or other forms of rule in which they are used to confine political prisoners, failing to recognize that they operate, however more subtly, in our own and all other modern societies, and therefore deserve thorough scrutiny in any science of politics in which power is central.

In societies that fancy themselves democratic, individuals are described polit- ically as citizens, who may or may not play active, participant roles in political parties, interest groups, or government. However, in many activities, one's status as a citizen matters little and confers no political power. In many cases, the in- dividual becomes not a citizen (more or less participant in the political process, with an armory of rights and protections), but a case—a social worker's case, a psychologist's case, a medical doctor's case, a lawyer's case.[3]

Although the individual remains an individual in the social worker's, psycholo- gist's, doctor's, or lawyer's file, he loses a good deal of his freedom in the process. As a citizen, the individual operates within a framework that allows him, within restrictions, to adopt a multiplicity of attitudes, opinions, actions, and activities, and even to change them. As a case, however, he is pinpointed, defined, clas- sified. His attitudes and opinions become not expressions of a political right or

---

[3] I am opposing here the idealized conception of citizenship against one actuality, the indi- vidual as a case. However, for Foucault, the category of citizen is also problematic (Finkle, personal communication). It calls up the idea of the active, engaged, free individual of an- cient Greece, whereas the modern liberal state creates the image of a free citizen-subject who is simultaneously the case-object of the disciplinary, normalizing practices of the "pastoral" state or what Polsky (see below) calls the "therapeutic" state (see Gordon 1991:8).

duty, but bases for making a judgment about him and whether the techniques of a body of knowledge or law need to be applied to him in order to train, correct, normalize, or exclude him from society (Foucault 1979:191) or, perhaps, whether they classify him as a victim denied his rights and, therefore, entitled to remedies. Those who exercise such techniques constitute an authority established not by democratic means but by induction. They occupy positions of power that are deemed legitimate because of their knowledge. They exercise that power through the examination by turning the individual from a citizen, who may belong to a broader group of like-minded citizens with potential influence in society, into an "effect and object of power" and of knowledge. The purpose of that power and knowledge is to establish "individual difference" (Foucault 1979:192) in order to treat, confine, or exclude individuals deviating from the normal.

These bodies of knowledge and the technologies of power associated with them arose at the very time that new conceptions of government were developing at the end of the age of absolutism. Indeed, the clinical sciences and practices of criminology, public health, medicine, and psychiatry flourished and entrenched themselves at the same time as did the democratizing movements that followed the French Revolution. Further, they became, in some respects, handmaidens to new systems of authority—first the centralizing absolutist state, then the democratizing state—that required detailed knowledge of their individual subjects/citizens to govern according to what were conceived as the new requirements of proper governance. These requirements included new systems of public health, means of keeping track of populations moving from the country to the city, means of detecting criminal elements in vast urban conglomerations, and so forth. All these new types of measures required bodies of knowledge to define the elements of the population, no longer demarcated into estates or classes, permanently settled in the countryside, but now seen as individuals on the move who had to be located, identified, and classified. They had to be located in order to be subject to surveillance; identified in order to be "known," so that authorities could anticipate their likely behavior (Clegg 1989:174, Foucault 1979:167); and classified as normal or abnormal according to the divisions of modern society, to determine whether they needed to be "trained or corrected" or "excluded" (Foucault 1979:191) and whether they belonged in the category of "ordinary criminals" or "monsters" (Foucault 1982:153,168).

The national census, among many other instruments of its type, became in the eighteenth and nineteenth centuries a vast source of knowledge of populations divided into the categories that most interested the authorities. In this way, newly disaggregated populations were reaggregated into objectified categories that served state interests, forming a body of knowledge concerning the individual subjects/citizens who composed the vast, amorphous public. Such populations were then controlled by being made known and accessible to government in their particularities rather than being controlled through "ostentatious signs" (Foucault 1979:220) of sovereign power manifested in brilliant displays of majesty, as well as violent displays such as public executions.

In the establishment of new systems of state surveillance and control of the population, the disciplines—that is, the bodies of knowledge operating through universities, professional associations, and public institutions—became, in effect, handmaidens of the state. Much of their knowledge was garnered through observations made in state institutions such as hospitals, asylums, and prisons. It then became incorporated into judicial institutions through which assignments to such institutions of confinement were made. It also extended more broadly into many aspects of public life, including the school, the factory, the military forces, the professions, and sports, all of which became permeated by tests, interviews, interrogations, and consultations. Some of the latter were used to permit or deny entry, whereas others were designed to deal with the psychological stress of the discipline and rigors imposed on individuals in these institutions, but all became, in effect, methods of referring "individuals from one disciplinary authority to another" (Foucault 1979:226–27). All these methods served the broad purpose of defining the range of behavior, attention to study, work ethic, and obedience to authority—of laws and persons—to be accepted as normal.

Individuals whose tendencies threatened to move them off the normal curve required care, healing, treatment to restore them to the normal range. Those who fell beyond the normal curve faced confinement in asylum or prison. The reigning term for the treatment rendered in some of these institutions became "correction." Institutions for the treatment of juvenile delinquency, for example, were called correctional institutions or reformatories. Foucault considered the establishment of the first such institution in France in 1840 as the beginning of a new era "in the normalization of the power of normalization, in the arrangement of a power-knowledge over individuals" (1979:296).

Ultimately, as we see today in American political life, a vast array of instruments for determining the beliefs, attitudes, desires, and aspirations of the entire population were developed. The daily accounting these instruments provide is used by the politicians, the governing economic bodies such as the Federal Reserve Board, and other agencies of government. In this vortex of information, which includes not only matters of public policy but also matters of private morality, the whole population—ordinary citizens, elected officials, and candidates for public office—is run through a sieve that sorts out the decent from the indecent, the holy from the unholy, the pure from the impure, the rational from the irrational.[4]

What are the implications of all this for the study of politics? The most stunning observation in Foucault's masterwork, *Discipline and Punish*, is the statement—in a book whose main apparent object of study was the formation of prisons, mostly in France, from 1770 to 1840—that all these connections between power and knowledge had led to the creation of a "carceral texture of society," in which the examination is the principal means of sorting individuals, just as the inquisition had been in its day (Foucault 1979:304–5). At the end of his book, Foucault was clearly

---

[4]One may doubt the relevance of the Federal Reserve Board in this list, but did not its chairman recently caution investors and the nation against their "irrational exuberance"?

talking about our present (and not only in France) when he referred to the contemporary state-society as a "carceral city." We live in no "city of God," no Jerusalem, no Athens, no democracy for that matter, but in a society composed of persons imprisoned in "walls, space, institution, rules, discourse" (Foucault 1979:307).

This modern society is something new in history, unprecedented. It flies in the face of what everyone in contemporary so-called democratic societies has been taught, namely, that the will of the people who formed a contract to establish a society based on participation of individuals, none of whom has any greater right to rule than any other, replaced the arbitrary rule of monarchs with rule of the people through elected representatives. We have been taught to believe that we live in democracies that more or less conform to this model. Political science has devoted itself overwhelmingly to discussions of how far our democracy does conform to such a model and how far it deviates from it. But the implications of what Foucault said in *Discipline and Punish* are quite radical and, for those who care to listen and understand, profoundly unsettling. One implication is that we have been unaware of the kind of society we live in, the ways in which our lives are organized, structured, and disciplined. We have been unaware of the confined, restricted, and ultimately inconsequential character of our participation in political life as citizens. Furthermore, the discipline of political science has virtually ignored these facts and has instead become implicated—indeed, has been implicated since its foundation—in fostering the governing myths of our political lives, our political selves.

If we do take to heart the implications of Foucault's comments on our "carceral city," what role can a political science play in its analysis? What mode of analysis can we adopt in the study of power relations, which used to be considered the very heart of the study of politics? Older definitions of power are of little use and older objects of study have been defined as either irrelevant or overstudied. That is, although Foucault used the term domination as an aspect of contemporary power relations, he told us there is no single center of power/domination, so we should not look for it in the state apparatus, which has already been overstudied. Do not look for it, Foucault advised, in acts of participation in politics designed to restore "power to the people" by reforming, controlling, and making accountable our elected officials and bureaucrats, for we and they are part of a broader network of power relations that operates almost independently of them. Do not believe that political science can demonstrate that power has been abused and that some movement of the people can restore power to them.

Yet, in the last sentences of *Discipline and Punish*, Foucault concluded:

> In this central and centralized humanity, the effect and instrument of complex power relations, bodies and forces subjected by multiple mechanisms of 'incarceration', objects for discourses that are in themselves elements for this strategy, we must hear the distant roar of battle.
>
> At this point I end a book that must serve as a historical background to various studies of the power of normalization and the formation of knowledge in modern society. (Foucault 1979:307)

What a curious way to end a book: an apparent call for—or at least a welcoming of—an historic battle to come, followed by the terse academic statement that he, in effect, hopes that his work will lead to further studies of the sort he has just concluded! A call to action and a call to scholarship.

One of the most remarkable features of commentary on Foucault, even by some writers otherwise sympathetic to his ideas, is the accusation that he was a nihilist, that his thought provides no basis for resistance, though the latter word is pervasive in his texts. In fact, it is evident from the sentences cited above that, just as—indeed largely because—there is no possible separation between power and knowledge, studies that seek to step outside contemporary forms of discourse cannot be separated from resistance to contemporary patterns of domination and unequal relations of power. Study and practice, political study and political practice, are inseparable.

Objects of Study for a Political Science

But what then are political scientists to study? The objects for our study have also been delineated in those last sentences: power relations, bodies, forces, and ourselves as "objects of discourse." But how to do it? Where is the framework, the methodological guidelines? In fact, there is no framework, for that would be inconsistent with the very scholarly and political enterprise that Foucault set forth, to escape from existing frameworks and to keep moving in such a manner that one does not get entangled in a fixed set of concepts that would then congeal into another imprisoning discourse.

Foucault's works are, however, full of methodological guidelines, some of them listed in a series of points. I do not outline them here because they too are not meant to be procedures of the type that our graduate students are taught—how to design a research project, how to elaborate an hypothesis or set of hypotheses, whether to use survey research, ecological data, in-depth interviews, or case studies, how to present the data, and so forth. Foucault also elaborated a method he called archaeology, by which he meant the analysis of layers and traces of thought and practice that link or separate discourses from one another in different historical periods combined with the analysis of the linkages among all elements of thought and practice across disciplines, even across lines that separate elite knowledge and popular knowledge in any era. But that too is a rather broad and comprehensive method that does not provide specific guidelines to a political scientist setting out to do a piece of research that is new and outside existing frameworks. Foucault summarized the archaeological method as follows: read everything that has been written, said, or otherwise preserved on the topic of your research in the time period pertaining to your research. The injunction to read everything does not mean to read the existing theoretical literature, digest it, regurgitate it, use it to structure your research and then read what relates to it. No, unfortunately, it means read absolutely everything, ignore nothing that might reveal the lines that connect your object of study with every other thought or practice of its time. It means avoid isolation of your topic, which would lead merely to some normalizing statement about human or institutional behavior as, for example, revealing the universality of self-interest or altruism or self-preservation. Instead, the aim is to identify the linkages among bodies of knowledge, institutions, and practices prevalent in society at a particular time that converge on your research topic and reveal its singularity.

At least, Foucault gave us in *Discipline and Punish* a set of objects for our studies, as noted above: power relations, bodies, forces, and ourselves as objects of discourse. However, these are all moving objects, not the fixed types to which we are accustomed in our social science disciplines, defined clearly, related to a model, a system, an order. Not power but power relations, not the body but bodies, not force but forces, and certainly not man but humanity. We cannot study such fixed objects as power or sexuality or force or man because such "grandiose objects do not exist" (Veyne 1997:176). Concepts such as the body, power, force do not exist independently of the discourses about them but are objects of inquiry constructed by and within particular discourses. Relationships occur, events happen, objects are constituted; these are the realities of existence, not some objectified concepts about reality.

Foucault made it clear that we ourselves are the most important objects in need of analysis. Before we can fully understand the complex relations between power and knowledge, we have to construct "the historical ontology of ourselves," how we have been "constituted as subjects of our own knowledge." We have to determine how we have become subjects of study, who both exercise and submit to power relations, and who also are "constituted as moral subjects of our own actions," beings possessed of knowledge that gives us power, subjects us to power, and makes us responsible in particular ways for what we do. This knowledge subjects us to discipline to ensure that we do not deviate from the normal curve, and subjects us to sanction, treatment, or punishment when we depart from it (Foucault 1997b:130).

With such vague guidelines—aside from the deeply threatening aspect of Foucault's thought—it is little wonder that political scientists have, with very few exceptions, not taken up the challenge. I refer later to some examples among the very few studies that have been undertaken that have been in one or another way inspired by Foucault's writings. But, first, I want to provide an example from Foucault's own work to illustrate some of the ways in which he himself moved, academically and strategically, to expose things previously hidden from view while challenging existing modes of thought. I want to show also how the scholarly and political functions merge in his work.

One of my favorite works in Foucault's corpus is *I, Pierre Rivière* ..., a text about a text. This book presents the dossier of a French parricide, who committed his atrocious acts of violence in 1835 and wrote a completely coherent account of the acts and his reasons for committing them. In addition to this text, Foucault's book includes all the commentary on it at that time (that time being a turning point in the history of the development of modern psychiatric thought and practice), including the statements of local people, newspaper reports, statements of local doctors, and statements from the leading Parisian psychiatrists of the day; and finally a set of commentaries by contemporary social scientists and historians. Foucault himself, however, kept strangely silent. He made no comment on Rivière's text. Instead he drew attention to the documents that commented on the text, in which he said he discerned a map that led to the rediscovery of the interaction of discourses coexisting at the time. He saw these discourses "as weapons of attack and defense in the relations of power and knowledge." He saw in those documents "a key to the relations of power, domination, and conflict within which discourses emerge and function, and hence provide material for a potential analysis of discourse (even of scientific discourses) which may be both tactical and political" (Foucault 1982:xi–xii).

There are several things going on here. Foucault's book consists of a text with commentary on it at the time and commentary on it today. The time then was a point of transition from one age to another when a battle among discourses was taking place. The time now is also a point of transition, according to Foucault (he did not say so in this book, but see Foucault 1989b:30). We are, in his mind, in the postmodernist age wherein another battle of discourses is taking place.

It is clear, therefore, that Foucault chose to analyze the discourses of the time of the murder and of the present, that is, 150 years later, not the text itself. Where is the "tactical and political" in it? Foucault revealed some years after the book was published that he wrote it as a deliberate challenge to "the shrinks," daring them to comment on it, daring them to apply their nosology to it. He claims that he won a victory because they all remained silent, "except for one fool, a psychoanalyst, who claimed that Rivière was an illustration of paranoia as defined by Lacan" (Foucault 1989d:132). The book, therefore, was put forth as a scholarly analysis of discourses on madness, but it is also a tactical, political statement directed against the criminologists, psychologists, and psychiatrists to demonstrate two things: that in 150 years, there had been no progress in the definition and nosology of mental illness, and, implicitly, that criminological and mental health professionals, who have so deeply penetrated our lives and our definitions of ourselves and who exercise powers and make use of powerful techniques in doing so, were fooling us and themselves. They have not been able to cross the boundary between reason and unreason that they themselves constructed. They have not been able to cope with the logic of the mad that contains understandings of reality that are inaccessible to our own reason because, if we stopped to think about them, they might cause our own ordered thinking about the world to crumble. The logic of the mad must, therefore, be defined as delusional, paranoid, and so forth.

What have madness and the violence of the mad got to do with politics? Nothing really. It is the way in which madness has been defined, that is to say, constituted through discourses, that is political. And what is political about those discourses is the establishment of difference, of divisions in society. The opposition between madness and reason is only one among many oppositions, for example, between peaceable citizens and delinquents/criminals, those who work and those who shirk, the moral and the immoral, majorities and minorities (especially ethnic minorities), those who have family values and those who do not. Is it not evident how far what we call politics in America today has been reduced to such empty oppositional categories? In short, Foucault's studies, however far removed they seem from the stuff of politics as political scientists have conventionally defined it, on the contrary go to the very heart of politics, to the ways in which political divisions are created and perpetuated in societies and to the power relations that sustain such divisions over time.

GOVERNMENT AND GOVERNANCE

The second great subject of political science stolen by Foucault is government and governance. As with all other topics that he touched, he treated these matters in utterly novel ways, introducing at the same time two further terms to encompass the subject matter he discusses, namely, governmentalization and governmentality. In his self-appointed role as "historian of the present," he went back to the sixteenth century to find out how governance came to take the form of the "relations of power and techniques which allow these relations of power to be exercised," which he studied in his other works. How were the mentally ill, the sick, the criminal and delinquent governed? How did the techniques used to treat them and separate them from society lead to methods of directing and controlling the daily behavior of entire populations (Foucault 1997c:156–57)?

Foucault argued that in the sixteenth century a process was set in motion, and with it a question, both of which have persisted into the present. The process was governmentalization, that is, the extension into society of new and more comprehensive means, modes, and methods of governing not only society but the individuals who composed it. As this process of governmentalization spread and, along with it, a "great preoccupation about the way to govern and the search for the ways to govern," a question arose alongside it, namely, how not to be governed. That is, "how not to be governed *like that*, by that, in the name of those principles, with such and such an objective in mind and by means of such procedures, not like that, not for that, not by them" (Foucault 1997a:28, italics in original). Within this dichotomy between new ways of governing, on the one hand, and the question of how not to be governed, on the other hand, was laid the foundation for critique. In effect, to use the other polarity in Foucault's political thought, as this process of construction of new modes of exercising power unfolded, new modes of resistance unfolded as well. In the midst of this process also there occurred the great transformation in modern thought that is designated the Enlightenment. Through his definition of the political and of critique, Foucault identified with Kant, the herald of the Enlightenment. "What Kant was describing as the *Aufklärung* is very much what I was trying before to describe as critique, this critical attitude in the Western world starting with what was historically, I believe, the great process of society's governmentalization" (Foucault 1997a:34).

But then, in this new space between governmentalization and critique of it, something strange happened that involved the persistence of ideas about governance and of knowledge about it drawn from medieval Christian thought and practices. The old idea that government meant "governing men," which in turn meant "to take them by the hand and lead them to their salvation through an operation, a technique of precise piloting, which implied a full range of knowledge concerning the individuals being guided, the truth towards which one was guiding" them (Foucault 1997a:70–71), was retained and transmuted. The essence of that process was retained, even if freed from the eschatological component, insofar as it involved a kind of earthly salvation to be achieved through a balance between necessary coercion and a process of constructing and modifying the self to conform not to religious law, belief, and practice but to the mandates of modern knowledge of what is good for man and for society (Foucault 1997d:181–82).

Methods derived from church practice of modulating conduct with "true knowledge" persisted while at the same time a vast expansion of the governmental occurred. Government, whose main function had been to collect taxes while the conduct of men and their acquisition of true knowledge was left to the church, now vastly expanded its functions in both the technical sense (dealing with sanitation, public health, control of large urban populations, public education, etc) and the pastoral sense of regulating individuals' daily behavior (Foucault 1997c:156) to conform to the needs of society. Regulating people's behavior required knowing them, teaching them, and disciplining them with the aid of new bodies of knowledge about the nature of man and his relation to his environment. To the governmental function of the modernizing state was added not only the pastoral function but an ancient "governmental function" previously confined to domestic relations, namely, training, education, and guidance (Foucault 1988:80).

It should be clear from Foucault's definition of the governmental and governmentality that he not only stole government from political science but also altered fundamentally the questions commonly directed to it and about it. Moreover, the questions about government derive from Foucault's radically different conception of power, power relations, and the technologies associated with power. The modern political science conception of power is primarily based on the notions of command and obedience and has been focused on the state's exercise of its powers of coercion in relation to individuals. The great theoretical and moral problem from this perspective concerns who governs, how much coercion is exercised in the process, and how to regulate this power and prevent its abuse of the rights of the people. In contemporary states defined as democratic, the leading question has concerned the distribution of power in state and society. It has been assumed for nearly two centuries that genuine rule by the people is an impossibility, that there is in all societies, democratic or otherwise, an uneven distribution of power. The question is how to describe it. For example, Dahl asks whether a single elite governs or whether there is a more pluralist distribution of power (Clegg 1989:53).[5]

Foucault's position is that this discourse of the state and of rights has ignored the more pervasive and insidious exercises of power not only by the state, but

---

[5]Dahl's answer, of course, is that the distribution is pluralist.

within society and virtually all public institutions. Foucault's questions are quite different. They pertain to "the practice of government (who can govern; what governing is; what or who is governed)" (Gordon 1991:3). This focus on the practice of government disregards for the moment the issue of who in fact governs—an elite, a class, an ethnic group, or whatever—for the questions common to all modern societies, namely, the vast extension of technologies of power that act on the bodies of persons seen not as citizens but as "subjects as members of a *population*," (Gordon 1991:5, italics in original), that is, both as individuals and as populations of individual bodies (Gordon 1991:36) to be socialized, disciplined, and normalized. The discourse on rights notwithstanding, these new domains of power have extended willy-nilly into the most intimate details of the person's and the family's life, including its sexual life and its child-rearing practices.

One of the great themes of both classical political philosophy and modern political science concerns legitimacy, the best government, the best form of government. Foucault, however, bypassed the question of legitimacy to ask how governing is actually done (Gordon 1991:7). What are the practices that are actually used in modern and contemporary states? For what purpose? It is not a question of whether democracy or constitutional government is better than autocracy, whether that government is best that governs least, whether a welfare state is better than a market-oriented state or a socialist state, but how all these governments actually govern in the spheres in which they undertake to govern. Further, Foucault argued that there are sets of practices that are common to all modern governments, however they are defined and classified, practices that are simultaneously individualizing and totalizing (Gordon 1991:8), capturing all in their net. Whatever distinguishes totalitarian regimes from representative regimes, it is not their governmental practices, which are the same, involving individualization, normalization, the disciplining of body and soul, confinement, and even execution. Of course, more people are brutalized, murdered, and confined in totalitarian regimes, but the methods are the same.

But it was not Foucault's purpose to compare states along some continuum of governance based on new criteria. His primary purpose, rather, was to show that all modern states have become—in an older sense of the term—police states. With or without the active involvement of state agencies, society as a whole and the individuals comprising it are subjected to intrusive, molding, disciplining, normalizing mechanisms accompanied by bodies of knowledge that create them, justify their use, and continue to perfect them, all for the good of the society. With the rise and consolidation of the modern liberal state, the central question of politics has become "not so much the justification of state action as the governability of the social" (Gordon 1991:34). It is now a question of governing large, amorphous populations, of maintaining order, of disciplining a population while dividing off the marginalized, dangerous, delinquent, and criminal elements. Although Foucault certainly opposed all forms of actual abuse of state power—all occasions in which the state acted like a police state in the direct, coercive sense of that term—his primary focus was on the consequences, or, in his terms, the effects of the everyday policing powers of the state in the form of its public services and of the social services in public health, mental health, and control of crime, delinquency, sexuality, and so forth. He thought that the exclusive focus by revolutionary and ideological movements on state powers in modern liberal states diverted our gaze from the everyday practices of state and social service institutions and of our own docility in relation to those practices.[6] Furthermore, he distrusted every revolutionary utopian movement, whose end result, he thought, could only be the reinstatement of old, or the development of new, disciplinary practices.

Finally, on this matter of policing and governing, Foucault intended not only to draw attention to those institutions and public services that are central in the disciplining of populations in modern states, but to draw attention to the internalization of practices of governing, to the policing of the self according to existing conceptions of truth grounded in domains of knowledge about the self. Foucault was interested ultimately in seeing "how men govern (themselves and others) by the production of truth," that is, by the production of knowledge systems that establish what is defined as true and false. Although the focus of his major works was on "'practices' like those of the sequestration of the insane, or clinical medicine, or the organization of the empirical sciences, or legal punishment" (Foucault 1991:79), his further aim was to consider how such practices and a host of others become embedded in rules of behavior for everyday life. How to live without neurotic fears and anxieties, how to follow a diet for bodily health, how to achieve sexual satisfaction, all these goals for a good life lead to an array of individual practices that affect our relations with others and that draw us into games of normalization, in which we determine who among us are truly fit, healthy, and happy. These games are also, of course, power games in which persons derive advantage or get what they want from others by manipulating the codes to their advantage, using them to determine what is "due" to one person from another.

Again comes that question of governance. How does one escape or resist those forms of governance of oneself by oneself or attempts by others to govern one according to truths whose validity one distrusts? It is evident from much of Foucault's writing, though not always directly, that he mistrusted many of the contemporary movements that appeared to challenge existing modes of governance. Many such movements, in fact, that spring up from the marginal sectors of the population simply demand that they themselves be integrated into the normalizing frameworks of contemporary society. The demand is not to do what one wants so long as it does not infringe on the rights or abilities of others to do what they want; the demand is instead that one's own definition of truth be integrated into the existing frameworks. Everyone must have orgasms, gay marriages must be recognized, individuals previously classified as perverts must be accepted as normal, all of us must discover our identity in our roots, and we must reveal our innermost thoughts and secrets

---

[6]"The fear (and hope) that the existing state will finally show its true colours as a police state blunts, he [Foucault] argued, our ability to perceive and refuse the unacceptable in what actually exists" (Gordon 1991:47).

so that we can see that we all are OK. [The fact that most of my examples of the striving for normality relate to sexuality reflects Foucault's view that all the moral problems of today "concern sex and politics exclusively" (Foucault 1989e:85).] In the process, the boundaries between the normal and the pathological are not eliminated; they are simply redrawn or moved outward a bit more.

I must come back now to the question of what relevance all this has to political science. When power and government were considered central to any conception of the appropriate subject matter for political science, it was commonly argued that power had to be defined precisely in order to avoid excessive broadening of the field to encompass family relations, sexual relations, doctor-patient relations, and so forth. But Foucault is telling us, in effect, that this avoidance was misplaced, that the study of power relations cannot be confined only to the power of governments and the power of citizens to influence their governors. Power is ubiquitous and universal, governance is personal as well as governmental, and all forms of power and governance are linked in contemporary societies.

The artificial demarcation of a sphere of political power attached to the questions of governance by governments has obscured from view most power relations in society. In fact, it has obscured from view the vast majority of life situations, including potentially life-threatening or life-constraining situations in which our ability to exercise self-determining power is sharply limited by the authority possessed by physicians, lawyers, psychiatrists, psychologists, social workers, teachers, etc, who are not agents of state power in any conventional sense but are licensed by the state because of their certified possession of a body of knowledge in their discipline. Although it is neither Foucault's intention nor mine to argue that all or even most interventions by such persons in our life situations are malign, it is certainly Foucault's intention to suggest that they all operate according to standards of truth and falsity that require scrutiny. These standards limit our powers excessively by penetrating our bodies so that we internalize norms of conduct that imprison us and lead us in circles of power relations that deny us the power to define ourselves.

Foucault's mode of analysis does not imply that political scientists should be framing research projects that analyze power relations between doctors and patients, husbands and wives, teachers and students. His injunction to read everything, study everything pertaining to one's subject of research does not require such a micropower focus.[7] What it does require is exploration of the networks of power relations in society that link individuals to other individuals to institutions to government proper. A micropower focus means that the researcher does not

---

[7]Foucault's writing does use the term micropower, in contrast to macropower studies that focus, for example, on the powers exercised by the state. A micropower focus, however, does not mean selecting the smallest possible site of personal interactions and examining it intensely, but rather extending one's gaze in all directions from that site. One examines the networks of power throughout society rather than those extending downward from some ultimate source or structure of power.

arbitrarily confine his research to a particular site of power relations but instead approaches any issue attuned to the linkages that may radiate out from or into a particular site of struggle.

Suppose one does want to pursue research of a more traditional kind that focuses on governance as a whole, that is, on the ways in which a society is governed or governs itself or, as Connolly puts it, on the "mode of governance" in a society that defines itself as democratic or is engaged in a process of "democratization" (Connolly 1995:154–55). Connolly, who has grappled with Foucault like Jacob with the angel for the past two decades, does indeed pursue that kind of research. Connolly has set his own idea of "essentially contested concepts" against Foucault's refusal to conceptualize in any conventional way and applied his notion to traditional concerns of political theory, such as the definition and meaning of power and freedom in democratic societies. Of particular relevance here is Connolly's discussion of power, which is treated in the next section.

FOUCAULDIAN FORAYS

Political Theory

Connolly is certainly the leading Foucauldian scholar in American political theory. However, he did not start out that way. Rather than survey his entire corpus, which has become increasingly consistent with Foucault's thought, I focus here on the changes that have taken place in his discussion of power. Connolly's struggle with Foucault on the subject of power demonstrates the challenge that Foucault's analytics of power presents to received conceptualizations of the central subject matter of traditional political science.

In his pre-Foucault *discursus* on power, Connolly (1974) effectively deconstructed prevailing notions of power, authority, and legitimacy—the rage of the age—demonstrating through a multiplicity of examples that it was impossible to arrive at any fixed, precise definitions of any of these terms and to build a science of politics on top of them. Instead, he used his analysis to demonstrate that power—and its associated terms—was an essentially contested concept, one indispensable to political science and to any meaningful study of politics in America, but also one that, by its very contestability, implied that whoever used that concept, political scientist or political practitioner, was himself involved in politics. In the process, Connolly revealed his own value preferences, presented as a model for democratic behavior, in which the "capacity for choice or action" was primary. In this model, revised only marginally in later editions of *The Terms of Political Discourse* while maintaining the "basic thesis" (Connolly 1993:2139), he established a continuum of forms of power that, however difficult to pin down precisely, worked more or less directly on the individual's capacities. At the virtuous end lay persuasion, at the other end threat, as methods of exercising power over another person (Connolly 1993:213–14). Democratic practices would have to be judged by the extent to which they imposed or refrained from imposing "limits or constraints on others" (Connolly 1993:216). Like Foucault, Connolly refuses to define power, but unlike Foucault, he presents a paradigm of power in which agents and recipients of power (in his terms) either have or lack access to resources that can limit or enhance the range of options over which the recipient can exercise autonomous choice (Connolly 1993:217). Outside the paradigm of power are those situations in which agents and recipients operate within structural and institutional constraints such that any action "will necessarily impose burdens on others" (Connolly 1993:218).

Connolly contrasts his conception of power with Foucault's, which he characterizes as "invested in institutions and divested from agents," who are artificially constituted subjects. Connolly uses the term power "for those contexts in which power can be said to be exercised." He uses the term structural determination for those situations "in which the constraints are so tight that there is no space for the exercise of power" (Connolly 1993:219). Despite his refusal to define power, Connolly's efforts to find a space for it and to differentiate it from other forms of exercising influence over others come quite close to a definition. He is especially keen, for example, to separate authority and persuasion from power (Connolly 1993:222–24). Connolly seems, in fact, to want to place power in an undemocratic rather than a democratic space; indeed, he characterizes most forms of power—"manipulation, coercion, deterrence, anticipatory surrender, force, and conditioning"—as immoral, whereas persuasion, which he insists is not a form of power, occupies the moral high ground in a democracy. Acceptance of authority also occupies a morally positive space, since he defines it as submission to "a command because one thinks it is the proper thing to do even if it is against one's interests" (Connolly 1993:109). Having presented a set of distinctions among various forms of power, authority, persuasion, and manipulation in which all the forms of power over other people are characterized as essentially immoral and undemocratic, Connolly reasserts the disarming position that his moralistic framework and definitions should be seen as essentially contestable, not dogmatic, fundamentalist, or otherwise immune from the democratic mode of argument and persuasion.

There is a considerable distance between Connolly's conceptualization of power (both in 1974 and later) and Foucault's. Foucault makes no distinction between good and bad, moral and immoral, or democratic and undemocratic exercises of power.[8] His focus is, as Connolly notes, "on the 'strategies' of power" (Connolly 1993:232–34), separated from concepts of agency and responsibility—although, contrary to almost everyone else who has written on this subject, I do not believe

---

[8]On the contrary, all forms of power are "insidious" to Foucault, the more insidious the more "invisible," including those exercises of power that fit none of Connolly's categories but "subtly penetrate ... an entire societal network" (Foucault 1977:207–8), such as the discursive practices that operate almost unconsciously, without anyone imagining that he is exercising power. However, there are some passages in Foucault's work that evoke a world without power, or at least a world in which power and fear are separated (see Foucault 1989c:130 for the latter).

that Foucault eliminates agency and responsibility from his perspectives on power. Strategies of power exist independently of responsible agents, but they obviously may be used consciously or unconsciously. I believe that the ideas of agency and responsibility, like so many other themes in Foucault's writings, are "bracketed," but they are not disowned.[9] What is most important for Foucault is first to identify the strategies, techniques, mechanisms, and instruments of power, leaving aside the question of the extent to which they are used or misused with perfect, imperfect, or no conscious knowledge of their effects.

A second distinction between Foucault's ideas about power and Connolly's relates to the relationship between power and authority. From Foucault's point of view, there can be no separation between power and authority, since all power rests on a base of knowledge that provides the authority for its exercise and the right of certain persons to exercise it.

Third, Connolly's text—if not Connolly now—remains caught in the traditional conceptions of power, authority, and legitimacy derived from Weber and extending through to Dahl. His text continues to talk about power over others and power to get something done in the form of A influencing B to do x (Connolly 1993:243fn). This A over B business is inconsistent with Foucault's kinetic conception of power. For Foucault, A's actions affect B, who resists, thus affecting A, in successive iterations, and all of this takes place in a context determined by discourse and practice. The parameters in which power is exercised are not on a continuum from persuasion to force but on a playing field where strategies of both power and resistance to power are exercised in a multiplicity of ways, including all the elements that Connolly wishes to exclude on moral, democratic grounds.

Finally, Connolly's conception of power and its exercise leads him to a statement concerning the relationship between political order and power that seems inconsistent with Foucault. "No order," says Connolly, "could sustain itself without power, though that will not be the *principal* basis of order in a well-ordered polity" (Connolly 1993:243fn, italics in original). Why do we need to go into this question of political order? This is another trap of the conservative bent of political science that Connolly otherwise resists vehemently in his writings. Radical political thought ought—to put it squarely in moralistic terms—not to be constrained by the fear of disorder or the delusion that there lies ahead "a well-ordered polity" of which power is not the principal basis. There can be no such thing for Foucault. A well-ordered polity is almost an oxymoron. It is impossible to envision one without engaging in some form of utopian thinking, anathema to Foucault.

---

[9]This is a debatable point. Both Polsky (1991) and I have identified specific persons, groups, and organizations, that is, various agents, responsible for actions, policies, and programs. I consider such identification necessary in empirical research. There is a diffuse societal responsibility for the predominant power practices in a society—on whichever end of Connolly's spectrum they lie—but there are also varying degrees of direct/indirect, conscious/unconscious involvement of agents in their perpetuation.

In the preface to his third edition of *The Terms of Political Discourse*, Connolly, now in his post-Nietzschean mode, challenges prevailing conceptions of moral order and calls for the destabilization of the "codes of moral order within which prevailing identities are set." It is evident that his later thinking also applies to the status of codes of political order and the need for their destabilization, but he allows himself an author's claim to consistency, stating that the conception of politics presented in the first edition of the book is "remarkably close" to that in the third edition (Connolly 1993:xii, xiii, xvii). Perhaps it is, but his work on power and authority, though it has succeeded in demonstrating the futility of the older distinctions that still prevail in the discipline, does not confront successfully the more difficult issues raised by the interplay of power and resistance that constitutes the core of Foucault's analysis of power relations.

Comparative Politics

An early work in comparative politics in the postmodernist mode is *Colonising Egypt* (Mitchell 1988). It is a book that crosses conventional disciplinary boundaries and the categories generally used in political science to discuss politics, political development, and political modernization. Mitchell discusses the "birth of politics" and the modern state in Egypt in terms of new concepts of knowledge, new practices made manifest in new institutions and arrangements of space, and an entirely new way of looking at the world. Many of Mitchell's ideas and arguments challenge some of the fundamental assumptions on which the discipline of political science is based.

Colonising Egypt is a strikingly unconventional re-presentation of the interaction between colonizers and colonized in nineteenth-century Egypt. The principal intellectual debt is to Foucault, but the author draws also from Derrida and Heidegger. Said's *Orientalism* (Said 1978) is a considerable influence on Mitchell as well.

Mitchell shows how Egyptians adopted the disciplinary mechanisms and the instruments of surveillance that had evolved in Europe in the preceding two centuries, as so well described by Foucault. He analyzes the spread of these mechanisms and instruments and their relationships to new systems of knowledge as well in the military, in the schools, in the villages, in urban planning, and in new forms of writing about Egypt's past. Some of the descriptions resemble a tracing out in Egypt of the European paths laid out by Foucault. Mitchell has, however, gone beyond such descriptions to make original contrasts between the distinctive approaches of traditional Arab/Muslim writers to words, language, texts, and knowledge and European approaches to them. The most novel parts of the work, however, are the interrelated discussions of the "world-as-exhibition," of enframing, and of the modern world as a world divided in two. Both Europeans and the Egyptians absorbed into this new, divided world create oppositions between reality and appearance, body and mind, text and world, authority and power, state and society, etc, and then seek the true relationships between the artificially separated entities. The false dichotomies lead us to perceive the world as an exhibition, never experiencing the reality but only the presentations and re-presentations of some imagined real world "out there." Hidden from perception are the disciplinary powers exercised by means of a reordering of space, enframing institutions and structures such as schools, factories, and barracks, as well as the land itself, and locating them on specific sites or grids in which individuals are "confined, isolated, combined together, and kept under surveillance" (Mitchell 1988:176).

This book provides a thoroughly innovative approach to the colonial experience. It avoids the developmentalist paradigm that focuses on modernization in colonial societies as a process of gradual adoption of western bureaucratic institutions, of value change from superstitious to rational, scientific ways of thinking and from religious to secular practices, and of the transformation of backward economies through the introduction of new means and modes of agricultural, industrial, political, and educational change. Instead, Mitchell (1988) focuses on the adoption, through the interaction between colonizer and colonized, of a division of the world into dichotomous categories that is characteristic of modernity, as Foucault has described it.

Two of my students have also adopted a Foucauldian perspective in their dissertations. Clea Finkle (*State, Power, and Police in Colonial North India*, unpublished thesis) focuses on processes of state formation in colonial northern India. She examines the spread of policing practices, in both the senses used by Foucault—that is, the establishment of a police constabulary as well as new practices of public health and sanitation. She too avoids the developmentalist paradigm and focuses instead on the ambiguities of relations of power and knowledge that developed between colonizer and colonized as the British sought to use the police as sources of both knowledge of local societies and control of the population. Far from seeing the establishment of a modern police force as an aspect of Indian bureaucratic development, Finkle examines the ways in which the British attempts to acquire both knowledge and control were constantly subverted and undermined by the local constabulary for their own purposes. In the process, she also exposes the unreality of the conventional distinction between state and society, the idea that modernization under colonial rule created a modern state above and separate from society. The Indian police, drawn from the local societies, never came to see themselves in such terms and were never integrated effectively into the neutral, hierarchical, bureaucratic police structure that the British imagined they were creating.

Kornmesser (*The Magical Rational Peasant*, unpublished thesis) takes off from a major debate in the literature on peasant politics in Asia, that between Popkin and Scott, (Scott 1976, Popkin 1980) concerning the economic "rationality" of the peasant. To what extent are peasants motivated in agricultural decision making by nonrational or extrarational considerations such as risk aversion (rather than profit maximization), moral relationships, and religious and ritual practices? Kornmesser transcends this debate and shows convincingly that such dichotomies do not hold up in the actual context of peasant productive decisions in which economically rational practices and magical, ritual, and religious practices cannot be separated.

Kornmesser's analysis of the power relations in which the peasantry are enmeshed is also quite original. He demonstrates that the category "peasant" is itself a construction that implicates the cultivators in systems of knowledge, external control, and decision making in which they are turned into objects rather than acting subjects. Power over their own lives and decisions is transferred to external agencies, whose understanding of the actual bases of peasant decision making is distorted and whose plans for changing that perceived behavior usually go awry.

In effect, Kornmesser revives a dormant debate on the issue of peasant agriculture and places it in the broader, more significant setting of the relationship of Asian cultivators to the contemporary state and international development agencies. This shift is of both theoretical and practical importance, since it draws attention once again to peasants—still most of the world's population—not as objects of study who need to be reformed and brought into a modern world, but as victims of a world development process that continues to claim many of them. Kornmesser's form of analysis, therefore, could be taken as a model to be extended to groups other than the peasantry.

My own recent work (Brass 1996, 1997) shows how a subject that clearly falls within the conventional domain of political science, namely collective violence, can be illuminated by adopting perspectives and modes of analysis influenced by Foucault. I should stress first, however, that I did not set out to make use of Foucault's ideas, methods, and modes of analysis when I began this work. Rather, I had been reading Foucault for years and his ideas simply subverted me as I worked simultaneously on issues pertaining to public violence, particularly riots, including Hindu-Muslim riots.

My work ultimately was influenced by those ideas in the following ways. First, I altered a method that I had been using from the beginning of my PhD research, that is, in-depth personal interviewing of politicians, bureaucrats, police, and other public figures, as well as ordinary people (nonpublic figures). In preference to seeking the causes of public violence with reference to existing theories on the subject, and mining my interviews for factually accurate and coherent explanations, I treated the interviews themselves as texts to be analyzed. I found, in the process, something akin to what Foucault presented in *I, Pièrre Rivière ...*, a multiplicity of voices, all speaking coherently within distinct, though not entirely separate, frameworks, narratives, or discourses about the same subject. They did not necessarily give different factual accounts, though some did, but interpreted the same events quite differently. Second, I found that each type of interpretation or explanation of events of collective violence suggested a different configuration of power relations among individuals, castes, religious groups, political rivals, and so forth. Third, I found that some of these narratives were incompatible, but others fit snugly inside each other. In the latter case, I realized that it was not possible to settle on a single explanation of large public events of this type, but that the explanations revealed processes, motives, and conflicts that hid behind other explanations.

The actual steps in the development of a riot, the persons, groups, and organizations involved, were hidden from view by certain types of explanations. Particularly obscuring were explanations that attributed riots to the spontaneous feelings of the people, especially to religious animosities. Fourth, I came gradually to the view that the very process of explanation constituted a form of blame displacement that contributed to the persistence of the violence "explained." Finally, on the specific question of Hindu-Muslim violence in India, I have concluded that there is in fact an overarching discourse of Hindu-Muslim relations in India that explains all incidents involving members of these two religious communities in terms of the eternal differences between them. That discourse is in itself really a subdiscourse of the modern nation-state, a discourse that contains a fundamental contradiction everywhere in the world, dividing every population that defines itself as a nation-state into majorities and minorities—those to whom the state rightfully belongs and those who are more or less tolerated, harassed, or discriminated against. Thus did I arrive from the ground up, as it were, from the smallest villages and towns in northern India to an understanding of how difference is created, sustained, and integrated into the very fabric of the modern nation-state in the contemporary world.

Public Administration

Two works on aspects of welfare policy in the United States that draw heavily on Foucault's ideas are by Polsky (1991) and Schram (1995). Although both deserve wide attention, I comment here only on Polsky's work.

The Rise of the Therapeutic State (Polsky 1991) is a model for the kind of political science research that responds to Foucault's call at the end of *Discipline and Punish* for further studies of the mechanisms, procedures, practices, and institutions of normalization in modern society. It also responds to Foucault's call for studies that constitute histories of the present, that is, for studies that ask, in effect, how we arrived at the current state of affairs with regard to instruments and institutional practices of normalization. Polsky traces the development and elaboration of such instruments, institutions, and practices with regard to a question of ongoing concern in American public policy, namely, the proper mode of providing relief to the poor, particularly to so-called marginal families, delinquents, and mothers with dependent children in families without fathers.

Polsky (1991) shows how, from the beginning of large-scale private philanthropic efforts in the 1870s, philanthropic societies introduced into the efforts to provide monetary relief to the poor and indigent a moral, normalizing concern. The aim was to bring the family up, through the care and instruction of caseworkers, to "meet the standards for normal family life" (Polsky 1991:80). This linking of normalizing care and treatment of the family through casework by philanthropic agencies was also picked up by the Progressive movement. Moreover, in the same period, the treatment and relief of the poor were linked for the first time with the judicial institutions in the establishment of juvenile courts to intervene in cases where the children were considered delinquent. Very early, therefore, such intervention was attached to state sanctions in a system that offered both rewards and punishments—economic relief for those families whose members adhered to the advice and instruction of the caseworkers, withdrawal of relief to those families that did not, and judicial intervention as the ultimate sanction that extended to the power of removing children from the mother's care to the care of the state in foster homes.

As the policy practice of providing relief to marginal families became entrenched, further linkages developed to create the modern system of public intervention. Schools of social work were founded to provide the personnel for casework-based relief to the poor. Schools of public administration were founded that provided the managerial techniques for the caseworkers and government officials to organize relief and treatment for the poor. Social science, particularly the discipline of sociology, provided the broad analytic framework for societal change and evolution into which the model of the well-adjusted family could be fit. Developments in modern psychiatry, particularly in psychoanalysis, were integrated into the training of social workers, adding to the armory of caseworkers the (pseudo)scientific findings of these bodies of knowledge to implement programs for the treatment and adjustment of marginal families to acceptable standards. Indeed, the intrusion of psychological and psychiatric knowledge into the therapeutic movement added a further demand on the welfare state as well as a further intrusion by the state into the lives of the poor in the name of relief, namely, the addition of professional counseling as a new "basic entitlement" of the poor in addition to their "right to the minimum standard of living" (Polsky 1991:200).

However, from its earliest stages up to the present, the therapeutic movement has failed to provide any evidence that its methods of diagnosis and treatment have had any salutary results (Polsky 1991:112–13 and elsewhere). The evidence that does exist suggests, in fact, that they have not produced such results. In the meantime, however, according to Polsky, the whole ideology of the therapeutic movement has been colonized by antidemocratic sentiments that deny agency to the poor to speak for themselves, to organize themselves, and to demand public relief free of the intrusive interventions of caseworkers (Polsky 1991:120).

The advance of the therapeutic movement, though it has succeeded in entrenching itself and its values into the systems of welfare for the poor, has not been achieved without struggle. In fact, it has faced resistance throughout its history, ranging from opponents of public relief to local communities to the poor themselves. The grounds for such resistance have included ideological opposition from the Right, the desire of state and local governments to receive the funds from the national government to distribute without therapeutic casework intervention, and the desire of the poor for the right to relief without the intrusion of caseworkers into their modes of living. Polsky's critique is clearly one from the Left that deplores the therapeutic movement's pretensions and failures, its antidemocratic character, its focus on the social and psychological adjustment of the family to societal norms, and the consequent avoidance of the structural and economic conditions that produce and reproduce poverty generation after generation in the country that prides itself in being the richest on earth. It is certainly not a call for the elimination of welfare, but rather for a reexamination of the conditions under which welfare is provided and the enormous waste of resources that is involved in such a system. It is not the welfare state that Polsky is criticizing, but the therapeutic state that is enfolded within it and that discredits the very goals of relief for the poor.

A study such as Polsky's clearly does not derive from the dominant methods and practices of contemporary political science. It crosses numerous conventional disciplinary boundaries: those between contemporary and historical analysis or between institutions and practices conventionally considered political (such as government agencies) and others considered nonpolitical (such as schools of social work and the techniques of psychoanalysis). It examines the role of the social and human sciences—particularly that branch of political science known as public administration—themselves in the failures of the therapeutic movement. It is based on the kind of comprehensive research that Foucault calls for in his injunction to read everything. Finally, while adhering to exemplary standards of empirical research that could be appropriated by persons and groups on the Right or Left for their own purposes, it stands on its own merits as a sharp, powerful critique of a major aspect of contemporary social policy.

CONCLUSION

The examples provided above are meant to illustrate how Foucault's ideas can provide new energy and direction to political science. For all its diversity, the discipline predominantly labors in traditional forms of hermeneutics in political theory and constitutional law; in state-centered studies of governance and intergovernmental relations; in analyses of the internal dynamics of political parties and their fates in the electoral process; in partisan discussions of contemporary policy issues such as affirmative action, race, and gender; in dissections of voter behavior; and so forth. I have argued and demonstrated that Foucault's work, and that of others who have headed in directions indicated by him or who have wrestled with or been subverted by his thought, can provide points of entry into new topics as well as new forms of theoretical, comparative, and policy analyses of subject matter that falls in the traditional domain of political science. But it would be a mistake to think that the discipline can profit much from the mere insertion of Foucauldian themes into political science or his resurrection in the form of a canonized theorist, whose works are to be dissected for their own sake or for the acquisition of his secret wisdom. Foucault was the most subversive philosopher–historian–political analyst of our present time. To read Foucault in depth and with understanding must be deeply disconcerting for those who have any doubts about the validity of their disciplinary enterprise, the methodologies they use and their rationalistic and mechanistic underpinnings, as well as their implication in existing power relations that are politically and academically conservative. A reading of Foucault may make one doubt the worth of everything that has been done so far, including one's own work, and challenge one to consider what is truly worth doing.

ACKNOWLEDGMENTS

Thanks, but no responsibility, are due to Clea Finkle, Margaret Levi, and Andrew Polsky for their helpful critical readings of the first draft of this article.

Visit the Annual Reviews home page at www.AnnualReviews.org

LITERATURE CITED

Brass PR. 1996. *Riots and Pogroms*. New York: New York Univ. Press

Brass PR. 1997. *Theft of an Idol: Text and Context in the Representation of Collective Violence*. Princeton, NJ: Princeton Univ. Press

Butler J. 1999. *Gender Trouble: Feminism and the Subversion of Identity*. New York: Routledge

Clegg SR. 1989. *Frameworks of Power*. London: Sage

Connolly WE. 1974. *The Terms of Political Discourse*. Lexington, MA: DC Heath

Connolly WE. 1993. *The Terms of Political Discourse*. Princeton, NJ: Princeton Univ. Press. 3rd ed.

Connolly WE. 1995. *The Ethos of Pluralization*. Minneapolis: Univ. Minnesota Press

Dumm TL. 1996. *Michel Foucault and the Politics of Freedom*. Thousand Oaks, CA: Sage

Foucault M. 1977. Intellectuals and power. In *Language, Counter-Memory, Practice: Selected Essays and Interviews*, ed. DF Bouchard; transl. DF Bouchard, S Simon, pp. 205–17. Oxford, UK: Basil Blackwell (from French)

Foucault M. 1979 (1975). *Discipline and Punish: The Birth of the Prison*, transl. A Sheridan. New York: Vintage (from French)

Foucault M. 1980a. *Power/Knowledge: Selected Interviews and Other Writings, 1972–1977*, ed. C Gordon, transl. C Gordon, L Marshall, J Mepham, K Soper. New York: Pantheon Books (from French)

Foucault M. 1980b. Body/power. See Foucault 1980a, pp. 55–62

Foucault M. 1980c. The politics of health in the eighteenth century. See Foucault 1980a, pp. 166–82

Foucault M, ed. 1982. *I, Pierre Rivière, Having Slaughtered My Mother, My Sister, and My Brother ... A Case of Parricide in the 19th Century*, transl. F Jellinek. Lincoln: Univ. Nebraska Press (from French)

Foucault M. 1988. *The History of Sexuality*, Vol. III: *The Care of the Self*, transl. R Hurley. New York: Vintage (from French)

Foucault M. 1989a. *Foucault Live (Interviews, 1966–84)*, ed. S Lotringer, transl. J Johnston. New York: Semiotext(e), Columbia University

Foucault M. 1989b. The discourse of history. See Foucault 1989a, pp. 11–34

Foucault M. 1989c. The politics of Soviet crime. See Foucault 1989a, pp. 121–30

Foucault M. 1989d. I, Pierre Rivière. See Foucault 1989a, pp. 131–36

Foucault M. 1989e. An historian of culture. See Foucault 1989a, pp. 73–88

Foucault M. 1991. Questions of method. In *The Foucault Effect: Studies in Governmentality: With Two Lectures by and an Interview with Michel Foucault*, ed. G Burchell, C Gordon, P Miller, pp. 73–86. London: Harvester

Foucault M. 1997. *The Politics of Truth*, ed. S Lotringer, L Hochroth. New York: Semiotext(e)

Foucault M. 1997a. What is critique? See Foucault 1997, pp. 23–82

Foucault M. 1997b. What is enlightenment? See Foucault 1997, pp. 101–34

Foucault M. 1997c. What our present is. See Foucault 1997, pp. 147–70

Foucault M. 1997d. Subjectivity and truth. See Foucault 1997, pp. 171–98

Gordon C. 1991. Governmental rationality: an introduction. In *The Foucault Effect: Studies in Governmentality: With Two Lectures by and an Interview with Michel Foucault*, ed. G Burchell, C Gordon, P Miller, pp. 1–52. London: Harvester

Mitchell T. 1988. *Colonising Egypt*. Cambridge, UK: Cambridge Univ. Press

Popkin S. 1980. The rational peasant: the political economy of peasant society. *Theory Soc.* 9:411–71

Polsky A. 1991. *The Rise of the Therapeutic State*. Princeton, NJ: Princeton Univ. Press

Said EW. 1978. *Orientalism*. New York: Pantheon

Schram SF. 1995. *Words of Welfare: The Poverty of Social Science and the Social Science of Poverty*. Minneapolis: Univ. Minnesota Press

Scott JC. 1976. *The Moral Economy of the Peasant: Rebellion and Subsistence in Southeast Asia*. New Haven, CT: Yale Univ. Press

Veyne P. 1997. Foucault revolutionizes history. In *Foucault and His Interlocutors*, ed. AI Davidson, pp. 146–82. Chicago: Univ. Chicago Press

Annu. Rev. Polit. Sci. 2000. 3:331–53

ASSESSING THE CAPACITY OF MASS ELECTORATES

Philip E. Converse

*Department of Political Science, University of Michigan, Ann Arbor,
Michigan 48105; e-mail: pconvers@umich.edu*

Key Words   elections, issue voting, political information, democratic theory, ideology

■ **Abstract**   This is a highly selective review of the huge literature bearing on the capacity of mass electorates for issue voting, in view of the great (mal)distribution of political information across the public, with special attention to the implications of information heterogeneity for alternative methods of research. I trace the twists and turns in understanding the meaning of high levels of response instability on survey policy items from their discovery in the first panel studies of 1940 to the current day. I consider the recent great elaboration of diverse heuristics that voters use to reason with limited information, as well as evidence that the aggregation of preferences so central to democratic process serves to improve the apparent quality of the electoral response. A few recent innovations in design and analysis hold promise of illuminating this topic from helpful new angles.

> Never overestimate the information of the American electorate, but never underestimate its intelligence.
>
> (Mark Shields, syndicated political columnist, citing an old aphorism)

INTRODUCTION

In 1997, I was asked to write on the topic "How Dumb Are the Voters Really?" Being revolted by the question formulation, I instantly declined to participate. Long ago I had written two essays (Converse 1964, 1970) to convey limitations on political information in the electorate. Consequently, I found myself typecast, in some quarters at least, as an apostle of voter ignorance. Hence my aversion. Shortly, however, I decided that with a change of title I could take the assignment.

The pithiest truth I have achieved about electorates is that where political information is concerned, the mean level is very low but the variance is very high (Converse 1990). We hardly need argue low information levels any more (e.g. Kinder & Sears 1985, Neuman 1986). Indeed, Delli Carpini & Keeter (1996) have recently provided the most sustained examination of information levels in the electorate in the literature, in an excellent and thoughtful treatment. They (and I) concur with Luskin (1990) that contrasts in political information have at least three broad sources: ability, motivation, and opportunity. "Dumbness" as commonly conceived is but a part of one of these sources. As this essay proceeds, the impoverishment of the question "how dumb are the voters really?" will become still more apparent.

The essay focuses instead on the second half of my characterization: the extreme variance in political information from the top to the bottom of the public. This is not controversial either. But the degree of this heterogeneity is widely underestimated, and the implications of that dramatic heterogeneity for research seem even less well understood. Hence, I discuss along the way some impacts of this heterogeneity on alternative methods of assessing voter capabilities.

This review emphasizes the relatively recent literature. It also clarifies, where relevant, what some authors still treat as residual mysteries in my two early pieces in the area (Converse 1964, 1970). Moreover, I import several findings from our large mass elite study in France, carried out in the late 1960s but not published until much later (Converse & Pierce 1986). This is an important study in the context of this review for two reasons: (*a*) It was the first study designed specifically to test the theories in those two early essays, since their hypotheses had merely been suggested by data gathered for other purposes; and (*b*) crucial results from the French project remain unknown to most students of American voting behavior, presumably because they were studied in a foreign electorate, and who knows what that might mean for external validity.

THE ROLE OF INFORMATION

When in the late 1950s I experimented with analyses stratifying the electorate into "levels of conceptualization" (Campbell et al 1960), I was impressed by the sharpness of the differences from "top to bottom" of the potential electorate in other respects as well. I came to feel that many empirical studies of voting behavior that did not routinely stratify the electorate in some such fashion were actually concealing more than they revealed. In recent research, some form of this stratification has become quite commonplace. The variable I originally thought was probably the clearest differentiator—formal education—had the advantage of being present in most political surveys. Although it is still used, and often to good purpose (e.g. Sniderman et al 1991), I later decided that it gave weaker results than multi-item measures of entities such as political involvement, provided these measures captured enduring interest and not merely the excitement of a specific election. The question of what predictor is best has remained alive, however, and authors using some shorthand for the core variation at issue choose among a wealth of terms to follow the adjective "political": awareness, attentiveness, expertise, informedness, interest, involvement, knowledge, or sophistication, to name a few. There are different nuances here, but a central construct lurks.

Zaller (1992:333ff) reviews a good deal of experimentation that has led him to prefer a broadly based measure of political information for the crucial discriminating dimension. I heartily applaud the choice. At a theoretical level, I had pointed to the "mass of stored political information" (1962) as a crucial variable in voter decision making, but I never had a good measure of political information to work with in the studies I used, all of which—including the French study—were designed before 1967.

The conventional complaint about measures of political information is that knowledge of minor facts, such as the length of terms of US senators, cannot address what voters actually need to vote properly. This is a tiresome canard. Information measures must be carefully constructed and multi-item, but it does not take much imagination to realize that differences in knowledge of several such "minor" facts are diagnostic of more profound differences in the amount and accuracy of contextual information voters bring to their judgments (Neuman 1986). Absent such imagination, scholars should review Chapter 4 of Delli Carpini & Keeter (1996) for extended proofs. In any event, measurements gauging what these authors denote as "political knowledge," i.e. "the range of factual information about politics that is stored in long-term memory," may be the most efficient operationalization of the latent dimension sought.

Evidence of Maldistribution

In my view, the maldistribution of information in the electorate is extreme. Yet Delli Carpini & Keeter, assessing the "Actual Distribution of Political Knowledge" (1996:153), find rather modest differences empirically. A Gini coefficient that I calculate from the distribution of respondents on their main measure (Delli Carpini & Keeter 1996:Table 4.6) shows a weak value of only 0.20. (The Gini coefficient norms between 0.00—when a resource such as information is equally distributed across a population—and 1.00, when one citizen possesses all of it.) This cannot reflect the actual maldistribution in the electorate, which would surely register a Gini coefficient over 0.60 and probably much higher.

At issue here is the easiness of the items making up these authors' test. It would be possible to devise a test on which everybody sampled could get a perfect score. This would produce a Gini coefficient of 0.00. It would also be possible to use items so arcane that only one person in the sample could get any correct answers, producing a coefficient of 1.00. (This would not mean that subject-matter experts could not answer those items but only that the sample contained at most one such expert.) Of course, no analyst wants to waste time asking questions that do not discriminate, i.e. that nobody or everybody can answer. Indeed, Delli Carpini & Keeter show that their median for correct responses is 49%, proof that the test is nearly optimal to sort on information levels for this sample. Their median does not imply, however, that this is how political information is naturally distributed.

Here is a thought experiment. The universe of all possible political information is, of course, huge and undefinable. But there are subdomains of this universe that are fairly concrete and listable. One of these is the set of political personages, defined as broadly as one wishes in time and space, such as US figures of the past 40 years. Let us lock up in a room with food and water a sample of respondents asked to list as many such personages as they can resurrect from long-term memory, provided they associate with each name some validating descriptor, however brief. There is reason to expect that, even in an adult cross section, the median number of names exhumed with proper "stub" identification would not be very large: twenty? Thirty? And a few would not get beyond two or three.

Let us now add a well-informed member of the same population—Nelson Polsby, for example. Even within the 40-year time window, the number of relevant subcategories is huge: the federal establishment, with administrations, agencies, and cabinets; both branches of Congress; the high judiciary; national party leaderships; state gubernatorial administrations and legislatures; city mayors and administrations; other influential party leaders; and so on. Nelson might well achieve a list of several thousand, or three orders of magnitude greater than the least informed citizen. If we relaxed the time limit, so that the whole history of the republic was eligible, Nelson's edge would simply grow larger still. Critics might say that no current citizen need know anything about earlier personages at all, but surely familiarity with the roles of John Jay, Boss Tweed or Joe Cannon enriches the context Nelson brings to current politics. But this is just the "who." Another simple category is the "where," since unit political interactions are enormously affected by geographic relationships. The National Geographic Society has found some respondents cannot even find their home state on a unlabeled US map, and the modal respondent cannot label very many states. Nelson could do the whole map in no time, and most of the world map, too, adding rich geopolitical lore on many subregions.

Yet "who" and "where" are the easy parts. We can move on to much more nebulous but profound contextual matters. "Rules of the game" for various significant agencies of the United States would be one of the simpler categories here. Tougher yet would be descriptions of actual process in Congress, for example, with the large range of parliamentary maneuvers that various situations can activate in both houses. Nelson could presumably write on this topic, from memory and without repetition, as long as the food held out, in contrast to most of the electorate, who would produce nothing at all. Of course Nelson Polsby is unique in many ways, but there are hundreds of thousands of citizens in the most informed percentile of the electorate whose "dumps" from stored political knowledge would have awesome dimensions, although it might take 10 or 20 national samples before as many as one such person fell in a sample. A small fraction of the electorate claims a large fraction of the total political information accessible in memory to anyone, hence the predictably high Gini coefficient.

Why such maldistribution? Downs (1957) pitted information costs against nearly invisible control over outcomes in order to explain low information levels. But to explain maldistribution we must add the aphorism "it takes information to get information." Consider Paul Revere watching the North Church steeple for the signal to begin his ride. This signal, in modern terms, transmitted only one bit of information, "one if by land, two if by sea." To digest that message, however, Revere had to know the code, as well as what it meant in context. So it took much more information to receive this one bit.

The same argument applies easily to much more complex transmissions. Stored information provides pegs, cubbyholes, and other place markers in the mind to locate and attribute meaning to new information coming in. The more pegs and cubbyholes one controls in storage, the lower the cost of ingesting any relevant piece of new information. This is a positive feedback system—"them what has, gets"—and it explodes exponentially, thus explaining extreme maldistribution quite simply. Perhaps people without much stored information on a subject are "dumb," but that is a rather primitive form of judgment.

Implications of Maldistribution for Research

The extravagant heterogeneity of information levels from top to bottom in the electorate should remind us to interpret research findings in terms of the layers of the electorate generating any particular body of data. There is some recognition of this fact; data on political information from college sophomores are acknowledged to lack external validity. But we too easily assume that "cross-section samples" are totally comparable. They are not.

For one thing, response rates have declined steadily over the past 40 years, and the cumulative difference between samples of the 1950s and those of today is sobering (Brehm 1993). The election studies of the 1950s routinely had response rate percentages in the mid- to upper 80s, and studies financed for exceptional follow-up efforts got as high as 92%. Well-financed efforts nowadays have trouble reaching 75%, and ordinary telephone interviewing response rates lie closer to 60%. I have seen hurry-up phone samples of which college graduates form the majority. This is the secular trend: For comparable levels of effort, nonresponse has approximately tripled since 1955. Within each period, of course, the effort to pursue respondents varies widely from one national study to the next.

When nonresponse grows, the least informed do not drop out en bloc. There is merely a correlation in this direction. Moreover, some surveys try to reweight their samples to restore proportions of the less informed, although it is not always easy to learn whether or not such adjustments have been made. And a recent view challenges whether nonresponse typically affects results much at all. (Evidence that it does not, however, comes mainly from checked-box "opinions," in which underlying quality of response is always well concealed, rather than from open-ended materials in which quality differences leap out.) In any event, the decline of response rates gives commendable pause to careful scholars such as Delli Carpini & Keeter (1996:66) in comparing measures of information in the electorate from five decades of national samples. All should be wary of the problem.

Outside the regimen of full cross-section sampling, it is even more important to "keep score" on the fraction of the public providing the bases for inference.

Memorable vignettes lead easily to working hypotheses, which in turn harden into convictions as to what goes on in the mind of "persons in the street." Popkin (1994) provides a charming discussion of some modes of "gut reasoning" about politics (which he sees in clinical settings, e.g. discussions with focus groups during political campaigns) that he calls low-information rationality. It is fun to read between the lines what types of citizens these insights come from. Most obviously, Popkin refers consistently to what "voters" do. Moreover, in context it is clear that these are serial voters, which dismisses roughly the bottom half of the electorate. Further, it turns out that these informants are disproportionately serial voters in presidential primaries, a much more exclusive set. Although voting in primaries is notoriously situational (Norrander 1992), it seems likely that most of the sources for Popkin's insights are part of, in information terms, the top quartile of the public.

This is no cavil at the Popkin (1994) description but rather a neutral effort to locate the discussion in a broader scheme. I heartily endorse the message that voters reason, and do so all the way down the information ordering of the electorate, in the simple sense of putting two and two together using the information accessible to them. Nor do I object to the label of low-information rationality just because of the high-information stratum of the electorate that Popkin seems to have considered. It takes information to generate new combinations of information, and this is true to the very top of the information hierarchy.

The moral of this section is humble. In the endless argumentation over the capacities of the electorate, the steepness of the information slope in the public means that data provenance must be kept in mind. Rancor sanctified by "data" is mindless when, as is not uncommon, contrasting results actually stem from differences in method.

THE RIDDLE OF RESPONSE INSTABILITY

Undoubtedly the greatest surprise in early survey research came when Lazarsfeld et al (1948) reinterviewed the same people at various points during the 1940 presidential campaign, using a design he christened a panel study. Although the study hinged on measuring preference shifts, it turned out that overall the preference distributions, or "marginals," rarely showed significant change; but there was a remarkably high rate of change caused by individuals shuffling back and forth across the available response space from one interview to the next, even though the intervals between measurements were very short, such as a few weeks. In sum, a great deal of gross change usually added up to little or no net change. This mystery was one of the factors that led Lazarsfeld to develop "latent structure analysis," grounded in the view that individual preferences were only probabilistic: Given a set of alternatives, the respondent could not be expected to choose any single one with certainty but had a range of probabilities of acceptance across those alternatives.

The Notorious "Black-and-White" Model

When our Michigan group did a panel study over the 1956, 1958, and 1960 national elections, the same mystery fell in our laps. There was variation in temporal behavior across political attitude responses. Party identification, for example, showed substantial stability as measured by correlations from one wave to the next. Moreover, the correlation of reported partisanship between 1956 and 1960 was not much greater than the product of the two two-year correlations, implying limited amounts of steadily progressive "true" change. On the other hand, eight items measuring the most gripping policy issues of the period showed little net change from election to election, and the temporal intercorrelations were also remarkably low. Furthermore, for these items, the four-year intercorrelations were barely higher than the two-year ones, a configuration thought to signal "no true change, all change is measurement error," or item unreliability. This high gross change without net change was the essence of response instability.

One of the eight issues was more extreme in all of these diagnostic particulars, and I began to consider it a pearl of great price as a *limiting case* of the response instability syndrome. This was the "power and housing" (P&H) issue, an agree-disagree item that read, "the government should leave things like electric power and housing for private businessmen to handle." The beauty of a limiting case, or boundary condition, is that in the midst of complex problems in which the unknowns outweigh the knowns, it often permits one to set a previous unknown to zero or a constant, thereby getting new leverage for inference. In this instance, if P&H were extreme enough, it would mean true change could be set to zero. And extreme it was: Four-year correlations were essentially the same as two-year ones, and more remote from the product of the two-year correlations (standard deviation = 3.20 in the mean and variance of the other items). As a bonus, the fraction of respondents who, when invited to participate, said they had no opinion on the issue was extremely high (standard deviation = 3.40).

Although it was troubling to posit no true change in attitudes between interviews on any item, it was clear that P&H was the best candidate of all the issues if such an assumption had to be made. The item aimed at measuring the central ideological divide between socialism and capitalism: nationalization versus privatization of industry. This issue had deeply polarized industrial states in the wake of the Great Depression, and nationalization had been ascendant in the 1930s and 1940s. The pendulum would later swing the opposite way, but in the late 1950s the issue was in a kind of repose. The politically attentive had long since chosen sides, while for the inattentive P&H remained a remote issue. Unlike the other issue domains measured, there were no major relevant events or even debates with any likely impact on P&H positions in the whole 1956–1960 period.

The black-and-white model took its name from the division of respondents into two groups: those with fixed true opinions pro or con, and those whose responses were totally unstable, "as though" random. This did not mean they were uncaused, to my mind. Indeed, in this period I enjoyed shocking students by pointing out that the results of coin flips were also caused. Given enough information about attendant conditions—exact thrust and spin, for starters—the head-tail outcome could be predicted. But it is the resultant of such a large number of forces that throws of an unbiased coin can be treated as random.

Since the proportion of these two groups could be defined between a first and second wave, it was possible to test the model with an independent prediction involving wave three. Changers between the first two waves were all of the error type, and the correlation of their responses between the second and third waves should be 0.00. The second group is a mix of stayers and changers, but in a known proportion, so we could predict that the correlation of their P&H responses between 1958 and 1960 would be 0.47. The observed correlations were 0.004 and 0.489, respectively, an amazing fit.

In presenting these findings I tried to make clear that the P&H issue was a limiting case, because of its location at the extreme boundary. Absent this extreme location, there was no warrant for assuming away true change, which could run in both directions and undoubtedly affected all the other issue items. My explanations clearly did not register. Some supporters wrote to entreat me to stop being so rigid and simplistic about a black-and-white model; if I would just lighten up and admit a range of grays, I would have a much more useful model of attitude change (but, alas, one which would be quite underdetermined for the information available!). Detractors, on the other hand, applied the simplistic model to the other issues despite my advice and, finding garbage results, used them to "prove" that my P&H inference must also be garbage. What both sides had in common was a basic incomprehension of the role of limiting cases in inquiry.

The success of the black-and-white model in illuminating response instability led me to ask whether anybody could answer these policy issue items without huge amounts of response instability. Happily, my colleagues Warren Miller and Donald Stokes had in fact just questioned a sample of US congressmen on these very issues. Considering item intercorrelations to be an indicator of how tightly structured or "constrained" (and free of casual response instability) the respondent's system of policy attitudes was on these items, I compared such intercorrelations for congressmen with those of the mass sample. The results (Converse 1964:Table VII) showed much higher intercorrelations for the elite respondents. This seemed to establish an extremely plausible direct relationship between information levels and reliability of response. Active politicians simply brought a lot more to the subject matter than many citizens did, and did not have to "guess" at the answers.

I reported these results to two audiences of different interests. The main essay (1964) was written for political scientists. But I read a shorter paper using these results to an International Congress of Psychology in 1963 (later published, 1970). Psychologists at the time were much more versed than political scientists in issues of measurement error, so there was no need to pull punches with them. The issue I wished to highlight stemmed from my student days in psychometrics. Stamping coefficients of reliability on psychological test batteries was then de rigueur, and I had been uncomfortable with the apparent precision of these coefficients. It clearly implied that reliability was a fixed attribute of the printed instrument, invariant over subjects. Of course, psychology was a different world, since for most items in such batteries, the wording was from daily life and the respondent was sovereign—"Do you like carrots?", "Are you uncomfortable in large crowds?" My data on political matters suggested that reliability could vary markedly with the amount of information brought to the subject matter of the test. My climactic statement was: "While the classical view of these matters took 'reliability' to be a property ... attached to the measuring instrument, we could not have a more dramatic example [than the black-and-white results] that reliability in our field of inquiry is instead a joint property of the instrument and the object being measured" (Converse 1970:177).

The phrase "what people bring to" a given subject matter is vague. But it refers to what has anciently been called the "apperceptive mass" in problems of perceptual recognition. In politics, it refers to the stored mass of knowledge mediating what respondents, answering on the fly as always, bring to their decoding of the question.

Critiques and Response

Having been away from this controversy for some time, I was interested in current views of response instability. Zaller (1992) has made major new contributions to the discussion (see below). But Zaller (1992), Page & Shapiro (1992), and others in the current decade conclude that a diagnosis of "just measurement error" seems to have won out over whatever it was that Converse was talking about. The latter is often left a little vague, but since I too was talking mainly about measurement error, I assume the discipline has decided that contrary to my demonstrations, information differences have no impact on measurement reliability. Supporting this verdict, it is true that Achen (1975) and Erikson (1979), frequently cited authorities, were unable to find such differences. But as Zaller has also pointed out, Achen and Erikson are in a minority in this regard. Others have found such differences easily, and in the French project (Converse & Pierce 1986), designed to study the question, they are large indeed.

I am also surprised by descriptions of the measurement-error interpretations of response instability as being relatively novel (Zaller 1992:31). Perhaps I misunderstand the referent, but the view that item responses are probabilistic over a range or "latitude of acceptance" is 70 or 80 years old in psychology, and "latent structure analysis" in sociology dates from the 1950s. That is in fact the view I teethed on, and my chief amendment has been that latitudes of acceptance are broader or narrower according to variations in what respondents bring to the items. Indeed, when I think of "attitude crystallization," the construct refers to the variable breadth of these latitudes. Nor is it true that correcting away error variance is novel. Joreskog has superbly dissected the many facets of error in LISREL, but the root calculation—then called "correction for attenuation"—originated in the 1920s. In fact, it is because of that correction that users of psychological tests by the 1930s began to require the printing of reliability coefficients on test batteries, so that results could be "corrected" up into more impressive regions. I knew that correction well when writing the "Belief Systems" material, and I momentarily considered applying it at least illustratively, but decided that it would willfully conceal exactly what was substantively important in the responses to issue items.

"Just Measurement Error"

The "just measurement error" folks present very appealing but misleading pictures of individual-level ranges of response. These probabilities are usually graphed as normally distributed, which is reasonable, except near endpoints. But the response probability distribution is rarely shown as straddling the midpoint between pro and con, which starts the reader wondering; and they typically take up rather small fractions of the possible range of responses (e.g. Page & Shapiro 1992:20). If latitudes of acceptance are on average as narrow as these authors depict, then the test-retest reliability of the item measured over short periods would have to be up in the 0.80s to 0.90s. But what I was talking about were issue items in which the apparent reliability never attained 0.60, averaged about 0.40, and at the bottom was under 0.30. This state of affairs can be diagrammed also, but the pictures look totally different from those used to advertise the plausibility of "just measurement error." Such realistic latitudes of acceptance sprawl broadly, with notable probability densities over the whole response continuum. In the P&H pro-con case, they show a rectangular distribution over the pro-con alternatives for much of the sample. What kind of issue "positions" are these? I thought I was providing solace by showing that where respondents were familiar with an issue, reliability of measurement was higher.

Achen (1975) and Erikson (1979), as mentioned above, are unable to find any impact of information differences on related measurement error. Their difficulty is worth reviewing in more detail. Both are in the awkward position of needing to disconfirm the substantive hypothesis of information effects on response error rates. This means failing to reject the null hypothesis of no differences in reliability as a function of information. A glance at the two terms in significance tests shows that it will be easiest to disconfirm if the natural variance of the independent variable can be artificially truncated and if the test Ns can be minimized. Neither author deals with the full range of variance; there is no elite stratum in their tests, and our French data (Converse & Pierce 1986) suggest that this by itself truncates the variance by about one third. Other steps are taken in the same direction. Most notably, for test purposes, respondents are required to have expressed substantive opinions on all three waves. As observed on the P&H issue, many respondents in any given wave have no opinion; to demand three consecutive opinions reduces test Ns dramatically. It also differentially discards cases at the least informed end of the electorate, so that the test variance is further truncated artificially. Thus, this editing gains two for the price of one in favor of disconfirmation.

Erikson's Critique   Erikson (1979) bears on the black-and-white model more directly than Achen (1975). Erikson's article is a masterpiece of organization, and the questions it asks of this model and the P&H issue in particular are entirely germane. It also shows that the black-and-white model is indeed a spectacular fit to the dynamics of the P&H issue. Erikson's main point, however, is that rival models produce equally good, and probably preferable, fits with the data. I beg to differ, mainly because crucial tests with the black-and-white model reduce to cross-time transition probabilities, and neither of his main challenges addresses this at all.

The first challenge is that a more likely model would not split error into a 0–100% contrast (the black-and-white way) but would instead spread it evenly over all respondents. This is the view that would preserve the practice of stamping reliability coefficients on measuring instruments. Erikson's Table VI is the proof of this contention, but it fails to represent transitions from one wave to the next, which is where the crucial test centers. We can try to finish the author's argument, however, to see where it leads. If reliability is equal for all respondents, then it must be 0.37, the overall average. If we then ask what the correlation of responses between the second and third waves looks like for Erikson, the answer is simple. For every possible bipartite division of the second-wave population (an extraordinarily large number), the correlation of responses between waves two and three must be 0.37. This is very different from the theory-driven prediction of the black-and-white model, which was a sharp bifurcation into temporal correlations at 0.00 for one subset and at 0.47 for the other. As mentioned earlier, the actual results were 0.004 and 0.489. It is not clear why the author claims his pair of 0.37s would fit the data equally well!

The author's second challenge has a different base, but it too ignores the fact that the crucial test hinges on intertemporal correlations. Erikson (1979:104) argues that if preferences for changers on the P&H issue are truly random (instead of "as though random"), then the responses cannot correlate with anything else. Since he shows nonzero correlations with other issues, our argument seems compromised. His premises are not correct, however.

First, what is randomly generated is a time path, such as the $r = 0.004$ between times 2 and 3. Second, we are not limited to randomness of the equiprobability kind here; within any given p governing the marginals, such as $p = 0.70$ or even $p = 0.9944$, there is a track that shows independence from one trial to the next and would produce a 0.00 correlation (the calculation of chi square "expecteds" goes exactly to this case of independence, for marginals of any lopsidedness). A metaphor for random time tracks where the options are not equiprobable is a sequence of flips of a biased coin. Other early analyses of these agree-disagree issue items had made clear that they were strongly influenced by response set effects of the "acquiescence" type. This response set effect is, of course, stronger for some respondents than for others. In the intertemporal case, this can be thought of as a set of respondents each flipping coins of different biases to answer the questions. Their responses would show temporal correlations of zero, but if the test were performed on two different issues, the correlations between items could be arbitrarily large. So the author's second challenge to the black-and-white model as a limiting case has no more merit than the first.

Erikson goes on to ask whether error in the issue items varies inversely with a multi-item index of information/involvement he labels political sophistication, as

I would predict. The results do not lead him to reject the null hypothesis. Here Erikson's independent variable is well conceived and apparently robust. However, his dependent variable, taken literally, seems not to be a measure of error variance alone but of total natural variance in the responses. If true, this is rather disconcerting. It would include true change, which is lively on some of these issues, and which other empirical work (most notably, Zaller 1992, also Converse 1962) has shown to be usually associated curvilinearly with the information/sophistication hierarchy. If so, then dull results with the author's linear analysis methods might not be surprising.

Achen's Critique   Achen (1975) tests the same hypothesis about information differences and error rates, and also fails to reject the null hypothesis. Any scholar addressing this debate should read three "communications" in the December 1976 *American Political Science Review* raising issues about the soundness of the Achen analyses. On the face of it, I prefer Achen's dependent variable for this test to Erikson's because it is an estimate of individual contributions to error variance. But the estimation process here is very murky. On the independent variable side, Achen tests my information-error hypothesis using a global analysis with 12 variables, most of which are face-sheet categories such as urban-rural residence and gender, which have no obvious connection to my theory and dilute the critical test with overcontrols. Only 4 of 12 predictors are in the highly relevant education/involvement department. With these measures predicting to each of the eight issue error variances, Achen reports that the "multiple R ranges from 0.11 to 0.19." This value is so low, he concludes, that response error can have no source in individual differences, such as political informedness. A communication from Hunter & Coggin (1976) points out that given details of its estimation, Achen's dependent variable—individual error variance—cannot even charitably have a reliability of more than 0.25. Noting that Achen wants to correct the issue item intercorrelations for attenuation, they ask why he does not correct his multiple Rs for attenuation also; they would rise to 0.45–0.75 and would be quite eye-catching, suggesting exactly the opposite of his conclusion.

I add that among Achen's 12 predictors, the political involvement/education nexus stands out in predicting even the dilute error variance, although Achen stresses that it does not. First, although Achen and Erikson had the same panel data from which to construct a robust variable to express information/involvement differences, Achen chose the three most feeble involvement measures available. Moreover, instead of combining them in a single index (standard social science practice to maximize their meaningful joint variance), he maintained them as three separate predictors in his array of 12, with the opposite effect of eviscerating that same joint variance. His Table 3 shows that in 7 instances, 1 of the 12 predictors relates to the error measure at a 0.05 level. Five of these seven instances involve an involvement/education predictor, despite the evisceration of those measures! With a more robust involvement variable, significant relationships would clearly have multiplied far enough to have made the disconfirmation verdict untenable.

Achen ends by famously noting that the reason I had showed much higher issue intercorrelations for congressmen than for constituents was that the questions asked of the elites on each issue were phrased differently than the versions designed for the mass sample. They were more elegant and incisive, whereas the mass items were vague and poorly worded, producing confused and ambiguous answers, full of response instability. It is true that the wordings were different. But Achen's view of the wording difference effects was pure conjecture, with no evidence offered. This conjecture has achieved great currency, but we already knew from our 1967 French data (Converse & Pierce 1986) that it was wrong.

Evidence from France

The conflict over error sources has sometimes been labeled as a problem in differentiating "errors in survey wording" from "errors in respondents." These labels are unfortunate because they imply that errors must arise from one side or the other, whereas I had argued that a joint interaction was involved. But so labeled, it has been suggested that the problem is fundamentally indeterminate. A claim of this kind underlies Sniderman et al's dismissal of the debate as "ontological" (1991:17). However, the problem is technically underidentified only for blind analyses of a grid of numbers. By "blind analyses" I mean number massaging in which side information about the substance of the variables is ruled out of consideration. For example, a parallel indeterminacy has dogged cohort analysis; it is crucial to distinguish conceptually the effects of age, period, and cohort, but with only two variables actually measured, no three-way assignment can technically be determined. But again, this is only true for blind inference from an unlabeled grid of numbers. Side information about the variables involved in such cases often shows that some rival "blind" inferences are, in fact, substantively absurd and can be discarded with a clear conscience (Converse 1976). The issue of error sources is formally equivalent to the cohort analysis problem. And the French study (Converse & Pierce 1986) casts this kind of side illumination on the issue with Achen/Erikson eloquently.

Two improvements on technical shortfalls in our earlier "Belief Systems" data were (*a*) the addition of a two-wave elite panel (French deputies) to parallel the mass panel, giving for the first time comparative mass-elite stability estimates; and (*b*) the use of identical wording for deputies and for their mass constituents on some issue questions. The results of the wording changes were directly opposite to the Achen conjecture: Elite responses to mass questions were brighter than elite discursive answers to more sophisticated, open-ended questions on the same policy debates. ("Brighter" here means showing larger correlations with obvious criterion variables.) This is no great mystery; given familiarly simple issue item wordings, our elites assign themselves more incisive and valid positions than remote coders can deduce for them from flowery and "two-handed" ("on the one hand; on the other") mini-speeches fingering the nuances of various component policy options.

For the French study, we routinely subdivided the mass sample into three strata defined on a very robust five-item measure of political involvement, yielding a

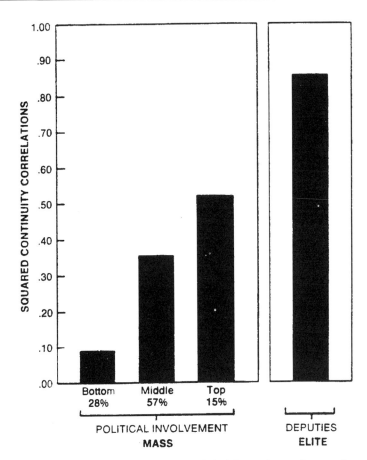

Figure 1   Stability of personal locations on the left-right continuum for mass (by political involvement) and elite, France, 1967–1968. (From *Political Representation in France* by Philip Converse and Roy Pierce, copyright © 1986 by the President and Fellows of Harvard College. Reprinted by permission of the Belknap Press of Harvard University Press.)

thin top (15%), a broad middle (57%), and a bottom (28%). When relevant, we superposed the elite stratum above the rest. Variability in both constraint and stability across these strata is typically sharp and, of course, neatly monotonic. Figure 7-3 from the main report (reproduced as Figure 1 in this chapter) the most dramatic of these displays, namely the stability of self-locations on the left-right continuum. (The item is identically worded for mass and elite.) In terms of theory, this should indeed be the sharpest display, because it involves the key ideological measuring stick or "heuristic" device that is so ubiquitous in informed political discourse in France, (but is about as weakly comprehended in the French public as the liberal-conservative dimension is in the United States, as probes of understood meaning have shown).

The differentiation here is indeed exquisite. Survey researchers are often forced to "prove" arguments with 5–8% differences and are thrilled to work with 20% differences, especially when demonstrating important theoretical points. In this display, which is of crucial theoretical consequence, the differentiation is nearly five times larger, spread out over most of the unit space. To be sure, "just measurement error" advocates could artificially remove chemical traces of error from the elite stratum, and 10 or 15 times as much error from the bottom stratum, thus smartly "proving" that even the most uninformed Frenchman has ideological self-locations just as firm and stable as those of his deputies. But such a calculation is ridiculous obfuscation, given a competing theory that predicts this near-total differentiation on grounds of information differences. And here, any alleged indeterminacy in the blind numbers is swept away by copious independent side information charting the steep decline in comprehension of the left-right continuum as political involvement declines. Again, "just measurement error" folks can assert that the question "where do you place yourself on this left-right scale?" is impossibly vague for *citoyens* who do not know what "left" and "right" mean anyway. But how does such an assertion prove that error variances show no interaction with information differences, as Achen and Erikson have convinced so many scholars?

Figure 1's display from France, 1967–1968, is neatly corroborated by data on "attitude crystallization" (stability) in ideological self-placement by political knowledge in the United States, 1990–1992 (Delli Carpini & Keeter 1996), showing the largest range also, despite lacking an elite stratum for comparison. Other French data relevant to this discussion are displays of factor-analytic structures of issue and ideology items for the elite and the three involvement strata (Converse & Pierce 1986:248). The left-right self-placements are dominant factors for the elite and the most involved 15% of the mass population; this role fades to fourth and fifth place in the broad middle and bottom strata, which display a scattering of much weaker factors [a parallel to Stimson's (1975) findings for the 1972 National Election Study]. Ironically, in both these lower strata, making up 85% of the electorate, the liveliest component of issue responses is a "methods effect," an artifact of question wording. Kinder & Sanders (1990) have put more meat on such bones, showing the susceptibility of low-information respondents to "framing" effects. And of course, although the French policy item responses show gradients less steep in both constraint and stability by involvement than gradients where an ideology measure is involved, the slopes are very impressive in their own right.

The Zaller "Receive-Accept-Sample" Model

Zaller's (1992) "Receive-Accept-Sample" (RAS) model is a pioneering effort to grapple substantively with the long-standing riddle of response instability. Better yet, it is not merely a theoretical argument. It reflects years of empirical probes to test the suspicion that response instability stems from the ill-prepared respondent's hasty weighting, under the pressure of an interview situation, of diverse top-of-the-head "considerations" that help him arrive at a quick, impromptu answer. Such a respondent does not, in my lingo, "bring much" to the question as posed; but Zaller has shown forcefully that most respondents at least recognize the topic domain and can intelligently bring to bear some relevant substantive considerations. This model is surely more useful than the "coin-flipping" metaphor. It does not turn response instability into some marvelously new stable base for democratic theory, nor does it claim to. But it gives a more penetrating view of response instability, and it lays out a platform from which a new generation of research can proceed, gaining incisiveness with a more substantive political base.

In one sense the "considerations" view is only a small part of Zaller's contribution, however. His persistence in stratifying the electorate in terms of very disparate information conditions produces dynamic time traces of opinion formation and change that are simply brilliant and make grosser analyses of the "electorate as a whole" look so clumsy and information-concealing that one wants to demand a recount. At points Zaller skates on very thin ice: Ns diminish rapidly in tripartite stratifications, and the only solution is more funding and larger samples, which is totally contrary to the tenor of the times. But his work is a centerpiece for the contention that new advances in this field are not cost-free.

HEURISTICS

Much progressive work in this area in the past decade or so, apart from Zaller's, has been engrossed in the issue of heuristics, the mental shortcuts by which modestly informed voters can bootstrap their contribution to democratic decision making. This use of shortcuts, which Simon terms "satisficing," is of course ubiquitous, although it does not compete intellectually (Luskin 2000) with the rich contextual information that some sophisticated voters bring to their voting decisions. All of the evidence reviewed above has to do with issue voting; competing candidates offer other attractions that can be assessed with less information, such as smiles and high sincerity.

Nonetheless, much can be said about heuristics that amplify even issue voting. Fair space was given to this subject in the "Belief Systems" essay (Converse 1964). Of first importance were cues about the party background of issue options. The second heuristic emphasized the liberal-conservative dimension. Another was "ideology by proxy," whereby an ideological vote may be doubled (or n-tupled) by personal admirers of a charismatic ideologue, or other "two-step flow" effects from opinion leaders (Katz & Lazarsfeld 1955). A fourth entailed reasoning that pivots on liked or disliked population groups other than parties; this heuristic was highly prevalent in the broad middle among both US and French voters. A fifth heuristic described in the "Belief Systems" essay involved the economies of restricted attention in the issue-public sense.

In the past two decades, some of the above themes have been greatly elaborated, and so many new heuristics devised that the list begins to rival the number of human instincts posited by psychologists early in this century. Fiorina (1981) does a marvelous job documenting one prime addition, labeled "retrospective voting," whereby voters simplify decisions by focusing on how well or poorly parties or candidates have performed in the past. Sniderman et al (1991) make other clever additions, such as the "desert heuristic." Furthermore, in an area where details of reasoning are hard to observe, Sniderman et al have attempted to infer them with intricate analyses. Again, in my opinion, their best insights come from stratifying by education or political sophistication.

In some of these instances, however—retrospective voting is a good example— it is not clear whether a given habit of reasoning has its most natural home among the more or the less sophisticated. As noted above, Popkin (1994) appears to have formed his impressions of heuristics in interactions with more informed voters. Indeed, when he lists what "the voter" will try to learn next (given a few impoverished cues), the very heftiness of the list bears little relationship to the political learning behavior of three quarters of the electorate. On the other hand, short-cut reasoning is not a monopoly of the poorly informed. It is an economy of the species, and it simply takes on different scales at different levels of information. Delli Carpini & Keeter (1996) ask how high elites can store such prodigious amounts of information, and the answer is twofold: nearly constant attention, along with various elegant heuristics for organizing and digesting information, such as an ideological continuum. This answer does not deny that under various circumstances, labels such as liberal or conservative take on huge affective charges with very little bipolar content (Conover & Feldman 1981). There are superb historical examples, including the antagonism of southern whites to "liberalism" in the first decade or two after World War II, when the term had come to mean efforts to protect the rights of blacks.

Sniderman et al (1991:272) conclude that political reasoning is not some generic process; rather, because it is a compensation for lack of information about politics, it depends on the level of information diverse citizens bring to the matter. Obviously I endorse this judgment, which is close to my own argument about response instability. If one reduces the matter to sufficient abstraction, then there are versions of syllogistic reasoning, or "putting two and two together," in which differences from high elites to citizens totally unaware of politics can be reduced to absurdity. Both do it! On the other hand, if we consider the different raw materials of information brought to the situation, then reasoning will indeed assume hugely different paths across these strata.

As far as I can tell, of the many varieties of heuristics discussed these days, an ideological criterion is the only one whose natural home is not disputed. It is always found among high political elites and remains robust within the most attentive tenth to sixth of the electorate, then weakens rapidly as we look lower in the information hierarchy, despite lingering affective residues (in the Conover & Feldman sense) that have real (but attenuated) effects elsewhere. Sniderman et al (1991) try to build a new synthesis about "ideological reasoning" by noting that both cognition and affect (two antitheses) are important in politics. They decide that the Michigan view of ideology was purely cognitive; and that Conover & Feldman's view is purely affective, so a synthesis is in order. Conover & Feldman can speak for themselves. As for the Michigan version, the superstructure constituted by the basic ideological dimension is indeed cognitive. But the personally selected locations on that continuum (which positioning is, after all, the main interest) are saturated in affect. In multi-party systems, the first enemies to be liquidated are the nearest neighbors (10 points away on a 100-point scale), before the party moves on to vanquish still purer evil across the aisle. No lack of affect here, for true believers. The terms of the proposed synthesis are strained from the start.

THE ELECTORATE COLLECTIVELY

Over the years, it has become increasingly clear that electorates grade out better in issue terms when they are viewed collectively, as aggregates, rather than as the sum of individuals revealed in sample surveys (Kramer 1971, Converse 1975, Miller 1986, Converse & Pierce 1986, Wittman 1989). Various revisionist analyses under the macro label, most notably MacKuen et al (1989), profit from the clarity of aggregation as well.

The most extensive recent demonstration of such aggregation effects comes from *The Rational Public* (Page & Shapiro 1992), which mines 50 years of sample surveys for trend data on American policy preferences. Its focus is totally on the electorate taken in the aggregate. Although the original data bases had individual data, the summarized data reported here are marginal distributions of preferences either at the level of the total electorate or, in one chapter, marginal distributions within the larger population groupings defined by face-sheet data. Some featured findings have long been familiar to survey scholars. For instance, aggregate divisions of issue preferences are nearly inert over long periods of time; where short-range shifts do occur, it is usually easy to see the events that putatively touched them off; for longer-range trends, as have occurred for example in race policy, the drift is attributable to turnover of the population more than to changing convictions of the same people, although the latter does occur as well; and when changes occur, most demographic groups respond in parallel to an astounding degree, rather than the more intuitive counterpoint of conflicting interests. It is a great contribution to show how these familiar features hold up in an exhaustive long-term array of survey data on issue items.

Of course, all of these observations have to do with net change; the method conceals gross change, including principally the Brownian motion of response instability. The authors are properly aware of what is hidden and conclude that it is "just measurement error" in the Achen/Erikson sense anyway, so nothing is lost by writing it off. They are also aware that almost all individual position change observed in panel studies, which absolutely dwarfs net change, is this kind of gross change, although they sometimes describe the features of "change" in policy preferences that are conceivably appropriate for net change, but exactly wrong if gross change is taken into account. In any event, since net change is what mainly matters in most political conflict, the findings of Page & Shapiro (1992) are another stunning demonstration of the more reassuring "feel" conveyed by the aggregated electorate. The authors describe this as a transformation "from individual ignorance to collective wisdom" (1992:15).

I quarrel only with interpretation. The authors see the net change as some proof of the rationality of the public. I prefer to see this type of change more modestly as "coherent," meaning intelligibly responsive to events. This is in part because of an allergy to the undefined use of the term rational, since most formal definitions involving the maximization of *expected* utility open the door to a tautology whereby any behavior, however self-destructive, is "rational" because the actor must have envisioned the option as personally useful in some sense or he would not have chosen it. But my objection also reflects doubt about all forms of post hoc "explanation." The epitome for me is in the nightly news' explanations of why the stock market rose or fell that day. I imagine a homunculus who culls market-relevant news all day, sorting the items into two piles: bullish and bearish. Then, whatever the net market change is at the close, it is clear which pile gives the "reasons." A real test for the authors (and the homunculus) is whether they could have predicted the amount and direction of change from the events alone, without peeking at the outcome first. Particularly in the more dramatic cases, I agree with Page & Shapiro that the public has shown coherent responsiveness, although I suspect that a real test over all significant net changes would be, as for the homunculus, a pretty mixed bag. It is unlikely that all significant net changes are in some sense inspired or reassuring.

My other concern has to do with the underlying model in our heads when we are pleased by the signs of enhanced competence of electorates in the aggregate. Miller (1986) relates such improvement to Condorcet's jury theorem; others have followed suit. The Condorcet model may well reflect one force behind gains in apparent competence through aggregation. But it surely is not the most telling model. It assumes, in Bartels's words (1996), that individuals contributing to the group judgment are "modestly (and equally) well informed." This does not seem a promising gambit for diagnosing the electorate, given the staggering heterogeneity of informedness across it.

I have thought for years in terms of a rival model, that of signal-to-noise ratios as developed in communications engineering. This is much better suited to electoral heterogeneity. The noise term fits neatly with the huge amount of gross change that has a net worth of zero. Aggregation isolates a signal, large or small, above the noise. The signal, thereby isolated, will necessarily be more intelligible than the total transmission. This smacks of the black-and-white model, although it easily encompasses "true change" as part of the signal and not the noise. The fact that it is still simplistic does not make it useless as a place to start; its complexity certainly advances beyond Condorcet's "one-probability-fits-all" thought experiment. It also fits the message metaphor: Voting and political polls all have to do with messages from the grass roots. A recent, homologous model of stock market decisions that distinguishes between two classes of participants, the expert traders versus the "noise traders," has been shown to fit reality better than the assumption of homogeneous information across traders.

Page & Shapiro (1992) imply by descriptions such as "the rational public" that contributions to the actual signal of net change can come equiprobably from any stratum of the electorate. At the same time, net change in policy positions is uncommon and usually limited in magnitude when it does occur. So such change need only involve a tiny minority of the parent population. At the same time, all data show that a small minority of the population is very well informed and attentive to events. It would be too simplistic to imagine that all net change comes from the most informed, although numerically this would usually be possible. But it would surely not be surprising if a disproportion of these observed net changes did come from those more attentive at least to particular issues, if not always more generally informed. This may be a minor gloss on the Page-Shapiro message. But it does suggest that the "magic" of producing "collective wisdom" from "individual ignorance" may not be the mysterious alchemy it appears, and that there is nothing here to overturn the long-standing picture of great information heterogeneity in the electorate. The fact of collective wisdom remains, however, reassuring for democratic process.

NEW DEPARTURES

A few new research gambits share the goal of improving understanding of the sources and implications of electoral capacity. Some of these may be the research future in this field.

New Issue Measurement

I have registered my doubt that mass publics have trouble giving stable responses to conventional policy issue items simply because questions are objectively vague or poorly worded. I doubt this in part because more informed voters understand the items easily, as do elites. I doubt it also because well-run surveys conduct extensive pretesting to spot confusing terms and to reduce the policy axes to simplest common denominators. None of this rules out, however, the possibility of finding other formats for policy questions that would address issues that matter more in people's daily lives. It is unfortunate that experimentation in this direction has been limited in the past half century.

I am intrigued by the work of Shanks on a new formatting of issue items, designed to help isolate what policy mandates underpin public voting results (a major focus in Miller & Shanks 1996). Five batteries of structured questions explore governmental objectives in as many policy domains as may seem currently worthwhile. These address (a) perceptions of current conditions, (b) the seriousness of problems by domain, (c) the appropriateness of federal action in the domain, and the relative priority of rival objectives as gauged by government (d) effort and (e) spending. The main drawback of these batteries is the time they take to administer. Nonetheless, a national pilot survey was mounted during the 1996 campaign (Shanks & Strand 1998), and initial results seem to show uncommon liveliness and face validity. Judgment of these innovations would be premature; we await such tests as panel data on short-term stability of responses. I would not expect this form of measurement to erase differences between information strata in matters of issue constraint or stability, but it might shrink the gaps in some reassuring degree. In any event, the effort bears watching.

Simulation of "Higher-Quality" Electorates

For decades, political pollsters have occasionally broken out estimates of "informed opinion" on various issues, simply by discarding substantial fractions of their respondents who can be considered "ill-informed" by some general (i.e. not issue-specific) criterion. In the past few years, much more elegant ways of simulating more informed electorates have begun to appear (Bartels 1996, Althaus 1998). These gain scientific credibility by isolating informed opinion within demographic categories that presumably reflect competing interests in the political arena, thereby preserving the actual numeric weight of those categories in their final solutions rather than distorting proportions by discarding larger fractions of less informed groupings.

There are enough intricacies underlying these simulations (e.g. adjustments linear only, or reflecting nonlinearities?) to encourage a fair amount of controversy. On the other hand, early findings seem to agree that information does matter, although it undoubtedly matters much more in some situations than others, with determinants yet to be investigated. It is not surprising that differences between actual and "informed" electorates are on average more marked with respect to policy issue preferences (Althaus 1998) than when vote decisions, with their grand compounding of often simpler decision criteria, are similarly compared (as in Bartels 1996), although information clearly matters even in the latter case. These are path-breaking efforts that should inspire a wider range of work.

Deliberative Polling

Fishkin (1991) is conducting a growing series of field experiments whereby proper national samples are given standard political interviews and then are brought together at a central location for further deliberation on one or more policy issues. The procedure has varied somewhat, but in the most extensive versions, the convened sample (or as much of it as can attend) receives a range of expert opinion on the topic(s) at hand and/or competing arguments from political figures. In all cases, the plenary sample is divided randomly into much smaller discussion groups that debate the topic(s) at length. In addition to "after" measures to capture attitude change, typically at the end of the deliberations, there are sometimes longer-range follow-up measures to gauge permanence of attitude change.

These field experiments are, not surprisingly, enormously expensive. They have attracted an astonishing barrage of hostility from commercial pollsters, who apparently feel that these funds would be better used to multiply the already overwhelming number of political polls, and who are affronted by the use of the "poll" name, fearing that the public will come to think of polls as a form of manipulation. The experiments also generate staggering amounts of data, not only through their panel waves but also through the material that monitors expert messages and the dynamics of group discussions, which can be seen as a large number of replications of parallel "deliberations." Material published to date barely scratches the surface of the findings (Fishkin & Luskin 1999).

However edifying these discussions may be to their immediate participants, they are unlikely to be replicated on any large scale, especially to cover the full range of issues that are likely to be debated in any national election campaign. But their scientific interest is wide-ranging, since they deal very directly with controlled (or at least carefully monitored) manipulation of information conditions affecting issue preferences in a proper microcosm of the natural electorate. Of course this is not the first time the field has profited from smaller-scale experimentation, some of which has been much more tightly controlled and hence incisive in areas such as attitude dynamics (e.g. Lodge & Hamill 1986, Lodge & Steenbergen 1995) or political communications (Iyengar & Kinder 1987). But for those interested in ideals of preference change through increased attention on the one hand, and democratic deliberation on the other, there are intriguing new empirical vistas here to be explored.

Visit the Annual Reviews home page at www.AnnualReviews.org

LITERATURE CITED

Achen CH. 1975. Mass political attitudes and the survey response. *Am. Polit. Sci. Rev.* 69:1218–31

Althaus SL. 1998. Information effects in collective preferences. *Am. Pol. Sci. Rev.* 92:545–58

Bartels L. 1996. Uninformed voters: information effects in presidential elections. *Am. J. Polit. Sci.* 40:194–230

Brehm J. 1993. *The Phantom Respondents: Opinion Surveys and Political Representation.* Ann Arbor: Univ. Mich. Press. 266 pp.

Campbell A, Converse PE, Miller WE, Stokes DE. 1960. *The American Voter.* New York: Wiley. 573 pp.

Conover PJ, Feldman S. 1981. The origins and meaning of liberal/conservative self-identifications. *Am. J. Polit. Sci.* 25:617–45

Converse PE. 1962. Information flow and the stability of partisan attitudes. *Public Opin. Q.* 26:578–99

Converse PE. 1964. The nature of belief systems in mass publics. In *Ideology and Discontent*, ed. DE Apter, pp. 206–61. New York: Free

Converse PE. 1970. Attitudes and nonattitudes: continuation of a dialogue. In *The Quantitative Analysis of Social Problems*, ed. ER Tufte, pp. 168–89. Reading, MA: Addison-Wesley

Converse PE. 1975. Public opinion and voting behavior. In *Handbook of Political Science*, ed. FW Greenstein, NW Polsby, 4:75–169. Reading, MA: Addison-Wesley

Converse PE. 1976. *The Dynamics of Party Support: Cohort Analyzing Party Identification.* Beverly Hills, CA: Sage

Converse PE. 1990. Popular representation and the distribution of information. In *Information and Democratic Processes*, ed. JA Ferejohn, JH Kuklinski, pp. 369–88. Chicago: Univ. Ill. Press

Converse PE, Pierce R. 1986. *Political Representation in France.* Cambridge, MA: Belknap Press of Harvard Univ. Press. 996 pp.

Delli Carpini MX, Keeter S. 1996. *What Americans Know about Politics and Why It Matters.* New Haven, CT: Yale Univ. Press. 397 pp.

Downs A. 1957. *An Economic Theory of Democracy.* New York: Harper. 310 pp.

Erikson R. 1979. The SRC panel data and mass political attitudes. *Br. J. Polit. Sci.* 9:89–114

Fiorina MP. 1981. *Retrospective Voting in American National Elections.* New Haven, CT: Yale Univ. Press

Fishkin JS. 1991. *Democracy and Deliberation: New Directions for Democratic Reform.* New Haven, CT: Yale Univ. Press

Fishkin JS, Luskin RC. 1999. Bringing deliberation to the democratic dialogue. In *A Poll with a Human Face: The National Issues Convention Experiment in Political Communication,* ed. M McCombs. Mahwah, NJ: Erlbaum

Hunter JE, Coggin TD. 1976. Communication. *Am. Polit. Sci. Rev.* 70:1226–29

Iyengar S, Kinder DR. 1987. *News That Matters: Television and American Opinion.* Chicago: Univ. Chicago Press. 187 pp.

Katz E, Lazarsfeld PF. 1955. *Personal Influence: The Part Played by People in the Flow of Mass Communication.* New York: Free. 400 pp.

Kinder DR, Sanders LM. 1990. Mimicking political debate with survey questions: the case of white opinion on affirmative action for blacks. *Soc. Cogn.* 8:73–103

Kinder DR, Sears DO. 1985. Public opinion and political action. In *Handbook of Social Psychology,* ed. G Lindzey, E Aronson, pp. 659–741. New York: Random House

Kramer GH. 1971. Short-term fluctuations in U.S. voting behavior, 1896–94. *Am. Polit. Sci. Rev.* 65:131–43

Lazarsfeld PF, Berelson B, Gaudet S. 1948. *The People's Choice: How the Voter Makes Up His Mind in a Presidential Election Campaign.* New York: Columbia Univ. Press

Lodge MG, Hamill RC. 1986. A partisan schema for political information-processing. *Am. Polit. Sci. Rev.* 80:505–19

Lodge M, Steenbergen M. 1995. The responsive voter: campaign information and the dynamics of candidate evaluation. *Am. Polit. Sci. Rev.* 89:309–26.

Luskin RC. 1990. Explaining political sophistication. *Polit. Behav.* 12:331–61

Luskin RC. 2000. From denial to extenuation (and finally beyond): political sophistication and citizen performance. In *Thinking About*

Political Psychology, ed. JH Kuklinski. New York: Cambridge Univ. Press

MacKuen M, Erikson RS, Stimson JA. 1989. Macropartisanship. *Am. Polit. Sci. Rev.* 83:1125–42

Miller NR. 1986. Information, electorates, and democracy: some extensions and interpretations of the Condorcet jury theorem. In *Information Pooling and Group Decision Making,* ed. B Grofman, G Owen, pp. 173–92. Greenwich, CT: JAI

Miller WE, JM Shanks. 1996. *The New American Voter.* Cambridge, MA: Harvard Univ. Press

Neuman WR. 1986. *The Paradox of Mass Politics: Knowledge and Opinion in the American Electorate.* Cambridge, MA: Harvard Univ. Press

Norrander B. 1992. *Super Tuesday: Regional Politics and Presidential Primaries.* Lexington: Univ. Press Kentucky

Page BI, Shapiro RY. 1992. *The Rational Public.* Chicago: Univ. Chicago Press. 489 pp.

Popkin S. 1994. *The Reasoning Voter: Communication and Persuasion in Presidential Campaigns.* Chicago: Univ. Chicago Press. 2nd ed.

Shanks JM, Strand DA. 1998. *Understanding issue voting in presidential elections.* Presented at Annu. Meet. Am. Assoc. Public Opin. Res., St. Louis, MO

Sniderman PM, Brody RA, Tetlock PE. 1991. *Reasoning and Choice: Explorations in Political Psychology.* Cambridge, UK: Cambridge Univ. Press

Stimson JA. 1975. Belief systems: constraint, complexity and the 1972 elections. In *Controversies in American Voting Behavior,* ed. RD Niemi, H Weisberg, pp. 138–59. San Francisco: Freeman

Wittman DA. 1989. Why democracies produce efficient results. *J. Polit. Econ.* 97:1395–424

Zaller J. 1992. *The Nature and Origin of Mass Opinion.* Cambridge, UK: Cambridge Univ. Press. 367 pp.

Annu. Rev. Polit. Sci. 2000. 3:355–77

Unions In Decline? What Has Changed and Why

Michael Wallerstein

*Department of Political Science, Northwestern University, Evanston, Illinois
60208-1006; e-mail: m-wallerstein@nwu.edu*

Bruce Western

*Department of Sociology, Princeton University, Princeton, New Jersey 08540;
e-mail: western@princeton.edu*

Key Words   collective bargaining, industrial relations, wage setting

■ **Abstract**   Between 1950 and 1980, labor markets grew increasingly organized in advanced industrial societies. Union membership in most countries expanded more rapidly than the labor force, centralized wage setting became more common, and union members became increasingly concentrated in a small number of large unions. Between 1980 and 1992, however, union density fell on average, and centralized wage setting grew increasingly rare. Only union concentration continued to increase in the 1980s. Existing theories of union organization and collective bargaining institutions are largely successful in explaining both the trends over time and much of the cross-national variation from 1950 to 1980, but they fail to account for the dramatic declines in union strength that some (but not all) countries have experienced since 1980.

INTRODUCTION

Unions are in big trouble, as everyone knows. Under attack by conservative politicians, battered by overseas competition, threatened by capital flight, bewildered by changes in the nature of work, and shackled by an outmoded egalitarian ideology, unions increasingly appear like large but aging dinosaurs struggling to adapt as the climate changes. The proportion of workers who belong to unions is in decline. Centralized systems of wage-setting are breaking apart. Incentive pay schemes and profit-sharing arrangements subvert negotiated wage scales. Wage inequality is growing while the median wage stagnates. Past achievements are under attack as European governments blame "labor market rigidities," i.e. the legal and contractual protections that current workers enjoy, for persistently high unemployment. Even the unions' traditional political allies, the social democratic and labor parties, are keeping their distance, having discovered that being too closely tied to the unions is a political liability.

As is usually the case, what everyone knows to be true is not completely wrong but not completely right either. In this paper, we aim to describe, as precisely as the data allow, what is and is not known about the changing terrain of industrial relations in advanced industrial societies in the postwar period. We survey the empirical research that seeks to explain cross-national and longitudinal variation in union organization and wage-setting procedures. We do not attempt to provide country-by-country descriptions.[1] Instead, we emphasize the patterns of change and stability in key aspects of labor organizations and wage-setting institutions across the major member countries of the Organisation for Economic Co-operation and Development (OECD). Although there is great interest in changes that have occurred in the recent past, the lags in data collection are such that we are forced to end our study in 1992.

Unions are heterogeneous institutions. The extent to which union-negotiated agreements determine the pay received by union members and by nonmembers, the participation of unions in aspects of the employment relation other than pay, and the involvement of unions in labor training and policy making vary across countries, across time, and frequently across industries within countries. Moreover, the sources of union power are equally heterogeneous across time and place. Unions, to varying degrees in different countries and different time periods, have become able to influence the terms of employment by threatening work stoppages, by participating in governmental bodies with statutory authority, by obtaining political support in parliament, and by offering employers services that employers value.

Within a short essay, we cannot hope to cover the full range of differences among unions as organizations. Instead, we concentrate on the core activity of unions in all advanced industrial societies, which is to represent workers in negotiations with employers concerning pay. We begin with a discussion of the share of the work force that belongs to unions and the share of the work force whose wages are covered by collective agreements. We discuss the extent to which wage setting is centralized through collective bargaining practices or through political intervention. We discuss the trend in union concentration. Each of these sections describes the fundamental facts concerning both cross-national variation and change over time. In addition, we summarize the evidence concerning the causal mechanisms that best explain the differences and changes that the data reveal. The essay concludes with a brief discussion of the impact of changes in union organization and wage-setting institutions on equality and economic performance.

---

[1] Several edited collections provide complementary overviews of the literature. Golden & Pontusson (1992), Kitschelt et al (1999), and Iversen et al (1999) all contain a mixture of case studies and quantitative studies of unions and collective bargaining in advanced industrial societies. Ferner & Hyman (1998 [1992]) contains an excellent set of country-by-country descriptions of industrial relations in Western Europe.

UNION DENSITY AND COVERAGE

To analyze cross-national variation in union organization, we follow Bain & Price (1980:2), who define a union as "an organization of employees which seeks to represent the job interests of its members to employers and in some circumstances to the state, but which is not dominated by either of them." This definition conveys the main idea of a voluntary organization of employees whose chief purpose is collective bargaining over wages and working conditions. Unions can then be distinguished from professional associations, such as the American Medical Association. Professional associations, though they do represent members' "job interests," generally include significant numbers of self-employed professionals in private practice. The Bain & Price definition excludes professional associations from union membership counts but includes organizations of credentialed wage earners such as teachers, nurses, or social workers.

The extent of union organization is typically measured by union density. Union density expresses the number of union members as a percentage of the number of people who could potentially be union members. This potential constituency usually includes all wage and salary earners and sometimes the unemployed. A distinction can be drawn between gross density statistics that count unemployed and retired members, and net density statistics that include employed union members only. Union members are defined as persons whom the unions count as members. In the case of employed workers, this is equivalent to persons who pay union dues.

Table 1 summarizes trends in gross union density through the postwar period for a group of 18 OECD countries (see also Visser 1991). The table shows three distinct patterns of variation. First, three groups of countries differ in their general level of unionization. Belgium, Denmark, Finland, and Sweden share very high unionization rates. By 1992, the total number of union members in these four countries nearly equalled or exceeded the total number of wage and salary earners. A large, heterogeneous group of countries unionized between a third and two thirds of their national labor markets. At the bottom of the scale, a group of six low-density countries organized less than a third of the work force in 1992.

Second, unionization in the industrialized democracies steadily diverged over the three decades from 1950. This divergence is reflected in the increasing standard deviation reported in Table 1. At the beginning of the postwar period, union density varied in a small band between about 30% and 60%. Unions—and industrial relations institutions more generally—showed much greater variation 30 years later, when the gap between the most and least organized countries had increased to 70 percentage points.

Third, the pattern of divergence in unionization that describes most of the postwar period was replaced by a convergent pattern of union decline during the 1980s. Although the average level of unionization dropped just three points between 1980 and 1992, some countries suffered spectacular declines. Falling unionization was especially severe in the English-speaking countries. Union density fell by 20 points in New Zealand, by 15 points in the United Kingdom, by

TABLE 1   Union density and labor market institutions[a]

	Density 1950	Density 1980	Density 1992	Level[b] 1965– 1992	Left[c] 1965– 1992	Ghent[d]	Coverage[e] 1990
High-density countries							
Belgium	36.9	76.6	80.5	0.50	0.23	Yes	90
Denmark	58.2	86.2	91.6	0.78	0.43	Yes	74
Finland	33.1	85.8	111.4	0.63	0.48	Yes	95
Sweden	62.1	89.5	111.3	0.85	0.73	Yes	83
Middle-density countries							
Australia	56.0	52.4	39.6	0.68	0.40	No	80
Austria	62.2	65.3	53.2	0.33	0.72	No	71
Canada	26.3	36.1	37.0	0.11	0.67	No	38
Germany	36.2	41.3	41.2	0.33	0.40	No	76
Ireland	38.6	63.4	53.5	0.54	0.15	No	
Italy	47.4	60.5	68.0	0.77	0.18	No	83
New Zealand	49.4	46.0	25.9	0.62	0.34	No	
Norway	53.8	65.3	67.7	0.91	0.56	No	75
UK	45.1	56.3	41.3	0.33	0.35	No	47
Low-density countries							
France	30.9	19.7	9.4	0.33	0.31	No	92
Japan	46.2	31.2	24.5	0.33	0.00	No	21
Netherlands	36.2	39.9	31.0	0.63	0.18	No	60
Switzerland	40.1	34.5	30.0	0.33	0.29	No	43
US	28.4	24.9	15.3	0.07	0.26	No	18
Mean	43.7	54.2	51.8	0.51	0.37		65.4
S.D.	11.4	21.5	30.7	0.25	0.20		24.7

[a]Union density taken from Visser's [1992 (unpublished), 1996] gross density series. Figures sometimes exceed 100 in 1992 because gross density here is defined on all wage and salary earners whereas union membership data include the retired and unemployed.

[b]Level is the 1965–1992 average level of collective bargaining, rescaled to vary from zero to one, measured by the scale of Golden et al (1999).

[c]Left is the 1965–1992 average of the proportion of cabinet seats held by left parties (see Western & Healy 1999).

[d]Ghent indicates countries with Ghent systems of unemployment insurance.

[e]Coverage refers to the share of workers covered by a collective bargaining agreement in 1990, taken from Traxler's (1994) unadjusted series.

12 points in Australia, and by 10 points in Ireland and the United States. Among non–English-speaking countries, Austria, France, and the Netherlands also suffered large declines in unionization. Out of all the industrialized democracies surveyed, only Finland and Sweden enjoyed strong union density growth through the 1980s.

Explanations of unionization should be able to account for these three patterns of union density variation. The dominant account of cross-sectional variation has emphasized the impact of labor market and state institutions (e.g. Visser & Ebbinghaus 1999, Western 1997, Rothstein 1989). The effects of leftist parties in government, collective bargaining centralization, and union-controlled unemployment insurance have received detailed empirical treatment. Labor and social democratic parties have been instrumental in expanding union rights and lowering the cost of unionization. In particular, leftist governments significantly facilitated public sector unionization in the 1950s and 1960s. In contrast, conservative parties have actively resisted unions through labor legislation and in industrial relations. Centralized collective bargaining is claimed to raise unionization by extending union agreements to nonunion workplaces, thereby defusing employer opposition to the expansion of union membership. Centralized union confederations also restrict interunion competition and coordinate organizing efforts among union affiliates. Finally, unions play a significant role in the distribution of unemployment benefits in the four high-density countries. The Ghent system, in which unemployment insurance is administered by the unions, enables union officials to protect union rates from competition from the unemployed through their discretion in the determination of the conditions under which unemployment becomes "involuntary" (Rothstein 1989). In addition, the Ghent system keeps workers in contact with their union during spells of joblessness.

Measures of leftist government, bargaining centralization, and the Ghent system are reported in Table 1. Bargaining level represents an index (described in more detail in the next section) of the extent to which wages are set at the level of the plant, the industry, or the economy as a whole. Leftist parties include socialist, social democratic, and labor parties, as well as the Liberal and New Democratic Parties in Canada and the Democratic party in the United States. Regressing 1992 union density on these two institutional variables and a dummy variable for the presence of a Ghent system yields the following estimates:

$$\text{Density} = 7.58 + 43.1 \text{ Level} + 31.9 \text{ Left} + 45.8 \text{ Ghent},$$
$$(0.8) \quad (3.1) \qquad (2.0) \qquad (5.5)$$

where t statistics are in parentheses, and $R^2 = 0.85$. This simple cross-sectional regression shows a close association between union organization and labor market and state institutions. The estimates indicate that a difference of about 40 points in union density is explained by the difference between national and local-level collective bargaining. About a quarter of the 85-point difference in union density between Sweden in Japan is attributed to variation in the electoral success of social democratic and socialist parties. In addition, Ghent system countries enjoy, on average, close to a 50-point advantage in unionization.

Although institutional conditions can explain cross-sectional variation in unionization, time-series variables are needed to explain divergence in union growth and union decline in the 1980s. The leading longitudinal explanation claims that workers convert market power into collective action in response to fluctuating economic conditions. In this business cycle account, poor economic conditions weaken labor's market power and increase employer resistance to unions. A strong economy improves labor's hand by increasing the benefits of collective action and lowering employer opposition. Operationally, the business cycle theory has taken many different forms, but the impact of two variables stands out. Union membership is positively related to inflation but negatively associated with unemployment. Relatively strong inflation and unemployment effects were reported in a large econometric literature that covered union membership trends in Australia, Canada, Sweden, the United Kingdom, and the United States (Hines 1964, Ashenfelter & Pencavel 1969, Sharpe 1971, Swindinsky 1974; also see the reviews of Bain & Elsheikh 1976:26–57 and Hirsch & Addison 1986:52–56).

Despite reasonable empirical results, the business cycle approach takes a thin view of labor movements. The key agents—workers and employers—respond to exogenously shifting market conditions. This approach discounts active efforts by workers to construct shared interests through mobilization. The strategic role of unions is also bracketed from analysis. In contrast to the business cycle approach, other researchers have focused on the mobilizing efforts of militant workers and unions. The role of worker militancy as a source of union growth was developed and largely abandoned by economists but rehabilitated by political sociologists. Dunlop's (1949) work on the early development of US unions associated spurts in labor movement growth with periods of intense strike activity. According to this analysis, the strike waves of the 1890s and the 1930s were critical moments. Comparative researchers observed that unions grew rapidly in the wake of strike waves, not only in the United States of the 1930s, but also in Sweden in the 1910s, in Italy after 1969, and in France for most of the twentieth century (Korpi 1978:211–12, Regalia et al 1978, Tilly 1986:369). In this political theory, strike activity raises unionization by mobilizing workers around a collective project. In some cases, strikes are explicitly intended to obtain union recognition and rights to collective bargaining (Griffin et al 1990:179).

The organizing problem of the union has been studied by examining effects of labor-force size and growth (Wallerstein 1989, 1991). In this perspective, the benefits of unionization depend on the proportion of the work force organized, but the cost of organization to the union depends on the absolute number of new union members recruited. As a result, the optimal level of unionization for the union falls as the size of the labor force increases. Although this idea was originally examined in a cross-sectional sample of 20 industrialized democracies, strong results were also found in time-series analysis (Western 1997:119). Estimates indicate that the union organizing task is more difficult when the labor force is growing quickly (Western 1997:119).

Longitudinal and institutional explanations can be combined in models that treat time-series effects as conditional on time-invariant institutional conditions. In this approach, institutions not only raise or retard unionization but also affect the strategic calculations of unions and the impact of labor market competition. Western (1997) followed a hierarchical approach in which he estimated

TABLE 2   Effects of labor market institutions on times series coefficients*

Time series coefficients	Intercept	Level	Ghent
Unemployment	−0.17	0.16	0.04
	(−0.21, −0.13)	(0.08, 0.24)	(−0.05, 0.12)
Strike volume	0.19	−0.12	−0.02
	(0.11, 0.27)	(−0.24, 0.00)	(−0.13, 0.09)
Leftist government	0.33	−0.28	−0.17
	(0.10, 0.56)	(−0.64, 0.16)	(−0.75, 0.39)

*The parentheses contain the 80% confidence intervals. The first row in the table gives the estimates obtained from the regression $b_{ui} = \gamma_{u0} + \gamma_{u1}\text{level}_i + \gamma_{u2}\text{Ghent}_i + \text{error}_{ui}$, where b_{ui} is the estimated coefficient for unemployment in country i derived from the regression of the change in union density on a constant, inflation, unemployment, strike volume, labor force growth, and leftist government. A similar procedure was followed for the coefficient on strike volume and leftist government. See Western (1997:109–21) for additional details. The coefficients for *level* differ from Table 7.3 in Western (1997:116) due to a rescaling of *level* so that it varies between zero and one as in Table 1.

country-specific coefficients in a time-series model of annual change in density for the period 1950–1985. Longitudinal predictors in this model included inflation, unemployment, strike activity, the growth of the dependent labor force, and leftist-party participation in government. The country-specific, time-series coefficients were assumed to depend on a measure of centralized bargaining and a dummy variable for the Ghent system of unemployment insurance. Table 2 reports Western's results, describing how the level of bargaining and the Ghent system affect the impact of unemployment, strikes, and leftist government on density.

Data from only 18 countries in a highly parameterized model with error at both the micro and macro levels yield only modest statistical precision. Nevertheless, the point estimates indicate that the effects of labor market institutions on the relationship between union growth and the economic environment may be substantial. Consider first the impact of unemployment on union density. According to the estimates in Table 2, the impact of unemployment on the annual change in union density is strongly negative in a country, such as the United States, that has decentralized bargaining (level ≈ 0) and a government-run system of unemployment insurance (Ghent = 0). In contrast, in such countries as Sweden or Denmark, with centralized bargaining (level ≈ 0.8) and a union-run system of unemployment (Ghent = 1), the rate of unemployment has almost no impact on the growth of union density [−0.17 + (0.16)(0.8) + 0.04 ≈ 0]. The key intuition of business cycle explanations ties the fortunes of labor movements to the fortunes of the economy, with unions growing when labor markets are tight and declining when labor markets are slack. The estimates reported in Table 2 (as well as in Pedersen 1982 and Freeman 1989) suggest that unions can maintain their memberships and even grow during periods of high unemployment when bargaining is centralized and unions administer the system of unemployment insurance.

Table 2 shows important institutional effects on the impact of industrial conflict and the partisan composition of government as well. In decentralized countries without the Ghent system, union growth is substantially higher when the volume of strikes is high. In countries with centralized bargaining, the volume of strikes is much less important for union growth. When bargaining is centralized, strikes frequently represent protests against wage restraint imposed by centralized agreements negotiated by the top union leadership. Finally, the partisan composition of government can have a large impact on union growth in countries with decentralized bargaining, where employers have a strong incentive to resist unions. With centralized bargaining, employers have less reason to resist unions, since the wages of union members and nonmembers are the same (Freeman 1989) and election results have little impact on union growth or decline. In sum, the vulnerability of unions to periods of high unemployment or government by parties with ties to business depends on the set of labor market institutions that unions and employers have established to regulate and moderate their conflicts.

To study the decline of union density in the 1980s, Western (1997:ch. 9) used the hierarchical model of union growth to form forecasts for the period 1974–1989. Where union density decline was modest—as in Canada, Norway, or Sweden—trends in unionization in the 1970s and 1980s were predicted accurately. The performance of the model for the healthier labor movements suggested a continuity in the statistical regime of union growth from the 1960s to the post–oil shock period. However, using information from the 1950s and 1960s provided little leverage on the major falls in union density of the 1980s. Where declining unionization was dramatic (as in the Netherlands, France, the United Kingdom, or Ireland), the model fared poorly. The declines in unionization are much larger than we would predict given the historical pattern of union growth in the 1950s and 1960s.

The failure of standard models to predict the large declines of union organization that occurred in a significant number of countries in the 1980s suggests that a new causal process may be driving the disorganization of labor markets in the industrialized democracies. Two explanations have been studied in some detail. First, a number of researchers have related union decline to declining employment in manufacturing industries (Bell 1973:137–42, Troy 1990, Visser 1991). However, the changing occupational structure does not fare well as an explanation of union decline. First, the timing is wrong. The employment share of secondary industries in OECD countries fell at about the same rate in the 1970s as in the 1980s, but unions generally grew in the 1970s and declined only in the later decade. Second, industry-level membership figures reveal large declines of union density within manufacturing in countries with large declines of union density overall (Western 1997:154). A successful account of contemporary deunionization must explain falling union density within industries where unions have traditionally been strong.

The second approach to union density decline has emphasized changes in the political and institutional environment. Howell (1995) emphasizes the importance of the Thatcher governments' labor law reforms in explaining the sharp decline of union membership in the United Kingdom between 1980 and 1992. Western (1997:ch. 11) examined the year with the greatest acceleration of decline in union density since the mid-1970s. Western found that the acceleration of decline was more likely to occur when the left had suffered an electoral defeat and when bargaining was decentralized. Such studies are suggestive, but we are still some distance from having an empirical model that can adequately account for the cross-national and longitudinal variation in union density since the mid-1970s.

A decline in the proportion of workers who belong to unions is not the same thing as a decline in the proportion of workers covered by union contracts. The last column of Table 1 displays the share of the work force who were covered by union contracts in 1990. In such countries as the United States, Canada, Japan, and the United Kingdom, the coverage of union contracts is roughly equivalent to the share of the work force who belong to unions. In English-speaking countries, apart from Australia, and in Japan, coverage has declined as density has fallen. In Australia and on the European continent, however, union contracts frequently cover far more workers than belong to unions. If countries are weighted by the size of their labor forces, the average density in Australia and continental Europe was 46.4 in 1990. The weighted average coverage rate for the same set of countries in the same year was 79.9. Outside of the United States, Japan, Canada, and the United Kingdom, four out of five workers are covered by a union contract, although less than half of the work force belongs to unions. Moreover, the share of workers covered by collective agreements remained roughly constant in continental Europe between 1980 and 1990 (Traxler 1994), even in countries where union density declined significantly.

The reasons for the difference between coverage and density are varied. In all countries, union and nonunion members who work side by side in the same plant receive the same wage. (Closed and union shops are rare in Europe. Thus, most plants have less than 100% union membership.) In Germany, the majority of workers are employed by members of an employers' confederation. In Austria, membership of employers in the relevant employers' confederation is mandated by law. In both Germany and Austria, the terms of wage agreements negotiated between a union and an industry-level employers' association are binding on all firms that belong to the employers' association, whether or not their workers belong to the union.[2] In France, Belgium and, to a lesser extent, the Netherlands, union-negotiated contracts are regularly extended by government act to cover all workers in the industry.

Falling union density is a major problem for unions, even when coverage remains high. A high level of coverage says little about the unions' financial health

---

[2] The dependence of coverage on employers' membership in the employers' association gives unions an important stake in the organizational health of employers' associations. See Thelen (1999) for a discussion of the depth of union concern in Germany with the declining organizational strength of German employers.

or ability to mobilize supporters in a conflict with employers. Yet, the high levels of coverage in Europe, outside of the United Kingdom, indicate that collective bargaining has declined much less than union membership has. In spite of the significant decline in union membership in some countries, the large majority of workers in Western Europe continue to work under conditions governed by a collective bargaining agreement.

THE CENTRALIZATION OF WAGE SETTING

Collective bargaining always entails a centralization of wage setting relative to a purely competitive labor market. At the very least, workers' pay and other aspects of employment are decided at the level of the plant or company when pay is covered by a collective agreement. However, pay may be decided at much higher levels. In most advanced industrial societies (albeit not in the United States, Canada, and the United Kingdom), a majority of workers are covered by multi-employer agreements negotiated at the level of the industry. In a few countries, multi-industry agreements covering the entire private sector have been the norm for substantial periods of time.

Why is the level of centralization important? The dominant understanding of the impact of the level of bargaining is as follows.[3] If wages are set at the plant or company level, unionization enables workers to obtain a share of the extra profit, or rents, that some firms enjoy by having lower costs than their competitors. If the product market is competitive, however, workers' possible wage gains are limited by the firm's inability to cover higher labor costs with higher prices. With purely local bargaining, collective bargaining changes the distribution of the firm-specific rents between workers on the one hand and management and shareholders on the other, but otherwise it has a limited impact on economic performance.

If unions set wages at the industry level, however, workers can raise wages throughout the industry. (The presence of foreign competition changes the argument, as discussed below.) If all firms in the industry face higher wage costs, the price of output is forced up. In effect, industry-level wage setters can exert monopoly power in the product market in a closed economy, with union members receiving monopoly profits in the form of higher wages. Employers may also benefit from industry-level bargaining, relative to local bargaining, since their ability to partially cover the higher wages with price increases lessens the negative impact of wage gains on profits. But now, there may be significant losses for groups who are not represented at the bargaining table. Wage increases that lead to price increases reduce the real income of workers in other industries. In addition, since higher prices imply lower sales and less employment, wage increases hurt workers who

---

[3]See Moene et al (1993) and Calmfors (1993) for surveys of the theoretical literature on the impact of centralized wage setting on economic performance. See Flanagan (1999) for a survey of the empirical literature.

are priced out of a job and hurt taxpayers who pay for the unemployment benefits received by workers who have been laid off. In sum, industry-level wage setting stands accused of allowing the externalization of the costs of higher wages and of generating an inefficient allocation of resources.

If, however, unions and employers centralize wage setting so that wages throughout the economy are set simultaneously, the wage agreement will be neutral with regard to relative prices. Workers' ability to exert monopoly power disappears. In other words, national wage setters internalize many of the externalities of industry-level wage setting, and thus, the theory goes, they would choose outcomes as efficient as decentralized bargaining (Calmfors & Driffill 1988). Moreover, if the central wage agreement contains an industrial peace obligation, i.e. a prohibition on strikes once the central agreement is signed and ratified, workers in low-cost firms are unable to obtain a share of firm-specific rents, as they could with local bargaining. Thus, fully centralized bargaining with an industrial peace obligation may result in the best possible outcome for employers, short of having no unions at all. However, since the determination of the wage distribution becomes an explicitly political decision with highly centralized wage setting, centralization may unleash forces that employers cannot control.

Whether or not centralized bargaining has a desirable impact on profits, wages, and aggregate economic performance is a subject of continuing controversy that we return to in the conclusion. In this section, our primary concern is to describe how centralization has changed during the postwar period. Table 3 presents data on the centralization of private-sector wage setting in 16 countries during 1950–1992. The main variable in the table is the country's score on a four-category scale of the level of wage setting. The four categories are (*a*) predominantly local or company-level wage bargaining, (*b*) predominantly industry-level wage bargaining, (*c*) national-level wage bargaining without an industrial peace obligation, and (*d*) national-level wage setting with an industrial peace obligation.

Wages can be centralized in two basic ways. The first is via direct negotiations between peak associations of unions and employers. The second is via government intervention. The scale of the level of wage setting combines both, but confederal involvement and government intervention can be examined separately. At the bottom of the table, we list the average scores on an 11-category scale of confederal involvement and a 15-category scale of government intervention.[4] The 16 countries have been coded on all three scales on an annual basis. The table reports the average scores during various time periods.

---

[4]Descriptions of the categories can be found in Wallerstein (1999) or in Golden et al (1999). Two limitations of the data should be noted. The first is that the data cover changes in wage-setting institutions in the private sector only. Wage setting in the public sector is usually organized differently. The other limitation is that the data refer only to wage setting, which may be centralized while other aspects of the employment relation that are covered by collective agreements are decided at the level of the firm or plant.

TABLE 3 The centralization of wage setting*

	1950–1959	1960–1972	1973–1981	1982–1992
Australia	0.67	0.67	0.67	0.70
Austria	0.47	0.33	0.33	0.33
Belgium	0.33	0.33	0.50	0.64
Canada	0.00	0.00	0.38	0.00
Denmark	1.00	1.00	0.92	0.52
Finland	0.73	0.74	0.63	0.58
France	0.33	0.36	0.33	0.33
Germany	0.33	0.33	0.33	0.33
Italy	0.67	0.67	0.67	0.88
Japan	0.00	0.24	0.33	0.33
Netherlands	1.00	0.81	0.79	0.48
Norway	0.87	0.95	0.96	0.82
Sweden	0.73	1.00	1.00	0.64
Switzerland	0.33	0.33	0.33	0.33
UK	0.00	0.40	0.50	0.00
US	0.00	0.14	0.00	0.00
Mean	0.47	0.52	0.54	0.43
S.D.	0.36	0.32	0.28	0.28
Confederal involvement				
Mean	0.30	0.35	0.32	0.26
S.D.	0.31	0.32	0.30	0.26
Government involvement				
Mean	0.30	0.33	0.39	0.31
S.D.	0.28	0.21	0.24	0.20

*The country data represent the scores on a four-category scale of the level or bargaining, described in the text. The confederal involvement and government involvement data represent the average scores on scales of confederal participation in wage setting and parliamentary participation in (private-sector) wage setting, respectively. All data have been scaled to vary between zero and one. The raw values for the three scales are taken from Golden et al (1999).

On average, the level of wage setting increased from the 1950s to the 1960s and increased again from the 1960s to the 1970s. After 1981, however, the average level of centralization has declined. Particularly sharp declines in centralization occurred in four of the 16 countries: Denmark, the Netherlands, Sweden, and the United Kingdom. However, not all countries moved in the same direction. In Belgium and in Italy, for example, the average level of wage setting was higher between 1982 and 1992 than at any earlier time in the postwar period. Overall, the estimated change in centralization from the 1970s to the 1980s is only −0.11 on the four-point scale—a marginally significant difference. Thus, without further analysis, the data provide some support for the argument that wage setting has become increasingly decentralized since the early 1980s (Lash & Urry 1987, Katz 1993, Katz & Darbishire 1999), and those who emphasize, instead, the continuing diversity of national experiences (Hyman 1994, Traxler 1995, Wallerstein et al 1997, Wallerstein & Golden 1997).

There is an interesting distinction between centralization via confederal involvement and centralization via parliamentary act. Whereas the average level of confederal involvement in wage setting was highest in the "Golden Age" from 1960 through 1973, government involvement increased sharply in the period between the two oil shocks. The initial response of many governments to the first appearance of rising unemployment and rising inflation was to seek greater control over the rate of wage increases. After 1982, however, both confederal and government involvement in wage setting declined significantly.

There are three approaches to explaining both the pattern of cross-national variation and change over time. The first approach might be labeled micro-Marxism. In the micro-Marxist approach, scholars have sought to explain the rise and decline of centralized bargaining institutions as the results of changes in technology and the organization of production. Ingham (1974) argued that centralized bargaining institutions arose in countries, such as Sweden, where industrialization was late and rapid. The consequence of rapid industrialization, according to Ingham, was a relative similarity of production methods and working conditions across factories and industries that made centralized bargaining feasible. Piore & Sabel (1984) and Pontusson (1991) emphasize the association of the establishment of centralized wage setting with the growth of "Fordist" methods of production, in which large numbers of workers are doing similar tasks.

The recent decline in centralized bargaining, according to the micro-Marxist approach, stems from the changes in technology and the organization of production that require greater flexibility and/or differentiation of work and terms of employment. Katz (1993), Streeck (1993), Pontusson & Swenson (1996), and Iversen (1996) argue that the rise of "diversified quality production" and "flexible specialization" necessitates greater differentiation of pay and a stronger connection between individual or team performance and rewards than centralized wage setting allows. A related explanation spotlights changes in the occupational structure. Hernes (1991) and Moene & Wallerstein (1993), for example, argue that the proliferation of small and highly specialized groups of workers with extraordinary market power had a destabilizing impact on the centralized bargaining systems in the Nordic countries.

The second broad approach to explaining the rise and decline of centralization focuses on the impact of international trade. Our discussion of the impact of centralization on collective bargaining outcomes rested on the assumption of a closed economy. In a small open economy, however, the prices of traded goods are independent of domestic wage costs. Thus, industry-level bargaining advantages workers in the sheltered sector relative to workers in the traded-goods sector. As a consequence, workers and employers in the traded-goods sector may form an alliance to centralize bargaining in order to restrain wage increases in sectors that do not face international competition. This, in brief, is Swenson's (1989, 1991) explanation of the establishment of centralized wage-setting institutions in Sweden and Denmark. Katzenstein's (1983, 1985) argument that centralized wage-setting institutions arise in small open economies as an adaptation to the risks associated with international openness has a similar flavor.

If the Nordic countries and the Low Countries adopted centralized bargaining institutions because of their high levels of trade dependence, it appears paradoxical that centralization is declining as economic openness increases. Wood (1994), Leamer (1993), Rodrik (1996), and McKeown (1999) offer a resolution of the paradox by arguing that increased international competition from rapidly industrializing developing countries, a new phenomenon, has reduced the demand for unskilled and semiskilled workers in advanced industrial societies while increasing the demand for their more skilled counterparts. To the extent that centralized wage setting prevents wages from falling at the bottom of the labor market, the argument goes, employers and governments increasingly seek decentralized alternatives. Although most observers argue that trade with the Third World has weakened unions relative to employers in recent years, Thelen (1999) makes the interesting argument that increasing international competition has weakened employers' associations most of all. As Thelen points out, centralized wage setting requires that both sides of the employment relationship are sufficiently organized to bargain collectively. If employers' associations collapse, so will centralized bargaining.

In yet another twist on the argument that globalization leads to decentralization, Lange et al (1995), Garrett & Way (1995), and Iversen (1996) point out that the unionized work force may be less dependent on trade today than in the early postwar period. Because productivity gains in the traded-goods sector outrun productivity gains in the sheltered sector, the share of workers who face international competition has declined even as the value of trade as a share of gross domestic product has increased. In particular, the share of union members who work in the public sector has grown in almost all countries. According to this line of argument, centralized institutions received widespread support among both unions and employers in the Nordic countries when the union movement was dominated by workers in the traded-goods sector. As sheltered-sector unions grew in size and influence in Northern Europe, the ability of employers in the traded-goods sector to restrain the wages of sheltered-sector workers through centralized bargaining declined. Whereas centralized wage setting functioned to restrain wages of sheltered-sector workers in the early postwar period, now employers seek to achieve the same goal of wage restraint through decentralization.

A third approach views centralization as a response to macroeconomic difficulties. In this argument, countries centralize wage setting to restrain wage growth in pursuit of greater price stability or lower unemployment (Headey 1970, Flanagan et al 1983, Martin 1984, Streeck & Schmitter 1991). The argument is transparent

TABLE 4   Ordered probit analysis of the level of wage setting[a]

Independent variable	Estimated coefficient	t-statistic	Mean of independent variable
Lagged dependent variable	1.29	14.1	0.688
Industry[b]	0.599	3.08	0.792
Authority[c]	0.424	6.79	0.794
Concentration[d]	−4.70	3.00	0.088
1982–1992[e]	−0.524	3.04	0.256
Lagged unemployment[f]	7.28	2.71	0.039
Lagged inflation[g]	2.43	1.70	0.052
First cut	1.752		
Second cut	3.010		
Log-likelihood index[h]	0.53		

[a]Dependent variable is a three-category scale of the level of wage setting as described in the text, with assigned values of one, two, and three. There are 630 observations (15 countries, 1950–1992). The countries are the same as in Table 3.

[b]Industry is a dummy variable equal to one if industry-level bargaining predominates in the absence of centralization.

[c]Authority is an index of the statutory authority of the employers' confederation.

[d]Concentration is the Herfindahl index described in Table 5.

[e]1982–1992 is a dummy variable equal to one for 1982–1992.

[f]Unemployment from the OECD. All other variables are from the Golden et al (1999) data set.

[g]Inflation data indicate the proportional change in the CPI from the Summers & Heston (1991) data set.

[h]Log-likelihood index is $1-(LL/LL_0)$, where LL is the log likelihood of the model and LL_0 is the log likelihood when the only independent variable is a constant.

when wage setting is centralized through the adoption of incomes policies. Even in the absence of incomes policies, unions and employers may adopt central-ized negotiations in order to collectively reduce wage growth in the face of high unemployment.

The view of centralization as a solution to macroeconomic problems receives support from the ordered probit regression reported in Table 4. Since we lack systematic data on the shift from industry-level bargaining to plant-level bargaining in the United States and United Kingdom, the dependent variable in Table 4 is a tripartite scale where the lowest level of centralization is either plant- or industry-level bargaining, the middle level represents national wage setting without an industrial peace obligation, and the highest level represents national wage setting with an industrial peace obligation. The independent variables are (a) the lagged dependent variable, (b) a dummy variable indicating whether industry-level or plant-level wage setting predominates when wage setting is not centralized at the national level, (c) an index of the statutory authority of the peak association for employers (described below), (d) the Herfindahl index of union concentration (described below), (e) a dummy variable for the period 1982–1992, (f) the rate of inflation from year t-1 to year t, and (g) the rate of unemployment in year t-1.

Countries are more likely to centralize wage setting when wage setting was centralized in the previous year. Countries in which industry-level bargaining predominates when not centralized are more likely to centralize wage setting than countries in which plant-level bargaining predominates. It is also not surprising that centralized wage setting is more likely to be adopted in countries in which the employer's peak association has substantial statutory authority over affiliated firms. The index of statutory authority is a threefold scale based on (a) whether the employers' confederation has veto power over wage contracts signed by members, (b) whether the employers' confederation can veto lockouts by members, and (c) whether the employers' confederation has its own conflict funds. It is interesting to note that the parallel index for the union confederation did not fit the data as well. The authority of the employers' confederation over its members appears to be more important for the success of centralized wage setting than the authority of the union confederation over its members. This could indicate that the employers are usually the driving force behind centralization, as Swenson (1991) argues, or that employers face a more severe collective action problem than unions do, as Thelen (1999) argues. The Herfindahl index is a measure of the extent to which the union movement is dominated by a small number of large unions, described below. The negative coefficient on union concentration may imply that centralization and concentration are substitutes. Countries with high levels of concentration, such as Germany and Switzerland, have less need for centralized procedures to coordinate wage setting.

The negative coefficient for the dummy variable for the period 1982–1992 implies a substantial decline in the likelihood of centralization after 1982. Before 1982, the probability of adopting centralized wage setting, with or without an industrial peace obligation, for a country at the mean of all of the other independent variables was estimated to be 0.48.[5] After 1982, the probability of adopting a centralized wage-setting procedure dropped to 0.28 (holding the other independent variables constant at their mean). The estimated impact of an increase in the unemployment rate of one percentage point, when all other variables are at their mean, is to increase the probability of centralization by three percentage points.

---

[5]The likelihood that a country adopts a decentralized system of wage setting in year t is $\Pr(\beta'x + u < \mu_1) = \Pr(u < \mu_1 - \beta'x) = \Phi(\mu_1 - \beta'x)$, where β is the vector of coefficients, x is the vector of independent variables for country i in year t, μ_1 is the first cut point, and $\Phi(\cdot)$ is the cumulative density function for the standard normal distribution. Thus, if all independent variables other than the dummy for 1982–1992 take their mean values, $\bar{x}$, we have $\Phi(\mu_1 - \beta'\bar{x}) \approx \Phi(0.055) \approx 0.52$ before 1982 and $\Phi(\mu_1 - \beta'\bar{x}) \approx \Phi(0.579) \approx 0.72$ after 1982. To calculate the impact of a marginal change in a variable x_i, we use $\partial\Phi(\mu_1 - \beta'\bar{x})/\partial x = -\beta\phi(\mu_1 - \beta'\bar{x})$. For unemployment, assuming all other independent variables take their mean values, we have $\beta\phi(\mu_1 - \beta'\bar{x}) \approx -(7.28)(0.398)$ before 1982 and $-\beta\phi(\mu_1 - \beta'\bar{x}) \approx -(7.28)(0.337)$ after 1982. In either case, the marginal impact of an increase in unemployment of 0.01 is to reduce the likelihood of decentralized wage setting by 0.03. The marginal impact of a change in inflation is calculated in a similar fashion.

Thus, if unemployment increased from 4% to 5% before 1982, and all other independent variables are at their mean, the probability that a country will adopt a moderately or highly centralized system of wage setting is estimated to increase from 0.48 to 0.51. An increase in inflation is estimated to have about one third the impact of an increase in unemployment. In other words, a three-percentage-point increase in the rate of inflation is estimated to have the same impact as a one-percentage-point increase in the rate of unemployment. Supplementary regression (not shown) revealed that measures of trade openness (imports plus exports over gross domestic product), size (the number of wage and salary earners), and the partisan composition of government (leftist-party participation in government) do not have significant effects on the likelihood of centralized wage setting after controlling for the variables in Table 4.

In sum, macroeconomic difficulties, in particular rising unemployment and rising inflation, are important determinants of the adoption of centralized systems of wage setting. Other explanations, however, are not necessarily wrong. There has been a significant decline in the reliance on systems of centralized wage setting to reduce unemployment since 1981. Whether that change is a consequence of changes in the organization of production, of increased international competition, or of a political shift to the right by social democratic as well as conservative parties is anybody's guess.

UNION CONCENTRATION

Even in the absence of centralized bargaining, industry-level unions may coordinate their demands and employers' associations may coordinate their responses. Alternatively, a union, such as the German metal workers, may act as the wage leader and negotiate a contract that is then copied in the other industries. If the German metal workers and metal-working employers understand that their contract will be copied by all, the result may be similar to what would be achieved by fully centralized bargaining [though Wallerstein's (1990) model demonstrates that the result with a wage leader may be very different from fully centralized bargaining]. Thus, Golden (1993) argues that centralization may be less important than concentration, where concentration refers to the extent to which union members are concentrated in a few large unions, as opposed to being divided into a large number of smaller organizations. If the number of actors is small enough, coordination of wage setting is likely whether or not wages are explicitly set in a centralized manner.[6] More recently, increasing concentration among unions in the English-speaking countries may capture an alternative dynamic in which unions

---

[6]Concentration might be measured between confederations (the degree to which union members belong to a single confederation) or within confederations (the degree to which union members belong to the same unions within the confederation). Since concentration between confederations is uncorrelated with all other measures of concentration and centralization (Golden & Londregan 1998), we focus on concentration within confederations.

TABLE 5 Herfindahl index of union concentration*

	1950–1959	1960–1972	1973–1981	1982–1992
Australia	0.014	0.018	0.019	0.017
Austria	0.088	0.099	0.103	0.105
Belgium	0.101	0.098	0.104	0.095
Canada	0.041	0.024	0.030	0.047
Denmark	0.148	0.130	0.123	0.118
Finland	0.062	0.088	0.068	0.076
Germany	0.120	0.144	0.159	0.158
Italy	0.097	0.075	0.073	0.073
Japan	0.111	0.089	0.097	0.078
Netherlands	0.108	0.115	0.181	0.157
Norway	0.045	0.055	0.079	0.114
Sweden	0.056	0.081	0.114	0.136
Switzerland	0.156	0.169	0.177	0.180
UK	0.046	0.050	0.053	0.046
US	0.025	0.018	0.019	0.025
Mean	0.081	0.084	0.093	0.095
S.D.	0.044	0.045	0.052	0.050

*Entries represent the average Herfindahl index for within-confederal concentration during the time period at the head of the column. The approximation formula is described in the text. In countries with more than one major blue-collar confederation, the data refer to the average weighted by each confederation's membership. Data are from the Golden et al (1999) data set. The raw data are available at five-year intervals. Missing values were added by linear interpolation.

merge to expand membership in a context where new organization has stalled (Chaison 1996).

To see how concentration has changed over time, we use the Herfindahl concentration index, defined as $H = \sum_{i=1}^{n} S_i^2$, where S_i is the share of confederal membership in the ith largest affiliate and n is the total number of affiliates in the confederation. The Herfindahl index represents the probability that two confederation members who are selected at random would belong to the same affiliate. Since we have membership data only for the three largest affiliates and for the total number of affiliates, we approximated the Herfindahl index using the formula $H^* = S_1^2 + S_2^2 + S_3^2 + (n-3)S_4^2$, where $S_4 = (1 - S_1 - S_2 - S_3)/(n-3)$. Table 5 presents the approximate Herfindahl indices for the main blue-collar confederations of 15 countries during the postwar period. In countries with more than one blue-collar confederation, we used a weighted average of the Herfindahl indices for each confederation, weighting each confederation by its relative size in terms of membership.

Within confederations, there is a trend toward greater concentration over time, as Windmuller (1981) observed almost 20 years ago. The mean Herfindahl index has increased steadily since 1950, although the change over time is small relative to the cross-national differences. Norway, Sweden, and the Netherlands show the largest increase in the Herfindahl index. If we measured concentration by the number of affiliates of the blue-collar confederations, Britain and the United States would show the largest increases in concentration (Golden et al 1999). For example, the British Trades Union Congress had 186 affiliates in 1950 and only 76 affiliates in 1990. In fact, the only countries whose number of affiliates has not declined over the postwar period are those whose number of affiliates was already small in 1950.

CONCLUSION

From 1950 to the 1970s, the average levels of union density, union concentration, and the centralization of wage setting were all increasing among advanced industrial societies. In spite of the diversity of national experiences, the general pattern is one in which the labor market was becoming increasingly organized and regulated. Since the early 1980s, however, most indicators of union strength and centralized wage setting have declined on average. Average density has declined since 1980 to a limited extent if each country is weighted equally. If countries are weighted in proportion to the size of their labor force, however, the fall in density is large. The decline in centralization, if judged from the raw figures, is not large. Controlling for macroeconomic conditions and the partisan composition of government, however, the likelihood of centralized wage setting declined sharply in the 1980s. The main exception to the trend toward greater decentralization is the steady but small increase in union concentration. Increased concentration, however, may reflect pressures to merge operations in the face of declining membership.

Does it matter whether union membership is falling and wage setting is becoming less centralized? The effect on equality is large. The more decentralized the system of wage setting, the more unequal the distribution of wages and salaries (Freeman 1988; Blau & Kahn 1996; D Rueda, J Pontusson, unpublished manuscript; Wallerstein 1999). Wallerstein (1999), for example, finds that the index of the centralization of wage setting, the Herfindahl index of concentration and union density, explains most of the cross-national and longitudinal variance in wage inequality among advanced industrial societies since 1980. But whether high levels of union density and centralized wage-setting institutions are associated with high or low unemployment is no clearer today than when Bruno & Sachs published the first systematic study of the question in 1985 [see, for example, the recent exchange between Siebert (1997) and Nickell (1997) on the causes of unemployment in Europe]. Part of the difficulty is that wage-setting institutions are only part of the institutional environment that may be relevant for macroeconomic performance. Lange and Garrett argued that what matters is not the centralization of wage setting but the interaction between the centralization of wage setting and the partisan composition of government (Lange & Garrett 1985, Garrett & Lange 1986, Garrett 1998). Hall (1994), Hall & Franzese (1998), Iversen (1998), and Soskice & Iversen (2000) argue that what matters is the interaction of the centralization of wage setting and the independence of the central bank. The number of countries is small enough that the number of interaction terms soon overwhelms the data. (Combining longitudinal and cross-national variation in pooled time series analyses does not help as much as might be expected, since there is strong dependence over time in the unemployment rate.)

Table 4 points to a different difficulty. If systems of centralized wage-setting are adopted, in part, as a response to macroeconomic difficulties, the system of wage setting is endogenous (as argued by Flanagan 1999). In order to estimate the impact of wage-setting institutions on macroeconomic performance, we need to simultaneously estimate the impact of macroeconomic performance on the choice of wage-setting institutions. Clearly, to jointly estimate the choice of wage-setting institutions and the impact of wage-setting institutions is a difficult task given the limited data available. But empirical studies of the impact of wage-setting institutions on macroeconomic performance that treat wage-setting institutions as exogenous, i.e. virtually all existing studies, are attempting to draw inferences from biased estimates. In spite of the large literature on economic performance and labor market institutions, we still know little about the magnitude of the tradeoff between equality and economic performance, or even whether a tradeoff exists.

ACKNOWLEDGMENTS

We thank Ernesto Calvo and Jomy Joseph Alappattu for research assistance. Financial assistance was provided by the National Science Foundation (SBR-9809014) and the Russell Sage Foundation. We thank Kathleen Thelen for helpful comments.

Visit the Annual Reviews home page at www.AnnualReviews.org

LITERATURE CITED

Ashenfelter O, Pencavel JH. 1969. American trade union growth: 1900–1960. *Q. J. Econ.* 83:434–48

Bain GS, Elsheikh F. 1976. *Union Growth and the Business Cycle.* Oxford, UK: Blackwell

Bain GS, Price R. 1980. *Profiles of Union Growth: A Comparative Statistical Portrait of Eight Countries.* Oxford, UK: Blackwell

Bell D. 1973. *The Coming of Post-Industrial Society: A Venture in Social Forecasting.* New York: Basic Books

Blau FD, Kahn LM. 1996. International differences in male wage inequality: institutions versus market forces. *J. Polit. Econ.* 104:791–837

Bruno M, Sachs J. 1985. *The Economics of Worldwide Stagflation.* Cambridge, MA: Harvard Univ. Press

Calmfors L. 1993. Centralization of wage bargaining and macroeconomic performance: a survey. *OECD Econ. Stud.* 21:161–91

Calmfors L, Driffill J. 1988. Bargaining structure, corporatism and macroeconomic performance. *Econ. Policy* 3:13–61

Chaison GN. 1996. *Union Mergers in Hard Times.* Ithaca, NY: Cornell Univ. Press

Dunlop JT. 1949. The development of labor organizations: a theoretical framework. In *Insights into Labor Issues,* ed. R Lester, J Shister, pp. 163–93. New York: Macmillan

Ferner A, Hyman R, eds. 1998 (1992). *Industrial Relations in the New Europe*. Oxford, UK: Blackwell. 2nd ed.

Flanagan RJ. 1999. Macroeconomic performance and collective bargaining: an international perspective. *J. Econ. Lit.* 37:1150–75

Flanagan RJ, Soskice DW, Ulman L. 1983. *Unionism, Economic Stabilization and Incomes Policies: European Experience*. Washington, DC: Brookings Inst.

Freeman RB. 1988. Labour market institutions and economic performance. *Econ. Policy* 3:64–80

Freeman RB. 1989. *On the divergence in unionism in developed countries. NBER Work. Pap. No. 2817*. Cambridge, MA: Nat. Bur. Econ. Res.

Garrett G. 1998. *Partisan Politics in the Global Economy*. Cambridge, UK: Cambridge Univ. Press

Garrett G, Lange P. 1986. Economic growth in capitalist democracies, 1974–1982. *World Polit.* 38:517–45

Garrett G, Way C. 1995. The sectoral composition of trade unions, corporatism and economic performance. In *Monetary and Fiscal Policy in an Integrated Europe*, ed. B Eichengreen, J Frieden, J von Hagen, pp. 38–61. Berlin: Springer

Golden M. 1993. The dynamics of trade unionism and national economic performance. *Am. Polit. Sci. Rev.* 87:439–54

Golden M, Lange P, Wallerstein M. 1999. *Dataset on Unions, Employers, Collective Bargaining and Industrial Relations for 16 OECD Countries*. http://www.shelley.polisci.ucla.edu/data

Golden M, Londregan J. 1998. *Globalization and industrial relations*. Presented at Annu. Meet. Am. Polit. Sci. Assoc., Boston, MA, Sept. 3–6

Golden M, Pontusson J, eds. 1992. *Bargaining for Change: Union Politics in North America and Europe*. Ithaca, NY: Cornell Univ. Press

Griffin LJ, McCammon HJ, Botsko C. 1990. The "unmaking" of a movement? The crisis

of US trade unions in comparative perspective. In *Change in Societal Institutions*, ed. M Hallinan, D Klein, J Glass, pp. 109–94. New York: Plenum

Hall P. 1994. Central bank independence and coordinated wage-setting: their interaction in Germany and in Europe. *Ger. Polit. Soc.* 31:1–23

Hall P, Franzese R. 1998. Mixed signals: central bank independence, coordinated wage-bargaining and European monetary union. *Int. Org.* 52:505–35

Headey BW. 1970. Trade unions and national wages policies. *J. Polit.* 32:407–39

Hernes G. 1991. The dilemmas of social democracies: the case of Norway and Sweden. *Acta Sociol.* 34:239–60

Hines AG. 1964. Trade unions and wage inflation in the United Kingdom 1948–1962: a disaggregated study. *Econ. J.* 79:66–89

Hirsch BT, Addison JT. 1986. *The Economic Analysis of Unions: New Approaches and Evidence*. London: Allen & Unwin

Howell C. 1995. Trade unions and the state: a critique of British industrial relations. *Polit. Soc.* 23:149–83

Hyman R. 1994. Industrial relations in Western Europe: an era of ambiguity? *Ind. Relat.* 33:1–24

Ingham G. 1974. *Strikes and Industrial Conflict: Britain and Scandinavia*. London: Macmillan

Iversen T. 1996. Power, flexibility and the breakdown of centralized wage bargaining: the cases of Denmark and Sweden in comparative perspective. *Comp. Polit.* 28:399–436

Iversen T. 1998. Wage bargaining, hard money and economic performance: theory and evidence for organized market economies. *Br. J. Polit. Sci.* 28:31–61

Iversen T, Pontusson J, Soskice D, eds. 1999. *Unions, Employers and Central Banks: Wage Bargaining and Macroeconomic Policy in an Integrating Europe*. Cambridge, UK: Cambridge Univ. Press

Katz HC. 1993. The decentralization of collective bargaining: a literature review and comparative analysis. *Ind. Labor Relat. Rev.* 47(1):3–22

Katz HC, Darbishire O. 1999. *Converging Divergences: Worldwide Changes in Employment Systems.* Ithaca, NY: Cornell Univ. Press

Katzenstein P. 1983. The small European states in the international economy: economic dependence and corporatist politics. In *The Antinomies of Interdependence*, ed. JR Ruggie, pp. 91–130. New York: Columbia Univ. Press

Katzenstein P. 1985. *Small States in World Markets: Industrial Policy in Europe.* Ithaca, NY: Cornell Univ. Press

Kitschelt H, Lange P, Marks G, Stephens JD, eds. 1999. *Continuity and Change in Contemporary Capitalism.* Cambridge, UK: Cambridge Univ. Press

Korpi W. 1978. *The Working Class in Welfare Capitalism.* London: Routledge

Lange P, Garrett G. 1985. The politics of growth. *J. Polit.* 47:792–827

Lange P, Wallerstein M, Golden M. 1995. The end of corporatism? Wage setting in the Nordic and Germanic countries. In *Workers of Nations: Industrial Relations in a Global Economy*, ed. S Jacoby, pp. 76–100. Oxford, UK: Oxford Univ. Press

Lash S, Urry J. 1987. *The End of Organized Capitalism.* Oxford, UK: Polity

Leamer E. 1993. Wage effects of a US–Mexican free trade agreement. In *The Mexico–US Free Trade Agreement*, ed. PM Garber, pp. 57–125. Cambridge, MA: MIT Press

Martin A. 1984. Trade unions in Sweden: strategic responses to change and crisis. In *Unions and Economic Crisis: Britain, West Germany and Sweden*, P Gourevitch, A Martin, G Ross, S Bornstein, A Markovits, C Allen, pp. 190–359. London: Allen & Unwin

McKeown T. 1999. The global economy, post-Fordism and trade policy in advanced capitalist states. In *Continuity and Change in Contemporary Capitalism*, ed. H Kitschelt, P Lange, G Marks, JD Stephens, pp. 11–35. Cambridge, UK: Cambridge Univ. Press

Moene KO, Wallerstein M. 1993. What's wrong with social democracy? In *Market Socialism: The Current Debate*, ed. P Bardhan, J Roemer, pp. 219–35. Oxford, UK: Oxford Univ. Press

Moene KO, Wallerstein M, Hoel M. 1993. Bargaining structure and economic performance. In *Trade Union Behavior, Pay Bargaining and Economic Performance*, RJ Flanagan, KO Moene, M Wallerstein, pp. 63–154. Oxford, UK: Oxford Univ. Press

Nickell S. 1997. Unemployment and labor market rigidities: Europe versus North America. *J. Econ. Persp.* 11(3):55–74

Pedersen PJ. 1982. Union growth in Denmark 1911–39. *Scand. J. Econ.* 84:583–92

Piore M, Sabel C. 1984. *The Second Divide: Possibilities for Prosperity.* New York: Basic Books

Pontusson J. 1991. *Fordism and social democracy: towards a comparative analysis.* Presented at Annu. Meet. Am. Polit. Sci. Assoc., Washington, DC, Aug. 29–Sept. 1

Pontusson J, Swenson P. 1996. Labor markets, production strategies, and wage bargaining institutions: the Swedish employer offensive in comparative perspective. *Comp. Polit. Stud.* 29(2):223–50

Regalia I, Regini M, Reyneri E. 1978. Labour conflicts and industrial relations in Italy. In *The Resurgence of Class Conflict in Western Europe Since 1968*, ed. C Crouch, A Pizzorno, 1:101–58. London: Macmillan

Rodrik D. 1996. *Globalization and labor, or: If globalization is a bowl of cherries, why are there so many glum faces around the table?* Presented at CEPR Conf. Regional Integration, La Coru, Spain, April 26–27

Rothstein BO. 1989. Marxism, institutional analysis and working-class power. *Polit. Soc.* 18:317–46

Sharpe IG. 1971. The growth of Australian trade unions: 1907–1969. *J. Ind. Relat.* 13:144–62

Siebert H. 1997. Labor market rigidities: at the root of unemployment in Europe. *J. Econ. Persp.* 11(3):37–54

Soskice D, Iversen T. 2000. The non-neutrality

of monetary policy with large price or wage setters. *Q. J. Econ.* 115: In press

Streeck W. 1993. The rise and decline of neo-corporatism. In *Labor and an Integrated Europe*, ed. L Ulman, B Eichengreen, WT Dickens, pp. 80–101. Washington, DC: Brookings Inst.

Streeck W, Schmitter PC. 1991. From national corporatism to transnational pluralism: organized interests in the single European market. *Polit. Soc.* 19(2):133–64

Summers R, Heston A. 1991. The Penn World Table (Mark 5): an expanded set of international comparisons, 1950–1988. *Q. J. Econ.* 106:327–68

Swenson P. 1989. *Fair Shares: Unions, Pay and Politics in Sweden and West Germany.* Ithaca, NY: Cornell Univ. Press

Swenson P. 1991. Bringing capital back in, or social democracy reconsidered. *World Polit.* 43(4):513–44

Swindinsky R. 1974. Trade union growth in Canada, 1911–1970. *Relat. Ind.* 29:435–51

Thelen K. 1999. Why German employers cannot bring themselves to dismantle the German model. In *Unions, Employers and Central Banks: Wage Bargaining and Macroeconomic Policy in an Integrating Europe*, ed. T Iversen, J Pontusson, D Soskice, pp. 138–169. Cambridge, UK: Cambridge Univ. Press

Tilly C. 1986. *The Contentious French.* Cambridge, UK: Belknap

Traxler F. 1994. Collective bargaining: levels and coverage. *OECD Employment Outlook* July:167–94

Traxler F. 1995. Farewell to labor market associations? Organized versus disorganized decentralization as a map for industrial relations. In *Organized Industrial Relations in Europe: What Future?*, ed. C Crouch, F Traxler, pp. 3–19. Aldershot, UK: Avebury

Troy L. 1990. Is the U.S. unique in the decline of private sector unionism? *J. Labor Res.* 11:111–43

Visser J. 1991. Trends in trade union membership. *OECD Employment Outlook* July:97–134

Visser J. 1996. Unionisation trends revisited. CESAR Res. Pap. 1996/2. Cent. Res. Eur. Soc. Ind. Relat., Amsterdam

Visser J, Ebbinghaus B. 1999. When institutions matter. *Eur. Sociol. Rev.*

Wallerstein M. 1989. Union organization in advanced industrial democracies. *Am. Polit. Sci. Rev.* 83:481–501

Wallerstein M. 1990. Centralized bargaining and wage restraint. *Am. J. Polit. Sci.* 34:982–1004

Wallerstein M. 1991. Industrial concentration, country size and union membership: response to Stephens. *Am. Polit. Sci. Rev.* 85:949–53

Wallerstein M. 1999. Wage-setting institutions and pay inequality in advanced industrial societies. *Am. J. Polit. Sci.* 43:649–80

Wallerstein M, Golden M. 1997. The fragmentation of the bargaining society: wage-setting in the Nordic countries, 1950–1992. *Comp. Polit. Stud.* 30(6):699–731

Wallerstein M, Golden M, Lange P. 1997. Unions, employers associations and wage-setting institutions in North and Central Europe, 1950–1992. *Ind. Labor Relat. Rev.* 50(3):379–401

Western B. 1997. *Between Class and Market: Postwar Unionization in the Capitalist Democracies.* Princeton, NJ: Princeton Univ. Press

Western B, Healy K. 1999. Explaining the OECD wage slowdown: recession or labor decline. *Eur. Sociol. Rev.* 15:233–49

Windmuller JP. 1981. Concentration trends in union structure: an international comparison. *Ind. Labor Relat. Rev.* 35:43–57

Wood A. 1994. *North-South Trade, Employment and Inequality.* Oxford, UK: Clarendon

Annu. Rev. Polit. Sci. 2000. 3:379–400

THE BRITISH CONSTITUTION: Labour's Constitutional Revolution

Robert Hazell[1] and David Sinclair[2]

[1]Constitution Unit, School of Public Policy, University College London,
29 Tavistock Square, London WC1H 9EZ, United Kingdom; e-mail: r.hazell@ucl.ac.uk
[2]McKinsey & Co., 1 Jermyn Street, London SW1, United Kingdom;
e-mail: david_sinclair@mckinsey.com

Key Words United Kingdom, constitutional reform, devolution, quasi-federalism

■ **Abstract** The Labour government elected in the United Kingdom in May 1997 has embarked on the country's biggest ever program of constitutional change. This chapter sets out the main constitutional measures adopted so far and identifies further changes that will need to follow in order to accommodate these early changes. The new constitutional architecture in the United Kingdom is a form of quasifederalism in which new institutions will have to be created to rebalance the political center if the Union is to hold together.

INTRODUCTION

Since its election in May 1997, the United Kingdom's Labour government has embarked on what Prime Minister Tony Blair, speaking to his party's conference in 1994, described as "the biggest program of change to democracy ever proposed." In its long first parliamentary session, the new government introduced 11 constitutional bills that on their own would transform Britain's constitution. Although each is discussed separately below, we first consider them together, to demonstrate the scale of the government's achievement. There were six devolution bills: first the referendum bills for Scotland, Wales, and later London; then the three main devolution bills for Scotland, Wales, and Northern Ireland; and finally a bill to establish Regional Development Agencies as a possible first step toward regional government in England. Two of the bills stemmed from the European Union: one to implement the Amsterdam Treaty, the other to introduce a proportional voting system for elections to the European Parliament. There was also a bill to register political parties, a side effect of introducing proportional representation; and last, but by no means least, there was a bill to incorporate the European Convention on Human Rights (ECHR).

Eleven constitutional bills in one session has to be a parliamentary record. The government's policy White Paper *Scotland's Parliament* (Scottish Office 1997) described these as "the most ambitious and far reaching changes in the British constitution undertaken by any government this century," and for once, it was not hyperbole. Four of the changes are really big: the Human Rights Bill and the three devolution bills to Scotland, Wales, and Northern Ireland. When these changes have had time to bed down, the United Kingdom will be transformed in a manner that will startle many of the ministers involved in putting these changes through. As one Whitehall insider observed, "Most senior Ministers involved in constitutional reform either don't believe in it, aren't interested in it or don't understand it" (quoted by Hennessy 1998). Blair is reported to have said in private discussions during the 1998 Party conference that the constitution was a "year one" issue—having legislated for it, the government can now move on.

However, the pace of reform has hardly slackened in the second session, with six constitutional bills coming before Parliament. The bill to introduce a proportional election system for elections to the European Parliament was reintroduced at the start of the session. It received its royal assent on January 14, 1999 after the House of Lords rejected it for an unprecedented sixth time, and the government invoked the Parliament Acts for only the second time since 1949. The Greater London Authority Bill will establish an elected authority for London, and the House of Lords Bill will remove the right of most hereditary peers to vote. The government has also introduced three draft bills: one on cabinet systems and elected mayors for local government, one on freedom of information, and one on controls on party funding.

These are very big constitutional changes whose impact will be greater than the sum of the individual parts (Hazell 1998). A highly centralized system of government is being replaced by a form of quasifederalism. This and other changes will lead to more checks and balances on the UK executive; parliamentary sovereignty is likely to be further eroded; there will be tighter rule of law, with a shift of power to the courts; and the British majoritarian, two-party system will be replaced by more pluralist forms of democracy.

DEVOLUTION AND DECENTRALIZATION

The previous Labour leader, John Smith, used to describe devolution as unfinished business from the Labour government of the 1970s. That government struggled for the whole of the 1974–1979 Parliament to get its devolution legislation onto the statute book. It eventually succeeded in the Scotland Act 1978 and the Wales Act 1978, only to see both measures fail in the referendums of March 1979. In Wales, the government's proposals were rejected by four to one.

Labour entered government in 1997 with two commitments that harked back to this bitter experience. The first was to legislate for devolution to Scotland and Wales in the very first year of a new Labour government. The second was to hold referendums before, and not after, introducing the devolution legislation. The Referendums (Scotland and Wales) Act 1997 therefore was introduced as the first bill of the new Parliament, guillotined, and passed unamended by the House of Commons after only two days in Committee on the floor of the House. The Act authorized the government to hold referendums asking the people of Scotland and Wales whether they approved of the devolution plans to be set out in respective White Papers. Scottish voters were asked, in addition, whether the Scottish Parliament should be able to vary the basic rate of income tax by up to three pence in the pound.

The White Papers on devolution were published at the end of July 1997, and the Scottish referendum was held on September 11. Of the 60% who voted, 74% supported the creation of a Scottish Parliament and 63% supported tax-varying powers for that Parliament. Two weeks later, the government's proposals for devolution in Wales were endorsed in the Welsh referendum, but only by a wafer-thin margin. On a turnout of 50.1%, only 50.3% voted in favor of a Welsh Assembly and 49.7% voted against it. The opposition could say that only one voter in four had supported the government's proposals for a Welsh Assembly; but once they had these verdicts, ministers repeatedly cited the endorsement of the people as a reason to disregard opposition concerns about the devolution bills. This approach had been foreshadowed in the government's manifesto: "Popular endorsement will strengthen the legitimacy of our proposals and speed their passage through Parliament."

The New Scottish Parliament

The major difference from the devolution legislation of the 1970s is that the Scotland Act 1998 does not specify the powers devolved to the Scottish Parliament. The 1978 Act included a schedule defining the powers of the Scottish Assembly in the smallest detail, and it gave the Secretary of State extensive power to intervene. The 1998 Act is a far more confident and generous measure. Following the model of the Government of Ireland Act 1920, the 1998 Act simply lists the powers reserved by Westminster, with all the remainder devolved to Edinburgh (Himsworth & Munro 1999). The reserved powers are limited to the constitution, foreign policy, defense and national security, immigration and nationality, macroeconomic, monetary, and fiscal policy, regulation of markets, employment and social security, and transport safety and regulation. In the new quasifederal system that is emerging, these are the matters reserved to the center. Devolved to Scotland are matters of health, education and training, local government, social work and housing, economic development and transport, civil law, criminal law, police and prisons, the environment, agriculture, forestry and fishing, sport, and the arts. These are very significant devolved powers; they constitute a sphere of legislative action comparable to that enjoyed by a state or province in a federal system. The only difference is that the Scottish Parliament cannot amend its own constitution as laid down in the Scotland Act; the parliament will continue to operate under the umbrella of Westminster sovereignty.

The government's large majority, and the authority it had gained through the referendum endorsement, meant that the bill emerged largely unscathed from the legislative process—another big difference from the 1970s (Bogdanor 1999). But Members of Parliament (MPs) and peers expressed concern about a number of areas, which may foreshadow future difficulties. One was over the future reduction in the size of the Scottish Parliament. It will start with 129 members: 73 constituency members, based on the existing Westminster constituencies, and 56 additional members from eight regional lists to ensure proportionality. But in recognition of Scotland's current overrepresentation at Westminster, the Scotland Act provides for the number of Scottish MPs to be revised in line with the electoral quota for England at the time of the next Parliamentary Boundary Commission review. It will mean a reduction from 72 to ~57 MPs. What has not been generally noticed are the knock-on consequences for the Scottish Parliament. There will be a corresponding reduction of 15 constituency Members of the Scottish Parliament, and a parallel reduction in the additional members. As a consequence, the Scottish Parliament is set to shrink at the end of its second term in 2007 from 129 to just over 100 members. Liberal Democrat amendments in the House of Lords sought to avert this consequence but were reversed in the House of Commons.

A further difference from the 1970s is the electoral system. In place of the majoritarian first-past-the-post, which would have helped to ensure Labour dominance, the government was persuaded by the Liberal Democrats and others to adopt a proportional voting system based on the additional member system used in Germany. Critics objected to the principle of the additional member system (largely because it involves creating two classes of Members of the Scottish Parliament) and to the details of the government's version. Particularly controversial was the choice of closed lists (i.e. voters vote for a party rather than a candidate) over open lists for the additional members drawn from the regional lists. The government was also criticized for its failure to provide, as many had hoped it would, for the Scottish Parliament to be composed of equal numbers of men and women.

The financial settlement was also criticized as inadequate and unsustainable. The government proposes to maintain the Barnett formula, a hangover from the previous Labour government's attempt at devolution, to determine changes in annual spending in Scotland (Kay 1998). The application of the formula has resulted in public expenditure in Scotland being ~25% higher than public spending in England. Because Scotland is now the third wealthiest region in Great Britain, English MPs in particular suggested that this could be a flashpoint for future conflict. Scottish MPs sought guarantees to protect future levels of public spending and complained that were the UK government unilaterally to revise the Barnett formula, Scotland would have little redress, because the Scottish Parliament would lack the power to summon UK Treasury ministers to explain their decision.

No devolution debate would be complete without Tam Dalyell, now MP for Linlithgow, raising the West Lothian Question, which was named in his honor after his former constituency. Simply put, the question asks why Scottish MPs at Westminster should have the right to vote on English matters when English MPs will no longer be able to vote on Scottish matters. Dalyell himself announced that he would no longer vote on English issues once the new parliament was up and running. The question was generally less prominent than it had been in the 1970s. But at the wider level, the West Lothian Question will not go away, because it is essentially a question about fairness—fairness in representation, in the distribution of public spending, in the sharing of political power. If in time the English regions feel that they are losing out because of Scotland's louder political voice and more generous levels of public spending, there will be strong pressures to redress the imbalance. Indeed, this pressure is already evident. In a speech to the Centre for Policy Studies in July 1999, opposition leader William Hague called for new parliamentary procedures to ensure that measures affecting England should only be voted on by English MPs.

A final area of concern was representation in Europe. This is bound to be a difficult issue, as it is in other European countries with a federal or regional system of government. The European Union will loom large for the Scottish Parliament because it is in precisely those areas where power has been devolved that so much legislation now comes from Brussels, namely economic development, agriculture and fisheries, the environment, training, and enterprise. The UK government held to the line that it is the United Kingdom, not Scotland, that is the member state of the European Union, and although Scottish ministers may be invited along as part of the UK delegation (e.g. on fishing), the role of Scottish ministers and officials will be to advance the single UK negotiating line. This will not prevent the Scots from lobbying the European Commission and the other member states, and the new Scottish government will open an office in Brussels just as regional governments from other European countries have done.

The first elections for the Scottish Parliament were held on May 6, 1999. On a turnout of 58%, Labour won 53% of the constituency seats and three of the top-up seats. The Scottish National Party (SNP) won 35 seats, 28 of which were top-up seats; the Conservatives won 18 seats, and the Liberal Democrats won 17. Donald Dewar was sworn in by the Queen as First Minister in Scotland on May 17. After a week of negotiations with the Liberal Democrats, he formed a coalition government of nine Labour and two Liberal Democrat ministers with 11 deputy ministers (including two more Liberal Democrats). Coalition government is a novel experience in the United Kingdom in the second half of the twentieth century, although it is not unknown from earlier years.

The coalition agreement between the parties was set out in a 20-page document entitled *Partnership for Scotland* (Dewar & Wallace 1999). The greatest stumbling block was student tuition fees, which the Liberal Democrats had pledged to eliminate in their election manifesto (as had the SNP and the Conservatives). The issue has been referred to an independent review body. But whereas Liberal Democrat backbenchers believe they will be allowed a free vote on the issue, Labour believes both parliamentary groups should support the decision of the coalition government. Failure to resolve this could bring down the coalition. The other key issue is proportional representation for local government, already being considered by the McIntosh Commission on local government reform. The coalition agreement states, "We will ensure that publication of the final McIntosh recommendations is followed by an immediate programme of change, including progress on electoral reform."

The Welsh Assembly

The Welsh Assembly set up under the Government of Wales Act 1998 is smaller and weaker than its Scottish cousin. It has just 60 members: 40 constituency members, elected from existing Westminster constituencies, and 20 additional members to provide a measure of proportionality. The Assembly has executive power and powers of secondary legislation only, operating within a framework of primary legislation laid down by Westminster and entirely dependent on Westminster for its annual block grant.

This model of executive devolution stems from continuing doubts within the Wales Labour Party about the merits of devolution. The party was deeply divided in the 1970s, when the "Gang of Six" Welsh Labour MPs (including Neil Kinnock) campaigned against their own government's proposals in the referendum. These divisions continued into the 1990s, and Labour's policy represents the most that Labour's Secretary of State for Wales, Ron Davies, could get his Welsh Labour colleagues to agree to.

This painfully constructed compromise represents little change from the Wales Act 1978, save in two respects. First, just before the election in March 1997, the Wales Labour Party agreed to a proportional voting system in order to make the Assembly more inclusive and less dominated by Labour (Welsh Labour Party 1997). Second, during the passage of the bill, the government moved amendments to substitute a cabinet system in place of a local government committee structure, so that executive power will now be vested in an identifiable executive (whose members will be known as Assembly Secretaries).

Despite these changes, questions have been raised about the durability of the Welsh model of executive devolution (Hazell 1996, Rawlings 1998). In particular, the Assembly will be dependent on the degree of discretion conferred by the Westminster Parliament. A well-intentioned Westminster might delegate broad powers, but sometimes Parliament will leave little or no room for local discretion or choice. Welsh legislation will have to take its chances each year in the long queue of measures put forward by Whitehall departments, only one quarter of which find space in Westminster's legislative program. Without legislative power, the Welsh Assembly will be unable to get around the Westminster logjam. It will be dependent on the legislation passed at Westminster and prepared by Whitehall, where the government will have a different agenda and other priorities. An Assembly with only executive powers risks incurring the worst of both worlds. It will create high hopes in Wales of independent action, which the Assembly may not be able to achieve, and it will be a permanent supplicant in Whitehall, leading to continuous tension between London and Cardiff.

But aside from these intrinsic difficulties there will be powerful external factors at work. The Scottish Parliament and the Northern Ireland Assembly will both have significant legislative power. The opposition parties in Wales will be able to point to their achievements and to contrast them with the subordinate position of the Assembly in Wales. It might be different if there were some quid pro quo that the leader of the Assembly could point to as an advantage of remaining tied to Westminster; but there is none. The application of the Barnett formula has not improved Wales' financial position. With identifiable public expenditure in Wales only 16% higher than in England, the Welsh benefit much less than the Scots and the Northern Irish do, even though Wales is significantly poorer than Scotland in terms of gross domestic product per capita.

The Welsh Assembly will not only feel like a poor relation; with just 60 members, it will also look like one. The small size is another product of Welsh Labour's ambivalence about having an Assembly, but it is beginning to look increasingly anomalous. Northern Ireland, with less than half Wales' population, will have an Assembly almost twice as large.

The first elections for the National Assembly for Wales also took place on May 6, 1999. On a turnout of only 45%, Labour won 28 seats, Plaid Cymru 17, the Conservatives 9, and Liberal Democrats 6. Here too most of the 20 top-up places from the regional lists went to the Conservatives (8 seats) and the nationalists (8 seats). The Welsh Labour leader, Alun Michael, decided to form a minority government rather than attempt to build a coalition.

Despite the differences between Scotland and Wales, there were important similarities. One is that in both countries there is a new two-party system, with the Conservatives displaced by the nationalists as the official opposition party. The electoral contest was regarded in each country as being between Labour and the nationalist party. That seems likely to continue, because the SNP came second in 54 constituencies in Scotland, and Plaid Cymru came second in 14 constituencies in Wales. They are unlikely to perform so well in general elections; but in Scotland and Wales it is not unrealistic for the nationalist parties to aspire to govern.

The Northern Ireland Assembly

As in Scotland and Wales, the form of devolved government adopted in Northern Ireland is not the product of a uniform pattern but is designed to meet the special circumstances of the province. In particular it is intended to allay the fears of two beleaguered communities: the nationalists, who are a minority in Northern Ireland, and the Unionists, who would be a minority in a united Ireland. The Northern Ireland Act 1998 seeks to implement the Belfast Agreement, which was endorsed in referendums held simultaneously on both sides of the border on May 22, 1998. In Northern Ireland, there was a 71% vote in favor of the agreement on an 81% turnout (the most vocal dissent coming from Ian Paisley and his fundamentalist Democratic Unionist Party); in the Republic, the agreement received the support of 95% of the 55% who voted. The agreement has six major strands. It formalizes the position of the British and Irish governments that the status of Northern Ireland can only be changed with the consent of a majority of the people living there; it provides for the devolution of a wide range of executive and legislative powers to a Northern Ireland Assembly; it sets up a new North-South Ministerial Council; it establishes a British-Irish Council (the "Council of the Isles"), bringing together representatives of the two governments and the devolved governments within the United Kingdom (Qvortrup & Hazell 1998); it replaces the Anglo-Irish Agreement with a new British-Irish Agreement (O'Leary 1998); and it enhances the protection of basic human rights with a new independent Human Rights Commission.

The Northern Ireland Assembly has 108 members, elected in six-member constituencies by the single transferable vote. The constituency boundaries are the same as those of the 18 Westminster constituencies. The Assembly has full legislative and executive authority with respect to the matters previously devolved administratively to the six Northern Ireland government departments. It thus has powers similar to the Scottish Parliament's, a Cabinet (the Executive Committee) with up to 12 ministers, and the capacity (by local agreement, and subject to Westminster approval) to expand its autonomy.

There are, however, special safeguards to ensure that all members of the community can be effectively represented in the Assembly, its committees, and the executive. This means that—unlike in Scotland and Wales—the executive will always contain ministers representing the minority community, in proportion to their parties' strength in the Assembly. (At present the nationalists are the minority community, but if demographic trends continue the Unionists may find themselves in the minority.) The Northern Ireland executive, as currently envisaged, will be broadly inclusive and operate without conventional collective cabinet responsibility. This plan will be strengthened by the creation of a novel dual premiership. The First and Deputy First Minister of Northern Ireland, who will have identical powers and capacities despite their different titles, will be elected in a manner that will require the endorsement of both Unionists and nationalists and will therefore require both candidates to be broadly acceptable as well as nationally representative.

Elections for the Assembly were held on June 25, 1998. The moderate nationalist party, the Social Democratic and Labour Party (SDLP), won 24 seats (on 22.3% of first-preference votes), although the largest party was the Ulster Unionist Party, which won 28 seats (on 21.3% of first-preference votes). In third place were the Democratic Unionists, who won 20 seats on 18.1% of the vote, narrowly beating Sinn Fein, which scored its best ever result with 17.6% of first-preference votes, giving it 18 seats. Overall, 58 members registered as Unionists, 42 as Nationalists, and 8 (from the Alliance Party and the Northern Ireland Women's Coalition) as "other."

For over a year after the election of the Assembly, devolution was stalled because the parties could not agree on election of the power-sharing executive. The Unionists linked formation of the executive with the decommissioning of terrorist weapons and refused to join an executive with ministers from Sinn Fein until the IRA engaged with the decommissioning process: "No guns, no government."

After several false starts, the deadlock was eventually broken after 11 weeks of talks in autumn 1999, with the help of former US Senator George Mitchell (who had previously helped to broker the 1998 Belfast Agreement). This led to the election of a power-sharing executive in December, with the Ulster Unionist leader David Trimble becoming First Minister and Seamus Mallon of the SDLP Deputy First Minister, and Martin McGuinness from Sinn Fein becoming Education Minister. Powers were immediately devolved to the Assembly and executive, and in December 1999 the first meetings were held of the British-Irish Intergovernmental Conference and the British-Irish Council, as part of the wider framework of inter-governmental support structures.

London and the English Regions

The fourth significant area of the country to which power is to be devolved is London. For most of this century, London has had a city-wide level of government, but it was abolished by the Thatcher government in 1988. The new government promised to restore city-wide government to London but with the innovation of a directly elected mayor. The Greater London Authority Referendum Act 1998 provided for a referendum to be held on the same day as the London Borough elections, May 7, 1998. Although only 34% of Londoners voted, 72% of those who did endorsed the government's proposals for a new regional authority, the Greater London Authority (GLA) comprising a directly elected mayor and 25 Assembly members. The mayor will be elected using the supplementary vote system, whereas the Assembly members will be elected using the additional member system with 14 constituency members and 11 top-ups. The first election for the GLA will be in May 2000. The GLA will not have tax-raising powers but will be allocated the budgets that central government and the London boroughs previously spent on the areas within its responsibility. It will also have powers to levy charges for parking and road use in order to reduce London's traffic congestion.

The mayor will run a mixture of new and old regional agencies: a London Development Agency, a transport authority, and a new authority to supervise the Metropolitan Police. As a directly elected politician with the largest personal constituency in Europe, other than the French President, he will also have an important political voice on the national and international stage, which may lead to tensions with central government. There is also the possibility of tensions between the mayor/Assembly and the London boroughs. Assembly members are likely to be full-time, salaried politicians, whose primary task is to act as a check on the mayor, but this may not happen. The mayor is likely to be a party political figure who will have the backing of his party in the Assembly; the Assembly's powers regarding the mayor are limited; and the mayor has important powers of patronage through appointing Assembly members to the executive agencies. The Assembly may wish to devote its time not to criticizing the mayor but to conducting broader inquiries into London-wide issues, and these are bound to trespass on territory belonging to the boroughs on the one hand, and to central government on the other.

In its July 1998 White Paper *Modern Local Government: In Touch with the People* (DETR 1998), the government indicated that it intends to facilitate the introduction of directly elected mayors in other parts of England. Local authorities will be given the opportunity to choose among three models of a more separate executive: a directly elected mayor; an indirectly elected mayor, elected by the other councillors; or a cabinet system. Should councils wish to introduce a directly elected mayor, they will have to seek endorsement in a local referendum. The likelihood is that most councils will opt for some form of cabinet system, but a petition of 10% of electors could then force them to hold a referendum on a mayor. The government intends to bring forward legislation to implement the White Paper and in 1999 published a draft Local Government Bill with a view to legislation in 1999–2000.

The new government has taken two very different approaches to regional government for the rest of England. They derive from separate strands developed in Labour's policy when in opposition, which appeared in separate chapters in Labour's 1997 manifesto. On the one hand, there was a policy of devolution on demand, developed by shadow Home Secretary Jack Straw. This started with regional chambers, building on the existing regional groupings of local authorities but moving on to become directly elected regional assemblies in those regions where there is demand, following a regional referendum. On the other hand, there was a policy of economic development, developed by Deputy Prime Minister John Prescott, with the English regions perceived as lagging behind not because of any democratic deficit, but because they lacked powerful development agencies of the kind Scotland and Wales have had for the past 20 years.

With John Prescott in the lead in government, as Secretary of State for the Environment, Transport and the Regions, the economic approach is in the ascendant. The Regional Development Agencies Act 1998 has created eight new regional development agencies (RDAs) for England, but as national bodies appointed by ministers and accountable through ministers to Parliament. The RDAs are to promote sustainable development, social and physical regeneration, and coordination of regional activity. They are business-led bodies whose members are appointed by central government to reflect the needs and perspectives of each region.

The eight new RDAs went live on April 1, 1999. Each has a board of 13 members, half from business and a third from local authorities. One of their first tasks is to prepare an economic strategy for the region.

One of the key stakeholders to be consulted is the Regional Chamber. The Regional Chambers are much larger nonstatutory bodies, with 40–120 members, of whom 70% are representatives from all the local authorities in the region. They can be designated by the Secretary of State if they meet central government standards of broad, cross-party representation, with nonlocal government members comprising no less than 30%. The RDA is then under a statutory duty to consult with its Regional Chamber. The first three Regional Chambers to be designated were in the North West, East Midlands, and West Midlands.

Several regions have ambitions to go much further. The North East is setting the pace. In an opinion poll conducted in March 1999 by MORI (Market and Opinion Research International), it showed the strongest support for an elected regional assembly (50% in favor, 27% against). The North of England Assembly is following the example of the Campaign for a Scottish Parliament, and in April 1999, it held the first meeting of the North East Constitutional Convention, a cross-party body charged with drawing up a blueprint for a directly elected regional assembly.

Not to be outdone, the North West Regional Assembly convened its own Constitutional Convention in July 1999. Another pace setter is the Regional Assembly for Yorkshire and Humberside. In January 1999, even the South East Forum changed its name to the South East Regional Assembly.

Despite choosing the name of Regional Assembly, none of these bodies is directly elected—yet. The test for each of them is to formulate a coherent set of functions for an elected assembly; to demonstrate to local authorities and to central government that it would add value; and then to persuade the people of the region, who will have to approve the proposals in a referendum. Richard Caborn, Minister for the Regions, said in a speech in Glasgow that devolution for the English regions should get under way immediately after the next election (*The Times*, 4 June, 1999). But in the government reshuffle of junior ministers in July, he was moved sideways to another department and replaced by Hilary Armstrong, the Minister for Local Government. She is unlikely to be as bold because local government itself is ambivalent about regional government, which it regards as a potential threat, and because the Prime Minister is lukewarm to hostile. Blair is skeptical about regional government for England because he is not persuaded that there is any demand for it. Further developments will depend on stronger demand prompted by devolution to Scotland and Wales, and on the power play within government between Blair and his Deputy Prime Minister, who is the main advocate of greater devolution to the English regions.

HUMAN RIGHTS

In its manifesto, the government pledged to incorporate the European Convention on Human Rights (ECHR) into UK law in order to "bring rights home," allowing access to the Convention in national courts. *Rights Brought Home* was the title of the July 1997 White Paper (Home Office 1997), followed by the Human Rights Act 1998. The Act incorporates the ECHR into domestic law so that the United Kingdom has a domestically enforceable bill of rights. Subordinate legislation—statutory instruments and all legislation from the devolved assemblies, primary and secondary—may be set aside by the courts if it is incompatible with the requirements of the ECHR. But in order to overcome concerns that the incorporation of the ECHR might dilute parliamentary sovereignty, the Act does not give the courts the power to strike down primary legislation from Westminster that is found to be incompatible with the Convention. Instead, the courts may make a declaration of incompatibility, which in effect invites Parliament to take remedial action. This can be done through amending legislation, which in urgent cases the government may introduce under a special fast-track procedure.

The impact of the Human Rights Act will be felt in every sphere of government: in Westminster, Whitehall, the courts, local government, and throughout the public sector. The Act applies to all bodies exercising public functions, so that even some private sector bodies (e.g. security firms running prisons) will be caught. To allow all public authorities time to prepare, the Act will not fully come into force until October 2000.

In Whitehall, the preparatory work has already begun. All bills are being "human rights proofed" so that ministers can certify, when introducing a bill into Parliament, that the bill is compatible with the Convention. But it is not simply new legislation that needs to be vetted for compliance; all policies and executive actions by the government are liable to challenge. The main difference following incorporation will be that decisions on human rights cases in the British courts will be much swifter than the five-year wait for a decision from the European Court of Human Rights at Strasbourg, so the government and Parliament will need to be more vigilant in ensuring that laws and practices comply with the ECHR before introduction, rather than rectifying matters afterward.

ECHR incorporation will be a significant check on the executive. British public administration has been characterized by a high degree of administrative discretion, with relatively light supervision by the courts. That has already begun to change with the steady growth of judicial review; but the Human Rights Act will lead to a much more tightly law-based system, in which the courts exercise significant new powers over the executive and over legislatures. The change is often portrayed as a shift in power from Parliament to the courts, but it is the executive's legislation that is presented to Parliament, and it will be the administrative actions and procedures of the executive that are challenged in the courts more often than its legislation. A deportation order, a parole decision, or discriminatory tax treatment will be the subject of ECHR challenge more often than will be the parent legislation. Judicial review has become a significant constraint on the actions of the executive; the Human Rights Act adds several more twists that will further constrain executive discretion.

Both the Human Rights Act and devolution will drag the courts into the political arena and throw the spotlight onto the judges. The Lord Chancellor announced in the first few months of the new government that he did not intend to take early action on Labour's plans for a Judicial Appointments Commission. But a few controversial human rights cases, or unpopular decisions on the devolution legislation, may revive calls for a judiciary drawn from a wider social background, with a proper territorial balance and a more transparent system of appointment.

ELECTORAL REFORM

In 1996, Labour and the Liberal Democrats established a Joint Consultative Committee on Constitutional Reform, which concluded that a commission on voting systems should be appointed early in the next parliamentary session to recommend an alternative to the current first-past-the-post system used for electing the House of Commons. The parties agreed that a referendum on the commission's proposal should be held within the first term of the new Parliament. In December 1997, as its manifesto had promised, the government set up an independent commission, under the chairmanship of Lord Jenkins, to recommend an alternative to first-past-the-post. The Jenkins Commission reported in October 1998 (Independent Commission on the Voting System 1998), recommending a hybrid system to be known as AV Top-up. Under this system, the House of Commons would include $\sim$500 constituency seats elected under the alternative vote system (in which voters list the candidates in order of preference) and $\sim$150 top-up seats. One member of the Commission, Lord Alexander, though accepting the broad thrust of the report, published a reservation arguing that the constituency members should be elected using first-past-the-post rather than the alternative vote system.

However, although Labour's manifesto included the Joint Consultative Committee pledge to hold a referendum on the Commission's recommendations, it contained no commitment as to when the referendum would be held. Some worry that the government will delay a referendum in the hope of killing off the proposals, although there are justifiable grounds for not rushing the process; educating the public so that it can make an informed judgment on AV Top-up is a task that will take years, not months. Furthermore, as the Jenkins Commission acknowledged, the need to redraw boundaries means that a general election under AV Top-up could not be expected before 2005.

By then, of course, the United Kingdom will have had considerable experience of proportional systems. As discussed above, the new assemblies in Scotland, Wales, Northern Ireland, and London all use proportional representation in varying forms. The government also followed through on the joint commitment with the Liberal Democrats to introduce proportional elections for the European Parliament. The European Parliamentary Elections Bill introduced a system of elections by regional lists, but the government opted for closed party lists rather than open lists, which enable voters to express a preference between individual candidates. In October and November 1998, the government was defeated five times in the House of Lords on its choice of closed lists for the European elections, and the bill fell right at the end of the session. It was reintroduced in the second session, and following a sixth defeat in the House of Lords, the government invoked the Parliament Act. The bill became law in time for the June 1999 European Parliamentary Elections.

The result of those elections—on a record low turnout of 23.3%, the lowest in the European Union—was that the Conservatives won 36 seats in the European

Parliament on 35.77% of the vote, Labour won 29 seats on 28.03% of the vote, and the Liberal Democrats won 10 seats on 12.66%. The Nationalist parties in Scotland and Wales won 2 seats each, the Green Party won 2 seats, and the anti-European Union UK Independence Party won 3 seats. The results were broadly proportional, and for the first time a minority party like the Greens was able to win seats in a nationwide election.

WESTMINSTER

Only a week after winning the 1997 election, Ann Taylor, the new Leader of the House, announced changes to the biweekly ritual of Prime Minister's Question Time. The changes were designed to fulfill the manifesto pledge to make Prime Minister's Question Time "more effective." Instead of two 15-minute sessions every Tuesday and Thursday, there is an extended 30 minute question time every Wednesday. Although the move was criticized, largely because it was imposed without consultation, it was softened by another change in the rules, which allowed MPs to ask an open supplementary question without first asking a question on the Prime Minister's engagements, effectively giving MPs more time to the question the Prime Minister.

Ann Taylor also became chair of the new Select Committee on the Modernisation of the House of Commons—a rare instance of a government minister chairing a Select Committee. In the 1997–1998 session, the committee produced seven reports on updating the procedures of the House. The most important was the first, on the legislative process, which recommended "programming" (i.e. timetabling) for all bills. The Scotland Bill and the Government of Wales Bill were the first two major bills in which programming (whereby a set number of clauses were debated on each day) was used instead of the guillotine to ease the parliamentary passage of the bill. However, on occasion the timetable adopted was too ambitious and time ran out, so that important clauses were passed without debate.

The Committee also recommended that more bills be published in draft to allow prelegislative scrutiny by Select Committees. The government announced that as a trial, seven bills would be published in draft. In the first session only three appeared, but in the second session six draft bills were published. Other key recommendations were that committees be able to reconvene to consider government amendments made in response to assurances given during the committee stage; that committees sit during recess; and that carry-over be introduced to allow bills that had not completed their parliamentary passage to survive from one parliamentary session to the next. In the other six reports, the Committee has considered conduct in the Chamber (recommending, for example, that Privy Councillors should not necessarily get precedence in debates), voting methods, and the scrutiny of European business.

Further reports have continued in this rather timid vein. The Procedure Committee's Report on the Procedural Consequences of Devolution (HC185) was published on May 19, 1999. Wishing to undertake a full review in due course, the Committee has initially recommended the abolition of the Scottish, Welsh, and Northern Irish Grand Committees and new rules restricting questions to the Scottish and Welsh Secretaries to matters relating to their reduced responsibilities. The Committee also proposed a new procedure for bills relating exclusively to one part of the kingdom, with a special Second Reading Committee, composed of a minimum of 35 English members for English bills, 18 Northern Irish members for Northern Irish bills, 20 Scottish members for Scottish bills, and 20 Welsh members for Welsh bills. The Committee discussed the possibility of Westminster committees holding joint meetings with committees of the devolved assemblies, and access for members of the devolved assemblies.   ·

The Commons Modernisation Committee has recommended a new committee (similar to the Australian Main Committee) to reduce pressure on debates in the chamber (HC194, April 13, 1999: Sittings of the House in Westminster Hall). Starting in the autumn of 1999, the new chamber will sit in the Grand Committee Room off Westminster Hall and provide more opportunity for adjournment debates, debating Select Committee reports, foreign affairs, etc.

The Joint Committee on Parliamentary Privilege, chaired by Lord Nicholls (a senior judge) delivered its report in April 1999 (HC214, HL43). It recommends updating the laws regulating freedom of speech in Parliament in a new Parliamentary Privileges Act and removing the change in the law that allowed Neil Hamilton MP to bring his libel action against *The Guardian*. It also recommends that all laws should apply to Parliament itself; the institution should cease to be a statute-free zone.

The biggest reforms at Westminster are promised for the second chamber. The government disappointed many supporters by failing to move swiftly in its first year to implement its manifesto commitment to reform the House of Lords. That has since been rectified in the second session with the passage of the House of Lords Act 1999, which removes the voting and sitting rights of hereditary peers. Labour's manifesto stated explicitly that this stage-one reform was self-contained and not dependent on having agreed what a fully reformed House of Lords might require. The Conservative leader in the House of Lords, Viscount Cranborne, acknowledged that despite his party's misgivings about removing the hereditary peers before agreeing on a replacement, it would observe the Salisbury Convention (devised by his grandfather Lord Salisbury during the postwar Labour government), which requires the Lords not to block or wreck a manifesto commitment. Despite this, the government supported an amendment—passed by 351 votes to 32—that would allow a total of 92 hereditary peers to stay on in the transitional upper house. The 92 would largely be elected from each party grouping of hereditary peers.

The government has also decided to set up a Royal Commission, going beyond its manifesto proposal of convening a joint committee of both Houses to consider the options for further reform. In a two-day debate in October 1998, the new Leader of the Lords, Baroness Jay, announced that the bill to remove the hereditary peers would be accompanied by a White Paper setting out the options for a new second chamber, and the establishment of a Royal Commission to consider those options and report by the end of 1999. Most importantly, the Royal Commission, which is chaired by the former Conservative Leader of the Commons and the Lords, Lord Wakeham, has been asked to consider the House of Lords in the context of the other constitutional changes set in train: devolution, closer integration with the European Union, incorporation of the ECHR, and any changes to the House of Commons which might result from a changed electoral system. If the Royal Commission fulfills that remit, it will become a commission not simply on Lords reform but on the Constitution. The Royal Commission is due to report in January 2000.

WHITEHALL

Since May 1997, a number of important changes to the organizational structures of government have been announced. The most visible changes were the creation of new ministries; a combined Department of the Environment, Transport and the Regions (DETR), headed by Deputy Prime Minister John Prescott; the Department for Culture, Media and Sport (formerly the Department of National Heritage) under Chris Smith; and the Department for International Development (formerly the Overseas Development Administration) headed by Clare Short. The government also appointed a Cabinet minister as minister for women: initially Harriet Harman (Social Security Secretary), and from July 1998 Baroness Jay (Leader of the House of Lords).

Less visible but no less important are the changes that have been made to the Cabinet committee structure. There are five new committees to deliver the constitutional reform program, including an overarching committee on constitutional reform strategy chaired by the Prime Minister. The Lord Chancellor helps to shape the strategy by chairing all the other Cabinet committees on different aspects of the constitutional reform program: the Committee on Devolution to Scotland, Wales and the English Regions, with 19 members; the Sub-Committee on Incorporation of the ECHR (17 members); the Sub-Committee on Freedom of Information (23 members); and the Sub-Committee on reform of the House of Lords, which has only seven members. Another constitutional innovation is a new Cabinet committee on cooperation with the Liberal Democrats, chaired by the Prime Minister. These committees are all supported by a new Constitution Secretariat in the Cabinet Office. Its role is to coordinate legislative and other action on the constitutional reform program, but the lead responsibility still lies with individual departments—the Home Office, Scottish Office, Welsh Office, Northern Ireland Office, DETR, Foreign Office, Lord Chancellor's Department, and Cabinet Office itself, which leads on House of Lords reform.

Further changes are coming. During the committee-stage debates on the Scotland Bill in the House of Lords, it was announced that a Joint Ministerial Committee would be set up as a forum for the UK government to meet with the devolved governments in Scotland, Wales, and Northern Ireland to discuss devolution matters. This committee is likely to become an important part of Britain's quasifederal constitutional settlement. In preparation for devolution, the Cabinet Office and Whitehall departments have also drawn up a series of concordats to cover the procedural aspects of the relationship—issues such as the sharing of information and data, confidentiality, and a liaison on EU matters (Cabinet Office 1999).

The constitutional reform process will develop a momentum of its own that will affect the central government in ways that are only beginning to be recognized. For example, the separate roles of the Secretaries of State for Wales, Scotland, and Northern Ireland will come under increasing pressure. The logic of devolution suggests that as their functions wither, these ministers should not continue to occupy separate seats in the Cabinet. In time they may be replaced by a combined Minister for Territorial Affairs, whose task will be to manage intergovernmental relations in the new quasifederal system.

EUROPE

Compared with the fireworks of Maastricht, the Treaty of Amsterdam may seem a damp squib. Certainly, its parliamentary passage was far calmer, a by-product of the government's large majority and its more relaxed attitude toward matters European. The European Communities (Amendment) Act 1998 gives effect to the Amsterdam Treaty, which seeks to ensure that decisions are taken "as openly as possible" and as closely to the citizen as feasible. The European Union is now declared to be founded on respect for human rights, democracy, and the rule of law; and member states that persistently fail to show sufficient respect for these ideals may have their rights (but not duties) of membership suspended. The treaty modifies the aims of the European Union, increasing the emphasis on environmental protection and job creation and adding the aims of fighting discrimination and promoting competition. The treaty also strengthens the role of the European Parliament.

The next major step in the long European march toward integration is Economic and Monetary Union (EMU). When the new government took office, its first major policy decision was to grant independence to the Bank of England, a policy later formalized by the Bank of England Act 1998. Within 100 hours of winning the election, the Chancellor of the Exchequer had announced that a new nine-member Monetary Policy Committee would take future decisions on interest rate levels, with the aim of meeting an inflation target set by the government while maintaining growth and employment. The members of the committee will appear before the Treasury Select Committee, where they can be called to account for their decisions. Although the government denied that granting independence to the Bank was part of a process of preparing to join the single European currency, critics were keen to draw connections. Certainly, the government's policy has evolved from its predecessor's "wait and see" to "prepare and decide," and greater independence for the Bank could be seen as part of the policy of preparation for EMU.

Should the government decide to join the single currency, it has pledged to hold a referendum to endorse that decision. The draft bill on the funding of political parties, which Home Secretary Jack Straw published in July 1999, contains proposals on the funding of referendums that may have a significant impact on any future referendum on the single currency. Under the proposals, the government would be able to spend money promoting its arguments until 28 days before any referendum. During the final 28 days, the government would give equal money to two designated umbrella organizations campaigning on both sides of the argument. These organizations would be allowed to spend up to £5 million. In addition, any political party with at least two MPs would be able to spend £5 million of its own money. This implies a potentially significant imbalance in the funding available to the pro– and anti–single-currency camps because only one parliamentary party, the Conservatives, would be likely to oppose entry.

FREEDOM OF INFORMATION

Labour's commitment to a Freedom of Information Act is the most longstanding of all its constitutional commitments, having appeared in every manifesto since 1974. Campaigners hoped for a bill in the first session, but with a new minister in charge (David Clark), the first Queen's Speech promised only a White Paper, to be followed by a draft bill. The White Paper *Your Right to Know* (Cabinet Office 1997), which appeared in December 1997 (Cm 3818), seemed to promise perhaps the most generous freedom-of-information regime in the world. There would be a right of access to documents or information from a very wide range of public bodies, including local government and the wider public sector; exemptions would be subject to the high threshold of a "substantial harm test"; and enforcement would fall to an Information Commissioner with the power to order disclosure. The only flaw appeared to be a wide exclusion for law enforcement information. It all seemed a little too good to be true, and underlying difficulties with Cabinet colleagues began to show when the draft bill, originally promised for April 1998, did not appear in the spring or the summer.

In July 1998, David Clark was sacked in Tony Blair's first reshuffle. Responsibility for the bill was transferred to Jack Straw in the Home Office, where a new team of ministers and civil servants had to grapple with the issues, particularly the interplay with privacy and data protection, recently updated by the Data Protection Act 1998. After a long wait, the Home Secretary published the draft Freedom of Information Bill on May 24, 1999 (Cm 4355). It represents a major retreat from the proposals in David Clark's White Paper *Your Right to Know*. The price of gaining support across Whitehall has proved to be a highly restrictive bill by international standards (Hazell 1999).

This is reflected in the exemption provisions—which include unnecessarily broad exemptions for policy advice, information about investigations, and commercial information—and the capacity to create new exemptions by ministerial order. In place of the overriding public interest test in the previous government's Code of Practice, authorities will merely have to consider the release of exempt information on a discretionary basis.

The bill relies heavily on publication schemes to be drawn up by each public authority, codes of practice from the Secretary of State, and a general responsibility on the Commissioner to promote good practice. The Data Protection Commissioner is to become the Information Commissioner. The estimated total cost of implementing the bill is £90 to £125 million per year, to be found within existing resources.

POLITICAL PARTIES

Political parties in Britain have been private bodies unregulated by law. That is about to change in two respects. The smaller change comes through the Registration of Political Parties Act 1998, which placed political parties for the first time on a legal footing. The Act was necessitated by the introduction of party list voting for the additional members in the devolved assemblies and the regional list system proposed for the European elections. Under both voting systems, electors will vote for parties rather than individual candidates. A party intending to field one or more candidates in an election may register its name and an emblem, and the registrar is to weed out names (such as Literal Democrat) that are likely to be confusing. To avoid establishing a separate office, the task of registration is given to the Registrar of Companies.

So far 80 parties have been registered, including those promoting the independence of East Cleveland and Morecambe Bay, along with the Pink Elephant Party, the Stoke on Trent Alliance, and the Witchery Tour Party. The most serious controversy was caused by parties in Scotland that wished to include the description "green" or "socialist," labels already registered by Great Britain–wide parties. Following the threat of legal action by the Scottish Socialist Party, the Registrar of Political Parties adopted a more lenient position, so that six parties now carry the "socialist" name in their title.

Much larger changes will flow from the Fifth Report of the Committee on Standards in Public Life (the Neill Committee; 1998) on the funding of political parties, published in October 1998. The report made 100 recommendations on party funding and related areas. Key recommendations were that an Electoral Commission be set up to oversee all future elections and referendums; that national spending limits be introduced for general election campaigns; that parties should not accept anonymous donations over £50; and that the names of those who give over £5000 should be disclosed. The report recommended the introduction of tax relief for donations up to £500 and a substantial increase in the amount of public funds made available to fund the work of the opposition parties in Parliament. This proposal, which did not require primary legislation, has already been acted on. From April 1999, public funding was increased by a factor of 2.7, with the bulk of resources being distributed according to the number of seats each party wins. The Conservative Party's allocation will increase from £1.25 million to £3.38 million per year. Although the allocative mechanism also takes into account the number of votes won, the financial results penalize the smaller parties.

The most controversial aspect of the report concerned the conduct of future referendums. The Committee was concerned to learn that the "no" campaign in the Welsh referendum had been financed on a shoestring budget, noting that since the result was so close, "a fairer campaign might have resulted in a different outcome." For the future, the Committee recommended that the government provide funding for yes and no campaigns to enable each to establish a small headquarters and staff, and to send out a mailing to every household stating their views. Although members of the government should be able to express their views, the government itself should remain neutral during a referendum campaign, in a manner analogous to a general election campaign.

These changes will have a big impact on the United Kingdom's party structure over the next few years, but other forces are at work too. The introduction of proportional representation, even if only at the European and subnational levels, will lead to greater fragmentation of national parties and the strengthening of regional parties. The Conservative Party has already loosened the ties, with separate party organizations and leadership to rebuild its fortunes in Scotland and Wales. The Labour Party may be forced to follow suit, as it is proving increasingly difficult to compete against the SNP and Plaid Cymru while being tied too closely to party headquarters in London.

MONARCHY

The most significant event for the monarchy since the 1997 election was the intense public reaction following the death of Diana, Princess of Wales, and the subsequent hints about repositioning and modernizing the monarchy. These have yet to yield anything of longterm constitutional significance. On the other hand, Lord Archer's Succession to the Crown Bill, which sought to remove sexual discrimination in the royal succession, has a relevance that could only be longterm. As Lord Archer stressed in the short debate that occurred before he voluntarily withdrew the bill, it would not take effect for 60 or 70 years, and might not affect the succession until the twenty-second century. Lord Williams of Mostyn, replying for the government, suggested that although the Queen was sympathetic to the bill, a government bill was the most appropriate way to deal with such matters—not least because the Statute of Westminster 1931 requires that changes to the succession receive the consent of the 15 other countries where Her Majesty is Queen.

THE NEW CONSTITUTIONAL SETTLEMENT

We will not see more years like 1998 and 1999. With 12 constitutional bills already on the statute book, the government can justifiably claim that it has embarked on the most ambitious and far-reaching changes in the British constitution this century. The scale and speed of the program is the government's main response to those critics who maintain that its constitutional reforms lack any coherent strategy or any clear vision of what the new constitutional settlement will be. It is too early to state precisely the nature of the new British constitution, but already we can discern some of its outlines, particularly as a result of devolution.

Devolution will introduce a form of quasifederalism. Its federal characteristics include (*a*) a formal division of legislative power, of the kind found in federal constitutions; (*b*) entrenchment, but by the political means of a referendum; (*c*) the creation of a new constitutional court, the Judicial Committee of the Privy Council, which is the body chosen to adjudicate in devolution disputes; and (*d*) formal machinery to handle intergovernmental relations, namely the new Joint Ministerial Committee on devolution.

The political drive and energy thus far has mostly gone into devolution and into the design and implementation of the new institutions in Scotland, Wales, and Northern Ireland. What has tended to be overlooked is the need for corresponding adjustments at the center. Devolution releases powerful centrifugal political forces, which will require rebalancing at the center if the new constitutional settlement is to rest on secure foundations and the Union is to hold together. This chapter has only hinted at some of the changes that will be required in all three branches of central government—in Westminster, Whitehall, and the courts. Many of these issues will surface more strongly as the devolution settlement starts to bed down and as the focus of the constitutional reform program shifts to the institutions of the center—starting with reform of the House of Lords.

Visit the Annual Reviews home page at www.AnnualReviews.org

LITERATURE CITED

Bogdanor V. 1999. *Devolution in the United Kingdom*. Oxford, UK: Oxford Univ. Press

Cabinet Office. 1997. *Your Right to Know*. London: Stationery Office

Cabinet Office. 1999. Memorandum of understanding and devolution concordats. Cm 4444. London: Stationery Off.

Committee on Standards on Public Life. 1998. *Fifth Report*. London: Stationery Office

Department of the Environment, Transport and the Regions. 1998. *Modern Local Government: In Touch with the People*. London: Stationery Office

Dewar D, Wallace J. 1999. *Partnership for Scotland*. www.scotlibdems.org.uk/docs/coalition.htm

Hazell R. 1996. *An Assembly for Wales*. London: Constitution Unit

Hazell R. 1998. *Constitutional Futures: A History of the Next Ten Years*. Oxford, UK: Oxford Univ. Press

Hazell R. 1999. *Commentary on Draft Freedom*

of Information Bill. London: Constitution Unit

Hennessy P. 1998. *Re-engineering the State in Flight: A Year in the Life of the British Constitution.* London: Lloyds TSB Forum

Himsworth C, Munro C. 1999. *The Scotland Act 1998.* Edinburgh: W Green/Sweet & Maxwell

Home Office. 1997. *Rights Brought Home.* London: Stationery Office

Independent Commission on the Voting System. 1998. *Report.* London: Stationery Office

Joint Committee on Parliamentary Privilege. 1999. *Report.* http://www.parliament.uk/commons/selcom/privhome.htm

Kay N. 1998. The Scottish Parliament and the Barnett Formula. *Fraser of Allander Q. Econ. Comment.* 24:32–48

O'Leary B. 1998. *The British-Irish Agreement: Power-Sharing Plus.* London: Constitution Unit

Procedure Select Committee of the House of Commons. 1999. *Report.* http://www. publications.parliament.uk/pa/c m/cmproced.htm

Qvortrup M, Hazell R. 1998. *The British-Irish Council: Nordic Lessons for the Council of the Isles.* London: Constitution Unit

Rawlings R. 1998. The new model Wales. *J. Law Soc.* 25:461–509

Scottish Office. 1997. *Scotland's Parliament.* Edinburgh: Stationery Office

Welsh Labour Party. 1997. *Preparing for a New Wales.* Cardiff, UK: Labour Party

Annu. Rev. Polit. Sci. 2000. 3:401–17

THE CONTINUED SIGNIFICANCE OF CLASS VOTING

Geoffrey Evans

Nuffield College, Oxford University, OX1 1NF United Kingdom;
e-mail: geoffrey.evans@nuf.ox.ac.uk

Key Words   method, measurement, theory

■ **Abstract**   Class voting is supposedly in severe decline in advanced industrial democracies. However, this conventional wisdom derives from research using problematic methods and measures and an overly simple model of political change. This chapter overviews past and current comparative research into changes in and explanations of class-based political behavior and argues for the continued significance of class voting and, by extension, class politics in contemporary democracies. I particularly emphasize the importance of using more appropriate methods and the application and testing of theories that integrate developments in this area with those in studies of voting behavior more generally. This translates into a need for the systematic testing of bottom-up/top-down interactions in the relations between social structure and political preferences and the precise specification and measurement of explanatory mechanisms that can account for the association between class position and voting.

INTRODUCTION

Some degree of class voting occurs in most democracies (Korpi 1983, Nieuwbeerta 1995), although it is as a rule less pronounced than political cleavages associated with religion and ethnicity (Lipset & Rokkan 1967; Lijpart 1979, 1984). However, it is common for political scientists' models of voting behavior to include measures of class position only as control variables, while focusing intellectual concern on the impact of other explanatory factors. Indeed, for many researchers it is apparently unnecessary to include class position in order to obtain well-specified models of voting behavior: Effective prediction can be obtained without it.

But is this really the case? I would argue not.

First, questions of causal order bedevil research based on perceptions and preferences: Does partisanship cause or reflect economic perceptions? Is party identity a running tally or an exogenous influence on vote? Are issue positions real and consequential or "nonattitudes"? In short, many cognitive and attitudinal constructs are so proximate to vote choice that they constitute part of what is to be

1094-2939/00/0623-0401$14.00   **401**

explained. In contrast, we can usually be confident that an individual's occupation and social background do not result from his or her partisanship. This greater distinctiveness from the dependent variable is one reason why holding "variable races" (King 1986) between measures of class position and measures of cognitive constructs makes little sense. Variance explained is no measure of causal impact.

Second, given that political perceptions and preferences are unlikely to be randomly distributed among the population, we must somehow account for their distribution. Why, for example, do some people endorse income redistribution while others do not? Why do some voters react more strongly to changes in unemployment levels and others to rates of inflation? Voters' locations in class structure can account for variations in these tendencies and, as the shape of the class structure alters over time, can account for changes in their relative importance. The potentially important role of changes in class structure for explaining long-term political change also points to the value of treating class position as a set of categories rather than as a unidimensional continuum. The use of meaningful categorical class distinctions is preferable to, for example, continuous prestige or status scales because it allows more effective comparison of the *sizes* of different categories over time and across nations.

So class may well be important, but only if it is effectively measured and modeled and is found to be meaningfully related to political preferences and, in particular, to voting. At first glance, the idea of class voting appears straightforward. It refers to the tendency for voters in a particular class to vote for a specific party, political candidate (or groupings of these), rather than an alternative option, compared with voters in another class or classes. In other words, class voting describes a pattern of association between class and vote. Yet this simplicity hides intricacy and ambiguity. The definition of social class in and of itself introduces much confusion; class is a much debated, even essentially contested, concept. The issues become still more complex when class concepts are translated into measures of class position that allocate voters to classes, and when attempts are made to summarize statistically the class-vote association. The explanation of observed patterns of class voting raises many more questions. All of these theoretical and methodological issues have been the focus of dispute. However, there is one major substantive question that has received more attention than all the others and has touched on all of them. Has class lost its role as a source of voters' political preferences?

For many recent (Beck 1992, Clark et al 1993, Pakulski & Waters 1996) and not so recent (Nisbet 1959) commentators, class position is no longer an important source of political preferences. Dalton (1996:186) describes the decline in the class basis of politics as the "new 'conventional wisdom'" of comparative electoral research. Where it does survive, class politics has in many cases been redefined so that race, gender, or "new politics" issues replace the economic conflicts derived from class-based divisions of interests (Eder 1993). Although some class analysts remain unmoved by these pronouncements (e.g. Vanneman & Cannon 1987, Marshall 1997), it appeared until recently that the debate over class voting was being resolved in favor of those who would declare it redundant—or at least in terminal decline.

Despite the appeal of these pronouncements, their empirical basis has not usually been subjected to rigorous scrutiny. The research that has purported to do so is rather flawed. This problem is compounded by frequent confusion in understanding advances in the measurement and statistical estimation of class voting. Inglehart, for example, concludes that "social class-based voting has declined markedly over the past 40 years" (1997:254) and asserts that opposition to this claim relies on obfuscatory measures of class and questionable statistical techniques. Particularly singled out in this respect are Hout et al (1993), and Inglehart's readers are instead referred to an analysis in which "Nieuwbeerta and de Graaf find a clear overall decline in class voting" (1997:255-56). Yet Nieuwbeerta & de Graaf (1999) use very much the same statistical techniques (loglinear modeling and logistic regression) as do Hout et al. They also use the same measure of social class—that devised by Goldthorpe (1980, Erikson & Goldthorpe 1992).

One of the aims of this review is to remedy such deficiencies in the comprehension of the relationship between substance and method. The chapter therefore involves two elements: first, a critical summary of themes and issues that have emerged from research on class voting, and second, a consideration of corresponding questions about method and measurement that underlie many of the theoretical and substantive debates. My focus is constrained by considerations of space, so although there are various qualitative studies (e.g. Halle 1984, McNall et al 1991) that provide illustrations of differences in politically relevant class-based experiences, and broad-ranging aggregate-level analyses (i.e. Bartolini & Mair 1990), I concentrate here on the quantitative survey research that provides systematic tests of substantive propositions and theories concerning class voting at the individual level. This encompasses research into intended vote and other expressions of party support as well as the act of voting per se, but inevitably it represents only one aspect of the relation between class and politics. My justification for this selectivity is the emphasis placed on the supposed weakening of the class-vote link by those who have argued either for or against the decline of class politics.

ORIGINS

Historically, interest in class voting arose in response to the failed agenda of Marxism. For classic texts in political sociology, electoral politics was an expression of "the democratic class struggle" (Anderson & Davidson 1943) that substituted, at least in the short term, for the predicted class-based revolution. This interpretation led to a focus on class voting as a dispute between only two classes, the working class and the middle class, and their representatives, parties of the left and right. Some of the early studies were merely impressionistic (Sombart 1976 [1906], Sorokin 1959 [1927]), whereas others relied on evidence obtained at the level of electoral constituencies (Siegfried 1913, Tingsten 1937). Given the well-known problems with inferring individual vote choices from aggregate data, these authors had to make assumptions about how voters in different classes actually voted. To help overcome this limitation, modern social scientific studies of class voting have relied on measurement through national surveys. From its postwar beginnings in national election studies in the United States and several other Western industrialized countries, the survey data base has expanded through time and space to create a large body of evidence on class voting that now informs academic debate.

Early studies in this genre found that in general lower class voters were more likely to vote for left-wing political parties than were those in higher classes. Substantial cross-national differences were also discovered, with Scandinavia and Britain having the highest levels of class voting and the United States and Canada the lowest. The early analyses of studies from different countries were inevitably restricted in their degree of comparability. For example, some studies used income to measure social and economic position, whereas others used education or occupation. Even when researchers used the same type of measure, classifications often varied from the very detailed to the very crude. In his comparison of Britain, France, and Italy, for example, Lipset (1981 [1960]) did not present any standardized measure of class voting. Similar limitations apply to the studies collated by Rose & Urwin (1969) and Rose (1974). Only since the 1970s have studies included comparable data, measures of class position, and measures of class voting from more than a handful of countries (Books & Reynolds 1975).

THE TWO-CLASS/TWO-PARTY ERA

The baseline for many current comparative studies of class voting was set by Alford's (1963, 1967) analysis of trends in class voting in four Anglo-American democracies (Australia, Britain, Canada, and the United States). He examined evidence covering the period from 1936 to 1962, using a measure of social and economic position in which occupations were aggregated to form a dichotomy of manual versus nonmanual classes and a similarly dichotomized measure of voting, left versus nonleft. He also introduced the most commonly used, cited, and criticized measure of the level of class voting, namely the "Alford index" (Alford 1962). The Alford index is the difference between the percentage of manual workers that voted for left-wing political parties and the percentage of nonmanual workers that voted for these parties.

The use of this index became standard practice in the cross-national and over-time analyses that followed, which usually concluded that class voting is in decline. Lipset (1981:505) presented evidence of a downward trend in Britain, Germany, and the United States between 1945 and 1980; Inglehart (1990:260 and above) found further evidence of a continuing decline from the early 1980s onwards; Sainsbury (1987) and Listhaug (1997) found a decline in class voting in the Scandinavian countries; Lane & Ersson (1994:94) found less class voting in nine Western industrialized nations in the 1970s and 1980s than in the 1950s and 1960s, and stronger class voting in only two of the nations (France and Italy). Nieuwbeerta's (1995) exhaustive review gives many more examples. On the basis of this sort of evidence, Clark & Lipset (1991:408) concluded by the start of the 1990s that politics is now "less organized by class and more by other loyalties."

This position was further endorsed by an extensive cross-national study of electoral change and the decline of cleavage politics between the 1960s and the 1980s compiled by Franklin et al (1992). This project modeled voting behavior (left versus nonleft) in no less than 16 countries, including as explanatory variables manual/nonmanual class position and social characteristics such as religion, trade union membership, sex, education, and issue/value orientations. It represents the culmination of the two-class/two-party approach to class voting. In his summary of the implications of the research reported in the book, Franklin (1992:385) observed that "almost all of the countries we have studied show a decline during our period in the ability of social cleavages to structure individual voting choice."

Unsurprisingly, then, whether class voting in modern industrial societies has declined is no longer an issue for many commentators. Some even go as far as to proclaim the "death" of class politics (Pakulski & Waters 1996). The question is *why*?

Explaining Decline

A plethora of explanations for this outcome have been proposed. At least five types are discernable (Goldthorpe 1996a, Manza et al 1995):

1. Social class has lost some or all of its importance as a determinant of life chances and in consequence its role as a source of divergent political interests. This has resulted from processes such as the "embourgeoisement" of the working class or the "proletarianization" of white-collar work, and from the presence of extensive intragenerational and intergenerational social mobility (cf Abrams et al 1960, Goldthorpe et al 1968).

2. New post-industrial social cleavages are replacing class-based conflict. The significance of class position for voting behavior has decreased as "new" forms of social differentiation have become more important for political interests—e.g. gender, race, ethnicity, and production and consumption sectors (cf Dunleavy 1980, Saunders 1981, Huckfeldt & Kohfeld 1989, Heath et al 1991, Saunders 1990).

3. Because of a general increase in levels of education and "cognitive mobilization," identity-based responses to class-based divisions of interest are being replaced by the expression of preferences that reflect voters' increasing ability to make electoral decisions that are calculative and issue oriented rather than being driven by collective identities (cf Franklin 1985, Rose & McAllister 1986, Dalton 1996, Heath et al 1991).

4. Values are becoming more important as a basis of party preference and are cross-cutting the impact of social class. In particular, the increasing influence of post-material values has led to a decline in the importance of the traditional, class-based, left-right political continuum for voting behavior. The new left draws its support from the middle classes, weakening the class basis of left-right divisions (cf Lipset 1981 [1960]:509–21, Inglehart & Rabier 1986, Weakliem 1991).

5. Finally, since the manual working class has declined as a proportion of the electorate, left-wing parties have had to direct their programs toward the concerns of the growing middle classes or face continued electoral defeat. They have therefore moderated the class character of their political appeals and weakened the class distinctiveness of the political choices facing the electorate (cf Przeworski & Sprague 1986, King & Wickham-Jones 1990).

None of these explanations has received unconditional support. Moreover, all of them assume that there is indeed a widespread decline in class-based voting that has to be explained. However, explanations of changes in class voting have been strongly influenced by choices of method and measurement, and the literature that followed Alford's work has shortcomings in both these respects (for critiques see e.g. Korpi 1972, Evans et al 1991, Goldthorpe 1996a). The application of more sophisticated methods and measures produces a somewhat different story.

RECENT METHODOLOGICAL INNOVATIONS

Operationalizing Class Position

One problem with the manual/nonmanual distinction is that it obscures variations in the composition of the manual and nonmanual classes. Any change in their composition may lead to spurious change in estimates of class voting. If skilled manual workers are more conservative than unskilled workers and the number of skilled workers increases, the difference between manual and nonmanual workers will decline even if the relative political positions of skilled, unskilled, and nonmanual workers remain the same. In recent years, therefore, the rather atheoretical manual/nonmanual representation of class voting has been largely superseded as researchers have taken into account more nuanced ideas about class structure. Most influential has been the class schema developed by Goldthorpe and colleagues (e.g. Goldthorpe 1980, Erikson & Goldthorpe 1992:36–42). First used to study patterns of class voting over time in Britain (Heath et al 1995), this instrument, unlike many other measures of class, has been empirically validated in that it has been shown to measure the theoretical construct underpinning the measurement instrument (e.g. Evans 1992, Evans & Mills 1998). The main classes identified by the Goldthorpe schema are the petty bourgeoisie (small employers and self-employed), the service class or salariat (professional and managerial groups), the routine nonmanual class (typically lower grade clerical white-collar workers), and the working class (foremen and technicians; skilled, semiskilled and unskilled manual workers). The principal distinction underlying the distinction among the employee classes in the schema is between a service contract and a labor contract. In a service contract, employees receive not only salaried rewards but also prospective elements—salary increments, job security and pension rights, and, most importantly, well-defined career opportunities. In a labor contract, employees supply discrete amounts of labor, under supervision, in return for wages that are calculated on a "piece" or time basis (Erikson & Goldthorpe 1992:41–42). Because the employment relationship of the service class is relatively advantageous in terms of employment and payment conditions, occupational security, and promotion prospects, its members have a stake in preserving the status quo. This leads Goldthorpe (1982:180) to expect that "the service class ... as it consolidates, will constitute an essentially conservative element within modern societies." In contrast, the disadvantages of the labor contract can explain why the working class provides a basis of support for the redistributive programs of the left.

Operationalizing Political Preference

This shift toward greater complexity in the measurement of class has been accompanied by a similar move away from the measurement of political choice as a dichotomy of left versus right (or left versus nonleft), toward a fuller representation of the voters' spectrum of choice at the ballot box. Apart from its simplicity, the main reason for the use of a dichotomy to represent voter choice seems to have been a desire to make systematic cross-national and over-time comparisons. Unfortunately, the selective nature of what is being compared undermines any true comparability. The problem is analogous to that faced in the analysis of class position, in that changes in the composition of composite categories such as left or nonleft may lead to spurious changes in estimates of class voting. The use of dichotomies to represent vote choices and social classes also precludes from observation any processes of class-party realignment. The concept of class realignment in voting implies a change in the pattern of association between class and vote without any change in the overall strength of this association, i.e. without class dealignment (or, of course, increased alignment). But realignment cannot be discerned if the distinction between realignment and dealignment is prevented by restricting the numbers of parties and classes to two (see Whitten & Palmer 1996).

Improved Techniques for Estimating Association

Another innovation of the last two decades is in the statistical measurement of the class-vote association, with a move from Alford-type indices to indices based on odds ratios. With the Alford and similar indices, e.g. Rose & McAllister's (1986:37–39) index of determination, the measurement of the class-vote association is vulnerable to confounding by changes in the shape of the class structure and in the general popularity of the parties. In other words, this type of index confuses differences in the marginal distributions of the variables with differences in the association it is supposed to measure. The same problem hampers apparently more sophisticated linear (ordinary least squares) regression techniques. These indices are not margin-insensitive (for further discussion see e.g. Evans et al 1991, Hout et al 1995). Thus, as Franklin et al are aware (Franklin 1992:435–36), the analyses reported in their 16-nation study should have used logistic rather than linear regression. The attempt to avoid the problems of bias in regression coefficients by emphasizing variance explained (Franklin 1992:436) not only fails to alleviate the technical and interpretative problems of using dichotomous dependent variables with linear regression models, it probably accentuates them (see e.g. King 1986). In contrast, odds ratios measure the strength of the relationship between class and vote independently of the general popularity of political parties or changes in the sizes of classes [Thomsen 1987; but see the dispute between Crewe (1986), Dunleavy (1987), and Heath et al (1987)].

The use of logistic modeling techniques originally imported into the analysis of class voting by Heath et al (1985) capitalizes on this basic feature of the odds ratio and allows the relationship between more complex class and party systems to be summarized, thereby facilitating greater sophistication in the representation of class and vote. Further refinements of the basic loglinear approach include the use of "log-multiplicative" (Xie 1992) or "uniform difference" (Erikson & Goldthorpe 1992) models that allow the complexity of changing strengths of association between categorical variables to be summarized using only a single degree of freedom. Disputes over analytical method remain, especially those concerning more inductive versus more theory-driven approaches to analysis. Examples of inductive approaches include association models (e.g. Weakliem 1991), and theory-driven approaches appear here in the form of topological models (Goldthorpe 1999). The relative appropriateness of these procedures depends somewhat on the degree to which expectations derived from theory can be assumed to be reliable and precise, although where relationships are robust they should not diverge much in their substantive conclusions (Weakliem & Heath 1999b).

CURRENT ASSESSMENT

Most contemporary comparative studies of class voting use some or all of the methodological advances described above. Much of this research comes to rather different conclusions than those in the two-class/two-party tradition.

The first wave of the new approaches to class voting (e.g. Heath et al 1985, 1991; Evans et al 1991) modeled class voting in Britain to examine whether trendless fluctuation, a linear trend, or one-off changes best described the pattern of association in class voting over time; subsequent analyses tested for evidence of trends using log multiplicative models (Heath et al 1995). These studies found little evidence of declining class voting and have concluded that trendless fluctuation, or at most a one-off change, in the 1960s best captures the pattern of association in class voting over time. Consequently, one recent study has focused on modeling the more invariant aspects of the relation between class and vote using topological models that show that not only the extent of class divisions but also their structure remain stable over time. The major changes over this period have been in the overall popularity of the main political parties (Goldthorpe 1999).

The United States, by contrast, has seen both class-party realignment and the growth of a class-vote cleavage between those who vote, i.e. the middle classes, and those who do not, i.e. the working classes (Hout et al 1995). The changing nature of the middle classes has received particular attention. Professionals and routine white-collar workers have shifted toward the Democrats, whereas the self-employed and managers have become more strongly Republican. In part, the interpretation of these changes depends on what is considered to be a class difference and what might reflect sectoral divisions within the professional and managerial classes (Heath & Savage 1995, Brooks & Manza 1997).

The most recent of these analyses (collected in Evans 1999) generally show that although there is evidence for a linear decline in traditional "left versus non-left" class voting in some of the 20 countries examined using various statistical approaches by Nieuwbeerta & de Graaf (1999), such a decline is not typical and is not replicated when party systems are modeled as more complex choices.

For example, Weakliem & Heath (1999a) combine data from sources such as Gallup and the US General Social Survey and extend their analysis back further than the standard national election surveys can. Their most striking findings are the differences between the three nations they study. Not only is there no convergence in levels of class voting over the period studied, but in some respects national differences are accentuated. Levels of class voting in Britain are found to have increased during the 1940s and 1950s before falling back in the 1960s. In France, levels of class voting have changed less markedly over time, and the only long-term realignment is the rightward shift of farmers. In the United States, Weakliem & Heath concur with Hout et al (1999), who argue that there has been significant realignment (but not dealignment) in class voting in American postwar politics, which cannot be explained by changes in compositional differences between classes—and that there has been a significant increase in class differentials in voter turnout. Even in Germany, where the new politics agenda that supposedly cross-cuts the old class cleavage has a marked presence, Müller's detailed multivariate analysis indicates "a quite astonishing constancy of the differences in party orientation among the antagonists of the classical class cleavage" (1999:178).

The one exception to this pattern is Ringdal & Hines' (1999) study of class voting in Norway between 1957 and 1989, which includes four party groupings (Socialist Left, Labor, Center, Conservative) to represent the main choices in the Norwegian multiparty system. These authors do find a decline in class voting, especially in the traditional axis of class voting between the service and the working classes. Much of this decline appeared during a relatively short period in the 1960s. Ironically, the reason for this change is probably the political success of class politics, in which universalistic welfare legislation has led to the erosion of middle-class opposition to social democracy (Esping-Andersen & Korpi 1984).

Post-Communist Class Conflicts?

A final area where changes in class voting are now under scrutiny is in new democracies. In contemporary Eastern Europe, the question is not whether class divisions have declined with the transition from industrialism to postindustrialism, but whether they have increased as the ex-communist countries undergo the uneasy transition from authoritarian command economy to free-market democracy. The very small amount of time that has elapsed since the commencement of glasnost in the 1980s, the "velvet revolutions" of 1989–1990, and the breakup of the Soviet Union in 1991 would appear to militate against any marked changes in the social bases of politics. Nevertheless, the dramatic disruption of voters' incomes, lifestyles, and futures in transition societies provides exactly the sort of impetus for the transformation of lines of division in political interests that may render established ideas about the glacial character of social change inapplicable (Evans 1997, Szelenyi et al 1998). Over a four-year period in which the costs of marketization became increasingly apparent to the Czech electorate, class voting realigned and polarized to approximate the left-right alignments observed in the West (Mateju et al 1999). Similarly, in an analysis of the emergence of class divisions to political preferences in Russia during the early and mid 1990s, Evans & Whitefield (1999) found evidence of both the economic basis of class polarization and the role of an increasing understanding of the socially differentiated costs and benefits associated with market economies.

From these recent analyses, I conclude that research does not support the thesis of a generalized decline in the class basis of voting in advanced industrial societies. Only in certain Scandinavian countries is there robust evidence of a decline from an unusually high degree of class voting to levels similar to those in other Western democracies. On balance, therefore, it might be just as plausible to argue that class politics is actually increasing as the marketizing former communist societies of Eastern Europe display signs of class-based political polarization along the classic left-right axis.

NEW DIRECTIONS

Top Down or Bottom Up?

The debate on class voting has been strong on evidence and weak on theory. Most scholars have assumed a sociological, relatively deterministic account of the transition to industrial and postindustrial politics, in which changes in the nature and structure of classes lead to changes in political competition. However, some have rejected this account in favor of more voluntaristic models. Kitschelt (1994), for example, argues that the electoral fortunes of European social democratic parties are largely determined by their strategic appeals rather than by secular trends in the class structure—a line of reasoning that echoes Sartori's (1969) and Przeworski's (1985) influential arguments on the importance of organization, and especially parties, in the creation of class constituencies. From this perspective there is reason to believe that, even in advanced industrial societies, class voting might increase as well as decrease. This argument also implies that the adoption of class-relevant policy programs should be associated with an increase in the class basis of partisanship. Evans et al (1999) present some evidence for this, showing a relationship over time between left-right polarization in parties' manifestos and the extent of class voting. Quaille Hill & Leighley (1996) provide further evidence, linking state-level left policy programs to class differences in turnout. The argument is developed by Hout et al (1999), who interpret class differentials in turnout and class-party realignment as a response to political parties' choices of policies and electoral strategies. Others, however, have found no such effects (e.g. Dalton 1996:175–76, Weakliem & Heath 1999a), and the sensitivity of class voting to party positions remains an area of conjecture.

Identifying the Mechanisms Through Which Class Leads to Vote

What is it about class position that leads to divergent political preferences? Lipset's (1981 [1960]:220–24) assertion that "in virtually every economically developed country the lower income groups vote mainly for parties of the left" is usually considered, in and of itself, sufficient explanation for class voting. It is a result of income differences. Consequently, the processes of individual vote choice that produce aggregate patterns of class voting are either left unspecified or inferred indirectly from observed patterns of changes over time in the class-vote association. Aggregate effects have been found for union density (Korpi 1983) and for the consequences of social mobility (e.g. de Graaf et al 1995). In general, however, attempts to model the effects of theoretically specified effects at the macro level have met with limited success (Nieuwbeerta & Ultee 1999). As a result, the individual-level mechanisms that account for observed patterns of class voting remain unclear.

There is, of course, relevant research. Some studies have tried to unravel why voters in different classes vote differently. *The American Voter* (Campbell et al 1960) and Butler & Stokes's (1974) British derivation of its approach, for example, placed considerable emphasis on class identity (Prysby 1977). Yet identity is not exogenous; class identity itself needs to be accounted for. Nor does it provide convincing explanations of changes in levels of class voting. Social context approaches, which place emphasis on friendship choices and interpersonal influence or on political context (e.g. Huckfeldt 1984), likewise incur questions concerning endogeneity and a need to show more precisely how political context affects the decisions of individual voters.

From a rational choice perspective, Weatherford's (1979) early work indicated the differential sensitivity of classes to economic events, thus pointing to plausible class differences in the voting decision calculus (see also Nagler & Niemann 1997). Weakliem & Heath (1994) directly confront and to some degree reconcile rational choice and identity-based approaches by providing evidence of the roles of both issue-based and inherited parental preferences in explaining class differences in vote. Evans (1993) models the effects of future expected rewards and the likelihood of promotion conditioned by position in the life cycle. He shows how promotion prospects can account for class differences among younger age groups, whereas aspects of current circumstance—institutional affiliations such as union membership and home ownership—are significant among older voters. Evans' (1993) argument is that the diminishing marginal utility of future rewards shifts the balance of interests to the present, and hence to class position and its associated resources. This tendency is reinforced by the greater degree of class structuring of such resources among older age groups.

Nevertheless, in general, theory has lagged behind measurement and modeling. This is one reason why much research into class voting has eschewed multivariate analysis. Most of the influential studies in this genre use relatively few independent variables, and many use only one: class position. Many variables routinely included in models of voting behavior—e.g. party identity, education, gender, political attitudes, party or candidate perceptions, economic judgments, and left-right self-placement—are often absent. However, whether this underspecification is a problem remains unclear. To the extent that the debate over class politics is concerned only with changes in the patterns of association between class and vote over time, it is not necessary to include other independent variables. If changes in these other variables affect the strength and/or pattern of the class-vote relationship, then this effect should be observed in the bivariate association. Even where explanation rather than description is the goal, the lack of well-established knowledge of how the effects of class position on voting might be mediated via experiences such as trade union membership, or orientations such as party identity or political attitudes, engenders caution in the specification of multivariate models. To go beyond the simplest level of analysis with confidence requires a more explicit link between models of class voting and theories of voting behavior. The integration of the micro-level logic of voting and the macro-level outcome of class politics is the most important focus for further development in this area. Our understanding of the latter depends on advances in the former (Goldthorpe 1996b, Sorenson 1998).

CONCLUSIONS

The debate over the supposed decline in class voting has changed as it has become clear that a model of secular decline does not account for observed patterns of change. The only consistent and robust evidence of declining class-vote relations is in Scandinavia, particularly in Norway, where high levels of class voting declined in the 1960s to become more like those of other Western European societies. In contrast, in postcommunist societies, class politics and class voting may well be increasingly significant as classes polarize in their economic circumstances and parties signal their relevance to differing class interests. Other countries, despite displaying similar characteristics of modernity and postmodernity, display varying patterns of change over time. There is also evidence that the effects of class position are robust despite changes in relevant characteristics such as trade union membership and postmaterialism, although some of the divisions found within the middle class are consistent with the postmaterialist account. In short, the patterns of constancy, dealignment, and realignment in class voting over time cannot be understood by generalized propositions about the effects of industrialism or postindustrialism. Thus generic theories of the decline of class voting and class politics in industrialized societies are empirically unsupported, as by extension are theories that claim that all social structural bases to politics are in decline.

A concern with bottom-up/top-down interactions now also informs debate and prediction to a greater degree. The notion that the changing shape of the class structure influences party strategy, which in turn affects the class-party association, is ripe for a theoretically informed examination of the relationship between the decision to vote and the choices available to members of different classes. So far, though, the empirical basis for such an approach is not well established. We might expect a decline in certain forms of class voting because parties on the left have adopted a "catch-all" strategy in response to the shrinking class basis of their support. In some systems, such moves leave space for left parties to attract support from marginalized working-class groups; in other, first-past-the-post systems, we might expect that the start-up costs for electorally viable left parties would be prohibitive. In the United States, there is evidence of the growth of a new class-vote cleavage between those who vote and those who do not. This "realignment" is not the same as the class voting of old, but it is a form of class voting. Also, the fact that the middle class has grown in size is not necessarily cause to forget class politics. Working-class politics is only one version of class politics. The strategic rationality of appealing to middle-class interests is simply a new take on an old theme.

There have also been various methodological insights. A focus only on traditional class voting, with a rigid specification of left and right, can be misleading if claims for its general relevance are overstated. It is legitimate to compare changes across countries over time, but important differences between countries need not be sacrificed in the effort. A trend is a trend whether it is based on the choice between ten parties or two. Obviously, with more parties there is more scope for realignment and the complexities of interpretation that might ensue, but the reality is that party systems are often complex. Given our current low levels of knowledge about the comparability of national political contexts, this complexity indicates that intensive national case studies sharing sufficiently similar frames of reference for the observation of common patterns provide the most reliable basis for theory building.

Research into the mechanisms that explain class voting is rudimentary, but it has turned up possibly useful theories, hypotheses, and models that might prove fruitful in further comparative analyses. One promising argument is that class divisions in political orientations may remain relatively constant, but that because of changing class sizes, parties change their strategies, which eventually changes class-vote relations. (It is important, however, to take into account sources of variation in the extent to which voters calculate returns to their investment rather than voting out of established allegiances.) Similarly, comparative research into new democracies indicates that different models are likely to apply at different points in the evolution of party systems. During periods in which alignments are first formed, voters' class-differentiated experiences, in conjunction with a learning and signaling process, do provide an explanation of cleavage formation—one that passes at least initial empirical testing and could therefore justify more detailed investigation.

Future research should more closely integrate models of individual vote choice and macro-level patterns of class voting. At the same time it should specify the contexts in which the relative force of sociological and political factors varies. Through these refinements we can develop an area of academic controversy that, despite a plethora of empirical findings, has not yet provided the evidential basis for the highly general claims of both sociologists and political scientists.

Visit the Annual Reviews home page at www.AnnualReviews.org

LITERATURE CITED

Abrams M, Rose R, Hinden R. 1960. *Must Labour Lose?* Harmondsworth, UK: Penguin

Alford R. 1962. A suggested index of the association of social class and voting. *Public Opin. Q.* 26:417–25

Alford R. 1963. *Party and Society: The Anglo-American Democracies.* Westport, CT: Greenwood

Alford R. 1967. Class voting in Anglo-American political systems. In *Party Systems and Voter Alignments: Cross-National Perspectives*, ed. SM Lipset, S Rokkan, pp. 67–93. New York: Free

Anderson D, Davidson P. 1943. *Ballots and the Democratic Class Struggle.* Stanford, CA: Stanford Univ. Press

Bartolini S, Mair P. 1990. *Identity, Competition and Electoral Availability: the Stabilisation of European Electorates, 1885–1985.* Cambridge, UK: Cambridge Univ. Press

Beck U. 1992. *Risk Society: Towards a New Modernity.* London: Sage

Books JW, Reynolds JB. 1975. A note on class voting in Great Britain and the United States. *Comp. Polit. Stud.* 8:360–76

Brooks C, Manza J. 1997. The social and ideological bases of middle class political realignment in the United States, 1972–1992. *Am. Sociol. Rev.* 62:91–108

Butler DE, Stokes DE. 1974. *Political Change in Britain: The Evolution of Electoral Choice.* London: Macmillan. 2nd ed.

Campbell A, Converse PE, Miller WE, Stokes DE. 1960. *The American Voter.* Chicago: Univ. Chicago Press

Clark TN, Lipset SM. 1991. Are social classes dying? *Int. Sociol.* 6:397–410

Clark TN, Lipset SM, Rempel M. 1993. The declining political significance of social class. *Int. Sociol.* 8:293–316

Crewe I. 1986. On the death and resurrection of class voting: some comments on how Britain votes. *Polit. Stud.* 34:620–38

Dalton RJ. 1996. *Citizen Politics: Public Opinion and Political Parties in Advanced Industrial Democracies.* Chatham, NJ: Chatham House. 2nd ed.

de Graaf ND, Nieuwbeerta P, Heath A. 1995. Class mobility and political preference: individual and contextual effects. *Am. J. Sociol.* 100:997–1027

Dunleavy P. 1980. The political implications of

sectional cleavages and the growth of state employment. *Polit. Stud.* 28:364–83, 527–49

Dunleavy P. 1987. Class dealignment revisited: why odds ratios give odd results. *W. Eur. Polit.* 10:400–19

Eder K. 1993. *The New Politics of Class.* London: Sage

Erikson R, Goldthorpe JH. 1992. *The Constant Flux: A Study of Class Mobility in Industrial Societies.* Oxford, UK: Clarendon

Esping-Andersen G, Korpi W. 1984. Social policy as class politics in post-war capitalism: Scandinavia, Austria and Germany. In *Order and Conflict in Contemporary Capitalism*, ed. JH Goldthorpe, pp. 179–208. Oxford, UK: Clarendon

Evans G. 1992. Testing the validity of the Goldthorpe class schema. *Eur. Sociol. Rev.* 8:211–32

Evans G. 1993. Class, prospects and the life-cycle: explaining the association between class position and political preferences. *Acta Sociol.* 36:263–76

Evans G. 1997. Class inequality and the formation of political interests in Eastern Europe. *Eur. J. Sociol.* 38:207–34

Evans G, ed. 1999. *The End of Class Politics? Class Voting in Comparative Context.* Oxford, UK: Oxford Univ. Press

Evans G, Heath AF, Payne C. 1991. Modelling trends in the class/party relationship, 1964–87. *Elect. Stud.* 10:99–117

Evans G, Heath AF, Payne C. 1999. Class: labour as a catch-all party? In *Critical Elections: British Parties and Voters in Long-term Perspective*, ed. G Evans, P Norris, pp. 87–101. London: Sage

Evans G, Mills C. 1998. Identifying class structure: a latent class analysis of the criterion-related and construct validity of the Goldthorpe class schema. *Eur. Sociol. Rev.* 14:87–106

Evans G, Whitefield S. 1999. The emergence of class politics and class voting in post-communist Russia. See Evans 1999, pp. 254–275

Franklin M. 1985. *The Decline in Class Voting in Britain: Changes in the Basis of Electoral Choice, 1964–1983.* Oxford, UK: Oxford Univ. Press

Franklin MN. 1992. The decline of cleavage politics. See Franklin et al 1992, pp. 383–405

Franklin MN, Mackie T, Valen H, et al. 1992. *Electoral Change: Responses to Evolving Social and Attitudinal Structures in Western Countries.* Cambridge, UK: Cambridge Univ. Press

Goldthorpe JH. 1982. On the service class: its formation and future. In *Social Class and the Division of Labour*, pp. 162–85, ed. A Giddens, G Mackenzie. Cambridge, UK: Cambridge Univ. Press

Goldthorpe JH. 1996a. Class and politics in advanced industrial societies. In *Conflicts about Class: Debating Inequality in Late Industrialism*, ed. DJ Lee, BS Turner, pp. 196–208. London: Longman

Goldthorpe JH. 1996b. The quantitative analysis of large-scale datasets and rational action theory: for a sociological alliance. *Eur. Sociol. Rev.* 12:109–26

Goldthorpe JH. 1999. Modelling the pattern of class voting in British elections, 1964–1992. See Evans 1999, pp. 59–82

Goldthorpe JH, with Llewellyn C, Payne C. 1980. *Social Mobility and Class Structure in Britain.* Oxford: Clarendon

Goldthorpe JH, Lockwood D, Bechhoffer F, Platt J. 1968. *The Affluent Worker: Political Attitudes and Behaviour.* Cambridge, UK: Cambridge Univ. Press

Halle D. 1984. *America's Working Man: Work, Home, and Politics Among Blue-Collar Property Owners.* Chicago: Univ. Chicago Press

Heath AF, Evans G, Payne C. 1995. Modelling the class party relationship in Britain. 1964–92. *J. R. Stat. Soc. Ser. A* 158:563–74

Heath AF, Jowell R, Curtice J. 1987. Trendless fluctuation: a reply to Crewe. *Polit. Stud.* 35:259–77

Heath AF, Jowell R, Curtice J, Evans G, Field J, Witherspoon S. 1991. *Understanding Political Change: The British Voter, 1964–1987.* Oxford, UK: Pergamon

Heath AF, Savage M. 1995. Political alignments within the middle classes, 1972–89. In *Social Change and the Middle Classes*, ed. T Butler, M Savage, pp. 275–92. London: Univ. Coll. London Press

Heath AF, Jowell R, Curtice J. 1985. *How Britain Votes*. Oxford, UK: Pergamon

Hout M, Brooks C, Manza J. 1993. The persistence of classes in post-industrial societies. *Int. Sociol.* 8:259–77

Hout M, Brooks C, Manza J. 1995. The democratic class struggle in the United States. *Am. Sociol. Rev.* 60:805–28

Hout M, Manza J, Brooks C. 1999. Classes, unions, and the realignment of U.S. presidential voting: 1952–1992. See Evans 1999, pp. 83–96

Huckfeldt R. 1984. Political loyalties and social class ties: the mechanisms of contextual influence. *Am. J. Polit. Sci.* 28:399–417

Huckfeldt R, Kohfeld CW. 1989. *Race and the Decline of Class in American Politics*. Champaign: Univ. Ill. Press

Inglehart R. 1990. *Culture Shift in Advanced Industrial Society*. Princeton, NJ: Princeton Univ. Press

Inglehart R. 1997. *Modernization and Postmodernization: Cultural, Economic, and Political Change in 43 Societies*. Princeton, NJ: Princeton Univ. Press.

Inglehart R, Rabier J-R. 1986. Political realignment in advanced industrial society: from class-based politics to quality-of-life politics. *Gov. Oppos.* 21:457–79

King D, Wickham-Jones M. 1990. Social democracy and rational workers. *Br. J. Polit. Sci.* 20:387–413

King G. 1986. How not to lie with statistics: avoiding common mistakes in quantitative political science. *Am. J. Polit. Sci.* 30:666–87

Kitschelt H. 1994. *The Transformation of European Social Democracy*. Cambridge, UK: Cambridge Univ. Press

Korpi W. 1972. Some problems in the measurement of class voting. *Am. J. Sociol.* 78:627–42

Korpi W. 1983. *The Democratic Class Struggle*. London: Routledge, Kegan Paul

Lane J-E, Ersson SO. 1994. *Politics and Society in Western Europe*. London: Sage. 3rd ed.

Lijphart A. 1979. Religious vs. linguistic vs. class voting: the "crucial experiment" of comparing Belgium, Canada, South Africa, and Switzerland. *Am. Polit. Sci. Rev.* 73:42–58

Lijphart A. 1984. *Democracies: Patterns of Majoritarian and Consensus Government in Twenty-One Countries*. New Haven, CT: Yale Univ. Press

Lipset SM. 1981 (1960). *Political Man: The Social Bases of Politics*. London: Heinemann

Lipset SM, Rokkan S. 1967. Cleavage structures, party systems and voter alignments: an introduction. In *Party Systems and Voter Alignments: Cross National Perspectives*, ed. SM Lipset, S Rokkan, pp. 1–64. New York: Free

Listhaug O. 1997. The decline of class voting. In *Challenges to Political Parties: The Case of Norway*, ed. K Strøm, LG Svåsand, pp. 77–90. Ann Arbor: Univ. Michigan Press

Manza J, Hout M, Brooks C. 1995. Class voting in capitalist democracies since World War II: dealignment, realignment or trendless fluctuation? *Annu. Rev. Sociol.* 21:137–62

Marshall G. 1997. *Repositioning Class*. London: Macmillan

Mateju P, Rehakova B, Evans G. 1999. The politics of interests and class realignment in the Czech Republic, 1992–96. See Evans 1999, pp. 231–53

McNall SG, Levine RF, Fantasia R, eds. 1991. *Bringing Class Back In*. Boulder, CO: Westview

Müller W. 1999. Class cleavages in party preferences in Germany—old and new. See Evans 1999, pp. 137–80

Nagler J, Niemann J. 1997. *Economic voting and economic status in U.S. presidential elections, 1960 to 1996*. Presented at Annu. Meet. Midwest Polit. Sci. Assoc., Chicago, IL, April

Nieuwbeerta P. 1995. *The Democratic Class Struggle in Twenty Countries, 1945–1990*. Amsterdam: Thesis

Nieuwbeerta P, de Graaf ND. 1999. Traditional class voting in 20 postwar societies. See Evans 1999, pp. 23–56

Nieuwbeerta P, Ultee W. 1999. Class voting in Western industrialized countries, 1945–90: systematizing and testing explanations. *Eur. J. Polit. Res.* 27:1–39

Nisbet RA. 1959. The decline and fall of social class. *Pac. Sociol. Rev.* 2:11–17

Pakulski J, Waters M. 1996. *The Death of Class.* London: Sage

Prysby CL. 1977. Psychological sources of working-class support for leftist political parties. *J. Polit.* 39:1073–81

Przeworski A. 1985. *Capitalism and Social Democracy.* Cambridge, UK: Cambridge Univ. Press

Przeworski A, Sprague J. 1986. *Paper Stones: A History of Electoral Socialism.* Chicago: Univ. Chicago Press

Quaile Hill K, Leighley JE. 1996. Political parties and class mobilization in contemporary United States elections. *Am. J. Polit. Sci.* 40:787–804

Ringdal K, Hines K. 1999. Changes in class voting in Norway 1957–1989. See Evans 1999, pp. 181–202

Rose R. 1974. *Electoral Behavior: A Comparative Handbook.* New York: Free

Rose R, McAllister I. 1986. *Voters Begin to Choose: From Closed-Class to Open Elections in Britain.* London: Sage

Rose R, Urwin D. 1970. Persistence and change in western party systems since 1945. *Polit. Stud.* 18:287–319

Sainsbury D. 1987. Class voting and left voting in Scandinavia: the impact of different operationalizations of the working class. *Eur. J. Polit. Res.* 15:507–26

Sartori G. 1969. From the sociology of politics to political sociology. In *Politics and the Social Sciences*, ed. SM Lipset, pp. 65–100. Oxford, UK: Oxford Univ. Press

Saunders P. 1981. *Social Theory and the Urban Question.* London: Hutchinson

Saunders P. 1990. *A Nation of Home Owners.* London: Unwin Hyman

Siegfried A. 1913. *Tableau Politique de la France de l'Oest sous la Troisieme Republique.* Paris: Colin

Sombart W. 1976 (1906). *Why is There No Socialism in the United States?* New York: Sharpe

Sorensen A. 1998. Theoretical mechanisms and the empirical study of social processes. In *Social Mechanisms: An Analytical Approach to Social Theory*, ed. P Hedstrom, R Swedberg, pp. 238–66. Cambridge, UK: Cambridge Univ. Press

Szelenyi I, Fodor E, Hanley E. 1998. Left turn in post-communist politics? Bringing class back in. *E. Eur. Polit. Soc.* 11:190–224

Thomsen SR. 1987. *Danish Elections 1920–79: A Logit Approach to Ecological Analysis and Inference.* Aarhus, Den.: Politica

Tingsten H. 1937. *Political Behavior: Studies in Election Statistics.* London: King

Vanneman R, Cannon LW. 1987. *The American Perception of Class.* Philadelphia, PA: Temple Univ. Press

Weakliem DL. 1991. The two lefts? Occupation and party choice in France, Italy, and the Netherlands. *Am. J. Sociol.* 96:1327–61

Weakliem DL, Heath AF. 1994. Rational choice and class voting. *Ration. Soc.* 6:243–70

Weakliem DL, Heath AF. 1999a. The secret life of class voting: Britain, France, and the United States Since the 1930s. See Evans 1999, pp. 97–136

Weakliem DL, Heath AF. 1999b. Resolving disputes about class voting in Britain and the United States: definitions, models, and data. See Evans 1999, pp. 281–307

Weatherford MS. 1979. Economic conditions and electoral outcomes: class differences in the political response to recession. *Am. J. Polit. Sci.* 22:917–38

Whitten GD, Palmer HD. 1996. Heightening comparativists' concern for model choice: voting behaviour in Great Britain and the Netherlands. *Am. J. Polit. Sci.* 40:231–60

Xie Y. 1992. The log-multiplicative layer effect model for comparing mobility tables. *Am. Sociol. Rev.* 57:380–95

Annu. Rev. Polit. Sci. 2000. 3:419–47

THE PSYCHOLOGICAL FOUNDATIONS OF IDENTITY POLITICS

Kristen Renwick Monroe, James Hankin, and
Renée Bukovchik Van Vechten

*Department of Political Science, University of California at Irvine, Irvine,
California 92697; e-mail: krmonroe@uci.edu*

Key Words   social psychology, self-categorization, self, intergroup relations

■ **Abstract**   This chapter reviews social psychological theories relating to political identity and group behavior. We define individual and social identity, examine the main social psychological explanations of social identity, and discuss work on intergroup relations, boundaries, and conflict. We suggest several particular substantive political debates that would benefit from knowledge of this literature.

INTRODUCTION

Identity as an explanatory concept is considered in many disparate fields within political science, from nationalism and ethnic conflict to group mobilization and electoral politics. Yet surprisingly little of this literature refers to the important work of psychologists interested in the internal dynamic through which identity and perceptions of self influence both individual and group behavior. This chapter reviews the most important social psychological theories relating to political identity and group behavior to demonstrate the relevance of this literature for political science. By focusing on the social psychological, we examine the immediate social influences that explain why, when, and how identity will affect political behavior; such influences include other people (their attitudes, behaviors, and relationship to the actor) and the actor's internal perceptions of others and the external world.

We concentrate on two main bodies of literature. The first concerns the social psychological explanations of identity, including the literature on social cognition, social roles, and social construction. The second includes work on intergroup relations, boundaries, and conflict—specifically psychodynamic approaches and work on symbolic racism, social dominance, realistic group conflict theory, and social identity theory. (Scholars tend to use the terms realistic group conflict theory and realistic conflict theory interchangeably and we will do so throughout this paper). We suggest several particular substantive political debates that would benefit from knowledge of this literature.

1094-2939/00/0623-0419$14.00

The paper has four main sections. The first section focuses on the definition of identity, both individual and social. How is identity formed, and how does social identity differ from personal or private identity? The second section examines the main social psychological explanations of social identity, with special emphasis on social cognition. The third section links work on intergroup relations, boundaries, and conflict and asks whether—and when—exclusion, prejudice, and discrimination occur as a result of group formation. Finally, we suggest how the social psychological literature could enrich political discussion in several substantive areas, from racism and ethnic conflict to electoral politics and social movements.

IDENTITY AS A CONCEPT

What do we mean when we speak of identity, of the self? Philosophers from Plato to Descartes have attempted to define what a person is and we can present only a brief overview here. Analysts typically follow one of two approaches to identity. The first is illustrated by the Aristotelian view that considers human beings as biological organisms or animals. The second conceptualization builds on the Lockean view of a person as a psychological entity, distinct from the biological organism and, at least potentially, separable from it. Elements of each approach are evident in the literature in social psychology.

Conceptualizations of identity or self most frequently encompass the idea of a sense, developed early in childhood, of oneself as both an agent and an object that is seen, thought about, and liked or disliked by others. This idea is implied both by Aristotle and by humanistic psychologists such as Maslow, who argue that people have both basic biological needs (e.g. food and sleep) and analogous social needs (e.g. desires for prestige, admiration, and security). The Lockean aspect of identity also appears in the work of most contemporary psychologists when they consider the self. This conceptualization defines a person as "a thinking intelligent being, that has reason and reflection, and can consider itself as itself, the same thinking thing, in different times and places" (Perry 1975:12). This early conceptualization illustrates what James (1983 [1890]) later characterized as the one-in-many-selves paradox, which refers to the apparent contradiction between individuals maintaining self-continuity over time while still acting out different roles and effectively changing personalities, situation by situation. The self as a complex and multifaceted identity is similarly understood by Mead as the "I" (the subject self) and the "me" (the object of consideration by others). Freud's work on the division of id, ego, and superego also recognizes the multiple self. Recognizing the multiplicity of identity is now commonplace in psychology.

The concern with others, and their impact on an individual's sense of self, is evident in the classic formulation of identity by Erikson, the theorist perhaps most intimately associated with identity. In Erikson's view (1980 [1959]), each person has (a) a conscious sense of individual identity, (b) the unconscious striving for a continuity of personal character, (c) an ongoing or developmental process of ego synthesis, and (*d*) maintenance of an inner solidarity with the ideals and identity of a group. We need both a sense of continuity or sameness within ourselves and the persistent sense that others share our concept of our essential character.

Little is known about the manner in which others' perceptions of who one is feed into one's own sense of self. Classical psychoanalytic approaches stress the family and critical others, often privileging early childhood experiences that construct one's basic personality, or at least provide critical shaping for any biologically determined personality predispositions.

Personal Versus Social Identity

An individual's identity is made up of a variety of different components or attributes. Broadly defined, social identity refers to the social categories, attributes, or components of the self-concept that are shared with others and therefore define individuals as being similar to others. In contrast, personal identity is made up of those attributes that mark an individual as distinct from all others. (For more detailed discussions of this distinction, see Weigert et al 1986, Reid & Deaux 1996, Turner et al 1994).

Prior to the 1950s, most conceptualizations of the self referred to personal identity. The concept of social identity appeared in the context of studies of group behavior, where identity is now taken to refer to that part of an individual's identity that is supplied by membership in a group or groups and is influenced by the values and emotions of that group (Fine 1986, Taylor et al 1997). Social psychologists explain behavior through a focus on the individual's interaction with others, and most have moved away from the psychoanalytic tradition and consider immediate contexts more relevant than the developmental aspects of identity theory. They try to accommodate more recent theoretical advances while retaining the spirit of Erikson's original conceptualization (Allen & Scheibe 1982).

Whereas psychological approaches to identity focus on the internal coherence and development of the psyche, social theorists such as Durkheim and Mead instead emphasize the influences of social structures and culture. Durkheim's approach (1982) was perhaps the most structuralist, considering the individual a determined product of social facts. Similarly, Marx considered individual identity and consciousness a product of a person's place in economic structures.[1] Marx, of course, focused on class location as determinative of identity (Marx &

---

[1] Unlike Durkheim's, Marx's approach to individual identity and consciousness is not strictly determinative, as he includes the possibility of "false consciousness," such as that which occurs among the working class when bourgeois ideology obfuscates their awareness of their class identity and interests. Similarly, the very possibility of revolution suggests that some individuals (primarily intellectuals acting on behalf of the working class) can counter determinative institutional positioning through action.

Engels 1989 [1947]); feminists substitute gender for class but utilize a similar logic (Hartsock 1991). Mead, on the other hand, suggested that identity has two parts, the "I" and the "me"—one as the subject self, the other as the object of consideration by others (Mead 1924, 1934). Of this bipartite self, Mead argues that the objectified part is most important to the individual's self-concept and behavior, because the internalized reactions and judgment of the "generalized other" are the source of self-consciousness (Mead 1924).

The above conceptualizations of identity form the foundation for most contemporary approaches to social identity, which draw on both psychological and sociological theory. Whereas sociology emphasizes structural influences on behavior, and psychology individual differences that affect action, social psychologists search for fundamentals of human nature that are then influenced by situational factors. But the individual self forms the basis for both personal and social identity, which rely on an identification in relation to others (Dobert et al 1977) in the particular social interactions and structures in which a person operates. Contemporary identity theory thus posits an interplay between cognitive processes and social or cultural influences.

How Conceptualization Influences Explanations of Identity-based Politics

Scholars since Aristotle have noted the human disposition for sociability and our capacity to form cohesive social groups (Howell & Willis 1989). But how is social identity constructed and maintained? This question is particularly important because the way in which theoretical models account for these processes tends to predefine the researcher's explanations for intergroup behavior and social change.

For example, if social identity is constructed in a relatively passive way (e.g. the learning of particular attitudes through socialization) and remains stable (as political culture theory tends to assume), then intergroup discrimination and prejudice might also seem to be latent, enduring, and stable. On the other hand, if social identity is actively constructed by individuals and if the attributes assigned to self and others are more flexible, then intergroup conflict might be more temporary, contextual, and transient than is often thought. We return to this issue throughout our review.

SOCIAL PSYCHOLOGICAL EXPLANATIONS OF SOCIAL IDENTITY

Social cognition research provides a number of models that explain the structure of social identity and stress the relationship between identity and behavior. Aside from attitudinal research, however, political scientists have not made extensive use of other potentially helpful cognitive models in explaining political behavior.

Schema theory, social attribution theory, cognitive dissonance theory, and social representation theory are four important models from social cognition that may be of use to political scientists. Two related themes that run throughout this literature are (*a*) the biases that result from selective information processing and (*b*) the motivations underlying individuals' attempts to maintain and validate their own identities. We argue that together, these models can help explain the processes and motivations that cause individuals to process information and act in accordance with the identity categories to which they belong and which are deemed salient by the context. (The role of context in establishing salient identity categories is critical and is discussed below.)

We begin with two models that provide a psychological location for identity, namely schema theory and social representations theory. Schema theory describes identity in terms of mental structures, and social representation theory assumes a more discursive and shared model of identity.

Schema Theory

Although political scientists have used schema theory, they have tended to conceptualize and measure it in much the same way as attitudes (Miller et al 1986). But schemata are more than simply attitudes; schemata are the highly organized and generalized structures in memory that guide cognition and memory recall (Morgan & Schwalbe 1990). These structures allow for efficient management of information by offering templates for interpretation that reduce the amount of cognitive processing an individual has to undergo in order to account for events. Schemata have been incorporated into identity research to account for the cognitive components and normative expectations that certain identities assume. In this sense, schemata that reflect the values and normative expectations of an individual's social group can be a useful way to conceptualize how social identities are cognitively organized.

For example, Markus & Nurius (1987) apply schema theory to identity, arguing that identity is a system of salient schemata about the self that are unique and fundamental self-defining elements. Once in place, schemata both define the self and maintain identity through selective processing of information. Based on their measurements of reaction times in response to identity-relevant questions, Markus & Nurius conclude that some individuals might have more schematic identities than others.

In a similar vein, Kihlstrom & Cantor (1984) argue that the self is represented mentally in a hierarchically ordered series of "context-specific self-concepts," each representing beliefs about the self in various social situations. People have categories for themselves, just as they have schemata for others. For example, a man might think of himself as a lawyer, a father, a friend, a soccer coach, and a cook. Having multiple schemata leads to "self-complexity" that may act as a buffer against threats to his identity. In other words, if he is threatened as a lawyer, he might cognitively compensate for the attack on his professional identity by conceptualizing himself as a superb cook, a great soccer coach, and a terrific father (Linville 1987). A person also may have negative self-schemata, however. These would consist of categories of negative traits that characterize the individual and may be more easily accessed than positive self-schemata (Wurf & Markus 1983).

Fiske & Taylor (1991:186) summarize the self-schema literature as follows: "self-schema is a familiar, affective, robust, complex, and possibly verbal self-portrait. Our schemas for others are less familiar, less accessible in memory, less affectively valenced, simpler, and may be more likely to be stored in image form."

The selective-perception element of schema theory offers one explanation for the apparent stability of individual social identity. Once activated or "cued," schemata can result in distorted perception because they offer ready-made pathways for interpretation of incoming stimuli. Neurobiologists now hypothesize that schema may actually form physical pathways of neurobiological material, making them akin to well-traveled roads (R Keller, personal communication). Events that fit an individual's self-schemata are more likely to be processed and accepted than contrary information, which may be distorted or even ignored. Individuals also may engage in distorted perception because they need to maintain self-esteem or a consistent view of self and others. This is critical for politics, since the terms in which political debates are structured often determine the outcomes.

Although research on schemata has much to offer the study of social identity, some argue that its North American versions suffer from an overemphasis on individual cognition and specific psychological processes (Morgan & Schwalbe 1990). This narrow focus, it is argued, leads to a conceptualization of the self and identity that is passively constructed (through learning or socialization) and static, because cognitive structures, once in place, produce largely automatic cognitive processes. In European social cognition research, a more social or collective approach to cognition can be found in models such as social representations.

Social Representation Theory

In contrast to schema theory, proponents of social representation research emphasize the collective nature of social cognition and the role of intersubjective interaction in the interpretation of events. Social representations are defined as the collectively held explanations of reality that are continually reproduced in interaction (Moscovici 1988). Though collectively held, social representations are an interstice between an individual's schemata and collective social knowledge because generally accepted truths about the social world (what Moscovici calls hegemonic social representations) become schematic or, in Moliner's terms (1995), become the "core" of a social representation. As such, hegemonic representations become the foundation on which new events are interpreted to produce more specific social representations.

This is a much less passive model of social cognition than is schema theory; even though hegemonic social representations may become nonconscious schematic frameworks, they still can be elevated to consciousness when an individual's understanding is challenged or when she is confronted with otherwise inexplicable social events. This model perhaps has more relevance for analysis of political rhetoric and discourse because it is able to capture the dynamics of ongoing constructions of meanings.

Social representations are useful to the extent that the researcher requires a more contextual, dynamic, and discursive psychological model of identity than schema theory. The models are to some extent complementary, however, because of their slightly different focus.

Let us now turn to two models of information processing: social attribution theory and cognitive dissonance theory. These models are useful because of their focus on two processes central to many identity theories, selective perception and the maintenance of self-esteem. Both social attribution theory (Kelley 1971, Weiner 1974) and cognitive dissonance theory (Festinger 1957) are models of information processing that highlight the motivational bases of identity.

Social Attribution Theory

Social attribution refers to the intuitive process by which individuals attribute causality to social events. Research in this area holds that when we make decisions on attribution, we consistently succumb to cognitive distortions, such as the self-serving bias and the actor-observer bias. The self-serving bias occurs when positive events are attributed to the observer's dispositional traits and negative events are attributed to situational factors; in the actor-observer bias, the same negative event is attributed to situational factors when it involves the observer and to dispositional traits when it involves an observed actor. Tetlock (1985) has suggested that social attribution can account for the mechanism by which the desire to maintain and enhance self-esteem operates on identity. The biases inherent in social attribution are not seen as the failure of an individual to correctly account for his or her social environment; instead, social attribution plays an essential role in maintaining and, indeed, defining positively, both personal and social identity.[2]

Cognitive Dissonance Theory

Cognitive dissonance theory is widely used in psychological accounts of identity, both explicitly and in rearticulated or parallel conceptions of identity crises, where conceptions of self are no longer validated during interaction with others. Identity theorists use cognitive dissonance theory (Festinger 1957) to argue that the motivation to change attitudes is based on the desire to relieve the tension one feels when (*a*) one holds cognitions that are inconsistent with each other or (*b*) one's

---

[2]Similar uses of social attribution are examined below in the context of situated identity (Alexander & Wiley 1981) and social identity theory.

cognitions and beliefs are inconsistent with one's acts (Sdorow 1990). As such, in instances where an individual's attitudes or schemata are highly salient, a conflicting cognition may itself be ignored or rationalized away in order to guarantee cognitive consistency.

Rosenberg (1981) incorporates cognitive dissonance into his model of identity, which he calls the self-concept. The self-concept is made up of attitudes that derive from an array of group statuses and social categories to which an individual belongs. Because the sources for identity are multiple, identity itself is a crystallization of more or less salient attitudes. Like Tetlock, Rosenberg argues that the key motivation for maintaining identity is self-esteem; individuals try to maintain a positive image of self in comparison with others. If, however, the salient attitudes that comprise identity are threatened in social interaction, a dissonance arises between self-image and social validation of that self-image. Rosenberg argues that in these instances, individuals attempt to achieve consonance through manipulative cognitive procedures, such as social attribution and social comparison.

Attitudes, schemata, and social representations all offer ways in which the definition of social identities of self and others might be conceptualized and provide the building blocks on which more detailed theories of social identity and prejudice are built. We now turn to these perspectives and review social role theory, models of self-presentation, and social constructionism.

Social Role Theory

Social role theories offer one perspective on social identity that might be useful for individual-level analyses of political behavior. These theories are drawn from symbolic interactionism (Mead 1934, Hewitt 1988) and micro-sociological traditions (Blumer 1969, Berger & Luchman 1966) that focus on the mutual construction of the self and social structure through interaction. Despite individual differences, social role theories are unified by the following propositions.

1. Society is differentiated into social roles.

2. Social roles prescribe behaviors that are considered appropriate by others.

3. Identity can be defined as the internalization of role designations by individuals.

Roles, in essence, are an analytical tool to describe how otherwise indeterminate social interactions become routinized into shared normative and behavioral expectations (Secord 1982). When applied to identity, social roles can be used to define the norms, values, and behavioral expectations that individuals face in organizations and particular routinized interactions.

Stryker's identity theory is one of the most influential attempts to apply role theory to symbolic interactionism in the explanation of identity and behavior. In Stryker's account (1987:84), roles are "symbols that designate relatively stable positions in social structure that carry shared behavioral expectations," and identity is comprised of the "internalized role designations corresponding to the social location of persons." It is on the basis of the shared behavioral expectations that Stryker attempts to predict an individual's behavior in particular interactional contexts, and this prediction is further specified by the concepts of identity salience and commitment. Identity salience refers to the way in which role designations are organized into salience hierarchies, i.e. the probability that certain role designations will be called into play. These salience hierarchies are constructed by an individual's commitment to the predictable behavior and self-esteem that are associated with certain roles (Stryker & Terpe 1982). Stryker's identity theory tries to account for an individual's behavior on the basis of that person's most salient role designations.

Some authors (Hogg et al 1995) argue that, beyond minimal descriptions of internalization of social roles, this perspective is not particularly psychological. However, other role theorists have incorporated more specific versions of social cognition into models of social roles. Alexander & Wiley (1981), for example, combine models of schemata and social attribution with roles to construct their model of "situated identity." The shared behavioral expectations and interpretations between parties in interactions are described as "dispositional schemata" (Wiley & Alexander 1987:107–9). Situated identity is made up of these dispositional schemata, which for any particular context define the self, others, and their expected behaviors. Dispositional schemata also provide the mode of interpretation that should be used to explain particular contexts. Alexander & Wiley (1981) suggest that social attributions become encoded in the dispositional schemata of individuals in shared social roles and as such are socially defined templates for interpreting the motivation of one's own and others' behavior.[3]

Social role theories also offer motivational explanations for why people act to maintain identity. The notion that successful interaction with others validates one's own conceptions of self is common in this and other identity perspectives (Stryker & Terpe 1982, Stryker 1987), as is the argument that people seek interactions to maintain a particular status (Sarbin & Schiebe 1983) or raise their self-esteem (Alexander & Wiley 1981).[4] Social role theories differ on the origin of the impetus; some stress the simple need to achieve cognitive consistency, whereas others stress the more active stance of seeking to maintain a positive sense of self. But most social role theories agree that despite the potential for failure in interaction, individuals

---

[3]Orwell's story about the Indian colonial officer shooting the elephant exemplifies the extent to which individuals can become trapped by the dispositional schemata associated with particular roles. Neither the colonial officer nor the local populace wanted to kill the elephant. But everyone felt obliged to act in a certain way, as specified by their dispositional schemata, and the elephant ended up being shot.

[4]Some empirical research has failed to support the theory that behaving in the service of one's self-esteem is a consistent universal. One view is that self-esteem is one of many motivating forces that is activated in varying degrees and is situationally dependent. See e.g. Lemyre & Smith 1985, Hogg & Turner 1985.

have surprisingly stable conceptions of identity (see Hogg et al 1995 and Robinson & Smith-Lovin 1992).

The Presented Self

In contrast to the concept of role, which tends toward a fairly specific and marked location in social structure, social psychologies in the presented-self tradition draw on Goffman (1973) and focus on the less rigid "performance" as the site of identity formation and maintenance (Baumeister 1986a,b; Schlenker 1986, 1985). Schlenker, for example, describes identity as "a theory about the self that is formed or maintained through actual or imagined interpersonal agreement about what the self is like" (1986:23). Identity is performed and maintained in particular contexts in which the individual, the situation, and one or more salient audiences combine to produce a consensually defined set of qualities that distinguish self from others. Since particular contexts have limited interpretations—and thus limit the identity possibilities available—identity will be as stable as the context allows. However, even in routinized forms of social interaction, failures can happen; in such cases, interrupted performances will produce attempts to explain/perform in ways that reinvoke identity and maintain self-esteem (Schlenker 1985). The presented-self literature could be useful in analyzing routinized performances, such as the parades in Northern Ireland where the Apprentice Boys of Derry commemorate the city's siege in 1689–1690. Another possible example is the State of the Union Address by American presidents, which is judged at least as much on the basis of style and performance as on substantive policy proposals.

Social Constructionism

Social constructionism takes a more extreme position than models on the presented self by dismissing the notion of a fixed identity and claiming instead that identity and social context are malleable and contingent. Social constructionism moves away from a concern with individual psychological processes or attempts to classify social context in terms of roles, schemata, or performance rituals, and instead focuses on the situational, linguistic, and narrative construction of identity. Social constructionism is perhaps the most post-structural perspective on identity that is still considered an empirically derived, scientific theory of psychology (see e.g. Gergen 1989, Billig 1987). From this perspective, identity is therefore a kind of discursive performance that occurs in reference to others in particular situations and can be conceptualized with terms such as self-narratives and social accountability (Shotter 1985, Harré 1987).

Self-narrative is a "linguistic implement constituted and reconstituted by people in relationships and employed to enhance, sustain and impede various actions" (Gergen & Gergen 1983:56). Self-narratives are akin to telling stories about who we are with the support of others as listeners. But self-narratives do not refer to or crystallize into a stable self-concept; instead, narrative can be seen as the capacity of people to represent themselves to others as if they do possess continuous and stable identities (Gergen & Gergen 1983:266). Indeed, narratives change, often as part of conflict resolution. (Witness the recent shifts in the narrative of Yugoslav identity).

Summary

Although the critique of passive individual-level models of social cognition and the recognition of the narrative role of identity constitution are important, all the above-discussed models are nonetheless worth considering if the goals are the depiction, measurement, and analysis of identity. Overall, these perspectives on the psychological aspects of identity range from the minimal (complexes of attitudes, schemata, or social representations) to the stable (role theory) to the most flexible and contingent (performed and socially constructed identity). These theories offer a variety of approaches that political scientists might use to account for political identity and political behavior.

INTERGROUP RELATIONS, BOUNDARIES, AND CONFLICT

Social identity sometimes becomes so salient that individuals excluded from the group are considered acceptable targets for discriminatory behavior. Why? Such questions require analyzing how the boundaries of social identity are formed, understanding why certain individuals are included or excluded, and asking what kinds of behavior members of one's own social identity categories can expect from outsiders. In this section, we review the social psychological theories that address these social identity processes in a manner most useful for political research. We begin with a brief discussion of two micro-level models of prejudice: psychodynamic approaches and models of symbolic racism. We then discuss a systemic account of prejudice—social dominance—before moving to two models of intergroup relations: realistic conflict theory and social identity theory.

Psychodynamic Approaches

A number of theories attempt to explain racism and discriminatory behavior based on the psychodynamic traits of individuals (Adorno et al 1950, Fromm 1965, Cash 1989). These theories essentially attribute discriminatory and racist behavior to the psychological structures of the unconscious.

The Authoritarian Personality (Adorno et al 1950) is the classic example of this type of research. Adorno argues that an individual's personality type predisposes him or her to particular types of political identity and behavior. These personality types in turn result from an individual's family structure. For example, a hierarchical and authoritarian family structure might cause a child to repress certain desires and drives. This repression produces anxieties, which in turn produce the authoritarian personality type, as defined by the following traits: intolerance of ambiguity, deference to authority, and the scapegoating of relevant out-groups.

As an explanation of why particular individuals and the groups to which they belong exhibit extreme political ideologies and discrimination, the authoritarian personality thesis is intriguing and has been applied in various ways to explain support for right-wing values (Altmeyer 1981, 1988). These approaches are limited, however, because group and societal explanations of authoritarianism must be extrapolated from the individual level. For example, to explain broad societal authoritarianism, researchers would have to claim that the culture of child-rearing practices was conducive to the development of authoritarian personalities.

Recent work (Cash 1989, 1996) builds on this approach by combining Kleinian psychoanalytic models with more social-structural accounts of ideology to account for social identity and prejudice. Cash defines both identity and group memberships by the ideological context of the day. Ideological structures are further invested with affect to the extent that when the boundaries, traits, and membership of identity categories are challenged, individuals face a crisis of meaning that is articulated through particular forms of anxiety. These forms of anxiety will in turn determine what forms of prejudice or ideological change will occur. In analyzing identity politics in Northern Ireland, for example, Cash argues that an ambiguous response is more likely to result in social change than a persecutory response, which would reinforce ideological prejudices and support the status quo.

Ross's (1995) work on ethnic conflict reflects another use of the psychoanalytic approach, one that privileges object-relations theory over the older, drive-based theories of psychodynamic functioning. Ross argues that the multiplicity of group memberships held by any one person reflects our multidimensional individual identities. It thus becomes critical to understand what makes one aspect of identity, and one particular group membership, so salient. Ross suggests that contemporary object relations theory, which links a person's inner and outer worlds, can explain the development of the intense social and political attachments to groups, since these groups provide shared identities. Object relations theory emphasizes the social basis of internalized images and identities, providing linkages between external events (or at least the constructed collective memories of these events) and individual internalization. The critical element is the external basis of internalized metaphors. Thus, Jewish images of the destruction of the temple, central European pogroms, and the Holocaust would be consistent with a shared worldview and identity that explains what outsiders will do if given the chance. In situations of ethnic group conflict, these group identities and history need psychic validation, even as a new and less conflictual identity is being formed (Kelman 1992).

Symbolic Racism

In contrast to psychodynamic models of social identity and prejudice, which focus on unconscious drives, attitudinal models assume identity results primarily from early socialization. One explanation for prejudice that draws on attitudinal research is the model of symbolic racism (Sears 1993, 1988; Kinder & Sears 1981). Sears and Kinder argue that white racism against African-Americans is based on symbolic dispositions learned early in life. In contrast to traditional racism, these symbolic dispositions are not overtly racist but are composed of feelings of "anti-black affect" and traditional Protestant values of individualism. The activation of these dispositions can lead to negative evaluations of African-American candidates and of policies aimed at benefiting African-Americans.

Most empirical evidence has supported the claim that anti-black affect does contribute to voting behavior and general evaluations of African-American candidates when measured on a hot-cold thermometer scale (Sears 1988, Sidanius et al 1992). On the other hand, empirical findings that covert racism is veiled in expressions of traditional values of individualism have been mixed at best (Sears 1988, Sniderman et al 1991). Sniderman & Carmines (1997) find that American reluctance to support policies in favor of minorities might actually be expressing an aversion to increasing governmental power.

The symbolic-racism thesis offers some interesting insights, particularly into the influence of political culture on the construction and maintenance of identity boundaries. Like attitudes, symbolic dispositions are presumed, for the most part, to be learned early in life and to remain stable over time. Although this approach also suggests that prejudice is stable and enduring over time, it is clear that extreme forms of overt racism are not acceptable in the contemporary American experience, and when prejudice and discrimination are recognized, public condemnation tends to be swift. But how are we to explain the occurrence and psychology of one group's specific expressions of prejudice against another? Beyond suggesting that symbolic dispositions become activated or are cued, the theory provides little detail as to how and why certain expressions of prejudice might occur.

Social Dominance

The same criticism applies to another social psychological perspective on prejudice: social dominance theory (Sidanius 1992, 1993; Sidanius et al 1994,b). Social dominance theory is an attempt to construct a grand theory of prejudice and discrimination in intergroup relations, drawing on the diverse theoretical sources of social psychology, elitism in political sociology, and evolutionary psychology of group conflict and ethnocentrism (Sidanius 1993). Symbolic predispositions are seen not as the cause but rather as the legitimizing myths that mediate more basic individual and group motivations into individual or institutionalized acts of discrimination.

This claim is based on the following theoretical assumptions. All societies are to some degree hierarchical. All societies have at least one hegemonic group and one subordinate group, with different behavioral expectations for each. Aggregated individual and institutional discrimination is a normal societal feature. These societal givens are maintained by individual and group identity processes, such as social comparison, social identification, and self-esteem maintenance (see "Identity as a Concept," above), which in turn lead to the "social dominance orientation." Social dominance orientation is a fundamental human desire to view one's own group as positive and occupying higher social statuses than other relevant groups.

In social dominance theory, then, an orientation toward social dominance constitutes a variable that is prior to symbolic racism, which is categorized in this model as a legitimizing myth or an ideological truism that supports widespread discrimination. For example, the traditional Protestant values of individualism and meritocracy, which are a component of symbolic racism, are for social dominance theory ideological supports that justify discrimination, which is at root caused by social dominance orientation.

Social dominance theory may be useful to researchers trying to discover the relation between certain orientations, e.g. social dominance, support for hierarchical, discriminatory societal structures, and political behavior. However, to claim that all societies are inherently hierarchical and discriminatory, albeit to different degrees, does not explain sudden eruptions of prejudice and discrimination; nor does it explain why prejudice and discrimination arise in specific situations or at different points in time. Certainly one could test for the existence of social dominance orientation or symbolic dispositions and correlate these findings with voting behavior and policy preferences, as proponents of these positions attempt to do. But what is missing is a more precise account of the specific psychological process that occurs when individuals display a particular social identity and simultaneously discriminate against others.

Realistic Group Conflict Theory

One model that does attempt to explain the actual dynamics of group identification and discrimination is realistic conflict theory, often called realistic group conflict theory. This theory rejects notions of symbolic dispositions or orientations and assumes group behavior and prejudice are based on individual rationality. Realistic group conflict theory (Campbell 1965, Sherif 1967, Insko et al 1992) adopts the basic premises of rational choice theory. It suggests that intergroup conflict is based on the perceptions of group members with regard to the real competition between groups for scarce resources. It posits that identification with in-groups and prejudice against out-groups are based on group members' perceptions of group competition for these resources. Like most economically oriented theories, realistic conflict theory assumes that individuals are selfish and are driven to maximize their own resources at the expense of others. When two or more groups are in competition for resources, realistic conflict theory assumes that conflict is inevitable and that group members, recognizing that their own self-interest lies with their group's success, will identify with their in-groups and begin to discriminate against the competitive out-group(s). The implication is that satisfying group needs will minimize, but not eliminate entirely, this natural conflict.

To illustrate, consider the well-known Robbers' Cave summer camp experiments, in which prejudice and stereotyping were created by instigating conflict and competition between 12-year-olds (Sherif et al 1961). In 1967, Sherif outlined the progression of group formation and group conflict as follows: groups form, develop in-group norms, and begin to stereotype and derogate members of the competitive out-group. Sherif argued that in order to reduce intergroup tensions, the intergroup dynamic should be restructured in such a way that superordinate goals, which require intergroup cooperation, replace the goal of intergroup competition. This redirection in perspective would reduce intergroup conflict and hostility and lead to the breakdown of group boundaries.

Realistic group conflict theory assumes that real conflict between groups produces the social psychological effects of in-group identification and stereotyping of the out-group. But this assumption seems to undermine the rational and material bases of the theory because, once in operation, group conflict operates at a psychological level that is far from rational and is in fact characterized by faulty, biased, and suboptimal decision making (see Janis 1983, Turner et al 1992). Further, as Taylor & Moghaddam (1994) point out, the solution of imposing superordinate goals that necessitate cooperation—as posited by Sherif and others—assumes a psychological shift in perception between groups and does not require a change in the initial conditions of competition. In essence, the functioning of group conflict and the solution to the conflict are framed in psychological terms that undermine the rational basis of realistic conflict theory.

Some realistic group conflict theorists would disagree with this, as do the authors of the behavioral interaction model (Rabbie et al 1989). One response (Insko et al 1992) has been to suggest that the initial phases of group conflict could be explained by realistic group conflict theory and later by theories such as social identity theory. Nevertheless, other psychological theories of intergroup relations—such as the ones discussed below—may be better equipped to account for the psychological processes by which individuals identify with groups and the development of discriminatory stereotypes of out-group members.

Social Identity Theory and Self-Categorization Theory

This literature suggests that perceptions of competition for scarce resources reinforce in-group/out-group distinctions but are not necessary conditions for in-group favoritism and intergroup discrimination. Although its foundations lie in individual psychology, social identity theory and its derivative, self-categorization theory, are attempts to construct a nonreductionist, cognitive, social psychological model of group identity and intergroup relations.[5] There are three basic tenets to this approach.

---

[5]There are alternative approaches to social identity theory. One is to view self-identity as an outgrowth of role theory. Other models of self-identity tend to complement the self-categorization approach to social identity. Sarbin & Scheibe (1983) suggest that social identity theory is a natural outgrowth of role theory, and that the latter should be considered a starting point for understanding social identity. Their model consists of three dimensions: (a) status or position in a social structure that conforms to a set of expectations held by members of a relevant society, a notion qualitatively different from role; (b) involvement, or the intensity with which a role is enacted; and (c) positive or negative valuation of these dimensions.

1. Social reality is definable as socially constructed categories that further define individuals, usually in terms of group norms.

2. Social identity is derived from an individual's self-categorization, the process by which the individual cognitively redefines the self in terms of group norms and the associated stereotypes of particular social categories (Hogg 1992, Oakes et al 1994, Turner et al 1994).

3. The assumption of "social comparison" suggests that because social identity is a source of positive self-esteem, there will be a tendency for members of the in-group to accentuate their similarities and to accentuate and negatively evaluate differences from out-group members, in order to achieve an intergroup evaluative advantage (Hogg & Abrams 1988).

Social identity theory has it roots in research based on Tajfel's "minimal group paradigm" (1970). Tajfel found that in situations of group decision making, people tend to favor their membership group (in-group) over out-groups, even when these groups are artificial laboratory constructions and competition for resources between groups is absent (Hogg & Abrams 1988). Unlike previous perspectives in group psychology, which explained group differentiation not only in terms of group cohesiveness but also in terms of real or perceived competition between the in-group and out-groups (Sherif 1967), Tajfel's research showed that the mere formation of otherwise meaningless groups produced in-group favoritism versus the out-group.

To account for this phenomenon, Tajfel argued that groups provide members with positive self-esteem, and that therefore group members were motivated to enhance their image of the in-group in relation to relevant out-groups (Hogg & Abrams 1988). Social identity theory takes Tajfel's insights further, arguing that because social groups provide members with social identities and because the desire to maintain positive self-esteem is a fundamental human motivation, derogation of out-groups is a likely outcome of in-group tendencies to enhance their self-evaluations (Hogg 1992).

Self-categorization theory extends the social identity theory paradigm to more precisely account for the cognitive bases of self-categorization and the relation/distinction between personal and social identity (Turner & Hogg 1987, Turner et al 1994). Self-categorization theory moves past social identity theory's binary distinction between personal and social identity, positing a self that is conceptualized at different levels of abstraction (Oakes et al 1994). For the sake of simplicity, these levels are designated as the interpersonal (or personal identity), the intergroup (an intermediate level of abstraction based on social identity derived from group membership), and interspecies (the superordinate level, or the self as human). Self-categorization theory is most concerned with the interplay between self-categorization at the personal and group levels; both involve a cognitive process in which the self is categorized as different from others (in the case of personal identity) or similar to group members (social identity). In the case of social identity, self-categorization theory builds on social identity theory by arguing that the self-categorization with a cognitive representation of the group results in the depersonalization of self and the homogenization of both the in-group and the out-group, based on dimensions that reflect the prototypicality or stereotypicality of members of each group (Hogg 1992).

The thousands of experiments underlying social identity theory have consistently shown that individuals identify with the in-group, support group norms, and derogate out-group members along stereotypical lines, even when there is no individual gain at stake (e.g. Gagnon & Bourhis 1996). Unlike realistic group conflict theory, social identity theory argues that the self-esteem that individuals receive from evaluating the in-group (and thus themselves) positively in relation to the out-group is enough to drive self-identification and intergroup discrimination. Further, social identity theory and self-categorization theory can more adequately account for the psychological processes by which the individual cognitively redefines the self in terms of the group norms and the associated stereotypes of particular social categories (e.g. Hogg 1992, Oakes et al 1994, Turner et al 1994). Such self- and other-categorizing along prototypical or stereotypical lines is a central tenet of social identity theory. Finally, the introduction of superordinate goals, which is posited as a solution by some realistic conflict theorists, can be seen as the cognitive reclassification of social identity by individuals into another social identity category.

Realistic group conflict theory and social identity theory are often seen as competing theories. Many social psychologists, however, see these models as complementary; for example, social identification may become more pronounced with more extreme in-group and out-group homogenization in cases where competition for real resources exists. However one views them, realistic group conflict theory and social identity theory can be useful to political scientists concerned with intergroup conflict, identity, and the allocation of resources between competing groups.

RELEVANCE FOR POLITICAL SCIENCE

Utilizing the psychological literature on identity could enrich many substantive discussions in political science, since much of politics concerns groups and our relations with others. In this last section we briefly illustrate how the knowledge of the psychology underlying identity could inform and enrich political discussion. We focus on two areas in some detail: (*a*) racism, ethnic violence, and genocide and (*b*) group politics in elections. We then suggest several other areas of potential interest.

Prejudice, Discrimination, Racism, Genocide, and Ethnic Violence

A traditional rational perspective on these subjects suggests that differential distribution of wealth or political resources, and the perception of competition for scarce resources, reinforce in-group/out-group distinctions and make them politically salient. A more troubling explanation comes from social identity theory, which suggests that genocide and racism may in fact be extreme manifestations of normal group identification and behavior.[6] These insights, though disturbing, help explain some of the cognitive and cultural processes involved in group identities and the ways that group difference can produce prejudice and intergroup conflict.

From this perspective, the critical shift in perception between self and other is due to individual self-identification at the group level. These critical perceptions of difference can become extreme enough to produce the complete distancing and dehumanization of the out-group based on the stereotypical dimension with which the out-group is defined. Browning's (1992) explanation of the mass killing of Jews by the Reserve Order Police Battalions during World War II suggests several possible social psychological explanations for this gruesome behavior, and points to several areas of inquiry that may prove more fruitful than merely explaining such behavior in terms of obeying orders or anti-Semitism.

To explain genocide, for example, a social psychological approach would focus not on the individual pathology of genocide (such as childhood abuse suffered from members of a particular ethnic group) but would instead ask what kinds of interpersonal situations might create the feelings of anger necessary to trigger or increase violent behavior that then turns into genocide. One social psychological explanation might be that frustrating situations, such as those imposed on the Germans by the Treaty of Versailles and the Depression, make people angry, thereby increasing their tendency to act aggressively. The frustration-aggression hypothesis (Festinger 1957) predicts that when people are blocked from achieving a desired goal (in this case a stable job that earns noninflating deutschmarks sufficient to care for their families), they become frustrated and angry. They then wish to lash out—at anyone. The frustration-aggression hypothesis focuses attention on the immediate social situation, the thoughts and feelings that the situation produces in people, and the overall effects of those subjective reactions on action. This example makes clear that there is considerable overlap among individual, societal, and interpersonal psychology.

Scholars then can move on to address some of the questions left unanswered by the social identity approach. For example, we know that not all identity differences become politicized or violent; in fact, wide ranges of group identities coexist peacefully in most times and places. Why? The social identity literature suggests that we need to understand more about the situational factors and processes that affect (*a*) which group categories form, (*b*) which group identifications become most salient in particular contexts and why, and (*c*) how these identifications

---

[6]This literature suggests that the critical shift in perception between self and other is due to individual self-identification at the group level. Group-level identification requires the perception of in-group similarity versus out-group difference, so social identity theorists assume that self and other are defined in terms of stereotypical similarity or distinctions. In this sense, social identity theory might lead us (*a*) to expect perceptual distance between self and other and (*b*) to find these perceptions of difference to be based on stereotypes.

escalate into violence. In order to explain what kinds of processes produce violent conflict from group identifications, we need to consider several other literatures: realistic group conflict theory, social representations, and post-structuralist theories of conflict.

Consider work that deals with racism and discriminatory behavior based on the models of symbolic racism (Sears 1993, 1988; Kinder & Sears 1981). These models draw on concepts from social psychology to argue that racism is based on symbolic dispositions learned early in life. These dispositions, though latent for the most part, can be elicited in certain contexts to produce racist attitudes and behavior. Because of their ability to account for the contexts in which symbolic dispositions become activated, theories of symbolic racism offer interesting insights and methodologies for the analysis of the critical shift of perception that occurs between self and other in cases of genocide and racism.

Sears and his colleagues, for example, have used the symbolic politics model to explain white resistance to public policies that might benefit African-Americans (Sears et al 1997, Sears & Funk 1999). Through statistical analysis of National Election Survey data, these authors argue that highly stable core dispositions comprised of negative affective responses to African-Americans and a commitment to traditional conservative values are key determinants of whites' support for racially targeted public policy. Such findings are useful in explaining racial bias in the absence of overt racism.

However, Sniderman and his colleagues question these findings. They suggest instead that one's commitment to values such as individual responsibility and achievement may be more important than whether one is politically liberal or conservative or harbors deep-seated biases against African-Americans (Sniderman et al 1991, Gilens et al 1998). Whites react negatively to racially based policies when they sense that African-Americans have violated particular "white" individualist values.

Also of interest is the work of social representation theorists (Moscovici 1988, Doise1988). This literature suggests that collective meanings are generated through the act of communication between individuals. It grants the validity of realistic conflict theory by agreeing that there is often a real material or political interest involved in intergroup conflict, but it argues that the "real" situation is less determinative of how people will behave than what people believe or perceive about the scarcity of resources. For this reason, it is also important to consider the production of beliefs in a particular society through symbols and systems of meaning. Moscovici (1988) suggests it is not objective phenomena but rather their representation that should be the focus of analysis about beliefs and social action:

> Social representations concern the contents of everyday thinking and the stock of ideas that gives coherence to our religious beliefs, political ideas and the connections we create as spontaneously as we breathe. They make it possible for us to classify persons and objects, to compare and explain behaviors and to objectify them as parts of our social setting. While

> representations are often located in the minds of men and women, they can just as often be found in the society as a whole and, as such, can be examined separately. (Moscovici 1988:214)

This theory suggests that when we represent the character and relation of identity groups in language and images, we actually help construct beliefs about them. Social representations might be identified in everyday language, media images, popular culture, or any other place where communication occurs. Because there are so many people talking and so many images around us, representations of identity groups are necessarily multiple and might not be shared by an entire society. At the same time, many representations become so common in a particular context that they have profound effects on popular perceptions and beliefs.

Consider how this theory might apply to the debate over why ordinary Germans participated in the mass killing of Jews. The popular representation of Jews in the interwar period in Europe as wealthy or connected to an international conspiracy made it vastly easier for the Nazis to exploit the generalized unrest resulting from Germany's loss of World War I and widespread economic distress resulting from the Depression. An individual's uneasiness at being unable to support his family could then be blamed on the Jews, who served as scapegoats for a situation whose causes lay in abstract, structural variables but whose immediate effect was painful and personal. While Hitler's propaganda machine certainly promoted the idea of the Jewish threat, Hitler did not invent this story, which had already become widespread through everyday channels. More detailed work that examines the social representations of Jews among differing groups might help explain the differential treatment of Jews and the shift in attitudes toward Jews among these groups.

Another example is found in the representation of freed slaves in the American South during Reconstruction. As in post–World War I Germany, generalized political disintegration, disruption of traditional patterns of elite dominance, and political influence were combined with widespread economic distress. Because material resources were scarce after the Civil War, individuals felt frustrated and wanted to blame someone. It was easy to perceive a conflict between whites, who felt entitled to land, jobs, and other resources, and newly emancipated blacks who were suddenly free to compete for these resources. But popular representations of blacks among white communities were particularly cruel at this historical moment. Blacks were portrayed not only as an economic threat, but also as criminal and sexual threats. As a result, racial violence resulting in black fatalities was arguably worse after the elimination of slavery, with the growth of the Ku Klux Klan and mob lynchings that reached their peak around the turn of the century. This perspective would suggest that in times of uncertainty (common to the documented cases of racism and genocide such as the Holocaust), social representations of self and other are intersubjectively constructed in order to produce shared understanding. Like theories of symbolic racism, social representations research is useful in alerting us to the contexts in which discriminatory stereotypes are generated.

Work on social dominance theory (Sidanius 1993; Sidanius et al 1994a,b) presents similarly troubling findings for those who are concerned about the fair and equal treatment of others. This literature explains racism in terms of sociobiology and evolutionary theory, arguing that the needs of certain groups to maintain the integrity of their gene pools cause racist attitudes and behavior. For example, Sidanius and his colleagues have operationalized the social dominance orientation through experiments and survey data in their attempts to explain attitudes towards interracial marriage (Fang et al 1998), differences in occupational status between genders (Pratto et al 1997), and differences between levels of punishment applied to blacks and whites in the criminal justice system (Sidanius et al 1994a,b). In each case, they argue that the social dominance orientation influences high-status groups to maintain a hierarchical advantage over disadvantaged groups.

Such an explanation does not explain the specific psychological processes that are peculiar to genocidal behavior. But when we combine findings in social dominance theory with the work in social identity theory, the implications for multiculturalism are disturbing. Relinquishing the myth of the melting pot in favor of a politics of multicultural group identities may accentuate group distinctions that then can further isolate us and result in increasing group tensions within society.

How would a social dominance approach explain the transformation of mere difference into intergroup conflict or violence? This literature tends to consider intergroup relations in highly contextual ways. That is, group identities form in historically specific ways, and then the social representations which foment conflict are also specific to a particular society.

Events in the former Yugoslavia provide an illustration. What is it that made "Serbianness" politically salient at a particular time and place, such that this Serb identity came to be understood as a basis for genocidal behavior?[7] Each Serb also had other identities that had the potential to be critical bases for differentiation: class, race, rural/urban, and even Yugoslavian status as opposed to some other national group. The first task in explaining Serb behavior would be to explain the politicization of Serb identity in Bosnia. The second would be to show how Bosnian Muslims came to be considered a critical out-group. Because group identities are relational, we might expect this process to be closely intertwined with the politicization of Serbian in-group identity. And finally, we would examine how Bosnian Muslims were represented in a manner that made it acceptable—even necessary—to kill them. What stories were in most frequent public circulation, and how might these have precipitated violence? A similar analysis could be performed for the other instances of ethnic violence, e.g. the Holocaust or the recent killings in Rwanda-Burundi.

---

[7]Here we simplify a very complicated historical situation for analytical purposes; other groups, e.g. Croats, were of course critical actors in the conflict. In addition, these questions are framed as if explaining Serbian behavior is the only concern, when in fact members of all involved groups committed acts of violence.

In some post-structural studies of group conflict, scholars have found the metaphors of representation an important component of the ensuing psychology of violence. For instance, consider the popular representation of the "dehumanized Other" as vermin, or as somehow so bestial that it is "life unworthy of life" (Glass 1997)—a group does not deserve human rights (Lerner 1992). Similarly, there might be a drive to eradicate the "morally bankrupt Other," lest they infest, defile, or pollute the healthy social body. This metaphor represents the in-group society as organic and the out-group as a source of impurity. Another specter is the "threatening Other" who will perhaps undermine the economy if left unchecked, who will kill us if we don't kill him first. In each of these situations, popular representations of the out-group reinforce the coherence and superiority of the in-group, as well as justify violent means to gain or maintain domination (Horowitz 1985). Such representations are commonly found in discussions of the Jews during the Holocaust, the Muslims during the Bosnian genocide, and immigrant groups or homosexuals in many times throughout history.

Group Politics and Electoral Behavior

The social psychological literature on identity also can be usefully applied to more conventional and less violent conflict that occurs within the context of democratic politics and elections. For example, ethnic identities are usually described in terms of broad categories whose members share common interests or belief systems. Explanations of conflict based on national or ethnic identities often rely on rational choice models of collective action or culturalist theories concerned with the shared cultural orientations of ethnicities and nationalities. But both modes of explanation could be enriched by the social psychological models discussed above.

Rational choice models of collective action have difficulty dealing with conflict based more on affective appeals and irrational hatred than on aggregated individual calculation or collective interest (Hardin 1995). The insights of realistic conflict theory and self-categorization theory might help overcome these difficulties. These social psychological models point out the importance of the lingering psychological effects of in-group homogeneity and intergroup conflict after intergroup competition over resources is under way. These models can account for the seemingly irrational stereotypes and hatreds that appear after the initial stages of conflict, conflict that indeed may have been based on real competition in its initial stages but whose objective competition for resources has long since vanished. Examples of this phenomenon include German fairy tales about the *Untermenschen*, depicted with "Jewish" physical characteristics; Soviet representation of Jews; and US colonial representation of Filipino natives. Continuing hatred after a war is a more general example. Witness the endurance of the Democratic South in the United States, 100 years after the Civil War had ended, or the refusal of some contemporary Americans to buy a Japanese car because of World War II.

Culturalist explanations (Almond & Verba 1963; Eckstein 1988, 1992) that assume that shared orientations or belief systems determine whether a society will function with or without political stability also can benefit from social psychological models. Because culturalist explanations assume passively socialized subjects, they have difficulty accounting for the rapid generations of meaning about self and other that occur when societies degenerate into identity-based conflict. Linking a model such as self-categorization theory to cultural explanations would ameliorate this problem, since the self-categorization explanations specifically concern the context in which group-based meaning and perception take over from political interactions based on personally held orientations. In this context, the culturalist emphasis on intermediate organizations to provide political stability and liberal democracy has some psychological support. Greater concern with the social psychological suggests that phenomena such as "cross-cutting cleavages" (Almond & Verba 1963), social networks and social capital (Putnam 1993), and formal power sharing structures such as consociational democracy (Lijphardt 1981) tend to deflect and diffuse contexts in which broad identity or ethnic categories might be called into play. By fostering multiple group memberships and interactions, intermediate organizations can limit appeals to perceive the world in simplistic social-categorical terms. Where these intermediate organizations and structures do not exist, there is higher potential for the eruption of political conflict based on broad ascriptive identity categories because there are no political or cultural limits to the broad categorization of self and others as different group members.

Beyond such instances of outright conflict, national and ethnic identity are also important in analyzing electoral campaigns, in which appeals to broad membership categories are commonly made by politicians. The analysis of group politics—long the staple of political scientists interested in elections and voting throughout the world—could benefit from knowledge of the models reviewed above, which can provide insights into the psychological processes that occur during campaigns. Campaigns not only draw on existing groups and group bias but also construct new coalitions from latent identity categories. Current trends in voting analysis focus on the interests of individual voters; however, political elites might also appeal to group-based categorization with the intention of mobilizing blocs of voters through the rhetorical or social construction of newly aware blocs. (For this reason, many contemporary studies on identity examine popular discourse and media as critical locations of the reproduction of social representations of identity groups). Although the use of divisive politics is widespread in electoral campaigns (Rudolph & Rudolph 1993), the psychological accounts of group perception offered by models such as self-categorization have been underutilized by political researchers.

The importance of latent groups is apparent in Bosnia. Such groups existed in the form of professional identities, social clubs, choral societies, and sports teams (Putnam 1993). Did these groups help keep ethnic conflict from erupting into violence? Was conflict avoided until these groups were collapsed into three separate categories—Bosnian Muslim, Serb, and Croat—which then annihilated intermediate intervening categories? These propositions are testable empirically and are the legitimate realm of examination for the political scientist. We are not arguing that this was in fact the case in Bosnia. Indeed, this example demonstrates the fragility of relying on such integrating groups for political stability, especially when broad structural conditions, such as economic deterioration or collapse of existing political structures, put the system under extreme stress (Monroe 1995). But we do suggest that scholars interested in this kind of analysis could enrich their work by introducing social psychological concepts into their empirical examinations.

The analysis of social movements presents another fertile area in which political scientists could apply social identity theory to better explicate group formation and behavior. For example, the intersection of religion and politics is a meeting place for theories about identity and group conflict. Religious elites may use salient religious symbols in public to reinforce group biases, often in response to the state's appropriation of moral issues that obscure group boundaries. For instance, the American Christian Right coalesced in response to the transformation of abortion and school prayer into legal questions (Van Vechten 1999). This might be interpreted through social identity theory as an instance of a group's response to perceived threats to its status. The added dimension of competition for resources, as analyzed in realistic group conflict theory, also could explain more militant expressions of religious fervor, such as the Taliban in Afghanistan or Islamic fundamentalist movements throughout much of the Middle East and Asia (Kreidie 1999). In those instances, theories such as social identity theory may account for prolonged mobilization better than do theories stressing access to resources or self-interest.

Elsewhere in the American politics literature, the concept of identity has been gaining currency. It is often operationalized in studies that consider demographic characteristics such as ethnicity and race (Morris 1984, Winant 1994, DeSipio 1996, Browning et al 1997, Ancheta 1998), gender (Bookman & Morgen 1988), religion (Wald 1997), class (Huckfeldt 1986), and sexuality (D'Emilio 1983) as independent variables. However, the theoretical application of concepts such as self-categorization or realistic group conflict theory has not yet gained much ground. Instead of applying these models wholesale, research that focuses on minority group members tends to rely either explicitly or implicitly on the developed social self-concept, as in studies of political participation that single out groups of voters for study. In these studies, one's identification as member of a group— Asian-Americans (Espiritu 1992), Chicano activists (Muñoz 1989), or a religious organization such as the Christian Right (Wald 1997)—is pivotal; such studies implicate identity but rarely take full advantage of developed psychological models. It is in this vein that the development of ethnic communities, the political assimilation of immigrant populations, the ideology of ethnic minority populations, the group consciousness of women, or the participation patterns of religious fundamentalists have been examined.

Other instances abound, ranging from Monroe's use of identity to explain altruism (1996) and moral choice during the Holocaust (1994, 1995) to Ringmar's (1996) critique of rational actor theory through his analysis of Sweden's participation in the Thirty Years' War and a burgeoning literature on the importance of identity in international relations (Mercer 1995, Bukovansky 1997).

CONCLUSIONS

These few pages have summarized a complex and vast psychological literature on identity. We hope our review will encourage other political scientists to examine a wider range of political phenomena using social psychological theories that deal with identity. The literature discussed above could help scholars address the next questions: Given the troubling implications of the above-discussed literatures on identity, what are the prospects for group identification without group conflict? And under what circumstances might identity-based conflict and violence be most—and least—likely to occur?

Visit the Annual Reviews home page at www.AnnualReviews.org

LITERATURE CITED

Adorno T, Frenkel-Brunswik E, Levinson DJ, Sanford RN. 1950. *The Authoritarian Personality*. New York: Harper & Row

Alexander CN, Wiley MG. 1981. Situated activity and identity formation. In *Social Psychology: Sociological Perspectives,* ed. M Rosenberg, RH Turner, pp. 269–89. New York: Basic Books

Allen VL, Scheibe K, eds. 1982. *The Social Context of Conduct: The Psychological Writings of T.R. Sarbin*. New York: Praeger

Almond G, Verba S. 1963. *The Civic Culture; Political Attitudes and Democracy in Five Nations*. Princeton, NJ: Princeton Univ. Press

Altmeyer B. 1981. *Right Wing Authoritarianism*. Winnipeg, Manitoba, Can: Univ. Manitoba Press

Altmeyer B. 1988. *Enemies of Freedom: Understanding Right Wing Authoritarianism*. San Francisco: Jossey-Bass

Ancheta A. 1998. *Race Rights and the Asian-American Experience*. New Brunswick, NJ: Rutgers Univ. Press

Baumeister RF. 1986a. *Identity: Cultural Change and the Struggle for Self.* New York: Oxford Univ. Press

Baumeister RF, ed. 1986b. *Public Self and Private Self.* New York: Springer-Verlag

Berger PL, Luchman T. 1966. *The Social Construction of Reality*. New York: Doubleday

Billig M. 1987. *Arguing and Thinking: A Rhetorical Approach to Social Psychology.* Cambridge, UK: Cambridge Univ. Press

Blumer H. 1969. *Symbolic Interactionism: Perspective and Method*. Englewood Cliffs, NJ: Prentice Hall

Bookman A, Morgen S. 1988. *Women and the Politics of Empowerment*. Philadelphia: Temple Univ. Press

Browning C. 1992. *Ordinary Men: Reserve Police Battalion 101 and the Final Solution in Poland*. New York: Aaron Asher/Harper-Collins

Browning RP, Marshall DR, Tabb DH. 1997. *Racial Politics in American Cities*. New York: Longman. 2nd ed.

Bukovansky M. 1997. American identity and neutral rights from independence to the War of 1812. *Int. Org.* 51(2):209–44

Campbell DT. 1965. Ethnocentrism and other altruistic motives. In *Nebraska Symposium on Motivation,* ed. D Levine, 13:283–311. Lincoln: Univ. Nebraska Press

Cash JD. 1989. Ideology and affect—the case of Northern Ireland. *Polit. Psychol.* 10(4):703–24

Cash JD. 1996. *Identity, Ideology and Conflict.* New York: Cambridge Univ. Press

D'Emilio J. 1983. *Sexual Politics, Sexual Communities: The Making of a Homosexual Minority in the U.S., 1940–1970*. Chicago: Univ. Chicago Press

DeSipio L. 1996. *Counting on the Latino Vote: Latinos as a New Electorate.* Charlottesville: Univ. Press Virginia

Dobert R, Habermas J, Nunner-Winkler G. 1977. *The Development of the Self.* Köln: Kiepenheuer & Witsch (In German)

Doise W. 1988. Individual and social identities in intergroup relations. *Eur. J. Soc. Psychol.* 18:99–111

Durkheim E. 1982. *The Rules of Sociological Method.* New York: Free

Eckstein H. 1988. A culturalist theory of change. *Am. Polit. Sci. Rev.* 82:789–804

Eckstein H. 1992. A theory of stable democracy. In *Regarding Politics*, pp. 179–228. Berkeley: Univ. Calif. Press

Erikson E. 1980 (1959). *Identity and the Life Cycle.* New York: Norton

Espiritu YL. 1992. *Asian American Panethnicity: Bridging Institutions and Identities.* Philadelphia: Temple Univ. Press

Fang CY, Sidanius J, Pratto F. 1998. Romance across the social status continuum: interracial marriage and the ideological asymmetry effect. *J. Cross-Cult. Psychol.* 29(2):290–305

Festinger L. 1957. *A Theory of Cognitive Dissonance.* Stanford, CA: Stanford Univ. Press

Fine R. 1986. *Narcissism, the Self, and Society.* New York: Columbia Univ. Press

Fiske S, Taylor S. 1991. *Social Cognition.* New York: McGraw Hill. 2nd ed.

Fromm E. 1965. *Escape from Freedom.* New York: Avon Books

Gagnon A, Bourhis RY. 1996. Discrimination in the minimal group paradigm—social identity or self-interest. *Pers. Soc. Psychol. Bull.* 22(12):1289–301

Gergen KJ. 1989. *Texts of Identity.* London: Sage

Gergen KJ, Gergen MM. 1983. Narratives of the self. In *Studies in Social Identity,* ed. TR Sarbin, KE Scheibe, pp. 254–73. New York: Praeger

Gilens M, Sniderman PM, Kuklinski JH. 1998. Affirmative action and the politics of realignment. *Br. J. Polit. Sci.* 28(1):159–83

Glass JM. 1997. *"Life Unworthy of Life": Racial Phobia and Mass Murder in Hitler's Germany.* New York: Basic Books

Goffman E. 1973. *The Presentation of Self in Everyday Life.* Woodstock, NY: Overlook

Goldhagen DJ. 1996. *Hitler's Willing Executioners.* New York: Knopf

Hardin R. 1995. *One for All: The Logic of Group Conflict.* Princeton, NJ: Princeton Univ. Press

Harré R. 1987. The social construction of selves. See Yardley & Honess 1987, pp. 41–52

Hewitt JP. 1988. *Self and Society: a Symbolic Interactionist Social Psychology.* Boston: Allyn & Bacon. 4th ed.

Hogg MA. 1992. *The Social Psychology of Group Cohesiveness: from Attraction to Social Identity.* New York: NY Univ. Press

Hogg MA, Abrams D. 1988. *Social Identifications: a Social Psychology of Intergroup Relationships and Group Processes.* New York: Routledge

Hogg MA, Terry DJ, White KM. 1995. A tale of two theories: a critical comparison of identity theory with social identity theory. *Soc. Psychol. Q.* 58(4):255–69

Huckfeldt R. 1986. *Politics in Context: Assimilation and Conflict in Urban Neighborhoods.* New York: Agathon

Insko CA, Shopter J, Kennedy JF, Dahl KR. 1992. Individual-group discontinuity from the differing perspectives of Campbell's realistic group conflict theory and Tajfel and Turner social identity theory. *Soc. Psychol. Q.* 55(3):272–91

James W. 1983 (1890). *Principles of Psychology: The Briefer Course.* Cambridge, MA: Harvard Univ. Press

Janis IL. 1983. *Groupthink: Psychological Studies of Policy Decisions and Fiascoes.* Boston: Houghton Mifflin

Kelley HH. 1971. *Attribution in Social Interaction.* Morristown, NJ: General Learning Press

Kelman H. 1992. Acknowledging the other's nationhood: how to create a momentum for the Israeli-Palestinian negotiations. *J. Palestinian Stud.* 22:18–38

Kihlstrom JF, Cantor N. 1984. Mental representations of the self. In *Advances in Experimental Social Psychology*, ed. L Berkowitz, 2:2–48. New York: Academic

Kinder DR, Sears DO. 1981. Prejudice and politics: symbolic racism versus racial threats to the good life. *J. Pers. Soc. Psychol.* 40(3): 414–31

Kreidie L. 1999. *Islamic fundamentalism: a new perspective.* Work. Pap., Univ. Calif. Irvine

Lemyre L, Smith P. 1985. Inter-group discrimination and self-esteem in the minimal group paradigm. *J. Pers. Soc. Psychol.* 49:660–70

Lerner RM. 1992. *Final Solutions: Biology, Prejudice, and Genocide.* Philadelphia: Penn. State Press

Lijphardt A. 1981. *Conflict and Coexistence in Belgium: the Dynamics of a Culturally Divided Society.* Berkeley: Inst. Int. Stud., Univ. Calif.

Linville PW. 1987. Self complexity as a cognitive buffer against stress related depression and illness. *J. Pers. Soc. Psychol.* 52:663–76

Markus H, Nurius P. 1987. Possible selves: the interface between motivation and the self-concept. See Yardley & Honess 1987, pp. 157–72

Marx K, Engels F. 1989 (1947). *The German Ideology: Part I.* New York: International

Mead GH. 1924. The genesis of the self and social control. *Int. J. Ethics* 35:251–77

Mead GH. 1934. *Mind, Self, and Society.* Chicago: Univ. Chicago Press

Mercer J. 1995. Anarchy and identity. *Int. Org.* 49(2):229–52

Miller AH, Wattenberg M, Malanchuk O. 1986. Schematic assessments of presidential candidates. *Am. Polit. Sci. Rev.* 80(2):521–40

Moliner P. 1995. A two dimensional model of social representations. *Eur. J. Soc. Psychol.* 25(1):27–40

Monroe KR. 1994. "But what else could I do?": a cognitive theory of ethical political behavior. *Polit. Psychol.* 15:201–26

Monroe KR. 1995. The psychology of genocide: a review of the literature. *Ethics Int. Aff.* 9:215–239

Monroe KR. 1996. *The Heart of Altruism: Perceptions of a Common Humanity.* Princeton, NJ: Princeton Univ. Press

Morgan DL, Schwalbe ML. 1990. Mind and self in society—linking social structure and social cognition. *Soc. Psychol. Q.* 53(2):148–64

Morris AD. 1984. *The Origins of the Civil Rights Movement: Black Communities Organizing for Change.* New York: Free

Moscovici S. 1988. Notes towards a description of social representations. *Eur. J. Soc. Psychol.* 18:211–50

Muñoz C. 1989. *Youth, Identity, Power: the Chicano Movement.* New York: Verso

Oakes PJ, Haslam SA, Turner JC. 1994. *Stereotyping and Social Reality.* Cambridge, MA: Blackwell

Perry J. 1975. The problem of personal identity. In *Personal Identity*, ed. J Perry, pp. 3–32. Berkeley: Univ. Calif. Press

Pratto F, Stallworth LM, Sidanius J, Siers B. 1997. The gender gap in occupational role attainment: a social dominance approach. *J. Pers. Soc. Psychol.* 72(1):37–53

Putnam RD. 1993. *Making Democracy Work.* Princeton, NJ: Princeton Univ. Press

Rabbie JM, Schot JC, Visser L. 1989. Social identity theory—a conceptual and empirical critique from the perspective of a behavioural interaction model. *Eur. J. Soc. Psychol.* 19(3):171–202

Reid A, Deaux K. 1996. Relationship between social and personal identities: segregation or integration. *J. Pers. Soc. Psychol.* 71(6):1084

Ringmar E. 1996. *Identity, Interest, and Action: a Cultural Explanation of Sweden's Intervention in the Thirty Years War.* New York: Cambridge Univ. Press

Robinson DT, Smith-Lovin L. 1992. Selective interaction as a strategy for identity maintenance: an affect control model. *Soc. Psychol. Q.* 55(1):12

Rosenberg M, Turner RH, eds. 1981. *Social*

Psychology: Sociological Perspectives. New York: Basic Books

Ross M. 1995. Psycho-cultural interpretation theory and peacemaking in ethnic conflict. *Polit. Psychol.* 16:523–44

Rudolph SH, Rudolph LI. 1993. Modern hate. *New Repub.* 208(12):24–29

Sarbin TR, Scheibe KE, eds. 1983. *Studies in Social Identity.* New York: Praeger

Schlenker BR, ed. 1985. *The Self and Social Life.* New York: McGraw-Hill

Schlenker BR. 1986. Self-identification: toward an integration of the private and public self. See Baumeister 1986b, pp. 21–62

Sdorow L. 1990. *Psychology.* Dubuque, IA: Brown

Sears DO. 1988. Symbolic racism. In *Eliminating Racism: Profiles in Controversy,* ed. PA Katz, DA Taylor, pp. 53–84. New York: Plenum

Sears DO. 1993. Symbolic politics: a sociopsychological theory. In *Explorations in Political Psychology,* ed. S Iyengar, WJ McGuire, pp. 113–49. Durham, NC: Duke Univ. Press

Sears DO, Funk CL. 1999. Evidence of long-term persistence of adults' political predispositions. *J. Polit.* 61(1):1–28

Sears DO, van Laar C, Carrillo M, Kosterman R. 1997. Is it really racism? The origins of white Americans' opposition to race-targeted policies. *Public Opin. Q.* 61(1):16–53

Secord P. 1982. The origin and maintenance of social roles: the case of sex roles. In *Personality, Roles and Social Behavior,* ed. W Ickes, ES Knowles, pp. 33–53. New York: Springer-Verlag

Sherif M. 1967. *Group Conflict and Cooperation.* London: Routledge & Kegan Paul

Sherif M, Harvey OJ, White BJ, Hood WR, Sherif CW. 1961. *Intergroup Conflict and Cooperation: The Robber's Cave Experiment.* Norman, OK: Univ. Okla. Press

Shotter J. 1985. Social accountability and self specification. In *The Social Construction of the Person,* ed. KJ Gergen, KE Davis, pp. 167–89. New York: Springer-Verlag

Sidanius J. 1993. The psychology of group conflict and the dynamics of oppression: a social dominance perspective. In *Explorations in Political Psychology,* ed. S Iyengar, WJ McGuire, pp. 183–219. Durham, NC: Duke Univ. Press

Sidanius J, Devereux E, Pratto F. 1992. A comparison of symbolic racism theory and social dominance theory as explanations for racial policy attitudes. *J. Soc. Psychol.* 132(3):377–95

Sidanius J, Liu JH, Shaw JS, Pratto F. 1994. Social dominance orientation, hierarchy attenuators and hierarchy enhancers: social dominance theory and the criminal justice system. *J. Appl. Soc. Psychol.* 24(4):338–66

Sidanius J, Pratto F, Mitchell M. 1994. In-group identification, social dominance orientation, and differential intergroup social allocation. *J. Soc. Psychol.* 134(2):151–67

Sniderman P, Carmines E. 1997. *Reaching Beyond Race.* Cambridge, MA: Harvard Univ. Press

Sniderman P, Piazza T, Tetlock P, Kendrick A. 1991. The new racism. *Am. J. Polit. Sci.* 35(2):423–47

Stryker S. 1987. Identity theory: developments and extensions. See Yardley & Honess 1987, pp. 89–103

Stryker S, Terpe RT. 1982. Commitment, identity salience and role behavior: theory and research example. In *Personality, Roles and Social Behavior,* ed. W Ickes, ES Knowles, pp. 199–218. New York: Springer-Verlag

Tajfel H. 1970. Experiments in intergroup discrimination. *Sci. Am.* 223:96–102

Taylor DM, Moghaddam FM. 1994. *Theories of Intergroup Relations: International Social Psychological Perspectives.* Westport, CT: Praeger

Taylor S, Peplau L, Sears D. 1997. *Social Psychology.* Upper Saddle River, NJ: Prentice Hall

Tetlock PE. 1985. Toward an intuitive politician model of attribution processes. In *The Self and Social Life,* ed. BR Schlenker, pp. 203–34. New York: McGraw-Hill

Turner JC, Hogg MA. 1987. *Rediscovering the Social Group: a Self-Categorization Theory.* New York: Blackwell

Turner JC, Oakes PJ, Haslam SA, McGarty C. 1994. Self and collective: cognition and social context. *Pers. Soc. Psychol. Bull.* 20(5): 454–63

Van Vechten R. 1999. *The Christian Right and American politics.* Work. Pap., Univ. Calif. Irvine

Wald K. 1997. *Religion and Politics in the United States.* New York: St. Martin's. 3rd ed.

Weigert AJ, Smith Teitge J, Teitge DW. 1986. *Society and Identity: Toward a Social Psychology.* New York: Cambridge Univ. Press

Weiner B, ed. 1974. *Achievement, Motivation and Attribution Theory.* Morristown, NJ: General Learning Press

Wiley MG, Alexander CN. 1987. From situated activity to self-attribution: the impact of social structural schemata. See Yardley & Honess 1987, pp. 105–17

Winant H. 1994. *Racial Conditions: Politics, Theory, Comparisons.* Minneapolis: Univ. Minn. Press

Wurf E, Markus H. 1983. *Cognitive consequences of the negative self.* Presented at Am. Psychol. Assoc. Meet., Anaheim, CA, August

Yardley K, Honess T. 1987. *Society and Identity: Psychosocial Perspectives.* New York: Wiley

Annu. Rev. Polit. Sci. 2000. 3:449–74

ELECTORAL REALIGNMENTS

David R. Mayhew

Department of Political Science, Yale University, New Haven, Connecticut 06520-830l;
e-mail: david.mayhew@yale.edu

Key Words   realignments, critical elections, presidential elections, cyclical theories

■ **Abstract**   American electoral realignment theory, as constructed in its classic form chiefly by Key, Schattschneider, Sundquist, and Burnham, can be sorted into 11 distinct empirical claims. These pertain to dichotomization of election types, periodicity, a cyclical dynamic, high voter turnout, durable new issue cleavages, ideologized elections, nationalization of issues, major changes in government policy, redistributive policy, effective and consequential voter voice, and the "system of 1896." These claims are assessed for their empirical validity and illuminative power.

INTRODUCTION

The study of US electoral realignments, which enjoyed its heyday in the 1960s and 1970s, was one of the most creative, engaging, and influential intellectual enterprises undertaken by American political scientists during the last half century. It rivaled the Michigan election studies. It offered certifiable science, in the sense of a conceptual scheme, a theory, and quantitative analysis; breadth, in tackling large political questions associated with all of American national history; and even an eschatology, in the sense that it has induced generations of students and others, armed with a key to historical development, to keep asking, "Is an electoral realignment about to happen?" or "Have we been witnessing an electoral realignment this year?"

Fundamental to the appeal and influence of the realignments enterprise was the talent of four major entrepreneurs during its creative early days. First came Key and Schattschneider, who contributed important groundwork, and then Sundquist and Burnham, who provided the principal statements in the genre. All four of these writers exhibited a prodigious, sure-footed command of the factual particulars of American political history as well as a rare capacity to generalize by detecting patterns. Small wonder that the genre made such a mark.

Here I address what might be called the classic phase of the realignments genre, which means chiefly works by these four writers. I touch on subsequent claims by Brady; I take up critical commentaries by the trio of Clubb, Flanigan, and Zingale, and by Bartels; and I refer to a few works outside the genre, but I do not address the rest of the now vast follow-up literature amending, extending, or critiquing the classical realignments genre as it emerged in political science, or the parallel literature contributed by academics in the history profession. The sideline topic of party identification is not touched.

I start by explicating the classic realignments genre and end by critiquing it. I briefly take up certain works by the four principal authors but then shift gears and consider what might be thought of as a fully fleshed-out, maximally ambitious version of the realignments perspective—an ideal type of a scholarship already featuring ideal types. This ideal version relies heavily on the work of Burnham, whose theoretical and empirical claims have been particularly ambitious, and on Schattschneider, whose claims were just as ambitious if less completely worked out. It relies somewhat less on Sundquist, who has been more cautious, and least of all on Key, whose claims were the most conservative. I risk misconstruing all four authors by adopting this course, but along the way I try to signal how the four have differed from each other. What I call the fully fleshed-out version of the realignments perspective has proven to be particularly engaging and influential.

THE CLASSIC REALIGNMENTS PERSPECTIVE

The Four Principals: Key, Schattschneider, Sundquist, and Burnham

The idea of realignments had been broached by earlier authors (see Schantz 1998), but it was Key who crystallized and popularized the concept. His 1955 article, "A Theory of Critical Elections," demonstrates the basic, trademark dichotomizing move of the realignments school—the idea of sorting American elections into two categories: a few that are critical elections, in Key's terminology, and a great residual many that are not. Critical elections are those "in which voters are, at least from impressionistic evidence, unusually deeply concerned, in which the extent of electoral involvement is relatively quite high, and in which the decisive results of the voting reveal a sharp alteration of the pre-existing cleavage within the electorate" (Key 1995:4). As "perhaps ... the truly differentiating characteristic of this sort of election," Key emphasized that "the realignment made manifest in the voting in such elections seems to persist for several succeeding elections" (Key 1955:4). Using data from townships in selected New England states, Key tagged the elections of 1896 and 1928 as critical elections that brought sharp and long-lasting changes in voting patterns. That was all. Not a word appears in Key's article about any critical elections prior to 1896, any possible periodicity in the occurrence of such elections, or any distinctive kinds of issue innovations or government policy results that might be associated with such elections. Also, Key seemed to back off critical elections somewhat four years later (Key 1959) by pointing up patterns of "secular realignment"—that is, gradual change—in voter coalitions. Still, in 1955, courtesy of Key, the idea of critical elections came out of the bottle.

Schattschneider weighed in with a different kind of contribution in 1956, which he reissued largely intact as a chapter in his *Semisovereign People* in 1960. This evocative framing of realignments was chatty rather than data-driven. Unlike Key's circumspect articles, it was laden with far-reaching if often elusive empirical and theoretical claims. Schattschneider zeroed in on the election of 1896, "one of the decisive elections in American history," which brought on a party coalitional alignment "powerful enough to determine the nature of American politics for more than thirty years." The realignment of 1896 was "perhaps the best example in American history of the successful substitution of one conflict [that is, one cleavage between opposing clusters of interests] for another"—a signature Schattschneider concern (1960:78, 81–82). Later, the "revolution of 1932" produced "the greatest reversal of public policy in American history" (Schattschneider 1960:86).

Key and Schattschneider provided materials to build with. A half generation later, Sundquist presented a large, well-worked-out construction entitled *Dynamics of the Party System* (1973, revised and reissued 1983). Probably most undergraduate students have learned about electoral realignments through this zestful, accessible volume that organizes so much of American political history so interestingly. Sundquist addresses realigning periods or eras rather than just single elections—a realignment "reaches its climax in one or more critical elections" (Sundquist 1973:294)—and he dwells on three such eras that by about 1970 had become canonical: the 1850s, the 1890s, and the 1930s. In Sundquist's account of voter realignments, as in Schattschneider's, the content of new voter cleavages (not just their statistical existence, as in Key's account) is the signal feature. However, in an updating touch, Sundquist indexes the cleavages according to opposing issue positions, not (like Schattschneider) according to opposing interests from which issue propensities could in principle be easily predicted. Sundquist is cautious. He is quick with a proposition or a generalization about behavior by voters or parties, but I find no claims in his work about the likely periodicity of voter realignments, or about the governmental policy consequences of realignments.

Of Burnham's many works on electoral realignments, the following three are perhaps the best guides to his thinking: his indirectly relevant, much-cited article "The Changing Shape of the American Political Universe" (1965), his chapter in the classic volume *The American Party Systems* (1967), and his *Critical Elections and the Mainsprings of American Politics* (1970). Burnham adopted the essentials set forth by Key and Schattschneider and pointed the realignments scholarship toward additional instances of realigning elections, toward periodicity throughout American history, and toward policy effects said to be systematically associated with realignments. With these extensions, the realignments genre at the level of graduate instruction became largely Burnham's.

The Most Ambitious Version: Eleven Claims about Realignments

A fully fleshed-out, maximally claim-laden version of the realignments perspective can be sorted into a series of distinct claims about reality. I present 11 such claims from the relevant literature. There is nothing magic about these particular 11; anyone else who happened to scrutinize the same literature would probably code it differently, though not radically differently. Any analyst approaching this literature can get tied up in knots over whether the features allegedly associated with realignments are causes, defining properties, concomitants, or consequences of them. I have devised my series of claims so as to try to bypass those knots, which probably cannot be untied. The 11 claims are all in principle empirically testable. The first ten are universalistic in form—at least across the domain of American national history. The eleventh is historical. The first three claims, taken together, sum to the appropriate kind of content of a cyclical theory of history—such as business-cycles theory.

1. National elections in American history can be sorted into two kinds: a few realigning ones and a great many nonrealigning ones. This is the genre's foundational claim. The terminology can be blurry; not all authors agree on the definitions of "critical" and "realigning." There is the messy matter of eras as opposed to single elections: 1860 often sprawls back to encompass most of the 1850s; 1896 is often joined to the sweeping congressional midterm result of 1894; 1928 and 1932 are variously treated as distinct and unrelated events, related events, or part of the same continuing event. For the most part, the literature addresses presidential elections only, but some authors take up congressional ones. Still, Key's 1955 claim has remained central: Voter alignment changes that are "both sharp and durable" are brought by some elections but not by others (Key 1955:11). There is consensus on the requirement of durability (Sundquist 1983:4; Burnham 1967:288–89, 1970:4–5). As for the elections in question, "There has long been agreement among historians that the elections of those of [sic] 1800, 1828, 1860, 1896, and 1932, for example, were fundamental turning points in the course of American electoral politics" (Burnham 1970:1)—a judgment that has not drawn much dissent within the genre.

2. Electoral realignments have appeared in patterns of regular periodicity. Key and Sundquist make no such claim, as noted above, but Burnham gives it prominence, titling a chapter "The Periodicity of American Critical Realignments" (1970:ch. 2). Burnham asserts that a realignment cycle emerges "approximately once every thirty years" (1967:288). "Historically speaking, at least, national critical realignments have not occurred at random. Instead, there has been a remarkably uniform periodicity in their appearance." "[T]his periodicity has had an objective existence..." (Burnham 1970:8). There has been a "periodic rhythm," a "cycle of oscillation" (Burnham 1970:181).

3. A dynamic exists that motors history through this pattern of cyclical oscillations into and out of realignments. This is Burnham's claim, with an assist from Sundquist. This line of thinking has relied on tantalizing suggestions and metaphors rather than sustained argument, but it has probably been no less influential for that, and the case for a dynamic is worth teasing out. In brief, political "stress" (Burnham 1970:4, 135) or "tension" (1970:10, 181) builds up over a period of roughly 30 years until it reaches a "flash point" (1970:10, 136) or a "boiling point" (1970:27), at which time a "triggering event" (1970:181) brings on an electoral realignment. The terms flash point and boiling point bear an Engels-like connotation of a change in quantity being overtaken by a change in quality.

To put it more elaborately, there exists a "dynamic, even dialectic polarization between long-term inertia and concentrated bursts of change" (Burnham 1970:27). Ordinarily, American institutions tend toward "underproduction of other than currently 'normal' policy outputs. They may tend persistently to ignore, and hence not to aggregate, emergent political demand of a mass character until a boiling point of some kind is reached" (1970:27). In another of Burnham's passages, "[T]he socioeconomic system develops but the institutions of electoral politics and policy formation remain essentially unchanged" (1970:181). Thus stacked up are "dislocations," "dysfunctions," and "increasingly visible social maladjustments" (1970:181, 135), which are not sufficiently attended to until the political system catches up with a lurch as "incremental bargaining politics" gives way to "nonincremental change" (1970:137).

Sundquist, reflecting the standard interpretation imparted by Progressive historians, gives a corresponding cast to the politics of the latter part of the nineteenth century leading up to the mid 1890s (Sundquist 1973:92–94, 144). "Patronage, rather than program, became the object of politics" (1973:93). For 20 years, the party system was based on "dead issues of the past," offering voters "no means of expressing a choice on the crucial issues of domestic economic policy around which the country had been polarizing" (1973:144). Then, with the nomination of Bryan in 1896, "the party system took on meaning once again.... The day of political unresponsiveness, of evasion and straddling on fundamental, burning questions, was over" (1973:144).

These first three claims offer a dichotomizing concept, periodicity, and a dynamic—the necessary components of a cyclical theory.

4. Voter concern and turnout are unusually high in realigning elections. This property could be tucked into claim #1 as an additional defining property, but on balance it is a recessive property in the literature, and there is probably no harm in considering it here as a distinct empirical claim. The idea goes back to Key, as noted above, and it is embraced by at least Burnham (1970:7–8): "The rise in intensity is also normally to be found in abnormally heavy voter participation for the time."

5. In an electoral realignment, a new dominant voter cleavage over interests or issues replaces an old one. This claim is central to Schattschneider's and Sundquist's work, though not to Key's. I do not see it as a clear, upfront assertion in Burnham's.

6. Politics at realigning junctures is exceptionally ideological. This is Burnham's idea. "The rise in intensity [during realignments] is associated with a considerable increase in ideological polarizations" (Burnham 1970:7). "In the campaign or campaigns [during a realignment]..., the insurgents' political style is exceptionally ideological by American standards; this in turn produces a sense of grave threat among defenders of the established order, who in turn develop opposing ideological positions" (Burnham 1967:288).

7. At least as regards the US House of Representatives, realigning elections hinge on national issues, nonrealigning elections on local ones. This claim is a recent contribution by Brady (1988) that I have not come across in any previous scholarship. "Certain elections, however, are dominated by national rather than local issues" (Brady 1988:14). "[D]uring realignments," Brady undertakes to demonstrate, "the House is elected on national, not local issues, thus giving a sense of mandate to the new majority party" (Brady 1988:18).

8. Electoral realignments are associated with major changes in government policy. This claim is absent from Key's work and recessive at best in Sundquist's, but it figures in both Schattschneider's and Burnham's, albeit complicatedly. Schattschneider finds it obvious that the 1932 realignment ushered in important changes in policy, and the voter alignment caused by the 1896 election no less obviously underpinned major policy results for a generation (1956:208, 205), but he stops short of asserting that the 1896 election brought about changes in policy—not least, evidently, owing to his judgment that the newly dominant post-1896 Republican party *"had no important positive program of legislation"* (italics in original). Catering to business interests that wanted the government off their backs, the party gauged its policy success "in terms of *what was prevented"* (italics in original)—not in terms of what was initiated or enacted (Schattschneider 1956:197–98). Burnham, in his more recent writings, has acknowledged this lack of post-1896 innovation: "Unlike the turnovers of 1828, 1860, or 1932, the realignment of 1894–1896 *did not* result in a major reversal of dominant public policy" (Burnham 1986:269, italics in original; see also Burnham 1981:175).

However, in the realignment genre's classic days, Burnham did not shrink from rendering bold, general, unasterisked assertions. A critical realignment constitutes "a turning point in the mainstream of national policy formation" (Burnham 1967:289). Critical realignments "are intimately associated with and followed by transformations in large clusters of policy" (1970:9). These assertions have had a life. Brady (1988) takes it as a given that the aftermaths of alleged realignments are times to canvass for successful major policy innovations. He examines the three chief canonical aftermaths (although no other times) and claims to detect such major innovations during those aftermaths. Through overcoming "policy incrementalism," his reasoning goes, "realigning or critical elections create conditions under which majorities are capable of legislating clusters of policy changes" (Brady 1988:4). "The Congresses of the Civil War, 1890's, and New Deal eras were responsible, in part, for outpourings of new comprehensive public policies" (Brady 1988:vii). Thus has the genre evolved.

9. Electoral realignments are distinctively associated with "redistributive" policies. This is a recent Burnham idea, building on Lowi's (1964) well-known three-category typology. There is no reason to expect distributive or regulatory policy making to map onto realignment cycles in any predictable way, Burnham states or implies, but "[m]atters become quite different when we turn to *redistributive policies*.... Such policies are the heart of critical-realignment periods and are among the most important of their 'symptoms'" (Burnham 1986:270, italics in original).

10. The American voting public expresses itself effectively and consequentially during electoral realignments, but not otherwise. This is an exceptionally large claim that capstones, and to some degree duplicates or incorporates, the rest (for example, claim #3), but it is worth stating independently. Note the language used in assertions such as the following: "[T]he voting public has made vitally important contributions to American political development approximately once in a generation" (Burnham 1967:287). That is, the public has done that on those occasions but not otherwise. Sundquist states that the public had "no means of expressing a choice on the crucial issues of domestic economic policy" for 20 years, but then in 1896 "the party system took on meaning once again" (Sundquist 1973:144). In Schattschneider's view, the voter alignment brought on by the 1896 election "determined"—an unusually strong verb—"the nature of American politics for more than thirty years" (1960:78). That is, voters could not or did not do anything effective or consequential thereafter for a third of a century.

11. There existed a "system of 1896." This historical claim figures so prominently in the work of both Schattschneider and Burnham—it is something like a large container packed with its own content yet snugly insertable into the general realignments vehicle—that it merits special mention. The "function" of the voter alignment struck by the 1896 election, Schattschneider wrote, using an explanatory style in vogue in the 1950s, was to award political and economic supremacy to the American business class—a result that stuck for a "determined" 36 years. The Republican party, "the political instrument of business," ordinarily ruled during that time (Schattschneider 1956:197). The sectional shape of the post-1896 alignment—that is, the newly accentuated one-party rule by Democrats in the South and Republicans in much of the North—was a key aspect of that hegemony. "Both sections became extremely conservative because one-party politics tends strongly to vest political power in the hands of people who already have economic power" (Schattschneider 1956:202). In addition, "the sectional

party alignment was unfavorable to the development and exploitation of new alternatives in public affairs" (Schattschneider 1956:205).

Insulation of the business sector from mass pressures has been a leading theme in Burnham's interpretation of post-1896 politics. By now the reader may be tired of quotations, but because they convey both content and flavor, here are a few more. Burnham claims that the 1896 alignment "almost certainly" depressed voter turnout for a generation or more, notably through depositing noncompetitive one-partyism across both North and South; accordingly, "the functional result of the 'system of 1896' was the conversion of a fairly democratic regime into a rather broadly based oligarchy" (Burnham 1965:23). In general terms, according to Burnham (1965:25), the realignment of 1896 "brought victory beyond expectation to those who had sought to find some way of insulating American elites from mass pressures." The "chief function" of the post-1896 party system was "the substantially complete insulation of elites from attacks by the victims of the industrializing process" (Burnham 1967:301). Burnham has "no doubts that *in general* the system established in the 1890s was in fact a political matrix which insulated industrial and finance capital from adverse mass pressures for a generation afterward" (1986:269, italics in original).

Let no one underestimate the intellectual aspiration of these Schattschneider and Burnham claims about the system of 1896. There is a line out to Barrington Moore: "The takeoff phase of industrialization has been a brutal and exploitative process everywhere, whether managed by capitalists or commissars. A vital functional political need during this phase [that is, during the early twentieth century in the American case] is to provide adequate insulation of the industrializing elites from mass pressures" (Burnham 1965:24). There is an answer to the question: Why is there no socialism in the United States? "One is indeed inclined to suspect that the large hole in voter participation which developed after 1900 roughly corresponds to the area in the electorate where a viable socialist movement 'ought' to have developed" (Burnham 1967:301). And there is an answer to the question: Why is there no European-style welfare state in the United States? "The accomplishments of the [post-1896] Republican party might be measured more accurately, therefore, by the gap produced between the social legislation of western European countries and that of the United States before 1932" (Schattschneider 1956:198).

Those are the 11 claims. I hope that I have stayed true to the texts and that I have expressed fairly the ambitions of the various authors.

A CRITIQUE OF THE GENRE

How does the realignments genre stand up at the close of the twentieth century, well past its historical evidence base and a generation or two beyond the main assertions by its chief exponents?

All the claims I have presented here can, in principle, be assessed for their empirical validity, and that assessment is my principal task in the remainder of this essay. In some instances, reasonably hard empirical information is available in published works and can be mobilized. In most instances, that course is not possible, and I resort to my understanding of the conventional wisdom piled up by generations of historians writing standard works about American political history. For recent times, I rely also on my own experience of living under and witnessing the American regime. These are fallible reliances, yet what are the options? It is bankrupt and irresponsible, as the realignment writers would likely agree, to throw up one's hands when confronted by provocative assertions on large, important, not easily tractable matters.

A second concern, beyond validity, is the illuminative power of the realignments genre. What has it added to the discipline? What would we be thinking about American electoral history otherwise? What did we think before the realignments genre came along? It has always been obvious that some American elections have surpassed others in engaging voters, generating a sense of high stakes among voters, shaking up received voter alignments, or causing important policy or other effects down the line. Elections are not all equal. Also, the Civil War and New Deal eras have always stood out for both their electoral turbulence and their policy innovations. It is reasonable to ask, what has the realignments genre fruitfully added beyond these baselines?

Probably the chief contemporary charge against the realignments genre is that is has ceased to be relevant. No certifiable realignment has occurred since 1932. A 68-year gap is a heavy cross to bear for a theory of 30-year electoral cycles, and it has been variously borne. The concepts of party "decomposition" and "dealignment" have been introduced. Burnham has argued that "there in fact *was* a critical realignment in the 1968–72 period. One of its essential features lay in the very dissolution of the traditional partisan channels that had been implicitly incorporated as a non-problematic part of the classic realignment model. People therefore looked for it with the wrong tools and in the wrong places" (Burnham 1991:107). Translation: For evidence of electoral realignments, don't bother to rely on patterns of election returns anymore. To support this point, Burnham draws on "the very perceptive political commentator Sidney Blumenthal" (Blumenthal 1982), with his idea of "the permanent campaign," who "was perhaps the first to get the basic story right" (Burnham 1991:107).

I do not wish to deal with the problem of a post-1932 absence of realignments here. The decomposition and dealignment ideas are not implausible, and, at any rate, a perspective that managed to illuminate the first century and a half of American political history, even if for whatever reasons it ceased to work in recent times, would be an impressive achievement.

But how does the realignment perspective stand up when applied to its apparently most favorable century and a half? Not very well, I argue here in assessing the empirical validity (and occasionally the illuminative power) of the 11 claims presented above. The genre's performance across the claims, which I take up one by one, ranges from mediocre to poor.

Dichotomization of Election Types

Of efforts to detect presidential elections in American history that have generated especially large and durable changes in voter alignments, I am aware of two sophisticated ones that were undertaken without regard for the conventional wisdom of the realignments genre about what results to expect. (Nardulli's 1995 work, with its inventive time series on subregions, does not seem to be "blind" in this sense.) No such work is unimpeachable. Countless decisions about data use need to be made; third parties are always a nightmare. Moreover, no one to my knowledge has used statistical methods to tackle the slippery and probably intractable task of detecting realigning eras as opposed to single elections. Still, impressive work has been done using data sets based on individual elections.

Clubb et al (1980; for a somewhat different version see Flanigan & Zingale 1974) were appropriately sensitive to two distinct connotations of the realignments genre. Using aggregate presidential election data by state, they probed for two kinds of electoral change: "surge," as when, in a limiting case, every state becomes 10% more Democratic in election year B than in previous election year A (a fitting accommodation of, for example, the election of 1932); and "interaction," as when, in a limiting case, half the states become 10% more Democratic and the other half 10% more Republican, yet despite the considerable disruption in cleavage there is no (necessary) net national party percentage change between election years A and B. Either kind of change is "realigning" if its end-state persists during a span of succeeding elections—again, a necessary requirement for the realignments genre. Otherwise, any A-to-B change is merely "deviating." Clubb et al proceed by analyzing successive election quadruplets (A through D, B through E, etc)—the logic being to situate each election in a context of both its predecessors and its successors. Their technology requires them to calculate results separately for each party (at least because of third parties, one major party's record is not simply the mirror of the other's). Calculations are provided for the Democrats from 1836 through 1976, the Republicans from 1868 through 1976.

Clubb et al's Table 3.1a (1980:92–93) warrants close inspection. For the Democrats, the notable realigning surge elections, in order of magnitude of change, are the following: 1932, +16.3% (a bull's-eye for the realignments perspective); 1948, –8.2%; 1868, +6.1%; 1848, –5.6%; 1840, –3.6%; 1920, –1.8%; 1876, +1.5%; 1960, +1.3%. The notable Democratic realigning interactive elections are as follows: 1836, 5.7%; 1860, 2.8%; 1964, 2.1%; 1928, 1.9%; 1864, 1.7%; 1948, 1.2%; 1904, 1.1%. (In these latter cases the values are absolute—that is, no directional plus or minus signs.) On the Republican side, the realigning surge elections are the following: 1932, –11.3% (another, or the same, bull's-eye); 1920, +7.7%; 1896, +5.2%; 1876, –4.7%; 1952, +2.5%; 1964, –2.5%. The Republican realigning interactive elections are as follows: 1952, 1.3%; 1936, 1.2%; 1964, 1.2%.

The election of 1932 performs spectacularly in these calculations. The election of 1860 is something of a washout, but that is understandable. No such comparative statistical analysis could adequately accommodate the breaking in half of the Democratic party that year (although note that the same thing happened to the Republican Party in 1912, and the 1912 election is not ordinarily regarded as realigning). But what about the unremarkable statistical performance of the election of 1896?

Bartels (1998), employing a more complex methodology, also relies on aggregate state-level election data and is sensitive to both surge and interactive types of change (though those are Clubb et al's terms) if they turn out to be durable. Tracked in the Bartels case, from 1868 through 1996—which rules out of bounds the election of 1860—is the Republican minus the Democratic percentage of the popular vote for president. The calculations allow a summary realignment score for each election. In Bartels' key Figure 8 (1998:315), the election of 1932 emerges a runaway winner in "average effect, 25-year horizon," but what then? An easy second-place finisher is the election of 1880, followed by, in order, those of 1920, 1972, 1936, 1876, 1912, 1896, and 1924.

From the viewpoint of the realignments genre, setting aside the anomaly of 1860, the problem posed here is that, confronted by the Clubb et al (1980) and Bartels (1988) analyses alone, probably not one reader in a hundred would seize on the election of 1896 as a realigning event. In Bartels' assessment (1998:316): "[T]he electoral pattern established in 1896 was much less durable than previous scholarship has suggested.... [T]he electoral impetus of 1896 was diminished by half within four years; the state-by-state voting pattern in 1900 reflected the divisions of 1888 ... as much or more than those of 1896." The 1896 result comes to look suspiciously like a deviating one.

At a more general level, Bartels casts doubt on the very idea of sorting elections into two types. "Rather than consisting of a few great peaks separated by broad plateaus reflecting long periods of political stasis, the distribution of long-term effects in Fig. 8 reflects a complex intermixture of large, medium, and small effects" (Bartels 1998:315).

In the face of such numbers, one way to try to keep 1896 on its pedestal is to argue that all such quantitative analysis is impeachable, and, at any rate, quantitative analysis is not enough. Relevant contextual information is needed, and certainly the decade of the 1890s offers a rich supply of it—the Populist revolt in 1892, the country's second worst depression in 1893, the astounding (still unmatched) 120-seat shift to the Republicans in the House elections of 1894, the fracturing of both major parties over silver and other questions in 1896, the capture of the Democratic party by anti–Wall Street insurgents, William Jennings Bryan's unprecedented nationwide campaign of speech making, Mark Hanna's mobilizing of the business community behind McKinley, and the Republican domination that resulted. It is a familiar and riveting story.

But there exist other riveting stories, even if, partly courtesy of the realignments genre, they may not be quite as familiar. In light of the impressive showings of the 1876 and 1880 elections in, respectively, Clubb et al's and Bartels' results, and in line with the realignment genre's practice of weaving narratives about short sequences of allegedly related elections (not just one election), consider the following three-paragraph sketch. It is a stylized account of the politics of the 1870s that I have composed for this occasion.

> In the 1874 congressional midterm election, spurred by Reconstruction fatigue and a poor economy, the American electorate rendered one of its most decisive results ever—a sweeping Democratic takeover of the House that rendered federal Reconstruction policy unsustainable. The state Republican regime in Mississippi soon crumbled, paving the way for the extraordinary election campaign waged by white "Redeemers" to take back South Carolina in 1876—a successful politicomilitary drive conducted largely by army veterans that featured guerrilla organization, intimidation, fraud, and murder (Zuczek 1996). It was an innovative mix that would be seen again in Germany and Italy after World War I. At the national level, the high-stakes presidential contest of 1876—which party would control the army?–ended in a hung result and, for the only time in American history, an extra-constitutional settlement. This cross-party, cross-regional deal involving an ad hoc commission has been brought to life in possibly the most distinguished work ever written about the events surrounding an American election— Woodward's *Reunion and Reaction* (1951). In effect, although the Republicans kept control of the presidency, southern Democratic whites gained control of their home affairs with a program of keeping whites on top, blacks down, and Yankees out. Full African-American disfranchisement came a generation later, but that was an afterthought. Redeemer governments came to enjoy solid control of the South by the late 1870s—notably of South Carolina (historically the deep South's style-setter), Mississippi, and Louisiana, which were the chief spots of contention because they had African-American population majorities or near majorities.
>
> In its southern aspect, the 1876–1877 settlement was so unusual that it has seldom figured in cross-national analysis. It featured constitutional politics for one race, but a caste system and suppression for another. The nearest analogy may be the South African Nationalist election victory of 1948. In terms of voting statistics, the full effect of the 1876–1877 settlement was not felt until 1880, when notably Louisiana and South Carolina, which had narrowly voted Republican at the presidential level in 1876—the beleaguered, biracial Republicans were still in control of counting ballots then at that office level—swung dramatically to the Democratic column, where they remained for generations. [Also, according to Bartels (1998:316), a lasting national pro-Republican thrust occurred in the 1880 election.] In major respects, the southern electoral victories of the mid 1870s determined (to use Schattschneider's verb, which works better here than in most contexts owing to the not easily reversible suppression of southern African-Americans) the course of American politics and society

for most of a century, until the civil rights revolution of the 1960s unraveled them.

One of the aftermaths of the 1876–1877 settlement was an abrupt shift in the national policy agenda. Reconstruction questions receded. The issue of civil rights was abandoned—not least by a Supreme Court that could read the election results. Presidents took to trying to modernize the executive establishment through civil service reform, wrestling with the tariff, and imposing order in industrial relations, as did the Republican Hayes by deploying federal troops in the national railway strike of 1877 and later the Democrat Cleveland doing the same in the Pullman strike of 1894.

The foregoing sketch is meant to be exemplary of ones that might compete with a sketch of the 1890s. The 1870s story, in my judgment, holds up well against the 1890s one, and, as reported above, the statistics for 1876 and 1880 dominate those for 1896. It seems a good bet that if the 1876 election had taken place 30 years after 1860 rather than when it did, we would have heard about it as a realigning election.

Periodicity

If the identities of realigning elections are in question, then their periodicity is in question. Above all, it is important not to let periodicity dictate identity. In this regard, it would be in order to take a close look at the election of 1828. Important though that contest was, exactly what justifies its reputation, as compared with other presidential elections perhaps in its vicinity, as a realigning election?

Stress, Tensions, Flash Points, Boiling Points

A long buildup of stress ending in explosion is a familiar idea and, sometimes at least, a plausible model of reality. One thinks of, for example, the growing intensity of discontent among African-Americans between the mid 1950s and the mid 1960s, or the anti–Vietnam War cause that accelerated between the mid 1960s and the early 1970s. Instances can be found on the realignments calendar, such as the growing tension between North and South between 1854 and 1860 (although that had evidently happened also between 1844 and 1850 without triggering a realignment or a civil war), and possibly the growing farmer discontent (though the pattern may not have been monotonic) in particularly the drier plains states west of Missouri and Iowa during the decade and a half or so leading up to the Populist movement around 1890.

But a general theory of periodic, 30-year-long stress buildups seems very dubious. For one thing, if the canonical realignment junctures are respected, it would have to be shown that politically relevant stress, somehow indexed or at least convincingly argued for, was abnormally high in 1892 and 1928. (Any society at any time is under some level of stress or tension.) Those were the years just before the onsets of the devastating and unquestionably stress-inducing depressions of 1893 (Hoffmann 1956) and 1929. Possibly abnormal stress existed in 1892 (even east of the plains and outside the cotton belt), but it is nearly certain that no "stress" case could be made for 1928, when an electorate wafted by record-shattering prosperity made it virtually impossible for Al Smith to gain issue traction. In effect, he had to wage an uphill struggle against burgeoning consumer durables, movie and radio entertainment, and stock prices. We have every reason to believe that, absent the abrupt economic downturn in 1929, voters would have kept on electing presidents like Coolidge and Hoover for quite a while.

At least one serious error lurks in the realignments genre's model of stress buildup—a tendency to elongate political troubles backward in time without warrant. To account for the Republican successes in 1894 and 1896, the 1893 depression is probably sufficient (although the apparently deviating shape of the 1896 result would no doubt have been different without a Bryan insurgency). To account for the Democratic successes in 1930 and 1932, the depression that started in 1929 is enough. In neither of these depression instances is a 30-year stress buildup required or in evidence.

Concern and Turnout

The concept of voter concern, though in principle distinct from turnout, may be intractable. Turnout is measurable. Lane (1959:19–20)[1] detected two spans of high turnout in presidential elections during the nineteenth century: 1840–1860 (the 1864 and 1868 elections are hard to deal with) and 1876–1900. In the former case, a band of values ranges from 14.5% (1852) to 17.0% (1860) of the total population with high readings also of 16.7% (1856) and 16.5% (1840). In the late nineteenth century, the band ranges from 18.3% (1876 and 1880) through 19.5% (1896) with a high reading also of 19.0% for 1884. Victories, albeit narrow ones, accrue here for the realignments perspective: the highest showings are 1860 and 1896. (As a side note, though, witness the modest levels of all these readings before women became part of the numerator in 1920.)

Yet no one examining a relevant time series for the twentieth century would categorize 1932 as a high-turnout election. It is not a close call (see Lane 1959:19–20, Burnham 1965:11). In the vicinity of 1932, what catches the eye is a nearly monotonic, rather steep rise in turnout between 1920 and 1940. In percentage of the total population voting, 1940 exceeded 1932 by a reported 37.8% to 31.9% (Lane 1959:19); in percentage of eligibles, by a reported 62.5% to 56.9% (US Bureau of the Census 1975, vol. 2, p. 1071). (The 1940 peak is thought-provoking. Was it the imminence of war that brought voters out?)

---

[1]Lane (1959) used total population as a denominator, rather than adult eligible voters; for elections prior to the mid 1860s, he considered the total non-slave population. The choice of technique makes little difference in this discussion.

New, Lasting Issue or Interest Cleavages

On the subject of the basic issue or ideological stances of the parties during the last two centuries, the most sophisticated and convincing work is by Gerring (1998), who used about 2000 texts to code rhetoric (including that in party platforms) emanating from candidates and other party figures during presidential campaigns from 1828 through 1992. One result is periodization (though not periodicity), as indicated in Gerring's chapter titles labeling "epochs." For the Whigs and then the Republicans, 1828–1924 was the "National Epoch," which featured emphasis on the work ethic, social harmony, neomercantilism, statism, order, Yankee Protestantism, and nationalism—above all, a quest for order over chaos (Gerring 1998:13–18). Then, at a hinge point in the mid 1920s, much of this assemblage of values gave way. A "Neoliberal Epoch" set in in 1928 that lasted through at least 1992 on the Republican side, featuring emphasis on antistatism, free market capitalism, right-wing populism, and individualism.

For the Democrats, a "Jeffersonian Epoch" lasting from 1828 through 1892 saw an accentuation of white supremacy, antistatism, and civic republicanism. Then, in an abrupt switch in the 1890s, a "Populist Epoch" began that lasted through 1948, bringing emphasis on egalitarianism, majoritarianism, and Christian humanism—above all, a championing of "the people versus the interests." The business sector symbolized by Wall Street (rather than, as earlier, an actually or potentially oppressive state) came to be seen as the chief political menace or enemy. (On this 1890s juncture, see also Huston 1993:1102–5.) Later, for the Democrats, a "Universalist Epoch" began in 1952 that lasted into the 1990s, featuring emphasis on civil rights, social welfare, redistribution, and inclusion. That is, around the middle of the twentieth century, after Harry Truman's "give 'em hell" campaign in 1948, the Democratic party

> discarded its abrasive, class-tinged ethos in favor of a *Universalist* [italics in original] perspective—the extension of rights to all aggrieved claimants and a general rhetoric of inclusion. Bryan, the evangelical crusader of the Populist era, was traded in for the moderate, ecumenical Lyndon Johnson. Party leaders now praised capitalism without qualification. Arguments for progressive social policies relied on empathy, social responsibility, and impassioned appeals for aid, rather than attacks on privilege and power. Postwar Democrats also reached beyond economic issues to address a wide range of "postmaterialist" concerns. (Gerring 1998:18)

[On this mid-twentieth-century juncture, see also Brinkley (1995), who documents the Democratic party elite's abandonment of "anti-monopolyism" as a credible policy stance a bit earlier, in the late 1930s and early 1940s.]

One clear bull's-eye emerges here for the realignment perspective—the Bryanization of the Democratic party in the 1890s—but otherwise there is a complete lack of correspondence between Gerring's coding and the realignments canon. Where are 1860 and 1932 in Gerring's calculations? I suspect that the problem stems at least partly from certain basic properties of electoral politics. Deep-seated, long-lived party issue stances of the sort discussed by Sundquist or documented by Gerring, important as they may be, are a long way from being hegemonic over voter choice. Even in the realm of "issue content," they supply a background to electoral politics but not ordinarily its foreground.

Instead, events, or the management of events, often generate the foreground issues, as in the following examples. In 1844: Should Texas be annexed? In 1854: What should be the reaction to the Kansas-Nebraska Act? In 1860: After John Brown's raid and the rest, what next? In 1864: Which should it be—clearcut military victory with Lincoln or a muddling compromise with McClellan? In 1866: How severe should Reconstruction policy be? In 1890: Have the Republicans gone overboard with their spending and regulatory schemes in the "billion-dollar Congress" under Benjamin Harrison? In 1894: Have the Democrats ruined the economy? In 1920: After two years of economic turmoil, frightening strikes, and international revolution, which party is a better bet for order? In 1932: Who can get the economy humming again? In 1938: After two years of sitdown strikes, Roosevelt's court-packing plan, allegations of Communists in the agencies, and another alarming economic downturn, is it time to curb the New Dealers? In 1952: Is Eisenhower the remedy for "Communism, corruption, and Korea" (the GOP slogan that year)? In 1968: What is the remedy for violence in the cities and a quagmire war? In 1974 and 1976: After Watergate, who can be trusted? In 1994: Can the ambitious domestic policy plans of the Clinton administration be trusted? In 1998: Should Clinton be evicted from office (see Abramowitz 1999)?

There is no way to prevent voters, politicians, or parties from dwelling on event-centered issues like the foregoing. Indeed, any democratic system that tried to do so—imagine a requirement that voters make decisions only by consulting party stances or cleavages of a sort that might last for 30 years—would probably collapse through rendering its elections irrelevant.

In sum, in the realm of long-term issue cleavages, the realignments perspective runs into problems of both validity (is the periodization correct?) and illuminative power (how much of politics and policy making can be accounted for by any kind of long-term issue cleavage?).

Ideology

Has ideological polarization, levered by the style of the insurgent side, been distinctively characteristic of realignments? Ideology is difficult to define, let alone measure, but let us say it is an ambitious, issue-laden, conflict-generating approach to politics wrapped in abstraction and not weighed down by pragmatism or opportunism. The 1896 election qualifies, as do several elections featuring slavery or Reconstruction issues from the 1840s through the 1870s (it is hard to know which ones to pick out), but how about in the twentieth century? Oddly, none of the New Deal–era presidential elections seems to qualify—certainly not 1928 or 1932. Al Smith's challenge was largely demographic, not ideological. In

1932, it would have been questionable tactics for the Democrats to conduct an ideological campaign, and they did not do so (any more than McKinley had in comparable out-party circumstances during a depression in 1896). There was much criticism of Hoover for not having balanced the budget. Some left-liberal rhetoric did emanate from Roosevelt in 1936, though probably not more than from Truman in 1948. [In actual voting behavior, 1948 was the standout "class cleavage" election between 1936 and 1960; 1936 was average for that time span (see Alford 1963:227).] And with Alf Landon in 1936, the Republicans were already half-way into their quarter-century-long "me-too" mode. In actuality, during the twentieth century, the presidential elections that best fit the "ideological" mold may be those of 1912 with its evangelistic crusade waged by the Theodore Roosevelt Progressives, 1964 with its hard-line conservative Goldwater Republicans, and 1972 with its McGovern Democrats. Possibly the Reagan election of 1980 qualifies.

Still, this is an unsatisfying apprehension of the 1930s, for the midterm elections should be examined also. It was the 1934 midterm that brought Upton Sinclair's "End Poverty in California" campaign, left-wing third-party victories in Wisconsin and Minnesota (the latter was a repeat performance), and, on impressionistic evidence, primary and then November victories by many left-liberal Democrats—for example, Maury Maverick (Democratic representative from Texas) and Joseph Guffey (Democratic senator from Pennsylvania)—who added a distinctive leftist tone to congressional politics for a few years (see Schlesinger 1960:142–44). A strong nationwide ideological impulse can infuse primary elections, November elections, and the ranks of officeholders without being easily readable off statistics on election results, major-party officeholding, or roll-call voting. That seems to have happened in 1934.

Yet to look beyond presidential contests raises the possibility of ideologized subpresidential elections besides 1934's. If a primary season tilting in one direction counts as indirect evidence of ideologization, consider the Progressive or insurgent victories in the Republican primaries of 1910. If the arrival of a class of particularly aggressive hard-liners in Congress counts as indirect evidence of an ideologized election, then the Republican-edged elections of 1980 and 1994 were arguably ideologized. So was the midterm of 1950—a kind of opposite bookend to 1934, since it came at the close of a decade and a half when (except during World War II) the question of a Popular Front, the muscular Congress of Industrial Organizations (CIO) with its many Communist organizers, or the fervent anti-Communism of that era seldom failed to intrude into American elections. Occurring at the height of the Korean War and McCarthyism, the election of 1950 was a disaster for incumbent politicians targetable as left-wingers. Down went Helen Gahagan Douglas in the so-called "pink lady" campaign in California. Out went, among others, Senator Claude Pepper (then sometimes called "Red Pepper") in Florida's Democratic primary, Senator Frank Graham in North Carolina's Democratic primary, Senator Glen Taylor (Henry Wallace's vice-presidential running-mate in 1948) in Idaho's Democratic nominating process, Senator Elbert Thomas in Utah, Senator Millard

Tydings in Maryland (Tydings was not a left-winger or even a liberal, but he had got on the wrong side of McCarthy), and the lone American Labor Party congressman, Vito Marcantonio of Manhattan. This 1950 purge—that is what it amounted to—was arguably an exercise of ideology.

It is not clear what to make of the ideological turbulence of the mid 1930s through the early 1950s. Its relation to the Democratic surge election of 1932 is uncertain. Much of Europe exhibited a similar pattern at the same time (Mayhew 1994). For an American analogy, it may be necessary to look back to the very beginning of national history; between roughly 1793 and 1812, during the height of the French Revolution and its aftermath, much of this country's political elite was comparably caught up in European ideological warfare.

National, Not Local Issues

That realignments have been distinctively dominated by national issues could hardly be claimed of elections at the presidential level. Since the presidency has the whole nation as its constituency, all presidential elections offer national issues.[2] But how about House elections? The point is important for Brady (1988:12, 14), who argues that a switch to "national rather than local issues" during realigning elections has generated party mandates enabling Congress to overcome "inertia" and "incrementalism" in the policy realm. But whether House elections actually sort this way is an empirical question—it cannot be settled by assertion or deduction—and, unfortunately, no sure measure exists to supply an answer. However, the case for thus singling out the elections of 1854–1860 (Brady 1988:33), 1894 (1988:61–63), and 1932 (1988:91) is far from clear-cut. For one thing, the elections of 1894 and 1932 (and also 1930) were classic "nationwide states of affairs" elections—that is, a poor economy everywhere favored the out party. That situation does make for "national" issues of a sort, yet many other House elections have borne, if in lesser degree, the same profile of a poor economy plus adverse voter reaction. Examples in recent decades include the elections of 1938, 1958, 1974, 1980, and 1982.

Beyond this, if one scans impressionistically for manifest national issue content in past House elections, other elections jut up. In the vicinity of 1894, for example, why should 1894 be said to dominate 1874, which featured Reconstruction issues as well as a poor economy; 1890, which brought an immense national seat swing in reaction to (it has often been casually claimed, although the matter has been understudied) the newly-enacted McKinley Tariff; or 1910, with its Progressive insurgency? The evidence is soft, yet the case for the distinctiveness of the canonical realigning junctures is certainly unproven and very likely weak.

---

[2]Oddly, if the history of presidential contests were seriously searched for elections with localistic aspects, the 1896 one might rank high. That year, a set of geographically concentrated special-interest tails—the silver industry plus cotton and high-plains farmers—managed to wag the huge Democratic dog.

Policy Innovations

Have electoral realignments ushered in "outpourings of new comprehensive public policies"? (Brady 1988:vii). No one has any doubts about the 1860s and the 1930s, but how about the 1890s? Not then, said Schattschneider, and now Burnham agrees.

This is the third rail of the realignments genre, and Brady was unwise to touch it. In the legislative sphere, policy innovations under McKinley during 1897–1901 probably rank in the bottom quartile of American history. There was the Dingley Tariff of 1897, but the Republicans had a habit of hiking the tariff just after sweeping into power—notably in 1861, 1890, and 1922 as well as 1897. (The Democrats did the opposite in 1894, 1913, and 1934). There was the Gold Standard Act of 1900, but that came after the inflation issue had lost its punch, and, at any rate, sturdy support for the gold standard had carried down from the Cleveland Democrats (they, not the Bryanites, had been running the country) through the McKinley Republicans. No other legislative policy innovations stand out. In the historical vicinity of the 1890s, Congresses can easily be found that were more innovative than either of McKinley's taken alone or probably together. Under Harrison in 1889–1891, the Republicans generated the McKinley Tariff (McKinley was a House member then), naval expansion aimed at making the United States competitive, the Sherman Antitrust Act, the Sherman Silver Purchase Act, and an expansion of Civil War pensions broad enough to help fuel recent discussion about a late-nineteenth-century American welfare state (Skocpol 1992:2). Under Theodore Roosevelt in 1905–1907 came a burst of regulatory activity—the Pure Food and Drug Act and the lengthily deliberated Hepburn Act regulating the railroads. Either of Woodrow Wilson's Congresses of 1913–1915 and 1915–1917 would outscore the 1890s on the "policy innovations" criterion. The McKinley era was not a fertile legislative one (see Mayhew 1996).

Recently, Burnham (1986:269–74) has reached for the business-friendly judiciary, as opposed to the legislative process, as the relevant policy-making arena of the 1894–1937 era. Although that may be justified, the claim at issue here involves change. It would have to be shown that the judiciary had been significantly more hostile to the business community during the generation before the mid 1890s than it was during the generation afterward. Burnham does not say or seem to imply that, and to demonstrate it would be a formidable task.

The 1890s pose a basic interpretive difficulty for the realignments genre. Policy change of turnaround dimensions favoring the business community is not to be found. The problem is the baseline. In the history of the world, when has a governmental environment ever favored private capitalism more than the American environment of the 1860s through the mid 1890s? On offer were high protective tariffs (on balance, they were arguably higher during 1861–1896 than during 1897–1930; see Hansen 1990:540), solid property and contract rights, huge free land-grants to the railroads, easy availability of an immigrant labor force from Europe, free trade across a continent, low taxes, a stable currency, little government regulation, and, in a pinch, presidents ready to send in federal troops to put down politicizing strikes, as in 1877 and 1894. How much more could be asked?

Redistributive Policy

Again, no one would hesitate to associate redistributive policy innovation with the 1860s (consider the Thirteenth Amendment abolishing slavery) or the 1930s. The case for the 1930s seems to become even better as new work appears emphasizing the decade's prodigious relief efforts (Amenta 1998:ch. 4, Amenta et al 1998, Kennedy 1999:ch. 9) and addressing the likely wealth-equalizing effects of various statutes (Shammas 1993:426–29). But I am not aware of any serious work attributing notable redistributive policy change, in either a progressive or a regressive direction, to the realignment of the 1890s. The tariff aside, there was little policy change of any sort after McKinley's election.

To dwell on alleged past realignments can exact costs—for one, neglect of other past junctures on which a spotlight might productively be flashed. In the redistributive realm, a good candidate would seem to be the immense increase in federal revenue and spending associated with World War II and the Korean War, which proved to be irreversible (Higgs 1987:ch. 2, Schultze 1992, Shammas 1993:426–29).

The Electorate Weighs in Consequentially at Realignment Junctures Only

Burnham (1967:287) claims that "approximately once in a generation"—i.e. at the canonical realignment junctures—"vitally important contributions to American political development" are made (Burnham 1967:287).

This is a large claim, and I believe a mistaken one. It is a basic theoretical error to associate changes in voting alignments, however lasting they may be, with attributes of the electorate's decisions (voter awareness, level of underlying concern, or consequentiality). As long as parties cater to the electorate, or else emanate from it—as do the American parties, with their widely participated-in nominating processes (even before the coming of direct primaries)—any contributions that the electorate wishes to make are likely to intrude into elections regardless of whether those elections feature realigning patterns. Notably, if both major parties accommodate such a contribution, it may come to dominate policy making without disturbing received electoral patterns at all. If, say, in the 1880s, the bulk of Americans had suddenly decided that the country should officially convert to Islam, that idea, if accommodated by both parties in an election campaign, might have come to pass through government action in short order without any electoral realignment. That would have been a major voter contribution. [Sundquist, in a discussion of nonrealignments, pursues this logic (1973:11–18).]

This is not a fanciful idea, perhaps particularly if one looks beyond issues that may last 30 years to ones that, let us say, just come up. Consider the election of 1940. Against a background of France having fallen to the Nazis in May and June and Britain imperiled, the Republicans opted in an open nominating process for a nonisolationist candidate (the surprising Wendell Willkie) without suffering serious defections then or afterward, and the Willkie-versus-Roosevelt November election, despite certain marginal late-season fudging by both sides, was readable as a victory for internationalism. How many election outcomes have been more important than that?

Or take the election of 1948, which generated at least four nontrivial results. An over-90% winner, courtesy of Dewey's carrying his party constituency with a "me-too" stance, was the heart of the domestic New Deal. Another bipartisan over-90% winner, in its first tryout in national nominating and general election processes, was the government's new stance of Cold War internationalism. Given a third-party choice for president—former Vice President Henry Wallace was still a major political property then—voters marginalized Popular Front politics with a devastating zero states and 2.4% of the vote. Also offered a choice, voters gave the Dixiecrat candidate Strom Thurmond four deep-southern states and an identical 2.4% of the vote—a non-negligible yet contained showing. All in all, few elections have been more consequential or information-rich than that of 1948, and it would be something of an insult to voters of that time to allege that they could not have been contributing, in Burnham's terms, to American political development just because they neglected to realign themselves. Approached in this way, the elections of 1940 and 1948 and probably many others will stand up against that of 1896.

The "System of 1896"

Was the American business community, as Burnham (1986) claims, insulated from mass pressures by a "system of 1896" for over a third of a century?

Probably not. First of all, as argued above, there is the problem of contingency. In any reasonably open polity operating in an event-packed world, no election result can program the future to that extent. Republican control of the national government crumbled in 1910 and 1912. Progressive-oriented Democrats came to power under Wilson and proved popular—a development passed over as an off-schedule intrusion by most realignments writers (Sundquist excepted). As of, say, 1916, the most likely electoral future was probably toss-up competition between the two major parties indefinitely. But then came act two for the Democrats, the management of World War I and its aftermath, which seems to have badly damaged them (in Britain, war management destroyed the Liberal party) and brought on their worst defeat ever in 1920. This is contingency. Electorates can key on wars and their aftermaths just as intently as on domestic socioeconomic programs. There is no good reason to credit the old 1896 realignment for the new postwar Republican hegemony that emerged as a "system of 1920" (the label is equally warranted) that lasted through 1930 and 1932. Note than in both the Clubb et al (1980) and Bartels (1988) calculations, 1920 earns a better license as a realigning election than does 1896, and an appealing 1876-like story could be composed about it.

Second, why should it be supposed that the American business community needed the alleged insulation after 1896? (The Schattschneider and Burnham "functional" argument is at issue here.) Certainly that community's practitioners had done well enough for themselves during the uninsulated decades of vigorous two-party competition, less accentuated sectionalism, and high (male) voter turnout before the mid 1890s. As for the American economy's presumably high-tension takeoff, that had occurred, according to Rostow's schematization (1960: ch. 4), between 1843 and 1860 under Presidents Tyler through Buchanan.

A major defect in the "system of 1896" line of thinking is that it ignores the extraordinary success, at least according to certain relevant indicators, of the American society and economy during the generations both before and after the mid 1890s. It seems not to have needed insulating. Real per capita income nearly tripled between 1870 and 1910; life expectancy rose dramatically (Bruchey 1988:67–69). The American economy grew at an estimated average annual rate of 4.3% between 1871 and 1913 (US Bureau of the Census 1975, vol. 1, p. 225). (Another estimate is 4.3% between 1973 and the mid 1890s and 5.6% between the mid 1890s and 1913; see Coppock 1961:227). Granted, short-term troubles could be severe, as in 1893, and sectors of the agricultural and blue-collar population could and did suffer, but everything we know about electoral behavior suggests that indicator readings like those above bring endorsements of regimes and the parties that manage them. Not least, in what was still dominantly a country of farmers, commercial agriculture grew and flourished. One firewall against Populism in the 1890s seems to have been indifference or antipathy to it among most farmers. Iowa, for example, always an agricultural showcase, stayed with the Republicans in both 1892 and 1896. (On the understandably limited appeal of Populism, see Hughes 1994.) In general, the threatening mass pressures of the "system of 1896" interpretation seem to have been drawn more from tracts than from reality. The best insulation is a 4–5% growth rate. As of the early twentieth century, the chief mass pressures of relevance to the United States were probably those associated with Europeans trying to immigrate here.

Did a "system of 1896" impede the development of a major socialist party in the United States? The case may be doubted. As Foner has pointed out (1984), this country did possess, in the early twentieth century, a nascent socialist party that "appeared to rival those in Europe, except the German, in mass support and prospects for future growth. Around 1910, the American Socialist party had elected more officials than its English counterpart" (1984:60). But the American party faltered in enrolling immigrant workers, and in World War I, "apart from the Russian Bolsheviks, the American was the party that remained most true to socialist principles" (Foner 1984:71–72). That is, it refused to back its own nation's military cause—a politically suicidal stance in the United States of 1917–1918. Again, contingency associated with World War I intrudes. In Britain, absent that war, the Labour party might never have catapulted to competitive status as one of that country's two major parties. On the subject of America's many nonvoters of the early decades of the twentieth century—leaving aside whether their nonparticipation had much to do with the realignment of 1896—the counterfactual question of how they would have voted if mobilized is unanswerable. The answer once would have been "as social democrats," but the full experience of the twentieth century has supplied too many competing answers. In various places at various times, widespread voter participation seems also to have helped liberalism, Toryism, nationalism, populism, Christian democracy, Communism, fascism, and racism.

CONCLUSION

The claims of the realignments genre do not hold up well, and the genre's illuminative power has not proven to be great. At an analytic level, the genre has proven vulnerable to at least three counterposing ideas: contingency, strategy, and valence issues.

Electoral politics is strongly influenced by the contingencies of unfolding events. To the extent that this is true, elections and their underlying causes are not usefully sortable into generation-long spans. Furthermore, victory-oriented strategy is plied by candidates and parties, both of which tend to cater to the electorate as well as emanate from it. (The two ideas are difficult to disentangle; I am emphasizing the former here.) To the degree that parties and candidates seek election victories above all else, courting the median voter, they will often accommodate major impulses from the electorate without telltale signs of realignment appearing in elections. Thus, the size of voter realignments cannot index the importance, innovativeness, and consequentiality of elections, nor the level of voter concern that underpins them.

If we consider the combination of contingency and victory-oriented strategy, certain results reported by Gans (1985) become understandable. In the sequence of presidential elections from 1856 through 1980, the distribution of victory "runs" by party (Carter, for example, was a run of one for the Democrats; Reagan's two victories and Bush's one made a run of three for the Republicans) did not differ significantly from the runs of heads and tails that would be expected from coin flips (Gans 1985:228–30). Also, in the absence of repeat major-party candidates (such as Reagan in 1984 or Bryan in 1900), a presidential election four years ago holds virtually zero predictive value for this year's election—either in predicting this year's victorious party or this year's party shares of the vote (Gans 1985:230–33).

The third idea that poses problems for the realignments genre is that of valence issues. The concept was introduced by Stokes (1966) and given major play, at least implicitly, in the sizable econometrics literature gauging the effects of ups and downs in the economy on elections. Unlike position issues, in which one party favors policy X and the other party favors policy Y—the staple kind of cleavage in the realignments genre—valence issues hinge chiefly on government management. Can another party manage the economy or the war, for example, better than the incumbent party has been doing? The more one examines American electoral history, the more it seems to tilt toward valence-issue as opposed to position-issue junctures. More than it did a generation ago, for example, the electoral turmoil of the 1890s seems to implicate the depression of 1893 as much as Bryan's insurgency. A poor economy figured in the critical 1874 midterm, and, according to one recent analysis, a quick nationwide economic downturn was a central ingredient in the Whigs' great victory of 1840 (Holt 1985). Valence issues, which also exemplify contingency and often bring into play opportunistic candidate or party strategies, are not friendly territory for the realignments genre.

It is not a minor matter that contingency, strategy, and valence issues tend to infuse elections. Blindsided by that threesome, for example, were Germany's Social Democrats and Communists in the early 1930s—brought up as they were on a script in which history would eventually favor their interest-based cause and they could simply wait. Politics cannot be about waiting—for electoral realignments or anything else. In the real world, voters are called upon to make judgments, not merely to register enduring interests or preferences—and to make them all the time.

In the ledgers of history and politics, perhaps the chief test for the realignments genre whether it successfully elevates 1896 to a level with 1860 and 1932. That seems to have been its chief aspiration, both as science (to wit, the alleged periodicity) and as political and historical assertion. The Bryan cause was so terribly important, after all. But it was a lost cause, if an interesting and important one, and as such it is a member of a large universe of not easily analyzable "roads not taken." History moved on, more or less seamlessly, and seamlessness does not easily rival the memorable undertakings of the Civil War and New Deal eras. Between these two eras, if one's concern is electoral turbulence, at least four junctures catch the eye. Choosing which ones to dwell on is largely a matter of policy interest. For race and section, there is the election sequence of 1874 through 1880. For center-periphery relations, there is 1892 through 1896. For Progressive state-building, there is 1910 through 1916. For US international involvement and the ricochet from it, there is 1916 through 1920.

ACKNOWLEDGMENTS

I am indebted to Bruce Ackerman, Robert Dahl, Alan Gerber, Donald Green, Matthew Green, Rogan Kersh, Joseph LaPalombara, Michael Layton, Harvey Schantz, Ian Shapiro, Steven Skowronek, and Rogers Smith for their helpful comments on this paper.

Visit the Annual Reviews home page at www.AnnualReviews.org

LITERATURE CITED

Abramowitz AI. 1999. *It's Monica, stupid: voting behavior in the 1998 midterm election.* Presented at Annu. Meet. Am. Polit. Sci. Assoc., Atlanta, GA

Alford RR. 1963. *Party and Society.* Chicago: Rand McNally. 396 pp.

Amenta E. 1998. *Bold Relief: Institutional Politics and the Origins of Modern American Social Policy.* Princeton, NJ: Princeton Univ. Press. 343 pp.

Amenta E, Benoit E, Bonastia C, Cauthen NK, Halfmann D. 1998. Bring back the WPA: work, relief, and the origins of American social policy in welfare reform. *Stud. Am. Polit. Dev.* 12(1):1–56

Bartels LM. 1998. Electoral continuity and

change, 1868–1996. *Elect. Stud.* 17:301–26

Blumenthal S. 1982. *The Permanent Campaign.* New York: Simon & Schuster. 336 pp.

Brady DW. 1988. *Critical Elections and Congressional Policy Making.* Stanford, CA: Stanford Univ. Press. 212 pp.

Brinkley A. 1995. *The End of Reform: New Deal Liberalism in Recession and War.* New York: Knopf. 371 pp.

Bruchey S. 1988. *The Wealth of the Nation.* New York: Harper & Row. 259 pp.

Burnham WD. 1965. The changing shape of the American political universe. *Am. Polit. Sci. Rev.* 59:7–28

Burnham WD. 1967. Party systems and the political process. In *The American Party Systems: Stages of Political Development,* ed. WN Chambers, WD Burnham, pp. 277–307. New York: Oxford Univ. Press. 374 pp.

Burnham WD. 1970. *Critical Elections and the Mainsprings of American Politics.* New York: Norton. 210 pp.

Burnham WD. 1981. The system of 1896: an analysis. In *The Evolution of American Electoral Systems,* ed. P Kleppner, WD Burnham, RP Formisano, SP Hays, R Jensen, WG Shade, pp. 147–202. Westport, CT: Greenwood. 279 pp.

Burnham WD. 1986. Periodization schemes and "party systems": the "system of 1896" as a case in point. *Soc. Sci. Hist.* 10:263–314

Burnham WD. 1991. Critical realignment: dead or alive? In *The End of Realignment? Interpreting American Electoral Eras,* ed. B Shafer, pp. 101–39. Madison, WI: Univ. Wisc. Press. 187 pp.

Clubb JM, Flanigan WH, Zingale NH. 1980. *Partisan Realignment: Voters, Parties, and Government in American History.* Beverly Hills, CA: Sage. 309 pp.

Coppock DJ. 1961. The causes of the Great Depression, 1873–96. *Manchester School Econ. Soc. Stud.* 29:205–32

Flanigan WH, Zingale NH. 1974. The measurement of electoral change. *Polit. Methodol.* 1(Summer):49–82

Foner E. 1984. Why is there no socialism in the United States? *Hist. Workshop* 17(Spring):57–80

Gans DJ. 1985. Persistence of party success in American presidential elections. *J. Interdisc. Hist.* 16:221–37

Gerring J. 1998. *Party Ideologies in America, 1828–1996.* New York: Cambridge Univ. Press. 337 pp.

Hansen JM. 1990. Taxation and the political economy of the tariff. *Int. Org.* 44:527–51

Higgs R. 1987. *Crisis and Leviathan: Critical Episodes in the Growth of American Government.* New York: Oxford Univ. Press. 350 pp.

Hoffmann C. 1956. The depression of the nineties. *J. Econ. Hist.* 16:137–64

Holt MF. 1985. The election of 1840, voter mobilization, and the emergence of the second American party system: a reappraisal of Jacksonian voting behavior. In *A Master's Due: Essays in Honor of David Herbert Donald,* ed. WJ Cooper Jr, MF Holt, J McCardell, pp. 16–58. Baton Rouge: Louisiana State Univ. Press. 297 pp.

Hughes JF. 1994. The Jacksonians, the populists and the governmental habit. *Mid-America* 76(1):5–26

Huston JL. 1993. The American revolutionaries, the political economy of aristocracy, and the American concept of the distribution of wealth, 1765–1900. *Am. Hist. Rev.* 98:1079–1105

Kennedy DM. 1999. *Freedom from Fear: The American People in Depression and War, 1929–1945.* New York: Oxford Univ. Press. 936 pp.

Key VO Jr. 1955. A theory of critical elections. *J. Polit.* 17:3–18

Key VO Jr. 1959. Secular realignment and the party system. *J. Polit.* 21:198–210

Lane RE. 1959. *Political Life: Why People Get Involved in Politics.* Glencoe, IL: Free. 374 pp.

Lowi TJ. 1964. American business, public policy, case-studies, and political theory. *World Polit.* 16:677–715

Mayhew DR. 1994. U.S. policy waves in

comparative context. In *New Perspectives on American Politics*, ed. LC Dodd, C Jillson, pp. 325–40. Washington, DC: Congr. Q. Press. 360 pp.

Mayhew DR. 1996. Presidential elections and policy change: how much of a connection is there? In *American Presidential Elections: Process, Policy, and Political Change*, ed. H Schantz, pp. 157–87. 258 pp.

Nardulli PF. 1995. The concept of a critical realignment, electoral behavior, and political change. *Am. Polit. Sci. Rev.* 89:10–22

Rostow WW. 1960. *The Stages of Economic Growth*. New York: Cambridge Univ. Press. 179 pp.

Schantz HL. 1998. *Realignment before V.O. Key, Jr.* Presented at Annu. Meet. So. Polit. Sci. Assoc., Atlanta, GA

Schattschneider EE. 1956. United States: the functional approach to party government. In *Modern Political Parties: Approaches to Comparative Politics*, ed. S Neumann, pp. 194–215. Chicago: Univ. Chicago Press. 460 pp.

Schattschneider EE. 1960. *The Semisovereign People: A Realist's View of Democracy in America*. New York: Holt, Rinehart, Winston. 147 pp.

Schlesinger AM Jr. 1960. *The Politics of Upheaval*. Boston: Houghton Mifflin. 749 pp.

Schultze CL. 1992. Is there a bias toward excess in U.S. government budgets or deficits? *J. Econ. Persp.* 6(2):25–43

Shammas C. 1993. A new look at long-term trends in wealth inequality in the United States. *Am. Hist. Rev.* 98:412–31

Skocpol T. 1992. *Protecting Soldiers and Mothers: The Political Origins of Social Policy in the United States*. Cambridge, MA: Harvard Univ. Press. 714 pp.

Stokes DE. 1966. Spatial models of party competition. In *Elections and the Political Order*, ed. A Campbell, PE Converse, WE Miller, DE Stokes, pp. 161–79. New York: Wiley. 385 pp.

Sundquist JL. 1973. *Dynamics of the Party System: Alignment and Realignment of Political Parties in the United States*. Washington, DC: Brookings Inst. 388 pp. Rev. ed. 1983, 466 pp.

US Bureau of the Census. 1975. *Historical Statistics of the United States, Colonial Times to 1970*. 2 vols. Washington, DC: US Gov. Print. Off.

Woodward CV. 1951. *Reunion and Reaction: The Compromise of 1877 and the End of Reconstruction*. Boston: Little, Brown. 263 pp.

Zuczek R. 1996. The last campaign of the Civil War: South Carolina and the revolution of 1876. *Civil War Hist.* 42:18–31

Annu. Rev. Polit. Sci. 2000. 3:475–508

POLITICAL TRUST AND TRUSTWORTHINESS

Margaret Levi
Department of Political Science, University of Washington, Seattle, Washington 98195;
e-mail: mlevi@u.washington.edu

Laura Stoker
Department of Political Science, University of California, Berkeley, California 94720;
e-mail: stoker@bravo.berkeley.edu

Key Words   public opinion, institutions, political attitudes, alienation, legitimacy

■ **Abstract**   After addressing the meaning of "trust" and "trustworthiness," we review survey-based research on citizens' judgments of trust in governments and politicians, and historical and comparative case study research on political trust and government trustworthiness. We first provide an overview of research in these two traditions, and then take up four topics in more detail: (*a*) political trust and political participation; (*b*) political trust, public opinion, and the vote; (*c*) political trust, trustworthy government, and citizen compliance; and (*d*) political trust, social trust, and cooperation. We conclude with a discussion of fruitful directions for future research.

INTRODUCTION

The social science literature on trust has grown enormously in recent years, partly in response to the perception that political and social trust, deemed essential to a good society, are in decline. There are now decades of responses to the same survey questions, which show diminished political and social trust in a number of advanced industrial democracies. These data have generated efforts to explain, and ultimately to reverse, these trends. Related arguments about the importance of social capital and the claim that it, too, is in decline have also inspired a renewed focus on trust.

In this chapter, we review micro-level research into citizen judgments about the trustworthiness of political officeholders, political organizations, and governments, as well as macro-level research into the attributes of politicians and governments that make them trustworthy. In joining these topics we are recognizing that trust and trustworthiness are what Weatherford (1992) calls multi-level concepts—concepts that are useful in organizing research on both individuals and aggregates such as bureaucracies or nations.

After clarifying what we mean by "trust" and "trustworthiness," we provide an overview of survey-based research on citizens' judgments of trust in governments

1094-2939/00/0623-0475$14.00

and politicians, and of historical and comparative case study research on political trust and government trustworthiness. Whereas the survey work tends to focus on the individual-level causes and consequences of political trust judgments, the historical and comparative case study work tends to focus on macro-level determinants and outcomes or on trust relations among elites. We then consider in more detail four topics that concern the consequences of political trust and trustworthiness: (*a*) political trust and political participation; (*b*) political trust, public opinion, and the vote; (*c*) political trust, trustworthy government, and citizen compliance; and (*d*) political trust, social trust, and cooperation. We conclude with a discussion of fruitful directions for future research.

DEFINITIONS

Although trust is a contested term, there appears to be some minimal consensus about its meaning. Trust is relational; it involves an individual making herself vulnerable to another individual, group, or institution that has the capacity to do her harm or to betray her. Trust is seldom unconditional; it is given to specific individuals or institutions over specific domains. For instance, citizens may entrust their lives to their government during wartime but not trust the bureaucracies that expend funds during peacetime. Trust is a judgment that can be conceptualized dichotomously (one either trusts or distrusts) or in a more graded fashion (one trusts or distrusts to a degree). Either way, there is the possibility that one neither trusts nor distrusts another. Trust judgments are expected to inspire courses of action. Distrust, for example, may inspire vigilance in and monitoring of a relationship, uncooperative behavior, or the severing of a relationship. The trust judgment reflects beliefs about the trustworthiness of the other person (or group or institution).

Trustworthiness is also relational but in a more limited sense. Even when there is no call for trust, a person or institution can possess the attributes of trustworthiness, which assure potential trusters that the trusted party will not betray a trust. These attributes fall along two dimensions. The first involves a commitment to act in the interests of the truster because of moral values that emphasize promise keeping, caring about the truster, incentive compatibility, or some combination of all three. When we call someone trustworthy, we often mean only this commitment, but there is in fact a second dimension, namely competence in the domain over which trust is being given. The trustworthy will not betray the trust as a consequence of either bad faith or ineptitude.

OVERVIEW OF SURVEY RESEARCH

Research on the United States

In 1962, Stokes introduced what later became known as the National Election Studies (NES) trust-in-government questions, which were designed to tap the basic evaluative orientations towards the national government. The criteria of judgment implicit in these questions were partly ethical, that is honesty and other ethical qualities of public officials were part of what the sample was asked to judge. But the criteria extended to other qualities as well, including the ability and efficiency of government officials and the correctness of their policy decisions. (Stokes 1962:64)

Stokes used these data to categorize survey respondents according to whether they held favorable or unfavorable evaluations of government. The concepts of trust in government or of political trust never figured into his analysis. It was subsequent developments that prompted work on political trust, or at least on political trust as labeled and measured by the NES.

The publication of Easton's (1965) *A Systems Analysis of Political Life* and of Gamson's (1968) *Power and Discontent*—at a time when sociologists were increasingly focusing on the topic of alienation (e.g. Seeman 1959)—catalyzed the analysis of political trust. Easton (1965) introduced the influential distinction between diffuse support (i.e. support for the system or regime) and specific support (i.e. support for the incumbent authorities). Gamson's (1968) theory of political mobilization and activism treated political trust as a central organizing concept.

A second development was the social and political unrest of the 1960s and early 1970s, involving race relations and the civil rights movement as well as the war in Vietnam. A third development was the dramatic decline over time in the percentage of US citizens giving trusting responses to the NES trust-in-government questions, particularly across the 1964–1972 period (Figure 1). Because of these developments, by the early 1970s there was an explosion of work addressing whether system support was in decline in the United States; if not, what was, in fact, declining; and how all of this related to the civil and political disruptions of the period.

One of the main preoccupations of this literature was measurement. Although scholars had begun to refer to the NES questions as measuring political trust or trust in government,[1] the measurement work did not focus on whether the NES items yielded a reliable and valid index of political trust or trustworthiness per se. Rather, it focused on whether the NES items tapped sentiments about current incumbents as opposed to judgments about the system or regime. Researchers compared the NES trust index to indices of alienation from the political system, debated whether and which incumbent-specific reactions were entering into the NES responses, and evaluated variants of the NES questions intended to direct respondents' attention away from current incumbents and toward the system as a whole (e.g. Miller 1974b; Citrin 1974, 1977; Muller & Jukam 1977; Abramson & Finifter 1981; Muller et al 1982; Feldman 1983; Seligson 1983; Williams 1985;

---

[1] Early studies that treat NES responses as measurements of trust include Aberbach (1969), Aberbach & Walker (1970), Miller (1974a), and Citrin (1974). Over the years, researchers have used other labels to describe what the NES questions were measuring, including political cynicism, disaffection, and alienation. See Citrin & Muste (1999).

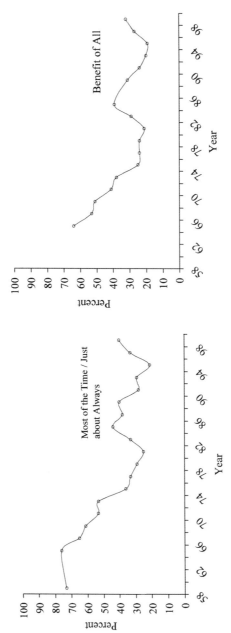

(a) How much of the time do you think you can trust the government in Washington to do what is right—just about always, most of the time, or only some of the time?

(b) Would you say the government is pretty much run by a few big interests looking out for themselves or that it is run for the benefit of all the people?

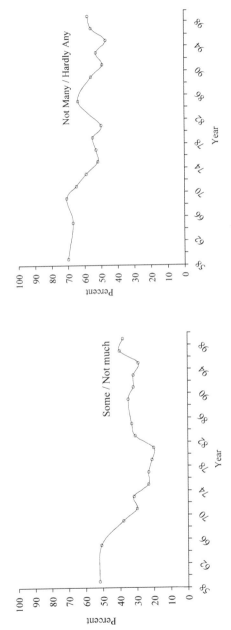

(c) Do you think that people in the government waste a lot of money we pay in taxes, waste some of it, or don't waste very much of it?

(d) Do you think that quite a few of the people running the government are crooked, not very many are, or do you think hardly any of them are crooked? (During 1958–1972, this question was worded as follows: Do you think that quite a few of the people running the government are a little crooked, not very many are, or do you think hardly any of them are crooked at all?)

Figure 1 Percentage of US citizens who gave trusting responses to the National Election Studies trust-in-government questions.

Citrin & Green 1986; Weatherford 1987; Jennings & van Deth 1989:ch. 11; Craig et al 1990. For more thorough reviews, see Craig 1993, Nye et al 1997, and Citrin & Muste 1999).

One way to make sense of this emphasis in the measurement literature is that the system versus non-system focus was important no matter what concept the index was taken to represent. Whether one accepted Easton's arguments about system support or Gamson's arguments about distrust and discontent or sociologists' work on the concept and consequences of political alienation, one could conclude that disaffection was bad for the society and polity only if it was focused on the system or regime. Thus, the critical question about the NES index—and, hence, about what meaning to give to the plummeting levels of trust-so-measured—was whether it was incumbent-oriented or system-focused.

Evidence from all sorts of studies, whether focused on this issue of measurement or on the causes of the over-time dynamics of trust/distrust, found the NES responses to have strong partisan and incumbent-specific components. For example, Democratic identifiers are more trusting if the president is a Democrat and less trusting if the president is a Republican (e.g. Citrin 1974); similar findings, though developed with respect to the parties who dominate governing coalitions, have been found in studies of Western Europe (e.g. Listhaug 1995). Trust judgments are also influenced by evaluations of the performance of the incumbent president or government, particularly in the economic realm; by evaluations of the leaders' personal qualities; and by dissatisfaction with the policies being promoted or implemented by the current government (e.g. Citrin 1974; Abramson & Finifter 1981; Weatherford 1984, 1987; Citrin & Green 1986; Miller & Borrelli 1991; Craig 1993; Orren 1997; Hetherington 1998, 1999). Studies examining related measures (e.g. confidence in political institutions) on US and non-US populations have uncovered evidence of these kinds of incumbent-specific and short-term influences as well (e.g. Lipset & Schneider 1983, Hibbing & Patterson 1994, Listhaug & Wiberg 1995, Mishler & Rose 1997, McAllister 1999, Miller & Listhaug 1999).

Further—and on this the evidence is less clear—those who express distrust in government appear to be more dissatisfied with the political parties or with the policy choices that the parties provide. This was a central argument in Miller's (1974a,b) early and influential articles, which developed the idea that distrust was most common among extremists of the left or right who were dissatisfied with the policy alternatives provided by the centrist American political parties (see also Miller & Listhaug 1990, and for a dissenting view, Citrin 1974). In more recent years, a new version of the argument has emerged; by the 1980s and 1990s, it was because the parties had become so politically polarized that the centrist American population was dissatisfied and hence not trusting (Craig 1996, King 1997).

If distrust reflects dissatisfaction with the positions taken by the political parties, this is evidence that trust judgments are not merely an amalgam of reactions to current incumbents but reflect deeper, and less readily reversible, dissatisfactions or concerns. Indeed, although the decline in trust from the 1960s to the 1970s was fueled by citizens' reactions to the war in Vietnam, Watergate, and civil rights initiatives (e.g. Abramson 1983, Markus 1979), trust did not rebound as the administrations associated with these events were replaced. Scholars have suggested a number of other forces that may have been at work over the decades to keep trust levels low or push them lower. These include the unrelenting string of political scandals over the years; the growth of television and its critical or cynical messages about politicians and government (Robinson 1976, Miller et al 1979, Patterson 1993, Capella & Jamieson 1997, Chan 1997); the public's perception, if not the reality, that American society was confronting but not solving a host of problems, including crime and family decline (Craig 1993, Mansbridge 1997, Hetherington 1998, PEW 1998; but see Bok 1997); Americans' increasing dissatisfaction with Congress, which fueled their distrust of politicians and government in general (Williams 1985, Feldman 1983, Hibbing & Theiss-Morse 1995, Hetherington 1998, Luks & Citrin 1997); and the fact that, for whatever reason, Americans had increasingly come to judge politicians as selfish and unresponsive to citizens' concerns (Craig 1993, Lawrence 1997). Evidence in support of these ideas comes from studies evaluating differences in trust levels across individuals as well as changes across time. A number of studies have developed these ideas through investigations of trust in local government as well (e.g. Litt 1963, Baldassare 1985, Beck et al 1990, Bobo & Gilliam 1990).

Nearly all of this research, whatever its specific conclusions, agrees on one point. Whether citizens express trust or distrust is primarily a reflection of their political lives, not their personalities nor even their social characteristics. Stokes (1962:65) observed that "one of the most arresting features of our empirical results is the similarity of these evaluations across a very wide range of social groupings in the United States," a point many recent authors have echoed (e.g. Craig 1996, Citrin & Muste 1999). Although blacks, for example, have at times been less trusting of government than have whites, the size and even the direction of the gap have varied with the federal government's efforts to ensure racial equality (Abramson 1983). Although citizens do not all agree about the trustworthiness of politicians and government, their disagreements reflect their varying political perceptions and values and the influence of their local social and political contexts.

Research Comparing Countries and Governments

Researchers have attempted to capture cross-national variations in citizens' trust in their governments and in citizens' perceptions of government trustworthiness. There seems to be a general belief that levels of political trust are declining across Europe. However, as Newton notes (1999), the sources for data are largely single-country surveys, which are not always or fully comparable. The World Values surveys included questions about trust of government or politicians only in 1990 and only for 12 countries; the Eurobarometer surveys have not included such questions. Authors who have attempted to make comparisons across countries using other survey data have not found support for the "across-the-board-decline" thesis. In his contrast of survey evidence from Norway, Denmark,

Sweden, the Netherlands, Germany, and Britain with evidence from the United States, Newton (1999) finds that not all countries have experienced a decline in political trust. Among those that have (e.g. Britain and Sweden), the timing and degree of decline are distinct from those in the United States (see also Listhaug 1995, Holmberg 1998, Miller & Listhaug 1999).

The World Values surveys do include questions concerning citizen confidence in certain public authorities and institutions, such as the police, the armed forces, and the Parliament. There is considerable variation both across institutions and across the 20 countries surveyed, although there is only one case (Korea in 1981 in regard to the armed forces) in which 50% or more of the respondents express a great deal of confidence. In most of these countries, confidence in political institutions declined between 1981 and 1990, the two years when opinions were asked (Listhaug & Wiberg 1995, Inglehart 1999:225–27). There is considerably more information about confidence in authorities generally, which seems to be declining, and about political participation, which seems to be increasing for activities other than the vote.[2]

Researchers are also beginning to explore what may account for variations in trust or "confidence" levels across countries, asking, for example, whether these differences can be accounted for by differences in the performance of governments or are due to characteristics of party systems and political institutions (e.g. Miller & Listhaug 1990, Mishler & Rose 1997, Norris 1999b). In an early comparative study, Hart (1978) used culture, or more precisely political consciousness, to account for variations in political trust. She attempted to link attitude surveys with historical evidence of popular political thought and behavior to account for variations in distrust of government by the British and Americans both over time and between the two countries. She concluded that distrust of politicians is intermittent in Britain but is the historical norm in the United States (also see Barber 1983), in sharp contrast to the claim of many contemporary analysts that distrust is the aberration.

Nor is the US citizenry unique in its relatively constant distrust of government. Pharr's (1997) analysis of Japanese data concludes that distrust of government and politics in Japan has been endemic since World War II. However, she finds the disaffection greater at the national level than the local level and more likely to focus on politicians than bureaucrats. Similarly, Jennings' (1998) analysis of American surveys finds variation in political trust across levels of government in the United States. Like Pharr, he finds greater confidence in government at the local level than at the national level—at least in recent years. He suggests that part of the reason is that the tasks of local governments are easier to perform and to evaluate, and that citizens find local government more responsive to their

---

[2]Inglehart (1997, 1999) attributes these apparent changes and variations to a shift from materialist to postmaterialist values. However, in the absence of data on the same questions over a long period of time, the World Values surveys cannot be said to document the trends Inglehart attempts to explain. Recognizing this problem, he uses other kinds of data to support his argument.

concerns (see also Craig 1993). Such an interpretation fits with Mansbridge's observations (1997) that increased public distrust of government has much to do with its declining performance due to burgeoning demands, rising expectations, and reduced resources.

Concluding Comments   The survey tradition in the United States became focused on (*a*) explaining variation across individuals and across time in the NES trust-in-government responses and on (*b*) tracing the behavioral consequences of trust so measured (to be described below). Although one important focus of this work concerned issues of measurement, almost none of that measurement work addressed the question of how political trust or trustworthiness should be measured. Researchers did not, for example, evaluate alternative survey indicators of political trust or introduce indicators representing different notions of political trust. This work did, however, emphasize the importance of distinguishing among various objects of trust or support.

In one sense, then, we have yet to question whether all of this research is really about trust or trustworthiness at all, as defined at the outset of this chapter. For now, we assume that this work is about political trust and that the NES questions capture trust judgments. Toward the chapter's end, however, we return to the issue of conceptualization and measurement, revisit the question of what the NES items are measuring, and urge survey researchers to ground their measures in a clearly articulated concept of political trust.

Still, we do know a lot. We know that there is a very strong individual-level connection between how citizens evaluate "government" or judge "politicians" and how they evaluate the performance of Congress, a finding that is demonstrated in comparable ways in research on other countries. We also know that there is a strong over-time correlation between political distrust and the perception that social problems are worsening or remaining unresolved and that politicians are unresponsive to citizens. These and other findings suggest that variations in political trust reflect more than incumbent-specific satisfactions or dissatisfactions. They mean that the behavioral and system-level consequences of distrust must be explored.

Finally, despite all the verbiage decrying the decline in trust, there is little actual evidence of a long-term secular decline, either in the United States or in Western Europe across the board. If it is true that political distrust is the norm for Americans, then surveys that date only since World War II may not be of sufficient duration to sustain the claim of a major and unusual decline. And even then, the time-series evidence available (Figure 1) suggests that trust levels have been moving both up and down since the mid 1970s. The evidence in other countries is generally of even shorter duration and depends on less comparable questions.

Overview of Historical and Comparative Case Study Research

Work in historical and comparative case study tradition primarily explores the attributes that render a government trustworthy and the extent to which trustworthy government causes or is caused by important economic, social, and political phenomena. This literature implicitly treats trust as a multilevel concept when it attempts to link institutions and behavior, especially when the behavior has micro foundations in individual perceptions, judgments, or dispositions.

Beginning with Gambetta's edited volume in 1988, there has been an industry of research on trust among comparative political scientists, political sociologists, and economic historians. There are essays on normative questions related to democratic governance; efforts by formal theorists, game theorists, and experimentalists to model relationships under conditions of trust and distrust; and empirical studies linking the levels of trust among citizens or political elites to how political institutions function. In addition, economists have continued to consider the ways in which trust facilitates economic exchange,[3] and sociologists have persisted in researching how trust facilitates social exchange.[4] These issues, though important, are not the focus of this chapter. What interests us here is comparative and historical research that links macro-level outcomes such as efficient government, political legitimacy, and democratization with the micro-level focus on individual choices and behavior.

If the essential tasks of government are to protect citizens from each other by providing justice and property rights and to protect citizens from external threats by providing national security, then the question immediately arises of how to prevent government from abusing the extraordinary power it possesses to carry out these tasks. In liberal political theory, or at least its Lockean variant, trustworthy government officials are a significant part of the answer (Silver 1985, Dunn 1988). From this perspective, government officials hold power and authority in trust to the people. Governors have both a legal and a moral obligation to those they serve, and it is expected that office holders will uphold their responsibilities— that is, prove their trustworthiness—or be removed. At the same time, in a tradition passed from Locke through Madison to many contemporary social scientists, the democratic project is one of "institutionalizing distrust" (Braithwaite 1998). As Barber (1983:166) argues, "a certain amount of rational distrust is necessary for political accountability in a participatory democracy" (also see Warren 1999b, Levi 2000, Tarrow 2000).

One of the most important concerns of the historical and comparative literature on trust is what makes for trustworthy political officials and, more generally, trustworthy government. The crucial attributes that scholars have identified are the capacities to make credible commitments, to design and implement policies nonarbitrarily, and to demonstrate competence. The morality of office holders

---

[3] Arrow (1974:23) characterizes trust as "an important lubricant of a social system" because it can enhance efficiency. Similarly, North (1981, 1990) considers trust a means for lowering transaction costs, as does Fukuyama (1995). Dasgupta (1988) picks up Hirschman's (1984) argument about trust as a resource and builds a model of trust as a commodity. Williamson (1993) is more skeptical of the role of trust.

[4] Luhmann's (1979) and Coleman's (1990) work is seminal, but there are also contributions by Giddens (1990), Eisenstadt (1995), Seligman (1997), and Misztal (1998).

can be an important source of political trustworthiness (Hardin 1996, Brennan 1998). A cumulative and positive research program has demonstrated that institutional arrangements play a significant role in making the commitments of public officials credible in the ways North & Weingast (1989), Root (1989), and Daunton (1998) stipulate. However, trustworthy government institutions must also be fair, transparent in their policy making, and open to competing views—propositions for which Tyler (1990), Levi (1997), and Daunton (1998) provide evidence in the domains of legal authorities, military service policy, and taxation.

Hardin (1998) argues that although governments may achieve the attributes of trustworthiness, it does not necessarily follow that citizens will possess sufficient knowledge to believe that any particular government actor will act in their interests. Hardin distinguishes between the basis for reliability or confidence, which is grounded in past experience, reputational factors, and regularity, and the basis for trust, which is grounded in a cognitive assessment of encapsulated interest. Other authors (Levi 1998, Whiting 1998) posit a somewhat broader definition in which the truster's knowledge of the institutions and reputation of the trusted may provide sufficient information for the truster to make a judgment about the trustworthiness of the trusted.

One of the biggest puzzles for students of politics is the appropriate basis for citizens' beliefs about when politicians are being trustworthy and acting in their interests or, at least, the public interest. Stokes' fieldwork on post-election policy switches by the leaders of several Latin American leads her to an ambivalent conclusion (Stokes 1999). Policy switches may be indicators of representative trustworthiness and accountability; the change may be intended to promote policies that better serve the citizenry. Alternatively, leaders' actions may reflect a lack of trustworthiness if during elections they provided erroneous information about the effects of policies in order to garner votes. Bianco's (1994, 1998) research on American congressional representatives combines a game theoretic model of trust (or, more accurately, the conditions under which citizens give their representatives leeway) with interviews and fieldwork. He argues that when constituents are uncertain about either policy outcomes or the motives of their representatives, when legislators are believed to possess private information, and when voters base their judgments on retrospective evaluations, legislators attempt to demonstrate their commitments to the common interest and thus to convince constituents of their trustworthiness. The problem, as in Latin American democracies, is normative as well as empirical. Electoral incentives may induce candidates and officials to misinform the public. Accurate assessment of trustworthiness is thus made difficult for the social scientific observer as well as for the voter, and representation may not always meet normative democratic standards.

The comparative and historical literature reveals key attributes of government trustworthiness and suggests reasons for variation in citizen trust of government across countries and over time. It also offers a normative argument for the importance of trustworthy government. But is there empirical evidence that it matters whether citizens trust government or whether government is trustworthy?

WHY DO TRUST, DISTRUST, AND TRUSTWORTHINESS MATTER?

Political Trust and Participation

The literature contains two different, and incompatible, claims about how trust influences political participation. One claim is that the trusting should be expected to participate to a greater extent than the distrusting, at least in conventional activities such as voting and campaign involvement. The idea that distrust might discourage political engagement was inspired by early theorizing about disaffection and alienation (Stokes 1962, Almond & Verba 1963, Finifter 1970) and by the fact that the over-time decline in US voting turnout coincided with the over-time decline in trust in government. This conjecture stimulated numerous studies and some very vehement statements of disconfirmation.[5]

> [T]he decline in turnout has not taken place as a consequence of declining trust or increased alienation; there is simply no direct causal link between the attitudes of trust in government and the decision to vote. (Miller 1980:24)

> [T]rusting citizens are *not* more likely to vote, *not* more likely to engage in campaign activities, and *not* more likely to be interested in political campaigns or governmental affairs. (Rosenstone & Hansen 1993:150, emphasis in original)

The second claim regarding trust and participation is that distrust, not trust, should stimulate political involvement—or, at least, distrust should stimulate political involvement among those who feel politically efficacious. This claim was articulated first by Gamson (1968, 1975), a political sociologist, and in a complementary way by Bandura (1982), a psychologist. In an often-cited passage, Gamson (1968:48) stated that "a combination of high political efficacy and low political trust is the optimum combination for mobilization—a belief that influence is both possible and necessary."

Over the years, this general claim has been tested, refined, and tested again. Early work looked at the effects of the conjunction of efficacy and distrust on conventional modes of participation, often coming away disappointed (e.g. Fraser 1970, Hawkins et al 1971). These early inquiries tended to examine participation

---

[5]The typical null finding concerns how the NES trust measure relates to vote turnout. Using survey data gathered in Mexico that carried both the NES questions and the questions comprising Muller's (1977) "Political Alienation-Support" (PAS) index, Seligson (1983) found the standard lack of a relationship between trust and vote turnout when using NES questions but a strong relationship when using PAS questions, where the more "supportive" citizens were more likely to vote. This, argues Seligson (1983), is strong evidence against the validity of the NES trust index as an indicator of diffuse support.

levels of people falling into different trust/efficacy categories without applying controls for other determinants of participation.

Drawing on Gamson's (1968) and Easton's (1965) ideas about the link between discontent and elite- or system-challenging behavior, scholars turned to the possibility that distrust spurred only unconventional participation. Survey research on non-US populations found mixed evidence for the hypothesis that distrust/alienation spurs protest activity (Muller 1977, Muller et al 1982, Pierce & Converse 1989). Authors trying to make sense of the turmoil of the 1960s and 1970s in the United States frequently discovered a link between distrust/alienation and either protest participation or approval of protest behavior (e.g. Jackson 1973, Sears & McConahay 1973, Abravanel & Busch 1975, Citrin 1977), although the relationships were sometimes weak or disappeared after the application of controls. Measurement questions were raised as well; some authors argued that only regime-oriented measures of alienation, and not incumbent-oriented measures of distrust, were strongly related to protest behavior or approval (e.g. Citrin 1974, 1977; Muller et al 1982).

Since many acts considered unconventional three decades ago have now entered conventional repertoires (Kaase & Newton 1995), arguments about the mobilization of discontent have come to rely less on this distinction. Shingles (1981), for example, has argued that the combination of efficacy and distrust should (and does) spur many different forms of participation as long as they are aimed at influencing the policy process. These participatory acts are often "conventional" but typically also require high initiative. Similarly, Inglehart (1997) has emphasized the importance of distinguishing participatory acts that are elite-directed and serve expressive functions (such as voting) from those that are citizen-directed and instrumental.

At the same time, new research has suggested that distrust may have come to inspire campaign-related participation in the United States in recent years. Analyzing NES data over time, Luks (1998) finds that in no election were the distrusting more likely than the trusting to vote, but they were more likely to engage in other forms of electoral participation in the late 1980s and 1990s. Atkeson et al (1996) suggest that the citizens who became involved in Perot's 1992 presidential campaign were much more distrusting than the national norm. Recent research in the "contentious politics" tradition also finds a link between activism and distrust of government. Tarrow (2000), for example, finds that activism is often a response to loss of confidence in government due to a protracted provision of misinformation; the British government's handling of the "mad cow disease" issue is a case in point. Even so, Tarrow suggests that those engaged in contentious politics may actually be building an antagonistic but "working trust" with government officials.

One theme that pervades this entire literature on distrust and political engagement is that the proper model linking the two is likely to involve complex interactions and contingencies. Distrust may, indeed, generate higher levels of participation but only under some circumstances, for some kinds of people, and with respect to some kinds of political activities. Gamson (1968) hypothesized that the kinds of activities people would engage in would vary depending on whether they were trusting, distrusting, or somewhere in the middle, a hypothesis later evaluated by Paige (1971). Finifter (1970), Schwartz (1973), Muller (1977), and Guterbock & London (1983), among others, developed typologies of political action types based on the combination of individual attributes. For example, Finifter (1970) considered the various high/low combinations of "normlessness" and "powerlessness," two "dimensions of alienation" that later came to be identified with political trust and political efficacy. Muller (1977) distinguished five types based on individuals' (*a*) level of diffuse support for the regime, (*b*) beliefs about the efficacy of past political aggression, and (*c*) beliefs about their own ability to be politically influential. Others have suggested that distrust encourages participation only or especially among those who are politically interested (Luks 1998), among those who lack other motivations to participate (Shingles 1981), among those who are both politically efficacious and dissatisfied with the policies of the current administration (Miller 1974b, Craig & Maggiotto 1981), among those who are highly educated (Citrin 1977, Chan 1997), among those who trust the opposition leaders (Nilson & Nilson 1980), and among those experiencing adverse personal circumstances (Aberbach & Walker 1970).

In short, scholars inspired to consider the consequences of trust/distrust (or alienation/allegiance or level of diffuse support) for political participation have generated a profusion of complex hypotheses. Perhaps because of this bewildering array, trust has not figured prominently in work that focuses directly on explaining participation (e.g. Rosenstone & Hansen 1993, Verba et al 1995).

Political Trust, Public Opinion, and the Vote

One idea found in the debates over the NES trust-in-government index is that distrust is not consequential if it simply reflects dissatisfaction with current incumbents or their administrations, whether that dissatisfaction concerns the personal characteristics of the leaders, the performance of the government in managing economic affairs or other matters, or the particular policies that the administration is supporting or implementing. Even if trust judgments are correlated with, say, the vote, this correlation would be a spurious reflection of the sentiments on which both trust judgments and vote choices are based.

Although there is strong evidence that people respond to the NES trust items with these kinds of administration-specific considerations in mind (Citrin 1974; Abramson & Finifter 1981; Citrin & Green 1986; Weatherford 1987; Craig 1993; Hetherington 1998, 1999), this cannot explain the long-term trends that are observed for the measure. Trust continued to decline throughout the 1960s and 1970s and, despite short periods of reversal (Citrin & Green 1986, Lipset & Schneider 1987, Miller & Borrelli 1991), into the 1990s. Reflecting on this fact, Miller

(1984:840) argues that the decline in trust reflects the accumulation of grievances across administrations. "People ... lost confidence because time after time political authorities, Democrats and Republicans alike, demonstrated through their decisions and actions that they were not competent, not efficient, not honest, not fair, and certainly not to be trusted to make the right policy decisions."

This thesis raises the possibility that the strong association between trust and evaluations of incumbent administrations, their performance, and their policies arises at least in part because distrust itself—now long-held, generalized, and based on the accumulation of grievances—shapes assessments of each administration.

One way to read this hypothesis focuses on the durability of distrust at the individual level. Only if a given individual has come to distrust many succeeding administrations, or has reached a generalized distrust of government through the accumulation of grievances over a long period of time, will distrust become an important, independent determinant of attitudes toward political candidates or public policies. This reading of the hypothesis has not been evaluated by survey researchers (since it requires long-term panel data), but it is an argument that Craig (1993) advances based on his analysis of in-depth interviews and focus groups.

Several other studies bear directly on this hypothesis. Hetherington (1998) estimated the reciprocal effects of distrust and evaluations of the incumbent president, finding that distrust was more important as a source of negative sentiment about the president than vice versa. He also modeled the relationship between trust judgments and evaluations of Congress as reciprocal, finding that although mutual influence was present, distrust was more a consequence than a cause in that case.

The experimental study of Sigelman et al (1992) also provides evidence that distrust stimulates negative assessments of political candidates or leaders. Their study was directed toward understanding how citizens react to representatives who vote (*a*) in accordance or in opposition to their constituents, (*b*) on the basis of principle or for reasons of expediency. The distrusting evaluated the politicians much more negatively than the trusting in all of the experimental conditions. The work of Sigelman et al supports Easton's (1975:447) contention that distrust of specific authorities can become generalized. "In time, disaffection may occur not because of what each succeeding set of authorities is perceived to have done but simply because they are perceived to be authorities—and authorities are no longer thought worthy of trust."

The arguments and findings reviewed thus far provide two different reasons for expecting trust judgments to be irrelevant to explaining citizens' vote choices. First, if trust judgments are simply a summary of citizens' assessments of current administrations (including their assessments of leadership qualities, performance, and policy directions) or the policy alternatives the parties present to them, then they should contribute nothing to an explanation of the vote once these other assessments are taken into account. Second, even if citizens' trust judgments independently affect their evaluations of politicians, this effect could leave a voter's relative evaluations of candidates intact, and, hence, render trust irrelevant to the vote. Even if voters who distrust politicians feel that they are choosing between two evils, what influences their vote choice is which of the two is judged to be worse.

Instead, however, the available evidence suggests that trust judgments do independently influence voters' choices. Studies have demonstrated that the distrusting are more likely than the trusting to vote in an anti-incumbent fashion in two-party presidential races and to support third-party or Independent candidates when they emerge as serious contenders, as did Wallace in 1968, Anderson in 1980, and Perot in 1992 and 1996 (Aberbach 1969, Rosenstone et al 1984, Hetherington 1999, Luks & Citrin 1997, Luks 1999). These effects have been observed in analyses that control for other plausible determinants of the vote.

According to Luks & Citrin (1997), whether distrust becomes consequential to the vote depends on whether one of the candidates emphasizes antigovernment themes. In other words, citizens' judgments concerning the trustworthiness of politicians and government are not always relevant to the choices they face. Only in some circumstances do those who judge the government untrustworthy have, or perceive, the option of supporting an "outsider" candidate. When such a choice is available, however, the behavioral consequences of distrust are revealed. This general idea also finds support in research evaluating how distrust shapes opinions on public policy and institutional reforms.

One set of studies focused on the Proposition 13 "tax revolt" in California in the 1970s. Both Sears & Citrin (1985) and Lowery & Sigelman (1981) emphasize the importance of distrust or disaffection as determinants of voter support for the property tax rollback (see also Beck et al 1990). As Lowery & Sigelman put it, "pro-tax limitation sentiments reflect a deeper disillusionment which is directed against government institutions and authorities" (1981:969). More recent work has focused on trust as a determinant of support for legislative term limits, another policy initiative associated with antigovernmental themes. Analyzing NES data and additional surveys carried out in Florida and Wyoming, Karp (1995) found that distrust was by far the most influential predictor of support for term limits, even in models that included evaluations of Congress or of the state legislatures, the very institutions where term limits were being implemented.

Much of the work on trust and public opinion or the vote has focused on citizens' judgments about the trustworthiness of "government" in general or of "most politicians," using the NES index or comparable measures. Yet some research is beginning to focus on the consequences of judgments about the trustworthiness of specific actors and institutions.

One line of work concerns judgments about the trustworthiness of one's own member of Congress, stimulated by Fenno's (1978) arguments about the efforts members of Congress undertake to ensure that they are judged trustworthy by their constituents. Parker's (1989) analysis used open-ended questions tapping what survey respondents like or dislike about their representative to form an index of how much they trust their representatives.[6] Parker found that this trust variable was a strong predictor of incumbent evaluation and vote choice, even stronger than party identification.

A second line of work focuses on citizens' assessments of environmental hazards and the siting of hazardous waste facilities. Several studies have identified trust as a crucial determinant of citizens' perceptions of risk or hazard, the degree of fear or distress they feel if living in proximity to a potential hazard, and their support or opposition to the siting of a hazardous waste facility in the area where they live (Flynn et al 1992, Goldsteen et al 1992, Flynn & Slovic 1993, Hunter & Leydon 1995; for a general review, see Citrin 1991). In these studies, researchers have focused on whether citizens trust the specific administrative agencies responsible for regulating or administering the hazardous waste facility. Even further, the questions gauging trust usually stipulate the domain of trust, asking respondents if they trust, say, the Department of Energy on the question of hazardous wastes—whether, for example, they will be told the truth, whether potential problems will be closely monitored, and whether public safety will be a priority.

Taken as a whole, research on trust and its relation to public opinion and voting suggests two major conclusions. First, judgments about the trustworthiness of government or of politicians are more than ideological or partisan reactions to specific incumbent administrations. They are generalized judgments that influence whether citizens endorse or reject existing authorities and public policy or institutional reforms. Second, general trust judgments about government or politicians are not the only trust judgments worthy of political study. Indeed, as we suggest toward the end of this essay, judgments about the trustworthiness of particular actors (in particular domains) may be of far greater consequence than the limited research to date would suggest.

Political Trust, Trustworthiness, and Compliance

One of the findings of the literature on government regulation is that the more trustworthy citizens perceive government to be, the more likely they are to comply with or even consent to its demands and regulations. This is one of the most important findings in Tyler's (1990, 1998) survey- and observation-based research

---

[6]Parker's categories were based on the content of the closed-ended NES trust-in-government questions. They referred to the following characteristics, among others: dependable, trustworthy, reliable, no one runs him, honest, sincere, keeps promises, man of integrity, man of high ideals, not just out for self. Roughly 20% of the respondents made at least one like/dislike response falling into these categories (Parker 1989:195). In another study, Parker & Parker (1993) analyzed the determinants of an index of trust in one's member of Congress formed from closed-ended questions that were developed after careful consideration of the concept of trust (a rarity in the literature). Both generalized trust in government and personal contact with the representative emerged as important predictors.

on citizen voluntary acceptance of court and other governmental authorities and of Levi's historical and political economy work on taxation (1988) and on military service (1997). Tyler focuses on the attribution motivations of the citizen and Levi on the actual attributes of government, but both attempt to show a link between the attitudes and decision making of the citizen being asked to comply and her perceptions of the trustworthiness of government. The difference between Tyler and Levi reflects the ongoing debate (see Brathwaite & Levi 1998) between authors who emphasize the social bonds or group identification between the truster and the trusted and those with a more interest-based account.

Although there is strong evidence for a link between perceptions of trustworthy government and citizen compliance, the interpretations of this evidence vary. Some accounts are explicitly based on institutional arrangements that ensure government actors are adequately constrained—that, as Daunton (1998:130) puts it, "Leviathan [is] chained." Majone (1997), for example, emphasizes the role of credible commitments in ensuring that the member states of the European Union comply with its rules.

Other accounts emphasize the psychological interactions between the governed and their governors. In a series of papers drawing on telephone surveys and a random sample of tax returns provided by the Internal Revenue Service, Scholz and his collaborators (Pinney & Scholz 1995, Scholz 1998, Scholz & Lubell 1998a,b) have investigated trust heuristics as cognitive shortcuts that affect tax compliance. Scholz argues (1998:157):

> In everyday situations, a number of attitudes toward potential "trustees" act as on-line processors that produce moving average measures of relevant information.... If the moving average works accurately, individuals learn to trust more trustworthy individuals. Trust then becomes a reliable guide to behavior in trusting situations.

When government is perceived as trustworthy, citizens are more likely to comply with its demands.

Ayres & Braithwaite (1992) also find that trustworthy government increases compliance, but they stress the importance of trust by regulators as a means of evoking compliance from the regulated. If regulators trust the regulated, "trust-responsiveness" (Pettit 1995), in the form of compliance, appears to result. This account of trust views the citizen as someone "who respects norms of trust as an obligation of citizenship in circumstances where it may or may not be rationally self-interested to do so" (Braithwaite & Makkai 1994) and implies that regulation will be most effective if it keeps punishment in the background and uses persuasion and trust to induce compliance (Ayres & Braithwaite 1992). Peel (1995) offers a fine and nuanced case study of the negative effects of government actors withholding trust or actively distrusting citizens in a working-class suburb in Australia, with the result that the citizens distrust government in return and are less likely to consent willingly to its bureaucratic requirements.

Those who study the relationship between trustworthy government and citizen compliance differ as to whether the source of trust is a social bond or some form of encapsulated interest. However, all agree that government officials who act in a trustworthy manner are more likely to elicit compliance, and virtually all agree that government regulators who trust the people they are regulating are more likely to evoke trustworthy behavior and compliance.

Government Trustworthiness, Social Trust, and Cooperation

What is the relationship between a trustworthy government and the interpersonal (or social) trust among strangers that is the focus of the social capital literature? It is conceivable that social trust and political trust are unrelated to each other, or related only spuriously. For Gellner (1988), following Ibn Khaldun, trust as social cohesion is possible only within a civil society where there are thick, embedded relationships. He questions the possibility of maintaining trust in a complex and anonymous society (also see Silver 1985, Williams 1988, Seligman 1997). We argue that there is indeed a relationship, as de Tocqueville (1990 [1840]) claimed in the nineteenth century and as Putnam (1993, 1995) claims today. But it is an empirical question whether a trustworthy government helps promote social trust and the cooperative behaviors that support democracy, or whether social trust is a necessary condition for democracy.

A close rereading of de Tocqueville reveals that he believed participation in political associations increases the probability of participation in civic associations and corporations. The reason has to do with the development of the capacity to trust, although he does not label it that way. He argues that individuals will risk joining a political association because they have little to lose from their participation; their money is not at risk. In doing so, however, they learn the advantages of combination. This makes them more willing to risk their possessions by engaging in what de Tocqueville terms civil partnerships, major examples being manufacturing and trading companies. Indeed, he hypothesizes that the existence of a democratic right of association accounts for variation in civil association. "I do not say that there can be no civil association in a country where political association is prohibited, for men can never live in a society without embarking in some common undertakings; but I maintain that in such a country civil associations will always be few in number, feebly planned, unskillfully managed, that they will never form any vast designs, or that they will fail in their execution of them" (de Tocqueville 1990[1840]:118).

A trustworthy government may actually generate the interpersonal trust that promotes a productive economy, a more peaceful and cooperative society, and a democratic government (Fukuyama 1995; Levi 1997, 1998), the reverse of the causal ordering suggested by Putnam (1993, 1996). Indeed, some scholars argue that the major source of social trust is government's credible commitment to uphold property rights and to protect constituents from each other. Weingast (1998:165) summarizes this position prefatory to his formal modeling of ethnic conflict, "Trust results when institutions make it far less likely that one group will be able to capture the state and take advantage of the other. Trust can therefore be constructed and institutionalized."

Others have reached similar conclusions. Without stable institutional arrangements for impartial regulation of the conflict among factions, medieval Genoa could not flourish (Greif 1994, 1999). Among contemporary Chinese townships (Whiting 1998) and among the developing countries more generally (Fukuyama 1995), variation in government capacity to uphold property rights and make fiscal commitments appears to be a major factor in explaining variation in economic development. What distinguishes all these arrangements is that they enable political actors to make credible commitments. Elster (1989:274–75) goes so far as to claim that credibility "captures most arguments about the causes and consequences of trust."

Other comparative and historical work suggests, however, that more than credibility of commitments is required in a state that engenders societal trust. Pagden (1988) argues that the Spanish rulers of eighteenth-century Naples demolished societal trust by controlling, destroying, and mystifying the information that individuals need if they are to trust each other and by changing customs, e.g. transforming the easy relations between sexes and among the various orders. "The degeneration of the necessary guarantors of the well-ordered community led inevitably to the collapse of the economy" (Pagden 1988:137). The Spanish created an aristocracy that replaced trust with honor, precisely the kind of government that Hawthorn (1988) claims is most likely to generate societal trust by producing a code by which individuals must live. He provides examples from the army and political parties in India and Korea, which also confirm his skepticism about the extent to which the aristocrats themselves can be trusted by those they govern. The disagreement between Pagden and Hawthorn over the role of honor largely reflects a difference in terms. More important is their consensus that the state plays a key role in creating values, which in turn generate and sustain social trust.

Scholars concerned with the growth of democracy as well as the economy in the post-Soviet countries also emphasize the importance of trustworthy government institutions for the development and maintenance of social trust (Rose 1994; Sztompka 1996, 1999; Offe 1999). All emphasize credible commitments, but Sztompka (1998) also emphasizes the creation of a "culture of trust" and Offe (1999) the importance of the values incorporated in the institutions of government.

Findings from survey research also address this question. Although researchers have long noted that survey measures of political and social trust are correlated, only recently have they tried to evaluate alternative explanations of how this connection might arise. Brehm & Rahn (1997) do so by estimating the causal interdependencies among social trust, confidence in government, and civic engagement. They find that the observed association between citizens' confidence in government and trust in their fellow citizens is largely a product of the influence of the former on the latter. In other words, whether citizens trust each other is strongly influenced by whether they have confidence in the government that they share. Yamagishi & Yamagishi (1994), also relying on survey data, find striking differences between social trust in the United States and Japan. They claim that the difference is at least partly caused by the greater distrust of government among the Japanese, which makes them less confident that the government will provide the institutional protections that facilitate generalized social trust.

All of this is not to deny that social trust may affect participation in and attitudes toward government. A huge literature, recently reviewed by Jackman & Miller (1998), makes precisely this claim. The literature discussed here reveals an important causal link in the other direction: A trustworthy government may facilitate the development of social trust and cooperation.

FUTURE DIRECTIONS

Political Trust: It Is Not Just About "Government"

At the outset of this chapter, we described the question of trust as arising when an individual finds herself in a relationship entailing the possibility of risk or vulnerability. If trusting, an individual is freed from worry and from the need to monitor the other's behavior or to extricate herself from the relationship. With that in mind, one way to think about where trust judgments will be most meaningful and influential is to ask such questions as: What relationships do citizens form with political authorities and political elites with each other? In what situations are citizens or elites potentially vulnerable to the actions of political authorities or institutions, so that they must confront the question of trust?

All citizens enter into a relationship with their national government in that they are bound by its laws. Still, the ordinary relationships that citizens have with political authorities are most likely to be local in focus. They involve local problems, if not local authorities, though perhaps usually both. As psychologists have emphasized, proximate judgments direct people's behavior (e.g. Fishbein & Ajzen 1974). Thus, for example, what should matter to whether people attend a local school board meeting is the extent to which they trust the school board with the education or even the safety of their children. What should matter to whether they join a local police watchdog organization is the extent to which they trust the local police to act competently, fairly, and honestly. What did matter to the distress felt by the residents living near Three Mile Island was whether or not they felt they could trust the Three Mile Island authorities (Goldsteen et al 1992), not "the government" or "political officials" in some more general sense. What mattered to the working-class residents in South Australia was whether particular bureaucrats were trustworthy and trusted them (Peel 1995). And what mattered to the meat eaters of Britain were very specific regulatory agencies (Tarrow 2000).

In cases like this, even if what people think about particular authorities is influenced by their perceptions of the trustworthiness of politicians in general, what presumably drives their behavior are their judgments concerning the particular authorities. If this is so, then trust of one's government or its institutions may be the most consequential judgment of trust, in the sense that if it is undermined then more cataclysmic or large-scale changes in a society or polity are possible. But in explaining everyday political behavior, distrust of government may not be as important as distrust of particular authorities. We urge scholars to expand their inquiries beyond the traditional focus on citizens' trust in "government" in general, by studying the causes and consequences of citizens' trust in specific political actors, organizations, or institutions.

There is the further question of trust among political elites. Larson (1997), for example, uses a psychological approach to trust to investigate the missed opportunities for international security agreements among heads of state. The literature on credible commitments, particularly if attuned to principal-agent problems, is especially sensitive to how political elites—governmental, bureaucratic, and societal—attempt to insulate themselves from harm that other elites may cause them. Distrust, usually mutual, generates the development of institutional arrangements that permit dominant factions to protect themselves from each other and from the state (e.g. Weingast 1998, Greif 1998) and that permit policy makers in democracies to protect programs from changes in government and from bureaucratic manipulation (e.g. Moe 1990). Work is yet to be done that adequately pulls together an emphasis on the qualities of particular actors and the institutional features of government that ensure trustworthiness. Such a research program might provide even greater understanding of when key political actors are likely to trust each other and with what political consequences.

Concepts and Measurement

In *The Malevolent Leaders: Popular Discontent in America*, Craig wrote:

> The subject of this book is political discontent. I want to be very careful with my terminology here so as to avoid getting bogged down in an endless review of the different concepts and measures that have been used to describe citizen attitudes toward politics and government (alienation, estrangement, disaffection, illegitimacy, etc.). Even where the same construct (e.g., alienation, or Easton's diffuse/specific support) is employed, its meaning and operationalization often vary so much from one study to the next that any possible common frame is lost. (Craig 1993:17)

Most researchers who have tried to grapple with the literature on alienation or distrust or discontent, including us, have also struggled with this profusion of concepts and of indicators. A recent volume reviewing survey indicators (Robinson et al 1999) includes separate chapters entitled "Political Alienation and Efficacy" and "Trust in Government," even though there is substantial overlap in the various scales that one encounters in each (as Citrin & Muste, authors of the "Trust in Government" chapter, wryly note).

Scholars have adopted a variety of strategies to cope with this problem. Craig's solution is to concentrate on variation in the objects of political support, "with support defined simply 'as an affective orientation to political objects ... and processes...', which can be positive, neutral, or negative'" (Craig 1993:17, citing Kornberg 1990:710). Citrin & Muste (1999) encourage researchers to distinguish both among the different objects of trust (e.g. particular institutions, politicians in general, the regime as a whole) and among different dimensions of appraisal. They emphasize the distinction between judgments of integrity and judgments of competence, although they also mention other dimensions, including fairness and responsiveness. When institutions are involved, they recommend distinguishing judgments about outcomes from judgments about processes. The authors contributing to *Critical Citizens* (Norris 1999) adopt a set of distinctions focused primarily on the object of support, distinguishing the political community, regime principles, regime performance, regime institutions, and political actors. The concept of trust is not central to this typology, although one of the authors (Dalton 1999) recommends a further distinction between "affective orientations" toward these objects and "instrumental evaluations" of these objects, and places trust judgments in the latter category.

This is not the place to interject our own recommended set of conceptual, and hence empirical, distinctions for understanding how citizens evaluate government. But we offer several comments on issues that particularly concern political trust. First, whatever differences remain, there is a consensus in the literature about the importance of distinguishing among the objects or targets of trust. This is eminently sensible and desirable. Second, it is clear that not every political object of assessment can be an object of trust. For example, one can have an attitude toward democratic principles, but one cannot be said to trust or distrust such principles. What is necessary for trust to be relevant to some political object is that the object be a political actor. Depending on one's conceptualization, this actor could be a person (e.g. one's Congressman), a group of individuals (e.g. the local school board or politicians in general), or even an institution (e.g. Congress or the Supreme Court). Finally, there is no agreement about the most fruitful way to distinguish among different dimensions of appraisal, although this is crucial to progress in thinking about the political consequences of trust.[7] Scholars need to develop a clear sense of how trust differs from other kinds of judgments about political actors or institutions. To accomplish this, they must first decide how to conceptualize and measure judgments of trust and trustworthiness.

This brings us back to definitions and to definitions of trustworthiness in particular. We see two possible approaches to defining trustworthiness, only one of which has been pursued in existing survey research. The first defines trustworthiness in terms of role responsibilities: those characteristics that are (ostensibly) morally entailed by the role that the political actor has assumed (Barber 1983). Miller &

---

[7]A review of existing literature suggests something approaching a consensus on what Citrin et al (1975) calls political alienation and what others (e.g. Norris 1999), following Easton (1975), describe as attachment to the political community. "[W]hat distinguishes the allegiance/alienation continuum from other attitudes toward the political system is the explicit reference to feelings of *closeness/distance, attachment/separation* or *identification/rejection*. To be politically alienated is to feel a relatively enduring sense of estrangement from existing political institutions, values and leaders" (Citrin et al 1975:3, emphasis in original; see also Sniderman 1981). If we recognize such distinctions, we may be able to make more sense of the perplexing features of the research literature on attitudes toward government that has developed over the past 30 years. Perhaps alienation, and not political distrust, discourages turnout; only the allegiant partake in the civic ritual of voting. And perhaps alienation, more than political distrust, is a consequence of social distrust.

Listhaug's (1990:358) definition of trust captures this notion well:

> Trust ... reflects evaluations of whether or not political authorities and institutions are performing in accordance with normative expectations held by the public. Citizen expectations of how government should operate include, among other criteria, that it be fair, equitable, honest, efficient, and responsive to society's needs. In brief, an expression of trust in government (or synonymously political confidence and support) is a summary judgment that the system is responsive and will do what is right even in the absence of constant scrutiny.

This is the conception of trustworthiness that underlies the NES trust-in-government questions, questions that ask whether respondents believe politicians are dishonest, do not know what they are doing, waste tax money, serve special interests and not the people, or try to do what is right. It is also the conception of government trustworthiness that underlies much of the work in the Lockean as well as current republican traditions of state theory (e.g. Braithwaite 1998).

The second approach would focus on whether the potential truster believes that the political actor or institution will act in his interests (or at least not against his interests). Although dominant in macro-level and elite-focused work on trust, this conception of trustworthiness has not figured into survey-based, micro-level work. To implement this approach in a survey project, one would first stipulate an objective account of interests, and then design survey questions that asked people whether they believed an actor was serving, or not obstructing, those interests. If, for example, one stipulated that people want (*a*) to be told the truth, (*b*) to be autonomous, (*c*) to be treated fairly, (*d*) to accumulate wealth, and (*e*) to live free from fear, then one would need to gauge whether a given political actor or institution was seen as protecting or harming those interests. Such questions would probe whether people felt the actor was working to protect/harm their own interests, not whether they thought the actor was working to protect/harm the interests of everyone.[8]

In contrast to both of these approaches, which begin with objective definitions of trustworthiness, is a third approach that leaves trustworthiness undefined, open to the interpretation of the potential truster. This is increasingly common in

---

[8] Several criteria would be common to the two approaches to trustworthiness. If, for example, political actors seek only to advance their own interests, this implies a disregard for the potential truster's interests and violates normative expectations. As well, both approaches are capable of representing the important distinction between process and outcomes, though in different ways. For example, whereas the role-responsibility approach would gauge perceptions concerning whether the political actor has generally treated people, in general, fairly, the interest-based account would focus on perceptions of whether the political actor has treated the truster fairly. Notice also that the interest-based judgments of trustworthiness will inevitably—and rightly—be colored by partisan and ideological sentiments as long as those partisan and ideological sentiments are themselves interest-based.

survey-based work on political trust. For example, in his survey of Russian citizens, Gibson (1999) measured political trust by asking, "What about the political leaders of Russia—can they be trusted, or do you have to be very careful when dealing with Russian political leaders?" In their study of trust in local government, Abney & Hutcheson (1981) asked: "How much of the time would you say you could trust city government?" And in their study of trust in former Communist countries, Mishler & Rose (1997) asked respondents to rate different political institutions on a scale that ranged from 1 = maximum distrust to 7 = maximum trust. In essence, all of these strategies involve asking respondents: "Do you, or how often do you, trust X?" This strategy builds in no assumptions about the kinds of considerations that may enter into judgments of trustworthiness, and hence, trust.

Quite apart from the issue of which conception of trustworthiness (if any) guides research on political trust is a second issue that concerns the domain specificity of trust and trustworthiness judgments. Most work in the survey tradition has gauged whether citizens trust political actors (or judge them trustworthy) in general, rather than whether citizens trust political actors with regard to particular domains or activities. Some exceptions, as we pointed out above, are found in studies of public opinion on the siting of hazardous waste facilities, where questions about trust in regulatory agencies are sometimes focused on particular policy arenas. Yet, as we noted at the outset of this essay, it is reasonable to think of political trust as domain-specific—one trusts a given political actor with respect to some problems, policies, or activities but not others. Thus, for example, one could trust the president on economic matters but not on matters concerning social policy, or one could trust the collective arms and agencies of government to provide an effective system of national defense but not to competently manage a health system.

Historical-comparative and other macro-level researchers have a somewhat different but related task than those doing micro-level work. Macro research requires, first, establishing the attributes of a trustworthy government and of political actors, but it also demands discernment of the domains in which citizens find that government and political actors meet these criteria and of the reasons why specific groups of citizens may vary in their perceptions. The extent to which governance accords to the rule of law and nondiscriminatory practices is a key attribute of trustworthiness, which macro-level researchers can use to evaluate government behavior and likely citizen responses in general and in specific domains. For example, even if an ethnic, religious, or linguistic minority group within the population believes government is generally trustworthy, it may find government lacks even-handedness and thus lacks trustworthiness in particular policy arenas, such as education or abortion. Thus, the group may not contemplate secession, but it will lobby and protest to achieve policy change.

Future work must grapple with these alternative approaches to conceptualizing political trust and trustworthiness, while being attuned to how trust judgments differ from other evaluations of political actors, organizations, and institutions— for example, judgments of "confidence" in institutions as gauged by the General Social Survey in the United States or by the World Values surveys, or feelings of "alienation." If researchers fail to do so, we will be left with the problem that has characterized previous research—that many different indicators, of potentially different concepts, have been employed by different researchers, making it difficult to draw conclusions across studies. This failure will also thwart the fruitful integration of micro-level and macro-level work, as we suggest below.

Micro-Macro Integration

Trust is what Weatherford (1992) calls a "multi-level concept." The trustworthiness of governments or other political actors can be important to researchers working with macro- and micro-level data and studying macro- and micro-level phenomena. Adopting Weatherford's argument, which he develops with respect to legitimacy, micro- and macro-level work on political trust can be integrated fruitfully only if scholars in both traditions share a common conceptual framework, in general, and a common conception of trustworthiness, in particular. Micro-level researchers would focus on citizen judgments about how well trustworthiness criteria are being met; macro-level researchers would seek data on governments and politicians gauging how well these criteria are being met. This means that micro-level researchers, rather than leaving open the question of what figures into trust judgments, must stipulate the attributes that, according to their definition, renders an actor trustworthy, and they must tap people's perceptions of these attributes. Similarly, macro-level researchers, including those doing historical and comparative research, must be clear about the attributes of trustworthy government and government officials but also must specify and measure expected outcomes in terms of both government policy and citizen behavior.

As we sketched out above, two different conceptions of trustworthiness have inhabited the research literature, one dominating the micro-level tradition (the role-responsibility conception), and one dominating the macro-level tradition (the interest-based conception). One consequence of this has been the development of micro- and macro-level literatures with few points of contact. Yet an integration of the two would be enormously helpful to understanding political trust at both levels. It would enable scholars to systematically address such questions as, "Do actual changes in government performance, and in institutional design, influence citizens' distrust in government? If citizens judge political actors trustworthy, does this affect how political institutions function or the policies that they produce?" To address such questions, scholars must bridge the micro-macro divide that currently characterizes research on political trust.

Gaining Leverage Through Experimental and Panel Analysis

As this review has described, many questions about the individual-level causes and consequences of political trust judgments, and about their over-time dynamics, still remain. The most persuasive and influential work in recent years has been notable in its attempts to model complex causal relationships. For example, Brehm & Rahn (1997) model the interdependencies between political trust and civic engagement, and Hetherington (1998) models the interdependencies between political trust and evaluations of the president. In these examples, the researchers gained leverage by working with large data sets and by estimating sophisticated statistical models. Although such studies represent an advance over those that build in dubious assumptions about one-way causality, they, like most of the micro-level research on political trust, are limited by the cross-sectional survey data analyzed.

To date, very few studies of political trust have employed experimental methods or the analysis of panel data, despite the power of such methods for studying questions concerning causal dynamics. One of the rare experimental studies (Sigelman et al 1992), as noted above, provides strong evidence that distrust of government, even if influenced by incumbent-specific evaluations, also encourages more negative evaluations of politicians. Innovative use of laboratory or survey-based experiments would certainly enhance our understanding of the causes and consequences of political trust. In addition, new light could be shed on unresolved issues about the over-time dynamics of political trust through analysis of the short-term 72-74-76 NES panel and the long-term panel found in the 1965–1982 Jennings/Niemi Study of Political Socialization (which includes measures of trust in government at each wave and for both Youth and Parent samples). Without stronger research designs, the indeterminacies left by past studies cannot be overcome.

CONCLUSION

Warren Miller was fond of describing trust in government as an independent variable in search of a dependent variable. One way to think about the consequences identified in this review is that the search has been successful. Whether citizens judge politicians or government trustworthy influences whether they become politically active, how they vote, whether they favor policy or institutional reforms, whether they comply with political authorities, and whether they trust one another. Still, perhaps because so much of the existing research, especially survey-based research, has focused on trust in government or politicians in general, we have not yet come to appreciate the full behavioral ramifications of political trust or distrust.

This is an interesting moment in scholarship on political trust and trustworthiness. Survey researchers are reevaluating the meaning of their concepts and indexes, and comparative and historical scholars are beginning to realize the need for understanding the role and attributes of trustworthy government. Both types of scholars recognize the need to improve their concepts and measurements. Both recognize the necessity of integrating the micro and macro levels to achieve more satisfactory accounts of the relationships among citizens, elected officials, and government agents, and of the consequences of those relationships for political, social, and economic outcomes.

ACKNOWLEDGMENTS

We thank Jacob Bowers and Theresa Buckley for research assistance and Don Green, Charles Stein, and Russell Hardin for helpful comments on an earlier draft.

Data for Figure 1 come from the National Election Studies Guide to Public Opinion and Electoral Behavior (http://www.umich.edu/~nes/nesguide/nesguide.htm), produced and distributed by the National Election Studies.

Visit the Annual Reviews home page at www.AnnualReviews.org

LITERATURE CITED

Aberbach JD. 1969. Alienation and political behavior. *Am. Polit. Sci. Rev.* 63:86–99

Aberbach JD, Walker JL. 1970. Political trust and racial ideology. *Am. Polit. Sci. Rev.* 64: 1199–1219

Abney FG, Hutcheson JD Jr. 1981. Race, representation, and trust: changes in attitudes after the election of a black mayor. *Public Opin. Q.* 45:91–101

Abramson PR. 1983. *Political Attitudes in America.* San Francisco: Freeman

Abramson PR, Finifter AW. 1981. On the meaning of political trust: new evidence from items introduced in 1978. *Am. J. Polit. Sci.* 25:297–307

Abravanel MD, Busch RJ. 1975. Political competence, political trust, and the action orientations of university students. *J. Polit.* 37:57–82

Almond GA, Verba S. 1963. *The Civic Culture: Political Attitudes and Democracy in Five Nations.* Princeton, NJ: Princeton Univ. Press

Arrow K. 1974. *The Limits of Organization.* New York: Norton

Atkeson LR, McCann JA, Rapoport RB, Stone WJ. 1996. Citizens for Perot: assessing patterns of alienation and activism. In *Broken Contract: Changing Relationships Between Americans and Their Government,* ed. SC Craig. Boulder, CO: Westview

Ayres I, Braithwaite J. 1992. *Responsive Regulation.* Oxford, UK: Oxford Univ. Press

Baldassare M. 1985. Trust in local government. *Soc. Sci. Q.* 66:704–12

Bandura A. 1982. Self-efficacy mechanism in human agency. *Am. Psychol.* 37:122–47

Barber B. 1983. *The Logic and Limits of Trust.* New Brunswick, NJ: Rutgers Univ. Press

Beck PA, Rainey HG, Traut C. 1990. Disadvantage, disaffection, and race as divergent bases for citizen fiscal policy preferences. *J. Polit.* 52:71–93

Bianco W. 1994. *Trust: Representatives and Constituents.* Ann Arbor: Univ. Michigan Press

Bianco W. 1998. Uncertainty, appraisal and common interest: the roots of constituent trust. See Braithwaite & Levi 1998, pp. 245–66

Bobo L, Gilliam FD Jr. 1990. Race, sociopolitical participation, and black empowerment. *Am. Polit. Sci. Rev.* 84:377–93

Bok D. 1997. Measuring the performance of government. See Nye et al 1997, pp. 55–66

Braithwaite J. 1998. Institutionalizing distrust, enculturating trust. See Braithwaite & Levi 1998, pp. 343–75

Braithwaite J, Makkai T. 1994. Trust and compliance. *Policing Society* 4:1–12

Braithwaite V, Levi M, eds. 1998. *Trust and Governance.* New York: Russell Sage Found.

Brehm J, Rahn W. 1997. Individual-level evidence for the causes and consequences of social capital. *Am. J. Polit. Sci.* 41(3):999–1023

Brennan G. 1998. Democratic trust: a rational choice theory view. See Braithwaite & Levi 1998, pp. 197–217

Capella JN, Jamieson KH. 1997. *Spiral of Cynicism: The Press and the Public Good.* New York: Oxford Univ. Press

Chan S. 1997. Effects of attention to campaign coverage on political trust. *Int. J. Public Opin. Res.* 9:286–96

Citrin J. 1974. Comment: the political relevance of trust in government. *Am. Polit. Sci. Rev.* 68:973–88

Citrin J. 1977. Political alienation as a social indicator. *Soc. Indic. Res.* 4:381–419

Citrin J. 1991. Political trust and risky policy. Unpublished

Citrin J, Green DP. 1986. Presidential leadership and the resurgence of trust in government. *Br. J. Polit. Sci.* 16:431–53

Citrin J, McClosky H, Shanks JM, Sniderman PM. 1975. Personal and political sources of political alienation. *Br. J. Polit. Sci.* 5:1–31

Citrin J, Muste C. 1999. Trust in government. See Robinson 1999, pp. 465–532

Coleman JS. 1990. *Foundations of Social Theory.* Cambridge, MA: Belknap Press of Harvard Univ. Press

Craig SC. 1993. *The Malevolent Leaders: Popular Discontent in America.* Boulder, CO: Westview

Craig SC. 1996. The angry voter: politics and popular discontent in the 1990s. In *Broken Contract: Changing Relationships Between Americans and Their Government*, ed. SC Craig, pp. 46–66. Boulder, CO: Westview

Craig SC, Maggiotto MA. 1981. Political discontent and political action. *J. Polit.* 43:514–22

Craig SE, Niemi RG, Silver GE. 1990. Political efficacy and trust: a report on the NES pilot study items. *Polit. Behav.* 12:289–314

Dalton RJ. 1999. Political support in advanced industrial democracies. See Norris 1999a, pp. 57–77

Dasgupta P. 1988. Trust as a commodity. See Gambetta 1988, pp. 49–72

Daunton M. 1998. Trusting Leviathan: British fiscal administration from the Napoleonic Wars to the Second World War. See Braithwaite & Levi 1998, pp. 102–34

de Tocqueville A. 1990 (1840). *Democracy in America*, Vol. II. New York: Vintage

Dunn J. 1988. Trust and political agency. See Gambetta 1988, pp. 73–93

Easton D. 1965. *A Systems Analysis of Political Life.* New York: Wiley

Easton D. 1975. A re-assessment of the concept of political support. *Br. J. Polit. Sci.* 5:435–57

Eisenstadt SN. 1995. *Power, Trust and Meaning.* Chicago: Univ. Chicago Press

Elster J. 1989. *The Cement of Society.* Cambridge, UK: Cambridge Univ. Press

Feldman S. 1983. The measurement and meaning of political trust. *Polit. Methodol.* 9:341–54

Fenno RF Jr. 1978. *Home Style: House Members in the Districts.* Boston: Little Brown

Finifter AW. 1970. Dimensions of political alienation. *Am. Polit. Sci. Rev.* 64:389–410

Fishbein M, Ajzen I. 1974. *Belief, Attitude, Intention, and Behavior.* Reading, MA: Addison-Wesley

Flynn J, Burns W, Mertz CK, Slovic P. 1992. Trust as a determinant of opposition to high-level radioactive waste repository: analysis of a structural model. *Risk Anal.* 12:417–29

Flynn J, Slovic P. 1993. Nuclear wastes and public trust. *Forum Appl. Res. Public Policy* 8:91–100

Fraser J. 1970. The mistrustful-efficacious hypothesis and political participation. *J. Polit.* 32:444–49

Fukuyama F. 1995. *Trust.* New York: Basic Books

Gambetta D, ed. 1988. *Trust: Making and Breaking Cooperative Relations.* New York: Blackwell

Gamson WA. 1968. *Power and Discontent.* Homewood, IL: Dorsey

Gamson WA. 1975. Political trust and its ramifications. In *Social Psychology and Political Behavior: Problems and Prospects*, ed. GA Soule, JW Soule, pp. 40–55. Columbus, OH: Merrill

Gellner E. 1988. Trust, cohesion, and the social order. See Gambetta 1988, pp. 142–57

Gibson JL. 1999. Social networks, civil society, and the prospects for consolidating Russia's democratic transition. Unpublished

Giddens A. 1990. *The Consequences of Modernity.* Cambridge, UK: Polity

Goldsteen RL, Goldsteen K, Schorr JK. 1992. Trust and its relationship to psychological distress: the case of Three Mile Island. *Polit. Psychol.* 13:693–707

Greif A. 1994. On the political foundations of the late medieval commercial revolution:

Genoa during the twelfth and thirteenth centuries. *J. Econ. Hist.* 54(4):271–87

Greif A. 1998. Self-enforcing political systems and economic growth: late medieval Genoa. In *Analytic Narratives*, ed. R Bates, A Greif, M Levi, J-L Rosenthal, B Weingast, pp. 23–63. Princeton, NJ: Princeton Univ. Press

Guterbock TM, London B. 1983. Race, political orientation, and participation: an empirical test of four competing theories. *Am. Sociol. Rev.* 48:439–53

Hardin R. 1996. Trustworthiness. *Ethics* 107:26–42

Hardin R. 1998. Trust in government. See Braithwaite & Levi 1998, pp. 9–27

Hart V. 1978. *Distrust and Democracy: Political Trust in America and Britain.* New York: Cambridge Univ. Press

Hawkins BW, Marando VL, Taylor GA. 1971. Efficacy, mistrust, and political participation: findings from additional data and indicators. *J. Polit.* 33:1130–36

Hawthorn G. 1988. Three ironies of trust. See Gambetta 1988, pp. 111–26

Hetherington MJ. 1998. The political relevance of political trust. *Am. Polit. Sci. Rev.* 92:791–808

Hetherington MJ. 1999. The effect of political trust on the presidential vote, 1968–96. *Am. Polit. Sci. Rev.* 93:311–26

Hibbing JR, Patterson SC. 1994. Public trust in the new parliaments of Central and Eastern Europe. *Polit. Stud.* 42:570–92

Hibbing JR, Theiss-Morse E. 1995. *Congress as Public Enemy: Public Attitudes Toward American Political Institutions.* New York: Cambridge Univ. Press

Hirschman A. 1984. Against parsimony: three easy ways of complicating some categories of economic discourse. *Am. Econ. Rev.* 74(2):89–96

Holmberg S. 1999. Down and down we go: political trust in Sweden. See Norris 1999a, pp. 103–22

Hunter S, Leyden KM. 1995. Beyond NIMBY: explaining opposition to hazardous waste facilities. *Policy Stud. J.* 23:601–19

Inglehart R. 1997. *Modernization and Post-modernization: Cultural, Political and Economic Change in 43 Societies.* Princeton, NJ: Princeton Univ. Press

Inglehart R. 1999. Postmaterialist values and the erosion of institutional authority. See Nye et al 1999, pp. 217–36

Jackman RW, Miller RA. 1998. Social capital and politics. *Annu. Rev. Polit. Sci.* 1:47–73

Jackson JS. 1973. Alienation and black political participation. *J. Polit.* 35:849–85

Jennings MK. 1998. Political trust and the roots of devolution. See Braithwaite & Levi 1998, pp. 218–44

Jennings MK, van Deth JW. 1989. *Continuities in Political Action: a Longitudinal Study of Political Orientations in Three Western Democracies.* Berlin: de Gruyter

Kaase M, Newton K. 1995. *Beliefs in Government,* Vol. 5. New York: Oxford Univ. Press

Karp JA. 1995. Explaining public support for legislative term limits. *Public Opin. Q.* 59:373–91

King DC. 1997. The polarization of American parties and mistrust of government. See Nye et al 1997, pp. 155–78

Larson DW. 1997. *Anatomy of Mistrust.* Ithaca, NY: Cornell Univ. Press

Lawrence RZ. 1997. Is it really the economy, stupid? See Nye et al 1997, pp. 111–32

Levi M. 1988. *Of Rule and Revenue.* Berkeley: Univ. Calif. Press

Levi M. 1997. *Consent, Dissent and Patriotism.* New York: Cambridge Univ. Press

Levi M. 1998. A state of trust. See Braithwaite & Levi 1998, pp. 77–101

Levi M. 2000. When good defenses make good neighbors. In *Institutions, Contracts, and Organizations: Perspectives from New Institutional Economics,* ed. C Menard, pp. 137–57. Colchester, UK: Elgar

Lipset SM, Schneider W. 1983. *The Confidence Gap: Business, Labor, and Government in the Public Mind.* New York: Free

Lipset SM, Schneider W. 1987. The confidence gap during the Reagan years, 1981–1987. *Polit. Sci. Q.* 102:1–23

Listhaug O. 1995. The dynamics of trust in

politicians. In *Citizens and the State*, ed. H-D Klingemann, D Fuchs, pp. 261–97. New York: Oxford Univ. Press

Listhaug O, Wiberg M. 1995. Confidence in political and private institutions. In *Citizens and the State*, ed. H-D Klingemann, D Fuchs, pp. 298–322. Oxford, UK: Oxford Univ. Press

Litt E. 1963. Political cynicism and political futility. *J. Polit.* 25:312–23

Lowery D, Sigelman L. 1981. Understanding the tax revolt: eight explanations. *Am. Polit. Sci. Rev.* 75:964–74

Luhmann N. 1979. *Trust and Power.* Chichester, UK: Wiley

Luks S. 1999. The consequences of trust in government for political participation and vote choice. Unpublished

Luks S, Citrin J. 1997. Revisiting political trust in an angry age. Unpublished

Majone G. 1997. Mutual trust, credible commitments and the evolution of rules for a single European market. In *The Evolution of the Single European Market*, ed. DG Mayes, pp. 253–74. Cheltenham: Elgar

Mansbridge J. 1997. Social and cultural causes of dissatisfaction with U.S. government. See Nye et al 1997, pp. 133–53

Markus GB. 1979. The political environment and the dynamics of public attitudes: a panel study. *Am. J. Polit. Sci.* 23:338–59

McAllister I. 1999. The economic performance of governments. See Norris 1999a, pp. 188–203

Miller AH. 1974a. Political issues and trust in government: 1964–1970. *Am. Polit. Sci. Rev.* 68:951–72

Miller AH. 1974b. Rejoinder to "comment" by Jack Citrin: political discontent or ritualism? *Am. Polit. Sci. Rev.* 68:989–1001

Miller AH. 1984. Review of *The Confidence Gap: Business, Labor, and Government in the Public Mind*, by Seymour Martin Lipset and William Schneider. *Public Opin. Q.* 48:838–40

Miller AH, Borrelli S. 1991. Confidence in government during the 1980s. *Am. Polit. Q.* 19:147–73

Miller AH, Goldenberg EN, Erbring L. 1979.

Type-set politics: impact of newspapers on public confidence. *Am. Polit. Sci. Rev.* 73:67–84

Miller AH, Listhaug O. 1990. Political parties and confidence in government: a comparison of Norway, Sweden and the United States. *Br. J. Polit. Sci.* 20:357–86

Miller A, Listhaug O. 1999. Political performance and institutional trust. See Norris 1999a, pp. 204–16

Miller WE. 1980. Disinterest, disaffection, and participation in presidential politics. *Polit. Behav.* 2:7–32

Mishler W, Rose R. 1997. Trust, distrust, and skepticism: popular evaluations of civil and political institutions in post-communist societies. *J. Polit.* 59:419–51

Misztal BA. 1998. *Trust in Modern Societies: The Search for the Bases of Social Order.* Cambridge, UK: Polity

Moe TM. 1990. The politics of structural choice: toward a theory of public bureaucracy. In *From Chester Barnard to the Present and Beyond*, ed. O Williamson, pp. 116–53. New York: Oxford Univ. Press

Muller EN. 1977. Behavioral correlates of political support. *Am. Polit. Sci. Rev.* 71:454–67

Muller EN, Jukam TO. 1977. On the meaning of political support. *Am. Polit. Sci. Rev.* 71:1561–95

Muller EN, Jukam TO, Seligson MA. 1982. Diffuse political support and anti-system political behavior: a comparative analysis. *Am. J. Polit. Sci.* 26:240–64

Newton K. 1999. Social and political trust. See Norris 1999a, pp. 169–87

Nilson DC, Nilson LB. 1980. Trust in elites and protest orientation: an integrative approach. *Polit. Behav.* 2:385–404

Norris P, ed. 1999a. *Critical Citizens: Global Confidence in Democratic Government.* Oxford, UK: Oxford Univ. Press

Norris P. 1999b. Institutional explanations for political support. See Norris 1999a, pp. 217–35

North DC. 1981. *Structure and Change in Economic History.* New York: Norton

North DC. 1990. *Institutions, Institutional*

Change, and Economic Performance. New York: Cambridge Univ. Press

North DC, Weingast BR. 1989. Constitutions and commitment: the evolution of institutions governing public choice in seventeenth century England. *J. Econ. Hist.* 49(4):803–32

Nye J, Joseph S, Zelikow PD, King DC, eds. 1997. *Why People Don't Trust Government.* Cambridge, MA: Harvard Univ. Press

Offe C. 1999. How can we trust our fellow citizens? In *Democracy and Trust*, ed. ME Warren, pp. 42–87. New York: Cambridge Univ. Press

Orren G. 1997. Fall from grace: the public's loss of faith in government. See Nye et al 1997. pp. 77–108

Pagden A. 1988. The destruction of trust and its economic consequences in eighteenth century Naples. See Gambetta 1988, pp. 127–41

Paige JM. 1971. Political orientation and riot participation. *Am. Sociol. Rev.* 36:810–20

Parker GR. 1989. The role of constituent trust in congressional elections. *Public Opin. Q.* 53:175–96

Parker SL, Parker GR. 1993. Why do we trust our congressman? *J. Polit.* 55:442–53

Patterson SC, Caldeira GA. 1990. Stand up for Congress: variations in public esteem since the 1960s. *Legis. Stud. Q.* 15:25–47

Patterson TE. 1994. *Out of Order.* New York: Knopf

Peel M. 1995. *Good Times, Hard Times.* Melbourne: Melbourne Univ. Press

Pettit P. 1995. The cunning of trust. *Phil. Public Aff.* 24:202–25

PEW Research Center for the People and the Press. 1998. *Deconstructing Distrust: How Americans View Government.* Washington, DC: PEW Res. Cent. People and the Press

Pharr S. 1997. Public trust and democracy in Japan. See Nye et al 1997, pp. 237–52

Pierce R, Converse PE. 1989. Attitudinal roots of popular protest: the French upheaval of May 1968. *Int. J. Public Opin. Res.* 1:221–41

Pierce R, Converse PE. 1990. Attitudinal sources of protest behavior in France: differ-ences between before and after measurement. *Public Opin. Q.* 54:295–316

Pinney N, Scholz JT. 1995. Duty, fear, and tax compliance: the heuristic basis of citizenship behavior. *Am. J. Polit. Sci.* 39:490–512

Putnam R. 1993. *Making Democracy Work: Civic Traditions in Modern Italy.* Princeton, NJ: Princeton Univ. Press

Putnam R. 1995. Bowling alone, revisited. *Responsive Comm.* Spring: 18–33

Putnam RD. 1996. The strange disappearance of civic America. *Am. Prospect* Winter: 34–48

Robinson JP, Shaver PR, Wrightsman L, eds. 1999. *Measures of Political Attitudes.* New York: Academic

Robinson MJ. 1976. Public affairs television and the growth of political malaise: the case of "The Selling of the Pentagon." *Am. Polit. Sci. Rev.* 70:409–32

Root HL. 1989. Tying the king's hands: credible commitments and royal fiscal policy during the Old Regime. *Rationality Society* 1:240–58

Rose R. 1994. Postcommunism and the problem of trust. *J. Democracy* 5(3):18–30

Rosenstone SJ, Behr RL, Lazarus EH. 1984. *Third Parties in America: Citizen Response to Major Party Failure.* Princeton, NJ: Princeton Univ. Press

Rosenstone SJ, Hansen JM. 1993. *Mobilization, Participation, and Democracy in America.* New York: Macmillan

Scholz JT. 1998. Trust, taxes, and compliance. See Braithwaite & Levi 1998, pp. 135–66

Scholz JT, Lubell M. 1998a. Adaptive political attitudes: duty, trust, and fear as monitors of tax policy. *Am. J. Polit. Sci.* 42(3):903–20

Scholz JT, Lubell M. 1998b. Trust and taxpaying: testing the heuristic approach to collective action. *Am. J. Polit. Sci.* 42(3):903–20

Schwartz DC. 1973. *Political Alienation and Political Behavior.* Chicago: Aldine

Sears DO, Tyler TR, Citrin J, Kinder DR. 1978. Political system support and public response to the energy crisis. *Am. J. Polit. Sci.* 22:56–82

Sears DO, McConahay JB. 1973. *The Politics of Violence: The New Urban Blacks and the Watts Riot*. Boston: Houghton Mifflin

Sears DO, Citrin J. 1982. *Tax Revolt: Something for Nothing in California*. Cambridge, MA: Harvard Univ. Press

Seeman M. 1959. Alienation studies. *Annu. Rev. Sociol.* 1:91–123

Seligman A. 1997. *The Problem of Trust*. Princeton, NJ: Princeton Univ. Press

Seligson MA. 1983. On the measurement of diffuse support: some evidence from Mexico. *Soc. Indic. Res.* 12:1–24

Shingles RD. 1981. Black consciousness and political participation: the missing link. *Am. Polit. Sci. Rev.* 75:76–91

Sigelman L, Sigelman CK, Walkosz BJ. 1992. The public and the paradox of leadership: an experimental analysis. *Am. J. Polit. Sci.* 36:366–85

Silver A. 1985. "Trust" in social and political theory. In *The Challenge of Social Control: Essays in Honor of Morris Janowitz*, ed. GD Suttle, MN Zald, pp. 52–67. Norwood, NJ: Ablex

Sniderman PM. 1981. *A Question of Loyalty*. Berkeley: Univ. Calif. Press

Stokes DE. 1962. Popular evaluations of government: an empirical assessment. In *Ethics and Bigness: Scientific, Academic, Religious, Political, and Military*, ed. H Cleveland, HD Lasswell, pp. 61–72. New York: Harper

Stokes SC. 1999. What do policy switches tell us about democracy? In *Democracy, Accountability, and Representation*, ed. A Przeworksi, SC Stokes, B Manin, pp. 131–53. New York: Cambridge Univ. Press

Sztompka P. 1996. Trust and emerging democracy. *Int. Sociol.* 11(1):37–62

Sztompka P. 1999. *Trust*. New York: Cambridge Univ. Press

Tarrow S. 2000. Mad cows and activists: contentious politics in the trilateral democracies. In *Disaffected Democracies: What's Troubling the Trilateral Democracies*, ed.

S Pharr, R Putnam, pp. 270–89. Princeton, NJ: Princeton Univ. Press

Tyler TR. 1990. *Why People Obey The Law*. New Haven, CT: Yale Univ. Press

Tyler TR. 1998. Trust and democratic government. See Braithwaite & Levi 1998, pp. 269–94

Uslaner EM. 1999. Democracy and social capital. See Warren 1999a, pp. 121–50

Verba S, Schlozman KL, Brady HE. 1995. *Voice and Equality: Civic Voluntarism in American Politics*. Cambridge, MA: Harvard Univ. Press

Warren ME, ed. 1999a. *Democracy and Trust*. New York: Cambridge Univ. Press

Warren ME. 1999b. Democratic theory and trust. See Warren 1999a, pp. 310–45

Weatherford MS. 1984. Economic "stagflation" and public support for the political system. *Br. J. Polit. Sci.* 14:187–205

Weatherford MS. 1992. Measuring political legitimacy. *Am. Polit. Sci. Rev.* 86:149–66

Weatherford S. 1987. How does government performance influence political support? *Polit. Behav.* 9:5–28

Weingast BR. 1998. Constructing trust: the political and economic roots of ethnic and regional violence. In *Where is the New Institutionalism Now?*, ed. V Haufler, K Soltan, E Uslaner, pp. 163–200. Ann Arbor: Univ. Michigan Press

Whiting S. 1998. The mobilization of private investment as a problem of trust in local governance structures. See Braithwaite & Levi 1998, pp. 167–93

Williams JT. 1985. Systematic influences on political trust: the importance of perceived institutional performance. *Polit. Methodol.* 11:125–42

Williams B. 1988. Formal structures and social reality. See Gambetta 1988, pp. 3–13

Williamson OE. 1993. Calculativeness, trust, and economic organization. *J. Law Econ.* 34:453–500

Yamagishi T, Yamagishi M. 1994. Trust and commitment in the United States and Japan. *Motiv. Emot.* 18(2):129–66

Annu. Rev. Polit. Sci. 2000. 3:509–36

CONSOCIATIONAL DEMOCRACY

Rudy B. Andeweg
*Department of Political Science, Leyden University, 2300 RB Leiden,
the Netherlands; e-mail: andeweg@fsw.leidenuniv.nl*

Key Words democracy, stability, social segmentation, elite cooperation

■ **Abstract** Consociationalist theory served initially as an explanation of political stability in a few deeply divided European democracies. It argued that in these countries, the destabilizing effects of subcultural segmentation are neutralized at the elite level by embracing non-majoritarian mechanisms for conflict resolution. The theory was extended as new consociational democracies were discovered, as the related but broader concept of "consensus democracy" was introduced, and as a normative component was added, recommending consociational engineering as the most promising way to achieve stable democracy in strongly segmented societies. Consociationalism has always been controversial, but rather than one great debate about its validity, there have been many small debates about the countries, the concepts, the causes, and the consequences associated with consociationalism. These debates can become more fruitful if consociational theory is formulated less inductively and at a higher level of abstraction, and if the critics of consociationalism focus more on its principles and less on the operationalizations provided by its most important theorist, Arend Lijphart. The erosion of social cleavages in many consociational democracies raises the question of whether the very logic of consociationalism should lead to a prescription of more adversarial politics in those countries.

THE PUZZLE OF STABLE DEMOCRACY

The puzzle of stable democracy is this: Stability is fostered by the absence of conflict in society, and thus by social and cultural homogeneity; representative democracy, on the other hand, presupposes at least a modicum of disagreement and contestation. The same conflicting views that are the lifeblood of democracy are also threatening to its stability (Diamond 1993:24,29–32). The pluralist theory of cross pressures provides an answer to the simultaneous needs for homogeneity and heterogeneity. Social cleavages can be rendered harmless by cross-cutting each other, i.e. social groups that are homogeneous with respect to one social cleavage are heterogeneous with respect to another. Thus, in his trade union a church member interacts with secular working-class comrades, and in his church he encounters upper- and middle-class brethren. The individual is pulled in different directions; he or she is cross-pressured, experiencing cross-cutting loyalties, which supposedly have a moderating effect on political views, in turn reducing the intensity of political conflicts. The existence of both centrifugal forces (social cleavages) and centripetal forces (cross pressures) at the mass level solves the puzzle of stable democracy.

Not all democracies meet this requirement. Sometimes, the social cleavages coincide and reinforce each other, as when, in the example above, all religious citizens belong to the working class and all secular citizens belong to the upper or middle class. In such a segmented or deeply divided society, the social groups are likely to develop into antagonistic subcultures. One way to avoid the breakdown of democratic stability that could result is for one social group to be able to dominate the others (Lustick 1979). This is a democratic option only if the dominant group is in a majority, but because social cleavages are relatively long lasting, it would condemn the minority groups to permanent exclusion from power, which hardly seems viable as a long-term solution to the puzzle of stable democracy. Yet, there are countries where stable democracy and social segmentation do coexist. The contribution of consociationalism to democratic theory is to explain these deviant cases by showing that social heterogeneity need not be balanced at the same (mass) level; it can also be compensated for at the elite level, by cooperation rather than competition between political elites. Both social segmentation and elite cooperation are continua, but when we dichotomize these two dimensions for the sake of presentation, four ideal types result (Figure 1).

The first solution to the puzzle of stable democracy, in which social cleavages do not reinforce each other and in which, therefore, political elites can be allowed to compete, is called centripetal democracy (Figure 1, *lower left*). The United Kingdom and United States are examples. Centrifugal democracy (*lower right*) is the situation in which deep social divisions are not compensated for by elite cooperation, causing deadlock in the short term and breakdown of democratic government in the long term. Weimar Germany and the French Fourth Republic are the historical examples that are referred to most often. If the elites cooperate although the social cleavages are cross-cutting, we find ourselves in a depoliticized democracy (*upper left*), a situation discussed at the end of this review. Finally, in a consociational democracy (*upper right*), elite cooperation prevents deep social divisions from destabilizing democracy. That situation is the topic of this review.

The two-by-two table in Figure 1 is adapted from the article that launched the term consociational democracy (Lijphart 1968). As Lijphart himself readily acknowledges, he was not the first to use the term; it had been introduced a few years earlier as one of three types of authority patterns in Africa (Apter 1961:4–7,24–25,474–78), and it was probably first used in 1603 by the German political philosopher Althusius [unfortunately, with few exceptions, the term has been translated in the recent English edition (Althusius 1995)]. Nor was Lijphart the first to describe what, through his publications, became known as consociational democracy; just before his description, Lehmbruch analyzed this solution to the puzzle

Mass Level

Cross-cutting
Cleavages   Segmented

		Cross-cutting Cleavages	Segmented
Elite Level	Cooperation	Depoliticized Democracy	*Consociational Democracy*
	Competition	Centripetal Democracy	Centrifugal Democracy

Figure 1 Lijphart's typology of democracies. (Adapted from Lijphart 1968:38.)

of stable democracy in Switzerland and Austria as *Proporzdemokratie* (Lehmbruch 1967) or *Konkordanzdemokratie* (Lehmbruch 1968). Lijphart also mentions Lewis (1965) and Ake (1967), both working on West Africa, as predecessors (Lijphart 1985:97).

CONSOCIATIONAL EXPANSIONISM

Broadening the Theory?

"Consociational democracy means government by elite cartel designed to turn a democracy with a fragmented political culture into a stable democracy" (Lijphart 1969:216). Most consociational scholars and their critics share this often-quoted core definition of consociational democracy, and it has remained unaffected by the evolution of the theory since the late 1960s.

All consociational analyses start with the destabilizing effect of social segmentation, whether because there are coinciding cleavages (e.g. Lijphart 1969:207–11), or because there is so little mobility between social segments that the usual democratic "game" of vote maximization cannot be played (e.g. Lehmbruch 1974:91), or because of what psychologists would call "ingroup-outgroup differentiation" (Nordlinger 1972:7, Steiner 1974:3).

An emphasis on the role of political elites is also characteristic of consociational analyses, although Huyse (1970:173–79) argues that political stability can be safeguarded as well if secondary cleavages cross-cut the social segments at the mass level. The central feature of consociationalism is that the elites eschew decision making by majority. Instead, they seek to accommodate political conflicts through compromise or amicable agreement. Finding a compromise can be facilitated by depoliticization, i.e. defining the issue as a technical (or economic or legal) problem rather than as an ideological conflict (e.g. Lijphart 1975a:129–30), or by (tacitly) agreeing to remove it from the political agenda altogether (e.g. Nordlinger 1972:26–27). Lehmbruch (1974:91–92) points out that in deeply divided societies, preferences are often incompatible and intransitive. Instead of a compromise in the sense of an intermediate solution, the negotiated agreement may therefore take the form of a package deal in which each social segment loses on some issues and wins on others. Another non-majoritarian mechanism for conflict resolution is to assign to the elite of each social segment its own sphere of influence, either territorially (federalism) or in the form of policy areas (functional decentralization). Nordlinger (1972:32), however, explicitly rejects such segmental autonomy as too strong an incentive for secessionist demands, and therefore threatening to the stability of the political system. In reply, Lijphart argues that it is not self-evident that separatism is encouraged more by federalism than by a unitary state. But even if Nordlinger's view is right, Lijphart argues, partition is an acceptable solution under certain conditions, e.g. when the social segments are geographically concentrated (Lijphart 1977:44–47). Some authors also mention mutual veto as a consociational device, implying that even non-decisions are preferable to decisions taken by majority (e.g. Lijphart 1977:36–38, Nordlinger 1972:24–26).

Non-majoritarian decision making is institutionally anchored by the inclusion of representatives from all social segments. Thus, consociational democracies are characterized by grand coalitions and by proportionality in the electoral system and in the distribution of public office and scarce resources. To Lehmbruch, widespread proportional patronage is such a distinguishing feature that it is reflected in his label for consociational democracy: *Proporzdemokratie* (Lehmbruch 1967:41–43).

Apart from differences in emphasis and differences of opinion on other aspects (e.g. the causes of consociationalism), these early formulations of consociational theory have in common the following idea: The threat to democratic stability by social segmentation is neutralized at the elite level by the use of various non-majoritarian mechanisms for conflict resolution, institutionally anchored by inclusive coalitions and proportionality in appointments. Later, Lijphart (e.g. 1977:25–47) singled out four characteristics (grand coalition, proportionality, mutual veto, and segmental autonomy) that must all be present if a political system is to qualify as a consociational democracy. Because Lijphart is also the scholar who has elaborated and defended consociational theory more than anyone else, and whom most critics of consociationalism have addressed, these four criteria have become the standard defining characteristics of consociational democracy. By insisting that all four should be present, and by ignoring other non-majoritarian mechanisms, Lijphart narrowed consociational theorizing unnecessarily.

On the other hand, Lijphart can also be said to have broadened the theory by introducing the concept of consensus democracy. Consensus democracy is characterized by institutional devices—first eight (Lijphart 1984a), now ten (Lijphart 1999)—that broaden the involvement in decision making as widely as possible. The opposite of consensus democracy, called majoritarian democracy, is

TABLE 1 The characteristics of majoritarian democracy, consensus democracy, and consociational democracy (adapted from Lijphart 1984a, 1989a:40, 1999)

Majoritarian democracy	Consensus democracy	Consociational democracy
1. Minimal winning cabinets	1. Oversized cabinets	1. Segmented society
2. Cabinet dominance over legislature	2. Separation of powers	2. Grand coalition
3. Two-party system	3. Multi-party system	3. Proportionality
4. Plurality system of elections	4. Proportional representation	4. Segmental autonomy
5. Pluralist interest group system	5. Corporatist interest group system	5. Mutual (minority) veto
6. Unicameralism	6. Bicameralism	
7. Unitary, centralized government	7. (Non-)territorial federalism and decentralization	
8. Flexible constitution	8. Entrenched constitution	
9. Parliamentary sovereignty	9. Judicial review	
10. Dependent central bank	10. Independent central bank	

characterized by an identical number of features that concentrate power in the hands of the majority (Table 1). Data on each of these institutional variables were collected for 36 countries and subjected to a factor analysis that clustered the first five characteristics in one factor (the executives-party dimension) and the remaining five characteristics in a second factor (the federal-unitary dimension) (Lijphart 1999:2–5,243–57). Table 1 shows that consociational democracy and consensus democracy are closely related. Lijphart uses Belgium, Switzerland, and the European Union, three polities from the set of consociational cases, as examples of consensus government. Yet, there are important differences. Austria, one of the core consociational countries, is classified as rather majoritarian, whereas Italy, regularly mentioned as a centrifugal democracy, ends up among the most consensual democracies. Such different classifications result from theoretical differences. The standard four characteristics of consociationalism are largely behavioral and broadly defined; they may find expression in the rather specific institutional arrangements of consensus democracy, but they are not confined to these mechanisms. Proportionality is not restricted to the electoral system, for example. On the whole, however, consociational democracy is the more narrowly defined of the two concepts. Although not mentioned explicitly among the standard four characteristics, a segmented or deeply divided society is an indispensable element in the definition of consociational democracy, whereas it is not part of consensus democracy. True, consensus government is also suitable for divided societies, but "[t]he difference between them is that consociationalism is the stronger medicine:

while consensus government provides many incentives for broad power sharing, consociationalism requires it" (Lijphart 1989a:41). Consensus democracy has not replaced consociational democracy: the debate over consociationalism has continued without reference to consensus democracy (e.g. Halpern 1986, Lustick 1997) and Lijphart himself has continued to apply the concept of consociationalism separate from that of consensus government (compare, for example, Lijphart 1996 and 1999).

The Expanding Consociational Universe

What started as a few country studies of deviant cases in the light of existing democratic theory has gradually expanded. The first countries to be identified as consociational were the Netherlands from 1917 to 1967 (see e.g. Andeweg 1999; Daalder 1971; Lijphart 1975a, 1989b; Mair 1994; Pennings 1997), Austria from 1945 to 1966 (see e.g. Lehmbruch 1967, 1974; Luther 1999; Luther & Müller 1992; Powell 1970), Belgium since 1918 (see e.g. Deschouwer 1999, Huyse 1970, Lijphart 1981b, Seiler 1997), and Switzerland since 1943 (see e.g. Daalder 1971; Hottinger 1997; Lehmbruch 1968, 1993; Linder 1998; Sciarini & Hug 1999; Steiner 1974). Luxembourg has also been regarded as a consociational democracy, although very little has been published on this country (but see Govaert 1997).

Soon, cases from outside Western Europe were added, notably Lebanon from 1943 to 1975 and since 1989 (see e.g. Dekmeijan 1978, Lehmbruch 1974, Picard 1997), Malaysia from 1955 to 1969 and since 1971 (see e.g. Case 1996, Von Vorys 1975), and Colombia from 1958 to 1974 (see e.g. Dix 1980). The most recent, but highly contested, claim for consociationalism regards India (from independence to the late 1960s), long considered the exception that proves the consociational rule that elite competition in divided societies threatens democratic stability (Lijphart 1996, but see Lustick 1997:113–17). Other countries have only briefly experimented with consociationalism, such as Cyprus from 1960 to 1963 (Lijphart 1977:158–61) and Czechoslovakia from 1989 to 1993, or are classified as semi-consociational because not all the characteristics are in evidence, such as Canada and Israel (Lijphart 1977:119–34).

Consociational aspects have been discovered in at least as long a list of other countries (Lijphart 1985:84, 1996:258). If we broaden the field to include consensus democracy, the list would probably grow significantly, but so far only 36 countries have been analyzed, and 24 of them have been classified as largely consensual on at least one of the two dimensions (Lijphart 1999:248).

It has also been argued that the political system of the European Union should be included in the consociational universe (e.g. Steiner 1974:281–83, Taylor 1991). Consociational theory has imported some aspects of international decision making into domestic politics; consociational scholars such as Lehmbruch and Lijphart draw explicit analogies between international relations and consociational practice (Lehmbruch 1974:92; Lijphart 1975a:123,131). To describe the European

Union as consociational thus provides a natural middle ground between international relations specialists, who characterize EU policy making as still primarily intergovernmental, and scholars in comparative politics, who proclaim it to be predominantly supranational. In the consociational interpretation of the European Union, the member states' societies constitute the separate social segments that make up EU society, and all four of Lijphart's consociational characteristics can be discerned: the European Council and the Councils of Ministers as grand coalitions; subsidiarity as segmental autonomy; the practice of decision making by consensus, even after the introduction of qualified majorities, as mutual veto; and proportionality (or even disproportionality at the expense of the bigger member states) in the composition of EU institutions. The position of the European Commission and the transnational party system that structures the elections to the European Parliament do not fit in this consociational interpretation. This has important consequences for the democratic nature (or future) of the European Union, according to consociationalist theory. People vote for parties in the EU elections, but the parties do not provide the elites representing the segments (nations) in the grand coalition. Addressing the democratic deficit by increasing the role of the European Parliament would destroy the European Union's consociational nature and would thereby threaten its stability, unless the cleavages that structure the EU party system replaced the boundaries between member states (see Chrysochoou 1994, Gabel 1998). If the European Union is a case of consociationalism at all, it cannot be regarded as a consociational democracy.

The set of consociational "sightings" may be growing, but some refer only to the past. Daalder noted back in 1974 that "[i]ronically, the consociational model is coming under considerable stress at the very moment at which it is belatedly recognized on the map of comparative politics" (1974:618). The dates mentioned above in connection with the core consociational countries (Lijphart 1996:259) indicate that consociationalism has largely disappeared in the Netherlands, Austria, India, and Colombia, and that it has failed at least temporarily in Cyprus, Lebanon, and Malaysia. In Czechoslovakia, the "velvet divorce" signaled the end of consociationalism and of the country. In Belgium, consociationalism has been transformed into federalism (Deschouwer 1999). It failed to take further root in the two semi-consociational countries (Canada and Israel). Only in Switzerland, regarded by many as a marginally (if at all) consociational democracy, do we see no evidence of change. For a model that is designed to explain political stability, such discontinuations and interruptions raise serious questions.

Lijphart argues that most of the discontinuations occur when consociationalism becomes the victim of its own success, and that most of the interruptions occur because relations between the social segments become embedded in an international conflict. The latter is most clearly the case in Lebanon, and to a lesser extent in Cyprus, although in both countries there were also flaws in the consociational design, such as fixed formulae for the representation of the segments that were actually disproportional (Lijphart 1977:147–61, 1985:91–93). The waning of Dutch and Austrian consociationalism should not be regarded as indications of failure because in neither country did it result in the end of stable democracy. "The cooption of minority groups helped to render the corresponding cleavages less and less virulent. This raises the question of whether consociationalism is not bound to disappear by rendering itself superfluous" (Lehmbruch 1993:56–57). Although I do not disagree with that conclusion, it does imply that consociational democracy itself is not a stable regime. It is a transitional phase in the slow process of social integration (Linder 1998:171–73). If consociational democracy is not to disappear altogether, it needs a constant supply of deeply divided countries converting to consociationalism.

From Explanation to Prescription

Such conversions are the objective of the next extension of consociationalism, from a purely empirical theory to one that is also strongly normative. Implementation of the standard four characteristics of consociationalism is recommended to deeply divided societies as the most promising way to achieve stable democracy (Lijphart 1977:223–38). Consociational engineering has been advocated for many countries, but the cases that have attracted most interest are Northern Ireland and post-apartheid South Africa. Northern Ireland is the case about which scholars have been most cautious with regard to consociationalism's chances of success (e.g. Barry 1975a, Lijphart 1975b, O'Leary 1989). Lijphart once suggested redrawing the boundary between Northern Ireland and the Republic, perhaps with some resettlement, as a possible solution (Lijphart 1975b:105–6) and argued that only the abhorrence of this alternative, along with continued British insistence on "power-sharing," might "still lead to a grudging acceptance of a consociational solution in the basically unfavorable environment of Northern Ireland" (Lijphart 1977:141). O'Leary reached a similar conclusion: "Immediate clarification of the choice between partition and power-sharing through the *threat* of partition just *might* produce a consociational settlement" (O'Leary 1989:603), but he was more hopeful than Lijphart that "coercive consociationalism" (i.e. a consociational solution imposed by Anglo-Irish cooperation, combined with institutional reform) could work. The 1998 Good Friday Agreement seems to indicate that events may indeed be moving in this direction. The agreement provides for power sharing (e.g. a dyarchy of Prime Minister and Deputy Prime Minister), minority veto power (i.e. complex rules requiring support for a proposal of both unionist and nationalist members of the Assembly), proportionality (in the electoral system and in appointments to the civil service, the police force, etc), and segmental autonomy (e.g. through equal funding of Protestant and Catholic schools) (O'Leary 1999).

In South Africa, consociational theory was misused (or at least grossly misrepresented) by the apartheid regime to defend its 1983 Constitution, but it also provided inspiration to apartheid's opponents, such as the Progressive Federal Party, and to the Buthelezi Commission of which Lijphart was a member. In 1977,

Lijphart was still quite pessimistic: "In the extreme cases of plural societies, such as South Africa, the outlook for democracy of any kind is poor, but if there is to be democracy at all it will almost certainly be of the consociational type" (Lijphart 1977:236). But in 1985 he vigorously advocated consociational engineering in South Africa, arguing that "while on the whole background conditions for consociational democracy are not exceptionally favorable in South Africa, they are not unusually unfavorable either—contrary to what is often assumed" (Lijphart 1985:126–27). Many of his critics have doubted Lijphart's conclusion, arguing that "he is constructing a myth of a peaceful democratic future rather than advancing a neutral science of cause and effect" (Laitin 1987:265; see also e.g. Horowitz 1991:137–45) and that neither the National Party elites nor the African National Congress leadership would accept consociationalism. Yet, they did, at least for the period of transition. The interim constitution of 1993, for example, contained many of the characteristics of consociationalism: a government of national unity, a proportional electoral system, and—less clearly—some provisions for segmental autonomy in education as well as a weak form of minority veto (qualified majority requirements for constitutional change). On the other hand, there can be no doubt that the Constitution of 1996 marks an erosion of consociationalism (especially the disappearance of the grand coalition), although there is still room for disagreement about how much of it is left and what prognosis this entails for stable democracy in South Africa (Hanf 1997 versus Lijphart 1997:692–95).

Thus consociationalism has expanded from an amendment to democratic theory intended to help explain the existence of democratic stability in a few small European countries, to a normative theory of consociational engineering in practically all deeply divided countries.

CONSOCIATIONALISM CRITICIZED

From the start, consociationalism has been a controversial theory, but instead of one great debate about its validity there are numerous small debates about various aspects and applications. Without any claim to being exhaustive, I offer a brief survey of the main criticisms with regard to the countries, the concepts, the causes, and the consequences associated with consociationalism.

Countries

Many of the classifications of countries as consociational democracies have been contested, sometimes for theoretical reasons, sometimes for factual reasons. Lijphart's original interpretation of Dutch consociationalism, for example, has been challenged on the grounds that Dutch society was not as deeply divided as Lijphart presents it to be; the subcultures (the *zuilen* or pillars) in Dutch society were not as far apart, the religious and class cleavages were actually cross-cutting, and the risk to political stability was relatively minor (at least with the benefit of hindsight). A grand coalition, including representatives from all segments, never existed at the level of the government (although most coalition governments were oversized), and Lijphart's identification of the tripartite Social Economic Council as a grand coalition overstates its importance. These are just a few of the objections to Lijphart's analysis of Dutch politics and society (for a more complete catalogue, see Van Schendelen 1984). Many of these criticisms are a matter of degree—more or less segmentation, more or less deference to the elites, etc. Together they present a much richer and more complex picture of Dutch political reality than the highly stylized and simplified version that Lijphart has painted, but they do not add up to a radically different image (Lijphart 1984b).

With regard to the Swiss case, however, the criticisms have found more acceptance. Critics have argued that Switzerland was never a deeply divided society, that religious and class cleavages cross-cut linguistic divisions, that linguistic groups had very few conflicting ambitions, and that partition into linguistically homogeneous and highly autonomous cantons and half-cantons took care of the few remaining conflicts. Others have gone further by suggesting that Swiss politics is not characterized by consociationalism—the Federal Council is not really a grand coalition because its members do not act as the leaders or representatives of the subcultures, and many decisions are taken by referendum, which is regarded as a majoritarian instrument (for a critique along these lines, see Barry 1975b).

Consociational scholars have been considerably more convincing in rebutting the suggestion that consociational practices are absent in Switzerland than in defusing the critique about the absence of deep social divisions. They have pointed out that elite cooperation does take place, albeit not exclusively in the Federal Council, and they have argued that the referendum acts as the functional equivalent of the minority veto, because elites will form inclusive coalitions to preempt the risk of one of the parties or groups calling for a referendum (e.g. Lehner 1984). Many scholars would share Daalder's conclusion about Switzerland (1974:618–19), that "politics in that country have traditionally been so flexible that one wonders whether it ever really fitted the consociational model: although it might have certain consociational practices at the elite level, it never had the tightness of segmented organizations which the model stipulates." But few have gone so far as to drop Switzerland from the list of consociational cases altogether, as Pappalardo (1981) has done, or to put it in a category of its own, as Hottinger (1997) proposes.

Concepts

Halpern complains that the debate on consociationalism is too focused on the countries, on the question of whether a particular political system can or cannot be properly classified as a consociational democracy. "The empirical inconsistencies within the consociational universe, and the debates engendered by them, are largely unresolvable since ... the disordered universe does not emanate from the cases but from the construction of the model" (Halpern 1986:182–83). She is not alone in criticizing the vagueness and elasticity of some of the core concepts used in consociational theory (e.g. Van Schendelen 1984, Lustick 1997). What, for example, is meant by a fragmented, a plural, a deeply divided, or a segmented society—and are these synonyms? "On the basis of which criterion can one say that some division is *not* a cleavage and that a cleavage is *not* segmental?" (Van Schendelen 1984:31). In response to such criticisms, Lijphart proposes four criteria of extreme pluralism: (*a*) the segments must be readily identifiable; (*b*) it must be possible to measure the size of each segment exactly; (*c*) the boundaries between the segments and between political, social, and economic organizations must coincide; and (*d*) the segmental parties must receive stable electoral support from the respective segments. Such an ideal-type segmented society may not exist, but the degree of pluralism can be measured by a society's deviation from these yardsticks (Lijphart 1981a:356). In earlier Dutch work he proposed five yardsticks to measure *verzuiling:* the role of ideology within the pillar, the size and density of the pillars' organizational networks, the cohesiveness of these networks through interlocking directorates and the like, the degree of "social apartheid," and the extent to which pillarized behavior is encouraged by the subcultural elite (Lijphart 1971). Such clarifications, however, highlight another problem. Some of the criteria to measure plurality and pillarization, such as the existence of subcultural organizations or the encouragement of social apartheid, indicate that cleavages are not pre-existing social realities that political elites find on their paths; they are social divisions that have been made salient by these political elites, and around which they have mobilized other people through political, social, and economic organizations. In other words, the political elites on whose prudence consociationalism relies to mitigate the destabilizing effects of segmentation are the same ones who created the problem in the first place. I return to this issue below.

The other central element of consociationalism, elite cooperation, is similarly contested. In 1969, Lijphart used the term elite cartel, defined not only by accommodative behavior but also by purposive leadership, characterized by commitment to maintenance of the system and by an understanding of the perils of fragmentation (Lijphart 1969:216, Lustick 1997:94–95). Later, this commitment and understanding are no longer mentioned, which may make the concept less precise but has the advantage that some possible causes of elite cooperation are removed from its definition. What remains is the essence of consociationalism: Political elites do not compete. However, when we try to assess whether elite behavior in a particular country complies with consociationalism's central prescription, we are likely to find that political elites exhibit behavior patterns that are mixed, with cooperation in some arenas on some issues some of the time, and adversarial behavior in other arenas (most notably the electoral one) on other issues at other times (see Halpern 1986:192–93). For that reason, Steiner (1981:348) has advocated that "decision modes about individual issues," not countries, should serve as the units of analysis. Lijphart (1981a:359) rightly counters that it would still be necessary to aggregate from such individual issues in order to "establish links between typical decision-making patterns of national political systems, the degree of pluralism of their societies, their political stability, their problem-solving capabilities, and so on," but this leaves unresolved the thorny issue of how to measure the degree of elite cooperation.

A related criticism refers to the concept of grand coalition. It seems to indicate an all-party coalition, but it is much more loosely defined, including oversized coalitions, all-party commissions, catch-all parties such as India's Congress Party (Lijphart 1996), and "diachronic coalitions" in which power rotates, as in Colombia between 1958 and 1974 (Lijphart 1977:31–36). Thus, according to Halpern (1986:190), "grand coalition becomes a catch-all concept, describing any joint governmental or quasi-governmental activity pursued by segmental élites whether they undertake that activity as bloc representatives or not, or engage at all in 'summit diplomacy.'" This may be valid literary criticism of some of Lijphart's writings, but it does not do much theoretical damage; consociationalism is characterized by intersegmental elite cooperation, and whatever institution, mechanism, or venue can be shown to have facilitated such cooperation fits the theory. The same response applies to similar criticisms of other characteristics of consociationalism: Functional equivalents to minority veto, proportionality, and segmental autonomy do not invalidate consociationalism simply because Lijphart fails to mention them.

The potentially most damaging criticism of consociationalism is that it is not a theory but a mere tautology. "'Consociational democracy' as conceptualized by Lijphart puts together in a package stability, dissensus, segmentation, elite accommodation and some mix of the 'consociational devices'" (Barry 1975b:480). Consociational democracy is defined by a deeply divided society and by elite cooperation; in other words, both the problem and its solution are part of the definition. Although it is true that Lijphart's writings sometimes explicitly suggest that democratic stability also defines consociational democracy, the more important criticism is that even without explicit incorporation into the definition, consociationalism practically implies stability. To say that elite cooperation leads to political stability is almost the same as saying that there will be no fights in the playground when the children stop quarreling (almost, because there still remains the possibility that the masses will revolt spontaneously against their cooperating leaders). In that sense, consociational democracy is not a theory of cause and effect but rather a descriptive category defined by a problem, the reaction to the problem by political elites, and the consequence of that reaction. However, this is not inevitable. Although there may not be much room for theorizing about the relationship between elite cooperation and stability, there is still much to be said about the relationship between social segmentation and elite cooperation. All that is needed is to remove the existence of deep social divisions from the definition of consociationalism, as Lijphart himself has done in his related work on consensus democracies. If consociationalism is defined as elite cooperation only (using the four standard characteristics or functional equivalents), there remains only the complaint that the theory "does *not* answer the vitally important question why and how such consociational systems developed" (Daalder 1974:609).

Causes

A Self-Denying Prophecy?   Twenty-five years after Daalder posed the question of causation, it has increased in importance because of consociationalism's expansion to prescription, but it has still not been answered satisfactorily. Lijphart's own answer stresses elite prudence. "[T]he essential characteristic of consociational democracy is not so much any particular institutional arrangement as the deliberate joint effort by the elites to stabilize the system" (Lijphart 1969:213). In his interpretation of Dutch consociationalism, he argues that, in the first decades of the twentieth century, the Netherlands was moving toward the category of centrifugal democracy, characterized by social segmentation and elite competition. The outlook was therefore one of immobilism and instability, but this prognosis turned into a self-denying prophecy when the elites realized these risks and set out to counteract the centrifugal tendencies by deliberate cooperation (Lijphart 1975a:182–84). If we assume that Dutch (or Belgian or Austrian) leaders are not inherently more farsighted or virtuous than their counterparts in Northern Ireland or the former Yugoslavia, the notion of a self-denying prophecy merely gives us a description of what happens, not why it happens. One possibility is that the danger of the country falling apart is so obvious that anybody with common sense would realize that the time has come to bury the hatchet (but then why would the masses not reach that same conclusion?). Another possibility is that favorable conditions facilitate the elites' decision to cooperate. Lijphart discusses this possibility in his comparative work, although he continues to insist, "The really crucial factor is the commitment and skill of the political leaders" (1985:127). The large variation in the lists of favorable conditions before 1985 (see Table 2) is probably explained partly by the "discovery" of new empirical cases, partly by the discussion of these factors by other scholars (notably Daalder 1974, Nordlinger 1972, Pappalardo 1981, Steiner 1974). It is not helpful, however, that Lijphart presents a new list of favorable conditions in 1985, while in the same publication reaffirming his full support for the conditions he had specified in 1977 (Lijphart 1985:115 fn).

Cross-Cutting Cleavages?   The status of some of Lijphart's favorable conditions is not clear. He argues that a multiparty system would contribute to consociationalism with reference to the desirability of each segment being represented by a party and the undesirability of one segment being in a majority, factors that overlap with other favorable conditions mentioned in Table 2. Lijphart does not reach a clear conclusion as to whether the degree of pluralism and cross-cutting cleavages have any bearing on the development of consociationalism. The mention of cross-cutting cleavages as a favorable condition for consociationalism (also by Steiner 1974:265–68) has resulted in considerable confusion because it seems to contradict the essence of consociationalism, namely to provide an avenue toward

TABLE 2   Lijphart's favorable conditions for the development of consociational democracy in divided societies (from Lijphart 1969, 1977, 1985, 1996)

Lijphart 1969:216–22	Lijphart 1977:53–103	Lijphart 1985:119–28, 1996:262–63
1. Multiple balance of power	1. Multiple balance of power	1. No majority segment
2. External threat	2. Multiparty system	2. Segments of equal size
3. Relatively low decision-making load	3. Small country	3. Small number of segments
4. Distinct lines of cleavage	4. Degree of pluralism (?)	4. External threat
5. Length of time a consociational system has been in operation	5. Cross-cutting cleavages (?)	5. Small population
6. Internal political cohesion of subcultures	6. Segmental isolation and federalism	6. Socioeconomic equality
7. Adequate articulation of the interests of the subcultures	7. Tradition of elite accommodation	7. Geographical concentration of segments
8. Widespread approval of the principle of government by elite cartel	8. Representative party system	8. Tradition of elite accommodation
	9. Overarching loyalties	9. Overarching loyalties

*Question marks indicate factors that Lijphart mentioned without definitely concluding that they are favorable conditions.

democratic stability when cleavages do not cross-cut. It is important to distinguish the level at which the cross-cutting cleavages operate. Some critics of Lijphart's interpretation of the Dutch case have argued that the country was not deeply divided because the class cleavage and the religious cleavage did cross-cut. This cannot be denied, but the associated moderating cross pressures were absent at the mass level, because religious workers were not members of "the" trade union, but of religious trade unions, etc. The cross pressures operated at the level of the leadership of the religious subcultures, who had to keep both their working-class and their middle-class rank and file on board. One might argue that this rather exceptional circumstance was most favorable to consociationalism because it kept elite attitudes moderate while keeping the subcultures isolated.

Since 1985, cross-cutting cleavages have been replaced by socioeconomic equality (in 1996, Lijphart mentioned the latter as the second most favorable condition), meaning that it is helpful when the class cleavage cuts across whatever other cleavage is salient. Great socioeconomic disparity between, say, linguistic or ethnic groups leads to demands for redistribution, which constitute the kind of zero-sum game that is a severe challenge to elite cooperation. Nevertheless, this new condition does imply that segmentation based on social class lends itself less easily to consociationalism. There is an added reason why this might be so: One of consociationalism's characteristics, segmental autonomy, seems less applicable to class-based segments. "For example, segmental autonomy does not afford a socialist subculture the power to own the means of production or set wage policies" (Halpern 1986:192).

Small Countries' Prerogative?   The small size of the country or the population is also contested as a favorable condition for consociationalism. Lijphart defends this condition on the grounds that "[i]n small countries political leaders are more likely to know each other personally than in larger countries, the decision-making process is less complex, and such countries generally do not conduct a very active foreign policy" (Lijphart 1985:123). These arguments have been convincingly criticized. Personal contact between leaders depends more on psychological than on geographical distance; the social segmentation that characterizes consociational democracies already multiplies the number of organized groups and makes decision making complex, so that the contribution of size in this respect can only be marginal; and the condition of a low foreign policy decision load contradicts another condition, that of external threat (Pappalardo 1981:375–79, but see Lijphart 1985:115–16).

A Tradition of Elite Accommodation?   Of particular theoretical relevance are the debates about the tradition of elite accommodation and multiple balance of power. Introducing a consociational tradition as a favorable condition only transforms the question about the origins of consociationalism into a question about the origins of the tradition of consociationalism, but even if the latter question can be answered, puzzles remain. In his debate with Lijphart about Dutch consociationalism, Daalder (e.g. 1989) argues that a tradition of elite accommodation actually predates the development of class and religious cleavages in Dutch society and that consociationalism therefore does not result from any self-denying prophecy. He draws attention to the striking similarities between the characteristics of consociationalism and the way politics was conducted in the much earlier days of the Dutch confederal Republic of the Seven United Provinces. The pillars replaced the provinces, but the emphasis on elite bargaining and compromise and on the autonomy of the constituent parts can be found both before 1795 and after 1917. The weakness in Daalder's explanation is the miraculous and timely reemergence of an elite culture that belonged to a political system of days long past. Even if socialization and selective recruitment allowed this culture to survive among the ruling establishment (see Lehmbruch 1967:26-29), it is not self-evident why the leaders of the new emancipatory movements of Protestants, Catholics, and the secular working class that came to form the pillarized segments would adopt the ways of those they were trying to replace. Lehmbruch's conclusion regarding Austria [accommodationist practices during the days of Empire (1967, 1974)] is similar to Daalder's on the Netherlands and can be criticized on similar grounds (Pappalardo 1981:386). The continuation of a tradition of elite accommodation deserves explanation as much as its origins.

Absence of a (Near) Majority?   The existence of a multiple balance of power among the social segments as a favorable condition for consociationalism implies several variables that Lijphart mentions separately in later work: the absence of a majority for any of the subcultures; the subcultures being of roughly equal size; and the number of segments being relatively small, between three and five. The most plausible of all the favorable conditions is the absence of a majority. Minority status for all groups means that militant intransigence not only threatens political stability (a leader may not recognize the danger or may not care) but also reduces a segmental leader's influence to that of a voice in the wilderness, whereas by sharing power at least something can be gained. From the opposite point of view, if political elites could count on a solid majority, why would they share power with and make concessions to the losing minority? It is not in their self-interest, democratic norms do not require it, and their followers may not accept it. The optimal situation seems to be one in which no party comes close to 50%, so that segmental leaders cannot entertain any hope that they might achieve a majority by competing a bit more vigorously.

The absence of this favorable condition might go a long way in explaining why consociationalism proves so difficult to achieve in Northern Ireland and why it broke down so quickly in Cyprus. However, in Austria, consociationalism succeeded even though there were only two *Lager* and it came into being at a time when one of the subcultural parties, the People's Party, had an overall majority in Parliament. Moreover, "[I]f the post-1945 Austrian consociation is compared with the deeply conflict-ridden experience of the First Republic, one immediately notices that whereas in the former there is two-partyism, in the latter there was multi-partyism, with two small German Nationalist parties actively involved in the coalition game between the wars" (Pappalardo 1981:368). In another core consociational democracy, Belgium, the Christian Democrats gained overall majorities in several elections, and were sufficiently close at other times to be tempted to switch to a more adversarial style. In Belgium, there are signs that consociationalism did indeed come under considerable stress at such moments, but not in Austria, at least before 1966. Pappalardo finds the Austrian exception sufficient grounds to dismiss the absence of a majority or near majority as a favorable condition. However, the Austrian case can improve our understanding. At a higher level of abstraction, the absence of a (near) majority is one example of a situation in which the costs of competition outweigh its benefits, while the benefits of cooperation outweigh its costs. There are other variations of the same calculation, as when stability has actually broken down and political violence is inflicting heavy casualties among members of the majority group. Just as legitimate hope of a majority is an unfavorable condition for consociationalism, well-founded fear of casualties is a favorable condition. If power sharing ever takes root in Northern Ireland, it may well be chiefly for this reason. In the admittedly more complex situation of South Africa during apartheid, "[t]he capability and desire of black groups to employ violence strategically, and in so doing threaten their own economic stake in the country, [was] a necessary condition for bringing the National Party into serious negotiations" (Laitin 1987:265). Laitin noted that, theoretically, "it is odd that such an important condition for the making of a consociational bargain is not discussed formally as a 'favorable' condition" (1987:265). In Austria, violence had not erupted when elite cooperation started, but the First Republic, which had ended in a civil war, was still a fresh memory. Similarly, in Belgium, a conflict over the monarchy led to violence in 1950. Such experiences may have led even majority leaders in these countries to calculate that the costs of competition were too high. Electoral chances and risk of casualties need not be the only types of benefits and costs: minority support may be indispensable to ward off a common enemy, or the minority may inflict economic damage on the majority or credibly threaten to do so (Nordlinger 1972:42–53).

The other components of "multiple balance of power"—segments of equal size and small number of segments—are less convincing as favorable conditions for consociationalism. Lijphart offers few arguments in support. He claims that equal size of segments facilitates negotiations, but it is not clear why this would be so, especially if the nonelectoral costs just mentioned are taken into account. Moreover, the rule of proportionality seems designed to facilitate elite cooperation between segments of unequal size. Lijphart points out that a small number of segments keeps transaction costs low and thus prevents negotiations from becoming complicated. This cannot be disputed, but such complications may also facilitate elite cooperation by obfuscating winners and losers in any package deal. For this reason Steiner (1974:268) asserts that the higher the number of subcultures, the more probable it is that amicable agreement is the typical mode of decision making. Theoretically at least, it is not self-evident what the optimum number of segments would be.

Lijphart's lists in Table 2 do not exhaust the number of favorable conditions for consociationalism mentioned in the literature. Pappalardo (1981:369–75), for example, argues that stability among subcultures rather than an equilibrium between them is a favorable condition. Such stability would reduce the uncertainty in the calculations of the costs and benefits of competition and cooperation referred to above. Furthermore, there is considerable evidence that subcultural stability is indeed associated with the existence of consociationalism, just as a subsequent decline of subcultural stability is associated with an erosion of consociationalism. However, this association seems to be of a different, almost tautological, nature. The existence of stable subcultures is the problem for which consociationalism provides a solution, rather than a favorable condition for its emergence. Subcultural stability is implied in concepts such as social cleavage, segmentation, or a deeply divided society. Consociationalism simply does not address the problem of conflict regulation in a society with groups of shifting membership that are divided by temporary differences of opinion.

The Nature of the Cleavages?   For most consociational scholars, the nature of the social cleavages is not among the favorable or unfavorable conditions for consociationalism.

Daalder's 1974 complaint is still valid: "Somewhat surprising (in view of the overwhelming and almost determinative importance ascribed to the existence of divisive cleavages), there is in this literature little systematic reflection on whether particular cleavages are more likely to lead to conflict or accommodation than others" (Daalder 1974:613). Some of the problems with divisions based on social class (by definition entailing socioeconomic inequality and limited scope for segmental autonomy) are mentioned above. In view of consociationalism's ambitions as a normative theory, however, the biggest question about its applicability is whether ethnic cleavages should be considered a favorable or an unfavorable condition.

The debate on this issue is muddled because the concept of ethnicity in this context is defined, implicitly or explicitly, in a variety of ways (e.g. Rabushka & Shepsle 1972, Horowitz 1985, McGarry & O'Leary 1993). For the sake of argument, let us use a most restrictive definition of ethnicity, including only race or phenotype, and contrast this with social segmentation based on ideology, with religious and linguistic cleavages at various points in between. Ethnic cleavages, it is argued, constitute an unfavorable condition for the emergence of consociationalism. First, ethnic conflicts are assumed to escalate more easily because there tends to be little effort involved in establishing someone's race, which facilitates ingroup-outgroup differentiation. "[I]t simply does seem to be the case that acts of gross inhumanity are more readily engaged in or supported when the victims are members of an ethnically-defined out-group than when the basis of differentiation is class or religion, especially when sympathetic identification is reduced by large physical or cultural differences" (Barry 1975b:502). Barry offers no empirical evidence for this broad generalization, and his comparison with the supposedly less violent nature of religious conflicts in particular is not self-evident. But even if further research supported Barry's contention, this greater risk of bloodshed is one of the types of costs that can bring calculating leaders to accept a consociational solution.

There seems to be more mileage in a second aspect of ethnic conflict mentioned by Barry as an obstacle to consociationalism. "[W]here the basis of the division is ethnic the question may not be how the country is to be run but whether it should be a country at all" (Barry 1975b:503). In an era when polities are defined as nation-states, this seems a plausible hypothesis. This is also why Nordlinger (1972:37–39) warns against attempts to overcome segmental conflicts by forging a national identity; such efforts are likely to make segmental symbols and traditions more rather than less salient. Lijphart counters Barry's argument by pointing out that the problem will hardly arise unless the segments are geographically concentrated (Lijphart 1985:96). However, even if few areas are ethnically "pure," geographical concentration seems more likely for ethnic groups than for ideological groups. Moreover, Lijphart's defense is at odds with his own listing of geographical concentration among the conditions that are favorable to consociationalism (see Table 2). Contrary to Barry, Di Palma (1977:224–25) argues that the ascriptive nature of ethnicity renders interethnic competition for mass support pointless and limits the ideological spread and polarization that characterize ideological divisions. This may be an underestimation of the potential of ethnicity for radicalization and extremism. However, the more important problem is that Di Palma's supposedly easier accommodation of ethnic conflict remains moot as long as Barry's question of national identification remains unresolved.

In addition, it has been suggested that ethnic leaders are less in control of their rank-and-file membership than are leaders of ideologically defined groups. First, leaders mobilize and control groups through organizations, but organizations are not needed to define membership of an ethnic group. "Whether these groups have an organizational embodiment is a contingent matter but in any case they do not need an organization to work up a riot or a pogrom so long as they have some way of recognizing who belongs to which group" (Barry 1975b:502). This hypothesis seems plausible, but no empirical evidence is offered. Second, whereas leaders may be needed to interpret Marx or the Bible, they are not needed to define what is in the collective interest of the ethnic group (Barry 1975b:502–3). As a consequence, leaders of ethnic groups are allowed less maneuvering room than leaders of ideological groups, and they are more vulnerable to competition from within the subculture. "The very act of forming a multiethnic coalition generates intraethnic competition" (Horowitz 1985:575).

These hypotheses lack more than empirical evidence. It is not clear why members of ethnic groups would be more astute than members of ideological groups or why ethnic leaders would run a greater risk of being outflanked when they seek accommodation than leaders of ideological groups. We should not assume that ethnic conflicts are inherently more dangerous simply because they refer to "primordial" or "pre-industrial" allegiances.

Two conclusions emerge from the debate on the prospects for consociationalism in ethnically divided societies. First, even though not all arguments for regarding ethnic cleavages as an unfavorable condition are convincing, it is hard to dismiss the suggestions that the question of national unity arises more easily when society is divided along ethnic lines, and that ethnic leaders are more vulnerable because organizations are a less effective means to control ethnic groups. Because ethnicity is a prominent cleavage in most deeply divided countries, addressing these doubts should be a priority for consociational theory if it is to remain of prescriptive value. Second, in concentrating on factors that facilitate intersegmental elite cooperation, the discussion of favorable conditions has somewhat neglected factors that facilitate intrasegmental elite control, regardless of whether the segments are ethnically defined.

Elite Security   "Elite predominance over a politically deferential and organizationally encapsulated following" is one of only two conditions that Pappalardo (1981:380–82) regards as unambiguously favorable to consociationalism. Mass political apathy features in several consociational analyses (e.g. Huyse 1970, Lijphart 1975a). The assumption behind this favorable condition is that segmental leaders may decide to cooperate with each other but that their followers never want them to switch from competition to cooperation. This is not necessarily so, not even in deeply divided countries, as the support in referendums for the 1998 Good Friday Agreement in Northern Ireland and the Irish Republic illustrates. But in general, it does seem more likely that followers will greet consociationalism less than enthusiastically. Social differences do not become divisive cleavages spontaneously; they are made salient by political entrepreneurs who use them to mobilize support. The more persuasive the politicians have been in this regard, the more difficult it will be for them to carry their followers with them when they start cooperating with "the other side."

Tsebelis (1990:160) models this problem as one of nested games, with sub-cultural leaders playing in the intersegmental (in his example, parliamentary) arena and simultaneously in the intrasegmental (in his example, electoral) arena. Cooperating in the intersegmental arena will hurt leaders in the intrasegmental arena unless the followers do not know what the leaders are up to, or unless there is no intrasegmental competition that provides the followers with an alternative. In Tsebelis' words (1990:171), "if elites enjoy a monopoly of representation within the pillar *or* if information costs regarding elite behavior are high ... then elites are less constrained by the electoral arena and play a chicken game. If there is elite competition within the pillar *and* information costs are low ... then elites have to conform to the demands of the masses, and a prisoners' dilemma or a deadlock game results." We have to turn principal-agent theory on its head and look for factors that maximize the risk of agency loss, to find the intrasegmental conditions that are favorable to the emergence of consociationalism.

Nordlinger (1972:78–87) lists four such conditions: "apolitical quiescence" among followers, "politically acquiescent" followers, "patron-client relations" between leaders and followers, and "mass parties with extensive organizational capabilities." The latter two institutional variables may even reinforce each other, as in Austria and Belgium, where dense subcultural networks of organizations have developed into political machines offering a whole range of services to individual members. Nordlinger places the political parties in the center of these organiza-tional networks, but a recent comparative study reports considerable variation in the position and role of the parties within the segments (Luther & Deschouwer 1999). The importance of organizations as instruments to insulate and control the subcultures has long been noted in the literature. It explains why social segmenta-tion often increases rather than decreases after the emergence of consociationalism. This increase in segmentation is not necessarily a sign of reverse causality between segmentation and consociationalism, as Daalder (1989:34) implies when he notes that, in the Netherlands, the problem (pillarization) became aggravated after the solution (elite accommodation). Nor is the increase in segmentation the result of elite efforts to prevent intersegmental hostility ("good fences make good neigh-bors") as Lijphart suggests (1985:106–7). Instead, increased segmentation after the beginning of consociationalism is probably motivated by the elites' desire to reduce their own increased intrasegmental vulnerability that is caused by their intersegmental cooperation.

The electoral system that is found most often in consociational democracies, Proportional Representation with party lists, on the one hand protects party leaders from within-party rivals (through their control over the ordering of the party lists), but on the other hand renders them vulnerable to new parties vying for their subculture's support. By tying itself to the subculture's organizations for many other social activities, the party reduces the attractiveness of its competition. Still, very little is known about patterns of elite recruitment and competition within social segments or about patterns of intrasegmental information and communication as they occur in deeply divided societies with and without consociationalism.

A final bone of contention with regard to conditions that are favorable to the emergence of consociational democracy is their importance (e.g. Bogaards 1998:486–93). Lijphart (1977:54) downplays it by warning that "[e]lite behavior seems to be more elusive and less susceptible to empirical generalization than mass phenomena" and that the favorable conditions "are helpful but neither indispensable nor sufficient in and of themselves to account for the success of consociational democracy." This hedging exasperates some of his critics, who argue that it renders the hypotheses untestable and allows Lijphart to recommend consociationalism whether the conditions are favorable or not (e.g. Lustick 1997:107, Pappalardo 1981:366, Van Schendelen 1984:34). In response, Lijphart points out that his propositions about favorable conditions are probabilistic in nature, as is "virtually all social science knowledge" (1985:115). This is fair enough, but the only way to test such probabilistic propositions is to study the correlation between supposedly favorable conditions and consociationalism in a fairly large sample of segmented societies, including both consociational successes and failures. Until such evidence is available, the cogency of the reasoning behind many of the favorable conditions could be improved by less post hoc and more systematic deductive theorizing.

Consequences

Consociationalism's intended consequence is stability, but if the leaders of the various segments cooperate, and if their followers allow them to cooperate, this is virtually a foregone conclusion. Meanwhile, there may be other, perhaps unintended, consequences. Lijphart himself warns that consociationalism may lead to indecisiveness and inefficiency. Elite bargaining within grand coalitions will slow down decision making; applying proportionality to the composition of the civil service interferes with merit appointments; segmental autonomy leads to a multiplication of agencies and facilities; and the mutual veto may produce deadlock, which Lijphart regards as the gravest problem of consociationalism (1977:50–51). When assessing the significance of these potential disadvantages, Lijphart continues, we should distinguish between short-term and long-term effectiveness. In the short term consociationalism may be less effective for the reasons mentioned, but in the long term it will be more effective than adversarial politics because of the stability and legitimacy consociationalism engenders in deeply divided societies (Lijphart 1977:51–52).

In addition to time span, the nature of the agenda is likely to make a difference. If issues of distribution dominate the agenda, consociationalist characteristics such as proportionality augur well for efficient decision making. If, on the other hand, the agenda consists largely of emotionally charged yes/no, black/white issues, the risk of immobilism is greatest because the very nature of consociationalism is the avoidance of zero-sum decisions. Little is known about the extent to which these potential disadvantages materialize in consociational democracies, but on the basis of Lijphart's related work on consensus democracies, the risks should not be overestimated. In a comparison of the performance of both consensus democracies (based on the executives-parties dimension) and majoritarian democracies with regard to economic growth, inflation, unemployment, the budget deficit, economic freedoms, strike activity, and the control of political violence, most correlations turned out to be statistically insignificant, disproving the suggestion that consensus democracies would be less effective in these respects (Lijphart 1999:258–74).

Several authors express concern about the consequences of consociationalism for the quality of democracy (e.g. Lustick 1997:104-5, Van Schendelen 1984:39–40). Absence of opposition, a predominance of elites, and mass political apathy do not suggest democratic vitality. Initially, Lijphart (1977:48) struck a rather defensive note when discussing these misgivings: "Under the unfavorable circumstances of segmental cleavages, consociational democracy, though far from the abstract ideal, is the best kind of democracy that can realistically be expected." In later work, Lijphart changed his mind: "There is nothing in consociationalism that true democrats have to be ashamed of" (1985:109). He bases his assertion on Dahl's ranking of countries according to their degree of democracy (defined as polyarchy). The countries that are commonly regarded as consociational all figure in the highest categories (Dahl 1971:231–48, cited by Lijphart 1985:110). Lijphart's adoption of polyarchy as his definition of democracy amazes Van Schendelen. "In a polyarchy competition between the elites is, more than anything else, essential; in a consociation basically the opposite, namely intense collaboration, is crucial" (Van Schendelen 1984:32). However, the puzzle is easily solved. Dahl (1971) defines polyarchy by two dimensions, competition and inclusiveness. He discusses institutionally guaranteed competition between the elites (1971:1–10), but he emphasizes electoral competition (the right to be eligible for office, the right to compete for votes, free and fair elections, etc), and the electoral arena has, with but few exceptions, been exempted from consociationalism's requirement that the elites cooperate (although this competition is intended to mobilize the faithful rather than to win over new converts). With a single exception, namely Dahl's requirement that institutions are responsive to votes and other expressions of preference, consociational democracies need not be inferior to adversarial democracies in this respect. Moreover, polyarchy's second dimension is inclusiveness, the proportion of the population entitled to participate in public contestation. Here, consociationalism may even outperform adversarial democracies, since its very aim is to prevent the permanent exclusion from power of any social segment. In his related work on consensus democracies, Lijphart even stakes out a claim that consensus democracy is of a higher quality and is a "kinder, gentler" democracy than majoritarian democracy. Again, most of the indicators used pertain to inclusiveness: women's representation, political equality, voter turnout, percentage of the vote on which the governing majority is based, etc (Lijphart 1999:275–300).

This is not to deny consociationalism's democratic credentials but to argue that there are different perspectives on democracy, and that consociationalism agrees more with one than with the other. If democracy is perceived as a device to keep political elites responsive and accountable to the masses, competition (and not just in the electoral arena) is essential, but if democracy is perceived as the avoidance of tyranny (including Madison's tyranny of the many over the few), inclusiveness is vital. Neither perspective is inherently more democratic than the other (cf. Huber & Powell 1994), but one may be preferable to the other in a given situation. Where the most salient distinction lies not within the masses, but between elites and masses, the need for competition may call for majoritarian or adversarial democracy; where the most salient distinction is between social segments of a relatively ascriptive nature within the masses, the need for inclusiveness may require a consociational or consensus democracy.

MIDTERM ASSESSMENT OR OBITUARY?

The problem of stable democracy in deeply divided societies is as relevant today as it was when consociational theory was first formulated three decades ago. Given the number and varied nature of the debates on consociationalism, it is difficult to arrive at an overall assessment. Lijphart's most comprehensive response to consociationalism's critics (1985:83–117) is both hailed as "very persuasive" (Mair 1994:122) and dismissed as evasive (Lustick 1997:109). The debates have two problems. First, because of Lijphart's prominent role in the consociational literature, many critics take aim at his elaboration of consociationalism, or at changes in his formulations over time. Some of their points are fair (such as the unnecessarily circular wording of consociational theory), but with all due respect for Lijphart's highly influential contributions, a valid criticism of some aspect of his work is not always a censure of the basic ideas of consociationalism. Second, the level of abstraction of many contributions to (and critiques of) consociationalism is rather low, perhaps because the theory has largely been developed inductively from empirical case studies. Lijphart (1985:88) rightly argues that "the crucial question is not whether propositions that specify relationships among variables are arrived at inductively or deductively, but whether they are empirically valid or not." However, an elaboration of these propositions at a higher level of abstraction would focus the debate on the principles rather than the operationalization of consociational theory. For some of the characteristics or favorable conditions of consociationalism that are now alleged to be missing from certain cases, functional equivalents may exist that would have been identifiable on the basis of more generalized hypotheses. Such a theory would also broaden consociationalism's applicability as a prescriptive theory. In future cases, consociationalism need not take exactly the same form and need not be made possible by exactly the same favorable conditions that can be discerned in historical cases.

This reformulation of consociationalism can build on the deductive work of scholars such as Nordlinger (1972), who essentially "theorized consociationalism as a Nash equilibrium" (Lustick 1997:99), Rogowski (1974), and Tsebelis (1990). The core of consociationalism remains that democratic instability resulting from social segmentation can be avoided when the segmental elites refrain from competition. This may take the form of Lijphart's four characteristics, but other nonmajoritarian mechanisms for conflict resolution (such as arbitration by a neutral judiciary, technocratic experts, etc) should not be excluded. The segmental elites will refrain from competition (*a*) when the conditions or institutional arrangements are such that they think it is beneficial and/or appropriate for them to do so, and (*b*) when their followers agree with them or, if they do not, when high information costs and lack of intrasegmental competition provide segmental elites with security. These conditions will include some of the "favorable conditions" discussed in this review, but here in particular consociational theory is not out of the egg yet, with important remaining questions about the impact of the nature of the cleavages and about intrasegmental elite-mass relations.

Meanwhile, it should be noted that consociational democracy seems to be retreating from its empirical region of origin, Western Europe. In such countries as Austria, Luxembourg, and the Netherlands, the social cleavages have eroded, and it may be that consociationalism itself has weakened the social segmentation to which it was a response. Where are these countries now in Lijphart's original two-by-two typology of democracies (Figure 1)? The answer depends on what happened to elite cooperation. If it has given way to competition again, the former consociational democracies can be classified as centripetal democracies, but if the elites have continued in a consensual style, these countries are now depoliticized democracies (i.e. government by elite cartel without social segmentation). At first, desegmentation seemed to be accompanied by more competitive elite behavior (e.g. a period of single-party governments in Austria, a shift toward minimum winning coalitions in the Netherlands), but today, the former consociational democracies appear to have retained many consensual characteristics (Lijphart 1989b, 1997:696). Meanwhile, other Western European countries, some of which never experienced social segmentation to any significant degree, are also moving toward a more consensual political style. Katz & Mair (1995:22), for example, observe a movement of political parties toward a position further away from civil society and closer to the state, but also closer to each other "as party programmes become more similar, and as campaigns are in any case oriented more towards agreed goals rather than contentious means." Katz & Mair call this process the emergence of the cartel party, and if that term alone does not provoke associations with consociationalism's government by elite cartel, they argue that "it is also a process that is likely to develop most easily in those political cultures marked by a tradition of inter-party cooperation and accommodation" (Katz & Mair 1995:17).

It is exactly what Lijphart foresaw in the same publication in which he first used the term consociationalism. "The model democracy of the New Europe is character-ized both by cultural homogeneity and by consociational patterns of government" (Lijphart 1968:37). Neither Lijphart nor Katz & Mair see this as a particularly positive development; the absence of true opposition within the system is likely to result in opposition against the system. This hypothesis perfectly fits the rise of populist parties of the radical right in recent elections in Austria, Belgium, and Switzerland. So far, the Netherlands escaped this fate; Luther & Deschouwer argue that the Dutch exception is explained by the early responsiveness of the po-litical system to anti-consociational challenges in that country (1999:259–63). As I noted above, if the main line of division in society is no longer between semiper-manent segments at the mass level but between elites and masses, democracy may be served better by a relative emphasis on competition. In this respect, an im-portant contradiction exists between Lijphart's work on consociational democracy and his elaboration of consensus democracy. Consensus democracy is advocated as a "kinder, gentler" democracy, not only in deeply divided societies, but also in culturally homogeneous countries (Lijphart 1999:302). The very logic of conso-ciationalism, however, inescapably leads to a prescription of more adversarial politics if social segmentation has vanished.

ACKNOWLEDGMENT

I wish to thank Sidney Tarrow for his valuable comments and helpful suggestions.

Visit the Annual Reviews home page at www.AnnualReviews.org

LITERATURE CITED

Ake C. 1967. Political integration and political stability: a hypothesis. *World Polit.* 19:486–99

Althusius J. 1995 (1603). *Politica.* Transl. FS Carney. Indianapolis: Liberty Fund. Abridged. 238 pp.

Andeweg RB. 1999. Parties, pillars and the pol-itics of accommodation: weak or weakening linkages? The case of Dutch consociation-alism. See Luther & Deschouwer 1999, pp. 108–33

Apter DE. 1961. *The Political Kingdom of Uganda.* Princeton, NJ: Princeton Univ. Press. 498 pp.

Barry B. 1975a. The consociational model and its dangers. *Eur. J. Polit. Res.* 3:393–412

Barry B. 1975b. Review article: political accommodation and consociational democ-racy. *Br. J. Polit. Sci.* 5:477–505

Bogaards M. 1998. The favourable factors for consociational democracy: a review. *Eur. J. Polit. Res.* 33:475–96

Case WF. 1996. *Elites and Regime in Malaysia: Revisiting a Consociational Democracy.* Clayton, Aust.: Monash Asia Inst. 300 pp.

Chrysochoou DN. 1994. Democracy and sym-biosis in the European Union: towards a con-federal consociation? *W. Eur. Pol.* 17(4):1–14

Daalder H. 1971. On building consociational nations: the cases of the Netherlands and Switzerland. *Int. Soc. Sci. J.* 23:355–70

Daalder H. 1974. The consociational democ-racy theme. *World Polit.* 26:604–21

Daalder H. 1989. *Ancient and Modern Pluralism in the Netherlands.* Work. Pap. Ser. 22. Cambridge, MA: Cent. Eur. Stud., Harvard Univ. 74 pp.

Dahl RA. 1971. *Polyarchy: Participation and Opposition.* New Haven, CT: Yale Univ. Press. 257 pp.

Dekmeijan RH. 1978. Consociational democracy in crisis: the case of Lebanon. *Comp. Polit.* 10:251–65

Deschouwer K. 1999. From consociation to federation: how the Belgian parties won. See Luther & Deschouwer 1999, pp. 74–107

Diamond L. 1993. Democracy as paradox. In *Israeli Democracy under Stress*, ed. E Sprinzak, L Diamond, pp. 21–43. Boulder/London: Lynne Riener. 385 pp.

Di Palma G. 1977. *Surviving Without Governing: The Italian Parties in Parliament.* Berkeley: Univ. Calif. Press. 299 pp.

Dix RH. 1980. Consociational democracy: the case of Colombia. *Comp. Polit.* 12:303–21

Gabel MJ. 1998. The endurance of supranational governance: a consociational interpretation of the European Union. *Comp. Polit.* 30:463–75

Govaert S. 1997. Le Grand-Duché de Luxembourg: une stabilité trompeuse? *Rev. Int. Polit. Comp.* 4:585–99

Halpern SM. 1986. The disorderly universe of consociational democracy. *W. Eur. Polit.* 9:181–97

Hanf T. 1997. De la dite concordance en Afrique du Sud et de son utilisation a des fins utiles. *Rev. Int. Polit. Comp.* 4:657–78

Horowitz DL. 1985. *Ethnic Groups in Conflict.* Berkeley: Univ. Calif. Press. 697 pp.

Horowitz DL. 1991. *A Democratic South Africa? Constitutional Engineering in a Divided Society.* Berkeley: Univ. Calif. Press. 293 pp.

Hottinger JL. 1997. La Suisse, une démocratie consociative ou de concordance? *Rev. Int. Polit. Comp.* 4:625–38

Huber JD, Powell GB. 1994. Congruence between citizens and policymakers in two visions of liberal democracy. *World Polit.* 46:291–326

Huyse L. 1970. *Passiviteit, Pacificatie en Verzuiling in de Belgische Politiek: Een Sociologische Studie.* Antwerp: Standaard Wet. Uitg. 225 pp.

Katz RS, Mair P. 1995. Changing models of party organization and party democracy. *Party Polit.* 1:5–28

Laitin DD. 1987. South Africa: violence, myths, and democratic reform. *World Polit.* 39:259–79

Lehmbruch G. 1967. *Proporzdemokratie: Politisches System und Politische Kultur in der Schweiz und in Oesterreich.* Tübingen, Ger.: Mohr. 58 pp.

Lehmbruch G. 1968. Konkordanzdemokratie im politischen system der Schweiz. *Polit. Vierteljahresschr.* 9:443–59

Lehmbruch G. 1974. A non-competitive pattern of conflict management in liberal democracies: the case of Switzerland, Austria and Lebanon. In *Consociational Democracy: Political Accommodation in Segmented Societies*, ed. KD McRae, pp. 90–97. Toronto: McClelland & Stewart. 311 pp.

Lehmbruch G. 1993. Consociational democracy and corporatism in Switzerland. *Publius* 23:43–60

Lehner F. 1984. Consociational democracy in Switzerland: a political-economic explanation and some empirical evidence. *Eur. J. Polit. Res.* 12:25–42

Lewis WA. 1965. *Politics in West Africa: The Whidden Lectures.* London: Allen & Unwin. 90 pp.

Linder W. 1998. *Swiss Democracy: Possible Solutions to Conflict in Multicultural Societies.* London: Macmillan. 210 pp. 2nd ed.

Lijphart A. 1968. Typologies of democratic systems. *Comp. Polit. Stud.* 1:3–44

Lijphart A. 1969. Consociational democracy. *World Polit.* 21:207–25

Lijphart A. 1971. Verzuiling. In *Verkenningen in de Politiek Vol. 2.* ed. A Hoogerwerf, pp. 24–37. Alphen aan den Rijn, Netherlands: Samsom. 211 pp.

Lijphart A. 1975a. *The Politics of Accommodation: Pluralism and Democracy in the Netherlands*. Berkeley: Univ. Calif. Press. 231 pp. 2nd ed.

Lijphart A. 1975b. The Northern Ireland problem: cases, theories, and solutions. *Br. J. Polit. Sci.* 5:83–106

Lijphart A. 1977. *Democracy in Plural Societies: A Comparative Explanation*. New Haven, CT: Yale Univ. Press. 248 pp.

Lijphart A. 1981a. Consociational theory: problems and prospects. *Comp. Polit.* 13: 355–59

Lijphart A, ed. 1981b. *Conflict and Coexistence in Belgium: The Dynamics of a Culturally Divided Society*. Berkeley: Univ. Calif. Press. 171 pp.

Lijphart A. 1984a. *Democracies—Patterns of Majoritarian and Consensus Government in 21 Countries*. New Haven, CT: Yale Univ. Press. 229 pp.

Lijphart A. 1984b. Time politics of accommodation: reflections—fifteen years later. *Acta Polit.* 19:9–18

Lijphart A. 1985. *Power-Sharing in South Africa*, pp. 83–117. Berkeley: Inst. Int. Stud. 178 pp.

Lijphart A. 1989a. Democratic political systems: types, cases, causes, and consequences. *J. Theor. Polit.* 1:33–48

Lijphart A. 1989b. From the politics of accommodation to adversarial politics in the Netherlands: a reassessment. *W. Eur. Polit.* 12(1):139–53

Lijphart A. 1996. The puzzle of Indian democracy: a consociational interpretation. *Am. Polit. Sci. Rev.* 90:258–68

Lijphart A. 1997. Changement et continuité dans la théorie consociative. *Rev. Int. Polit. Comp.* 4:679–97

Lijphart A. 1999. *Patterns of Democracy: Government Forms and Performance in Thirty-Six Countries*. New Haven, CT: Yale Univ. Press. 351 pp.

Lustick IS. 1979. Stability in deeply divided societies: consociationalism versus control. *World Polit.* 31:325–44

Lustick IS. 1997. Lijphart, Lakatos, and consociationalism. *World Polit.* 50:88–117

Luther KR. 1999. Must what goes up always come down? Of pillars and arches in Austria's political architecture. See Luther & Deschouwer 1999, pp. 43–73

Luther KR, Deschouwer K. 1999. 'Prudent leadership' to successful adaptation? Pillar parties and consociational democracy thirty years on. See Luther & Deschouwer 1999, pp. 243–63

Luther KR, Deschouwer K, eds. 1999. *Party Elites in Divided Societies: Political Parties in Consociational Democracies*. London/New York: Routledge. 291 pp.

Luther KR, Müller WC, eds. 1992. *Politics in Austria: Still a Case of Consociationalism?* London: Cass. 226 pp.

Mair P. 1994. The correlates of consensus democracy and the puzzle of Dutch politics. *W. Eur. Polit.* 17(4):97–123

McGarry J, O'Leary B, eds. 1993. *The Politics of Ethnic Conflict Regulation*. London: Routledge. 321 pp.

Nordlinger EA. 1972. *Conflict Regulation in Divided Societies*. Cambridge, MA: Cent. Int. Aff. Harvard Univ. 133 pp.

O'Leary B. 1989. The limits to coercive consociationalism in Northern Ireland. *Polit. Stud.* 37:562–88

O'Leary B. 1999. The nature of the British-Irish agreement. *New Left Rev.* 233:66–96

Pappalardo A. 1981. The conditions for consociational democracy: a logical and empirical critique. *Eur. J. Polit. Res.* 9:365–90

Pennings P. 1997. Les Pays-Bas: déclin partiel de la démocratie consociative? *Rev. Int. Polit. Comp.* 4:561–83

Picard E. 1997. Le communautarisme politique et la question de la démocratie au Liban. *Rev. Int. Polit. Comp.* 4:639–56

Powell GB. 1970. *Social Fragmentation and Political Hostility: An Austrian case study*. Stanford, CA: Stanford Univ. Press. 176 pp.

Rabushka A, Shepsle KA. 1972. *Politics in Plural Societies: A Theory of Democratic Instability*. Columbus, OH: Merrill. 232 pp.

Rogowski R. 1974. *Rational Legitimacy: A Theory of Political Support.* Princeton, NJ: Princeton Univ. Press. 313 pp.

Sciarini P, Hug S. 1999. The odd fellow: parties and consociationalism in Switzerland. See Luther & Deschouwer 1999, pp. 134–62

Seiler DL. 1997. Un système consociatif exemplaire: la Belgique. *Rev. Int. Polit. Comp.* 4:601–23

Steiner J. 1974. *Amicable Agreement Versus Majority Rule: Conflict Resolution in Switzerland.* Chapel Hill: Univ. No. Carolina Press. 312 pp.

Steiner J. 1981. The consociational theory and beyond. *Comp. Polit.* 13:339–54

Taylor P. 1991. The European community and the state: assumptions, theories and propositions. *Rev. Int. Stud.* 17:109–25

Tsebelis G. 1990. *Nested Games: Rational Choice in Comparative Politics*, pp. 159–86. Berkeley: Univ. Calif. Press. 274 pp.

Van Schendelen MPCM. 1984. The views of Arend Lijphart and collected criticisms. *Acta Polit.* 19:19–55

Von Vorys K. 1975. *Democracy Without Consensus: Communalism and Political Stability in Malaysia.* Princeton, NJ: Princeton Univ. Press. 443 pp.

SUBJECT INDEX

A

Abandonment
  costs of, 69
Abolitionist movement
  success in changing public
    opinion, 32
Accessibility models
  applications of, 8–9
Accountability
  system transformation and
    democratic, 163–64
Achen, CH, 342–43
Acid rain
  cases involving, 36, 41
Action-reaction logic, 253–54
Actor-observer bias, 425
Adaptation
  benefits of emotions in, 226
  institutional, 153
Adult preferences
  based in development of
    preferences in childhood,
    6
Advocacy networks
  transnational, 156
Affect
  defining, 225–29
  and group reactions, 231
  as information, 229–31
  mediating judgment,
    232–33
  vs. cognition, 231–32
Affection
  sensory basis of, 5
Agenda setting
  by nongovernmental
    organizations, 156–57
Agreements
  See International
    agreements; Regulatory
    agreements

Alford index
  of class voting, 404
  moving beyond, 407
Alienation, 496
  measures of, 487
Alignments
  distinguishing from
    alliances, 64–65
Alliances
  conditions activating, 67
  costs of, 65, 69–70, 80–81
  defining, 63–64
  deterrent effect of, 68–69
  distinguishing from
    alignments, 64–65
  domestic politics and,
    79–80
  duration of, 78–79
  future of, 80–81
  military coordination in, 70
  need for ongoing
    management of, 78–79
  symmetric vs. asymmetric,
    79
  writing down, 63–83
Allies
  vs. arms to enhance
    security, 76–77
Ambivalence
  important in experience of
    emotion, 236
Amendment rules
  affect on incentives of
    committee specialists, 18
American National Election
    Studies (ANES),
    191–95, 197–98
Amnesty International
  consulting at the United
    Nations, 157
Amsterdam Treaty, 379, 395

Analysis
  of arms races, 268–69
  of latent structure, 336
  of ourselves, 313
  See also Policy analysis
APEC
  See Asia Pacific Economic
    Council
"Apperceptive mass"
  in perceptual recognition,
    339
Appraisal
  See Emotional appraisal;
    Reflectivist appraisal
    processes
Aristotle
  advice to leaders, 222
Arms
  vs. allies to enhance
    security, 76–77
Arms agreements
  political economy view of,
    39
Arms control
  reducing probability of
    war, 251–52
Arms races
  causes of, 251–59
  consequences of, 259–66
  formal models of, 269–71
  when states should engage
    in, 266–71
Asia Pacific Economic
    Council (APEC)
  as a forum for US foreign
    policy objectives, 109
Asian economic crisis
  rethinking, 85–115
Asian economic miracle
  viewed as a threat, 89–90
Asian model, 85–115

537

in consociational
expansionism, 527–29
Emerging markets
impact of booms on, 95
lack of transparency in,
90–92
multinational forums for
opening to free capital
mobility, 109
Emotional appraisal
neuroscience of
independent, 229
Emotional reactions
generated by political
institutions, 228
to groups, 229
using startle reflex to
ascertain, 235
Emotions
anchoring behavior and
attitudes, 225–29
defining, 223–25
enabling contemporary
responsiveness, 229–33
importance of ambivalence
in experiencing, 236
methodological quandaries
over, 235–36
in politics, 221–50
possible adaptive benefits
of, 226
role in moral socialization,
228–29
strategies for studying, 225
structure of, 233–35
theoretical models of,
233–37
Empirical validity
assessing claims for
realignment genre for, 457
EMU
See Economic and
Monetary Union
Endogeneity
compliance problems
posed by, 32–33
Endorsers

influence on perceived
believability, 16–17
Enforcement mechanisms
criticism of
transformational design
view, 31
principle of omitting in
transformational design,
29
English regions
devolution of power to,
387–89
Entrapment problem
in commitment, 69, 72–73,
81
Environmental regimes
constructing effective,
25–42
constructivist perspective,
27–30, 32–39
impact of size of, 27
modest contributions made
by, 40–41
political economy
perspective, 30–32
Equilibrium
punctuated, 287
Equilibrium selection
determined by cultural
beliefs, 143
Erikson, R, 340–42, 420–21
Ethnic conflicts
defining, 526
social psychological
insights into, 435–40
Ethnic nationalisms
vs. civic, 125–27
Eurobarometer surveys, 481
European Convention on
Human Rights (ECHR)
British bill to incorporate,
379, 389–90
European Parliament
proportional voting system
proposed for, 379, 391
European Parliamentary
Elections Bill, 391

European polities
reforms in the British
constitution involving,
395–96
risk aversion of, 299
European Union (EU)
budget deficits in, 291–92
consociational
interpretation of, 515
effects on economic voting
nationally, 213
evolution from Coal and
Steel Agreement, 31
Labour government's
response to, 379
studies of the, 151, 162–63
Evaluation
as affect, 227
based on beliefs, 4
critical, 14
of foreign policy, 168–70
of government, 483
origins of, 4–6
of politicians, 483
running counters in, 10
Expansionism
consociational, 511–17
Experimental analysis
gaining leverage through,
500–1
Experimental and panel
analysis
gaining leverage through,
500–1

F

Falklands War variables
eclipsing economic voting
effects, 205–6
Federal theory, 512
rejuvenation of, 129–30
Federations
ethnically based, 130
Russian, 129–32
Financial fragility
in the East Asian economic
crisis, 102–4